FRANCE

A HISTORY OF NATIONAL ECONOMICS

1789 - 1939

FRANCE

A HISTORY OF
NATIONAL ECONOMICS

1789-1939

By

SHEPARD BANCROFT CLOUGH

Assistant Professor of History
Columbia University

CHARLES SCRIBNER'S SONS · NEW YORK
Chicago · Boston · Atlanta · San Francisco · Dallas

PREFACE

WHAT ails France today? What attempts have been made by France to increase its economic power? These are the questions which this book tries to answer for the layman, the student, the statesman, and the scholar.

The order is a large one, but the filling of the order is larger still. By analogy, French economic policies and French present-day problems throw much light upon the difficulties of nearly all the countries of western Europe.

The search for answers to the initial questions has been centered around one of the major problems of contemporary times—national economics or, as it is called in America, economic nationalism. Although it is realized that national economics is not always the prime mover in recent history, it is believed that this basic issue furnishes an excellent opportunity to treat economic development, class interests and conflicts, political controversies, and international rivalries. A survey of all these matters provides a veritable "inside story" of France a story that aims to be penetrating in its analysis and free from the superficiality which sees profundity in mere personal intrigues.

That the national problems of France are discussed in their historical setting is clear from the title. This is important, because no cross-section investigation of present-day France would furnish an understanding of the dynamics of the past which will certainly protrude into the future.

This brief justification for bringing another book into the world is predicated upon the belief that man can do something about contemporary difficulties if he understands them. Without this faith, the writing of such books would be only an idle pastime.

In this place I wish to express my gratitude for the encouragement that has been given me by my friends in making this study. To Professor Carlton J. H. Hayes I owe an intellectual debt that I shall never be able to repay. To the memory of the late Professor Henri Sée I pay homage for the kindness with which he gave freely of his time and

v

great learning to my endeavors. To Professor Charles W. Cole I am a debtor for a friendship that has been as intellectually refreshing as it has been pleasant.

Furthermore, I am deeply grateful to several persons who have had a hand in the preparation of the manuscript. I am especially appreciative for the criticism of the first three chapters by Professor Georges Lefebvre, of the Sorbonne, and by Professor Sée; of the last seven chapters by Professor Georges Weill; of the last two chapters by Professor Eli Heckscher; and of the entire manuscript by Professor Hayes. Sincere thanks are also extended to Doctor George Woodbridge, of Columbia University, for the hapless job of reading proofs and for his many helpful suggestions. To Columbia University I desire to express my gratitude for having awarded me a Cutting Travelling Fellowship that enabled me to spend over a year of study in France and for a grant from the William A. Dunning Fund that made possible what was a third trip to Europe in the search for necessary materials. I want to acknowledge further my great appreciation to Charles Scribner's Sons, and especially to their editor, Doctor W. D. Howe, for their friendly co-operation and their belief in the wisdom of placing scholarly works upon the American market. Finally, I want to testify to the inspiration and joy which I have received from my colleagues and my students. To the latter I dedicate this volume.

S. B. C.

CONTENTS

FRANCE

A HISTORY OF NATIONAL ECONOMICS

1789 - 1939

CHAPTER I

NATIONAL ECONOMICS[1]. THE PROBLEM AND ITS BACKGROUND

WHAT IS NATIONAL ECONOMICS

To say that national sentiment is one of the most distinguishing characteristics of present-day society has become commonplace, and yet it is a triteness the importance of which can scarcely be exaggerated. On every hand there is copious evidence of its overwhelming force. The national flag, the symbol of the nation, is displayed generously in public places. An elaborate ritual has been developed for the worship of that symbol. Hymns to the nation, ranging from the more austere *God Save the King* to the revolutionary *Marseillaise* and the ponderous *Deutschland über Alles,* have been devised. Public schools teach devotion to the nation; patriotic societies, national holidays, a nationalist press, and a blatantly national radio keep aroused national emotion and sentiment. The national army requires even the supreme sacrifice of all citizens.

The force of national patriotism has conquered Europe and the Americas and bids fair to master the East. It has outmoded established religions as the object of greatest loyalty; it has outdistanced humanitarianism; it has outstripped individualism; and it has conditioned socialism.[2] This all-conquering force has moulded and fashioned the institutions of nationalities—politics, society, and philosophy—but perhaps no branch of human interest has been more profoundly influenced by the national concept than has economics. The national economic systems that have grown up in the course of the last four centuries have been at once the reflections and the promoters of national sentiment. Love of country has led to a desire for national power and the process of securing that power has intensified national patriotism.

The theory upon which national economic strength is at present based is the theory of productivity. The strength of a nation is to be gauged, so it is believed, by a nation's ability to produce goods within its own borders or within its easily accessible colonies. This doctrine is fundamental. It applies both to those countries which seek to achieve economic self-sufficiency and to those which concentrate on the production of a few specialties and on the exchange of them with foreign powers.

Hence modern national economic policies aim to develop productive capacity. To this end nations give subsidies to infant, unacclimated, or ailing industries; they seek new supplies of raw materials; and they encourage the adoption of new techniques. Because production is directly conditioned by demand, nations endeavor to secure markets for their citizens. The home market is protected by tariffs and is widened by the construction of railways, canals, and roads. Invasion of foreign markets is facilitated by government-subsidized dumping, by guaranteeing credits of exporters, by granting preferential railway and marine rates, and by giving assistance to merchant shipping. Because production cannot thrive without workers, nations adopt elaborate codes of social legislation to insure not only better conditions for labor but also an ample and capable supply of hands. Similarly, because the productive process requires capital, nations frequently pledge support to their citizens who borrow abroad, and conversely oppose those who wish to export capital. Nations build up empires for the purpose of securing supplies of raw materials, markets for manufactured goods, and areas for the investment of "surplus" capital. Today nations go so far as to manipulate currency for the express purpose of decreasing debts, of increasing exports, and thereby of increasing production.

The spirit behind such measures has been well stated in Fascist Italy: "Labor in all forms, intellectual, technical, and manual, is a social duty. . . . The whole body of production is a single unit from the national point of view; its objects are summed up in the well-being of producers and the development of national strength."[3] Moreover, the national state cannot entrust the task of national economics to unbridled private initiative. "The strong State intervenes [in economic affairs] with its labor courts to correct eventual disequilibrium [between labor and capital] and to alleviate hardships in the field of production. . . . The

State traces the great lines which production must follow, calls to duty the slackers, and holds in check the intemperance of those who consider wealth as an end in itself and not as a means for the amelioration of individuals and for the strengthening of the nation."[4]

In this regard Italy is not an exception. Germany has adopted a similar position. Great Britain, the traditional home of *laisser-faire,* has made frequent suggestions for guiding private business and has often lent a helping hand to agriculture and industry. The United States of America has accepted the responsibility of keeping going the private capitalist economic order. And France, as will be shown in detail in this work, has done much to build up the economy of the state. National economic policies have led to such a high degree of governmental intervention that nations seem to be speedily reaching a condition in which they will control and partially own their economic machines. When such a position is attained, nations will undoubtedly compete with one another for business, as present-day private enterprises do. Then direct economic interests will be added to the already long list of causes of international friction. Despite the great economic interdependence of nations, there are many signs that this acme of national economics is not far off.[5]

In an historical study of national economics, it is obvious that the primary task is to describe those state policies which aim to increase the economic power of the nation. But it is necessary for a real understanding of the problem to do more than this. It is essential to investigate the forces at work in the formulation of economic policies. In the ensuing pages an endeavor will be made to discover what economic classes or groups control the politics of the state and to what degree that control is used for selfish purposes. At the same time attention will be turned to economic history and to the relative economic position of various states. Furthermore, consideration will have to be given to economic theory, foreign relations, and the intensity of national patriotism. Finally, and perhaps most difficult of all, an effort will be made to evaluate the results of national economic policies in order to determine whether or not they accomplish their appointed purposes. It is to these questions, as exemplified by the history of France since 1789, that the present work is devoted.

THE FOUNDATIONS—THE NATIONAL STATE, TRADE, CAPITALISM

The historical origins of the contemporary national economic system are rooted deep in the past. They can be traced back through the industrial expansion, the empire building, and the national productivity theories of the nineteenth century to the mass of economic theory and practice which has unfortunately been indiscriminately lumped together under the generic term of mercantilism. They can be seen in their heterogeneous beginnings in the economic phenomena of the late Middle Ages, and they could probably be run to ground only in the most primitive governments, when political organizations first interested themselves in the economic needs of their citizens. It would be too arduous a task to discuss in detail the long evolution of national economic theory and practice as a simple introduction to a history of French national economics in the nineteenth century, but a brief glance at its development is almost a *sine qua non* for an intelligent understanding of the present study.

In the early part of the medieval period those institutions upon which modern national economics is based—national states, trade over large areas, modern capitalism, and the mechanization of industry—did not exist or were in an embryonic stage. Lay political organizations were limited to small areas or exercised but a tenuous authority over their subjects. The Roman Catholic Church cut sharply across national lines and was a counterweight to state power. Relative economic self-sufficiency of the manor or of the district was the rule and the small amount of trade between distant places did not require much economic regulation. Wars were likewise usually of a local character and what general strife there was did not have the complexion of national warfare. Finally, capital in its modern form—a mobile surplus that may be readily used for the production of more surplus—was in its infancy.

In those centuries after the Crusades, however, the institutional foundations of national economics began to take shape. Characteristic of the trend was the appearance of the national state. This singular political entity seems to have resulted from the amalgamation of people who were drawn together by the centripetal forces of a common language or closely related dialects, a homogeneous culture, historical traditions, similar customs, and economic interests.[6] In the process of the territorial unification of national states, authority usually became concentrated in the hands of one feudal lord who, as king, extended his sway over other feudal lords. The onerous and difficult task of political unification was facilitated in England and France by peasant uprisings and by feudal struggles. Inheritance and marriage accelerated also the process of state-building, sometimes operating so rapidly that unification was finally effected within a generation. Foreign wars, such as the Hundred Years' War, resulted in the establishment of strong national armies, the centralization of authority, and the birth of lively historical traditions. Lastly, the need of a centralized authority for protecting and regulating economic enterprise speeded up the process of state-formation.

In the realm of trade the need for political intervention gradually became pressing. After the Crusades the demand for Eastern fineries, like silks, spices, and tapestries, the trade of the Baltic, the shipment of wool from England to Flanders, and the sending of Flemish cloth to Florence to be dyed resulted in long-distance commerce of a new magnitude. Then with the opening of the route to India around Africa and the discovery of America, trade developed still larger proportions. Rivalry for the rich plums of business was keen and success hinged frequently upon the strength of the respective competitors. If one nation was fortunate enough to get control of trade in a given area, a strong central authority was needed to regulate it and to guard it from the encroachments of others.

With the growth of commerce there developed the institution of modern capitalism which was to place its imprint upon national economics. In medieval times the Church preached that the possession of great wealth was sinful and frowned upon the taking of large profits. The charging of interest was prohibited, for money was considered sterile—a theoretical conception that had some factual foundation in a society which used a portion of its currency for spendthrift show.[7] With the development of trade, however, money became extremely useful, if not necessary, in facilitating the exchange of goods. Tremendous supplies of bullion from the New World and the development of banking and credit gave to capital a fluidity, mobility, and usefulness hitherto unknown. In view of the changed conditions, the Church altered its position on money, and the Protestant ethic made no serious objection to the accumulation of riches.[8] The amassing of wealth was not only condoned but even encouraged, and money was regarded as endowed with intrinsic virtue. Getting rich became an important goal in life, and logically enough political authority was enlisted to help people attain that goal. States became agents of businessmen and expanding business provided a reason for the formation of states. Capitalism and the capitalist spirit were vital factors in this process and conditioned deeply the nature of state economics.[9]

In the course of time the development of industry was, along with trade and capitalism, to cast its shadow across the course of national economics. When industrial production was geared to the satisfaction of local wants and when markets were not expanding with any rapidity, the gilds provided an organization sufficient for the needs of manufacturing. But as trade grew and markets were opened up, industry took advantage of the golden opportunity to meet the new demands for goods. Machines were gradually introduced into the productive process and the mechanization of industry presented new problems that required the intervention of political authority. It was necessary to secure ample supplies of raw materials, to keep pace with technological advances, to have a good labor supply, and to have markets in which to sell the finished products. States aided manufacturers in solving these problems and at the same time did their best to develop their capacity for producing industrial products.

With the growth of trade, capitalism, and industry, western European states began to formulate definite economic theories and policies. They endeavored to get control of trade for the benefit of their citizens. Venice engaged in an expansionist program and obtained outposts in the Near East for its merchants. In such places she maintained *fondachi,* which were combination warehouses, countinghouses, and inns, and by them endeavored to monopolize the traffic.[10] States also adopted "provisioning" measures, for certain goods were so badly needed for consumption or manufacturing that it was thought unwise to permit the export of them. Grain was frequently subjected to such rules and sometimes local supplies of metals or wool were required to be worked within the confines of the state.[11] Some of these early economic rules had as their object the prevention of abuses—monopoly, forestalling, regrating, short measures, bad quality, and the like. Others aimed to secure an immediate diplomatic advantage, and still others were dictated by the needs of war.

From an early time, moreover, efforts were made to draw precious metals to the territory of the homeland. Money was needed to grease the wheels of production and exchange, and to fill war chests for the payment of mercenary soldiers.[12] Francesco Guicciardini, the Renaissance historian of Florence, stressed the importance of hard cash by maintaining that it was easier to get soldiers with money than it was to obtain money with soldiers.[13] Such an important rôle did money play in the warfare of the late Middle Ages that it was referred to as the sinews of war—*pecunia nervus belli*.[14] Precious metals began to be considered indispensable to the life of states and the "bullionist theory" came into existence.[15] It was maintained that the wealth and strength of a state were in direct proportion to the amount of gold and silver within its territory. To get precious metals became, therefore, a primary concern of state interest. In France a royal order of 1443[16] aimed to keep close at hand a ready supply of bullion, and in England the financial drain of the Hundred Years' War was so great that three officers of the mint stated the principle of the balance-of-trade theory—that more merchandise must not be imported than is exported—in order that bullion, the sinews of war, would not flow out of the country.[17]

Thus the rising national monarchs, employing the methods of obtaining wealth which were suggested to them by the activity of private entrepreneurs, feudal lords (among whom they were little more than *primi inter pares*), gilds, and city states, formulated empirically a theory of state economics. They believed in economic regulation to foster their own industries, to do injury to their enemies, and to keep bullion within their territories. Economics was not a separate science, but a part of statecraft, and from the seventeenth to the late nineteenth century was known as *political* economy.[18]

State economics on a large scale did not develop, however, until the expansion of Europe overseas resulted in an increase of bullion in Europe, in the extension of foreign trade, and in the augmentation of national rivalry. Then a more persistent and definite attempt was made to construct strong states. With the ever greater centralization of power in government, at the expense of towns and provinces, an effort was made to create real political economies with more and more unity[19]— an ideal that ultimately was to come close to realization.

MERCANTILISM OR ECONOMIC STATE BUILDING

To the economic state-building of the period from approximately 1500 to 1800, Adam Smith in his *Wealth of Nations* gave the name "mercantile system." This was undoubtedly a misnomer, but it, or its equivalent, mercantilism, has stuck. More misleading still is the fact that mercantilism has been reduced in the popular mind to hard-and-fast concepts—bullionism, favorable balance of trade, protectionism, the exploitation of colonies for the benefit of the mother country, and navigation acts. As a matter of historical record, states were highly empirical in adopting economic plans. Their policies varied greatly; they were not systematic; and the mercantile, that is, the commercial, aspect of them was not always dominant. The crux of the whole phenomenon was the desire to strengthen the political organism and to aid the capitalist class. Within the space of three hundred years can be found nations that were struggling for supremacy by following widely opposed policies. Some stressed bullionism, others productivity; the ones placed emphasis upon free trade, the others, upon protectionism. But whatever the course adopted, it is erroneous to believe that the state-economic-building aspect of mercantilism came to an end at the beginning of the nineteenth century. The national phase of political economy today is a continuation of earlier theories and practices and is more alive, more vigorous, and more intransigeant than ever before.[20]

PORTUGAL, SPAIN, AND THE NETHERLANDS STRESSED TRADE AND BULLIONISM

A glance backward at the experience of Western European states from 1500 to 1800 will give confirmation of these facts. Portugal, the first state to rise to economic primacy in the modern period, was perhaps the most typically mercantilist.[21] She had the good fortune to discover the water route to India and bent her energies to amassing bullion from the profits of Oriental trade. She declared a royal monopoly of the commerce with the East and did her best to keep out interlopers. For a time all went well. Profits were large and bullion was drawn to the country. But all branches of economic activity except trade were sadly neglected and in the end great stores of precious metals did not result in national strength. The purchase abroad of consumers' goods proved too easy and the fabric of Portuguese supremacy was eaten away. The Dutch and the English made inroads in the trade by going themselves to the East, and the Portuguese did not have the military strength nor the economic power necessary to keep them out. From 1580 to 1640 Portugal was a Spanish province and as such became involved in a long series of expensive and disastrous wars. When she regained her independence, she had become definitely a third-rate power.

The successor to Portugal as the leading economic power in Europe was Spain.[22] The Spaniards, like the Portuguese, were pioneers in overseas exploration, and like their Iberian brothers discovered lands of immense wealth. But, whereas Portugal discovered a route to a country that offered great opportunities for trade, Spain found a land that was semi-waste and that was peopled by natives who produced little which could be sold in Europe. For this reason Spain's Empire in the New World looked for a moment like a white elephant with a tapeworm. In a short time, however, this beast turned to gold. For a century *conquistadores* marched and countermarched through the country, plundering and robbing as they went. Cortez stripped the Aztecs in Mexico of their hoards; Pizarro pillaged the Incas in Peru; and their followers worked the natives to exhaustion in fantastically productive mines.

Spain went precious-metal mad. If bullion were the sinews of war and the basis of national wealth, Spain was to rise to unknown eminence. Sums of gold and silver never before equalled in the history of Europe were imported. Bullion could not legally be taken from Spain and all manner of means to prevent its escape was resorted to.[23] Nor could foreigners go to the Spanish New World to obtain part of the treasure, because trade there was declared a national monopoly. Consequently, Spain amassed great hoards of bullion that had the effect of reducing the purchasing power of gold and silver. This is indicated in part by a rise of prices of over four hundred per cent from 1501 to 1601.[24]

After a temporary stimulus to production, bullionism seems to have helped undermine Spanish economy. Work in Spain was decidedly unfashionable. All aspired to be *caballeros* or *hidalgos*—gentlemen who spent their time in tilting with windmills and wooing "Lady Dulcineas" rather than in pursuing economically productive trades. Land began to go out of cultivation after the middle of the sixteenth century, and manufacturing fell off. The government, in order to obtain the necessaries of life, had to wink at foreign smugglers and to let them reap rich profits from their illicit trade.[25] Unemployment, which is reflected in the reports of vagabondage and begging, became rife. Finally, when Spain became engaged in foreign wars, in which leading industrial and commercial nations always have become involved, she did not have the economic stamina that was required for victory. Her economic policy of hoarding bullion did not produce the national power that had been anticipated, and she was forced to make economic concessions to her rivals. By the treaty of Münster (1648), when the Dutch were given the privilege of trading in the West Indies, and by the Treaty of Utrecht (1713), when the English were granted a monopoly of the slave trade to Spanish colonies and were allowed to send annually one merchant vessel to Puerto Bello, the commercial monopoly of the American empire was broken. A tardy attempt to overcome Spanish economic difficulties is seen in the writings of Don Gerónimo de Uztáriz, an official of the eighteenth century, who pleaded for greater productivity in Spain, for renewed commercial endeavors,[26] and for the establishment of commercial companies to prevent encroachments of England and the Netherlands. But, in spite of his efforts, Spanish industry was not rejuvenated, and "shortly before 1740, the English alone are said to have had as much share in the Spanish colonial trade, in ways prohibited, as the Spaniards themselves had in authorized ways." The Spanish national economic theory of bullionism was not sound, but Spain realized the error of her ways too late.

Unlike Spain, most of the nations of Western Europe did not succeed in obtaining colonies that had great stores of bullion which could be appropriated, or rich mines that could be exploited. They had to build up their national wealth in other ways. Their methods differed some-what, because they were confronted with various economic problems and inherited divers economic traditions, but three fairly definite pos-sibilities were open to them. They could gain bullion by engaging in trade and take profits from carrying, as had the Portuguese; or they could produce and, in selling abroad, reap a harvest of precious metal; or they could do both, which England and France endeavored to do, but in which only the former was highly successful. The simplest of the three manners of obtaining bullion, and the most strictly mercantile, was undoubtedly the first. It was in the carrying trade that the Nether-lands, the first of the western European states north of Spain to achieve a position of economic primacy, found the goose that laid golden eggs.

At the close of the Middle Ages the Netherlands enjoyed an economic development superior to that of nearly all other sections of Europe.[27] Her industry was well advanced; her herring fishery was prosperous; and her trade was expanding. To the Netherlanders fell, moreover, the remunerative business of selling the products of the North to the South of Europe and, on the return trip, of merchandising at high prices the Eastern products which were picked up at Lisbon. This happy existence was seriously endangered in the late sixteenth century by the attempt of Spain, to whom the Low Countries belonged, to suppress by force the fast-spreading Calvinist heresy of the Dutch. The war sapped the strength of the Netherlands and split the country into two parts. The South remained under Spain and accompanied her in decay; the North was left to continue the struggle alone. As a consequence of this situa-tion, Spain closed her ports and, after 1580, Portuguese ports, to the Netherlanders. For a moment the Dutch commercial star lost its bril-liance, and appearances indicated that it would become gradually lustre-less. But in the darkest days, individual Dutch traders went to the source of Oriental products and established trading posts in the East. Thus was brought into the Dutch commercial orbit a trade that was to lift the Netherlands upon one of the greatest waves of prosperity that modern history has known.

The Dutch, like the Portuguese, took measures to protect and foster trade. A monopoly of commerce was maintained in so far as possible by semiprivate and public organizations—the Dutch East India Company, the Dutch West India Company and the Boards of Directors of the Levant Commerce and Navigation in the Mediterranean. The exchange of goods was facilitated by the almost complete absence of customs tariffs. The Dutch needed to obtain wares from the Baltic and German states in return for overseas articles and did not want to jeopardize this commerce by levying irritating duties. It was not until the 1770's that the Netherlands adopted protectionist tariffs,[28] and by then her period of supremacy had passed. The Dutch burghers in the seventeenth century were bent on trade. The greatest of the Dutch sailors of the period, De Ruyter, fought for Netherlandish commercial interests[29] and the greatest of Dutch legal minds, Hugo Grotius, to clear the waves for Netherlandish commercial and fishing fleets, argued for a *mare liberum* against the English contention of territorial waters.

Great prosperity was attained by the Dutch through trade, and their commercial activity became the envy of all Europe. The ever augmenting amount of commerce increased the stores of bullion in the Netherlands and stimulated production, particularly in the shipbuilding and allied industries. The Netherlands looked as though they might remain on the economic pinnacle of Europe indefinitely, but such was not to be the case. The Low Countries formed a small country whose possibilities for production were limited and whose population was too small to cope successfully for long with the onslaughts of jealous neighbors. With all states following the policy of desiring to do their own carrying and being willing to fight for the privilege, it was only a matter of time before the Netherlands would succumb to stronger powers. From the middle of the seventeenth century onward, Dutch merchants were forced to withstand the continued attacks of the English, French, and Portuguese. They were driven from Brazil in 1661, from the New Netherlands in 1667, and from Ceylon and the Cape Colony during the Napoleonic Wars. In the Far East, their trade fell off, for, although they maintained their hold on their East Indian possessions, the narrow policies of the East India Company led to its disintegration and final dissolution in 1798. By the eighteenth century, the Dutch had suffered a tremendous relative, although not an actual, decline in commerce. Dutch economic supremacy, built on overseas trade, lasted scarcely more than a century.

ENGLAND STRESSED TRADE AND PRODUCTION

Neither Portugal, Spain, nor the Netherlands stressed or had the capacity for great national production. This was not true, however, of the two states which ascended rapidly the scale of economic prominence upon the decline of Dutch power. Both England and France were to place great emphasis on productivity. In the England of the sixteenth century the need for such a policy was great. Industry was not highly developed; agriculture was upset by enclosures; and foreign commerce was comparatively meager. William Cecil, later Lord Burghley, Secretary of State and Lord Treasurer in the reign of Elizabeth,[30] resorted to all manner of expedients to foster industry. He introduced new industries, and in order that England might be literally more powerful, he stimulated the manufacture of munitions and ammunition by giving exclusive rights to those who would undertake mining operations or the production of sulphur and saltpeter. He paid the salaries of foreign workers who had to be brought to England to teach the natives tricks of the metallurgical trades. In order to build up England's shipping industry, he saw to the preservation of forests along the seacoasts, encouraged the cultivation of hemp and flax and the manufacture of canvas, improved harbors, and insisted that Protestant England eat fish on Friday and all through Lent. By the Statute of Artificers (1563) Lord Burghley made labor practically obligatory on a national scale and provided machinery for keeping wages down. He gave also his attention to trade, for an unfavorable balance "robbeth the realm of England" of its money, but his main stress was upon the production of staple goods. This was important, for it was upon such common articles as iron, steel, coal, and textiles that England's economic and political primacy was ultimately to be based.

In the seventeenth century the English placed relatively more emphasis upon trade than they had during Lord Burghley's period. They endeavored to secure more overseas commerce by making war on the Dutch,[31] by establishing the Navigation Acts,[32] by founding the monopolistic East India Company and other trading concerns of a similar nature,[33] and by opening new markets in divers parts of the globe. Even though it looked for a moment as though the business of the East India

Company would be cramped by the feeling against the export of bullion,[34] supporters of the Company, with their arguments that the true goal of trade was a general favorable balance of trade[35] and that this goal could be most easily attained if there were leniency in the traffic of gold and silver,[36] obtained essentially free trade in precious metals (1663). Nevertheless, sight was not lost of the productivity theory of national wealth. English manufactured and agricultural products were heavily protected by tariffs and the East India Company exported woolen goods to the East at a loss in order to pacify woolen manufacturers who complained of the importation of calico prints.

In the eighteenth century the development of trade went hand in hand with the growth of industry. By the Methuen Treaty in 1702, an advantageous exchange of English woolens for Portuguese wines was effected. The treaty of Utrecht of 1713 with Spain granted England the right to send one merchant ship a year to Puerto Bello in Spanish America and gave her a monopoly of the slave trade. As a result of the Seven Years' War, England obtained Canada and a predominant position in India; and although she lost the American colonies in the Revolutionary War, she increased her trade with them after the peace. Then, to add to this extension of the market, England adopted a policy of paying a bounty for the export of goods which she had in such abundance that prices of them were extremely low—a policy which found concrete expression in the corn law of 1689 that provided an export bounty on grain.

Simultaneously England did her utmost to stimulate industry. Throughout the eighteenth century she maintained high import duties or prohibitory regulations on the goods of her greatest economic rival, France, and on the products of all competitors. In 1721, the Calico Act forbade the importation of cotton stuffs on the ground that these cheap and very popular fabrics from the Orient were ruining woolen manufacturing. Then came the invention of machines which were introduced especially widely in the cotton-textile, metallurgical, and later in the woolen trades. Gradually power was applied to the machines; and soon England found herself in the throes of an *industrial revolution*. The ideal of eighteenth-century economic theorists for great productivity as a basis for national wealth was realized, then, under a system of protection—a vital historical point that modern economists might do well to bear in mind. Owing to the industrial revolution's developing first in Britain and the tremendous commerce that the English built up, Great Britain was able to rise to the first economic and political place among the nations of the world.

The national economic theories and practices of England after the advent of machine industry on a large scale were conditioned greatly by Adam Smith's *Wealth of Nations* (1776). He paid his homage to production in the following passage:

"The annual labour of every nation is the fund which originally supplies it with all the necessaries and conveniences of life which it annually consumes, and which consists always either in the immediate produce of that labour, or in what is purchased with that produce from other nations. According therefore as this produce, or what is purchased with it, bears a greater or smaller proportion to the number of those who are to consume it, the nation will be better or worse supplied with all the necessaries and conveniences for which it has occasion."[37]

As a general rule, Adam Smith believed that a nation should produce what it was best suited to produce and that it should exchange the surplus of its specialty for goods to meet its other wants—a process that should be allowed to operate without the impediment of tariffs. Although Smith made several qualifications to this international division-of-labor theory—qualifications and exceptions which had to do especially with measures for national defense or punishment of a foe[38]—he thought that its application would result in greater wealth and hence greater economic strength. From this point of view *laisser-faire* or free trade may be considered a national economic policy. At all events, Great Britain did not adopt free trade until she had such technological advantages over her competitors that they were unable to sell in her markets. When she did apply this doctrine, she endeavored to convince other nations of the wisdom of pursuing the same policy in the hope that the removal of trade barriers would allow her to sell to them.

As long as Britain maintained her industrial superiority, she retained first place among the nations of the world. Gradually, however, when other nations surpassed her agriculturally, drew abreast of her industrially, and took away some of her markets she began to experience an economic struggle with equals. Moreover, she had unwittingly developed a new form of hoarding wealth, which might be called "foreign investmentism." The surplus capital which came to her, especially in the early days of the industrial revolution, was invested in productive enterprises abroad. She thus helped to build up competitors in other lands and she lived, in part, on the "tribute" (interest) that came from her investments.[39] National fears were felt for the future of a nation built on such an economic foundation, and many Englishmen with King Magnus, the hero of George Bernard Shaw's *Applecart,* trembled at what would happen if foreigners stopped paying tribute. In the last years of the nineteenth century a serious movement got under way for a return to governmental regulation in an effort to keep up production. After the World War England did go back to her eighteenth-century stand that national wealth and strength are dependent upon production and that the government's duty is to foster industry and trade.[40]

FRANCE TEMPERED BULLIONISM WITH PRODUCTION AND TRADE

In the midst of the national economic policies and practices surveyed in the last few pages, French state economics was bred. French opportunities for establishing great wealth in early modern times were unlike the Portuguese in the sixteenth century or the Dutch in the seventeenth. The French had no exceptionally remunerative carrying trade;[41] nor were their opportunities like the Spanish, after that nation's expansion overseas, for France did not obtain, as a result of the early explorations and discoveries, rich colonies with mines to be exploited or with natives to be robbed. France's position was more closely analogous to that of England's under the Tudors. It was necessary for her to work out her economic salvation from native resources and, although covetous glances were cast in the direction of her more favored neighbors—glances that were reflected in economic theory and national economic practice—French national economy may be characterized by its continued dependence upon native resources for its prosperity. Because of this comparatively great economic self-dependency, French national economy has always reacted sensitively both to internal political or social factors and to governmental aid. The intervention of the state in economic affairs has for these reasons been invited, and governmental paternalism has played a large rôle in national economics.

A belief in the necessity of production for national strength and wealth has been strong throughout French economic history. In the sixteenth century, to be sure, the bullionist theory was taken seriously, but straight bullionism was usually tempered with "productionism." An ordinance of 1540, frequently reiterated thereafter, forbade the export of bullion as tending toward "the impoverishment of our subjects,"[42] and there was legislation to suppress luxuries, for by their purchase "great sums are drawn from our kingdom by foreigners."[43] But it was recognized that the storing of bullion was dependent upon foreign commerce and that foreign commerce in turn was dependent upon production. An ordinance of 1572 forbade the importation of woolen, silk, and linen fabrics and the exportation of raw wool, flax, tow, and other articles. It definitely stated, moreover, that the purpose of the regulation was to increase manufacturing in France and to keep the profit of such work within the kingdom.[44]

The French Government of the sixteenth century also offered direct aid to private enterprise in order that production might be stimulated. Subsidies, tax exemptions, grants of monopolies, loans, and patents of royal manufactories[45] were employed to develop and extend such industries as glass making, sugar refining, tapestry weaving, and woolen, silk, and linen textile manufacture.[46] Toward the close of the century, Sully, an "agricultural bullionist,"[47] placed credence in bullionism, but thought that "feeding flocks and working the land are the two sources of French nourishment—the real mines and treasures of Peru"; and Henri IV, in whose service Sully was, complemented that gentleman's economic interests by occupying himself with the development of industry. Emphasis was also placed upon the building-up of commerce. Henri IV gave serious attention to the improvement of communications, and Richelieu (Minister from 1624 to 1642) did his utmost, although in large part for political purposes, to establish trading companies[48] and to construct a merchant marine.[49] Commerce, according to the French, was the handmaiden of industry and a necessary part of the state's economic interests.

The chief writers on economic subjects in this period immediately prior to the advent of Colbert voiced opinions which harmonized with the economic practice already mentioned. Jean Bodin (1520–96),[50] one of the first to point out that the amassing of bullion in Spain had resulted in a rise of prices rather than in the expected economic strength, seems to have been primarily concerned with the increase of production and with state measures to effect that increase. To the end of greater national production, he advised the charging of high export duties on French products without which foreigners could not do, the prohibition of the export of raw materials, the importation of raw products at low rates, and the levying of high duties on foreign imports. With all his seeming liberalism, he was primarily a productionist.

Of a similar mind was Barthelémy de Laffemas (1545–1611),[51] tailor and valet to Henri IV and later Contrôleur-Général de Commerce. He based his economic thinking on a conviction that France needed gold and silver—"two noble metals, . . . the principal muscles that sustain" the state. In order to get more bullion in France it was necessary to prevent its export and to encourage its import. To effect the latter *desideratum,* supervision of commerce was essential to insure that each individual foreign transaction brought gold into the country and did not take it out. French merchants should be made to exchange their goods for bullion or raw materials, but never for manufactured articles. For two reasons, therefore, it was necessary to stimulate French industry, first, that France would have the wherewithal to sell abroad, and, secondly, that she would not be forced to rely upon foreign importation to get articles for her own consumption. Manufacturing and agriculture were the real gold and silver mines of France. The king should, therefore, supervise production. He should revive the gilds in order to keep quality at a high level and to attract foreign buyers; he should secure the services of foreign workers to teach French artisans new trades; and he should put all Frenchmen to work producing something. Opponents of this system and national slackers would certainly crop up, but no mercy should be shown them. They should be hanged or strangled.

The summary execution of those who refused to obey national economic regulations would probably have been welcomed by Laffemas' contemporary, Antoine de Montchrétien (1576–1621).[52] This economist, tragic poet, swordsman, duelist, industrialist, adventurer, and seditionist, who is reminiscent of Cyrano de Bergerac, wrote a *Traité de l'économie politique* (1615)—the first time that the expression "political economy" was used—in which he advanced economic ideas similar to those of Bodin and Laffemas. Like them he understood the usefulness of gold and silver, "those two great and faithful friends which supply the needs of all men and are honored among all peoples," but he recognized that "it is not the abundance of gold and silver, the quantity of pearls and diamonds, which makes states rich and opulent, [but rather] the supply of things necessary for life. . . ." He therefore urged state self-sufficiency of both agricultural and industrial products and, although he held a brief for the international division of labor, he advocated the removal of all foreign competition by state action. He was, moreover, the champion of foreign commerce. Trade, he claimed, provides the best way for securing gold and silver; it contributes, as was amply proved by the example of the Netherlands, to the strength and power of the state; and it furnishes goods which cannot be produced at home and which have come to be recognized as necessities of life. France must get a share of the Far Eastern trade; she must develop fisheries so that sailors will be trained; and she must establish colonial settlements throughout the world—New Frances—that will keep up the traditions of the motherland. These inroads into the commercial field will not be wrought without conflict, said Montchrétien, for what is one state's gain is another's loss. But with all its accompanying dangers, commerce leads to wealth, greatness, and glory. Economic strength, then, depends upon abundant natural resources, a large and industrious population, a thriving agriculture, a vigorous industry, and a great commerce.

COLBERTISM

The climax of French economic statism in the period before the Revolution, which was gradually worked up to by the policies of Sully, Henri IV, and Richelieu and by the writings of Bodin, Laffemas, and Montchrétien, came during the administration of Jean Baptiste Colbert (1619–83), in the reign of the great Roi Soleil, Louis XIV. Colbert,[53] the son of a cloth merchant of Rheims, after having served an apprenticeship in matters of state under Mazarin, was made economic adviser to Louis XIV. He was primarily interested in state economics, and so great was his activity in such matters that historians have named his particular system "Colbertism." For pure theory he had no bent; he was a practical man who was faced with the problem of securing money for his king in a period of rising prices.[54] He based his moves on the doctrines of others—particularly on those of Montchrétien. Like his predecessors, he acknowledged the rôle of bullion in a nation's life and was inclined to make it the basis of his structure. "But this principle, in itself narrow and *mesquin,* became great on account of the things accomplished in its name."[55] To obtain bullion it was necessary to build up the entire productive and commercial machinery of the country; and, to this cause, Colbert devoted his entire life.

Colbert held that gold would pour into France if great quantities of goods were produced, enough to supply France completely and to effect a surplus; if the goods were of such a high quality that foreigners would find purchase of them irresistible; and if France had the means of transporting them abroad. To foster industry he gave subsidies to manufacturers, carried the policy of royal manufactories much further than it had been carried previously, and did his best to introduce new industries. That there might be a sufficient labor supply, he forbade the emigration of French workers and stimulated the immigration of foreign skilled laborers; he encouraged boys to marry before they were twenty and exempted families of ten or more, if none of the children became priest or nun, from paying taxes; and he carried on bitter campaigns against begging, charity, and general indolence.[56] That the quality of French products might be kept up, he took a leaf out of the book of the gilds and established rigorous regulations for manufactured products—three hundred and seventy-one articles in an edict of 1671 pertained to the dyeing of cloth.[57] In the interests of domestic commerce he built roads, bridges, and canals. To do away with the annoying provincial customs barriers within France, he did his best to unite all districts into a customs union and, although he failed, he found the way for a reform that was accomplished in the French Revolution.

In the interests of foreign commerce, Colbert's acts were legion. They were characterized by a conviction, borrowed from Montchrétien, that there is a given quantity of trade in the world and that, if France increased her share, some other nation must lose a proportionate amount. "Commerce," he wrote in 1669, "is carried on by 20,000 vessels and that number cannot be increased. Each nation strives to have its fair share and to get ahead of the others. The Dutch now fight this war [of commerce] with 15,000 to 16,000 vessels, . . . the English with 3000 to 4000, . . . the French with 500 to 600. The last two countries can improve their commerce only by increasing the number of their vessels and can increase this number only . . . by paring away from the 15,000 to 16,000 Dutch ships."[58]

He, therefore, took a hostile attitude toward his prosperous neighbors, consented to Louis XIV's first war on the Netherlands, and gloated over the fact that in 1669, "this state [France] is prosperous not only in itself, but also in the condition of want which it has created in the neighboring states. Extreme poverty appears everywhere; only Holland still resists."[59] In order that France might get some of this Netherlandish trade, he adopted in 1664 comparatively low customs rates, thinking that "free trade" would achieve his purpose, but after he had heard the complaints of industrialists, he established a high tariff in 1667. He sponsored trading companies, particularly the French East India Company (founded 1664), which he hoped would wrest oriental trade from the Dutch and English, and he gave subsidies to the merchant marine. Finally, he exerted a special effort to secure colonies and to settle those which had already been obtained. He sent colonists to Canada at governmental expense. When it was found that women, among other things, were lacking in the new settlements, he characteristically wrote to his agents in Canada saying, "We prepare one hundred and fifty girls, mares, horses, and sheep [to send to you]" and ordered that soldiers marry within fifteen days of the arrival of the shipment.

With such drastic measures and with a comprehensive program, Colbert aimed to push France to the fore of all nations. That his efforts were crowned with unqualified success, it would be difficult to maintain, but that they bore no fruit is incorrect. In the luxury trades and in certain other industries, much progress toward the final goal was realized. His general plan, however, suffered much from Louis XIV's

wars of glory and conquest. The treasury could not stand the burden
of large military establishments and of aid to industry and commerce,
nor were the energies of the French people sufficient to carry on
grandiose economic enterprises and war at one and the same time.
French commerce suffered because of hostilities and, although the
French merchant marine did become a strong second to England in the
eighteenth century, the events of the seventeenth century indicated that
France would probably have to rely on her own native resources, on
agriculture and industry, and not on commerce, for her economic
strength.

STATE INTERVENTION IN FRENCH ECONOMICS DURING THE EIGHTEENTH CENTURY

France continued to make a strong bid for primacy in agriculture,
industry, and commerce throughout the eighteenth century, and emphasis continued to be placed upon production and trade as the touch-
stones of national wealth. Unanimity of opinion did not exist, however,
as to the best course to pursue to attain economic power. There were
those who believed that the most rapid development of France's economy would result from a policy of governmental "hands off"—of
laisser-faire—and there were those who thought that most could be expected from a rational policy of state aid and intervention.

Among the latter there were in the early part of the century the
so-called "neo-mercantilists," most prominent of whom were John Law,
François Mélon, Dutot, and François Véron de Fortbonnais.[60] They
wanted to increase production and commerce of France and believed
that it could be done automatically by augmenting the amount of
money, whether in the form of metallic coin or of paper, in circulation.
John Law (1671-1729),[61] a Scottish banker, maintained that "wealth
depends upon commerce, and commerce depends upon circulation."
The problem for national states to solve was how to increase the amount
of money in use in the economic system. This could be done, Law
believed, by issuing paper certificates. Unable to sell his ideas to his
Anglo-Saxon compatriots, he went to France where he was given an
opportunity to practice his magic. He founded a bank, put paper money
into circulation, and established his schemes to gain a control of

practically all the colonial trade of France. But his undertakings were unsuccessful. After a short time people lost confidence in his paper, and his system fell with a resounding crash in 1720.

Made cautious by the results of Law's inflationism, his followers approached more closely the Colbertian idea of money. Mélon held,[62] and Dutot and Fortbonnais were in substantial agreement with him, that wealth consists in consumptible goods, but that money is representative of wealth and is an indispensable instrument of exchange. An abundance, but not an excess of money, which may, in part, be paper, is vital to the life of a nation. But from this point on Mélon and his followers tended to separate from Law and to drift toward Colbert; they stressed the importance of production and governmental regulation. Mélon, to be sure, contended that commerce could thrive best under a régime of liberty, but, being unwilling to repudiate Colbertism, he interpreted liberty in government "not as a license to do as one wishes, but [to do] only that which is not contrary to the general interest [of the nation]. . . ." In the name of this brand of liberty, the state should develop production by prohibiting the importation of manufactured products and the exportation of raw materials; by regulating industry (even going so far as to consider the advisability of re-establishing slavery in Europe in order that every one may be made to produce); and by doing everything possible to improve agriculture. The state should do approximately what Colbert had attempted:—stimulate production in order to advance commerce; advance commerce in order to secure a favorable balance of trade; and secure a favorable balance of trade in goods in order that the difference may be paid in bullion.

In French eighteenth-century economic practice, the doctrines of Colbert and his followers were closely reflected in the continuance of state aid to industry and in the elaboration of state regulation for the production of quality goods. Rules, which became a positive nuisance to manufacturers and a hindrance to industry because of their excessive number and meticulousness,[63] were put on the defensive in the years just prior to the Revolution, but public assistance to manufacturing suffered no decline. The industrial development of England, particularly in the second half of the century, encouraged the French state to come to the aid of its nationals. The process of introducing into France

—of grafting onto a foreign organism—the machines that had sprung spontaneously from fertile soil across the Channel was an artificial one, and one in which the hand of the government was ever visible.[64] The state's attitude toward the importation of skilled artisans is shown, for example, in the bestowal of bounties and the title of "Inspector of Foreign Manufactures" upon John Holker, an Englishman of Rouen, who later became a French citizen. He brought in English workers and introduced into France many of the secrets of Manchester.[65] Ever on the alert to attract English inventors, the state gave to John Kay, after his flight from England, not only harbor, but also an annual subsidy and the exclusive right to make his machines in France;[66] and it did its utmost to persuade Watt and Bolton to migrate to France.[67] In order to learn new manufacturing methods, the state sent spies abroad. One of them, Gabriel Jars, learned the English method of smelting with coke and, by teaching it to his compatriots, contributed an enormous service to French industry.[68] The state granted subsidies to entrepreneurs who undertook machine production; gave money aids to French inventors, like Jacquard;[69] held exhibitions of new mechanical contrivances;[70] and set up institutions to train laborers to work the machines. The tariff system, too, was employed to protect the industries that were striving so desperately to withstand English competition. France tried to quarantine herself from English goods and to immunize herself against them by inoculations of industrialism.

CRITICS OF STATE INTERVENTION

Such attempts to raise French economy by governmental action to a level with or to a stage superior to that of other states were not without their critics in the eighteenth century. Pierre le Pesant de Boisguilbert (1646–1714)[71] believed that nature should be allowed generally to take its course in economic affairs. If this were done, French manufacturing would be relieved of its burden of regulations, commerce would grow, and agriculture would be improved. There would thus be established a healthy equilibrium in international economics and simultaneously a more vigorous national economy. Richard Cantillon (1680–1734), an Irishman in the banking business in Paris and for a time connected with Law, likewise looked upon Colbertian economics as futile. In his *Essai sur la nature du commerce en général*,[72] he maintained that a nation is at its greatest economic strength when it has a surplus of production and a favorable balance of trade, but he denied that this condition could be permanent. As the supply of bullion in a country increases, prices go up until they are too high to attract foreign buyers. The balance of trade then becomes unfavorable, bullion is exported, prices decline, and the process begins all over again. The strongest nation must inevitably, and by the very nature of things, suffer a decline after it has reached a peak of prosperity. There are cycles of national economic supremacy which are controlled by "economic law." To fly in the face of this "law" is both foolhardy and useless.

Important as such attacks were on state interventionism, the hardest blows were delivered by the Physiocrats. Under the leadership of the redoubtable Doctor François Quesnay, they contended that agriculture was by nature the basis of prosperity and of wealth; that it would be futile to try to circumvent natural law; and that nations should pursue a policy of *laisser-faire* in economic matters. Although they did not stress patriotism, less prominent members of their group claimed that they wished to make French subjects patriots and farmers, and to clarify the true interests of the nation. Commercial men, artisans, and *rentiers* were, according to them, cosmopolites and not integral parts of the state. Only landed proprietors were true citizens.[73] But Physiocratism was not strongly patriotic; it was capitalistic, agricultural, and anti-proletarian. It preached *laisser-faire*, not only because it was the best policy for France, but also in order that the wealthy classes might continue unhampered their happy existence.[74]

At the end of the *ancien régime*, some of the leading statesmen who were believers in Physiocratic doctrine endeavored to put their theories into practice. Trudaine,[75] director of commerce in 1759, and the ministers of Louis XVI, Turgot[76] and Necker,[77] relaxed enforcement of onerous, industrial regulations in the hope that French production, freed from its shackles, would take a new lease on life. The right to export precious metals was granted in 1755 and a movement to free domestic commerce from its many barriers, especially from provincial and city customs duties and from tolls, got under way. The necessity of reform was indeed apparent, for local imposts had become so numerous that wine coming from Roanne, on the Loire River, to Paris was subjected in 1755 to eleven customs duties and twelve tolls.[78] Moreover, France did not have a common customs tariff for foreign goods. The *Cinq Grosses Fermes* had one tariff, each of the *Provinces Réputées Étrangères* (the provinces of southern France, Brittany, the Franche Comté, Artois, and Flanders) had its own, except for a limited number of goods on which the tax was the same as that for the *Cinq Grosses Fermes,* and the *Provinces d'Étranger Effectif* (Labourd, Gex, Lorraine, Alsace, and the three Bishoprics) as well as the Free Ports (Marseilles, Bayonne after 1784, Saint-Jean-de Luz, Lorient, and Dunkirk) had the right to trade freely with foreign nations, but not to export goods to the rest of France without paying the general customs rates. Necker found trading conditions, and particularly taxes, so complicated that "only one or two men in each generation entirely succeed in understanding them."[79]

Trudaine, Necker, and Turgot applied themselves to this problem, which was "monstrous in the light of reason"—but without much success. Trudaine never got beyond the stage of studying what should be done; Necker issued a decree, August 15, 1779, suppressing all tolls, but it was never enforced;[80] and Turgot established, but could not maintain, freedom of commerce in grain.[81] The tax farmers opposed reforms that injured their collections; provinces were jealous of their fiscal prerogatives; and the fear of local famines, because of bad harvests, counterbalanced the economic hopes of the adherents to the principle of *laisser-faire.*

The most noteworthy economic change wrought under the ægis of Physiocratism concerned foreign, rather than domestic commerce—and more particularly trade with England. Throughout most of the eighteenth century there existed between France and England a trade war that made legal commerce difficult in times of peace, and practically impossible in times of war. An agreement between France and England, drawn up as part of the Treaty of Utrecht, had provided for the importation of French wines into England on the same footing as those of Portugal, and for some degree of reciprocity. This draft treaty had never been ratified by the British because of fear of French industrial competition.[82] This non-ratification had led to French reprisals that prohibited the importation of most English cotton and woolen goods, leathers, hardware, clocks, tin, and lead. These, in turn, had caused England, for her part, to enforce rigorously her navigation acts and to place high taxes on French products, particularly on wines.[83] Finally, after the War of American Independence, it was proposed that the two nations enter into negotiations with the view of putting an end to the commercial *impasse* that had lasted so long.[84]

After lengthy discussions, the treaty was signed, September 26, 1786.[85] Its provisions followed in general the abortive commercial section of the Treaty of Utrecht. England consented to make an exception to the navigation acts in regard to French shipping, and France agreed to change her policy of prohibitions concerning English products. It was stipulated that each country should charge the other on linen goods no more than it charged the Dutch, and on cottons, hardware, chinaware, pottery, and glassware about 12 per cent *ad valorem*. This meant that England, with her superior industrial equipment and cheaper costs of production in many lines, would be able to rout her French competitors in the home markets—a situation that both the English and French negotiators understood,[86] but which the former desired and the latter did not seem to fear. France, for her part, secured favors concerning agricultural products only, goods ever dear to the hearts of Physiocrats. The English agreed to charge French wines no more than Portuguese wines paid at the time of the signing of the treaty (a provision which allowed shortly afterwards a one-third reduction of the English tax on Portuguese wines); they consented to lower the tax on vinegar by one-half, the tax on brandies by about one-third, and to allow the importation of olive oil on the basis of the most-favored-nation treatment. But they refused to allow, under any conditions, the importation of French silks, the only industrial product that could be exported to England with real profit.

In England the treaty was welcomed with enthusiasm, especially by manufacturers, and received severe criticism only from the political opponents of the Pitt government.[87] In France the pact was regarded with dismay by industrialists and by artisans, who prophesied that French manufacturing would be ruined. Their expectations were not entirely realized, but according to Arnould, formerly director of the Bureau of the Balance of Commerce, the value of English-manufactured goods imported into France jumped from 13,000,000 livres in 1784 (to which he added 10,000,000 livres as an estimate for contraband) to 58,500,000 livres in 1787.[88] The actual effects of the treaty, however, are difficult to estimate. French students of the period have for the most part let their judgments of it be conditioned *a priori* by their economic theories.[89] But the most serious economic historians are, in general, of the opinion that the treaty delivered French industry a severe blow; they leave to the prophets the prediction of what might have happened had not the French Revolution come to change the commercial relations of the French and English.[90] It is certain, moreover, that the experience obtained from the treaty made France wary of an international division of labor and turned her again towards a policy of economic self-sufficiency—a policy of state-aided productionism.

TREND TOWARD INTERVENTIONISM ON THE EVE OF THE FRENCH REVOLUTION

The efforts of the *laisser-faire* school to realize reforms were not crowned with success in eighteenth-century France. The Eden Treaty of 1786 was unpopular; the removal of impediments to internal commerce was not extensive; and there was an admitted need for state aid to industry to keep France abreast of England. Moreover, during the eighteenth century, France had become involved in disastrous wars which injured her shipping, destroyed her chances for a large colonial empire, and retarded the development of her commerce. From the War of Spanish Succession through the Napoleonic struggles, she fought England in six wars, but only in two was she victorious, and then her triumphs were short lived. At the beginning of the reign of Louis XV, France's foreign commerce amounted to 215 millions of livres, of which 93 millions were imports and 122 millions exports, according to inexact, but relatively correct, statistics;[91] to 616 millions as an annual mean for the years 1749-1755; to 323 millions as the mean during the Seven Years' War; to 725 millions during the period 1764-1776; to 683 millions during the American War of Independence;

to 1061 millions in 1784; and to 1153 millions for 1787, of which 611 were imports and 542.5 exports. There was thus an expansion of French foreign commerce during the eighteenth century, which was less in actual goods than these figures show because of an increase of 63.7 per cent in prices from the period 1726-1741 to the period 1785-1789.[92] With the increase in the total amount of commerce, it should be noted that there was a decline in the proportion of exports to imports—a falling off of a favorable balance of trade. This may explain, at least in small part, why there was not an increase in wages in proportion to the increase in prices, why there was so much unemployment (one of the direct causes of the French Revolution),[93] and why the proletariat leaned toward principles of protectionism.[94]

Theorists, too, added their bit to the cause of economic statism, for, although Physiocrats may have dominated economic thought for a moment, it is a grave error to believe that their doctrines received unanimous approval in France. Étienne de Condillac (1715-1780) frowned upon the idea of an international division of labor, whereby each nation produces only those things for which it has a special aptitude and imports the rest, but advocated diversification within national limits and economic self sufficiency.[95] Arnould, director of the Bureau of the Balance of Commerce, was convinced of the importance of a favorable balance of commerce for the welfare of national economy,[96] and G. J. A. Ducher, who played a rôle in preparing the foreign commercial policy of the Revolution, was an ardent supporter of the theory that national power is based on production.[97] There was also the Abbé Galiani (1728-1787), secretary of the Neapolitan embassy at Paris, the most widely read of the opponents of Physiocratism during the *ancien régime*. In a brilliant style that put to shame the plodding expositions of the Physiocrats, he attacked the search for economic laws which might be applied to any country under any circumstances, and made a strong plea for a pragmatic approach to economic problems. The economic ideal for a nation is not to develop its agriculture at the expense of its industry, or *vice versa,* he said, but to build up simultaneously all branches of production in order that it may support a greater population.[98] "Galiani prepared the way for national economy: he maintained, refined, and purified the mercantilist point of view: his doctrine forms a link in the chain which stretches from Montchrétien to Frederick List."[99]

On the verge of the French Revolution, there was in France a reaction from free trade and a movement toward national economics. The Revolutionary and Napoleonic Periods, by endeavoring to establish a closed economic system, gave impetus to this movement. The years from 1789 to 1815 are a high-water mark in French national economics.[100]

From this rapid survey of state economic policies, it should be clear that the usual condensation of them to fit into the ordinary presentation of mercantilism is erroneous. Portugal sought wealth and prestige in Oriental trade; Spain strove for economic glory in hoarding the gold and silver of the Americas; the Dutch attained the heights on trade; England rose first on production, then on commerce, and finally on a combination of the two; and France, after attempting to ride both horses, got astride one and rode it for all it was worth. Government policies, too, varied according to time, place, and circumstances. The Portuguese maintained a close monopoly over their trade with India, but encouraged foreigners to come to Lisbon to get Oriental products for distribution in the north, thus combining monopoly with free trade; the Spaniards reserved for themselves the exploitation of their empire as long as they could; the Dutch adopted free trade to encourage shipping; the English, after employing a careful system of protection and shipping regulation, resorted to *laisser-faire* when there was no longer any danger of competition; and the French throughout their history pursued a policy of paternalism toward agriculture, commerce, and industry. It is unsatisfactory to devise a simple formula which will fit the economic practice and theory of all European nations from 1500 to 1800. *Fundamentally they sought to effect state-wide economic unification and to acquire economic strength.* Their approach to the problem and their means of solving it were empirical and varied. In so far as the measures which were taken facilitated business, these policies benefited particularly the wealthy classes. In desire for state power, in empirical methods, and in private or class interests of statesmen are to be found the keys to national economic history of this period and of more recent times as well.

CHAPTER II

THE REVOLUTION—ECONOMICS OF UNIFICATION AND DEFENSE

CHARACTER OF NEW FRENCH NATIONAL ECONOMICS

FRENCH national economics of the nineteenth and twentieth centuries is a direct descendant of the French state economics of the sixteenth, seventeenth, and eighteenth centuries—and its inherited characteristics are very marked. It has acquired from its parent the theory that the strong state must be a great producer, and the corollaries of that doctrine—protectionism, colonialism, and state aid to business. But these inherited characteristics have been conditioned by a changed environment—especially by a new kind of national patriotism, by the rise of the bourgeoisie and its acquisition of political power, and by the tremendous advances that have been made in economics.

In the earlier period, national sentiment was moderate in comparison with its present-day intensity. It usually took the form of personal allegiance to a national monarch, and was seldom, if ever, an overwhelming passion and an all-consuming love for everything of the nationality (for its language, literature, history, traditions, population, economic interests, and territory).[1] If mild expressions of such "modern" national feeling can be found before 1789, it will be discovered that they were limited to a few intellectuals (much as in some present-day minority movements)[2] and were never, as in the case of contemporary patriotism, the property of the masses. The intensifying of sentiment for the nationality and the instilling of that sentiment into the heart of every man, woman, and child have of necessity conditioned national economics—have made it more intolerant and more the concern of all citizens.

In the earlier period, also, economic policy was determined usually by kings and their advisers from the landed nobility. Although at times the monarchs allied themselves with the bourgeoisie against the nobles, as did the Tudors in England and Louis XIV in France, and royal economic edicts were issued for the benefit of commercial and industrial interests, the large property owners were most frequently favored. It took a long time to unseat the landed aristocracy from its high social and political position, but the bourgeoisie, raised to a new position of importance by its increasing economic strength, fought for, and finally obtained, control of the state. The governing bourgeoisie in France expanded gradually to include all wealthy persons —those who had their fortunes in agriculture as well as those whose capital was in commerce or industry. As this wealthy class represented a broader stratum of economic interests than did the ruling nobility of the *ancien régime*,[3] national economic legislation of recent times has had a tendency to be broader and more inclusive than that of the period before the French Revolution.

Finally, the contemporary brand of national economics in France has had to adapt itself to an environment of increasing industrialism, of closer international commercial ties, of ever more complicated and intricate economic processes, and of an increasing division of labor and a specialization of production. It has therefore become more detailed and more flexible, and has invented ways of realizing its aims which had never been dreamed of before the industrial revolution. Thus French national economics has evolved under the influence of intensified national sentiment, capitalist control of politics, and of greatly increased industrialization. While its species may be ascertained by studying its predecessors, as was attempted in the preceding chapter, the real nature of the beast can be known only by a case study—a study which is the object of the succeeding chapters.

CLASS ALIGNMENT FOR REVOLUTION

Two of the fundamental factors in the new environment to which national economics had to become acclimated—intense national patriotism and great political influence of the middle class—mark their rise from the French Revolution. It is with the Revolution and, more specifically, with a consideration of the issues that resulted in the outbreak of trouble in 1789, that our story properly begins.

Complicated as are the issues that preceded the French Revolution, more recent historians of the closing years of the *ancien régime* are generally of the opinion that there was a real struggle between the privileged classes (the clergy and the nobility),[4] on the one hand, and the bourgeoisie, on the other, for control of the government. The outcome of the struggle of these two groups was of the greatest import for the development of national economic theories and practices. The privileged classes, who had a quasi-monopoly of the government and who administered public affairs in their own interests, were not especially concerned with the economic welfare of society or in the economic strength of the nation. Their own incomes, with which they were largely concerned, depended almost exclusively on the immediate production of their estates; other economic matters gave them little worry. The bourgeoisie,[5] however, was vitally interested in general prosperity, and in the development of the state as an economic unit, for only under favorable conditions would its goods be consumed, and only the state could keep out foreign competitors or aid in extending French affairs abroad. It was clear that if bourgeois got political power, they would use their position to stimulate economic activity in France. The coming to power of the middle class meant a new era in the economic policies of the state.

The crusade of the bourgeoisie for a voice in government was supported (singularly enough to those who have grown up in the environment of twentieth-century class struggle) by the rural and urban proletariats. The former of these groups was numerically the most important class in France, and the latter, although a small minority, was in large part strategically located at Paris where it could bring direct pressure to bear upon the government. Each of these classes was discontented with the existing state of things. Agriculturalists rejoiced that serfdom, as regards personal freedom, had been practically abolished, but were resentful because they were still obliged to fulfill many feudal obligations and to pay heavy taxes.[6] And those artisans who had once had their work protected by gilds but had now become day laborers working for a wage, joined the unskilled workers in lamenting long hours and low wages. Just was their complaint, for between the periods 1726-1741 and 1785-1789 the salaried proletariat had suffered a 25 per cent reduction in real wages.[7] Under the circumstances, both peasants and urban workers criticized the government and hoped to benefit from the revolutionary events. During the Revolution they rendered the middle class indispensable support. In return for their aid, they persuaded the bourgeoisie at times to give state economic measures a democratic turn.

The press of inequality and injustice, from which French society of the *ancien régime* suffered, came to a head during the economic depression of 1787–1789 (one of the worst of several crises in the eighteenth century).[8] So directly did it influence events that leading historians of the period have ventured to suggest that, had it not taken place, the Revolution might have been postponed indefinitely.[9] But be that as it may, it is certain that the depression, by its severity, increased the misfortunes of the non-privileged classes and, by its scope, affected every one. It was felt almost simultaneously by those engaged in agriculture and those in industry and commerce. In 1788, spring frosts, an early summer drought, and heavy rains at the time of ripening injured the crops. In some localities, the yield was only one-half of normal and, although prices on grain were greatly increased, the farmers lost heavily. At about the same time, a multitude of unfortunate events was befalling industry. Decline in the purchasing power of farmers and of city workers, who were obliged now because of dear bread to put more money into food, impaired the domestic market;[10] the silk industry was suffering from a series of bad worm years;[11] Spain put up a tariff against French goods;[12] money was hoarded, thus reducing purchases; and English competition, that had been a mere threat after the signing of the Eden Treaty, had become a real menace upon the application of the treaty's provisions, May 10, 1787.

Sedan, which in normal times worked 1000 looms and employed 15,000 workers (three-fifths of the population of the city), had 9000 unemployed in January, 1787, and was forced in April to ask the government for aid in relieving suffering.[13] Troyes' 3000 looms were reduced to 1157 at the end of 1787; and Bourges and Amiens witnessed, from 1785 to 1788, a 50 per cent reduction in the looms employed within their walls. By the end of 1788, every textile and hardware district in the country had been affected; there were some 200,000 unemployed, numerous bankruptcies, and pleas on every hand for governmental relief. By arousing the discontent of the bourgeoisie and the anger of both city and agrarian workers, the depression brought these groups together. Consequently "it was the entire Third Estate that rose to demand the abolition of the privileges enjoyed by the aristocracy, the admission of all men to all positions, and, in the rural sections, the destruction [of the remnants] of the manorial system. . . . The non-privileged classes . . . realized that they had the same demands to make . . . and the same abuses to combat. That is the reason why the lower classes, forming a bloc against the upper classes, came to feel that they truly represented the nation."[14]

Although the business depression united the bourgeoisie and proletariat and forged their temper for a war on privilege, it was the crisis in the state's finances that provided the occasion for governmental reforms and, ultimately, for the triumph of the middle class. The origins of French financial difficulties reached back into the reign of Louis XV, whose expenditures were so large that allegedly he prophesied, *"Après moi, le déluge"*—meaning, in part, perhaps, a flood of debts—and whose extravagance failed to provoke an immediate catastrophe only because of the strict economy of his minister, the stern Abbé Terray.[15] The flood of debts went on, too, during the reign of Louis XVI, whose treasury was a veritable sieve in normal times and, in such periods as the War of American Independence, a funnel.[16] In 1789 the public debt, having tripled in the previous fifteen years, had mounted to 4,500,000,000 livres, and the interest on it had risen from 93 millions at the death of Louis XV to 300 millions in 1789, which was three-fifths of the total national budget.[17]

Against the rising tide, the ministers of finance[18] were as powerless as King Canute against the sea; it would, in truth, have taken a wizard with a Midas-like gift to have stemmed the waters. More debts kept rolling in; the limit of the power to tax the Third Estate was reached; and the court and the *Parlements* were at swords' points over legal matters of taxation. Under the circumstances, the only possible dike against impending disaster seemed to be a tax upon the nobility and the clergy. But when an Assembly of Notables was called to discuss the possibility of such a radical departure from *ancien-régime* routine, the nobles, with cryptic criticism of the court, rose as one man to deny the King the luxury of taxing them. The court was sorely troubled and played its last card; it called, as is frequent in cases of financial crises in despotisms, a meeting of representatives of the state[19] to see what they would do to save their nation. The King's party believed that this action would automatically place the financial problems upon the shoulders of the people, and that it would demolish the spontaneous alliance of bourgeois and noble against the court. It did, in truth, immediately accomplish these *desiderata,* but it led to what was entirely unexpected—to the overthrow of the monarchy, to the rule of the bourgeoisie, and to the establishment of a state economic policy in the interests of the nation and of the middle class.

PREREVOLUTIONARY NATIONAL ECONOMIC DEMANDS

Before the Estates General actually met, abuses and grievances were discussed and programs of reform were formulated. On the condemnation of absolutism and despotism (but not of monarchy), there was general agreement; but on measures to be taken for the improvement of economic conditions there was great difference of opinion. The nobility wanted the state to follow the economic doctrines of the Physiocrats; the peasants wanted the abolition of seigniorial dues; the rich artisans wanted their gilds strengthened; wage workers wanted the right to organize and to bargain collectively; and the bourgeois wanted the state to support their interests. Of all these demands, only those of the middle class were placed on national rather than on social grounds. To strengthen the state economically, but also to feather their own nests, the bourgeoisie suggested (1) that France be made an economic unit; (2) that all impediments to commerce within the country be abolished; (3) that French industry be allowed to develop freely by the application of a governmental "hands-off" policy; (4) that the state give subsidies to needy businesses; and (5) that foreign industrial and commercial competition be curbed by protective tariffs and navigation acts.

The details of these economic proposals of the bourgeoisie were presented in various ways, but perhaps most clearly and completely

in the *cahiers,* those memorials of grievances and of platforms which
were drawn up prior to the meeting of the Estates General. From the
mass of evidence contained in these documents, the primary concern
of the members of the middle class seems to have been the elimination of impediments to trade within France. They suggested that the
physical difficulty of transportation be minimized by the construction
of new roads and canals,[20] arguing that thereby commerce should be
better served, and that the averting of such national calamities as the
recent famine would be made possible by the ability to transport large
quantities of grain from regions of plenty to regions of want.[21]
They also proposed that all man-made hindrances to domestic commerce, such as tolls[22] and octrois,[23] be abolished, and that difficulties
arising from local usage in such matters as law and weights and
measures be overcome by the adoption of national systems.[24] Most
significant of all from a national point of view, they demanded that all
internal customs barriers be done away with, and that all provinces—
the *Cinq Grosses Fermes,* the *Provinces Réputées Étrangères,* the
Provinces d'Étranger Effectif, and the Free Ports—be joined in a customs union.

For these projects most regions voiced their hearty approval. Only
concerning the customs union was there any dissident opinion, and
it came from the *Provinces d'Étranger Effectif,* whose customary commerce with foreign nations would be impaired by the moving of the
customs barriers to the political boundaries of the nation. Lorraine,
especially, which was an entrepôt for trade in the Germanies and
whose industry was oriented toward the north, opposed such a reform.[25] But opposition was not general and reflects, perhaps, a local
rather than a national sentiment on the part of the Lorrainers. Franche
Comté, a *Province d'Étranger Effectif* which might have suffered from
the change because of trade with Switzerland, although it had been
forced to adopt some of the customs duties of the *Cinq Grosses Fermes,*
regarded the reform as the "fundamental basis of national prosperity."[26]
The majority of the provinces agreed that internal customs form a
"ridiculous line which seems to divide France into two hostile camps.
Because of them the different parts of a single nation seem to be
rather in a state of permanent warfare than to be governed by one

king and one law."[27] For the nation the *cahiers* demanded commercial, as well as political, unity. They preached the doctrine of "one God, one king, one law, and one system of weights and measures!"[28]

The commercial unification of France was to be accompanied by the creation of a new tariff that would protect national industries, insure work for labor, and guarantee a favorable balance of trade. The first step in the realization of this characteristically national economic reform was to be the denunciation of the Eden Treaty. Ever since the publication of this document, criticism of it had been particularly severe. The Chamber of Commerce of Rouen[29] had thrown up its hands in despair when it contemplated the terms on which Norman cotton manufacturers would be forced to compete with those of Manchester. An anonymous tract of 1788 had prophesied the immediate ruin of the hardware trade of St. Etienne because of English competition. The Bureau of Commerce, a governmental commercial and industrial agency, placed the blame for the industrial depression upon the treaty,[30] although, as we have already seen, the crisis began before it went into effect.[31] Even the Physiocrats admitted that the treaty was a severe shock to French industry, although Dupont de Nemours maintained with shameless optimism that it would teach the French to keep abreast of the times in machine production.[32]

Then the *cahiers* of the Third Estate came to add fuel to the fire that roasted this commercial agreement with England. "We see with sorrow," said one of them, "that the English are exporting to France all kinds of goods and are carrying home the money of the kingdom. This has diminished French production . . ., which has caused, in turn, the ruin of several business men. . . ."[33] "The treaty is," claimed another, putting forward the case of labor as well as that of capital, "very detrimental to business men and to the common people of the kingdom, and notably to those of Picardy and of Artois. . . . It has resulted in England's buying great quantities of raw materials in France and in working them up in England to the great detriment of manufacturers of this country and also of an infinite number of laborers who earn their livelihood by working for industrialists and who are now without employment, on the streets, and reduced to the lowest misery."[34] Even the name of the minister who proposed the treaty, charged a third, "ought to be blotted forever from the memory of men. His sinister projects have ruined part of France; he has cut the throat of the nation; and he has fooled his king. . . . Before this event, [France had] a thrifty population and plenty of work . . . today what a horrible change! No more commerce, no more work, no more bread."[35]

In the popular mind, at least, the Eden Treaty had brought only misfortune to France: protectionism, it was thought, was necessary for national well-being.[36] The *cahiers* definitely stated that every new tariff should aim to increase the productive power of the state. The same energy should be employed to prevent foreign nations from selling their goods as would be employed to prevent them from breaking the arms of French workmen.[37] No tariff, moreover, should be made without consulting the business interests of the nation as represented in chambers of commerce. Many districts listed in their memorials their particular products as unquestionably requiring the protection of a high tariff.[38]

In addition to customs protection, the *cahiers* demanded that everything possible be done to rejuvenate the economic life of the nation—to keep manufacturing establishments and commerce going and growing. They requested that the practice of granting subsidies to industries be continued and that the tax burden on manufactures be reduced.[39] They demanded that labor organizations, which cause strikes and raise wages, be legislated against.[40] And they suggested that people be encouraged to "Buy French"—the example to be set by the king and his court.[41] If these measures were taken, the domestic market would be completely captured by French goods and productive enterprises would become powerful enough to enter foreign markets with their wares. Therefore, it was stated, efforts should be made to increase the merchant marine in order to provide French bottoms for the new trade. To this end a navigation act, similar to the one that Cromwell had decreed in 1651, should be adopted. It should reserve all French commerce to French vessels; it should relieve French shippers from paying port dues; and it should prohibit foreign-built ships from sailing under the French flag.[42] Finally, trade with the colonies, which had been partially opened to foreigners in 1784,[43] should be given exclusively to French merchants.[44] The dream of French bourgeois for an economic paradise envisioned a nation economically self-sufficient, free from foreign competition, and great because of its economic power.[45]

ECONOMIC REFORMS—ECONOMIC UNIFICATION

That the economic demands of the middle class would have a chance of being realized was evident early in the course of revolutionary events.[46] To the Estates General, the Third Estate was allowed to send as many representatives as the other two estates combined. Its delegation was composed almost exclusively of members of the middle class —lawyers, publicists, professional men, merchants, and industrialists— and there were no peasants in its ranks.[47] At first, to be sure, there was grave danger that the voting in the Estates would be by class rather than by head, and that the bourgeoisie would thus be in an eternal minority. The final decision to vote by head not only placed the Third Estate on a numerical par with the nobility and clergy, but actually gave it an advantage over the other two classes, for to its ranks came some of those aristocrats whose minds had been turned by the enlightenment of the eighteenth century, and several of the lower clergy who had at heart the interests of the lower classes.

There was also the danger that the King would repent of having called the Estates General and would suppress it altogether. But, when it seemed that he was about to do this, the people of Paris, by a display of force, defended the Estates. Henceforth the bourgeoisie knew that it had a powerful ally on whom it could depend when the Revolution was in danger. Thus protected, the middle class controlled the Estates General and was responsible for the transformation of that body into a constitutional convention, the Constituent Assembly, which ruled France from 1789 to September 30, 1791. It placed its mark, moreover, on the famous Declaration of the Rights of Man, which held that "private property is an inviolable and sacred right," and upon the constitution under which France was governed from October 1, 1791, to September 20, 1792, a document that provided for a bourgeois Legislative Assembly in a limited monarchy.[48] Finally, it took upon itself the task of putting into effect the economic program which had been presented in the *cahiers*.

The most pressing economic problems which were inherited from the *ancien régime* were the peasant question[49] and the bankruptcy of the state. The former matter the middle class, many of whom were themselves landholders, would gladly have pushed into the background, but the peasant uprisings and the destruction of property brought it to the fore.[50] Forced to act, the government endeavored to temporize. Although it abolished feudalism[51] in 1789, it made the removal of the most burdensome dues subject to the payment of large indemnities. Consequently peasant revolts were numerous, and it was not until 1793, when all seigniorial dues were suppressed without remuneration, that large numbers of peasants were finally won to the support of the nation in revolt.[52]

Financial difficulties, too, the bourgeois government would gladly have evaded if evasion had been possible, but this problem, like that of peasant reform, was one that could not be dodged. Since it was absolutely necessary to deal with the problem of public finance, the middle class accepted the inevitable with philosophical resolve. Acting upon the suggestion of Abbé Talleyrand, that greatest of all political chamelions, it confiscated church lands. With this property, enhanced by sequestered holdings of *émigrés*,[53] as security, it issued paper money (the *assignats*). So successfully did these measures provide temporary relief that the government abused the use of the printing press, as is often the case when expenditures continually exceed receipts. *Assignats* were issued in great quantities. Soon they began to lose value; in 1795 they were worth but 5 per cent of par, and in 1797 were repudiated as worthless. Inflation, however, had bridged the swamp of bankruptcy and had dried up the financial morass of the public debt. Although many members of the middle class lost heavily, they came out of the experience comparatively well.[54]

Having thus dealt with peasant reform and inflation, the bourgeois government devoted itself to the economic reforms that it wanted. In agreement with the demand of the *cahiers* for the abolition of state impediments to business, regulation and inspection of industrial products were done away with;[55] privileged companies, such as royal manufactories, were deprived of their grants; and all forms of workingmen's associations, including the gilds,[56] were suppressed.[57] In order to unify France economically, the collection of provincial customs duties was ended and tariff boundaries were moved to the foreign borders of the country;[58] seigniorial tolls were abolished;[59] a commission was appointed to propose plans for a unified system of weights and measures;[60] laws forbidding the free circulation of all goods were annulled;[61] and roads, which suffered from the suppression of the corvée, were repaired with money diverted from funds for charity and for the relief of unemployment.[62] Finally, to curb foreign competition with French goods on the domestic market and in the colonies, a new protective tariff was adopted (1791); trade with the colonies was forbidden to foreign nations; duties on colonial goods coming to France were reduced;[63] export taxes on French goods destined for colonial consumption were abolished;[64] and later, under the Convention, all customs duties between the motherland and her oversea foundlings were suppressed.[65]

While the national implications of all these measures are obvious, the passage of the tariff law provides an insight into the workings and motives of the bourgeoisie. Long before the Revolution, plans had been made for higher protective customs rates,[66] but these had been rejected by the aristocratic Assembly of Notables in 1787. Not content to let the tariff situation remain as it was, the bourgeois of the Constituent Assembly appointed a committee of three business men to draw up a bill for greater protection. In presenting his proposition for reform to the Assembly, the chairman of this "tariff commission," a silk manufacturer of Lyons, voiced the état d'esprit of his class.

"Your Committee," he said, "admires the theory of free trade, but we have not thought it wise to adhere to it exclusively. To do so would be to effect the destruction of our industry. I come to ask freedom of you. Freedom is the motto of commerce and of industry, but freedom is incomplete without protection and safety. . . . I ask you to grant a higher freedom to business—the freedom to exist. The protection and safety that you owe industry cannot be had in our present European system without a combination of import and export duties. These will draw to France everything to aid national industry, and will increase exportation to the highest possible degree."

There were, however, in the Constituent a few Physiocrats to whom such doctrine was an anathema. They managed to have the tariff bill referred to a committee composed of the tariff commission and the committee on taxes. The chairman of this latter body was the ever-present free trader, Dupont de Nemours. Although this boded ill for the future of protection, the committees, after consultation with commercial and industrial groups, presented a revised bill that provided for customs rates only slightly inferior to those of the original version.[67] Goods were divided into eleven categories, ranging from raw materials to finished products. Duties were graduated, running, for imports, from free entry to the payment of a 15 per cent tax *ad valorem,* or to absolute prohibition; and, for exports, down the scale from prohibition to leave the country for certain raw products to free exit for manufactured articles. This scheme, that fitted well into the bourgeois theory of national production and with their own interests, was accepted by the Assembly and became the Tariff of 1791.[68] While not all that the bourgeoisie wanted, this tariff was a break from the "international division of labor" theory that had conditioned the signing of the Eden Treaty, and was an indication of the direction in which the tariff policy of France was to go.

WAR AND THE INTENSIFICATION OF NATIONAL ECONOMICS

From the beginning of the Revolution national policies were energetically pursued, but they did not attain their height until the Revolution had become endangered by foreign wars, the King had been overthrown, the bourgeoisie had been firmly established in power, and a spirit of intense national feeling had seized the masses. The succession of events that led to these developments began when the King was brought into patriotic disrepute by conniving with foreign powers to deliver him from the revolutionaries and, after the declaration of war on Austria, April 25, 1792, by his refusal to take measures for the vigorous prosecution of the conflict. In the moment of crisis, the radical bourgeoisie, which wanted to abolish the monarchy, secured the support of the proletariat, which was suffering from the high cost of living. It was only a matter of time before they struck at the King and took the government into their own hands. During the Festival of the Federation, July 14, 1792, they held themselves in check with difficulty, but after the Manifesto of the Duke of Brunswick, who threatened Paris with pillage if Prussia and Austria were prevented from delivering the King and Queen, they could restrain themselves no longer. They suspended the King by the Revolution of August 10, 1792; they overthrew the Legislative Assembly; and they proceeded, by universal suffrage, to the election of a constitutional Convention which met for the first time on September 21, 1792 —the new year's day of the Year I of the First Republic. In this assembly, a group of radical bourgeois, the Mountain, gained control and, what was more, remained in power, supported by the people of Paris, so long as *la patrie* was in peril.

The patriotism of these Jacobins was not based upon allegiance to a king, as had been the patriotism of the *ancien régime,* for the King was no more. It was founded upon the democratic principle that the people are the nation, and that all citizens should contribute to its well-being. At first, too, their patriotism had a cosmopolitan complexion and the revolutionaries earnestly believed that the oppressed people of other nations would join them in a general war on tyrants. On this last score, they were to be sadly disappointed. Not only did the Austrian masses remain loyal to their commanders in the war on France, but so did other peoples—the English, the Hanoverians, the Prussians, the Sardinians, the Spanish, the Neapolitans, and the Dutch —as one state after another joined the First Coalition against France. Thus the revolutionary war—beginning partly as a class struggle, in that it was fought by aristocracies for the suppression of revolution in France; partly as a political war, in that it aimed to make France respect international treaties; and partly as an economic war, in that England wanted to maintain the balance of power on the Continent and to assure herself of the supremacy of the seas—became the bitterest of national struggles. The French Jacobins forgot their cosmopolitan mission when their own Revolution was endangered by foreign oppression.[69] In the moment of greatest peril, they declared *la patrie en danger, la patrie* of liberty, equality, and fraternity, and bent all their efforts to save it. It was to this end that they placed dictatorial powers in the hands of the Committee of Public Safety; that they weeded out traitors and rebels by means of the terror; that they de-

declared a *levée en masse* of all able-bodied single men between the ages of eighteen and twenty-five; that they whipped up to a frenzy national sentiment by means of ceremonies, societies, public meetings, and the press; and that they capped all with a more vigorous economic policy than had been witnessed hitherto—a policy that was highly *national*.

At first the economic platform of the Convention and of the Committee of Public Safety had but two main planks: (1) the continuation and development of the protectionist program of the Constituent and of the Legislative Assemblies, and (2) the harnessing of the economic resources of the nation for war. As part of the former policy, the Convention, after the declaration of war on Great Britain (February 1, 1793), annulled the Eden Treaty.[70] A few months later[71] it prohibited *in toto* the importation of a large number of English specialties, such as textiles, metals, and earthenware, and required evidence that imports did not come from an enemy country.

"But these laws were a mild warning in comparison with the outbreak of fury, harmonizing completely with the spirit of the Reign of Terror, which appeared in the form of a statute of October 9, 1793, bearing the title: *Loi qui proscrit du sol de la république toutes les marchandises fabriquées ou manufacturées dans les pays soumis au gouvernement britannique.*" Every owner of British goods in France was obliged to declare and to surrender them to public authorities; any customs official found guilty of laxity in enforcing the law, or any person trafficking in these goods was liable to twenty years in irons; anybody who wore or used British goods fell under the "laws of suspects"; and any advertisement of British articles was to be suppressed and the person guilty of such offence imprisoned for twenty years. With this measure, there seems to have been added to the general desire for protection the belief that, because of her extensive commercial activities, especial injury could be done to Britain by the prohibition of her goods. This was the beginning of an economic warfare *à outrance* which was to continue well into the Napoleonic era and to prove a test of the economic strength of France and of Britain—a test in which England had the advantage because of her superior staples industry and her control of the seas.

In addition to these regulations against British goods, the Convention took equally harsh measures against British shipping. For some time the adoption of a French navigation act had been under consideration. Upon the renewal of hostilities with Britain, the idea was brought by brilliant publicists forcefully to the attention of statesmen.[72] The need for such an act from a national point of view was great, for of the 16,225 ships that did French carrying, only 3763 were French-owned. Two-fifths of French sea commerce was carried in British ships; two-fifths in the ships of other states; and but one-fifth in national bottoms.[73] The efficacy of a navigation act was certain, it was pointed out, for in England at the time of Cromwell's famous measure, one-half of English shipping was in the hands of the Dutch, while now (1791) only one-fourteenth fell to foreign powers. The political wisdom of such an act could not be questioned either, for, whereas previously an act of navigation would possibly have let loose the dogs of war and would, therefore, have been injudicious, now the "dogs" were barking at French heels. In fact, everything was to be gained and nothing to be lost by confining French carrying to French ships. Thus it was decreed on September 21, 1793, that all shipping should be done in French bottoms, exception being made in the case of vessels importing to France the products of their own countries;[74] but even under these conditions foreign vessels were subject to a surtax per ton—*droit de tonnage*.[75] This measure, it was believed, was double-edged. By reserving all carrying to herself, France would, on the one hand, build up a thriving merchant marine, create shipbuilding yards, stimulate the consumption of domestic products, multiply her industries, increase her profits, and augment her population, and, on the other, destroy British prosperity. As Barère, the great tribune, stated before the Convention, "Let us decree a solemn navigation act and the isle of shopkeepers will be ruined." "Carthage will thereby be destroyed."

"Carthage," however, was not to succumb without a struggle. Rising to the challenge, Pitt retaliated with equally vigorous measures. He hastened destruction of French credit by printing counterfeit *assignats* and putting them into circulation. He struck at France's shipping by ordering her coasts blockaded. He declared not only arms and ammunition contraband of war, but also grain.[76] He encouraged members of the Coalition to stop exporting goods to France. For a short time in the summer of 1793, he ordered fleet commanders and privateers to search ships bound for France, and authorized, for a few months in the winter of 1793–94, the seizure of neutral vessels carrying French colonial products.[77] Unlike a modern blockade, however, these measures aimed neither to starve France into submission[78] nor to deprive her of imports, other than war materials. The embargo was placed on grain simply because England needed foodstuffs for her own famine-stricken people; other measures were taken to secure more business for British shipping and industry at the expense of her allies and of neutrals.[79] England, in fact, was the first to supply the wants of her enemy. In spite of the French Tariff and Navigation Act and her own blockade, her trade with France and the Netherlands declined only from fifteen per cent to twelve per cent[80] of her total trade. Although England seemed, from the first, capable of withstanding French sallies against her commerce, the idea of destroying the "isle of shopkeepers" by hitting at its trade lived on in France and became the very essence of the Continental System—the economic phase of the struggle to the death between Napoleon and Great Britain.

HARNESSING THE NATION'S RESOURCES FOR WAR

The French Navigation Act and Tariff Laws were adopted in the interests of the bourgeoisie as well as in the interests of the nation. Fortunately for the Revolution, however, the economic program of the state was not completed with them, but included another kind of activity—the harnessing of the nation's resources for war. In the face of the threatened invasion of Coalition armies the French banded together in a co-operative endeavor to save *la patrie* as they could never have done in peace times.[81] The Convention, which, in a normal period, would have favored a policy of *laisser-faire* as regards domestic economy, was forced by the danger to the nation to go far along the road of state control and to interfere in business. The *levée en masse* in drafting men to fight in the army furnished a logical basis for the conscription of men, women, and children to do war work and for the requisitioning of everything necessary to the economic life of the nation. Popular enthusiasm for the conflict made possible the application of the logic. As Barère exclaimed:

"Liberty has become the creditor of all citizens. Some owe her their industry, others their fortune; some their advice, others their arms; all owe her their blood. Thus, all French people of both sexes and of all ages are called upon by *la Patrie* to defend liberty. All moral and physical faculties, all political and industrial talents belong to *la Patrie;* all metals and elements are hers. Let every one take his post in the national and military movement that is in preparation. The young men will fight; the married men will forge arms, transport baggage and artillery, and provide subsistence; the women will work at the soldiers' clothing, make tents, and become nurses in the hospitals for the wounded; the children will make lint out of old linen; and the old men, again performing the mission that they had among the ancients, will be carried to the public squares, there to inflame the courage of the young warriors and propagate the hatred of kings and the idea of the unity of the republic. The houses of the nation shall be turned into barracks, the public squares into workshops, the cellars into factories of gunpowder; all saddle horses will be requisitioned for the cavalry, all carriage horses for the artillery."[82]

As Barère urged, so the Convention ordered. On August 23, 1793, it decreed that single men should go to war and married men should make arms and carry supplies; that public buildings should be turned into barracks and public squares into manufactories of arms; and that all guns, except hunting pieces, be sequestered for use in the army. Moreover, upon the shoulders of the Committee of Public Safety it placed the colossal task of organizing and administering the economic life of the nation.[83]

The most pressing need, at first, was for arms and ammunition, since the *levée en masse* had provided an army larger than France had ever known, the supplies in the arsenals were insufficient to equip the men. To be sure, the revolutionary soldiers were ready to rush the enemy with pikes and pitchforks, but these weapons, even in the hands of the bravest, were no match for rifles, as experience proved. To meet the shortage of arms, the Committee of Public Safety stimulated production in the seven munition plants of the provinces and set up new rifle factories in such public places at Paris as the Invalides and the Jardin du Luxembourg.[84] These establishments furnished for the Parisians an example of febrile activity to save the nation and developed a greater monthly production than all the old munition factories combined.[85] The Committee of Public Safety founded, moreover, shops for the manufacture of swords and bayonets, and forced cutlery workers to turn their hands to the manufacture of these articles. It established seventeen new foundries for the manufacture of bronze cannon for land artillery, which supplemented the production of the older foundries at Douai and Strasburg by about 14,500 cannons a year. It put new life into the private manufacturing of cast-iron cannon for the navy, increasing the production from 900 to 13,000 per year.[86] It drafted labor, trained unskilled workers, and looked to the provision of raw materials.

To secure iron and steel, the Committee ordered the seizure in each town of iron from confiscated property and the amassing of all other iron which could be obtained by requisition or request.[87] It took analogous measures in order to secure copper, tin, bronze, steel, and lead. Bells of town halls were taken down; metal fences around lordly estates were razed; iron ornaments on public and private edifices were confiscated; and decorations of churches were made to yield their quota—those of the Cathedral at Rheims alone were reported to have produced 150 tons of iron. Agents were sent from Paris to all the metallurgical centers to urge on manufacturers and workers. The Government printed handbooks for the popularization of the latest methods for producing steel; it commissioned agents to find new sources of coal; it advanced money to plants and paid high prices for finished products; it sent into the factories German and English prisoners who were metal workers; and it secured special rations of food for laborers, that they might not succumb to the fatigue of their industry or yield to the discouragement of their conditions.

Thus the Committee of Public Safety attempted to meet the economic emergency of war, to produce those things which France had the "unhappy habit of receiving from her neighbors," and to augment her economic self-sufficiency. And what was perhaps of greatest moment, it called, in democratic fashion, every active person in France to serve the national cause. By making them work, it brought home to the people the fact that they were the nation.

The economic activity of war that reached deepest into the hearts of the masses and spread to all the extremities of the state was the production of saltpetre. Cut off by the blockade from the ordinary supply from India and America, France was thrown upon her own resources. In the emergency, an order was given for each individual to wash his cellar, stable, and any other place where saltpetre might collect, and for each town to provide kettles and fire to boil down the liquor, that the precious deposit might be obtained. The campaign was launched with a vigorous appeal to nationalist sentiments.

"To arms, citizens! To arms! Immediately forges, shops rose everywhere. Under the régime of Liberty everything lives, everything grows. The cutlery worker makes swords; the clock-maker, machines of war; guns are born by the thousand; the soil of liberty is transformed into tyrant-killing metals; earth changes into iron, iron into steel, and steel into swords. All bronze becomes cannons—and church bells, tired of vainly pleading for justice, themselves kill off brigands and tyrants. . . . But it is not enough to have cannons: one must also have the charge. Nature has deposited it in saltpetre: it is the soul of guns and of cannons. . . . Each individual must say to himself, 'The salvation of the human race is perhaps in the last pound of saltpetre that remains in my house.' "[88]

Thus the people went at the laborious task of soaking the earth of their cellars and stables in water, and of evaporating the water to get the deposit that was to carry destruction to the enemies of liberty and of France. Refineries were set up in large buildings and the stolid Abbey of St.-Germain-des-Prés, which had become a Temple of Reason, was employed, like many other churches, for this purpose. On the doors of those houses in which the people performed the assigned labor was tacked a notice, which read: "To kill tyrants the citizens living in this house have furnished their quota of saltpetre"—just as Americans pasted in their windows during the World War signs indicating that they had subscribed to Liberty Loans, or had sent a son to war. Various sections of Paris presented the first of their saltpetre production to the

Convention in a solemn ceremony, which was described by a contemporary as follows:

"Drums announced a military procession. Artillerymen came first; armed citizens followed them. With their flags they marched in order to the accompaniment of martial music. In the middle of the procession, citizens came forward, carrying great containers filled with saltpetre. . . ."[89]

And after the offering had been blessed, there might perchance have been chanted this hymn to saltpetre:

> "Descendons dans nos souterrains,
>   La Liberté nous y convie;
>   Elle parle, Républicains,
>   Et c'est la voix de la Patrie (bis).
>
> Lavez la terre en un tonneau
> En faisant évaporer l'eau
> Bientôt le nitre va paraître,
> Pour visiter Pitt en bateau,
> Il ne nous faut que du salpêtre (bis)."[90]

The Revolutionary Government left no stone unturned in its efforts to increase the fighting strength of the country. As well as forcing the masses to labor on war work, it drafted the services and resources of scientists and, to some extent, those of capitalists. Among the contributions of the former may be numbered new kinds of shells, with which experiments were made in a laboratory at Meudon, where Berthollet was counted among the specialists; a semaphore telegraph system, which was perfected by Chappe and which was installed between Paris and the front; captive observation balloons which were developed and used in battle; and a new method of making gunpowder which reduced the time required for its preparation. Of capitalists, the Committee required the production of specified articles and the surrender of goods that were subjected to requisition; it cut the profits of some entrepreneurs by fixing prices and increasing taxation; and it virtually established a national monopoly of foreign commerce.[91]

"All France presents today," wrote a representative of the Convention on a mission to the provinces, "the aspect of a great factory, where each one works for the Republic. On the frontiers, it looks like a great fortress, bristling with arms and covered with the children of Liberty, who burn with the desire to become heroes. All the hands, all the knowledge, all the talents, all the useful resources [of France] have been requisitioned for *la Patrie.* . . ."[92]

THE CONVENTION'S SOCIAL PROGRAM

On account of bad times, the Government was forced to go a step farther in its economic policy—to undertake a social program. In industry the depression was largely a continuation of the crisis of 1788, aggravated by events of the Revolution. The luxury trades were practically ruined because of the emigration of nobles, the impoverishment of churchmen, and the suppression of the court; and the manufacture of colonial products, such as sugar, was curbed because of the inability of French ships to bring raw materials through the English blockade. In agriculture, insufficient crops in 1791 caused much suffering and led to bread riots. The following year the filling of empty storage bins, large orders for the army, and the holding of grain for speculation, resulted in continued high prices. The conditions of city workers were pitiful, and were made worse by the continuous fall of *assignats.*[93] Prices rose steadily, and wages failed to keep pace with them, as is always the case in periods of inflation. In some places during the winter of 1792–93, urban laborers were paid, for a day's work, only enough to buy one pound of black bread. Since labor unrest was rampant, the bourgeois members of the Mountain realized that they had to come to the rescue of the masses who supported them. On September 29, 1793, they voted a law, "the general maximum," which fixed wages and prices for staple goods. By thus putting a legal curb on what was closest to the hearts of most members of the middle class—the liberty to make all the money they could—they brought on their heads the wrath of the more conservative members of that class.

Once embarked on the road of governmental paternalism and pushed on by the masses, the Mountain found it difficult to turn aside or to arrest its course. Forced to go on, it provided immediate food relief by requisitions at home and purchases abroad; it endeavored to increase agricultural production by draining marshes and clearing waste land; and it ordered the turning of Parisian flower gardens, like the Tuileries, into vegetable plots. Finally, in Ventôse, 1794, at a time when there were some 300,000 suspects, it went further than the bourgeoisie could allow—it voted laws aiming to divide among the poor the property of the "enemies of the Republic."

As the value of this prize was too great to be permitted to slip through the fingers of the members of the middle class, they began a devastating attack on the régime of the Mountain, now led by Robespierre. Their cause was aided, happily for them, by a combination of events that placed the Government in an almost inescapable predicament. In the first place, victories of French arms had freed the Republic from the danger of immediate invasion and had thus removed the *raison d'être* for such severe measures as the Terror and the forcing of people to perform war work. Moreover, there was growing disapproval of the Government because of its seemingly dictatorial policies and its excesses in employing terrorist methods. Labor, too, was made discontent by continued suffering and the way in which the "law of the maximum" was enforced. It complained, and with justice, that wages were kept down to the legal limit, but that prices were allowed to soar high above those stipulated by the Government.[94]

Before all this opposition, Robespierre's authority weakened, and he was finally overthrown, 9 Thermidor, Year II (July 27, 1794). With his fall there was a gradual disintegration of the nationalist economic structure erected by the Committee of Public Safety. The production of war materials became less feverish; the search for saltpetre practically ceased; fixed prices were not adhered to; and steps were not taken to give the property of suspects to the poor. Under the threat of invasion, the Committee of Public Safety had accelerated the national economic machine to a breakneck speed. With the victories of French arms, the nation wanted to slow down to a more agreeable pace. The bourgeoisie, especially, wished to return to its favorite policies of *laisser-faire* in domestic business and national protection in foreign trade.

THE DIRECTORY—ECONOMIC WAR ON BRITAIN

After the fall of Robespierre, the middle class, freed from the dictates of the Parisian masses, once more got control of the French state. Its representatives prepared hurriedly a new constitution that placed political power in its hands—the Constitution of the Directory, under which France was governed from 1795 to 1799. Having thus provided for the framework of government, the bourgeoisie turned its attention toward the establishment of conditions that would allow it to carry on the activity dearest to its heart—the business of making money. Its cry was for "normalcy," for peace with foreign powers, for quiet at home, and for regular functioning of France's economic machinery.

To realize this plan almost insurmountable obstacles had to be overcome. In the first place, the ever-present question of the *assignats* had to be dealt with. The Government decided, once for all, that the paper money could not be continued. It proceeded rapidly to increase the amount in circulation and then suddenly ordered that no more be issued.[95] The *assignats* fell greatly in value, finally became practically worthless, and were suppressed by the Directory, May 21, 1797. Thus ended the chapter of inflation in the Revolutionary period—an inflation which along with the "two-thirds bankruptcy," had made it possible to relieve France of its tremendous public debt and to finance its foreign wars.[96]

The rapid inflationary policy of the Directory, the suppression of maximum prices and wages,[97] and the consequently sharp increases in the cost of living augmented the hardships of labor and caused urban workers to show that they were not ready to yield to capital without a tussle. In fact, a movement toward economic egalitarianism, developed under the leadership of Babeuf, became important enough to be suppressed by force. The supporters of the old régime also asserted themselves, thinking that they could get into power on the wave of reaction that followed the fall of Robespierre. So eminently successful were they in the elections of 1797 that the Directors resorted to coercion to keep the legislative bodies in line. From all sides return to normal conditions seemed to be threatened, but at home the Directory succeeded in maintaining order.

Internal peace did not, however, usher in a golden era of business. Peace abroad, it appeared, was necessary for real prosperity, and foreign war still sapped the strength of the population. By highly successful military victories France had eliminated (1797) all her enemies of the First Coalition except Great Britain. To Britain overtures had been made, but the English, encouraged by French royalists,[98] stuck tenaciously to their guns. This tenacity was exceedingly embarrassing to the French, for, although they had succeeded in putting into the field an irresistible land force, they had been unable to cope with the English on the seas.

It was thus necessary for them either to take the offensive against their opponents with arms in which they were admittedly inferior, or to choose new weapons. France's choice was naturally the latter, and her weapons were two. First, she prepared to send Bonaparte to Egypt to obtain a valuable colony for France,[99] to threaten British hegemony in the East, and, by establishing trade via the Isthmus of Suez, to undermine British commerce around the Cape of Good Hope. Secondly, she decided to renew war on the economy of Great Britain in order to ruin British commerce, industry, and credit. The former arm, like a slender rapier of poor steel, broke at once—the Egyptian campaign ended in a complete disaster. The latter, like a tremendous broadsword, was waved around for sixteen years, but not once was France able to deliver Britain a really mortal blow. In the end, she fell exhausted from her own exertion. The history of this latter duel constitutes a dramatic chapter in French national history.

The economic attacks that France made on Great Britain were conditioned by traditional, national, economic theory and practice, and were in line with the blows that had been directed at England during the Reign of Terror. France proposed to defeat her enemy by a boycott —by refusing to take English goods, or goods which were important in British trade. Such a policy, it was believed, would force English ships to wander over the seas in futile search for a market, and would, as Barère had prophesied in the Convention, destroy "Carthage." It would ruin English shipping; it would cause the bankruptcy of her industry; it would force Britain to resort to paper money; and it would knock down, like a house of cards, Britain's credit system throughout the world.[100] With Britain's credit destroyed, that nation would no longer be able to subsidize France's enemies on the Continent, and peace, victorious peace, would be won.

To realize this beautifully logical dream, stern measures were necessary, but the Directory did not flinch from taking them. On October 31, 1796, it passed a tariff law which was much harsher and more inclusive than that of 1793. It not only prohibited the importation of British goods, but also ordered the exclusion of a long list of products which were claimed to be always of British origin. It hit at all goods on which the British could possibly make a manufacturing or commercial profit. So conscientiously was this policy applied that Geneva watches were not admitted into France because of an alleged small quantity of British steel which was employed in their construction. Moreover, France, except for smuggling, cut herself off from British shipping. Reaffirming the Navigation Act of 1793, she declared a veritable war on British and neutral carrying by laying down the rule[101] that any ship coming from an English port or any English possession, regardless of the ownership of the vessel, was liable to confiscation with all its cargo; that any ship which had touched at a British port (and the British had required this procedure for all ships carrying colonial goods unless the ship touched at its homeland) should not enter French ports; and that the nationality of a vessel should be determined by the origin of its cargo.

For two years these rules were rigorously enforced. Put into effect without warning, they were applied to British and neutrals alike, with the utmost disregard of justice. The rule that the nationality of a vessel was determined by the origin of its cargo was so interpreted that, if anything English was found on a ship, the ship was declared to be British and confiscated on the spot. "A woolen blanket on the skipper's berth, a few sacks of British coal for the ship's stove, British earthenware used by the crew, the English metal buttons on the skipper's coat, etc., were sufficient to lead to confiscation."[102] Thus the French, without securing any compensation, except perhaps increased protection for their industries and carriers, banished neutral shippers from their shores at a time when the British had driven all French vessels from the seas. Because of their blind faith in the efficacy of their mercantilist measures, the French unwittingly destroyed the only bridge over which could come the goods, especially the raw materials, that they were certain to need. The blows which they aimed at the British injured themselves as much as they injured their adversary.

The French were slow in coming to a realization of their lack of wisdom,[103] for there was some evidence that the policies pursued were having their desired effect. British exports to France and British shipping in French ports had certainly diminished; the British public debt was rising, going from £230,000,000 in 1793 to £507,000,000 in 1802;[104] and the resources of the Bank of England had fallen so low that, in 1797, gold payments had been suspended.[105] But there was also evidence that Britain was not in imminent danger of being pinned to the mat. Pitt had taken advantage of Bonaparte's difficulties in Egypt to secure the alliance of Austria and Russia in the Second Coalition (1798) and had lavished subsidies upon his allies. The French, in view of these facts, came finally to believe that if their economic measures against Britain were to be really effective, they must be applied by countries other than France.[106] The French did what they could for the moment in this respect by prohibiting British goods on the Left Bank of the Rhine (1798) and by ordering French envoys to persuade Hamburg to boycott British products. The root of the idea for an economic blockade of the entire Continent against Britain was present in these measures— a root that was to grow under the assiduous culture of Napoleon Bonaparte.

CRISIS—THE DIRECTORY DISAPPEARS

The economic war on Britain did not bring prosperity to French industry or commerce, and it was in prosperity that the bourgeoisie was largely interested. The depression continued in spite of a slight amelioration of conditions.[107] At Lyons, of the 9000 silk looms in operation in 1788, only 3500 were worked during the Directory; and similar conditions existed in practically all industries, except those which produced goods for the armies.[108] Trouble in the colonies following the freeing of the slaves, the subsequent intervention of the English, and the British blockade made the trade in colonial raw products almost impossible. Foreign commerce declined from a billion *livres* at the end of the *ancien régime* to an average of about 550 millions for the years 1797–1799.[109]

Cognizant of these conditions, the Directory desired whole-heartedly to improve them. It was as generous in the giving of subsidies to ailing industries as a precarious financial situation would permit.[110] It spread knowledge concerning new methods of manufacture and to this end encouraged the use of machines by offering prizes for new inventions, of which one of the most interesting from a national point of view was for a machine that would cause the greatest loss to British industry.[111] An attempt was also made to improve roads, for, as was stated in a circular issued by the Government,[112] "to destroy the roads of an empire is to cut the veins of Hercules, and it is to this condition that France has almost been reduced." Toll roads, in partial imitation of the English turnpikes, were established, but, although they improved matters, they were not eminently successful. These efforts on the part of the Directory had an almost insignificant effect upon the general economic situation. Business was poor and continued to be poor. The bourgeoisie became more and more restless, and, as is often the case when things go wrong, responsibility for the depression was placed upon those in power.

For other reasons, too, bourgeois discontent with the Government was growing. The object of the Directory, from its very inception, was to steer France safely between the Charybdis of Royalism and the Scylla of extreme Jacobinism—a very difficult task. The Thermidorian reaction brought *émigrés* back to France and emboldened Royalist sentiment. To curb this rising tide of the "right," extra-legal methods were used on 18 Fructidor, Year V (September 4, 1797) and on 22 Floréal, Year VI (May 11, 1798)—incidents that have been glorified by the title *coups d'état*. Aspirations of the "left" were also highly exalted, and, although the movement led by Babeuf was suppressed by condemning its leaders to death, Jacobinism awaited an opportunity to return to power. Its chance came in the spring of 1799, when France was threatened with military invasion. Successful in the elections held in the midst of the crisis, Jacobins secured control of the legislative bodies and forced the dictatorial Directors out of office, 30 Prairial, Year VII (June 18, 1799).[113] Then they began to put their ideas into practice.

Freedom of the press was re-established; no one was permitted to evade the draft because of wealth, position, or rank; and a "forced loan," which was in reality an income tax amounting to seventy-five per cent in some instances, was instituted as an initial attack on large fortunes. In Jacobin clubs there were appeals for land bonuses to war veterans and laws against war profiteering. Finally, the "law of hostages" of July 12, 1799, which aimed to suppress the attacks on the property and persons of purchasers of national land, allowed the seizure of four nobles as hostages for every Royalist murder or uprising in the provinces. This measure angered Royalists and forced them to sympathize with the bourgeois class in its desire to overthrow the Directory.

Under these circumstances a movement for a change got under way. Its most prominent leader was Siéyès. He was much disgruntled because he had not been allowed to draft the constitution for the Directory in 1795, and he wanted now to become the great law-giver of France by writing a new charter for the country. Cognizant that the military desired order and discipline at home and that the army could be used for effecting a *coup d'état,* Siéyès sought the support of a military leader. He and his supporters decided upon Joubert, but he was soon killed in battle. Then they turned to Napoleon Bonaparte, who was not at all averse to their plans. Funds for the move were provided by wealthy capitalists and promises were made that in case of success the forced loan would be abolished and provisioners of the army would be treated better. The stage was set, and on 18 Brumaire, Year VIII (November 9, 1799), the Directory was overthrown. This *coup d'état* of Brumaire was, in principle, nothing more than another attempt to attain the "juste milieu." It was effected by a minority of parvenus of the Revolution, but was founded, this time, on a general need of order and of peace and backed by the "connivance of capital."[114] Bonaparte's Consulate (1799–1804) was another attempt at bourgeois government.

CHAPTER III

NAPOLEON'S NATIONAL AND WAR ECONOMIC POLICIES[1]

BONAPARTE, BOURGEOISIE, AND BUSINESS

ONCE in power, Bonaparte received the general approbation of the French bourgeoisie, for his military gifts indicated that he would be able to conquer France's enemies and restore the peace and prosperity that had eluded the Directory. Also, upon investigation, his economics were found to be satisfactory. He had come from a good family, and, although he had tasted the bitterness of poverty, he had fallen into the soft lap of Parisian *salons* and had displayed a sympathetic attitude towards the aims and desires of his benefactors. The world of business believed that it could depend upon Bonaparte to keep the government from interfering in their affairs, to get state aid for industry, and to pursue a protective policy. Moreover, it thought that it would be able to manage this young man and would find in him no obstacle to its plans.

The bourgeoisie, however, did not really know Bonaparte. It little realized the strength of his dictatorial character and the power that he would assume once firmly seated in the saddle. It never imagined that he would busy himself with the smallest detail of government and would dictate economic policy to business. Still less could it foresee that Bonaparte was to bring to France not peace but the sword, nor that he was to engage in an economic struggle with England which was to jeopardize the very life, to say nothing of the profits, of more than one business enterprise in France. Bonaparte's economic heart was in the right place, but military and political necessity and ambition frequently dislocated it. This fact got him into serious difficulties and finally, when defeat bore down upon him, a discontented capitalist class could only rejoice at his going.

When, on the 18 Brumaire, Year VIII (November 9, 1799), Bonaparte took the helm in France, the ship of state was being severely battered by a storm of war. His departure for Egypt had been the signal for the formation of the Second Coalition, composed of Great Britain, Austria, and Russia,[2] against France, and his long absence had allowed the allies to register important military victories. It had been news of these happenings that had decided the young general suddenly to abandon his ill-fated Egyptian expedition and to return to defend the nation. Upon his arrival in Paris, he lost no time in executing his *coup d'état* and then turned to face France's foes. Russia was eliminated from the Coalition by a stroke of diplomacy, and Austria, by a brilliant use of arms.[3] Then he concentrated his efforts on subduing Great Britain.

The task of bringing England to her knees was a difficult one, for, while France had complete military mastery of the Continent, Great Britain had absolute control of the seas. The two powers stood glaring at each other across the Channel. Neither knew how to strike the other, and neither took the initiative in making peace. France's territory, increased by the annexation of the Belgian Netherlands, of Nice and Savoy, and of the Rhineland, France's strength, augmented by treaties of alliance with the Batavian, Helvetic, Ligurian, and Cisalpine Republics and with Spain,[4] and France's armies still in possession of Egypt, upset England's traditional ideal for Continental politics—the balance of power—and made her averse to the cessation of hostilities on the basis of the *status quo*. On the other hand, Great Britain, by having taken Martinique, Saint Lucia, Tobago, Saint Pierre, Miquelon, and Malta from France, Trinidad and Minorca from Spain, the Cape of Good Hope from the Dutch, and by having driven out all powers from India, had raised herself to a colonial eminence. This was a position that would not be tolerated by France and her allies. Both countries feigned to desire peace, but they wanted it on their own terms.[5] As selfish as their demands were, however, they managed to come to an agreement on all points except on the fate of Egypt and Malta, on which depended the control of the Mediterranean.

Finally, the capitulation of France's armies in Egypt and the fright that the British received from Bonaparte's threatened descent on their island stronghold from Boulogne[6] paved the way for peace. The British accepted extraordinarily harsh terms. They promised to restore all colonial conquests made during the war, except Ceylon and Trinidad; they agreed to evacuate Malta; and they were forced to leave unaltered the Continental arrangement whereby the mouths of the commercially important Scheldt and Rhine Rivers and Italy were under French influence. By the signing of peace on these conditions (Treaty of Amiens, March 27, 1802), Bonaparte finished the task that had been placed upon him after his seizure of the government on the 18 Brumaire. By bringing the last of France's enemies to terms, he made the peace that the bourgeoisie had so ardently desired and paved the way for a return to business prosperity.

Bonaparte did not consider his mission complete with the signing of peace, however, and devoted his energies to the ushering in of the golden era that would at once strengthen the nation and enrich the bourgeoisie. There was indeed room for improvement, for bad times had accompanied Bonaparte's seizure of power. Poor harvests in the years VIII and IX made bread dearer than it had been in 1789 and had led the First Consul to provision the people of Paris at reasonable prices in order to keep them favorably inclined towards him. The finances of the state were also in a precarious position. Bonds issued by the Directory in 1797 were exchanged at one-half their value after March, 1801 for new 5 per cent bonds, that in turn fell to one-half their par after the Peace of Amiens, or for public lands. Nor did the future of the public finances look brilliant, for Bonaparte's grandiose projects required large sums and the costs of government were increasing with the rising price level. Conditions of the time required vigorous action; they explain, in part, Napoleonic economic measures.

As part of an attempt to realize the middle-class demands to make France an economic unit, he established commissions to prepare unified codes of law for the nation, and saw to it that they favored the bourgeois class.[7] He put down the last vestiges of trouble in the Vendée and the *Chouannerie* in Brittany, thus making these regions safe for business, and he suppressed brigandage on the highways. He tried to improve roads, replacing the onerous tolls with a salt-tax,[8] and he began the construction of those great military and commercial routes that, radiating from Paris, were to reach Hamburg to the north and were to pierce the Alps to the south.[9] He balanced the national budget by the careful collection of taxes, rigid economy, severe punishment of corrupt officials, and the policy of making the conquered territories support his armies. He encouraged the founding of the Bank of France,[10] which, as its act of association testifies, was looked upon from the first as a national economic institution. He himself held that the Bank "does not belong exclusively to the stockholders; it belongs also to the State, for the latter gives it the privilege of striking money."[11] He created schools of arts and crafts. He endeavored to improve the quality of French wool by establishing breeding stations for merino sheep. He offered prizes in conjunction with the Société d'Encouragement pour l'Industrie Nationale for new inventions. And he held industrial exhibitions for the propagation of mechanical information.[12] So well disposed did he appear to be toward business that a wave of great prosperity was expected by all. Chaptal, Minister of the Interior, a chemist and industrialist, expressed well the general, over-optimistic opinion in a letter which he wrote to Napoleon after the industrial fair of 1802.

"Citizen, Premier Consul, in visiting the exhibitions which contain precious products, you questioned a great number of manufacturers from all parts of France. Their replies proved to you what a difference there is between the actual state of our industry and that in which it has been in all former times. Already commerce is picking up on all sides. The activity will soon be as great at Lyons as it was in 1788. The north of Europe, Italy, the Near East demand silk goods of this city, famous for its industry. The exportation of linens and batistes from Flanders increases every day. The making of lace takes on new life in the departments of Orne and Calvados; the cloth of Brittany is being sent once again to Spain, Peru, and Mexico. And manufacturers of Carcassonne, who are in a position to provide the Near East with woolens, receive new orders every day."

BONAPARTE'S COLONIAL AND COMMERCIAL PLANS

Bonaparte was also interested in colonies, which, he was firmly convinced, were a great asset in developing a nation's strength. He believed, as Colbert had believed before him, that overseas possessions should provide the metropolis with raw materials and that they should consume the products of the homeland—especially manufactured articles. In this exchange of goods, there would be reciprocal economic advantage, but for the colonizing power there would be an especial gain, for it would increase the homeland's resources and augment its productive ability. In the first two years of his rule, Bonaparte had no opportunity to put his colonial theories into practice, because England had either occupied French colonies or had prevented French ships from reaching them. With the signing of the Treaty of Amiens in 1802, however, this situation was changed. Although powerless on the seas, Bonaparte succeeded in securing the return of the French colonies which had been taken in the recent struggle and in establishing a peace that would permit French ships to sail the seas unmolested. His first task was to suppress the anarchy and disorder that had decimated the colonies during the Revolutionary Era.

Of conditions in the colonies, he was kept vividly aware, not only by official reports but also by letters from Josephine's relatives and friends in Martinique. He was convinced that most of the ills came from the lack of authority of French officials and from such innovations as the freeing of the slaves. He determined, therefore, to re-establish the colonial legislation of the *ancien régime,* even to the extent of restoring slavery in all the American colonies where it had previously existed, except in Santo Domingo, and to send out new officials backed by the force necessary to support them.

He dispatched his brother-in-law Leclerc to Santo Domingo to deal with the insurrectionary Negro leader, Toussaint L'Ouverture—an ill-fated expedition, which cost the lives of 33,000 men[13]—and he sent smaller forces to other places. He encouraged French planters to live on their land in the colonies and to attend personally to the exploitation of their holdings, and he reserved colonial trade to French carriers. By maintaining his alliance with Spain, he hoped to form an economic and military unit of the Antilles, Mexico, Louisiana, and Guiana, in order to prevent England's seizure of these colonies in case of another war.[14] Ambitious also to add to France's colonial empire, he had designs upon certain possessions of his ally, Spain. He planned to establish French rule in the Spanish part of Santo Domingo and actually forced Spain to cede Louisiana to him.[15]

Like nearly all his other plans, his colonial schemes were grandiose and, like many of the others, were doomed to failure. Scarcely had he begun to carry them out when war was renewed with England, and French ships were swept off the seas. From time to time in subsequent years, Bonaparte endeavored to establish contact with his overseas possessions, but the French navy, as he well knew, was no match for the British. For fear of losing Louisiana to the English, he sold it to the United States, exclaiming as he did so, "This increase of territory insures forever the greatness of the United States. I have created [by the sale of Louisiana] a maritime rival to England which sooner or later will lower her pride."[16] His colonial program proved abortive, but he attached to colonies a greater importance, and showed a greater interest in effecting a national exploitation of them, than perhaps any other French colonizer from Colbert to the present time.[17] They formed an integral part of his national economic thinking.

Furthermore, in order to build up the economic power of France, Bonaparte desired to increase her foreign commerce. He believed that trade abroad stimulated production at home and, for political as well as economic reasons, he wished that the statistics of foreign commerce, one of the few, and hence extremely significant, mathematical indices of business prosperity in those days, be favorable. According to his economic concepts, it was necessary that the trade with other nations should show a favorable balance, for an excess of imports over exports would drain the country of its precious metals, destroy its credit, and deprive the public treasury of much needed funds. His policy, then, was to encourage exports and to prevent imports. This he did until he fell in 1814. When he had first come to power, he had begun negotiations with nations that were likely purchasers of French manufactured articles, and had signed treaties with several of them—with Naples,[18] Spain,[19] Portugal,[20] Russia,[21] and Turkey.[22] Zealous in keeping British goods out of France, after the signing of the Peace of Amiens, he refused English demands to renew the already-expired Eden Treaty. Some goods continued to be prohibited and others were subjected to a new protective tariff, April 28, 1803.[23] This measure did not apply exorbitant rates except on cotton textiles and refined sugar, but they were high enough to win the general approval of the business classes. It formed part of Napoleon's plan to build up French commerce and manufacturing at the expense of the English.

TRADE RIVALRY—RENEWAL OF WAR

During this period of peace, French foreign trade prospered. It increased from 553 millions in 1799 to 790 millions in 1802. Moreover, a fifteen per cent rise in the re-export of foreign goods and a twenty-three per cent increase in the exportation of colonial products were registered. So great was the development of French trade that the English did not think that they were getting their fair share of the business. The British envoy in Paris is said to have complained to Talleyrand that "His Majesty's subjects [have been unable] to reap the advantages common to, and always expected from, a state of peace." Bonaparte's schemes seem to have begun to have their desired effect, but war came to interrupt their development before they could be carried to full fruition.

The fundamental reasons for the short duration of the peace were largely economic. Bonaparte was discontented because England would not fulfill her pledge to evacuate Malta.

"If," he said, "besides the important possession of Gibraltar, England wants to maintain another foothold in the Mediterranean, this would evidently be an announcement of her plan to unite to her practical monopoly of trade with India, America, and the Baltic, that of the Mediterranean; and of all the calamities which could come to the French people, there could be none comparable to this."

The English, for their part, were dissatisfied because the peace had not allowed them to benefit from trade with France as much as they had hoped. They had not expected that their enemy would continue her vigorous war-time economic policy, nor that she would embark upon ambitious colonial projects after the peace had been signed. Moreover, they had never looked with favor upon France's predominant political position on the Continent, upon her occupation of Antwerp, nor upon her place in the councils of the Batavian Republic. In view of Britain's traditional Continental policy, it was difficult to believe that she would be content with the maintenance of the *status quo*. War was in the air during most of the period of peace. Bonaparte undoubtedly wanted peace, but on his own terms. He demanded the impossible—that England should be abased economically to the profit of France. Many are those who consider that he was unwise not to have consolidated his gains and to have made the sacrifices that would have been necessary to appease England.[24] Such a policy, however, was not compatible with Bonaparte's character; the most that he offered was to allow British occupation of Malta for ten years.[25] This was not enough; hostilities began in May, 1803.

With the plan of attacking England directly, Bonaparte mobilized an army at Boulogne. He whipped up enthusiasm for the struggle by occupying the ports of Hanover, the Papal States, and the Kingdom of Naples, and by closing them to the British; he renewed his alliance with Spain; and he strengthened his position among his fellow-countrymen by assuming the title of Emperor.[26] But in spite of all his efforts, things went wrong. The "Boulogne Campaign" was a failure, and a Third Coalition, composed of Britain, Russia, and Austria, formed against him. Then the bourgeoisie, as it had little faith in Napoleon and feared that the renewal of war on land would end the "wavelette" of prosperity, became panic-stricken. Rumors were abroad that Napoleon, upon his departure for the Austrian front, carried the gold reserves of the Bank of France with him. As a result, such a run developed on the Bank that the Government had to intervene.[27] Finally, as a crowning misfortune, a combined French and Spanish fleet was decisively defeated at Trafalgar (October 21, 1805), and the English became complete masters of the seas.

Out of this morass there was only one way—the way of victory. With swift, hard blows, Napoleon overcame Austria at Ulm and Austerlitz, and forced her to sign the Treaty of Pressburg (December, 1805). Then turning on Prussia, which made the unhappy choice of joining Russia and Great Britain in the Fourth Coalition against France, he defeated her at Jena and Auerstadt (1806). And he overcame Russia at Friedland (1807). By his lightning successes, he restored the confidence of the bourgeoisie and raised his person to even greater heights of glory than he had previously enjoyed. He failed, however, to deal England a serious blow for her machinations against him. Since he was powerless to hit at her directly, it was necessary for him to revive plans to subdue her with economic rather than with military weapons. The story of his efforts makes an important chapter in the history of French national economics.

ECONOMIC WAR ON ENGLAND—THE THEORY

The fundamental principles upon which the Convention's and Directory's economic war on England was based were kept steadily before French statesmen during the Consulate and the first years of the Empire. Three of the outstanding proponents of a renewal of these measures were Montgaillard, whom Napoleon charged with several diplomatic tasks; F. L. A. Ferrier, who was in the customs service; and a certain Chevalier De Guer, the author of many articles on economic subjects, one of which Bonaparte caused to be inserted in *Le Moniteur* in 1803. The first of these men held that:

"England is lost if her territorial power in Asia is lessened, if the prohibition of her merchandise is successfully established in Europe, if her commercial outlets are closed, and if the necessary measures are taken to weaken her naval strength. . . . It is by attacking her commerce that it is necessary to strike at England. To allow her to reap her profits in Europe, Asia, and America is to allow her to keep all her arms and to render conflicts and wars eternal. To destroy Britain's commerce is to strike England to the heart and, at the same time, to attack her alliances and her continental intrigues."[28]

De Guer argued that, when England cannot pay subsidies to her allies on the Continent by exporting goods and by maintaining a favorable balance of trade, she will be placed in an inescapable economic dilemma. She will either have to export gold, which will force her off the gold standard and ruin her bank of issue, or she will be obliged to pay subsidies in paper money, which will cause the rate of exchange to go against her and her trade to decline.[29]

Such arguments convinced Napoleon that he could defeat England by making war upon her exports. He believed that by means of a blockade, not of Britain, but of Britain's markets, England would see "her vessels laden with useless wealth wandering around the wide seas, where they claim to rule as sole masters, seeking in vain from the Sound to the Hellespont for a port to open and receive them."[30] The British Bank Restriction Act of 1797, limiting the redemption of paper money with gold, had given him grounds to think that British credit was in a precarious position,[31] and that it could easily be upset by injury to British trade. Once Britain failed to sell abroad, she would be unable to subsidize her Continental allies. Thus France would be relieved of the danger of war. He reasoned, moreover, that, if Britain were unable to sell her wares abroad, overproduction would result, manufacturing establishments would shut down, labor would be out of employment, and both workers and bourgeois would join together against the government, as they had done in France during the Convention, and force it to make peace. His economic plan for the destruction of Britain was double-barrel; either he would upset Britain's credit or ruin her economy.

No matter how imperative the felling of Britain was, Napoleon could not ignore France's economic development. He hoped to combine his plans against Great Britain with a scheme to build up, first, agriculture, France's greatest economic concern; secondly, manufacturing; and, thirdly, commerce, "as an aid to the functioning of the other two branches," and not as an end in itself.[32] The two principal axioms in Napoleon's economic thinking were that a state cannot be strong unless it has great productive power, and it cannot be powerfully productive without protection. Between the idea of protection for French goods and the desire to prevent Britain from selling her products on the Continent, there was close affinity. It was from this affinity that Napoleon constructed his blockade theory. At first thought, indeed, the prohibition of English goods was the complement of the idea of increasing France's productive power, but as practiced during the Empire, it contributed to the destruction of the blockade system.

ECONOMIC WAR ON ENGLAND—THE PRACTICE

With the outbreak of war between Great Britain and France in 1803, there was a renewal of the commercial conflict on a large scale. At the beginning of hostilities, the English seized the French and

Dutch ships which were in their ports. Napoleon retaliated by the imprisonment of English travelers on the Continent and by the confiscation of their goods. This preliminary skirmish, which roused illfeeling on both sides of the Channel, was followed by the "battle of the blockades" that lasted throughout the remaining years of Napoleon's reign. The French "blockaded" themselves from British goods; the English "blockaded" the mouths of the Elbe and Weser,[33] and, in 1804, all the French-controlled ports on the North Sea and the Channel.[34] If they maintained control of trade to French ports, the English expected that they would be able to reserve for their own nationals a considerable part of the commerce; and the French believed, as we have already seen, that, if they did not purchase British goods, they could undermine the power of their rival. There was little thought of depriving the enemy of imports, as in the case of modern blockades. All attention was given to the workings of national economic theory.

The French went into the fray with confidence, and early measures were tinged with the mildness that accompanies certainty of success. They prohibited the importation of British colonial and industrial goods and, to stop up an obvious loophole, ordered that neutral vessels carry French consular certificates showing the origin of their cargoes.[35] Gradually they were forced to make their regulations more rigid, for Britain failed to succumb as rapidly as had been hoped. The French extended the list of prohibited articles, refused to allow vessels which had put in at a British port to dock in France, and in 1805 declared general prohibition of articles, no matter what their origin, for fear that British goods would be disguised as neutral.[36] The import taxes on colonial goods were increased in order to deprive England of carrying profit. The rate on coffee, cocoa, and sugar was raised 350 per cent; that on cotton from one or three francs to 60 francs per 100 kilograms, or to about 10 per cent of its value; and cotton products were either prohibited or heavily taxed. Step by step, France erected against foreign goods a system that brought no more injury to Britain than to industrialized regions of the Continent, like the Grand Duchy of Berg (the Ruhr),[37]—a system that provided heavy protection for her own products. Unfortunately, it cut her off from raw materials, especially raw colonial products, but she believed that she could meet all such *lacunae* by a more versatile domestic production. She confidently expected that she could make herself economically self-sufficient.

THE BLOCKADE EXTENDED

The French, also, began a policy of forcing other states on the Continent to adopt measures against British goods. This policy led to the establishment of what Napoleon himself called the "Continental System." When Hanover, an English possession, was taken, these repressive measures were extended to this territory and to Hamburg and Bremen. Meppen on the Ems River was occupied to prevent the passage of goods to Frankfort-on-the-Main. The Kingdom of Italy, in the northern part of the Italian peninsula, of which Napoleon was the ruling monarch, was required to exclude a long list of articles, unless they came from France. The Kingdom of Naples, ruled by Joseph Bonaparte, prohibited the importation of goods of British origin and seized British property within its borders. The subservient Helvetic Republic, too, was forced to bar all British goods except cotton yarns.

These measures comprised an economic war *à outrance* between France and Great Britain. Armed hostilities might cease between them, as Napoleon hoped they would after the defeat of Austria in 1805, but economic peace seemed out of the question. The Emperor himself declared on March 4, 1806:

"Forty-eight hours after peace with England, I shall proscribe foreign products and shall promulgate a navigation act that will permit the entry to our ports of only French ships, constructed of French timber, and manned by a crew two-thirds French. Even coal and English 'milords' will be able to land only under the French flag."[38]

In view of this attitude, the peace overtures that he made to England at the time failed, and he was convinced that further war was necessary to secure peace with economic victory.

With the formation of the Fourth Coalition in 1806, Napoleon had to direct his energies towards war, but after the conquest of Prussia he devoted himself to his economic struggle with Great Britain. It was from Berlin, whither he had gone after the battle of Auerstadt, that he issued the decree of November 21, 1806[39]—a landmark in his economic conflict with Britain. The Berlin Decree summed up the arguments for the prohibition of the importation of British goods and reiterated many of the measures that had already been taken. Once again, all trade with the British Isles was declared prohibited; all commerce in English products was forbidden; and all ships, British or neutral, coming from Britain or her colonies, or calling at a British port, were refused admittance to blockaded ports. The decree introduced only two new features into the already well-established Continental System: (1) it declared the British Isles in a state of blockade, and (2) ordered all Englishmen on the Continent arrested and their property confiscated. But neither of these measures was particularly important. As Lord Erskine said in the House of Lords, Napoleon might as well have declared the moon in a state of blockade as the British Isles, for he was in an absolutely impotent position to enforce his order; and the practical effect of interning Englishmen and of seizing their property was limited to the moment of application. The real significance of the Berlin Decree was not in its novelty or even its provisions, but in the fact that it indicated that old edicts would be enforced strictly and over a large area. "And it was now, too, that [the System] was made the central point in the entire internal and external policy of France, around which everything else had to turn in an ever-increasing degree."[40]

The English met Napoleon's new thrust by a series of confused and self-contradictory Orders in Council, the most important of which were issued November 11, 1807. First, they declared a blockade of all ports from which Englishmen were excluded and outlawed all ships which attempted to run the blockade. Then, by a subsequent decree these measures were made a little less rigid. Permission was granted to neutral countries to carry on direct trade with enemy colonies. Prohibitions were placed, however, upon direct trade between enemy colonies and the enemy homeland and upon direct trade between neutral countries and enemy ports. If neutral vessels wished to trade with the enemy, they had to touch at a British port and unload their cargoes. Thus the French boycott of British goods was answered by an English blockade-boycott of French goods. The English did this to control Continental trade for the benefit of their own commerce. They collected heavy harbor dues and taxes from non-British ships and prohibited the exportation to France of certain products, like raw cotton and Jesuit's bark (quinine), for which the need was great. Finally, the British gave warning that their ships would examine merchantmen on the high seas and would seize vessels that endeavored to evade British rules.

Napoleon, in anger, countered these orders with the Milan Decree of December 17, 1807.[41] He declared that any ship and its cargo which submitted to examination by the British, called at a British port, or paid a duty in Britain became denationalized, and was a lawful prize on land or sea. Napoleon thus reversed the policy that he had adopted at the beginning of his régime of allowing neutral shipping to come to France. Like the Directory, with its Nivôse Law of 1798, he attacked neutral carrying at a moment when it was important in provisioning him with goods. The fact that the sales of Americans to France had increased from $20,000,000 in 1794 to $94,000,000 indicates how significant the commerces of neutrals had become. But now all caution was thrown to the winds. With Napoleonic logic, the Emperor ordered that foreign ships in French ports be seized, for, in view of English orders, they were either English, and therefore should be taken, or they were the ships of neutral or allied powers and would be captured by the English when they set sail. He placed on neutrals the responsibility for maintaining the nationality of their flags, and, as this was impossible because of English rules and the Milan Decree, there were, as far as Napoleon was concerned, no more neutrals.

Not only by edicts, but also by the extension of his system of prohibitions to an ever-widening circle of states on the Continent, did Napoleon intend to obliterate neutrals. His extraordinary military successes made it possible for him to extend his system to almost the entire Continent. His brother Louis, now King of Holland, his brother Jerome, King of Westphalia, his brother Joseph, King of Naples, and his stepson Eugène Beauharnais, Viceroy in his own Kingdom of Italy, were forced, not without difficulty, to join in the blockade of English goods. He imposed his measures upon Hamburg and Bremen, upon his brother-in-law Murat in the Duchy of Berg, which was incorporated in the Confederation of the Rhine in 1807, upon the Confederation itself, and upon his ally Spain. They were adopted, at least nominally by Austria, Turkey, the Barbary States, and even Persia. Denmark applied them after the bombardment of Copenhagen in 1807, and, at Tilsit, Prussia was forced to acquiesce in their enforcement.[42] Moreover, Russia promised her co-operation. In the secret clauses of the Franco-Russian Alliance, it was stipulated that, if England had not made peace by December, 1807, Russia would join France in her economic war on Britain.

Content with his exploits, Napoleon had reason to expect an early defeat of his enemy. He announced to his soldiers, "The peace of Tilsit puts an end to the operations of the *Grande Armée*. . . . It is probable that the Continental blockade will not be an empty word."[43] But England did not yield, and Napoleon persisted in the extension of his system. Most of the Adriatic coast was closed to English goods; the Papal States, Venetia, and Etruria were annexed to the Kingdom of Italy; Eugène was ordered to close Leghorn, Città Vecchia, and Ancona; Portugal was forced to shut her harbors; Sweden, attacked by Russia and France, was brought into the orbit of the Continental System;[44] and in 1812 the United States was manœuvred into a war with Great Britain. Napoleon almost carried out his threat to close to British ships all ports from the Hellespont to the Sound. He made his system veritably Continental.

ADVANTAGES OF THE BLOCKADE TO FRANCE

The object of this *machine de guerre* was, as has been mentioned above, not alone to force England to abase herself before France, but also to build up French industry and to win the markets of the Continent for French products. Napoleon counselled:

"You must never lose sight of the fact that British commerce is triumphant on the sea because the English are the strongest there. Hence it is right, inasmuch as France is strongest on land, that she make her commerce triumphant there. Unless this is done, all is lost."[45]

It was this national economic point of view that made Napoleon further the economic interests of France, even at the expense of his vassals and allies, when, if he had been solely bent on the destruction of England, his policy should have been to harness the forces of the Continent and to form a Continental economic union regardless of national aims.[46] But Napoleon was too strong a national patriot to embark upon a Pan-European economic adventure, or even to treat all of his subjects the same. Only after the interests of the "old" provinces of France had been taken care of did he show favors to his other possessions; even the treatment that was meted out to them was graduated in accordance with their importance to France. Italy's economic welfare was given first consideration after that of France, and then followed in order the interests of the Belgian departments, of the Netherlands, of the Hanseatic towns, and of the Illyrian provinces.[47]

To be even first after France during the Napoleonic régime, however, was a hardship. In Italy, the annexation of some districts to the French Empire and the erection of others into the Kingdom of Italy placed customs barriers between provinces, like Lombardy and Tuscany, that had been economic complements. This made it easier for French industrial products to capture the markets. As King of Italy, Napoleon made laws to the detriment of his Italian subjects and to the benefit of his French ones. Among other things, he prohibited the exportation of raw silk except to France[48] and by declaring a number of articles to be British, no matter whence they came, he struck a severe blow at the centuries-old German-Swiss trade with Italy.[49]

If to be first after France in the heart of Napoleon was a disadvantage, to be in a lower position in his scale of economic loves was almost a calamity. Switzerland was forced to import cotton goods from France and to import nothing from Britain;[50] Holland, although annexed to France in 1810, was brought into the French customs union only to the extent of allowing French industrialists to export freely to the Netherlands, but not of allowing the Netherlands to export to France without the payment of customs duties;[51] the industrialized Grand Duchy of Berg was cut off from the Baltic and the Netherlands by high tariff walls in order to curb its competition with France;[52] agricultural districts, like Russia, were prevented from getting rid of their surplus crops because of the ban placed on shipping with Great Britain;[53] tariff concessions were demanded of German states;[54] and customs rates were dictated to Spain.[55] As Paul Darmstädter has well said, "Frankreich über alles! das war die Devise, die Napoleon bei seiner Handelspolitik befolgt hat."[56] Unfortunately for France the

Continental System neither lasted long enough to allow French industry to get a firm hold on the markets that were opened to it, nor did it react entirely to France's benefit. There were weaknesses in it that proved to be its undoing.

By the end of 1807, the issue between France and Great Britain was closely joined. Napoleon was endeavoring to break England's power by cutting her off from Continental markets, and Great Britain was defending herself by doing everything possible to introduce her goods to the Continent and to destroy the commerce of her competitors. By the Berlin Decree, all commercial relations between the British Isles and France or France's allies were forbidden; by the Milan Decree, neutral trade with Britain was attacked; and by Napoleon's conquests, these orders were forced upon almost the entire European Continent. The struggle was one in which France's ability actually to deprive Great Britain of markets and her power to supply the needs of the Continent were pitted against Great Britain's skill in forcing goods through the blockade to Continental customers and in cutting France off from the most important colonial raw materials—cotton, sugar, and dyes.

WEAKNESSES OF THE CONTINENTAL SYSTEM

Early in the history of the Continental System, there appeared in the blockade fundamental weaknesses that augured ill for an ultimate French victory over Britain. In the first place, there was great laxity in the enforcement of Napoleon's orders, especially on the part of his allies and satellites. Smuggling in foreign countries was not only winked at but even encouraged, and corruptibility of customs officials became almost a requirement for office. As time went on, the desire for the rigorous application of the System continually diminished, for France's vassals became ever more cognizant of France's desire to supplant British goods with her inferior and dearer products, which were shipped by expensive overland routes. Secondly, Napoleon's attempts to enforce the economic blockade by arms involved him in wars that were too overwhelming even for his genius. Thirdly, the Continental System, in conjunction with other causes, led in France to an economic crisis that was almost as severe as the one Napoleon had expected to create in Britain. The Continental System, like many of Napoleon's schemes, had a germ of possibility in it, but in actual operation it proved to be unrealizable.

Perhaps the greatest weakness in Napoleon's blockade was the laxity with which his measures were enforced. The English were past masters in the art of smuggling and, save for a short time after the issuance of the Berlin Decree, they maintained a brisk commerce with the Continent. Their main points of entry up to 1808 were the Netherlands and the Hanseatic towns, Hamburg and Bremen, which were reached via Heligoland. From the issuance of the Berlin Decree to August 1, 1807, there arrived in Hamburg 1475 vessels with 590,000 tons of merchandise, most of which was English; and, in the same period, Bremen earned the reputation of being a "smuggling metropolis."[57] Napoleon's agent in Hamburg at this time was so dishonest that the Emperor called him the "undaunted robber," and Bernadotte, who was sent to improve conditions, was alleged not to have been above taking bribes.[58] Ironically enough, too, the French ordnance department bought in Hamburg English cloth and leather with which to provide clothing and shoes for the French armies that were extending the Continental System by force.[59]

It was only gradually that enough pressure to stop the leaks at Hamburg and Bremen was brought to bear, and, as it was applied, the British shifted the center of their illicit traffic to the Baltic. They made of Gothenburg in Sweden a smuggling *entrepôt* comparable to that of Heligoland; they extended their activities so much that their exports to Sweden more than doubled in 1808; and they maintained their commerce there even after Sweden was forced to declare war upon them.[60] Holland, too, was a breach in the Continental System. Although King Louis pretended to erect a blockade against English products, he had little sympathy for the System. In a letter to his brother Joseph, King of Spain, he said:

"Far from settling down, matters get more and more tangled. Perhaps I speak too much like a Dutchman, but I find something revolutionary in the way in which war is made on commerce. It seems to me that they will never attain the object that they have set before them. . . . For a chimerical system, the whole continent is losing its trade and shipping, while that of England grows prodigiously."[61]

Napoleon criticized bitterly the state of affairs in Holland, but Louis was loath to improve them. Thinking that the Emperor demanded the impossible, the King replied to one of his many abusive complaints about Dutch smuggling, "You might as well prevent the skin from sweating" as to stop the entry into Holland of British goods.[62] This impudence, on top of Louis' coolness to the Continental System, was more than Napoleon could endure. He closed the Dutch frontier to France on September 16, 1808; he shut Dutch ports to almost all outside commerce on October 23, 1808; and, after giving Holland, in 1809, another chance to play France's game, he concluded that the Dutch were incorrigible and annexed their country on July 9, 1810.

The fate that befell Holland should have befallen all of Napoleon's vassals, if he had been logical, for they were all more or less guilty of breaking his commands. In the Kingdom of Naples, Murat managed to evade the Continental System to the extent of shipping his country's olive oil and grain overseas every year,[63] and in Switzerland corruption flourished so much that, in seven months, eighty customs officials at Geneva had to be discharged for dishonesty. It was only in France that some semblance of strict enforcement of the blockade was maintained, and even here there were many leaks. At Strasburg, there was a company that made a business of insuring smugglers' goods, charging but 30 per cent on cargoes destined for France. British goods bearing a "made in France" tag were to be found in all important cities. English textiles were especially in demand, and the story is told that, in the course of a trip with Josephine, Napoleon discovered that the Empress had filled her trunks with stylish British stuffs, which, incidentally, he caused to be destroyed. To be sure, British exports to France decreased—French customs receipts fell from 51,200,000 francs in 1806 to 11,600,000 francs in 1809—but some of this loss was owing to the growth of illegal trade. Save for France, the blockade was not highly efficacious, and a ditty of the time, addressed to Napoleon, mocked its existence.

> "Votre blocus ne bloque point,
>   et grace à votre heureuse adresse,
>   ceux que vous affamez sans cesse
>   ne périront que d'embonpoint."

Although the blockade did not "'block" absolutely, it was effective enough to exasperate the states that were supposed to adhere to it. They railed against a system that was aimed at increasing France's economic power at their expense, and, when conditions became really bad, they were ready to cross arms even with Napoleon to obtain their economic freedom. Although it would be incorrect to attribute the wars that fell like an avalanche upon Napoleon in the closing years of his reign exclusively to the Continental System, there is no question that they were caused in part by the blockade. The purpose of the Emperor's war on Portugal in 1807 was to bring that country into the orbit of the Continental System, and his seizure of Spain and the raising of his brother Joseph to the Spanish throne in 1808 were, at least partly, for the purpose of enforcing the blockade more strictly in the Iberian Peninsula. It was on account of these high-handed measures in the interests of the French economic war on Great Britain that the Spaniards revolted against Napoleon and that, aided by the British, they fought continuously for their freedom until the end of the Empire. It was the Spanish national insurrection, in turn, that gave Austria courage to join Spain and Great Britain in the Fifth Coalition against France, and it was Napoleon's departure from Spain to subdue his new foe—which, incidentally, he did with comparative ease (Treaty of Schönbrunn, October, 1809)[64]—that made possible the success of the Anglo-Spanish troops in the south. It was partly the Continental System which destroyed the Franco-Russian Alliance[65] and led the Emperor to undertake the disastrous Moscow campaign. Finally, it was the economic war that kept Great Britain in the field against France and that urged her to engineer the formation of the last and great Coalition which was to undo Napoleon altogether.

Another important weakness in the Continental System was that, although created for the benefit of France's economy, the blockade reacted unfavorably upon French foreign commerce, upon certain French industries, and upon those agricultural districts that customarily raised produce for Great Britain. The blow to France's foreign trade was particularly hard. Statistics show a decline from 933 million francs in 1806 to 705 million in 1810, despite the greater size of the Empire at the latter date.[66] The American Consul at Bordeaux wrote on March 26, 1808: "Grass is growing in the streets of this city. Its beautiful port is deserted except by two Marblehead fishing schooners and three or four empty vessels that still swing to the tide."[67] Other testimony fully corroborates this view. The Napoleonic policy was undoubtedly injurious to French commerce.

The injury to agriculture was not so severe as to commerce, but Lower Brittany had, in the fall of 1808, great stores of grain which it was anxious to export, and Guyenne was virtually swamped with surplus stocks of wine. The blockade also worked a hardship upon some industries, like the woolen textile business of Carcassonne, by cutting off oversea markets, and upon others, like the cotton cloth and sugar-refining businesses, by stopping the supply of raw materials. The number of pieces of cloth manufactured in a good year in Carcassonne before the Revolution was 60,000, but in the early years of the Consulate this number had been but 18,000, and was at that figure in 1810.[68] The price of raw cotton was always higher in Paris and Ghent than it was in Leipzig and London. The difference between that of Paris and of the latter city was 15 per cent in 1806, 480 per cent in 1808, and 100 per cent in 1810.[69] These fluctuations in prices made cotton manufacturing extremely speculative.[70] The high cost of the raw material in France made difficult competition with foreign countries, including France's vassals, which benefited by extensive smuggling. During his wedding trip with Marie Louise in the spring of 1810 along the coast from Le Havre to Antwerp and to northern industrial towns, Napoleon recognized that the blockade was causing hardships that must be alleviated.

If the need for altering the Continental System to relieve certain businesses seemed wise in normal times, it must have appeared absolutely imperative during the crisis that began in 1810 and lasted, with only slight amelioration, until Napoleon's fall. In addition to the aforementioned ills, which were besetting French industry, there were numerous others. The high protection afforded by the blockade at home and the opening up of new markets abroad had encouraged the leaders in some trades, especially in cotton manufacturing, to expand their activity more than conditions warranted. The result was that in 1810 such businesses were in bad straits. The silk industry, which usually sold ten million francs' worth of cloth to Russia every year, had its entire Russian market cut off at the end of 1810 by an embargo.[71] Bad harvests, high prices of grain, and increased cost of colonial goods decreased the purchasing power of the people for industrial products. The widely varying prices of goods from overseas led to wild speculation, which resulted at times in abnormal profits and at others in great losses. The bankruptcy of a Lübeck concern had an almost immediate repercussion on Amsterdam and on Paris. Discounts of the Bank of France declined from 843 millions in 1810 to 506 millions in 1811;[72] at Rouen the spinning mills employed in 1811 but one-half of the laborers who had been given work in 1810;[73] the great Richard-Lenoir textile company of Paris was only saved from bankruptcy by Napoleon's aid;[74] and as late as 1813 an official report estimated that there were in the cotton industry 600,000 unemployed who had to choose between begging and ending their misery on the battlefield.[75]

ATTEMPTS TO OVERCOME WEAKNESSES OF THE CONTINENTAL SYSTEM

To cope with the difficulties besetting French economy, Napoleon concocted many schemes. In order to procure colonial goods, he offered subsidies and soldiers to shippers who would run the English blockade and establish trade with France's colonies[76] and, when that plan failed, he conceived of the equally impossible expedient of using government ships for the same purpose.[77] He experimented with the growing of cotton in Southern France and in Italy, and endeavored to secure supplies of Levant cotton by an overland route. When these projects proved of little success, he started a campaign to make France independent of cotton goods. He abolished their use in all imperial palaces[78] and offered a prize for a flax-spinning machine. At the same time, and most inconsistently, he gave subsidies to the ailing cotton textile plants and to other industries that were hard pinched, disbursing, according to Chaptal, sixty-two million francs in all.[79] And finally, in order to improve the economic situation and to curb smuggling, he made exceptions to the Continental System.

The first departure[80] from the rules laid down in the Berlin and Milan Decrees was taken in the spring of 1809 by granting licenses to

Breton farmers to export their surplus stocks of grain.[81] Once embarked upon, the policy of making exceptions to the blockade was rapidly extended. The list of goods for which licenses could be granted was lengthened in 1809 and 1810;[82] prize goods captured from the enemy by war vessels or licensed privateers were allowed to be imported to France on the payment of 40 per cent duty;[83] certain French ports, among which Dunkirk was the most important, were permitted to receive smugglers if they would export French goods or Dutch gin and bring back precious metals;[84] and trade permits were granted to Americans in the hope that France would thus be provided with sufficient supplies of colonial raw products.[85] These measures, the work of an opportunist, were taken to meet specific exigencies and hence were subject to sudden changes. Because of bad crops in 1810, the exportation of grain was prohibited and licenses were issued for its importation. It often came about that the articles for which licenses were granted were determined by underground negotiations with England as the British showed great leniency in 1811 in allowing the importation of French goods.

The economic activity that resulted from opening these gaps in the wall of the Continental System was turned as much as possible to the benefit of France. In a letter dated August 20, 1810, Napoleon pointed out that the shipping to which the licenses gave birth was reserved to French bottoms:[86]

"I do not grant licenses," he said, "to other than French vessels. Briefly, I will not hear of any neutral vessel, and as a matter of fact there is no such thing, for they are all vessels which violate the blockade and pay tribute to England. As to the word *foreign,* that means foreign to France. Thus foreign vessels cannot trade with France or leave our ports, because there are no neutrals."

On the trade opened up by licenses, extraordinarily high customs rates were imposed by the Trianon Tariff of August 5, 1810, in order to increase France's revenue and to protect her products. The taxes on colonial goods were made especially exorbitant, the rate on cotton being increased from 60 francs per hundred kilograms to between 200 and 800 francs according to its place of origin. The impost on indigo was augmented from 15 francs to 900 francs, for, as Napoleon wrote,

"The interest of France, which has no colonies, is to restrict as much as possible the consumption of colonial products."[87] New efforts were expended, also, to prevent illicit trade which, if continued, would have made the measures for legitimate commerce of no avail. By the Fontainebleau Decree of October 18, 1810, smuggled colonial goods were to be confiscated and sold at auction every six months, smuggled manufactured articles were to be burned, and smugglers were to be branded and sent into penal servitude for ten years. In order that France might benefit to the full from the opening up of trade, Napoleon intended that his vassals adopt the restrictive measures, but that they should not give licenses in return, and he actually forced Russia and Italy to apply customs rates similar to those contained in the Trianon Tariff.

The license system had the virtue of opening up trade and of increasing the revenue of the state. From August, 1810, to approximately November 25, 1811, licenses to the number of 1153 were signed[88]—a transaction which netted the treasury 828,430 francs.[89] The customs receipts increased from 11,600,000 francs in 1809 to 105,900,000 francs for the period from August, 1810, to the end of 1811, and the revenue from auctions amounted to 150,000,000 francs from October 18, to the end of the year 1810.[90] To offset these advantages, however, there were numerous disadvantages. Corruption was more widespread than ever, and Napoleon's officials became so incorrigible that he made them turn a part of their graft into the state treasury.[91] Various documents required for trade were forged wholesale, and the fires that were supposed to consume confiscated goods were usually made of straw and cheap cloth, unwound to give the impression of great quantity. The expenses of enforcing the blockade were greatly increased, and the harshness and selfishness of the new system antagonized France's allies. King Louis of Holland tried to issue licenses on his own authority, but with little success. When finally licenses were granted to France's satellites, they were of a nature to aid French shipping and industry rather than the economy of the dependent states.

Most important of all, the new measures weakened the original scheme of bringing Britain to her knees by closing the Continent to her goods. In later years at St. Helena, Napoleon lamented to his secretary Las Cases, "The system of commercial licenses was no doubt mischievous. Heaven forbid that I should have adopted it as a principle. It was the invention of the English; with me it was only a momentary resource."[92]

Official documents from the early part of 1812 indicate that the French believed that the Continental System was having its desired effect.[93] The willingness of the British to receive French goods and the Luddite riots in English industrial centers led the French to extravagant appraisals of Britain's abasement.

"England flattered herself with controlling the commerce of the world, but now her commerce, become a mere stock-jobbing affair, is carried on only by means of 20,000 licenses delivered each year. Forced to obey the laws of necessity, she thus renounces her Navigation Act, the real foundation of her power. She aspired to universal dominion of the seas, yet now navigation is forbidden to her vessels which are repulsed from all the ports of the Continent. She wished to enrich herself with tributes from Europe, but Europe has escaped not only from her injurious pretensions but likewise from paying tributes to her industry. Her manufacturing cities have become deserted; distress has succeeded to prosperity. . . . The alarming disappearance of specie and the absolute privation of business daily interrupt the public tranquillity."[94]

COLLAPSE OF THE CONTINENTAL SYSTEM

If all this was true, the French argued to themselves, there was obviously no reason why the license system should not be rapidly extended. Accordingly, in 1812, licenses were granted in large number and in 1813, wholesale. By the latter date, however, the entire Continental System had been undermined. Russia's disaffection from the blockade, that had been apparent since 1810, was a factor in Napoleon's decision to undertake a great campaign against her.[95]

On the very day, June 16, 1812, that he crossed the Russian border, England's misfortune seemed really overwhelming. At that moment the United States declared war on Great Britain, because the Orders in Council had not been repealed, although at almost the same hour those very Orders were revoked to avert a conflict with America. If Napoleon had not been so precipitant and had known of these acts, he might never have gone to Russia. As it was, however, he went; but he found upon his return a defeated Continental System. Enforcement of its decrees became almost inexistent where French authority was not felt, and where it still did exist, the blockade was turned into a machine to provide money for Napoleon. The Emperor's scheme of making his army live on his conquered enemies had worked in times of victory, but in moments of defeat, it was useless. "Undoubtedly it is still necessary to harm our foes," he wrote in 1812, "but above all we must live."[96] As Heckscher has brilliantly written:

"In the rush of more pressing claims that now came upon him, it exceeded even Napoleon's ability to devote to the enforcement of the system the superhuman energy which, even under more favorable auspices, would have been necessary to prevent it from falling asunder. Moreover, the falling away of his compulsory allies cost the system its continental extension . . . and with the advance of the allied armies into France, there also followed whole swarms of forbidden goods. Finally, the Continental decrees were formally rescinded immediately after Napoleon's abdication in April, 1814. With that the system passed into the realms of history."[97]

The Continental System came to grief for very practical reasons. It was never so rigidly enforced as Napoleon had intended that it should be. Smuggling and corruption of officials provided many leaks, and France found herself unable to hold all European governments to a strict application of her decrees. But in spite of the laxity of enforcement, the Continental System had patent weaknesses. Napoleon was forever vacillating from one policy to another and never stuck to one line of action long enough to effect logical results. From France's point of view, too, the blockade acted not only as a boon, but also as a handicap. It cut France off from raw materials that were vital to her industry; it stopped the exportation of French products to the British market; and it prevented her from shipping by sea to other countries. Moreover, the political hostility which the blockade aroused abroad led to political and military complications that completely entangled France and caused her to disperse her armies to all points of the compass at once. Finally, too much was expected of the Continental System from the first. It was almost incredible that, in any length of time in which it could conceivably be enforced, the blockade would have the effects on which Napoleon counted.

INFLUENCE OF THE CONTINENTAL SYSTEM ON FRENCH ECONOMIC LIFE

Before the death-knell of the Continental System sounded, it exerted a profound influence upon French economic life although it failed to bring Britain to her knees. It acted as a gigantic protectionist wall, and yet it did not follow to the letter traditional protectionist theory. In its attempt to humble Britain, it cut France off from raw materials and overseas markets.[98] As compensation for these definite losses, France was obliged to find substitutes for the raw materials, or new sources of supply, and to seek new markets on the Continent. In judging the purely economic results of the Continental System from the point of view of national production, then, it is necessary to ascertain as closely as possible how beneficial the abolition of English competition was to French industry, how successful the French were in obtaining raw materials from new sources, and whether the new markets opened up on the Continent were as rich as the one that was closed to France by England. Moreover, difficult as it may be, it is necessary to disentangle causes and effects and to attribute to the Continental System only its just due.

The blockade delivered a severe blow, as we have already seen and upon which we shall not dwell further, to all those engaged in export businesses, particularly to Breton agriculturalists, to Bordeaux wine growers, and to shippers. The luxury industries did not thrive during the Napoleonic era, except in moments of imperial extravagance, and undoubtedly suffered from the closure of the British market. The silk industry, which was affected especially, was one of the first to benefit from trade licenses. It did its utmost to make up for the loss of British trade by developing the markets of the Continent, and it persuaded Napoleon to secure for it a large portion of the cocoons that were produced in Italy. But when Continental anger rose against France, one of the first measures of foreign states was to tax, or to prohibit the importation of, French silks.[99] Woolen manufacturing, which had fallen to a low mark during the Revolution, was only able to attain a figure of production slightly in excess of that of 1789, and the linen industry, which Napoleon hoped in the closing years of his reign would supplant the cotton industry, made comparatively little progress. The metal trades profited from the abolition of English competition but did not develop rapidly enough to satisfy foreign demands. The Cockerill company in Liége, which was to become one of the world's most famous metallurgical organizations, was founded during the Napoleonic era. Coal production increased from 250,000 tons in 1794 to 900,000 tons in 1814. The Anzin mines were models of exploitation, and after the Saar valley had been carefully surveyed, mining in it was also begun. In the production of iron, France was behind both Germany and Sweden and sold her products at from 30 to 40 per cent dearer than they. In the chemical industry, she was ahead of all other nations, but her advantage came not from the Continental System, although that helped, but rather from the successful researches of her chemists.

The industries to be most profoundly affected by Napoleon's economic measures were dye, cotton, and sugar refining, for the raw materials essential to them were largely cut off. To save these industries from extinction, it was necessary to find new supplies of raw products or to produce domestic substitutes, the latter policy being one that would increase the economic self-sufficiency of the nation. To replace indigo, the growing of pastel was attempted, but the results were poor and years were yet to pass before coal tar products were to be substituted for Oriental dyes. To take the place of cane sugar, beet sugar was produced successfully, its production in 1813 amounting to 1,100,000 kilograms. Although all beet sugar factories were forced to close in the face of competition with colonial sugar after 1814, the beet sugar industry had been given a start and with continued protection was, in the course of the nineteenth century, to make France sugar-self-sufficient.

To find a substitute for cotton or to produce cotton in Europe[100] was, perhaps, the most imperative need that was created by the closure of the Continent. In the early years of the blockade, the absence of English competition had given a great impetus to the cotton industry. At Paris, the firm of Richard-Lenoir employed in its balmiest days as many as 14,000 persons; at Mülhausen, birth was given to one of

Alsace's most important industries; at Ghent, Liévin Bauwens developed such a thriving manufactory that the English Court of King's Bench condemned him to death *in contumaciam* for having robbed Britain of her cotton trade, "the apple of her eye"; and at Jouy-en-Josas near Versailles, Oberkampf built up such an important cotton-printing establishment that Napoleon is reported to have said to him, "We are both carrying on war against the British, but your war is the better."

The hopes of cotton manufacturers were raised to great heights by early successes, but as their demands for raw cotton increased and the supplies diminished, their discouragement was pitiful. Attempts were made to grow cotton in Europe, Naples being selected as the tropical element in the Continental System;[101] and efforts were expended to obtain supplies from the Levant. But never more than 12 per cent of the total needed was procured in these ways.[102] For these reasons, Napoleon, despairing of the cotton industry, advised that, "It would be better to use only wool, flax, and silk, the products of our own soil, and to proscribe cotton forever from the Continent . . ."[103]—and he did banish it from his palaces. The cotton industry thus waned in the closing years of Napoleon's rule. When thrown into competition with the English in 1814, all of the large cotton concerns went into bankruptcy. Nevertheless, the foundations of the cotton industry had been strengthened, and on these foundations a strong structure was built in the succeeding years.

Final judgment of the Continental System must take into consideration its merits and its demerits. Chaptal,[104] a keen observer and one of the best sources for the economic history of the Napoleonic era, was extravagant in his praise of it, but he saw only one side of the question. "It was during [Napoleon's] reign," he said, "that we freed ourselves from the tribute which we had up to that time paid foreigners. It was during his rule that we saw for the first time all our industrial products compete favorably, both as to price and to quality, with the goods of the most advanced industrial nations in all the markets of Europe."[105] He failed to consider that not once during the Napoleonic period did French foreign trade or French exports equal those of 1789. A more sober estimate would, in addition to lauding Napoleon's measure, demonstrate that the semi-hermetical closure of the Continent inflicted injuries on certain trades that the Emperor was powerless to heal.

Whatever history's ultimate judgment of the System may be, however, it is certain that Napoleon brought neither peace nor lasting prosperity to France. This fact accounts in large part for the enthusiasm with which a restoration of the Bourbons was welcomed in 1814. With Napoleon's fall capitalists felt that they had been relieved of an overzealous taskmaster.

DEFEATED FRANCE NOT DESPOILED

Napoleon's defeat placed France in a precarious political position. The conquerors of the "Little Corporal" were, after years of struggle, the masters of Europe and, if they had so desired, could have made France atone for the ills from which they had suffered during the long struggle. Among the victors there were those who advised a partial dismemberment of their victim, a long military occupation, and an indemnity so heavy that she would be weighted down by her burden. There were others, however, who were in a much less revengeful mood and fortunately for France their counsel prevailed. The Allies had so often reiterated the statement that they were working solely for the overthrow of Napoleon and not for the annihilation of the French that to have reversed their position now would have been to show extraordinarily bad faith. Moreover, Talleyrand, the French negotiator of the peace, that political chameleon whom Napoleon called a "silk stocking filled with mud," employed cleverly the doctrine of legitimacy, of a return to the *status quo ante,* whenever there was question of despoiling France.

The Allies were not altruistic, but neither Great Britain, Austria, nor Russia desired to see the political balance on the Continent upset by the Prussian proposal, made prior to the second peace of Paris, for the dismemberment of France.[106] The victorious Continental powers ultimately got territorial advantages elsewhere in Europe, and Great Britain, France's greatest economic rival, was satisfied with the acquisition of important colonies overseas and with the thought of her industrial superiority. Thus it was that France was not severely punished economically for her past sins. Her boundaries were fixed by the Congress of Vienna to correspond approximately to those she had had in 1791;[107] all the colonies which she had possessed in 1789 were returned except the Ile de France (modern Mauritius) in the Indian Ocean and the French part of Santo Domingo,[108] which had revolted, and its dependencies Saint Lucia and Tobago in the West Indies; and the indemnity that she was forced to pay was so small that by internal and foreign borrowings she was able to settle it by 1818.[109]

The Allies, and especially Great Britain, as Napoleon characteristically remarked, neglected their opportunity at Vienna of suppressing France economically. France was free after 1814 to develop her national economy as she saw fit, unimpeded by the dictates of her conquerors.

CHAPTER IV

ESTABLISHMENT OF THE ULTRA-PROTECTIVE SYSTEM UNDER THE RESTORATION[1], 1815-1830

ECONOMIC POSITION OF FRANCE

THE France that went down to defeat with Napoleon and that was spared the ravages of omnivorous victors at Vienna was, in economic affairs, essentially the France of the *ancien régime*. Neither the social legislation of the Revolutionaries, nor the Continental Blockade, nor the paternalism of the government had effected a fundamental alteration of her economic structure. Important as were such changes as the freeing of peasant property from seignioral dues, the sale of church and noble lands, the growth of certain industries, the establishment of a national customs union, and the suppression of the gilds, agriculture, industry, and commerce were carried on in 1815 much the same as they had been in the latter part of the eighteenth century.

France was still predominantly an agricultural country with approximately 75 per cent of the population living in rural districts[2] and with the greater part of the national wealth in farming.[3] Changes in landholding were also much less revolutionary than might be imagined. The large estates of the Church and of many nobles had been confiscated and sold, but so many had been purchased by bourgeois that the general aspect of the countryside had been only slightly altered. Small holdings in the hands of peasants and medium-sized farms in the possession of lesser bourgeois had increased, but not all Frenchmen had received title to rural property—there was a large, landless, agricultural proletariat.[4] Agriculture was carried on with few exceptions in the time-honored manner of the three-field system without the use of any except the more rudimentary tools and machines. Only after the middle of the century did fundamental changes become general.[5]

In industry, methods of production were also similar to what they had been in the eighteenth century, except that the domestic or merchant-employer system seemed to be losing its vitality and that there was a trend toward concentration, especially in mining and textile manufacture. How meager the industrial changes were may be gathered from the fact that only fifteen establishments had steam engines in 1814, and most of these were mines where the power was used for pumping water. France produced only a million tons of coal, while the Kingdom of the United Netherlands, which included Belgium, produced nearly four times that amount. And France had no cities whose population showed an increase in the Revolutionary and Napoleonic periods at all comparable with those of Manchester, Leeds, and Birmingham.[6] In the field of foreign commerce, France had definitely lost ground. Official statistics, which are only approximately correct, show that France's total foreign commerce decreased from 1,017,564,000 francs in 1789 to 621,000,000 francs in 1815.[7] Much of this loss had been Great Britain's gain and that nation's export trade showed an increase from £16,845,000 in 1788 to £51,600,000 in 1815.[8] Ample data can be provided to show that France had failed to keep pace with her most formidable economic rival of pre-Revolutionary days and that her inferiority to Britain in industry and commerce was hardly contested on the threshold of the Restoration. For these reasons, France's national economic problem in 1814 was to develop her industry and commerce to a position of at least equality with Britain's and in the meantime to protect her domestic market from British products.

The danger of the new situation was apparent upon the retreat of Napoleon to Paris. Close on the heels of the advancing allied armies came British merchants with goods that had been amassed in large quantities during the Continental Blockade and which the owners were willing to dump at bargain prices. The disrupted French customs service found it impossible to levy the legal duties on these goods and large supplies of certain products were imported to sell for less than had formerly been paid for customs. Thus British sugar sold in Paris for 1.80 francs a pound, while the normal protective rate was 2.20 francs, and beet sugar had cost about 6 francs a pound in the last years of the Napoleonic *régime*. Raw cotton and coffee fell about 50 per cent in price and both textiles and iron products, which had to meet the competition of British and Belgian manufacturers, became considerably cheaper.[9]

The predicament in which French merchants and manufacturers thus found themselves was only made worse by the policies pursued by the Restoration Government in the first days of its existence. The Comte d'Artois, brother of Louis XVIII, who had taken charge of affairs at Paris while the King recovered from an attack of the gout in England, was moved by his English backers[10] and by the apparent impossibility of collecting the existing customs duties to abolish some of the machinery for tariff enforcement, to replace the almost prohibitive rates on coffee and sugar by moderate ones, and to establish practically free trade in raw cotton.[11] The effects of the unbridled competition of the English that followed these measures were disastrous to the French, who had become accustomed to the protection of the Continental System and to the foreign markets that Napoleon's victories had given them. There were several bankruptcies, including one of the most important of the cotton manufacturing concerns, Richard-Lenoir, which had seven factories and employed 11,000 workers. All of the sugar-beet factories were forced to close their doors and many a merchant who had stocked up with raw cotton, sugar, or coffee at the high prices prevailing in 1812 and 1813 was pushed to the wall. As usual, business men in their extremity looked to the state for aid. Cotton manufacturers of Lille, Paris, Saint-Quentin, and Rouen asked for the restoration of prohibitive duties on cotton goods and for an indemnity of 30,000,000 francs as recompense for the losses that they had sustained because of the fall in prices.[12] The Rouen Chamber of Commerce wrote to the King, May 27, 1814, "A prohibitive tariff is a political and social right. From the manufacturer to the worker all demand, and doubtless rightly so, the privilege to meet exclusively the needs of the country in which they live."[13]

Such appeals moved the Government to send out a circular to the Chambers of Commerce stating its belief in a temperate tariff and a reciprocal exchange of goods with foreign nations and inviting business men to express their desires concerning customs duties.[14] With few exceptions manufacturers voiced approval of prohibitive rates or high protection on manufactured goods, low rates on raw materials, and government aid to further the exportation of their products. The General Council of Manufactures[15] and the General Council of Commerce,[16] advisory bodies to the government through which passed most economic legislation, received numerous pleas for the erection of a high tariff wall. The former became a stanch supporter of that policy. In a *mémoire* to the Duchess of Angoulême, daughter of Louis XVI, it prayed her Highness to buy French goods, for to purchase foreign products is "to deprive France's unfortunate laborers of work." And in a petition to the King the same Council urged on him the policy of Henry IV and Louis XIV.[17] The Chamber of Deputies made known its position in favor of high protection, even going so far as to advocate a return to Napoleon's policy of prohibition of foreign goods from France. Before such determined opposition the Government decided to modify its position. It agreed to establish moderate rates temporarily, but warned that it hoped to reduce them in the not distant future.

RULE OF THE RICH

Thus before the Restoration was a year old, France was in the throes of a debate on the question of protection, and more generally on the problem of national economics. To understand the outcome of that debate and why the nation adopted finally a policy of ultra-protectionism, it is necessary to consider briefly the political structure of the state and the alignment of political parties. From the point of view of national economics, perhaps the most fundamental political feature of the restored monarchy was the placing of power in the hands of the wealthy, in the hands of nobles and rich bourgeois. According to the terms of the Charter granted by Louis XVIII, the Chamber of Deputies was chosen through an indirect election system of two stages by those who paid direct taxes of at least 300 francs, while eligibility for membership in the Chamber required the payment of a thousand francs in direct taxes. Thus the legal-political life of the country was limited to not more than 88,000;[18] the lesser bourgeoisie and the poorer classes were excluded from a voice in political affairs. But even with these provisions the King might have reserved power for himself, for he appointed members to the House of Peers and according to the Charter had the right to formulate and execute laws while the legislative bodies were to make suggestions and to ratify royal proposals. He thought evidently that it was a wiser policy to allow the Chamber to play a large rôle in the government and after the first year selected his ministers from the benches of the majority in the lower house. So conscientious was he in the pursuit of this policy and so firmly did he establish the principle of ministerial responsibility that the Comte d'Artois, who became king as Charles X in 1824, was powerless in his attack against it.

The wealthy classes directed in practice the policies of government through their control of the Chamber of Deputies. But they were badly divided among themselves into three parties—Ultra-Royalists, Royalists, and Independent or Liberal. The essential division between the extremists was based on whether France should develop the traditions of the Revolution and of Napoleon or whether she should return to the traditions of the *ancien régime*. The Ultra-Royalists, who were led by the Comte d'Artois and whose strength came from *émigrés* and the clergy, insisted that the formalities of the old order be followed, that land which had been confiscated during the Revolution should be returned to its former owners, and that the position of the Church should be elevated. The Liberals, who were bourgeois, military officials, and anti-clericals, favored the guarantee to purchasers of *biens nationaux* of titles to their new property and the maintenance of the Church in the position to which the Revolution and the Concordat had relegated it.

Most of the nation was divided between these two groups—a division so fundamental that it still persists today—but there was a small group of Royalists led by Louis XVIII who endeavored to steer a middle course between the extremists. The King's policy of compromise led him to adopt measures favorable to the Ultras or the Liberals but not to push an aggressive personal program. He tried to pacify the Ultras by adopting the white flag, regarded as traditionally monarchist, by using the title of Louis XVIII, "King of France and Navarre by the *Grace of God*" rather than "by the will of the people"; by dating his reign from the death of his unfortunate nephew; and by

placing many of the *émigrés* in traditional administrative positions at
the court. On the other hand, to placate the bourgeoisie and the people, he guaranteed to them their greatest material acquisitions of the
Revolutionary era—title to land which they had purchased and the
abolition of seigniorial dues.

ULTRA-PROTECTIVE TARIFFS

Because he favored compromise, he did not insist on his avowed
policy of low tariffs, but allowed the Chamber to deal with the problem as it saw best. Such an attitude could only invite high protection,
because both the Ultras and Liberals had interests which were directly involved. The former desired to increase the income from their
lands and accordingly favored the protection of agricultural products;
the latter wanted to augment their profits on manufactured articles
and therefore labored for prohibitive rates on industrial goods. . . .
"Thus two hostile political parties found in a tariff system which prevented foreign competition an equal guarantee of riches. They allied
to defend and to develop it."[19] It was this condition that established between 1814 and 1826 the ultra-protective tariff system of the Restoration which continued in force with but little change until the Second
Empire.

The tariff bill, which first gave evidence of the alliance between
agriculturalists and manufacturers for higher duties, became a law in
December, 1814. Although this was the work of Louis XVIII's first
Chamber of Deputies, the same body that had sat as Napoleon's *Corps
Législatif,*[20] it reflected the political alignment of the wealthy against
the King's policy of moderate tariffs. The Government had thought
to satisfy the bourgeoisie by proposing a bill that provided for the
free transit of foreign goods through France, a small surtax on foreign shipping, and a partial restoration of the rates that had been reduced by the Comte d'Artois in April. With such a proposition the
Chamber was not satisfied, and, as at that time the King's ministers
were not members of the Chamber and rarely appeared before it, they
failed to sense correctly the temper of that body. The deputies proceeded, with unaccustomed audacity, to give the Government a lesson
in national economy.

Working on the theory that "customs are established to guarantee the prosperity of manufacturers and to enhance national industry" and that tariffs are not really national until they have established economic self-sufficiency of the nation,[21] the Chamber adopted the principle of free transit of non-prohibited goods;[22] approved, as in all the tariff legislation of the Restoration, a provision for a surtax on foreign shipping in order to satisfy French carriers; prohibited the importation of refined sugar, and increased the tax on French colonial sugar and the surtax on foreign sugar; raised the rates on linens and hemp products, and on iron from 10 to about 50 per cent *ad valorem;* and, most important of all, prohibited the importation from all nations of the long list of goods, including cottons, which had been prohibited only from England by the law of October 31, 1796.[23] Thus was established and made general in a period of peace a system of prohibition and protection that had been adopted by the Directory and Napoleon[24] largely as a weapon of war against England. It was the first important victory of the protectionists after the coming to power of Louis XVIII; it was the initial move in the construction of an ultra-protectionist tariff system.

Upon the foundation thus established, successive Restoration Chambers, whether controlled by Ultras or Liberals, built a customs fortress around France. The *Chambre introuvable,*[25] the extreme royalist body that was elected in the midst of the reaction to the Hundred Days and in the heat of the White Terror, added to the structure by the law of April 28, 1816. The cabinet presented a bill providing for higher rates with an eye to increasing the much-depleted revenue of the state. But as in 1814, the Chamber was not satisfied with the official proposals, and vested interests vied with one another to secure protection that would be advantageous to them. A spokesman of manufacturers of white lead stated that this product should be highly taxed, for, although the French produced the best in the world, the common people preferred foreign brands; and a representative of wine growers made a plea for a heavy duty on tea, because "this drink destroys national character in that it develops in those who use it frequently the cold nature of northerners, while wine expands the soul with a sweet gaiety and hilarity which helps to give Frenchmen that friendly and witty character that distinguishes them from the citizens of other nations." All interests could not be satisfied, but agriculturalists obtained the privilege of exporting hides and the prohibition of all brandies except those made from wine, and manufacturers the right to have prohibited stuffs sought for from house to house and seized by government officials—a right that still existed in 1860.

To these measures, the Chamber made no important additions in 1817 and 1818,[26] expending much of its energy in the eternal fight between the Right and the Left. In this struggle, the Liberals were momentarily successful, increasing their representation from twenty-five in 1817 to ninety in 1819[27] and electing that notable regicide Abbé Grégoire who had once said, "Kings are in the moral order what monsters are in the physical." With the Liberals in the ascendancy attention was centered in 1819 on securing legislation favorable to grain growers—evidence that the economic interests of bourgeois were not limited to commerce and industry. Agricultural protection was comparatively a new phenomenon, for in the *ancien régime* France was not much bothered by foreign competition in farm products. The principal regulation in the commerce of grain before 1789 was the rule, established because of fear of famine, against exportation. Attacks on this restriction by farmers and speculators were numerous, and in 1814 it was abolished.[28] But with exportation of grain came also importation; on April 28, 1816, grain was allowed to come in practically free. As fate would have it, however, the crops failed in 1816 and there was a shortage in 1817. Prices soared and suffering followed. Serious riots and fighting took place in the winter of 1816–17 and the spring of 1817.[29] The events alarmed the government and generous subsidies were offered for the importation of grain.[30] Under these conditions, wheat began to come to France from the Ukraine—800,000 hectoliters from the port of Odessa in 1817. The tapping of this abundant source and good crops in 1818 forced the price of wheat down from 36.16 francs a hectoliter in 1816–17 to 18.42 francs in 1819. First the poor crops and then the cheap prices of agricultural products reduced the purchasing power of the farmers, which in turn contributed to bringing on a general economic crisis in 1818. There were many bankruptcies, especially among wheat growers. In their consternation agriculturalists placed the blame for their predicament on Russian wheat, which they claimed could be delivered in France for from 12 to 13 francs a hectoliter while French grain of the Midi could hardly be produced for 23 francs,[31] and they clamored for the security to be obtained only from a protective tariff. The Government hastened to give them satisfaction; by the law of July 16, 1819, it established a sliding-scale duty on grain in imitation of the English corn laws. The country was divided into three zones and the import duty was fixed at 25 centimes per hectoliter for wheat imported in French ships, or at 1.25 francs if imported in foreign ships, when the price was at or above 23 francs for the first zone, 21 francs for the second, and 18 francs for the third. The customs rate was increased by one franc for every franc decrease in the price of grain until prices reached or fell below 20, 18, and 16 francs for the respective zones.[32] When these prices were attained, importation was prohibited.

High agricultural rates were thus added to the system of industrial protection. Ample as the customs tariffs of the time appear to the scientific investigator to have been, they satisfied only temporarily the voracious desires of the immediate recipients of benefits. In 1820 the assassination of the Duc de Berri, the only member of the Bourbon family that seemed likely to produce an heir, but who, ironically enough, was the father of a posthumous son, aroused sentiment against the Liberals. The Ultra-Royalists were carried to power on a wave of reaction and fortified their position by a law, the law of double vote, that allowed 25 per cent of the voters paying the highest taxes to choose 172 of the 270 deputies. The election of the reactionary *Chambre retrouvée* in 1823 and the succession of the Comte d'Artois to the throne as Charles X in 1824 consolidated power in the hands of the Ultras until 1827. This new governing group attempted to outdo its opponents in tariff legislation. By the law of June 7, 1820, the Chamber increased the tax on steel from 45 to 60 per cent *ad valorem* and that on raw wool to 5 per cent, prohibited the importation of Indian silks and placed a high rate on all silks, and, to appease woolen manufacturers for the tax on raw wool, established export subsidies as a kind of drawback on finished woolen goods. On July 4, 1821, the large landed proprietors, whom the new electoral law had helped to power, voted a still higher protection on grain than had been afforded them in 1819. After the erection of the first sliding scale, farmers had planted large acreage of wheat in the belief that prices would be high. An abundant crop in 1820 kept prices down and an appeal was made for higher rates even though an investigation showed that but 700,000 hectoliters had been imported within the year. Now France was divided into four zones and the basic prices of the original scheme were considerably raised. French agriculturalists were made indisputably safe from foreign competition—prices were high enough to allow importation for only one month in the remaining years of the Restoration. But in spite of this fact, wheat remained cheap, selling at a mean price of 15 francs 74 in 1825. Farmers were irritated at conditions, but could no longer vent their wrath on the tariff.

The work begun thus by the Ultras was carried to completion by the laws of July 27, 1822, and May 17, 1826. The rates were increased on practically every important article of foreign commerce or national production. The surtax on foreign sugar was increased from 33 per cent to 50 in the interests of colonial planters and the rates on domestic animals were more than doubled for the benefit of farmers who were suffering from the low price of meat. The customs on wool were doubled and then raised to 30 per cent of their value and the export subsidies on woolens were correspondingly augmented. The tariff on iron was fixed at the equivalent of 120 per cent *ad valorem* in 1822 (this seemingly exaggerated rate was established in view of the fact that imports from England had grown from 800,000 to 7,000,-000 kilograms in six years), and the tariff on steel was raised to about 100 per cent in 1826. Duties on hops, dried vegetables, blankets, pen quills, linens, and on rice, which France did not produce, were either established or greatly increased; surtaxes on goods imported in foreign ships were made higher, and when the application of the new rates seemed to endanger export trade, export subsidies were accorded manufacturers. The Ultras outdid themselves in establishing rates to satisfy every one; they brought to completion the most impregnable protective system that France had from the Continental Blockade to the World War—one that was without a rival in Western Europe.

THE COLONIAL COMPACT

Protectionism did not complete, however, the plan of national economy during the Restoration; it had two important complements—the colonial system and the navigation acts. Towards her colonial empire, which had been returned at the Congress of Vienna much as it was in 1789[33] and in which the French people took much national pride,[34] France adopted a policy which was essentially that of the colonial pact, or of the *exclusif*—that colonies must supply the mother country with those raw materials in which she is deficient and purchase all their manufactured articles from her.[35] As a guarantee that this policy would be strictly carried out, no self-government was granted the colonies and jurisdiction over colonial affairs was placed in the hands of a group of shippers from Bordeaux, led by Baron Portal, who had an interest in continuing the economic interdependence of the colonies and France.[36]

For the proper functioning of the colonial policy that was adopted, it was necessary that each colony produce some article that would enter easily into international trade. French West Indies had already satisfied this requirement by growing sugar, but Senegal and Guiana provided real problems. The latter was comparatively barren, and the former was forbidden, by an agreement signed at Vienna, to traffic after 1820 in its most lucrative article of commerce—slaves. Abolition of the slave trade deprived Bordeaux shippers of a profitable business and they cast about for a plan to restore trade with Senegal to its former prosperity. In their search for a scheme of exploitation, they found that the Dutch had been successful in growing industrial crops in the East Indies.[37] They, therefore, decided to try a similar scheme in their undeveloped tropical possessions. With the aid of government subsidies, cotton, indigo, and coffee culture was attempted in Senegal, and, in like manner, expeditions were sent out to Guiana and Madagascar to colonize and to raise commercial crops.

Laudable as these experiments in colonization were, they were not destined to succeed during the Restoration. All kinds of hazards had to be overcome—hostility of the natives, unfriendly climate, inability to secure French colonizers, and heavy first costs. The failure to realize an immediate triumph dampened popular enthusiasm for the experiments. In 1821 the Bordeaux group fell from control of colonial affairs with the coming to power of the Ultras, and with the change of administration there was a decided relaxation in the vigor with which the projects were carried out. Discouragement and apathy followed the let-down, and, toward the close of the Restoration, it was decided to abandon the attempt to raise industrial crops in Senegal. With the decline in rubber production, that colony became little more than a trading post. The penetration of Madagascar by means of settlement and agriculture was also given up and the exploitation of Guiana was considered hopeless.

In view of these failures, it is little wonder that France did not undertake a vigorous campaign of colonial aggrandizement during the Restoration. The only conquest of any importance was of Algiers and that cannot be explained in the light of national economics. To be sure, Algerian pirates were obnoxious and the Bey of Algiers was insulting over minor matters, but both the Villèle and Martignac cabinets had refused to become embroiled with him. The main reason that the expedition was undertaken was because Charles X, on account of his autocratic rule during the Polignac Ministry, needed military glory to win support for his domestic policies.[38] The economic potentialities of Algeria, to say nothing of its geography, were unknown; and in wealthy circles the campaign was unpopular. Even when news of the taking of Algiers reached Paris, quotations on the Bourse fell.[39] But in spite of the non-economic origin of the extension of the French colonial empire in North Africa, Algiers, and eventually all Algeria, became a French possession. To future governments was left the problem of working out an economic program for salvaging the new acquisition.

The colonies from which France received her greatest economic benefits during the Restoration were her more civilized and better established possessions in the West Indies. Here the old colonial system was applied in its more pristine form. In them, manufacturing, even sugar-refining, was forbidden; trade with foreigners was prohibited; and shipping was reserved for French bottoms. Nor were these mere paper rules: save for minor exceptions they were enforced strictly.[40]

The major product of the French West Indies was sugar and the history of this article illustrates well the functioning of the colonial system in its application to other colonial goods such as spices, dye-wood, quinine, cocoa, and coffee. All during the Revolutionary and Napoleonic periods, intercourse with the colonies had been spasmodic, so that the lot of planters was not happy. They looked to peace for their salvation, but the first act of the Restoration was, as we have seen, to allow sugar and other colonial products to come to France from foreign nations. This the colonies resented. They demanded clamorously the reciprocal benefits of the colonial system. If they had to purchase all manufactured articles in France, France ought at least to buy colonial products exclusively from them. This argument won the Chamber to their support and in 1814 a preferential tariff was established on sugar—a tariff that was raised by the law of April 28, 1816. These duties cut foreign importation of sugar to about two and a half million kilograms out of a total consumption of 50,000,000 kilograms. But still colonists were not satisfied. The tax on sugar from India had been kept purposely low to encourage French shippers to maintain contacts with the East—to keep up the "long haul"—and although the quantity of sugar from this source was not large, planters in the West Indies demanded a tax that would wipe it out. Such a tax was established on June 7, 1820, but it had to be raised on July 27, 1822, to be absolutely effective. The price of sugar increased and colonists revelled in their trade. Only when cane sugar became so expensive that the beet sugar industry was revived, was their joy restrained.

Thus did colonists become bedfellows with industrialists and agriculturalists in the French national economic system of the Restoration. It remains for us only to place shippers alongside their colleagues to have the picture complete. No special legislation was enacted at the behests of labor; and consumers,[41] if there be any such in the pure form, were practically ignored during the Restoration.

AID TO THE MERCHANT MARINE

The chief aid given to French carriers during this period consisted in advantages similar to those granted during the Revolution. The Navigation Act of September 21, 1793, was,[42] in fact, the basis for regu-

lating shipping to and from France from 1814 to 1861. The terms of
this act provided originally for the importation of goods to France only
in French ships, or in the ships of the country in which the goods carried originated. Foreign ships had, however, to pay a surtax—a tax
known as the *droit de pavillon*—on the ordinary customs of the goods
they imported. This restrictive legislation was mitigated somewhat by
the law of April 28, 1816, which allowed foreign carriers to import
into France all goods irrespective of their origin. This advantage was
minimized by augmenting the *droit de pavillon;* by re-establishing the
droit d'entrepôt—used in Colbert's time—which was a surtax on non-
European goods that were imported from a European country rather
than directly from overseas; and by maintaining *droits de tonnage*—a
tonnage tax on foreign ships—established by the Act of Navigation of
1793.[43] Foreigners were prevented, moreover, from securing the privileges granted to French carriers by registering their vessels in France,
for from 1793 to 1866, it was provided that vessels of French registry
had to be constructed in France and to be owned completely by
Frenchmen, except that after 1845 one-half ownership in France was
sufficient to satisfy the requirements for sailing the French flag.
Finally, coastwise shipping, *la grande pêche*[44] and colonial commerce
were reserved exclusively for French bottoms.

The nature of the navigation laws of the Restoration was restrictive:
shipping was to be developed by keeping the foreigner out rather than
by building up the industry by direct subsidies. It was not until steam
navigation developed that it was deemed advisable to grant money
aids to the marine industry to help it compete with England.[45] In the
meantime, it was hoped that protective navigation legislation would
be sufficient to quiet the opposition of French shippers to high tariffs
and to provide France with a strong navy. In these matters the nationalist argument was a powerful one, for the nation was dependent
upon a strong marine force in case of war. Only could this be provided, if shipbuilding and carrying prospered. National navigation
laws remained the law of the land until late in the history of the Second Empire.

The fact that shippers were afforded protection, as protection was
afforded industrialists, agriculturalists, and colonials, provides addi-

tional evidence to the already abundant proof that the national system of economics during the Restoration was the creation of the capitalist class. Through its control of the legislature, this class could pass any bill which it believed was to its advantage, for, although its members were divided badly among the Ultra, Royalist, and Liberal parties, they agreed perfectly on the principle of advancing their own interests. The national economic system developed on the basis of greed, a fact that was recognized generally in the first part of the nineteenth century, but, that the greed might seem less brazen, the system was cloaked in an elaborate *rationale*—in a philosophy of economy in which national welfare was writ large. But national sentiment played a much less important rôle in peace-time economy than it had in war-time. From war, however, capitalists had learned of ways to use the nation for their benefit.

NATIONAL ECONOMIC THEORY

Among the theorists who contributed to the doctrine and propaganda of national economy during the Restoration three names predominate: Charles Ganilh, whom Roscher called the Friedrich List of France,[46] F. L. A. Ferrier, one time General Director of the Customs, and Louis Say, the brother of the better-known free-trade economist, Jean Baptiste Say. In the writings of all of these men, the theory that national strength and greatness depend on a nation's capacity to produce looms large. Nearly all their theoretical writings are merely variants of this central theme. Ganilh (1758–1836),[47] one of Bonaparte's supporters in the *coup d'état* of Brumaire, who devoted much of his time to economic writing after he fell out with his master in 1802, stated categorically that national greatness depends on production: and production, he continued, is the result of all the forces, all the faculties, and of all the power of the nation for work. To judge the wealth of a nation, a measurement of the goods that are consumed should not be taken, but rather a measurement of the ability of the nation to produce these goods. A purely agricultural nation cannot rise to the heights of power among the states of the world: it must become industrial and commercial. To attain these ends, an agricultural state, supposedly like France, should protect and give subsidies to its industries and pass navigation acts to develop its merchant marine until those branches of national production reach their maturity. When the period of full development has been attained, nations will not be completely self-sufficient. Then foreign commerce should take the form of the interexchange of what each nation has in surplus. At this point tariffs and subsidies should not be excessive; they should be moderate and "scientific."

In a similar vein were the arguments of the politician Ferrier (1777-1861),[48] General Director of the Customs from 1812 to Napoleon's downfall. His *Du gouvernement considéré dans ses rapports avec le commerce,* one of the best defenses of national economics written during the Restoration and a book that sold approximately as well at the time as the popular free-trade works of Jean Baptiste Say, begins with a statement of faith—that the author's economics is concerned with France "because France is my fatherland and because to be able to aid her to increase her well-being is my sole desire." Ferrier maintained that a nation could not be happy unless it were independent; that independence depended on force, and force on wealth. The more consumable goods a nation produces the wealthier it is, and hence the more powerful it is. Therefore nations should look to their production. They should stimulate industry and exports, but imports should be curbed because they reduce production at home. A nation should do its own carrying, which may be aided by navigation acts if necessary, and should have colonies to assure a diversified production. Barriers to commerce within the boundaries of a nation impede the exchange of goods which individuals have in surplus and are on this account undesirable, but barriers to imports are necessary, for an unfavorable balance of trade deprives the nation of capital for its development. Ferrier's theories fitted well with the economy of the Restoration; he was one of its most enthusiastic admirers.

Louis Say (1774-1840),[49] who had a sugar-refining business at Nantes, was, unlike his brother, a stanch protectionist. Doubtless his interests in seeing foreign sugar excluded from France conditioned his economics, but his arguments for protectionism were invariably nationalist. The wealth of a nation depends upon the consumable goods that it possesses, according to Say, but only on the condition that they are not too unequally distributed. Goods may be obtained by violence, by gifts, by exchange, and by production, but by production is the best way. The greater the production of a nation, the greater is the usefulness of goods, because even in case of surplus the excess may be exchanged for what the nation lacks. A gauge which indicates whether these conditions are being met is provided by the balance of trade statistics which should always be favorable. To insure a favorable balance in foreign commerce, a nation should have an efficient government and a strong enough military force to maintain its independence. The government should take measures to prevent the purchase of foreign goods even at low prices, when similar goods may be had at home, because purchases abroad reduce national production and deprive workers of their means of subsistence. Such a policy may result in higher prices within the state, a burden that falls particularly on the bourgeoisie, but it provides work for labor and allows an increase in population. That national production cannot be speeded up to satisfy the wants of a growing population, as held by Malthus, is false. The nation can and must increase its production. Increased production results in a large population; and these two factors are fundamental in the creation of a strong state.

Such were the ideas frequently expressed in writings of a great number of national economists during the Restoration. J. A. Chaptal (1756–1832), chemist, chemical manufacturer, and economic adviser to Napoleon, lauded the effects of the Continental System and praised protectionism in his *De l'industrie française;*[50] Comte Destutt de Tracy (1754–1836), a member of the House of Peers, stressed the importance of production and of a large population in his *Traité d'économie politique;*[51] and Alexander Moreau de Jonnès (1778–1870),[52] a statistician and economist, in an essay for a prize established by the Academy of Marseilles on the subject "Causes for the loss of commerce and the remedies therefor," held that the main causes for decline were revolutions and wars and that the remedies were increased production and the *mise en valeur* of colonies. Of a similar mind was Comte de Vaublanc[53] (1756–1845), a politician and publicist. In spite of all arguments for free trade, a nation that has a decidedly favorable balance of trade has an advantageous economic position. England attained her industrial and commercial superiority under a system of protection and France must have recourse to the same instrument in order to build up her productive power. England's superior position furnishes now ample protection; France's inferiority requires a policy of employing every means to augment her economic strength.

Even among economists who were inclined to approve of the doctrines of the English school of economics, there was a feeling that some virtue was to be found in national economy. Charles Dupin (1784–1873), mathematician, statistician, and professor at the Conservatory of Arts and Crafts, was critical of the traditional balance-of-trade theory but recognized the importance of national economy. After making an elaborate statistical survey of France and Great Britain,[54] the sources of which are obscure and were in some instances probably in his imagination, Dupin concluded that France was in a comparatively precarious position and that she was losing ground. If France were to improve her position, she must develop more highly her resources. "As in Rome, in time of great public need, all party discord and all sentiment of hate must be forgotten. Our only thought must be of national salvation, of the grandeur and glory of the country and of the monarchy."

Among business men and public officials expressions of national economy were frequent. One of the outstanding representatives of their position was the Baron de St. Cricq, General Director of Customs during those years when the ultra-protective system was established. His frequent speeches in the legislative bodies reflect an early sympathy for low tariffs, but a growing support for protectionism. Whether economic theorists approved of protection or not, he held, protection was the rule applied by all European governments to increase home production to its highest point and must be employed by France.[55] France must protect those infant industries that laid their foundations during the Continental System.

"It is not the government who will say to the proprietors of industries which were built up because of the greatest sacrifices: 'If a tariff of 20 per cent does not suffice to protect you, perish!' Foreign industry with immense capital is present to advise this position, to say: 'You have taken the wrong road, carry your ruins elsewhere.' [Shall we say] to thousands of cotton workers: 'Your goods are too dear, break your looms!' To our metal workers: 'We can buy for 15 francs what you sell for 25: Put out your fires!' To millions of hands in all industries: 'Find work which does not have to be protected' . . . In economics . . . all interests must be respected. . . .'"[56]

EFFECTS OF THE RESTORATION'S NATIONAL ECONOMIC POLICIES

The effect of the "respect" that was paid to all economic interests by the closed economic system that was developed during the Restoration is extremely difficult to measure. In economics there are myriads of causal factors of which state action is but one. To segregate one cause from all the others and to estimate its influence irrespective of all other causes is a very delicate if not impossible task. So complex is the undertaking, in fact, that it has usually been in attempting it that economists have made their worst blunders. Instead of dealing exclusively with fact in making an analysis of the results of protective legislation, students of economics have all too frequently become lost in a sea of detail and have fallen back upon theory. Free traders have thus found ample evidence to confirm their opinions and national economists have interpreted their findings to fit their views. From experience, the scholar is wary of taking at face value the estimates of writers on the subject of protection and always seeks in advance to ascertain what bias the author he is reading may have. But difficult as it is to isolate the cause-and-effect relationship of economic legislation, it is a matter that the economic historian cannot well ignore. To evade it is to lose the greater part that history can teach.

One of the most obvious and immediate results of French protective legislation from 1815 to 1826 was the reprisals of foreign nations. Few countries were willing to accept the restrictive legislation of France without retaliation. Such was the mind of the United States, which complained especially of the surtax *de pavillon*. Unsuccessful in attempts to obtain relief through diplomatic channels, the young American republic placed a surtax on goods imported in French bottoms. The French parried this blow by raising their rates still higher, but so burdensome did the respective charges become that the importation of raw cotton to France was seriously hampered. This condi-

tion could not be allowed to continue, and the French offered to negotiate. It was agreed that goods imported to France in American
bottoms should pay less than the regular tax *de pavillon* and that not
more than this new rate should be the basis for the American tax on
French vessels carrying cargoes to the United States.[57] American carriers thus secured an advantage over other shippers, but the English
soon complained and obtained by a reciprocal agreement the same
privileges that were granted to Americans. In like manner, Sweden
placed especially heavy duty on French wine because of the prohibitive rates on iron; the Netherlands prohibited the importation of
French woolens and of French wines, and they placed a hundred per
cent duty on French pottery; Spain struck at French manufactured
articles because of the tax on her wool; and Russia and several German states took similar action. Whatever the general effect of French
national economics may have been in increasing production at home,
it is certain that it tended to force other nations further along the
route of closed economy.

Another obvious and direct result of the high duties and prohibitions was smuggling. This was not a new practice, especially to those
Frenchmen who had lived during the Continental Blockade, but instead of waning, it continued to flourish. How important it was
in French economy, however extensively carried on, or how organized are not well known, and perhaps can never be accurately ascertained. But certain internal evidence can be obtained to show that it
was highly developed. One of the best examples is that concerning
the manufacture of muslins, percales, and tulles. The weaving of
these cotton cloths required a fine thread, the importation of which
was prohibited and the spinning of which hardly existed in France.
Yet these cloths were manufactured in relatively large quantities, for
entire towns lived on that particular industry. Smuggling was obviously resorted to in this case, and it is said that regular rates, ranging
from 20 to 50 per cent according to the dangers involved and the dis-
tances covered, were established for the service, consumers of the
finer yarns being informed of current smuggling charges in advance
of the delivery of the goods. The fact that laws had to be passed
allowing house-to-house search for and the seizure of contraband

articles and the hauling of large groups of smugglers into court, gives additional proof that illicit trade was common. However important it may have been in counteracting French national economics, it is significant in reading trade statistics of the period. Undoubtedly the item was large, and it was "invisible."[58]

The effect of the French protective system during the Restoration on foreign trade is much more difficult to evaluate than its effect on smuggling and on retaliatory legislation. In international exchange not only all the factors regulating the nation's economy came into play, but also the economic conditions in foreign lands. Judging from official customs statistics, it would seem that the legislation of the Restoration aided in limiting imports and perhaps in increasing exports. The total foreign commerce increased from 585 million francs in 1814 to 1201 millions in 1825, which surpassed for the first time the foreign commerce of France in 1788. With this growth, a general favorable balance was maintained.

FOREIGN COMMERCE OF FRANCE
DURING THE RESTORATION[59]
(Millions of Francs)

Year	General Commerce			Special Commerce		
	Imports	Exports	Total	Imports	Exports	Total
1814 ...	239	346	585	"	"	"
1815 ...	199	422	621	"	"	"
1816 ...	243	548	791	"	"	"
1817 ...	332	464	796	"	"	"
1818 ...	336	502	838	"	"	"
1819 ...	295	460	755	"	"	"
1820 ...	335	543	878	"	"	"
1821 ...	394	405	799	"	"	"
1822 ...	426	385	811	"	"	"
1823 ...	362	391	753	"	"	"
1824 ...	455	441	896	"	"	"
1825 ...	534	667	1201	401	544	945
1826 ...	565	561	1126	436	461	897
1827 ...	566	602	1168	414	507	921
1828 ...	608	610	1218	454	511	965
1829 ...	616	608	1224	483	504	987
1830 ...	638	573	1211	489	453	942

But the favorable evolution of French foreign commerce may have been more apparent than real, for the official statistics are open to severe criticism. One of their greatest weaknesses was their failure to establish the correct value of imports. The value on which the duty was levied was determined by the price of goods in the country of their origin. But as imports were generally cheaper in the lands whence they came than in France, there was a tendency to underestimate their worth. Indigo, for example, cost 9 francs a kilogram where it was bought and 15 francs in France; it was valued by the customs service at 9 francs or 40 per cent of its real value. For exports, the customs service levied duties according to weight, and, while this system was not liable to much error on staple products, it was far from correct when applied to goods of varying quality like guns, Chinaware, or pianos. Furthermore, the customs made no distinction between general commerce on all goods which were exported and imported, and special commerce—goods of French production which were exported and goods which were imported solely for French consumption.

The Balance of Commerce Bureau of the Ministry of the Interior endeavored to make corrections for some of the errors, especially for smuggling and for the value of imports and exports, and consequently presented statistics at great variance with the customs' figures. In 1820, the official statistics showed a large favorable balance of trade, while the Balance of Commerce Bureau declared that it was only 13 million; the difference between the two statistics in 1821 was 29 millions; and in 1824 the difference in one item, silk, was 44 millions. Thus customs' statistics came in for much criticism and an attempt was made in 1826 to correct the abuse of erroneous evaluation and to distinguish between general and special commerce. In that year, a fixed value was established for various articles[60]—a value that was maintained without change until 1847—and a separate set of statistics was drawn up to show what imports were for French consumption and what exports were simply re-exports.

A still more serious charge against official statistics was that they were altered for political purposes. A contemporary, the Comte de Vaublanc,[61] and a modern writer, Professor S. Charléty,[62] have maintained that whenever a campaign was launched for a high tariff, statistics were made to show a very small favorable or an unfavorable balance of trade. Thus the excess of exports over imports was 223 millions in 1815 following the tariff of 1814; it remained rather stable during 1816 and 1817, when tariff increases were voted, and improved in 1819 and 1820 with the establishment of the grain laws; but it became very small in 1821 and turned into an excess of imports over exports in 1822. Then the tariff of 1822 improved conditions until 1824, when a new campaign was waged that resulted in the tariff of 1826. Furthermore, it has been said that the statistics were arranged to show a favorable balance of trade in order to secure popular support for the régime and approval of the Restoration economic policy.

Internal evidence is not sufficient to prove the case, nor does the fact that the statistics were compiled under the direction of a protectionist make it conclusive. Nevertheless, other evidence seems to indicate that there may have been tampering with or at least serious error in the official trade statistics. According to these figures, French imports nearly doubled from 1820 to 1828, but the duties collected in this period increased only from 70 to 104 million francs and this in spite of higher tariffs. Similarly, from 1821 to 1829 exports were shown to have increased from 405 to 610 million francs but the small export tax, levied to cover the cost of statistics, decreased from 2,671,202 francs to 1,394,613 francs. And furthermore, statistics showing capital transfers do not indicate extraordinary payments to France in settlement of a large favorable balance of trade in goods. These facts have led Professor Charléty to conclude that from 1814 to 1829 imports to France probably remained stationary and that exports from France actually diminished.[63]

Whatever the truth may be, enough doubt has been cast on the official statistics to make the historian cautious in generalizing about them. Nevertheless, an analysis of the figures which show trade between France and individual countries and the kind of goods exchanged throws some light upon the effect of the tariff. According to the statistics, France had a favorable balance of trade with England, and, if they may be trusted to show relatively the commercial transactions between the two nations, it would seem that the protective system was successful in keeping out manufactured articles. With the exception of machines, the leading imports from England were raw products. Even in textiles France exported to her competitor more than she imported, although some goods were for re-export. Her greatest trade was with the Kingdom of the United Netherlands, and, although this commerce resulted in an unfavorable balance for her, the only manufactured articles which she imported in large quantities were cheese and lace. To the United States, Switzerland, and Sardinia she exported more than she imported; to Russia, Austria, Sweden and Norway, and Prussia she imported more than she exported. In general, she sold more manufactured products abroad than she did raw materials and imported small quantities of finished products in comparison with goods destined for production or consumption. After allowing for all other factors, such as the industrialization of France, it would seem that the tariff must have had some effect upon the nature of French imports and exports.

GROWTH OF DOMESTIC COMMERCE AND PRODUCTION

It would seem, also, that there may well have been some increase in foreign trade, for there was a decided growth of internal commerce. All available statistics indicate an augmentation of business activity. The operations of the Bank of France, a good index of conditions at Paris if not in France, increased in paper discounted from 209 million francs in 1815 to 426 millions in 1816 and to 727 millions in 1818; fell off to 390 millions in 1819 as part of the economic crisis; and recovered to 822 millions in 1826, preceding another depression. There was also an increase of the Bank's current accounts from 25 millions during the Empire to an average of 56 millions between 1820 and 1830.[64] Transactions on the Bourse at Paris more than doubled and the value of the stocks and bonds quoted almost tripled from 1820 to 1830.[65] The number of passengers carried in public vehicles and the number of letters distributed by the postal service practically doubled from 1816 to 1828; and in the same period indirect taxes increased from 140 to 212 million francs.

With this growth of internal commerce, there was an increase in production. How great it was is almost impossible to estimate, for official statistics are lacking in most industries and figures amassed by private individuals reflect more often fancy than fact.[66] Likewise, it is difficult to judge the general effect of the national economic system on production, which according to protectionist theory should have been great. In some industries, however, adequate information is available to allow some generalization and particularly is this true of metallurgy. At the beginning of the Restoration, the tariff on iron and steel was comparatively small and although it was increased in 1814 and again in 1820, imports of pig iron grew from 800,000 kilograms in 1815 to 7 million kilograms in 1821.[67] In answer to the demands of metallurgists, the duty was raised in 1822 to the equivalent of 120 per cent *ad valorem,* which was sufficiently high to keep out English and Swedish products. As a reaction to the abolition of foreign competition, iron prices went up until they were more than double those in England. The high prices in turn tended to keep alive a great number of small charcoal furnaces; three-fifths of French production came from them as late as 1846.[68] The extensive use of charcoal raised the price of wood, much to the delight and benefit of landed proprietors. The increased cost of wood led in turn to the introduction of more coke blast and reverberating furnaces, and the new equipment to some concentration of production, as at Le Creusot, the iron-works of Fourchambault near Nevers, and the establishments of de Wendel in Lorraine. Behind the tariff wall, French ironmongers raised their output from 114,000 tons of pig iron in 1818 to 220,000 tons in 1828,[69] an amount approximately sufficient to satisfy the demands of the home market. The increased use of coal, a product in which the natural resources of France are deficient, caused its price to double from 1819 to 1828. Prices of coke were especially high, being 130 francs a ton in the metallurgical district of Saint Étienne and only 65 francs in England. Under the pressure of increased consumption and high prices, production of coal grew from one million tons in 1814 to 1,774,000 tons in 1828, but this amount was not adequate to meet internal requirements.

High prices of coal and iron caused iron and steel products to be dear. Not only tools but also machines, that were necessary for an industrial revolution, were expensive. Steam engines of thirty horsepower cost 45,000 francs in France and 30,000 in England and for this, in addition to other reasons, were adopted much less rapidly in the former country than in the latter.[70] The state endeavored to popularize the use of machines by holding industrial fairs and by furnishing technical training in the Conservatory of Arts and Crafts (established 1820), and in the Central School of Arts and Manufactures (established 1829), but its efforts were hardly sufficient to offset the economic handicaps. In the metallurgical industries, then, protectionism seems to have had the effect of reducing imports, of alleviating social hardships caused by sudden technological changes abroad, and of increasing national production and employment. But all this was realized at the expense of high prices and tardy technical improvements.

In the cotton-textile industry the effects of the tariff were similar to those in metallurgy. Under a system of prohibition of imports of cotton goods, the importation of raw cotton increased from 10,500,000 kilograms in 1812 to 30 millions in 1827, and in 1829 finished cotton cloth was one of France's leading exports. Industrialization of the cotton industry was less slow than that of iron; mechanized spinning machines and power looms were introduced in fair numbers. Some towns like Roubaix[71] near Lille and Mulhouse underwent real industrial revolutions. The power loom was adopted in the latter place more rapidly "than anywhere in Europe not excluding Lancashire."[72] But generally in France mechanization was slower than in England. Moreover, cotton prices did not soar. The index for cotton goods was 34 in 1847 as compared with 100 in 1826.[73]

The woolen industry changed much less than did the cotton in the first half of the nineteenth century, for, as it was an old and well-established industry, new methods of manufacture were introduced only with great difficulty. Therefore, there was little mechanization and no great growth in exportation, although there was a decrease in price. Perhaps the most noteworthy development in the industry during the Restoration was the improvement of raw wool produced in France. A protective tariff on wool and state-subsidized breeding stations aided the country in partially freeing itself from dependence on Spanish merino wool. In the silk industry, France had a favored position from earlier times, but prohibited the importation of Indian silks in 1820 and placed a high duty on all others. With this protection, French silk manufacturers prospered—silk goods enjoyed a virtual monopoly of the home market and were one of France's leading exports. The industry grew—417,150 kilograms of raw silk were worked up at Lyons in 1814 and 587,137 kilograms in 1829. Because of the increased production substantial quantities of raw silk had to be imported from abroad. In spite of the lack of foreign competition, mechanization of silk manufacture developed; 1200 Jacquard looms were in operation in 1819 and 4202 in 1825.[74]

The effect of the tariff system on the sugar industry is much more precise than on the woolen or silk trades. Here not only the question of national production—both industrial and agricultural—but also the problem of the colonial system came into play. As has been explained above,[75] the importation in 1814 of cane sugar from foreign countries spelled disaster for the nascent beet-sugar industry and aroused the wrath of French colonial planters. To satisfy both groups and to supply the treasury with a substantial revenue, a duty was placed on French colonial sugar, a very high surtax on foreign sugar, and, to please refiners, an export bounty was established on refined sugar. Much to the joy of French colonists, this arrangement practically eliminated the importation of foreign sugar and allowed them to charge such a high price for their product[76] that sugar was grown at the expense of other crops. But to their detriment, the high prices and the fiscal duty on French colonial sugar revived the beet-sugar industry. And the export bounty, provided to offset the import duty on colonial sugar, proved to be a tremendous boon to beet manufacturers. In 1828 there were fifty beet-sugar factories with a production of six and a half million kilograms of sugar a year.[77] The beet sugar industry, with all its ramifications in agriculture and manufacturing, was destined to grow until France was practically self-sufficient in the production of sugar. For this product, the duties of the Restoration had ultimately quite other consequences than those envisaged.

While the rôle that the tariff played in some phases of agricultural production, like beet sugar, is comparatively well delineated, it is not so clear in many others, and the complete absence of reliable agricultural statistics makes an attempt at analysis almost futile. The grain laws excluded in practice the importation of foreign-grown grains; the tax on wool helped to improve the quality of sheep; the duties on animals were a source of great satisfaction to farmers generally and more specifically to those who lived in frontier departments; and the customs on flax and hemp allowed France to produce what otherwise might have been purchased abroad. But what the actual increase of the production of these goods was or how many persons were given employment because of protection, it is impossible to ascertain. In some lines, the tariff seems to have effected an increase in price; in others, there was a definite reduction in spite of the absence of competition. In some, there was an improvement in agricultural methods; in many, no progress at all. In others, like wine, export trade was injured by retaliation that the protective tariff evoked. Much depended in agriculture, as in industry, on whether or not France could adequately meet demands of her home market for those goods which were excluded. If she could, either by the expansion of productive forces or by the introduction of new techniques, the results were not generally harmful, except to her surplus products. If she could not easily supply the demand, new productive machinery might be set up that could increase employment and the strength of the nation, but high prices, with all their attendant consequences, usually resulted.

On shipping, the effect of the Restoration's national economic policy does not appear to have been either felicitous or efficacious. The curbing of foreign commerce by the erection of high tariff barriers had a direct and detrimental effect on the carrying trade, because, before the advent of railways, about 72[78] per cent of France's exchange of goods with other nations was by water. In the face of this fact, the reserving of colonial trade to French bottoms and the flag surtax on goods brought in by foreign ships availed but little. There was but slight increase in the tonnage passing through French ports and of this French carriers managed to handle only 36 per cent of the imports and 42 per cent of the exports, while in England, British shippers controlled about 75 per cent of the nation's foreign-trade tonnage.[79] Of this condition French shipping interests were well aware, and of it they complained. Their attempts at developing trade in the East were unsuccessful because of the lack of permanent establishments or representatives and their trade with French colonies was not as remunerative as it should have been. The colonists were all too prone to smuggle in cheap English goods rather than buy in France and this practice left French shippers in the predicament of having full cargoes of sugar from the Antilles but empty holds on the trip out. What the shippers wanted was reciprocal trade agreements with the young nations of the western hemisphere so that they could carry them the innumerable articles they needed and return to France with full loads of colonial produce. To this suggestion colonial interests were inalterably opposed and reciprocity agreements were not negotiated. Hence, shippers, along with vintners, were the sharpest critics of the Restoration's national economics.

ECONOMIC DEPRESSION AND CRITICISM OF THE PROTECTIVE SYSTEM

In times of business crisis, attacks on the protective system became severest and the rival interests of bourgeois became clearest. Particularly is this true of the depression which began in 1826 and continued almost unabated until 1830. After a period of excessive credit expansion and of high prices, a reaction of low prices, stringent credit, and reduced business activity set in. As is frequent in such cases, the cause of all the trouble was sought in the policies of the state. Cotton manufacturers complained of the iron duty that resulted in the high price of machines; makers of woolen cloth criticized the tax on raw wool; producers of silk claimed that protection had caused a rival silk industry to spring up in England; metallurgists complained of the high price of coal and charcoal; but in each instance the critic would suffer no alteration in the protection of his particular product. With the original champions of protectionism thus divided, shippers, wine merchants, and a few free-trade theorists succeeded in having the Government appoint in 1828 a commission to study the effects of protection and to make recommendations. The investigation was duly carried out and expanded by cotton industrialists who organized an *enquête* on their own initiative. After testimony had been taken from businessmen in various lines, the commission came to the conclusion that protectionism as a system should not be destroyed; but that in certain details customs duties might be reduced.[80] It was suggested that the import taxes on sugar, silk, and iron might be pared down without injury. The Government did not follow the recommendations of its commission to the full, but did draw up a bill providing for a reduction on iron duties.[81] With the fall of the

Martignac Ministry and the coming to power of Polignac, the bill was dropped without ever being debated by the Chamber. The protective system of the Restoration seemed inviolable.

OVERTHROW OF THE RESTORATION GOVERNMENT

Much more secure were, indeed, the national economic policies of the Restoration than the Restored Monarchy itself. Louis XVIII had lived out his reign by pursuing a policy of compromise, but Charles X was destined to end his life in exile because he antagonized the Liberal bourgeoisie. The very year that Charles became king, 1824, he showed definitely that he was to continue to champion the cause of the Ultras, as he had done when his title was merely the Comte d'Artois. As evidence of his "imperturbable incorrigibility"—the words are of Pozzo di Borgo—he insisted that his coronation be held at Rheims in the traditional monarchist manner. Then with the "crown over his eyes," blind to the antagonism of the Liberals, he marched to disaster. One of his first acts was an attempt to re-establish a modified form of primogeniture. He saw in the continual partition of estates through inheritance a weakening of the economic basis of the very class which supported the monarchy, and he planned to put a stop to it. To this policy the bourgeois were opposed, for not only did it fortify their opponents but it made the acquisition of land more difficult. When the King's plan finally failed, there was great rejoicing in Paris.

Less was the joy of the bourgeoisie, however, when the King succeeded in realizing another of his pet projects—the securing of an indemnity for the *émigrés* whose land had been confiscated during the Revolution—for not only was the rising middle class opposed to the measure in principle, but it had to share much of the cost.[82] The "billion of the *émigrés*," as the indemnity was called, was to be paid in state bonds bearing interest at 3 per cent. Payments were to be made in five annual equal instalments. Funds to meet interest charges on these bonds were to be obtained from the budget, the amortization fund, and the saving effected by an optional exchange of government 5 per cent bonds for government 4½ per cent bonds issued at par and redeemable in ten years or for government 3 per cent bonds issued at seventy-five. The success of this refunding operation depended naturally on the rapid rise of the new 3 per cent bonds. The Government used all its influence to effect this rise, but without avail. A decline set in which caused a loss to bourgeois bankers particularly, who had speculated on the rise, and which prevented *émigrés,* who wished to sell their newly acquired bonds, from selling them at par. The failure to convert a sufficient amount of the 5 per cent bonds to 3 per cent placed a heavier interest burden upon the budget than had been anticipated, a burden that had to be met by taxation, and the expected rise in real property, resulting from land purchases by *émigrés,* and consequently larger income from property taxes, did not take place immediately. The indemnity did provide a final settlement for a very vexing question and brought undoubtedly the "two Frances"—the France of the Revolution and the France of the old régime—closer together. Even the bourgeoisie was ultimately to rejoice over the fact that the "billion" of the indemnity cost the state only about 629,721,315 francs, largely because of the ability of the government to amortize the bonds at an average of 72.73 francs.[83] For the moment, however, opponents of the King made capital of the entire undertaking for their attacks upon his régime.

The antagonism of the bourgeoisie to the King, aroused by the measures in favor of nobles, was made much more intense by the Government's pro-clerical policies. The influence of the Church in education was increased; a Catholic organization—the *Congrégation*—was allowed a voice in naming administrative officers of the state; and a law providing capital punishment for profaning a Catholic Church was passed. All this the bourgeois resented, for while many of them were Catholics, they did not approve of putting "religion to the service of politics or politics to the service of religion."

Opposition to the King grew rapidly and found expression in the Chamber, in newspapers, in pamphlets, in political meetings and in secret organizations. The King tried to calm his opponents by placing Martignac, who favored a policy of conciliation, at the head of the government (January, 1828). Charles endured the program of this Ministry until August, 1829, and then in utter disregard of the doctrine of ministerial responsibility, he reverted to a cabinet of Ultras, led by the Prince de Polignac. This action, which was contrary to established practice, enlivened the opposition. Knowing this, the King did not convoke the Chamber until March, 1830, and when he did, it censured him in no uncertain terms. Whereupon Charles dissolved his lower house and called for new elections. But the new elections did not increase the King's strength in the Chamber; and Moderates who had led the opposition were returned in a body.

Undaunted the King resorted to the power of the royal prerogative —to what the Liberals called force. On July 26, 1830, he issued four famous ordinances. He dissolved the new Chamber before it had ever met; he suspended the liberty of the press and required that newspapers renew every three months their authorizations to publish; he reduced the number of deputies and altered suffrage qualifications in such a manner that many bourgeois would be deprived of the franchise; and he called for more elections. This was an ill-fated move, because it called for retaliation in kind, and, although the nation as a whole was not aroused to action, bourgeois were. With the aid of the Parisian populace, they overthrew the object of their hate—the dynasty. Once again the struggle between the forces of reaction and the rising capitalist class had turned on the use of direct action and again the bourgeoisie was victorious.

CHAPTER V

OPERATION OF THE ULTRA-PROTECTIVE SYSTEM UNDER THE JULY MONARCHY, 1830-1848[1]

THE POLITICAL RESULTS OF THE REVOLUTION

THE revolutionaries who effected the *coup d'état* of July, 1830, acted with little thought of the morrow. Uppermost in their minds was the overthrow of the Bourbons and the strengthening of the state; concerning a successor to Charles X there was no general opinion. As events developed, however, the two groups who had joined forces against the dynasty formulated two plans for the future. One group, made up of bourgeois, under the leadership of the banker Laffitte and a few other ex-deputies, wanted to give the crown to the Duke of Orleans, head of the younger branch of the Bourbon family. The other, composed of students, young intellectuals, and the lower classes of Paris, dreamed of a republic with Lafayette as president. Conciliation between these divergent programs seemed difficult, but it was achieved with one of those comic-opera scenes with which French history is filled. The Duke of Orleans went to the Hôtel de Ville in Paris, center of the republican district, and appeared on a balcony with Lafayette before a throng of republican sympathizers. Both men were draped in an enormous tricolor flag—popular symbol of Revolutionary France. As the people waited for developments, the aged Lafayette kissed the Duke on both cheeks. The people roared approval. If Lafayette favored a king, they would be content. As Chateaubriand said, "The republican kiss of Lafayette made a King."

In the new monarch, the bourgeois thought that they had made a splendid choice. To their eyes he was one of them. He had fought in the Revolutionary armies, and, although he had emigrated, he had never borne arms against France. He had lived long years in England on a subsidy provided by the British Government and he had adopted bourgeois clothes and bourgeois manners. Like the bourgeois themselves, "he loved order and work; like them, he was preoccupied with money matters; like them, he looked down on the lower classes."[2]

But bourgeois did not rely exclusively upon the selection of the right person as king for a continuation of their predominance in politics. Before the Duke of Orleans was allowed to mount the throne as Louis-Philippe, he had to accept changes in the Charter. No longer was the monarch to be King "of France," but King "of the French"; no longer was the white flag to be employed, but the tricolor of the Revolution; and no longer was Catholicism to be the religion of the state, but the religion of "the majority of the French." Liberty of the press was guaranteed and laws were promised establishing ministerial responsibility, public education, and the abolition of the "double vote." The King was deprived of the right to issue ordinances for the "safety of the state," although he could still issue them concerning the execution of laws, and the right to initiate laws was transferred from the crown to the Chambers. Heredity of the peerage was abolished, since peers were appointed in the future for life only. The age of eligibility to the Chamber of Deputies was reduced from forty to thirty years and the financial requirement from 1000 francs in direct taxes to 500. The electorate was increased from about 80,000 to between 200,000 and 240,000 persons by reducing from 300 to 200 francs the amount of direct taxes that had to be paid to receive the franchise. And that the new order might have the support of a devoted armed force, the national guard, organized in 1831, was limited to the well-to-do by the requirement that all members must furnish the necessary equipment at their own expense.[3] The bourgeoisie believed that with these measures its position was secure, but if it could have looked into the future, it would have seen many dangers ahead. Louis-Philippe nourished at least an ambition to rule as well as to reign, and large elements of the population were dissatisfied with the new régime.

The political parties that formed on the morrow of the July Revolution gave voice to the discordant political views of the nation. On the extreme right, a small group of Legitimists looked upon the new King as a usurper and labored, although unsuccessfully, for a re-establishment of the Bourbons. On the extreme left, there were the Republicans, young intellectuals and some workers, who considered that the King had been chosen illegally and that they should have had a voice in the selection of a successor to Charles X. To them the July Revolution was "The Two Weeks Comedy."[4] Intelligent and energetic, the Republicans made successful use of secret societies, of political meetings and of the press for their propaganda, and their numbers increased steadily. In the first years of the July Monarchy, they attempted several *coups,* in which the red flag was used widely for the first time. In the center, bourgeois, who had conducted the revolution, were divided into two parties—the Party of Movement (later known as the Dynastic Left), and the Party of Resistance. The latter looked upon the July Revolution as little more than a ministerial crisis and desired that all change be limited to a change in the head of the state. The former looked upon the overthrow of Charles X as only a beginning; they advocated an extension of the suffrage and the support by armed force of revolutionary movements in Belgium, Poland, and Italy. From out of these political divisions, complicated later by the appearance of Catholic and Socialist parties, came a government of bourgeois parties that lasted until 1841. In that year the King began an era of personal rule supported by the right wing of the Party of Resistance led by Guizot. The main elements of the bourgeoisie suffered this arrangement until 1848 and then sent Louis-Philippe on his travels as, in 1830, Charles X had been sent.

The bourgeois character of the July Monarchy has never been seriously questioned and there seems to be no reason why it should be. The old aristocracy found itself supplanted in the government and at court by a new aristocracy of wealth. All testimony of the period indicates a preponderance of middle-class influence in public affairs. De Tocqueville, writing about the bourgeois monarchy in 1847, said:

"Master of everything in a way no other aristocracy had ever been, the middle class, once in control of the government, took on the character of private industry.... Posterity will perhaps never know to what degree the government of that time was a capitalist enterprise in which all action is taken for the purpose of profit for its members."[5]

Guizot, in a letter of 1840 to Palmerston, expressed much the same opinion.

"Another class, that of great manufacturers, metallurgists, and merchants is favorably disposed toward the government of the King and has supported it and continues to support it on every possible occasion with its energy, its intelligence, its wealth, and its social influence. It is impossible for the government of the King not to be attentive to the interests and desires of the class of the population which has become attached to it. . . ."[6]

An analysis of the Chamber in 1836 shows that 206 of the deputies were employees of the state and hence controlled by the government. Of these 50 were cabinet ministers, general directors, or mayors; 96 were judges, 47 were officers; and 13 were either attached to the court or to the diplomatic corps. Of the other 257, 45 were industrialists, bankers, or commercial men; 116 were rentiers or proprietors, 56 were lawyers or physicians, and 37 general counsellors.[7] The significance of the preponderance of bourgeois and of governmentally controlled deputies in the Chamber had lost much of its importance in matters economic, however considerable it may have been in other questions. As during the Restoration, so during the July Monarchy and the rest of contemporary French history, the distinction between capitalists who had their wealth in land and possessed a title and capitalists who had their fortunes invested in factories, merchandise, or securities tended to disappear. According to Proudhon,

"The clergy, nobility and the serfs represent no longer castes. By bourgeois is understood today every individual who lives from the rent of his lands or his houses, the interest of his investments, the profits from his business; by plebeian, or proletarian, each individual who has only his labor as a means of subsistence."[8]

This being the case, it was to have been expected that the national economic system as set up during the Restoration would be kept virtually intact and that it would be developed further for the profit of men of wealth. This is, indeed, the history of French national economics from 1830 to 1848.

ATTACKS ON THE ULTRA-PROTECTIONIST SYSTEM WITHSTOOD

Immediately upon the establishment of the new régime, the questions that had troubled the last years of the Restoration reappeared—

should France maintain the actual prohibition of goods, refuse to make reciprocity treaties with foreign nations, continue tariff duties that resulted in high prices, and support numerous unnecessary practices that irritated foreigners? Among those who desired a change, wine-growers, shippers, consumers of large quantities of iron and steel, and academic economists appeared to be most numerous and to take the most advanced stand. Opposed to them were the manufacturers and agriculturalists who had something to protect. The Government's attitude was one of conciliation; it wanted the political support of both groups. It was willing to free the protective system of many of its useless and exaggerated features, but it was strongly opposed to adopting freedom of trade. It kept its political ear to the ground in the hope of knowing just what moves were safe to make. This task was facilitated by a new and more representative system of selecting members to Chambers of Commerce, the establishment in 1831 of general advisory councils for agriculture, commerce, and manufacturing, and the appointment of a Superior Council of Commerce.[9] With this machinery the Government thought that it would be able to charter a sane and popular course.

At first, it seemed as though events might play into the hands of those who wanted to attack the ultra-protectionist system. The business crisis that accompanied the political turmoil in 1830 saw the price of wheat go so high that the Government was concerned. In the extremity, the tariff on grain was reduced for one year to allow the importation of some foreign wheat. Then to improve the carrying trade, the free transit through France of almost all goods, even those on the prohibited list, was permitted,[10] and bonded warehouses were established in several cities to allow the storing of foreign merchandise.[11]

Innocuous as such tamperings with the tariff were, they evoked opposition. It was felt that the lowered grain duties might become permanent and that dutiable goods might leak from the transit trade into the domestic market. Officials were inclined to minimize such opinion, but when the Comte d'Argout[12] and Adolphe Thiers,[13] successive Ministers of Commerce under Louis-Philippe, endeavored to make some further and very minor reductions, largely for the purpose of discouraging smuggling, they met with defeat. Not able to get reforms through Parliament and yet convinced that its proposals were sound, the Government played its trump card—it made tariff changes by decree.[14] In this way a few prohibitions were replaced by high duties,[15] but nothing fundamental was accomplished.

Criticism of the Government's action was, however, so sharp that a new Minister of Commerce, Duchâtel, decided to undertake one of the numerous *enquêtes* which are to be found throughout French nineteenth-century economic history. His investigation of 1834 was the most thorough of any that had been made up to that time, although its scope was limited to the question of prohibitions.[16] From it the Government learned little of a general nature that was not already known, but many a loose impression received substantial confirmation. The *Enquête* showed definitely that tariff opinion was formed by the usefulness of customs duties to private interests and only incidentally by thought of the general welfare of society or of the nation. Chambers of commerce in wine-growing districts and in ports expressed themselves unalterably opposed not only to prohibitions but to protection in general, although, despite an obvious inconsistency, they disapproved of the transit of wine through France and favored navigation acts.

A few manufacturing districts, like Arras, Sedan, Metz, Strasburg, and Lyons, that represented well-established industries, had no objection to replacing prohibitions with high duties. But the majority of industrial centers disapproved of any change. Lille, Louviers, Elbeuf, Roubaix, Tourcoing, and Rouen were especially strong in their sentiment. They advanced in favor of protection the arguments of national strength, the welfare of workers, and their own advantage. Rouen endeavored to answer the current free-trade doctrine, imported from England, that competition from abroad stimulates technological progress at home, by saying:

"Given the frequent communications with our neighbors, the ease of visiting their establishments and of buying their machines, is not the severe competition within France enough of a stimulant and force over manufacturers to mechanize in every imaginable way in order to produce at the lowest possible price?"[17]

And the Lille district went so far as to threaten the régime:

"To the King whom we love, we pay [taxes] without a murmur.

. . . We do not refuse to give our sons to the nation; our means of labor, respect them. . . . Above all remember that low wages have twice caused revolts at Lyons."[18]

These opinions caused the Government, in order to avoid a fight, to relax for the time being its campaign of tariff reform. It limited its action in 1834 and 1836 to a slight reduction by decree of the rates on coal, raw wool, and pig iron. Feeling more courageous in 1836, it presented a bill for the approval of its decrees and for the further reduction of some rates. This bill was reported favorably to the Chamber by a tariff commission packed with deputies from the wine-growing and shipping district of Bordeaux. After a bitter fight, it became law July 2, 1836, thereby reducing the rates on silk, hides, and lumber, and substituting a duty for an import prohibition on woolen yarn.

Again, these minor reductions in the tariff put the protectionists on their guard. In 1840 they defeated overwhelmingly a bill to reduce the duty on livestock and were even hesitant about ratifying a treaty with the Netherlands[19] that facilitated the shipping of raw cotton to Alsace and the transportation of French wines down the Rhine! In 1841 they managed to raise enough rates to offset reductions on cashmeres and linen thread and the free importation of steam engines destined for ships in foreign trade. And in 1842, when the Government asked the General Council of Manufactures if the iron and steel industries could get along with less than the 70 and 110 per cent *ad valorem* duties, respectively, then in force, protectionists replied with such an emphatic *"no"* that all thought of change was abandoned.

For three years there was no alteration of the tariff,[20] but the spell was broken in 1845 by the concerted efforts of the flaxseed and poppy-seed interests of Flanders and the olive-oil producers of Provence. They were perturbed because the soap industry at Marseilles was using fats from Indian sesame, and proposed that the duty on this product be increased tenfold. Their wishes were granted, even though it was proved that prices of their fats had suffered no decline!

Yet the protectionists did not have everything their own way. In the law of 1845 Indian silks were removed from the prohibited list and duties on machines were reduced. But much more significant than this was the fact that the Government proposed a bill in 1847 to abolish fifteen prohibitions and to place 298 of the 666 items of the tariff on the free list, among the latter being iron, copper, zinc, and ship-building materials. This was a bold and inauspicious project. Louis-Philippe's personal rule ended before it ever came to debate.

Thus all serious attempts to change the ultra-protectionist system of the Restoration came to naught during the July Monarchy. What successful attacks there were upon the tariff structure were of a very secondary nature. Only the fact that there were assaults upon the al-most insurmountable customs barrier is of real significance.

The only alteration in the French tariff from 1830 to 1848 of any importance concerned sugar. The July Monarchy had inherited from the Restoration a system of sugar duties that was decidedly favorable to the beet industry. High import rates on colonial sugar and still higher ones on foreign sugar resulted in prices that not only made the fortune of many a colonial planter but resurrected the beet industry from the collapse it had suffered with the overthrow of Napoleon. More-over, an export bounty, that had been established originally to offset the import duties on cane sugar, was collected on beet sugar and proved to be extraordinarily remunerative. The beet-sugar industry grew so rapidly under these conditions that the importation of colonial sugar fell from 80,000,000 kilograms in 1830 to 57,000,000 in 1837. This state of affairs required remedial legislation and the Government was anxious to act, because the decreasing customs collected on cane sugar and the increasing export bounties paid on beet sugar were burden-some for the treasury. The situation provided a nice problem in na-tional economics. To favor cane rather than beet sugar meant a les-sening of national production; to aid the beet industry rather than the cane would be to attack the colonial compact.

A solution to this dilemma was difficult to find and recourse was had to the trial-and-error method—most of which was error. In 1833, the Government, in order to obviate the evil which affected the treasury, replaced the export bounty by a sum equivalent to the import duty actually paid, which excluded beet sugar from collecting anything be-cause it paid no import tax, and reduced the duty on foreign sugar enough to allow it to compete with French colonial and beet sugar on the French market.[21] This arrangement was not satisfactory. Beet-sugar interests disapproved of the abolition of the bounties; colonial planters did not receive enough protection against either foreign or beet sugar; and shipping interests wanted colonial sugar favored in order to do the carrying. It was necessary to find some other means of effecting equality of price between beet and colonial sugar, and to exclude foreign sugar. The Government began, then, to consider seriously levying an internal-revenue tax on beet sugar. An attempt at establishing such a tax had been successfully resisted in 1832, and was again fought off in 1835, but when beet-sugar production showed an increase from 35,000,000 kilograms in 1835 to 45,000,000 in 1836, colonists and shippers forced the issue. In 1837[22] a law was passed establishing a tax on beet sugar, that was to be raised by one-third in 1839. Almost conjointly the duty on cane sugar from the colonies was reduced.[23] It was now the turn of the beet-sugar interests to complain. The smaller establishments closed their doors amidst much wailing and the large concerns, in which the industry was becoming concentrated, were loud in their criticism.

The Government tried unsuccessfully in 1840 to appease all the parties involved by establishing new rates, but with no success.[24] Shipping centers began a campaign for the total abolition of the beet-sugar industry, with an indemnity, and some beet-sugar interests favored the same scheme. Heeding these opinions, the Government presented a bill in January, 1843, to carry out this proposal. It set the sum to be paid to the beet-sugar industry at 40,000,000 francs. Such a project was impracticable; beet sugar was too well established—it had a "mania for living." The idea of suppressing the beet-sugar industry was given up and a new solution for establishing equality between the beet and the cane was sought. After much discussion, it was finally decided (1843)[25] that the only way to cut this knotty problem was to place an internal-revenue tax on beet sugar equivalent to the import duty on sugar from the French West Indies. This was done; the tax on the beet product was increased gradually until by 1847 it equalled that on cane sugar. At first, it was believed that the beet industry would not be able to compete with the cane on equal terms, but, contrary to expectations, it did. The importation of cane sugar jumped from 851,000 quintals in 1840 to 1,025,000 in 1845, and the production of beet sugar, from 237,000 quintals in 1840–41 to 563,000 in 1847–48. By the compromise of 1843, the colonial compact and national production were allowed to work in harmony.

RECIPROCITY DEFEATED

As difficult as was this comparatively satisfactory settlement of an essentially "national" economic problem, it was easy compared with the adjustment of commercial questions between France and her neighbors. Protectionists guarded carefully against the negotiation of treaties that might lessen customs duties. Agreements with Switzerland and Piedmont which reduced the rates on domestic animals were about all that could be pushed through the bourgeois Chamber of Deputies. France had, however, at least two attractive opportunities to extend by treaty her commercial dominion during the July Monarchy. One was with Bavaria and Würtemberg; the other with Belgium; both were missed.

The opportunity of establishing a favorable tariff arrangement with Bavaria and Würtemberg presented itself because of fear of domination by Prussia.[26] The French minister to Munich informed his country that a customs union under Prussian leadership was not popular in South Germany, and that French co-operation with Bavaria and Würtemberg might prevent it. French tariff relationships with these two states had not been exceptionally friendly in the recent past, for the tariff of 1822 had prevented a traditional exportation of cattle to Alsace and attempts to alleviate the difficulty had been repulsed. Now, however, there seemed to be a strong motive for France to make reciprocal concessions. The question was taken under consideration by the French Superior Council of Commerce, but it refused to recommend a change in tariff policy toward South Germany. Across the Rhine, hope was not given up for collaboration with France. In 1832 a newspaper of Stuttgart made a plan for it and, although there were opponents to this scheme in Würtemberg, a large element, including the King, approved it. Again the French Government took the matter under advisement and asked its chief commercial committee for an opinion. Again the Council disapproved. Before a year had elapsed, Bavaria and Würtemberg had joined Prussia in the *Zollverein*—a union that was full of economic, as well as political, importance for both France and Germany. Although it would be gratuitous to conclude, as did the French minister to Berlin in 1844, that the failure of the French to make the most of this opportunity caused the formation of the *Zollverein,* it is certain that France might have made the formation of that union more difficult and might have delayed it for some time.

The opportunity granted France to effect a commercial agreement with Belgium was even more promising and more concrete than that with South German states. The erection of the German *Zollverein* filled both France and Belgium with apprehension for their commercial futures. Exactly what effect it was to have on them, they were not quite sure, but both thought that it would be to their disadvantage. Their common fear, their territorial proximity, and rumors that the *Zollverein* hoped to include Belgium and Switzerland, led the two countries to consider the possibility of forming in their turn a customs union.[27] Negotiations to such an end were begun in 1835, and the whole question became one of prime importance in 1837 with the publication of an article by Léon Faucher in the *Revue des Deux Mondes* entitled "L'Union du Midi."[28] Faucher pointed out the advantages, such as an enlarged market and cheaper raw materials, of a customs union of France, Belgium, Spain, and Switzerland, and suggested that the first step should be an agreement between France and Belgium. Exchanges between the governments quickened and definite proposals were made. The French suggested a plan that was highly favorable to their interests. They wanted the customs line between France and Belgium abolished and French tariffs applied to Belgium's non-French frontiers. The receipts of this customs union would be divided proportionately between the two nations according to population. Tariff changes should be made conjointly by the two states, except that in case of difference, France would have the deciding vote.

This proposition was refused by King Leopold, but with it as a basis negotiations continued. From 1837 to 1842, the two governments endeavored to overcome the obstacles to the conclusion of an agreement. The task was a difficult one; on both sides the desires of vested interests complicated the work. In Belgium, the textile centers approved a customs union with France and the metallurgical centers, although unenthusiastic, were not strongly opposed to it; but the port of Antwerp, much of whose shipping came from the German *hinterland,* and Belgian patriots, who felt keenly for the independence of their newly created state, were firmly against it.[29] In France, opinion concerning the union was conditioned almost exclusively by economic interests. Bordeaux was the strongest protagonist of the scheme, for it saw in Belgium a lucrative market for wines and in Belgian foreign trade increased carrying for its fleets. Paris, textile centers, and the metallurgical district of St. Etienne, which was well removed from Belgian producers, were mildly favorable to the plan. Unalterably opposed to it were French metallurgists and coal-mine operators of the North, for they feared that France would be inundated with Belgian coal, iron, steel, and machinery. Even foreign nations intervened to make the negotiations more difficult; both the *Zollverein* and Great Britain placed their weight in the scales of opposition. The British made the claim that a Franco-Belgian customs union would be an attack on Belgian independence and contrary to the neutrality treaty of 1831. Never would Britain condone the presence of French customs officials in Antwerp;[30] and in this the Germans felt much the same. Great pressure was brought to bear on both the French and Belgian governments to give up their plan, and, in the end, they did. French metallurgists considered that they had won an important victory. In a public statement, one of their number said:

"We felicitate the government for having understood the real interests of the country; for not having wished to increase its sufferings; for having known that to unify France and Belgium by effacing with a stroke of the pen that line of customs, encouragement, guarantee, and protection of our industry was to kill the forges of Flanders, the Ardennes, the Vosges, the Moselle, and Champagne. Such action would have ruined our manufacturers of woolens, of linens, and of cotton; it would have been a sad blow to our agriculture. What compensation would we have found in such a disaster? Would it have been in a new market? No, for Belgium, which has so many products to sell to us, has little need of buying from us. She produces like a country of thirty million inhabitants; she consumes like a country of four millions. But, you might object, France would have increased her territory? Gentlemen, of what good is it to increase one's territory if it does not augment prosperity? It is a course of weakness, not one of greatness."[31]

The interests of Bordeaux were, on the other hand, much chagrined at the outcome of the affair. They complained that if France had conquered Belgium by force of arms, all France would have applauded enthusiastically the acquisition of a rich territory and an intelligent, laborious people. Every one would have considered that France had become more powerful by the augmentation of her material forces.[32] France was not governed in the interests of the nation; the real government of France were the metallurgists. Greed dictated French economic policy.

Those in favor of the customs union hoped that something might be salvaged from the wreck—that a commercial agreement might be made by the two countries which would accomplish much that union had aimed to do. Here again they were subjected to disappointment. A treaty was negotiated, but it provided only for a reduction of the duties on French wines and on Belgian linen and hemp cloth. So great was the opposition to any economic *rapprochement* to Belgium, however, that the Government did not have the courage to present this harmless document to the Chamber for ratification until two years (1844) after it had been negotiated. And then the Chamber refused to approve it for more than one year. The power of the bourgeois protectionists in the Chamber was still supreme.

FREE-TRADE THEORY

As powerful as the protectionists were during the July Monarchy, they were not without their free-trade adversaries, as the foregoing survey of French tariff history from 1830 to 1848 shows. In some circles economic *laisser-faire* was popular; among intellectuals it was making steady progress towards its ultimate triumph. The influence of the Physiocrats was still felt in some quarters; Adam Smith's *Wealth of Nations* was from the first widely read in France, four translations of it being made from 1779 to 1802;[33] and French economic theorists were writing elaborate treatises on the virtues of the facile exchange of goods and the international division of labor. Among these writers Jean Baptiste Say (1767–1832) was for many years pre-eminent. In 1816 Say gave what was probably the first course in political economy in France. His teaching proved popular and won for him the approval of the Government. In 1819 a course in "industrial economy" was established for him and in 1830 he was given the first chair of economics at the Collège de France. From the authoritative position of the academy, he taught with only slight variations the doctrines of Adam Smith.[34] He won many men to his beliefs and influenced many more—persons like Pellegrino Rossi (1787–1848), his successor at the Collège de France;[35] Michel Chevalier (1809–79), successor to Rossi in the same chair and about whom we shall hear more later on; Charles Dunoyer (1786–1863);[36] and Frédéric Bastiat (1801–50).[37] This rising tide of economic liberals, with their *Journal des Economistes* (founded 1841) that has remained to the present day one of the principal organs of free-traders in professional ranks, swelled the current of free-trade thought in France and events in England increased it to almost flood proportions.

The tariff reforms of Huskisson, the agitation of Cobden and Bright, and the repeal of the Corn Laws by Robert Peel encouraged French reformers to take action. Bastiat, who came to Paris and into the public eye in 1845 and who died in 1850, thus cutting short a career of promise, organized the forces of free trade. With the aid of the Mayor of Bordeaux, he founded in 1845 the Association pour la Liberté des Echanges.[38] Branches were established at Bordeaux, Paris, Marseilles, Lyons, Le Havre, and Rheims, and attempts were made to ape the propagandist methods of the English Anti-Corn Law League. Large gatherings were harangued by free-trade spell-binders; a paper *Le Libre Echange* was founded (1846); and Cobden was fêted as the messiah of a new economic era.[39] With all its propaganda the Association was not able to develop a large popular movement as did the Anti-Corn Law League in England. The arguments that a greater exchange of goods would increase industrial production and that the abolition of agricultural protection would reduce the price of bread seemed less convincing in France than they did in England. About all the Association succeeded in accomplishing during the July Monarchy was to throw a scare into the camp of the protectionists.

PROTECTIONIST THEORY

Fright did actually seize the champions of protection and they prepared for battle. They founded an organization for propaganda bearing the euphemistic title, Committee for the Defense of National Labor. An organ, *Moniteur Industriel,* was established and public meetings were held. A placard was sent by the Committee to manufacturers with the request that it be posted so that it might be seen by workers. It read:

"There is no need to be cunning to understand that free-traders only wish to favor England and to ruin France in order that the English may reign over our country. It is not necessary to starve the French in order to nourish the English."

In an appeal to the Government, the Committee warned:

"Do not hasten by your silence, which cannot be justified by any serious motive, the crisis which menaces. Do not prolong the uncertainty which is gaining ground among us all and which unsettles all convictions. Do nothing to arm your enemies against those who wish to aid you in contributing to the prosperity of the country."[40]

In support of this protectionist agitation, there was a contemporary version of national economic theory, albeit not so abundant as liberal theory nor having the prestige enjoyed by the latter that comes with speaking from halls of learning. Among statesmen, the leading national theorist was perhaps Adolphe Thiers, Minister from 1832 to 1837 and Premier in 1836 and 1840. Although he wrote little on the subject, his speeches reflect a well-developed system.[41] Bred in the economic tradition of Baron Louis, first finance minister of the Restoration, and of Baron Saint-Cricq, a director of the customs, Thiers was firmly grounded in national economic principles. He believed that no nation could be really great unless it produced the basic products of national consumption—food, raw materials, fuel, and iron. A nation should aspire to economic self-sufficiency; it should not consume more than it produces. In case of war or foreign economic crisis, autarchy is essential. Only a great political power with control of the seas (and here Thiers had England in mind) may dare to rely upon foreign lands for supplies. Inasmuch as this is the case, France must always strive to increase her production. She must employ customs duties to stimulate new industries which cannot be created without protection. This practice will undoubtedly increase prices, but high prices are not necessarily disadvantageous to the consumer. Consumers are also producers and it is more essential for them to have work than to have cheap bread. Protection assures work; free trade puts it in jeopardy. Moreover, the international exchange of goods on a free-trade basis tends to establish monopoly of production in certain nations and once this monopoly is firmly entrenched prices may be raised to excessive heights. Protection must not, however, be employed unreasonably. It would be foolhardy to try to grow bananas in Paris behind a tariff wall. Absolute prohibition, Thiers believed, has little to recommend it and perhaps protection is not a satisfactory theory for every time and place.[42] For France, however, at least moderate protection is the wisest policy to pursue.[43] It is the one which Thiers supported during the July Monarchy, during the rule of Louis Napoleon, and during his Presidency after 1870.

Important as was the concept of the nation in the economic philosophy of Adolphe Thiers and of the protectionists of the Restoration, it became increasingly strong as time went on. The French Revolution and Napoleonic times marked a high-water point in national economics; after Napoleon national economic theory seems to have been put on the defensive by the rise of liberal doctrines. As political patriotism developed,[44] however, there appears to have been a recrudescence of that national exuberance which was so common in the Revolutionary period. The transition was not an abrupt one, but became evident toward the middle of the century. Be that as it may, however, it is certain that national love burned fiercely in a minor economic theorist, Lestiboudois, when he wrote toward the end of the July Monarchy his *Economie pratique des nations*.[45] Unlike the free-trade theorists of his day, Lestiboudois was not an academic economist; he was, rather, a physician, agriculturalist, deputy, and member of the Institute. His active life in public and political affairs turned his attention toward political economy; his love for France directed the course his economics took. He believed that as long as society was divided into numerous and distinct nations, all rivals and enemies, among whom conquest was still a part of public law and of actual practice, the prime necessity for a nation was to become strong.

"The grandeur of the nationality is the holiest obligation and the profoundest sentiment of all citizens. Obviously the first condition, the supreme task of economic theorists is to preserve, consolidate, and develop national strength. . . . It does not suffice to have material goods; there are others much more precious. The history, the fame, the independence, the intellectual grandeur, the ties of parenthood, of neighborliness, and of country are more dear and more sacred than those which satisfy physical needs. All this is found in nationality—in the idea of love for *la patrie*."[46]

As a means of fortifying economically the "sacred nation," Lestiboudois relied on the perennial argument of the national theorists—protection. Goods are paid for with goods; goods represent labor. If a nation imports more than it exports, it is using up labor that was expended long ago. It is not keeping pace with its rivals. Free trade is only feasible for nations like England which have a superior industrial position. For France, protectionism is the only course. If free trade were adopted under actual conditions, France could not escape a fall. In surrendering her industrial lines of defense, she would be enslaved more certainly than if she surrendered her fortresses and her arms."[47]

Like Lestiboudois, Mathieu De Dombasle[48] (1777–1843) attacked the doctrine of free trade and the international division of labor. Speaking with the authority of a man who had made a reputation by introducing a system of crop-rotation on his model farms and by activity in the sugar-beet industry, Dombasle attracted considerable attention by his economic writings. Whether or not his praise of national economic principles was influenced by his desire to protect his own sugar interests against the encroachments of colonial sugar is difficult to ascertain, but it is certain that he produced a strong argument for a closed national economy. The word nationality, according to Dombasle, is not a vain word—it signifies a living reality. A nationality is formed undoubtedly by the ties of a common language, common customs, common religions, and, most important of all, by common economic interests. Between citizens of one nation and those of another, there cannot be the economic bonds that bind the citizens of one nation so closely together. Citizens of France should be cognizant of these bonds. The production of goods within the boundaries of the nation has a beneficial effect throughout the entire structure of society. Increased production furnishes wages to laborers and profits to capitalists, which permit them to buy articles they had previously never been able to afford. This increased consumption gives birth to new industries and not only to those producing the goods in question but also to those which furnish machines and buildings for the new enterprises. The greater the production, moreover, the greater is the population. Through increased production the nation becomes stronger and raises its standard of living. Of what advantage is it, indeed, for a Frenchman to buy cotton cloth in England rather than in France, even though it be cheaper, if by so doing he deprives himself of work and the wherewithal to buy bread for his children? If goods are bought with goods, as the classical economists teach, then a nation must produce more and export more in order to import more. Moreover, in the exchange of goods between nations, the state that receives capital goods for consumers' goods is at an advantage, for consumers' goods are soon used up, while capital goods increase production. If all this is true, relative economic self-sufficiency, guaranteed by protective tariffs, is the soundest policy for national states.

Less impassioned in love for France than Dombasle and Lestiboudois, but no less impressed with the importance of the nation was the German Frederick List (1789-1846).[49] Although not a French citizen, List was widely read in France. His *Das nationale System der politischen Ökonomie* was published in 1840, and proved popular enough to be translated into French in 1851 by H. Richelot, an official in the Ministry of Commerce.[50] As the translator explained in his preface, List placed the idea of nationality in sharp relief. He held that the wealth of nations rested less in the mass of exchangeable goods than in productive power; that protection is a justifiable instrument for increasing production; and that among all the economic units of the nation there is a solidarity of interests which should lead them to work for economic prosperity. These ideas were not essentially new, but they were presented with such force and clarity that List has gone down in economic history as the founder and chief exponent of national economy.[51] They had been expounded even earlier in France by List himself in an article entitled *"Idées sur des réformes économiques, commerciales, et politiques applicables à la France"* for *La Revue Encyclopédique*.[52] List had explained that, although he was by principle a cosmopolite and full of faith in the utopia of perpetual peace, he did not believe that in the actual condition of the world a nation should demolish its fortresses nor neglect its defense. He understood that the abolition of provincial tariffs in France had had a beneficial effect, but the abolition of national tariffs was another matter. That would not be possible until the "political condition and the industry of nations should advance so much and become so much alike that their union would be useful to each one of them, as the union today of the twenty-four states of North America is advantageous to each of them." In France, it might be wise to reduce the customs duties on raw materials. France should negotiate reciprocity agreements for trade in goods that could not be produced at home. Most important of all, however, France should undertake the construction of a vast network of railways. Then Paris would rival London.

"The French railway system should reach out to Belgium, Italy, Switzerland, Germany, and to the Iberian peninsula. It would carry everywhere commercial, moral and political influence from its point of control. France would conquer the European continent not by arms but by civilization. She would not demand indemnities of war but would expand her industry. . . . She would introduce the only true continental system capable of consolidating her moral, political, and commercial ascendancy over the nations of Europe without fear of the opposition or of the naval power of England or of the vengeance and jealousy of other nations."[53]

THEORY OF STATE INTERVENTIONISM—POSITIVISM AND SOCIALISM

In addition to the work of the national economic theorists, the July Monarchy produced two other currents of thought that contributed, although indirectly, to national economics; these currents were positivism and certain branches of socialism. Both of these movements were *étatist;*[54] they placed great emphasis upon the rôle that the state should play in economic matters. Auguste Comte, father of positive philosophy,[55] preached a system in which the state would be all-powerful in directing society for the common good. Controlled by "the competent men" the Comtian state was, according to John Stuart Mill, "the most complete temporal and spiritual despotism that was ever conceived by the brain of man." Among socialists there were differences of opinion concerning the power of the state. Some, like J. P. Proudhon, believed in anarchy, but many others favored a strong state. Saint Simon,[56] from whom Comte got many of his ideas, held that in order to give to "each one according to his capacity, to each according to his works," the state should own all property and "direct production to harmonize it with consumption." "A nation is nothing more than a great industrial enterprise." Louis Blanc[57] appealed to the state to establish his "workshops," and to regulate the relations among the shops, and to manage banking and distribution. Pecqueur[58] and Vidal[59] preached a national collectivism that should ultimately become cosmopolitan. Simonde de Sismondi[60] and later Dupont-White[61] advocated the intervention of the state in economic matters to assure a just relationship between capital and labor. Villeneuve-Bargemont, the Catholic socialist, and other members of the same school, urged laws of social reform. These appeals for state action were not in themselves national; in fact most socialists, though not all, prided themselves on their cosmopolitanism.[62] But "state-ism" was, according to the writers mentioned, to be applied in the nation—France. It was almost inevitable that the state, running the economy of a nation, would develop national policies.

In at least one other respect—in the matter of social reform—socialism has contributed something to the national system of economics. The socialist plea for better working conditions and for healthier living quarters for labor has been based not exclusively on the ground of justice and humanity but also on the argument that as citizens of the nation workers should be physically sound and mentally alert. It was largely by this reasoning that the French bourgeoisie was won to a support of the first labor law in 1841. Although this legislation provided only that no children under eight years of age should be employed in a factory, that children from eight to twelve should work only eight hours a day, and those from twelve to sixteen twelve hours a day, it was a beginning. The chief argument for the law seems to have been, "The first duty of a government is to see that the children of the country are healthy, robust, intelligent, and moral."

STATE INTERVENTION—ROADS AND RAILWAYS

State intervention in economic affairs was an old institution: the state had for years taken upon itself the protection of private property, the construction of roads and bridges, and the building of canals. This form of statism was pushed forward energetically during the July Monarchy. Great efforts were made to improve the national equipment (*outillage national*) of France. From 1830 to 1847, 1538 millions of francs were expended by the state on public works. The mileage of royal roads (*routes royales*) in good condition was more than doubled, and on them 18 bridges were repaired or constructed. The mileage of departmental roads was increased by one-third; 287 new bridges were built; and the cost of upkeep was more than doubled. Town roads and streets were similarly increased and bettered. These improved communications made possible a reduction in stage-coach schedules as compared with those of 1814 of one-half, a reduction in the cost of travel by one-third, considerable increase in traffic, and a doubling of the postal business. In order to accelerate communications, the government began in 1845 the construction of electric telegraph lines to replace its semaphore system. Furthermore, the state expended large sums to better the waterways of the nation.[63] Two thousand and forty-one kilometers of canal were constructed during the July Monarchy, as compared with 921 during the Restoration, and the navigability of rivers was so improved that 8255 kilometers were in use in 1848. The Marne was connected by water with the Rhine, the Rhine with the Rhône, and Nantes with Brest. These improvements facilitated the transportation of heavy goods that the growing industry of the nation was turning out in an ever increasing quantity and they opened up France's internal market.

The most important problem of national equipment and state intervention during the July Monarchy was, however, the construction of railways.[64] As in England, so in France the first railways were short industrial lines constructed for the purpose of connecting industrial centers with waterways. In 1823, a concession was granted for a *"chemin en fer"* from the metallurgical district of Saint Etienne to the Loire, and in 1831-32 locomotives replaced horses on the line between Saint Etienne and Lyons. France thus got started in railway building nearly as soon as did England (the railway between Manchester and Liverpool was opened in 1830), but she failed to maintain the pace that was set by her rival across the Channel. Until 1842 she built only lines of local interest; at that date Great Britain, the United States, Germany, and Belgium had surpassed her in railway construction.[65]

In the decade of the 1830's, France was entirely cognizant of her growing inferiority in railway equipment, but opinion was divided as to whether or not this was an advantage or a disadvantage. Adolphe Blanqui, professor of economics at the Conservatory of Arts and Crafts (who should not be confused with Auguste Blanqui, the socialist agitator), never so much as mentioned railways in his lesson on transportation until 1838. When he did discuss them, he thought that, in spite of the attractiveness of their speed, they would be too costly to carry freight and that they would never prevent peasants from continuing to travel on foot, their sacks on their backs.[66] Adolphe Thiers, although fundamentally in favor of railways,[67] saw many impediments to their realization. Customs duties on iron and steel prohibited the use of these products in large quantities and he did not believe that the French metallurgical industry was in a position to furnish the necessary materials.[68] Concerning the proposed line from Paris to Saint Germain Thiers said, "We shall have to give it to Paris as a plaything, but it will never carry a single passenger or a single trunk." Even Arago, that famous popularizer of scientific discoveries and political ally of Louis Blanc, believed that the transportation of soldiers by rail would make them too effeminate for fighting and that persons given to perspiring would catch "lung trouble, pleurisy, and colds" in the tunnels.[69]

In favor of railways were most of the business interests of the nation. Industrialists, agriculturalists, and bankers saw in them a great technical advance. The Saint-Simonians carried on an active propaganda for railway building in their organ, *The Globe*,[70] and in public meetings. The praise of railways was sung in music halls.

> "Grâce à la nouvelle voiture,
> Quand un convive sonnera
> Pour commander une friture,
> De l'océan, le poisson sortira,
> En un quart d'heure à Paris il viendra.
> Sans s'informer des trésors de la Halle,
> Chacun se met à table et le garçon
> S'en va, pendant qu'on débouche un flacon
> Chercher des huitres à Cancale."[71]

Professor Perdonnet, of the Central School for Arts and Manufactures, believed that railways would add to the productive power of France and guarantee to her "long peace and a prosperity whose limits cannot be imagined."[72] Dufaure, illustrious deputy and minister, considered railways a benefit to the economic life of France and a unifying force in the nation:

"Nothing could contribute more actively [toward national unity] than great railway lines, these marvelous means of communication, which, by their rapidity, encourage our populations to exchange and mingle the products of their districts and of their labor. The extremities of France will be more closely drawn together and more united. . . . And is it unimportant to have a means of carrying in an instant our troops, fresh and ready for combat, to the frontiers of our kingdom— from Paris to the banks of the Rhine, from Lyons to the foot of the Alps?"[73]

The poet-politician Lamartine was characteristically flowery in his portrayal of the value of railways:

"We are dealing with one of the greatest questions that a country has ever had to settle—with the creation by iron routes of a political, commercial, military, and industrial condition whose importance no one here can calculate. It is the conquest of the world, of distance, of space, of time. It will multiply to infinity human forces and industry. . . ."[74]

National security was jeopardized by the tardiness of railway construction. A call went up on the floor of the Chamber for the immediate building of a line from Paris to Strasburg. "The German confederation is concentrating a formidable network of railways on the Rhine and in two days an army of 400,000 men could cross our frontier through the breach between Thionville and Lauterbourg."[75] This warning of military invasion, which was a prophecy of the events of 1870, added a terse argument for more rapid railway construction.

The forces of delay were, however, potent. Opposition to railways was reflected in parliamentary lethargy, which the Government had difficulty in overcoming. Official commissions were sent to England and America[76] to study the railway systems of these countries, and a special commission worked out a plan, that was ultimately followed in its general aspects, for a network of trunk lines which would radiate from Paris to the various frontiers. The Government did succeed, moreover, in enacting a law to facilitate the expropriation of land for railways[77] and in transferring the power to grant concessions for railway constructions from the King to Parliament.[78] But when it came actually to the question of granting concessions, real trouble was encountered. In 1835, Thiers proposed lines from Paris to Le Havre via Rouen, for which the state would subscribe one-fifth of the stock and receive no interest until private investors were receiving 5 per cent, and from Paris to Saint Germain, which would be built by a company financed by Emile Pereire, banker, and by Baron Rothschild. For many reasons, one of the most important of which was that the deputies did not want the state to aid in railway building, the bill for a line to Le Havre was defeated; the other was passed by an overwhelming majority,[79] in order, it was argued, to have a successful railway under the nose of Paris that would encourage investors to place their capital in railways.

This move forward was followed in 1836 by a concession for two lines to Versailles, one of which was granted to Pereire, and for one from Montpellier to Cette. In 1837, the Government advocated that the state subsidize private construction of an entire network of railways and showed especial concern for the building of the Paris-Belgium line, for the purpose of knitting the economic life of that nation more closely to France, as the proposed customs union, which was then being discussed, proposed to do; but the Chamber defeated this bill. Not being able to secure the support of a majority of the deputies for these state-subsidized schemes, the Government suggested in 1838 that the state itself should construct four lines—Paris-Belgium, Paris-Rouen, Paris-Orleans, and Marseilles-Avignon. This bill gave rise to an important debate in which Lamartine was the leading protagonist for the statist point of view. He held that the existence of great private companies would make them dominant in political affairs which would be incompatible with the doctrine of liberty. Moreover, "Nothing great, nothing monumental has ever been done in France, and I shall add in the world, except by the State. How can it be otherwise?" Besides, what is the modern state? "[Today] governments are only the action of all citizens centralized in power. The government is the nation in action."[80] Railways should be constructed by the people and for the people. But in spite of Lamartine's oratory and his social political philosophy, the Government's bill was defeated. The project for state-constructed railways was given up and a return was made to the system of concessions to private companies. The right to build lines from Paris to Le Havre, Paris to Orleans, and Strasburg to Basel was granted in 1838.[81] The companies concerned were soon, however, in hot water. The economic crisis of 1837-39 made financing difficult and the costs of construction exceeded the estimates. It was necessary for the state to step in to save the situation. The company that was to have built a line to Le Havre broke its contract and a new company was formed, aided by government subsidies, to construct a railway to Rouen; the Orleans company obtained aid from the state in the form of a guarantee of interest to private investors at 4 per cent;[82] and the Strasburg-Basel company had to be given a loan from the treasury to permit it to carry on.[83]

For twelve years, the French Government and parliament struggled with the railway question. From the experience which it gathered, it was evident that private enterprise could not, or would not, construct railway lines so fast as public opinion demanded. State construction was likewise impossible, for parliament was opposed to it and huge expenditures for armaments and defense in 1840 and 1841 made state financing unfeasible. So a new scheme was worked out for the cooperation of private industry and the state. The Government was to obtain the necessary land, build the roadbed, bridges, and tunnels,[84] lay down the geographical plans, and control the railway rates, while private enterprise was to furnish rails, ballast, stations, rolling-stock and working capital. The state agreed to lease its property without charge to private companies with the understanding that upon the conclusion of the contracts it could take over the railways upon payment for the companies' property. This plan proved generally acceptable to all and was passed by the Chamber in 1842.[85] Those who believed in state ownership and operation saw in the scheme a possibility for the eventual realization of their dreams; capitalists believed it an opportunity for reaping a golden harvest at little risk; and the public thought that it would result in the rapid construction of railways without great increase in taxation.

Under this new arrangement, concessions were granted in quick succession and construction was started. France began to arise from the morass of inaction into which she had sunk as regards railway development. By 1848, France's railway system had grown from 38 kilometers in 1831 to 1921 kilometers of roads in use and 4000 kilometers more under construction or planned. This was not great in comparison with England's 6349 kilometers and Prussia's 3424, but the growth after 1842, in spite of the economic crisis of 1846–48,[86] was encouraging. The ultimate realization of the 1842 plan cost 2270 million francs, of which private industry furnished 1051 millions. The state's share seems inordinately high, but railways were of such great national importance that the Government had to provide bounteous assistance and encouragement to private capital. It was a national necessity to have railways to provide rapid transportation of troops to the frontiers of France, to open up new internal markets, and to furnish a means of cheap transportation of freight and passengers.[87] France's tardiness in railway building made it imperative for the state to act to save the nation from being outdistanced militaristically and economically by her neighbors. In matters of national interest, the nation intervenes to accomplish what private initiative fails to do.

STATE AID TO THE MERCHANT MARINE

As important as railway development was, the merchant marine continued to be the main means of carrying on foreign commerce, about three-fourths of the goods in this trade being shipped by water.[88] The merchant marine retained thus an important place in national economics during the July Monarchy. The navigation laws of the Restoration remained in force, but their action was considerably diminished by treaty. The *droit de pavillon,* which had aimed particularly at foreign competitors, had been practically removed by treaties with the United States and England during the Restoration and now similar treaties were negotiated with twelve other countries,[89] among them the leading carriers of the world.

The loss of this protection undoubtedly injured French shipping, but the state endeavored to offset it by other advantages. With the development of steam shipping, France exerted herself to keep pace with the English. In order that her carriers might not have to suffer from the high price of iron goods and steam engines, duties on these articles, that were intended for use in ships for her merchant marine, were not collected after 1836, and, for use in ships to be employed in international commerce, a subsidy of 33 per cent of their value was given to shipbuilders after 1841.[90] The Government encouraged the establishment of regular shipping services by awarding attractive postal contracts to carriers, but, when this system proved unsuccessful, the state itself went into the shipping business. In 1835 six state lines were established in the Mediterranean, which cut the time from Marseilles to Constantinople and return from fifty to twenty days, and in 1840 the first French postal line on the Atlantic, between Le Havre and New York,[91] followed soon by lines to Mexico and Brazil, began to function. Moreover, the state reserved trade between France and Algeria to French ships and forced foreign vessels trading with that colony to pay a *droit de pavillon,* manipulated the sugar duties to favor trade with the West Indian colonies, and spent huge sums for the improvement of French ports.

In spite of all this aid from the state, the French merchant marine failed to expand. It was outdistanced by the English after steam shipping began to develop and fell hopelessly behind with the coming of iron vessels.[92] The high cost of coal, iron, and machines in France, the comparative slowness of industrial development, the lack of extensive colonial exploitation, and a thousand and one other factors were greater handicaps than a mild form of state aid could overcome.[93]

EXPANSION OF THE COLONIAL EMPIRE

Although France's merchant marine failed to keep pace with commercial growth during the July Monarchy, her colonial empire, that was eventually to be a lucrative source of carrying for French shippers, was considerably expanded. The colonial policy of Louis Philippe was, however, not one of expansion. The foreign policy of the July Monarchy had two main tenets—peace and friendship with Great Britain. Neither the King nor his subordinates would take any action that would disrupt these two principles, which at first view appear to be absolutely incompatible with conquests overseas. But in spite of this fact, the course of events seems to have forced a timid government to be audacious.

The most important extension of colonial holdings in the period from 1830 to 1848 was the conquest of Algeria. The Algerian adventure had been undertaken, as we have already seen,[94] during the Restoration for political reasons. The Liberals had been opposed to it, and, when they obtained power after the Revolution, many favored renouncing the whole thing. One of the proponents of this policy said:

"We are beginning to see that colonies cost more than they profit us. They have even seen that in England. In truth, an extension of territory is not an advantage unless it furnishes men and money to the conquering nation. Well, Algeria, far from supplying these things, will require them. But let us suppose that Algeria was colonized and produced quantities of colonial products. For what purpose increase the production of these goods? They are found in abundance in every land. The universe is gorged with them. . . ."[95]

This "Little France" opinion, which had its counterpart in the contemporary "Little England" movement, had, however, its opponents. Marshal Gérard, Minister of War in 1830, saw in Algeria an outlet for France's surplus population, an argument that was particularly impressive in view of current Malthusian doctrines; others believed that Algeria would be an important market for French goods; Guizot maintained that France should take the colony for national reasons, because "The abandonment of Algeria would be a notable weakening of France's reputation and morale," and another deputy, taking the same stand, affirmed even more strongly the importance of occupying the colony:

"I consider this possession so very important to the interests of France under the present circumstances that the minister who would sign an order to evacuate it should, to my mind, be brought to the bar of justice as guilty of high treason to the State. . . . It is possible that this conquest will lead us into diplomatic complications, but let us act like the English and say that what is good to take is good to keep."

These arguments led the hesitating Liberal Government to calm its fears and to continue the conquest of Algeria. It was a long and arduous task that was not entirely accomplished during the July Monarchy in spite of the surrender of France's most bitter enemy, Abd-el-Kader, in 1847. Just how valuable the colony was no Frenchman knew in 1830 and as time went on many doubted the wisdom of colonial expansion in North Africa. In 1834, there were only 8000 Europeans in Algeria, not all of whom were French; and few new colonizers were entering the country because of native hostility. Marshal Bugeaud, governor from 1841 to 1847, who believed that the only way to conquer the country was to colonize it, expended much effort in establishing settlements. He attempted military colonization, without much success, although he gave land to some of his soldiers and went so far as to bring a boatload of women from France to marry them. But his civil colonization, that got under way in 1842, produced real results. Settlers were allowed to buy twelve hectares of land at advantageous terms on the condition that they would not sell their holdings for three years. With this scheme in operation and with the country relatively pacified, Europeans began to emigrate to Algeria in increasing numbers. By 1847 there was a European population in the colony of 110,000, of whom about half were French; roads had been built, and schools with an attendance of 7000 had been established.

Efforts were made, moreover, to control the growing commerce of Algeria for the benefit of the mother country. The first tariff, established in 1835,[96] allowed the importation of French goods free of duty, while foreign goods were taxed. The "flag surtax" was placed on foreign shipping to the colony, and trade between Algeria and France was reserved for French carriers. Algeria proved, as had been prophesied by those in favor of conquering the colony, to be an important outlet for French goods. In 1835, the "special commerce" statistics between France and Algeria showed that France exported to the colony seven million francs' worth of goods, the leading item of which was textiles, and imported materials to the value of one million francs; in 1847, general commerce with Algeria was 106,700,000 francs' worth of goods exported from France, and 3,800,000 francs' worth of goods imported. This was a tremendously favorable balance of trade, enough to gladden the heart of the most skeptical anti-colonist. The only "fly in the ointment" was that many of the goods sent to Algeria were for French armies and for French colonists who made their purchase with capital from France. The real value of Algeria was to be realized after the passing of the July Monarchy.

In other colonial fields, French activity was less sensational than in Algeria. We have already considered the case of the West Indies, France's most valued overseas possessions, and seen how at one moment it was proposed to abolish the beet-sugar industry in France to protect the major industry of the islands, but how ultimately cane sugar and beet sugar were placed on what was presumed to be an equal footing. On the west coast of Africa, France established trading posts from Senegal to Gabon and strengthened her position in Senegal. In Madagascar, France made no progress; and in the Far East, although she obtained in 1844 the same privileges at Canton that the English had secured by the Opium War and became the defender of the Roman Catholic faith in China, which gave her a handy excuse for intervening at any time, she failed to establish a base for expansion as had the English at Hongkong. In the Pacific Ocean, France obtained a protectorate over Tahiti in 1847, but only after a severe crisis with England, with a loss of face, and the surrender of ambitions for other islands. This colonial record is not illustrious. The bourgeois government was not enthusiastic about engaging in expensive expeditions of questionable profit. What colonial expansion there was, however, during the July Monarchy was colored with a desire for national economic advantage.

DOMESTIC ECONOMIC EXPANSION

Another reason why French expansion overseas was not pressed more vigorously during the 1830's and 1840's was because domestic economic expansion was monopolizing the energies of the nation. Bourgeois had enough opportunities for making money at home without venturing abroad. Industrialization was moving steadily ahead, although not so swiftly as in England.[97] The number of steam engines increased from 525 in 1832, representing 900 horsepower, to 4853 in 1847, with a horse-power capacity of 62,000, which was little compared with England's 375,000 horsepower as far back as 1826. The production of iron ore grew from 741,000 tons in 1833 to 1,658,000 tons in 1847; the amount of coal mined jumped from 1,500,000 tons in 1829 to 5,153,000 tons in 1847; and cast-iron production increased from 221,000 in 1828 to 591,-000 tons in 1847. Despite these gains in the metallurgical industries, France labored under a handicap. Iron and coal were not produced in sufficient quantities to satisfy adequately the needs of the country and their cost was high. Bar iron brought 30 francs per hundred kilograms at Paris, while at Cardiff its price was only 15 francs; coal cost about ten times more in the woolen textile district of Rheims than it did at Leeds. Because of this condition, machines were much more expensive in France than in England, a fact which served to diminish their use. There was, nevertheless, a marked improvement in the technical equip-ment of France. Puddling machines increased in number from 184 in 1834 to 456 in 1847; steam hammers and rolling mills were put in use; the sugar industry became more highly mechanized; power-driven printing presses began to replace hand presses; and paper machines in-creased from four in 1827 to about a hundred in 1847.

The most noteworthy mechanical advances were, however, to be found in the textile industries. Improvements were made on cotton machinery so that production was increased 50 per cent during the July Monarchy and the spinning of fine threads for the better stuffs, that had been almost an English monopoly, was developed until in 1848 French weavers no longer had to depend on England for their supply of yarns. Cotton weaving by machine spread, also; and the Jacquard loom was employed for cotton as well as silk. With these improvements, the con-sumption of raw cotton in France increased from 28,000,000 kilograms in 1831 to nearly 65,000,000 in 1846. As earlier, mechanization of the woolen, flax, and hemp industries progressed slowly, although there was some advance, while that of silk moved steadily forward. The lathe was widely adopted during the July Monarchy; artificial dyes were invented; photography was developed; improvements were effected in soap and candle making; galvanoplasty was invented; and the method for vulcanizing rubber was applied industrially. Finally, there was a notable concentration of the more basic industries.

With all this industrialization, however, France was still at the very beginning of the industrial "revolution"; she remained largely an agricultural nation. In 1846, only 25 per cent of her population lived in towns of 2000 or more inhabitants, and whereas this was a considerable increase in urban population, the corresponding percentage for 1830 having been 15, it was not enough to change much the general aspect of the land. French agriculture was striving to keep pace with industry. In the North and in the valley of the Garonne, the agricultural revolution was well under way. In these districts, the three-field system, with one-third of the land being left fallow every year, was disappearing. Farmers endeavored to keep up their land by rotating crops and using fertilizers, and to winter their livestock on forage crops. Although these new agricultural methods were not adopted in their entirety in other parts of France, their influence was gradually being felt.

The state approved of these changes and did much to popularize agricultural knowledge. In 1838 agricultural courses were instituted in normal schools and at about the same time the "principal facts of agriculture" were added to the curriculum of elementary schools. No state agricultural schools were established in this period, but to advance technical information and to propagate its use financial and moral support was given by the government to private institutions and to agricultural societies. Finally, the state set up a General Council of Agriculture in 1831 and a Ministry of Commerce and Agriculture in 1832 to deal with the legislative and administrative problems of farming.

But with all this effort, it was difficult to penetrate the vast mass of small peasants and *métayers* with new ideas, and the state did nothing to overcome one of the worst obstacles to advance—the lack of capital. Nevertheless, there was an increase in agricultural production from 1830 to 1848. In 1840 France grew 96,000,000 hectoliters of potatoes as compared with 21,000,000 in 1815; wheat production increased from 52,000,000 hectoliters in 1829 to 90,000,000 in 1847; the sugar-beet industry was greatly developed; the production and consumption of meat increased, although this article had not yet come within the reach of all; vegetable growing became more general; and wine registered a moderate gain.

GENERAL ECONOMIC EXPANSION

All the evidence that has been presented thus far concerning agriculture, industry, and transportation indicates a steady increase in national production—a condition dear to the hearts of national economists. Nearly all the statistics available confirm this tendency—that France was steadily strengthening herself economically, albeit she could not pull herself up to the level of Great Britain. France's population during the July Monarchy grew from 32,569,223 in 1831 to 35,401,500 in 1847, a growth that is not without significance, although reputed at the time to have been the slowest in all Europe. In banking, there was a notable increase of activity. Fifteen new branches of the Bank of France, six departmental banks, and several private banks were founded from 1830 to 1847. The current accounts of the Bank of France increased in these years from 4635 million francs to 6315 millions and its discount business from 481 millions to 1816 million francs. The departmental banks similarly augmented their activity. Two important private institutions were set up, the *Caisse Centrale du Commerce et des Chemins de Fer* in 1843 and the *Caisse Générale du Commerce et de l'Industrie* in 1837, which, under the direction of Pierre Laffitte, endeavored to extend banking services to the lesser bourgeoisie. Even the state entered, although indirectly, the banking fields; it advanced 30 million francs during the crisis of 1830 for the establishment of the *Comptoir d'Escompte* at Paris and for facilitating discounting among commercial banks in the provinces. Stock companies multiplied also. In 1831 only forty-four stocks and bonds were listed on the exchange in Paris; in 1847 the number had increased to 198. On this list were some foreign securities and, although France had not secured yet the financial importance of England, the Netherlands, or even Belgium, she had gone forward in the game of lending abroad. From a national point of view, this was a dangerous practice, for while it might lead to an extension of France's colonial empire, it aided in financing the productive development of

France's economic rivals. It was not until much later that the real significance of this fact was realized.

Parallel with the growth of capitalism and the credit system during the July Monarchy—both important assets of economic nationhood—was an increase in France's foreign commerce. Official statistics show that in 1829 imports were valued at 483 million francs and exports at 504 millions, while in 1846 corresponding figures were 920 millions for imports and 852 for exports.

FRENCH IMPORTS AND EXPORTS FROM 1829 TO 1847 IN MILLIONS OF FRANCS

Year	General Commerce Total Exports and Imports	Special Commerce			Capital Transfers	
		Imports	Exports	Total	Imports	Exports
1829 ...	1224	483	504	987	148	66
1830 ...	1211	489	453	942	221	60
1831 ...	1131	374	456	830	221	29
1832 ...	1349	505	507	1012	133	111
1833 ...	1459	491	559	1050	200	160
1834 ...	1435	504	510	1014	192	97
1835 ...	1595	520	577	1097	136	83
1836 ...	1871	564	629	1193	117	102
1837 ...	1566	569	515	1084	199	59
1838 ...	1893	656	659	1315	173	57
1839 ...	1950	651	677	1328	175	78
1840 ...	2063	747	695	1442	217	73
1841 ...	2187	804	761	1565	187	73
1842 ...	2082	847	644	1491	147	65
1843 ...	2179	846	687	1533	169	104
1844 ...	2340	868	790	1658	168	80
1845 ...	2428	856	848	1704	117	88
1846 ...	2437	920	852	1772	190	77
1847 ...	2339	956	720	1676	159	119

These figures, like those of the Restoration, must not be accepted uncritically. The customs receipts, paid mostly on imports, increased

only from 104 millions in 1828 to 155 millions of francs in 1846, a jump
of about one-half, while the above trade statistics show a growth of
nearly 100 per cent. The trade statistics were figured on the price base
established in 1826, but since that date prices had decreased—the index
figure for 1847 being 97.5 for raw materials and 87 for manufactured
articles. This fact would tend to decrease the official returns, particularly on some of the more important imports like cotton, whose price
index at the close of the July Monarchy was at 34.[98] But whatever the
actual value of France's foreign trade was, it increased considerably
from 1830 to 1848, although it far from equalled England's 4597 million francs' worth of foreign commerce of 1840. Of France's leading
clients, the United States, having nosed out the divided Kingdom of
the United Netherlands, took first place in the seventeen years following the establishment of the July Monarchy. England came second;
Sardinia third; Belgium fourth; and the Zollverein fifth. France continued to import chiefly raw materials, of which the most important
were cotton, grain, raw silk, lumber, and sugar, while she exported
manufactured articles, silk, cotton, and woolen textiles, wine, and luxury articles.

The difficulties of estimating the influence of the tariff, as well as
that of the entire national economic system, on France's foreign trade
were pointed out in the last chapter.[99] They were not mitigated by time.
It is probable that during the July Monarchy, as during the Restoration, the nature of France's trade abroad was conditioned by customs
duties. The only sound impression of their conditioning force and of
the influence of all governmental economic measures can be obtained
by a study of individual cases. An extensive use of this method is almost
impossible of accomplishment in such a work as this, but the cases of
sugar, of spinning fine cotton threads, of the merchant marine, and of
agriculture, treated alone, furnish illuminating evidence. Such a study
indicates that what is *prima facie* a struggle for national interest is usually a fight by bourgeois to gain personal advantages. Perhaps in the
July Monarchy the only outstanding exception was the railways. Yet
even here, railway construction on a large scale was not undertaken
until the state had offered capitalists exceptionally favorable terms and
had demonstrated that in case of crisis, investments of financiers would

be safeguarded. Such was possibly inevitable under modern capitalism. But the fact remains that in working for their private advantage, bourgeois developed or tended to create a national economy.

ECONOMIC CRISIS, 1846–1847

The nation's productive powers grew during the July Monarchy—as national economists would have had them grow, but the growth was halted at times by economic reverses. Reference has been made already to the crisis at the end of the Restoration, that was prolonged by the effects of revolution, and to the depression of 1837. The worst crisis of the July Monarchy was, however, that of 1846–47. The crops in 1845 were mediocre and in 1846, the rains that "washed away the Corn Laws" in England and that rotted potatoes in Ireland until the Irish were reduced to starvation, fell also in France. Agricultural production, especially that of wheat and potatoes, went far below normal. As a result, prices advanced, the cost of wheat went from about 19 francs a hectoliter to a high of 37 francs 88, although the mean price for the two years was 27 francs 90. Reduced agricultural production lowered the purchasing power of the farmers, and the high cost of living prevented the industrial population from buying much else than food. Like most of the business crises of the latter part of the nineteenth century, the one of 1846–47 was preceded by a large extension of credit, especially for railway construction and industrial development. When the crops failed, fear seized ambitious entrepreneurs, bankers, and the people. Runs on banks developed, the deposits in the Bank of France fell from 320 millions in June, 1845, to 57 millions in January, 1847.

In this process of deflation, industrial workers suffered probably more than any other class, and their lot was not an enviable one even in normal times. Their real wages had increased very little, if at all, since the Restoration; in fact, in the cotton-textile industry, there had been an actual decrease.[101] Living conditions of industrial workers had obviously taken a turn for the worse. The total population of towns of 3000 or over increased by 2,000,000 in the period of 1840–48; infant mortality in fourteen of the most highly industrialized departments as compared with all France was in the ratio of 121 to 41; and the number of foundlings increased 30 per cent from 1820 to 1848. Diet consisted mainly of soup, bread, potatoes, and milk; green vegetables and meat were considered luxuries. Hours of labor were long, averaging eleven a day in Paris and over thirteen in the provinces.

As industrial workers became more and more urbanized, they became more dependent upon their daily wage as a means of livelihood; they were deprived of those small plots of land which had served to tide them over in earlier periods of stress. To improve these conditions, French workers were almost powerless. Labor unions were prohibited by law,[102] and workers were kept on their good behavior by the *livret,* a small book which contained a record of the worker's activity and which had to be presented on application for a new position. Striking was not an efficient weapon, for there were women and children available to fill the places of men at from one-half to one-third their wages, and besides strikes were vigorously repressed. In spite of all these handicaps, however, the workers did form protective societies of one kind or another. *Compagnonnage,* a hang-over of the *ancien régime,* persisted in a declining state until after 1848; mutual-aid societies developed, numbering 200 at Paris in 1840; *résistance* organizations were founded, like the *Chambre Syndicale des Typographes de Paris;* and workingmen's political groups and labor papers were established. But prior to the crisis of 1846, all that the agitation of the lower classes effected as regards action by the state was the passage of a child-labor act in 1841 that was meager in its restrictions and *nil* in its enforcement.

Thus the crisis of 1846 found the workers helpless, unorganized, and, in some localities, absolutely desperate. Riots broke out among them in industrial centers. Grain warehouses and bake shops were looted; châteaux were pillaged; peasants were robbed; and, in at least one place, the wrath of the poor was wreaked on the *"mauvais riches."* The government did little to alleviate the suffering except to reduce customs duties on food and the charges on canal transportation of foodstuffs. These measures were not sufficient to cope with the situation; it was only with the somewhat better crop of 1847 that the depression began to wane. The experience was, however, a lesson to the proletarians. They became to a greater degree class-conscious; they realized that they could expect little from the July Monarchy; and they began to crystallize schemes of social reform.

Contrary to what might be imagined, the economic ills of 1846–47 do not seem to have occasioned any serious political agitation for a change of *régime*. Political parties of the opposition did not make capital of the economic trouble, and the few evidences of hostility to the King to which the crisis gave rise did not awake the masses to action. Yet while it is true that the opposition which led to the overthrow of Louis-Philippe was mostly political, the effect of economic distress should not be ignored. It is undoubtedly true that hard times aroused the discontent of the proletariat—a factor which conditioned the course and events of the Revolution of 1848 after it got started.[103]

REVOLUTION OF 1848

Leaders of the political attack on the July Monarchy were bourgeois. That they might rule, they had overthrown the military régime of the Empire and they had cast out the autocratic Charles X. In Louis-Philippe, they believed that they had found a man whom they could handle—a man who was a compromise between democratic republicanism and absolutist Bourbonism. Gradually they had become disillusioned. Little by little, Louis-Philippe had taken authority into his own hands; he had ruled since 1840 through Guizot and Soult. These men had been maintained in power by a system of corruption and restricted franchise. In the Chamber of 1836, 206 deputies were functionaries of the state whose votes could be controlled by the party in power; in the Chamber of 1840, 166 deputies held government posts; and in that of 1842, 149. From 1831 to 1847, eighteen bills to eradicate this evil were killed. The electoral system, moreover, had such a narrow base that the King seemed to be able to control a majority—a majority that was no longer representative of the bourgeoisie that industrialization was creating. Bourgeois, who did not share in the government, believed that the only way to get power back into their own hands was to extend the franchise to all members of their class.

"Reform" became the rallying cry of the malcontents. The personal rule of the King had antagonized many groups beside the bourgeoisie —proletarians, liberal Catholics, and some conservatives. Of the nature of "reform," the opponents of Louis-Philippe were not certain. Ledru-

Rollin, lawyer from Le Mans and leader of the Radicals, wanted universal suffrage, and although he was the only deputy to take such a stand, he expressed the wishes of a large element in the nation. Most of the opposition political leaders desired an extension of the suffrage just wide enough to awaken the Government from its political lethargy and to get political power into their own hands. Proponents of this scheme were to be found among all the parties in the Chamber. Lamartine, sympathetic to the masses but loyal to the monarchy, De Tocqueville, Conservative, Odillon Barrot, leader of the Left, and Thiers, chief of the Dynastic Left, supported it—and worked for it.

Numerous were the demands for "reform," but scarcely a voice was raised for "revolution"—for the forceful overthrow of the King. Nevertheless, attacks on the Government, fired by proof of bribery among ex-ministers, became ever sharper and more bold as the year 1848 approached. The reformers maintained that a broader franchise was the only cure for corruption. The enlightened bourgeois elected to office under a new system would, moreover, pursue a more vigorous foreign policy—one that would not sacrifice the liberals of Italy, Switzerland, and Poland to the conservatives; one that would not allow England to insult France's national honor as she had in the Near Eastern affair of 1840, in Tahiti, in the question of the Spanish marriages, and in the right to search French ships for slaves; and one that would not make France the pawn of the Holy Alliance. A more representative bourgeois parliament would take in hand the government's financial difficulties—a necessary step in the light of an enormously increased public debt—and it would pursue an economic policy that would result in something besides a few concessions for railway construction.

In spite of all their campaigning, however, the reformers lost to Guizot in the elections of 1846—the King's supporters securing a greater victory than they had scored in 1842. The King felt reassured. To one of his aides, then forty years of age, he confided patronizingly, "Don't fear, young man; France is a country that can be controlled by functionaries," and to the Prussian ambassador he said, "Tell your master that two things are in the future impossible in France—Revolution and war." Many of the King's counselors sensed the danger in the situation; among them were his own sons. But to all pleas for concessions, the King remained adamant. Guizot promised that there would be no reform, and with his majority defeated easily proposals for a change.

In the impasse, the reformers could do only one thing—carry their cause to the country in a great number of political meetings. Banquets were held, which, according to the lights of their organizers, whether Republican, Dynastic Left, or Conservative, were occasions for preaching reform. Few persons in authority believed that this agitation would lead to revolution, but Leopold I of Belgium prophesied correctly when he said, "My father-in-law will soon be chased out like Charles X." The crisis came when one of the banquets in Paris was prohibited by the Government. Its organizers obeyed the official injunction, but some enthusiasts decided, nevertheless, to demonstrate. The demonstration led more or less accidentally to bloodshed. The revolution was on. The lower classes, as in 1830, rallied against the troops and even the bourgeois national guard took arms against the King. Louis-Philippe had to cede. The propaganda of liberal bourgeois had started a movement that went further than they had desired—it overthrew the "bourgeois" government. Once again men of wealth were confronted with the problem of salvaging their political supremacy from the Parisian mobs.

CHAPTER VI[1]

NAPOLEON III: PATERNAL AND LIBERAL ECONOMIST

BOURGEOISIE AND PROLETARIAT FIGHT FOR CONTROL OF THE REVOLUTION

THE Revolution of February, 1848, was not conducted according to any preconceived plan. It occurred unexpectedly and spontaneously. Parliamentary agitation against the King and Guizot was transformed haphazardly into a revolt that had neither been foreseen nor desired by a majority of the French.[2] The bourgeoisie and proletariat of Paris had joined arms to cast out an unpopular monarch, but once their immediate task had been accomplished, the disjointedness of the entire undertaking became apparent. What course was the Revolution to take? Who were to be its leaders? To these questions the two co-operating groups did not have a common answer. Each was anxious to secure power for its own advantage; each was bent on realizing its own program; and each had its own leaders. Strife soon developed between these two factions, and the subsequent history of the Revolution of 1848 is largely a history of the fight between bourgeois and proletarians for control of the state. The outcome of this struggle is significant, because a victory of the lower classes would have meant a new orientation of national economics—an orientation characterized by policies aimed to benefit the proletariat. The course of the fight is also important, for, complicated as it was by economic depression, it was replete with state interventionism to save the national economic structure from collapse.

The first round of the battle between the two groups that had effected the downfall of Louis-Philippe took place on the morrow of the revolution and resulted in a victory for the bourgeoisie. In the offices of the moderate and middle-class republican newspaper, *Le National*—the source of orders for the conduct of revolutionary activity on February 23—a list of names for a provisional government was drawn up. This list, with few changes, was accepted by the mob in the Chamber and received popular approval, according to revolutionary custom, at the Hôtel de Ville.[3]

Proletarians of Paris did not accept, however, this first defeat as a conclusion to the fight for control. For eighteen years they had felt that they had not profited from the Revolution of 1830 in spite of the important rôle which they had played in it—that it had redounded exclusively to the benefit of the wealthy—and now they did not intend that such a result should be the outcome of the overthrow of the July Monarchy. They forced the acceptance of four new members, including Louis Blanc, upon the provisional government[4] and the issuance of a decree that France was a republic. Encouraged by these successes, the mob appeared on February 25 in order to secure concessions for the improvement of its material conditions. One of its members, a Fourierist, made his way into the presence of the provisional government to demand, not the abolition of private property, but simply a guarantee for the right to work and state assistance in case of sickness or disability. Obviously embarrassed but impotent before the crowd, the government had to bow before these requests; and Louis Blanc worked out a formula with the people's delegate guaranteeing work and recognizing the principle that workers ought to form producers associations in order to benefit by their labor—a solution that was ultimately to be reduced to the principle of labor on public works, that is, employment in the so-called national workshops.[5] Scarcely had the proletariat won this concession, before it demanded adoption of the red-flag-symbol of the democratic and popular cause. This demand was not granted,[6] but not disheartened the mob gathered again around the Hôtel de Ville (February 28), to insist on[7] a ten-hour day, a ministry of labor, and the abolition of a peculiar and obnoxious labor abuse called *marchandage*.[8]

Louis Blanc was sympathetic to such reforms and in the government waged a battle for the establishment of a ministry of labor with himself in charge. His propositions fell on hostile ears and he threatened to resign. His loss at this moment of crisis would have turned the mob against the provisional government and his colleagues endeavored to satisfy him with a compromise. It was decided that a commission should be created to discuss and propose solutions for social questions and, to increase its prestige, that it should meet at the Luxembourg Palace and that its members should sit in the seats of the peers. Blanc was at first opposed to such a makeshift compromise, but finally agreed to accept it. The announcement, February 29, of the creation of this "Commission of Luxembourg,"[9] as it came to be called, calmed the restless masses before the Hôtel de Ville.

GOVERNMENT MEASURES TO OVERCOME THE ECONOMIC CRISIS OF 1848

Up to the first of March, the struggle between the bourgeoisie and the lower classes had resulted in a victory for the former as regards personnel of the provisional government, and in success for the latter as regards promise of the right to work and the establishment of the Luxembourg Commission. The proletarian triumphs indicated that national economic policy might take a swing toward social reform; a bourgeois victory meant that the new government would continue to protect business interests. There was obviously much to be done in both these matters, for the economic life of the country, which had showed some signs of improvement prior to the events of February, took a turn for the worse. State bonds fell precipitously[10] and the Bourse closed its doors. Runs on banks began and banks which had large quantities of state bonds in their portfolios were unable to meet their obligations. Several were forced to close and this made it difficult, if not impossible, for commercial houses to discount their bills or notes. Industry was in turn affected and unemployment consequently increased. Paris, with a total male laboring population of about 200,000 at the beginning of 1848 and with 7000 or 8000 unemployed on the eve of the revolution, had, according to an official estimate, 17,000, or, according to other sources, 49,000 unemployed on March 1.[11] The increased seriousness of the depression led the provisional government to intervene in economic matters with a vengeance.

Under these conditions the Luxembourg Commission held its first meeting.[12] Its task was to cope with the immediate problems of labor and to prepare a social program for the constitutional convention which was to be called in the near future. The work of the commission began auspiciously, for it was decided that *marchandage* should be abolished and that the length of the working day should be reduced from eleven to ten hours in Paris and from twelve to eleven in the provinces.[13] On March 2 representatives of employers accepted these reforms and the provisional government gave them the sanction of law. This action was significant, for it was the first time in the nineteenth century that the French state had legislated for the improvement of adult laboring conditions and because it indicated one direction in which the lower classes would move, if they obtained control of the government. The Luxembourg Commission, then, concerned itself especially with relations between employers and employees[14] and was so successful in dealing with strikes that Louis Blanc in a moment of enthusiasm exclaimed, "Employers and workers come to the Luxembourg by different routes, but nearly always they leave by the same path."[15]

The happy beginning of the Luxembourg Commission was hardly duplicated in the case of the provisional government's other instrument of social improvement—the national workshops. From the first, Louis Blanc's idea[16] of the establishment of producers' co-operatives was sabotaged. Marie,[17] a lawyer and Minister of Public Works, to whose lot it fell to administer the workshops, was not a socialist nor a believer in the wisdom of Blanc's plan. He therefore ignored the principle of co-operation and simply endeavored to care for the unemployed on public-works projects. Already several cities, including Paris, had resorted to this procedure with their *chantiers de charité* and it was only necessary to expand the system to weather the crisis. This Marie began to do, putting the men to work on street improvements, on grading around the Gare Montparnasse, and on levelling the Champ de Mars. The men were paid at the beginning 2 francs a day, when they worked, and 1.50 francs on days off.[18] Because of lack of funds the latter rate was reduced to 1 franc March 15 and for lack of work the men were employed only two days a week after April 16. The remuneration which they received was therefore hardly sufficient for bare subsistence.

Moreover, chaos ruled supreme in the workshops. Even after Emile Thomas,[19] brilliant young engineer, assumed direction of them (March 9) and endeavored to rule them by a semimilitary organization, complete control over the men was never established. Work was not efficiently performed; the men on their days off talked politics, caroused, or played cards; and an accurate record of attendance was not kept. In spite of everything, however, unemployed workers flocked to Paris from the provinces. The number of men registered in the workshops increased rapidly to about 120,000 in June,[20] and by that time nearly 50,000 had been refused admittance.[21] It was obvious that the national workshops were mitigating the trials of unemployment, but it was also clear, at least to the shrewd, that they were sabotaging Blanc's dream of producers' co-operatives and that they were at best a temporary expedient. They were really only keeping the workers pacified while the bourgeoisie established its control over the situation caused by the revolution. They were not a fundamental and far-reaching institution for improving the status of labor in the nation.

While these things were being done to handle the labor situation, the provisional government was engaged in trying to find a solution to the sad condition of state finances and in helping business to weather the storm. In order to get funds to run the affairs of state, an attempt was made to float a 5 per cent loan at par, but this move met with little success because other state 5 per cents were selling as low as 70. Consequently other schemes were resorted to, such as a patriotic call for gratuitous contributions, paying a part of savings accounts of over 100 francs deposited in government banks in state bonds valued at par instead of in currency, increasing taxes, and requiring the Bank of France to issue paper money that was to pass as legal tender.[22] In order to help the businessman, the provisional government aided in the establishment of *Comptoirs d'Escompte* (discount banks) in Paris and in the provinces.[23] These institutions helped considerably in providing working capital, but as further assistance of a similar nature the state set up storehouses in which *entrepreneurs* might place their goods and get a receipt which might be surrendered to the purchaser of their stock or which might serve as security for loans.[24] Finally the provincial banks of issue were united with the Bank of France so that henceforth the nation might have a more highly centralized fiduciary system.[25]

BOURGEOISIE GAINS CONTROL OF THE REVOLUTION

These measures, characteristic of state action during economic crises, assisted the nation in pulling out of the depression and allowed the bourgeoisie time in which to consolidate its forces for the struggle with the proletariat for control of political power. The plan of the middle-class members of the provisional government was to hold the election for the constituent assembly, which was to draft a constitution for the republic, on April 9 in the belief that the interim would be too brief to allow the proletariat to mobilize its political strength or to groom political leaders, and that bourgeois candidates would be swept into office. As a concession to the lower classes, however, it was decided to establish universal manhood suffrage (an increase in the electorate from 240,000 to 9,000,000)[26] and to return to the revolutionary principle of financial remuneration for governmental representatives.[27]

Neither the bourgeoisie nor the proletariat was completely satisfied with these measures; the former feared that it would be swamped by the large popular vote and the latter that it could not prepare for the elections in the limited time available. For this reason the lower classes essayed a *coup* on March 17 and were strong enough to have taken matters into their own hands, but Louis Blanc dissuaded them from doing so.[28] All that their efforts accomplished was the postponement of the election to April 23—a delay that was of little advantage. March 17 marked a turning point in the Revolution; thenceforth there was little possibility of steering the course of events toward socialism.[29]

In the meantime the provisional government was fortifying its position by opening up the ranks of the National Guard to all electors and furnishing equipment to the newcomers;[30] by enrolling the proletarian youth of Paris in the newly formed Garde Mobile;[31] and by massing troops of the regular army in the vicinity of Paris.[32] These measures were wise ones from the viewpoint of the provisional government, for workingmen were preparing, under the guidance of Louis Blanc,[33] for a new demonstration that took place on April 16. On this occasion the National Guard was called out and the demonstrators were unable to reach the Hôtel de Ville and had to file ignominiously through lines of taunting guardsmen.

The impression resulting from this event, that the middle classes were firmly in the saddle, was driven home by their overwhelming triumph in the election for the constituent assembly, April 23,[34] a victory that eliminated all but a handful of workers from direct participation in the drafting of the new constitution.[35] Further to fortify their position, the wealthy elements in the assembly voted to place executive power in the hands of a commission of five, for although members of this body were to be selected from the provisional government, the numerical restriction made it possible to eliminate Louis Blanc and the worker Albert from positions of authority. This move angered proletarians and once again they endeavored a *coup de force*. They struck on May 15 and succeeded in invading the Palais Bourbon and voting the dissolution of the constituent assembly. They named a new provisional government and started to consecrate it at the Hôtel de Ville when they were met by the National Guard and dispersed. The leaders of the uprising, including the socialist Blanqui, were arrested and condemned to perpetual imprisonment.[36]

The gradual intrenchment of the middle class in power was accompanied by a liquidation of the social policies of the provisional government. The Luxembourg Commission, whose members had been influential in organizing the uprising of March 17, was rapidly reduced to a debating society. Its suggestions were ignored or suppressed. Louis Blanc, in delivering, as he himself said, a course of lectures on the subject of hunger to a starving audience,[37] was deprived of an active rôle in the provisional government.[38] After April, the commission spent its time in drawing up an *exposé général* of Louis Blanc's ideas[39] and after the *coup* of May 16 did not meet at all.[40]

As regards the workshops, the provisional government exerted its every effort to use them as a weapon against the proletariat. They were brought under the influence of the moderate political views of the government and large numbers of their members were enrolled in the National Guard.[41] The presence of some laborers from the national workshops among the demonstrators on April 16 indicated that there was a real danger in having so many semi-employed men in Paris.[42]

The termination of the workshops was discussed and decided upon prior to May 15, but the rioting of that day hastened the execution of the decision. On May 17 orders were given to stop enlistments and on May 24 Emile Thomas, the director, was instructed to begin the gradual liquidation of the enterprise.[43] After a partial victory for the workers' list in a bye-election at Paris (June 4),[44] it was decided to vote only 1,000,000 francs for the national workshops at a time, thus placing the finances of the enterprise in jeopardy and finally on June 21 to dissolve the workshops completely. Such a move was too much to be tolerated by the proletarians; they made one last, desperate resort to force in order to save the situation. The government determined to put an end to these sporadic uprisings, which had occurred every month since February. Executive power was placed in the hands of General Cavaignac, a man trained in the harsh school of Algerian experience, who adopted the plan of letting the insurrection ripen and then of eradicating its very roots. By June 26 the opposition had been crushed.

A wave of reaction, that boded no good for the workers, now swept the country. The leaders of the insurrection were taken prisoners. About 15,000 were thus held, and the more dangerous ones were either killed, banished to Algeria, or, like Louis Blanc, forced to flee. Workingmen's clubs and newspapers were suppressed, and the lower classes were virtually deprived of political power. As a sedative to proletarian sentiment a credit of 3,000,000 francs was set up (July 5, 1848) to make loans at 5 per cent to producers' co-operatives. This was a small sum and some of it went to *entrepreneurs*. Although fifty-six associations benefited from it, only fourteen of this number were still in existence in 1855.[45] The gesture was a feeble one; it was apparent that nothing far-reaching would be done to turn national economy into socialist channels.

NAPOLÉON LE PETIT—IL VOIT EN GRAND

The victory of the bourgeoisie was complete after the June insurrection. It remained to be seen how that victory would be used. It lies outside the scope of this study to trace the drafting of the republican constitution that provided for universal suffrage, a unicameral legislature, and a popularly elected executive; and that declared the state to be founded on the basis of work, private property, and public order.[46] Nor is it important to investigate the political jockeying for the election of president. Suffice it to say that Louis Napoleon, nephew of the great Emperor, secured the support of the Party of Order, composed of Legitimists, Orleanists, and Catholics, and was overwhelmingly victorious. Nearly 75 per cent of those who voted cast their ballots for him;[47] the masses and to some degree the wealthy supported "Napoléon le Petit." Now, as after the Directory, capitalists were faced with the problem of controlling a new leader with Corsican blood in his veins. They succeeded little better than had their predecessors in handling Napoleon Bonaparte. By a series of adroit political moves and the use of force, Louis got absolute control of power December 2, 1851, and established a dictatorial empire with himself as Emperor Napoleon III, December 2, 1852.

With power thus concentrated in his own hands, Napoleon III aimed to divert the attention of the French from politics to economics. He hoped to inaugurate a period of prosperity hitherto unknown in France. Just what his economic policies would be, it was difficult to judge from his record.[48] Reared haphazardly in political exile by a wayward mother, he wandered in his youth from place to place and from interest to interest. He was involved as a Carbonaro in the Italian insurrection of 1831; he studied in Switzerland; he attempted two unsuccessful *coups d'état* in France and spent six years in prison; and he wrote numerous pamphlets to further his political fortunes. From his writings, the impression is obtained that he sought support among all classes and all interests. He preached military glory and an authoritarian government which should derive its power from the people;[49] he maintained that vassals, freed by the Revolution, were being created anew by industrialism; he held that education ought to be placed in the hands of the church; and finally he advocated grandiose schemes, such as a transcontinental canal through Nicaragua, and promised economic prosperity and the extinction of poverty.[50] These views, as well as his pre-election promises,[51] gave little indication as to what his constructive program would be. It was only apparent that he would provide a strong government and pursue a personal policy.

Dictators cannot act, however, in a void; they must seek to win approval and to satisfy their subjects, if they are to remain in power. Napoleon III, in searching for an economic formula that would gain general approbation, decided that prosperity, the *sine qua non* of successful economy, could best be attained by developing the productive resources of the nation and by accelerating the speed of its economic activity. The roots of such a concept of national economy went deep into France's past, as we have already seen, and they were to be found in the Napoleonic tradition. Napoleon III wanted to use them to make France economically great. *Il a vu en grand*.

Most significant of all, perhaps, was the fact that these ideas of national economy had their strong advocates in Napoleon III's own time. They formed, as it were, a veritable economic *Zeitgeist*. Representative of those persons who urged industrialization and increased economic activity was Michel Chevalier. He had been a follower of Saint Simon and had caught from his master an enthusiasm for action and for industrial development. He had also an admiration for authority, a respect for the leadership of the "wise men," and, as he had abandoned the Saint Simonian socialist ideal, he was able to pledge his allegiance to Louis Napoleon after the *coup d'état* of December 2, 1851, and to continue to give this *leader* the prestige of his support. From his chair of political economy at the Collège de France, to which he had been appointed in 1840, Chevalier taught[52] that the source of social evils was to be found more often in production than in distribution. Well-being can be obtained by seeing to it that there is always an increasing amount of goods for the same number of people. The state can lend its weight toward the end of greater production by perfecting the means of communication, developing credit institutions, constructing public works, and providing professional training. It should not condone high prices and antiquated technological methods resulting from protective tariffs, but should embark on free trade as a sound national policy.[53] Finally, the state should not regard nationalization of property as an end; it should intervene in economic affairs only when general national interest is at stake.

BANKING DEVELOPMENT

Napoleon III seems to have admired Chevalier and his economic theory. He appointed the economist to the *Conseil d'État*[54] and went ahead, although perhaps not consciously or directly influenced by Chevalier, in putting the above-mentioned concepts of national economy into practice. One of the Emperor's first concerns was the extension of the banking system, for ample credit facilities seemed fundamental for developing productive enterprises. *La haute banque,* that had survived the crisis of 1848—the banks of Rothschild, Heine, Mallet, and Hottinger—specialized in government loans and investments rather than in commercial banking and short-term loans to industry. It catered to a rich and conservative clientele rather than to forward-looking and active entrepreneurs, and was considered by many to be moribund.

Napoleon wanted this situation corrected and gave encouragement to all types of banking enterprise.[55] He gave his blessing to the *Comptoir d'Escompte,* founded to meet the crisis of 1848, and extended the term of the bank's charter in 1850 and 1857. His confidence seems to have been well placed, for the *Comptoir* grew prodigiously. Its capital was increased from the original 6,500,000 francs to 80,000,000 francs by 1866, and at the end of the empire it was doing an annual business of over 3,000,000,000 francs.[56] Its prosperity had allowed it to pay back to the state in 1854 the 3,000,000 francs advance which had been granted to it and to free itself, except in the matter of dividing profits and in making very large loans, from governmental control. Yet the bank was an important adjunct to the designs of Napoleon III—it not only performed well the services of a commercial bank but, by engaging actively in colonial and Far-Eastern affairs, became a valuable economic instrument of penetration.

The commercial banking needs of France were thus well taken care of by an institution that had been founded by governmental initiative to meet a crisis. In other fields of banking, however, there was ample opportunity for state action, the most fertile one being mortgage banking. The only important institution doing this kind of business had closed its doors in 1848 and French property owners were having extreme difficulty in securing new funds upon their holdings. They were already heavily mortgaged, for perhaps as much as eight billion francs in 1851, and ordinary banks were loath to extend them new financing except under the most onerous terms. To ease this situation, R. Louis Wolowski, economist and adviser to Louis Napoleon, proposed the establishment with state aid of a new mortgage bank. The president approved the suggestion and on August 3, 1852, the Crédit Foncier came into being.[57] Later the Empire gave it a legal monopoly of mortgage business—a monopoly that it retained in practice under the Third Republic—gave it a subsidy of 10,000,000 francs, and retained for itself the power to appoint its governor and two assistant governors.[58]

From its very inception, the bank, enjoying governmental prestige, did an important business in granting mortgages on easy terms. It helped finance the transformation of Paris, which was done so extensively and with so much *éclat* under the direction of Haussmann during the Second Empire,[59] aided in the financing of railways, assisted towns in making municipal improvements, furnished capital for land reclamation, and finally extended its activity to Algeria.[60] Contrary to original plans, it did not engage extensively in farm mortgages and for this reason set up an affiliated bank—the *Crédit Agricole* —to ease agricultural financing.[61] Unfortunately this institution ran soon on the shoals of bankruptcy, owing to an ill-advised loan of 168,000,000 francs to the Khedive of Egypt, and had to be absorbed by its parent bank (1876). Despite some loss, the *Crédit Foncier* weathered the storm and grew to be one of the most important financial institutions of France.

In the creation of these semistate banks Napoleon III obviously played an important rôle and although he was less directly concerned in the establishment of private banks during his régime, he seemed nevertheless to impart to them his desire to stimulate the economic activity of France. The most notorious of these banks was the *Crédit Mobilier*,[62] founded by Émile and Isaac Pereire. These brothers, like Chevalier, had been connected with the Saint Simonian movement and were imbued with the idea *de faire en grand*. They established their stock bank with some gusto and, free from government control, plunged into investment banking. They organized a construction company, lent large sums to the railways, subscribed heavily to state bonds during the Crimean War, founded the French Line (*Compagnie Transatlantique*), and invested in Austrian, Spanish, and Russian railways. At first success was theirs; in 1853 they paid dividends of 40 per cent and by 1866 their capital had been doubled. But their prosperity was short-lived; in 1867, with their credits frozen, they were forced to begin liquidation. Of almost an equal wild-cat nature were the banks presided over by J. I. Mirès, which, like the *Crédit Mobilier,* plunged into investment banking and came to early ruin.[63] Of a less dramatic and more substantial character were the *Société Générale,*[64] founded in 1864, and the *Crédit Lyonnais,* set up in 1863 —banks that grew by relatively conservative practices until they became leaders in French banking circles.[65]

PARIS MONEY MARKET—FOREIGN INVESTMENTS

All of these banking enterprises served the national economic purpose of amassing capital—even the savings of the proverbially thrifty French peasant—and of making it available for productive enterprises. Paris grew rapidly as a money market, at times even rivalling London as a European center. Limited-liability stock companies, favored by imperial legislation,[66] increased in number from 118 in 1851 to 307 in 1869 and in the same period the value of their stock on the Bourse rose from 11 to 33 billion francs.[67] This expansion was accompanied by considerable speculation, encouraged by the practices of the *Crédit Mobilier,* and from 1852 to 1856 the Bourse enjoyed a veritable golden age. So much business developed that the central exchange had to delegate a large portion of it to the less conservative *coulisse* (curb). The mania for speculation at times exceeded all bounds and gave rise to criticism in which the Emperor shared.[68] But notwithstanding some mad adventures, the money market of Paris grew rapidly in size and strength. During the Crimean War it was able to lend the government one and a half billion francs without exhausting its resources, and it was the center of the Latin Monetary Union, established in 1865 for the purpose of maintaining the same metallic content in the coins of France, Belgium, Italy, and Switzerland.[69]

The quantity of capital available was so great, in fact, that French financiers began to invest their funds abroad in search of more remunerative interest rates than obtained at home. Foreign loans had been prohibited by the decree of August 7, 1785, and, although they were negotiated after Waterloo, they were not made legal until 1823.[70] They remained fairly insignificant during the July Monarchy, being considerably overweighted by British loans to France,[71] and it was not until the Second Empire that they came to be of real importance. In 1870 France had between ten and fourteen billion francs in foreign investments,[72] most of which was in railways, canals, mines, and government bonds.

The economic advantage to the nation of these loans was hardly questioned at the time, nor has it been until very recently; foreign investments were considered to be national assets, if they were sound from a financial viewpoint. Politically they seemed to be desirable, for, controlled as they were by the government of the Second Empire, they could be used to secure and bind international friendships or to punish national enemies. In this regard it is interesting to note that most of the capital was placed in Russia, Italy, Spain, and Austria-Hungary, and that very little was invested in Germany or in England.[73] Moreover, capital investments gave France an opportunity to extend its influence imperialistically. By loans for the construction of the Suez Canal, France had a loud voice in the conduct of the enterprise, and later on, an opportunity that was not exploited, of extending her influence in Egypt. French loans to Mexico, moreover, were the excuse given for intervention there and so deeply was the government involved that, when the project ended in disaster and Mexican bonds went into default, the state had to pay an indemnity to holders of these securities.[74]

One angle of the national implications of foreign investments that does not seem to have been considered at the time was that French capital was being used by rival nations to develop production—the basis of national economics. This anomaly of national interest is obviously explained by the fact that capitalistically minded persons were interested in making money and preached national economics when the idea could be used to support their plans for greater profits. In other instances, they did less thinking, or altered their views. They thought no less of exporting capital than they did of exporting productive machinery, even if these practices were to create economic giants with whom France would have to compete.

INTERNAL IMPROVEMENTS—RAILWAYS

Foreign investments were but an offshoot of banking development; the main purpose of harnessing capital was, as has already been stated, to give new life to the economy of France. Government use of capital for economic development was by no means neglected. Improvements were made on internal waterways; the projects begun under Louis-Philippe were carried to completion; and new enterprises were undertaken. Government rates were reduced by one-half in 1860 and lowered still more in 1867. Shipping in the port of Paris more than doubled during the Empire.[75] The telegraph system was extended to cover all France and in 1869 four million private messages were sent over it.[76] But railways were looked upon by the Empire as of most vital concern to the nation; governmental energy was devoted to them rather than to other kinds of *outillage national*.

At the middle of the century, France was decidedly behind her closest competitors in railway construction. She had only about 3000 kilometers in operation as compared with Germany's 6000, the United Kingdom's 10,500, and Belgium's 900. Reasons for this backwardness have already been discussed—they were indecision as to whether the state, private initiative, or a combination of the two should build the roads, disaccord concerning routes, parliamentary haggling, and lack of capital. Most of these problems had been solved by the agreements of 1842[77] and railway construction had gone forward. But new and serious problems arose to complicate the situation, as they always will. Overspeculation, strict governmental control, and concessions too short to allow companies to plan for the distant future[78] impeded progress. During the crisis of 1848 many of the lines went into bankruptcy and the Government felt it incumbent on itself to take matters into its own hands. State ownership was discussed, and for a moment it looked as if it would be adopted.[79] But after the insurrection of June, 1848, this project was given up on the ground that it was an attack on private property and too great a financial burden for the state to assume at the moment.[80]

Thus matters stood[81] when Louis Napoleon seized dictatorial powers by his *coup d'état* of December 2, 1851. Immediately he took measures to accelerate railway construction. The granting of concessions was hastened by eliminating competitive bidding, and the Government aided companies by offering them long-term contracts. Financial support was also forthcoming from the state, as it had been in the past. Up to the end of 1851, one and a half billion francs had been spent on railways, two-fifths of that sum having been furnished by the Government.[82] Napoleon seemed willing at first to maintain this pace and into most of the new contracts was written a state guarantee of interest at 4 per cent as return on the capital invested. Under these favorable conditions, concessions were made in 1852 and 1853 for a mileage much superior to all that had been granted up to 1850. The Empire encouraged also the merging of railways into large companies in order to improve their financial standing and to make the remunerative main lines pay for branch railways. Concentration would, moreover, minimize overhead and trans-shipments; and it would cut down foreign purchases by small coastal lines, for the larger networks would be able to carry over their own rails French products from distant points of manufacture.[83] As a result, the number of companies was reduced from thirty-three in 1846 to six in 1859, namely, the *Nord, Est, Midi, Ouest, Orléans,* and *P. L. M.*[84]

Mergers were considerably facilitated by the crisis of 1857, for many of the weaker railway companies found themselves in narrow straits. As usual in bad times, the railway companies appealed to the state for aid, and got it in the form of new contracts—the so-called Franqueville Conventions of 1859.[85] According to these new agreements, railways were classified into "old" and "new" networks. The "new" network consisted largely of subsidiary lines and, as they were not deemed to be especially profitable, it was agreed that earnings on the main lines in excess of a specified sum should be allocated to the "new" network. If, however, the "new" lines did not earn 4 per cent, the state guaranteed that amount for a period of fifty years. The Government would, in turn, be reimbursed, if the earnings of the old lines exceeded 8 per cent and of the new lines 6 per cent; but it could receive no refunds prior to 1872.[86] The state believed that an increase in business would in the long run free it from any financial obligations to the roads. But that was a long-time view, and for the moment it trusted that its concessions were sufficient to stimulate construction. They were not, however, for the companies refused to build lines that they did not consider to be remunerative. The state built some of them on its own account, and then in 1863 made new agreements with the railway magnates which called for state advances of capital for the "new" networks and in some cases for a re-valuation of property and increased capitalization that made the terms of the 1859 conventions less onerous.

Under the stimulus of governmental action, railway building went rapidly forward under the Empire. In 1870 France had in operation about 17,500 kilometers, as compared with 19,500 for Germany, 24,500 for the United Kingdom, 3000 for Belgium, and 6000 for Italy. In 1847 12,800,000 passengers and 3,600,000 tons of freight were carried by French railways, as compared with 111,000,000 passengers and 44,000,-000 tons of freight in 1869. Speed was increased, and railway construction, it was said, would be considered by posterity to be one of the most remarkable feats of the century.[87]

From a national economic point of view, if production be taken as a criterion, railways were of tremendous importance. They gave direct impetus to many industries whose products they employed in construction and indirect stimulus to many more. They hastened the mechanization and concentration of industry, for with cheap transportation goods could be taken to distant markets, and the better equipped and more economically managed factories could force weaker ones out of existence. Railways practically abolished famines in France; and they contributed to the standardization of prices throughout the country. Agriculture profited by being able to transport cheaply its heavy produce to market and to get artificial fertilizers at reasonable rates. The country dweller was now in a position to receive urban niceties and the city dweller was able to get such perishable farm products as fresh milk and vegetables.

Internal trade was increased by the supplying of articles to meet new wants and by the opening of hitherto inaccessible regions. Export trade, facilitated by special rates, was broadened, and it was hoped that this trade, made possible by railways, would allow France to extend its influence in Italy, Spain, Belgium, and Luxembourg.[88] Perhaps, indeed, contemporary opinion was not exaggerating the importance of railways, when it said that posterity would consider their construction to be the paramount achievement of the nineteenth century.

FREE-TRADE THEORY AND NAPOLEON III

In attempting to accelerate economic activity by means of railway building, extension of the banking system, and other governmentally encouraged projects for national equipment, Napoleon III seemed to be paralleling, if not following, the national economic theory of Michel Chevalier. How firm a grip the economic doctrines preached by this ex-Saint Simonian had on the Emperor was speculated about during the first years of the Second Empire; people wondered whether or not Napoleon III would go the whole distance with Chevalier and adopt free trade as an important phase of his policy. There was a strong force, liberal economic theory, at work to lead him to adopt such a line of conduct; and Napoleon III was partial to theories. In addition to Chevalier, J. A. Blanqui, a disciple of Jean Baptiste Say, and Louis Wolowski were preaching free trade from academic chairs; and the Association for Free Trade, created by Bastiat, brought together numerous publicists and a few businessmen for the propagation of the same doctrine.[89] Their argument was that if tariffs were abolished, prices would fall; competition would stimulate production and result in technological improvements; each nation would produce what it was best suited to produce; and an era of international peace would be guaranteed. This ideology, raised almost to the level of a blind faith, dominated the economic thought of most intellectual circles.

During the Second Republic a deputy, Sainte-Beuve, presented the case for free trade to the Legislative Assembly (December 30, 1850), and thereby provoked a debate in which he promised the millennium if his theories were put into practice. Thiers opposed him with vigor and invoked God as a proponent of protectionism. Upholders of the tariff system called for the dismissal of Chevalier and Blanqui from their professorial positions and carried on in the press a virulent attack on liberal economics. The Government did not join them in their campaign, but did make a statement that, although protectionism was necessary for French industry, there was need of tariff reform.[90]

This episode indicated that the forces of protectionism were still strong in the country. Industrialists, most of whom manufactured for small local markets, were more concerned with keeping foreign goods out of their districts than they were with expanding their affairs to compete abroad. Peasants as well as large landholders felt it was to their advantage to have duties on the products of agriculture. And workmen now became vocal in their approval of a system of tariffs, because their greatest fear was lack of employment.[91]

The national economists had an able theorist in Charles Gouraud,[92] who answered all the free-trade arguments with apparent persuasion. To the contention that increased competition would improve the technical equipment of the nation and encourage the production of what France was best able to produce, he countered with the suggestion that a backward nation might never be able, on an equal basis, to compete successfully with states that were better equipped or more bountifully endowed by nature than it. Such a nation would become an economic vassal to stronger powers and sooner or later would become a political vassal as well. He held, therefore, that there is no guarantee of peace in free trade; to the contrary, there is promise of bondage. Neither is there a guarantee of cheap prices. What good are low prices on foreign goods to the worker, if he has no work? Will foreigners continue to sell at reasonable sums after they have gained monopolistic control of a market? History teaches otherwise. Production must be maintained and in France it cannot be kept up and developed without customs duties.

To these arguments many a politician lent an attentive ear, but whether or not Napoleon III was among them in the early years of the Empire is difficult to state. In his youth he had been an avowed protectionist and when the fight between cane and beet sugar was on, he wrote a pamphlet that would have been worthy of Napoleon I:

"If in France the partisans of free trade dared to put into practice their sinister theories, France would lose in wealth a sum of at least two billions; two million workers would be without employment, and our commerce would be deprived of the benefit which it secures from the immense quantity of raw materials which are imported for our factories. The history of the birth of all industries in France, the example of all peoples, finally the precepts of all eminent men who have been at the head of governments, are in accord on this point, that the existing industries of a country ought to be protected as long as they have need of protection. Even the celebrated minister Huskisson, although a disciple of Smith, declared that 'it is not necessary to put national industries in competition on the home market with foreign rivals unless the former can withstand the struggle.' "[93]

Whatever may have been Napoleon's convictions, no one knew exactly where he stood. As Théophile Gautier said of him, "He turned to the right and then to the left and one could never tell where he was going." But that he had once held protectionism so dear and that he lauded so heartily the policies of his uncle indicate that probably he favored at least moderate tariffs. At all events, although he appointed a strong minority of free traders to the *Conseil Supérieur du Commerce, de l'Agriculture, et de l'Industrie,* he curbed them by naming a majority of stanch protectionists.

REDUCTION OF CUSTOMS RATES

Real apprehension was felt by national economists, however, when the Emperor obtained the right to lower customs rates by treaty without legislative approval.[94] Complaints of protectionists elicited from the president of the Senate a declaration against free trade, but no promise was made against reductions. The Government began soon a program of tariff reform. In 1853 harvests were poor and to meet the emergency of high prices, the sliding-scale corn laws were suspended as were the *droit de pavillon* and the *droit d'entrepôt* on grains.[95] Imports of wheat bounded from 232,000 quintals in 1852 to 4,428,000 quintals in 1854, yet the sliding-scale duties were not re-established until 1859. Other decrees lowered the rates on livestock, coal, iron and steel, cottons, machines, raw materials for shipbuilding, wool, and hides; and the prohibition on ships was replaced by a 10 per cent *ad valorem* tax.[96] These changes, coming as they did in a period of relative prosperity for industry, although not for agriculture, were less hostilely received than they would have been in bad times. They were ratified by a sullen legislature in 1856 and 1857.[97]

It was apparent that Napoleon III, if not an advocate of absolute free· trade, was at least interested in tariff reform—that he had succumbed, in part, to the liberal economic theory of his day. He and his advisers were, in fact, planning more drastic measures. In 1852, the Government submitted to the Council of State a project for abolishing sixteen prohibitions on imports and practically all those on exports, for allowing 241 articles to come in without paying a levy, and for reducing the duties on 97 others. Although there was so much disagreement in the Council concerning this plan that no action resulted from it, the Government continued to nourish ideas of tariff reform. It wanted to put its theories to a test—to show France that her industry and agriculture could compete with foreign goods.

An opportunity to do this on a small scale, it was believed, was presented by the Paris Exposition of 1855. The Government granted foreigners the privilege of sending articles on the prohibited list to the fair and to sell them in France, subsequent to the exposition, upon payment of a customs duty of 22 per cent. Of 22 million francs' worth of goods thus admitted, only 2,500,000 francs' worth were purchased by Frenchmen; therefore, the Government thought that its case for free trade was proved.

Encouraged by this test and enjoying political prestige upon the favorable conclusion of the Crimean War, the Government submitted (1856) a revised plan for the abolition of prohibitions—a plan that substituted high duties for actual proscription. A bill incorporating this change was introduced to the *Corps Législatif* on June 9, but the moment was not propitious. The legislature was still sulking from having been forced to ratify the decrees for reducing rates. So bitter was opposition to the bill, that the Government amended it by increasing certain rates and finally withdrew it altogether. But the fight was not over. The Government appointed promptly a committee of the *Conseil Supérieur du Commerce* to study French industries and to make proposals concerning the need of prohibitions and protection. Agitation even against this move was so vigorous that once again the Government retraced its steps and informed the public that it had prepared a new bill which provided for the repeal of prohibitions only after July 1, 1861.[98]

This reprieve for protection only served to stimulate the opponents of reduction. The Committee for the Defense of National Labor, the chief protectionist organization, and its organ, *Le Moniteur Industriel,* worked overtime in awakening the country to the disaster to which it felt the Government was leading France. It nipped in the bud another official attempt in 1859 to hold an investigation and succeeded in getting the grain tariffs restored instead of abolished, as was the Government's wish. Again circumstances favored opponents of tariff reform, for it was apparent that Napoleon could not risk an internal upheaval over tariffs when he was about to engage Austria in the war of Italian liberation.

THE COBDEN TREATY, 1860

These various attempts of the Government to reduce customs duties indicated that Napoleon was definitely bent on tariff reform—the abolition of prohibitions and the reduction of the high protective rates. His every move had been thwarted by the *Corps Législatif* or by propagandists. But he had one recourse for circumventing his blocking legislature—he could reduce rates by treaty. Much earlier his friend and adviser Chevalier had toyed with the idea of concluding a general low-tariff treaty with Great Britain. He had already gone so far as to correspond with Richard Cobden concerning it. In 1856, hoping to cement the military alliance of the Crimean War with economic mortar, these two free traders, on Chevalier's initiative, had endeavored to push their plans to realization, but Prime Minister Lord Palmerston would not listen to their project because it meant a reduction in Britain's revenue.[99]

A more propitious moment had to be awaited. In 1858, the Orsini plot against Napoleon, which had been hatched in England, aroused antagonism between the two countries. The English thought that the Emperor of the French was planning to invade their isle and went so far as to organize volunteer corps and to vote money for defense. The French, for their part, were angry because the plot had originated in England and because a bill against foreign intriguers, which aimed to appease French sentiment, was defeated. No efforts were made to relieve the tension until John Bright proposed to the House of Commons that French passions be mollified by reducing the tariff on wines (July 21, 1859). This was the cue for Chevalier to renew with Cobden his plan for a treaty. Gladstone, Chancellor of the Exchequer in Palmerston's new ministry, gave Cobden his approval of negotiations. Cobden then met Chevalier in London to work out a campaign of action. They easily obtained English support; then they moved on Paris. Chevalier got a favorable hearing from some of Napoleon's ministers; but those who were known to be unalterably opposed to tariff reform, like Walewski, were kept completely in the dark concerning the proceedings. Finally the two plotters approached the Emperor himself just at the time when negotiations were being conducted at Zurich for French annexation of Nice and Savoy—a territorial acquisition to which England was opposed.[100] Napoleon lent an attentive ear to their proposal; he was pleased by its economics and grateful for the opportunity it gave to disarm English hostility to his imperialistic ambitions in the south.

With these preliminaries concluded, unofficial negotiations were entered into by the two powers. Obstacles such as lack of support of those French ministers who had been kept in ignorance of the Chevalier-Cobden scheme and the opposition of protectionists had to be overcome. Napoleon himself created a serious problem to the free traders, for he hesitated and procrastinated and appeared never to be ready to take the bull by the horns. Gradually some of the protectionist ministers were won to the plan because of a belief that the treaty was the only way of averting war over the Italian question. Eventually, Napoleon was encouraged to make a final decision by Cobden's insistence. On January 15, the Emperor made public a letter to one of his ministers in which he declared his intention of reforming the tariff by treaty in order to allow French industry to profit from the stimulating effort of foreign competition.

This statement cast the die, but it aroused also the wrath of industrialists. Napoleon realized that this would be the case and endeavored to take the wind out of their sails. He promised that financial assistance from the public treasury would be forthcoming for those industries which suffered from the reductions[101] and he agreed, upon the demand of his protectionist ministers, to hold a hearing at which industrialists might present their views. This *enquête* was held, but it was limited to two days. Those few who testified were carefully chosen from among tariff reformers and were received privately by the Emperor.[102] This procedure did not pacify protectionists. Petitions were sent to Napoleon; and manufacturers, especially those from Normandy, Picardy, and Flanders, swarmed to Paris. The leading industrialists of Rouen chartered a special train to take them to the capital. Lobbying was of little effect, however, and finally a petition, signed by nearly 1400 manufacturers, was drawn up which recalled the dire results of the Eden Treaty of 1786 and threatened, "We must choose between an alternative. Either we must submit to the disastrous consequences, or we must go to war and destroy the treaty by cannon fire. It is with this terrible alternative that you [the Emperor] have faced us." The *Moniteur Industriel* was seized for publishing this petition and those manufacturers who threatened to shut down, so that their workers would be forced to violent action against the state, were told that they, rather than their workers, would be held responsible for any untoward action. The Government remained adamant and the treaty was signed on January 23, 1860.

By the terms of this document France agreed, as regards British goods, to abolish her prohibitions by October 1, 1861 (the Emperor did not feel that he could do this sooner because of his promise of 1856 not to abolish them for five years), and to reduce her tariff schedule to a maximum of 30 per cent within two years and of 25 per cent within five years. Upon the insistence of Gladstone for some immediate favors to aid in securing the ratification of the treaty by the English Parliament and as a sign of good faith, France granted reductions on coal, coke, iron, steel, machines, and tools to go into effect during the course of 1860.

For her part, Great Britain pledged, in accordance with her general free-trade policy, to allow nearly all French products to enter without customs charges, to reduce the rate on French wines from 15 shillings a gallon to a scale from 1 shilling to 2 shillings, and to grant a reduction on brandies of about 40 per cent.[103] Export prohibitions and duties were to be abolished by both contracting powers, but in reality this was a British concession and concerned particularly coal. France was a large importer of this commodity and had once had to pay a "tribute" to the English in the form of an export tax; she even feared that in case of war her supply might be entirely cut off. The treaty included, moreover, the most-favored-nation clause, a provision that the accord should run for ten years and then annually unless denounced by either party upon twelve months' notice, and an agreement that supplementary conventions should change the *ad valorem* figures into specific duties.[104]

The signing of the treaty created a favorable feeling in England toward France and may have averted war.[105] Napoleon used it adroitly to this end, making public his intention of annexing Nice and Savoy after the treaty had been submitted to the Commons for ratification. His move caused considerable excitement in England and strengthened the Tory opposition to the treaty. It was criticized on both political and economic grounds, but it was finally ratified.

LOW RATES FIXED—EXTENDED BY MOST FAVORED NATION TREATIES

In France, hostility toward the treaty continued almost unabated. Inasmuch as opponents of the agreement had failed to thwart the Government's action, they criticized it severely in the *Corps Législatif*[106] and endeavored to obtain the establishment of the 30 per cent maximum rate on all goods of importance. The Government refused to grant their demands and proceeded to an investigation of prices in France and England for the fixing of specific rates. The *Conseil Supérieur du Commerce*, now with a majority of free-trade members, was instructed to hear evidence in order to ascertain price levels during the preceding six months and to collect information concerning the actual need of French industries for protection. The seven volumes[107] that contain the evidence taken by the Council form a study in the perfidy of vested interests. British manufacturers swore that in some lines they could not compete with the French; the French swore that in the same lines they would be ruined by the British. Both sides cited facts and figures to substantiate their views.

Little head or tail could be made of the mass of material which was compiled, but that mattered little, for the Government had already determined the course to be pursued. It had appointed special commissioners, who were free traders, to negotiate with the English, and their decisions were presented without discussion to the Superior

Council of Commerce. The final conventions, signed October 16 and November 16, 1860, provided for French duties on British goods that were much inferior to the maximum of 30 per cent. The rate on cotton yarn averaged between 8 and 10 per cent *ad valorem;*[108] on cotton cloth between 10 and 15 per cent; and on cutlery 20 per cent. The duties on iron and steel were so low that great quantities were imported in the following decade for railway construction. France had not established absolute free-trade, as had Britain, but she had gone far enough to facilitate greatly the international exchange of goods.

This system of liberalized international commerce was obviously pleasing to Napoleon III. It was now apparent to all that he had not agreed to the proposition of Cobden and Chevalier for purely political purposes, and that he believed emphatically in the virtues of low tariffs. Import duties on a certain number of raw materials were abolished by the law of May 5, 1860; rates on coffee, sugar, and other colonial products were reduced at about the same time;[109] the sliding-scale taxes on grain were replaced by an insignificant statistical tax, June 15, 1861; and other reforms, including the abolition of export and transit duties, were effected in 1863 and 1864. Still more important changes were wrought by commercial agreements with Belgium, the German Zollverein, Italy, Switzerland, Sweden and Norway, the Hanseatic towns, the Netherlands, Spain, and Austria.[110] In each of these treaties was written the most-favored-nation clause which meant that those states secured the rates granted to Great Britain and would obtain the benefits of any new reductions. Thus by the end of the Second Empire there were no export duties; raw materials and foodstuffs were allowed to enter free or upon payment of very low rates, and manufactured goods for import faced no longer absolute prohibitions or excessive protectionist tariffs. Napoleon III brought France as close to free trade as she has ever come.

PRIVILEGES TO SHIPPING ABOLISHED

The Emperor's schemes for economic reform were not, however, complete with these measures. He considered the development of the merchant marine essential to the economy of France. It was obvious that something needed to be done in this direction, for the percentage of tonnage entering French ports in foreign ships had increased from 51 in 1820 to 73 in 1840,[111] and the total mercantile tonnage on the national registry was 688,000 in 1850 as compared with the United Kingdom's 3,565,000.

In the first part of his reign, Napoleon III endeavored to improve these conditions by his general plan of increasing credit facilities and more specifically by subsidies. The *Compagnie des Messageries,* which had been engaged in transporting post and freight on land and had begun to see its business vanish with the coming of the railways, decided that it should extend its operations to water carrying. In 1851, the company, henceforth known as the *Messageries Maritimes,* agreed to buy the money-losing Government ships on the Mediterranean and to carry the mail from Marseilles to Constantinople and Alexandria for an annual subsidy of 3,000,000 francs.[112] In 1860 it undertook the operation of mail lines to South America for a subsidy of 4,700,000 francs and in 1861[113] to the Far East for state aid that amounted in 1869 to 10,503,383 francs. The success of these mail routes was not duplicated in the case of The Havre-New York run, for the company subsidized in 1857 to ply between these ports was unable to fulfil its contract. The Government therefore turned to the *Compagnie Générale Transatlantique* (French Line), recently established by the daring *Crédit Mobilier* of the Pereire brothers, to handle mail traffic in the North Atlantic and secured its agreement on the condition that the state grant it a substantial loan.

Napoleon III was not satisfied with the results of this form of assistance to shipping; when he began to prescribe liberal economic doctrines for France, he decided to give the nation a complete treatment—to extend his policies to the merchant marine. Although he did not abolish subsidies, he did make the French shipping industry compete with foreign lines. Until the Crimean War French shippers were prohibited from purchasing foreign-built vessels. But during the war, a temporary exception was made upon the payment of a 10 per cent *ad valorem* tax. The way was thus paved for the negotiators of the Anglo-French treaty of 1860 to abolish the prohibition and this they did. Ships built in England might be nationalized French by paying 70 francs a ton for iron vessels and 25 francs for wooden ones—sums that were to be reduced to 60 francs and 20 francs, respectively, in 1864, or to about 5 per cent *ad valorem*.

French shipbuilders denounced this change and became particularly vehement in their complaints after the privileges were extended to countries other than Great Britain.[114] They secured the ear of the Government who gave them the satisfaction of an *enquête*.[115] As usual, contradictory evidence was heard, but on the basis of it the *Conseil Supérieur du Commerce* recommended the free importation of materials for ship construction and the abolition of the *surtaxes de pavillon et d'entrepôt* and of the *droits de tonnage*. A bill to this effect, which was submitted to the *Corps Législatif,* gave rise to vigorous opposition by the protectionists. Thiers argued that because France did not have bulky articles for export her merchant marine would be unable to withstand competition with the entire universe. Pouyer-Quertier, an important cotton manufacturer of Rouen and stanch believer in tariffs, offered in evidence the results of the Cobden treaty on French industry as an indication of what would befall French shipbuilding and carrying if the bill were accepted.

In spite of this reasoning and these dire prophecies, the bill became the law of May 19, 1866. Foreign-built ships were henceforth able to become French on the payment of the insignificant sum of two francs per ton, foreign shipbuilding materials could be imported free of duty, and no subsidy was to be granted, as formerly, for the use of French rather than foreign goods in construction. Moreover, the *surtaxe de pavillon* and *droits de tonnage* were abolished; a move that was of some importance, for, although they had been wiped out by treaty with most of the important carrying nations of the world, they encouraged, if not forced, certain countries, especially those of South America, to send their goods to France in French bottoms. France relinquished also her monopoly of the carrying trade between the motherland and Algeria, as she had already surrendered it for Guadeloupe, Martinique, and Réunion in 1861,[116] a reform that was extended to other colonies in 1869;[117] and she gave up her *surtaxe d'entrepôt*.[118] Thus were removed practically all the privileges which the merchant marine and the shipbuilding industry had previously enjoyed.

NAPOLEON III'S IMPERIAL POLICIES

In imperialism, the Second Empire sought to find opportunities for the development of French shipping which would compensate it for the abandonment of "navigation acts." Colonies would, moreover, round out Napoleon's general plan of national equipment—they would provide markets for France's fast-developing industry and places for the investment of her capital. In the conquests of backward areas, Napoleon would win at slight expense that military glory which he coveted so much and he would be able to let shine the civilizing rays of French culture and of Catholicism on barbarous peoples.

Thus it was that during the Second Empire colonization took on new life; there was imperialist activity reminiscent of the times of Colbert and Napoleon I. Algeria was "pacified," which made settlement there more attractive, as is shown by the fact that the number of Europeans in the colony doubled between 1848 and 1870. Senegal was explored in order to learn its true economic wealth. When reports indicated great possibilities there, if a strong government were established, the French under the able leadership of Faidherbe[119] began its conquest (1855). Cochin China was conquered (1865), following the massacre of French missionaries, and Cambodia fell to France as a protectorate (1863), when that country sought refuge from a much-feared Siamese domination! New Caledonia was taken in 1854 (the cause for intervention was the protection of missionaries), and a protectorate was established over the eastern coast of Madagascar in 1862 and 1868. A Red Sea trading station (Obock) was obtained from Abyssinia in 1862 and Japan was opened to French merchants by two naval demonstrations (1854, 1864). Napoleon had ambitions for obtaining a foothold in China comparable to the English port of Hongkong, and although he was unsuccessful in attaining his goal, he profited from the opening of seven ports which followed the Anglo-French march on Peking (1860). Finally, the Emperor supported the attempt to set up Maximilian in Mexico, which, if it had succeeded, would have given him control over a vast area in the New World. In spite of this failure, Napoleon's imperialist record was remarkable; he added to French territories lands of great economic potentiality and he won thereby a little of the military glory that he was less successful in securing from his Continental wars.

The policy that was adopted toward these new acquisitions, as well as toward the old colonies, was decidedly liberal. The measures taken by the provisional government of the Second Republic to free the slaves in the Antilles were not undone.[120] This inroad on the old colonial system, which was founded on the belief that colonies existed for the sole advantage of the mother country, indicated the lines along which Napoleonic colonial policy would move. The prohibition against importing refined colonial sugar was removed in 1852;[121] and in 1854 Martinique, Guadeloupe, and Réunion were granted a measure of self-government.[122]

As the ideas of the liberal English economists began to win favor with the Emperor, it became more and more evident that he approved their views regarding colonial policy. After the signing of the Cobden treaty, with its articles allowing the importation of foreign colonial products free or almost free of duty, it seemed iniquitous to force the colonies to trade exclusively with France—to bear the burdens of a system from which they derived no benefits.[123] Hence there was good reason for the law of July 3, 1861, which permitted Martinique, Guadeloupe, and Réunion to buy and sell all kinds of merchandise with foreign nations and to employ foreign ships for the carrying of all their goods on payment of the usual navigation surtaxes—surtaxes which were abolished in 1866.

Furthermore, the three "old colonies" were in the same year granted the privilege of establishing their own wharfage fees and in co-operation with the Conseil d'État of fixing their own customs duties (decree of July 4, 1866). This privilege gave them what amounted to tariff autonomy, for they abandoned regular customs duties and used wharfage fees for fiscal and protectionist purposes—fees which fell with equal force on French and foreign goods. Trade with Algeria was facilitated by allowing Algerian products into France free of duty and by granting preferential rates to French goods imported into the colony.[124] Other French colonies had their tariffs cut to the bone and their ports opened to foreign ships. By these measures the old colonial system, along with high protective tariffs, was thrown into the discard by the Second Empire. Napoleon III wanted a great colonial empire, but he believed it would develop best under a régime of liberal economics.

EFFECTS OF NAPOLEON III'S ECONOMIC POLICIES

The effects of Napoleon III's policies on the economy of France are, as is always the case, difficult to ascertain with any degree of accuracy. The period of the Second Empire was one of economic expansion; the production of coal and lignite increased from 5,153,000 tons in 1847 to 13,464,000 tons in 1869; that of iron and steel increased by 32 per cent, and that of pig iron by 100 per cent.[125] The number of bales of cotton imported went up from 467,470 in 1855 to 762,593 in 1868;[126] total imports of special commerce rose from 765,100,000 francs in 1851 to 3,153,100,000 francs in 1869, and total exports from 1,158,-100,000 francs to 3,074,900,000 francs.[127] Napoleon III was fortunate in coming to power when business was at the bottom of its cycle, for he was able to gain prestige by the normal upward swing. The discounts of commercial paper by the Bank of France in Paris, which had declined from 1329 millions in 1847 to 256 millions in 1849, rose steadily to 1753 millions in 1856.[128]

These were prosperous years for industry and commerce, but Napoleon could not guarantee a golden age—in 1857 there was a severe depression. In fact, the second decade of the Empire's existence was much less brilliant economically than the first. The Italian war, the Civil War in America, the Mexican expedition, and the Seven Weeks' War contributed much to upsetting business conditions. In 1861 there was a financial crisis caused by the demands of the United States for silver to finance the war; in 1864, there was another financial crisis caused by the exportation of silver to India and Egypt to pay for cotton; and in 1866 there was a business depression brought on by overspeculation and overexpansion from which France did not fully recover during the remaining years of Napoleon III's reign.

There was a tendency on the part of business men to attribute the cause of this economic instability to Napoleon's liberal economic measures. This problem is worthy of consideration: were his policies sound ones from the national point of view? The results of the commercial treaty with Great Britain, which were submitted to the sharpest criticism, indicate that different industries were variously affected. In the iron industry, there was a considerable increase of British imports from 1861 to 1863, but then they fell off to approximately normal amounts. This was attributed to the fact that iron imports in these years exceeded the immediate demands and that the specific duties on iron and steel, which ranged from 29 to 38 per cent *ad valorem,* were in effect protective. The treaty hastened, however, the transformation of the metallurgical trades. Already there had been a move to abandon charcoal smelting in widely scattered districts and to concentrate activity in large plants which made use of coke and improved machinery. This process was eccelerated, and many of the small producers who were pinched in the change placed all blame for their misfortunes upon the treaty.[129]

In the cotton industry, there were, as in iron, large imports immediately after 1860, a reduction of prices, and then an ebbing of the flood. Subsequently, the diminished supply of cotton from America, owing to the Civil War, upset the industry so badly that it is difficult to arrive at a correct appreciation of the effect of Napoleon's policies on the industry. Nevertheless, the tariff on coarse yarns was sufficient to prevent an inundation of the market, although France developed a decidedly unfavorable balance of trade with England in cotton goods.[130] The coal industry, which was less able to compete with English exports than were the iron and cotton industries, saw after 1860 imports increase at a greater rate of speed than its production. Shipbuilding suffered also from the new order of things. French construction fell from 63,189 tons in 1865 to 47,312 in 1869 and the importation of ships increased by more than 100 per cent, which was, however, not enough to make much difference in France's total tonnage. The percentage of shipping to and from France carried in French vessels declined from 39.75 to 34.77, although the volume of total tonnage increased by over one third.[131] Woolen and worsted manufacturing, on the other hand, expanded during the decade of the 1860's, owing chiefly to the cotton shortage; the exportation of silk goods grew rapidly, although they never flooded the British market; and

French wine sold to Great Britain increased from 44,000 hectoliters in 1858 to 157,000 hectoliters in 1864.

The experience of individual industries indicated, as was to be expected, that those trades which had little to fear from British competition, like silk and wine, profited from the free-trade agreement. Some, like the iron and steel businesses, which were granted a small degree of protection, improved their plants and suffered very little. Others, like shipping, that could not stand before British rivalry, were definitely harmed. The steady growth of production in practically all industries except cotton and shipbuilding after 1860 was hailed by free traders as proof of the validity of their theories. But it should be borne in mind that expansion took place more rapidly in the first decade of the Empire under high protection than in the second decade. The general unsteadiness of business in the 1860's was pointed to by protectionists to indicate the proof of their contentions, but here political conditions played an important rôle.

These facts tend to show that tariffs may be much less significant in a nation's economy than other forces, such as extension of credit, growth of markets, development of means of communication, technological improvements, discovery of new supplies of raw materials, and favorable political conditions. This is especially true in periods of economic expansion; it is probably much less so under static or semi-static conditions. A consideration of the total foreign-trade statistics for the decade of the 1860's indicates, however, that the new tariff régime was not without its effect. In 1859 French imports[132] amounted to 1,640,700,000 francs and exports to 2,266,400,000 francs; in 1869 the respective figures were 3,153,100,000 francs and 3,074,900,000 francs. Thus what had been a very "favorable" balance of trade became slightly "unfavorable" and this excess of imports over exports continued to grow until the tariff of 1881.

Classical economists would maintain that there is no significance to changes of this nature and yet they would have to admit that a continually growing unfavorable balance of trade indicates that a nation, perhaps because of the absence of tariffs as well as for other reasons, is less able to compete with foreign countries than it had been formerly. This in turn would mean a proportional reduction in production—

the very crux of the system of national economics.[133] A more detailed analysis of trade statistics indicates that for all France and all industries this theoretical conclusion is probably correct: French exports of manufactured articles remained almost stationary from 1860 to 1870, while the importation of manufactured products increased nearly 500 per cent. The exportation of raw materials and foodstuffs approximately doubled and the importation of raw products for industry increased by 44 per cent.

ATTACKS ON NAPOLEON III's LIBERAL MEASURES

In view of these facts, industrialists and national economists had undoubtedly a case for attacking the low-tariff policies of Napoleon III. From the first it was realized that their opposition would be stern and an attempt had been made to disarm them by providing a fund of 40,000,000 francs to alleviate the stress caused by the Anglo-French treaty. This plan, which was suggested by Michel Chevalier, stipulated that those industries which suffered from increased competition because of the new policies would be granted credit from the fund at a rate of interest lower than the prevailing commercial rates. Iron, coal, and cotton industries received most of the loans that were made before the sum was exhausted in 1865. How much of this money was granted to companies that were actually in narrow straits as a result of tariff reductions, how much was used for ordinary expansion or to refund outstanding obligations, and how much was never repaid is impossible to tell because of the lack of official data on the subject. It is certain, however, that the fund did serve to sweeten the attitude of many an industrialist toward free trade. Yet the fund was too small to make any appreciable difference in the condition of French production or of French foreign trade or to win over all protectionists.[134]

Although criticism of the low-tariff policy of Napoleon III always continued, a vigorous campaign for its abolition began in 1868. The moment was opportune, for France was suffering from bad times and the Emperor's political position was weakened by the results of his Italian and Polish policies, the Seven Weeks' War, and the Mexican misadventure. Du Mesnil-Marigny published a scathing denunciation of Napoleon's economic measures and a bold attack on dictatorial governments.[135] Adolphe Thiers, prominent in public affairs for more than thirty years and an opponent of Napoleon III, questioned the Government on its economic policies in May, 1868. He attributed to protection all the economic gains of France, and to low tariffs most of her ills.[136] He was joined by Pouyer-Quertier, an effective speaker in debate, and by Baron Lespérut, who proclaimed that January 23, 1860, the day on which the treaty went into effect, was the saddest in French history since the revocation of the Edict of Nantes. Although the Government was sustained in a vote taken at the end of the debate, the opposition was large enough to shake the complacency of the régime.

In the next year, Thiers returned to the attack, seeking abrogation of the treaty. He failed in his immediate objective, but his opposition was instrumental in the Emperor's decision to resign his powers of making treaties without the sanction of the *Corps Législatif*. Thiers was also influential in securing an investigation of the results of the Empire's liberal trade policies. Napoleon III announced that the *Conseil Supérieur du Commerce* had been directed to conduct hearings on this subject. When several leading manufacturers, including Schneider of Creusot, refused to co-operate because the council was packed with free traders, the Government yielded more ground and consented to allow the investigation to be made by a parliamentary committee. This committee, composed of twelve free traders, seventeen moderate protectionists, and seven extreme protectionists, held hearings from March to July, 1870, when their activities were interrupted by the outbreak of hostilities with Prussia. The testimony that was taken, although relatively not very extensive, indicated clearly the protectionist bent of French industrialists.[137] The tide of protectionism was coming in and it would undoubtedly have washed away the treaty had the Empire lasted longer.

OPPOSITION TO NAPOLEON III

Napoleon III's large expenditures also came in for criticism in the last years of the Empire. His civil list, that carried important items for friends, his costly wars, and his elaborate plans of national economic equipment added tremendously to the expenses of government. From

1853 to 1860 state expenditures exceeded receipts by 2,878,333,000 francs and from 1861 to 1867 by 1,000,000,000 francs. The average budget under Louis Philippe was 1,300,000,000 francs; under Napoleon III, 2,200,000,000 francs.[138] Even granting that some of this money was used to improve economic conditions, the bourgeoisie had to face the fact of increased taxes and the possibility of inflation.

This condition, combined with many others, put the Government on the defensive. Already in 1860, Napoleon III had granted the *Corps Législatif* the right to vote an annual address to the throne, to amend bills, to publish its minutes, and to vote the budget by sections. It had seemed only logical that some liberal concessions should be granted to Frenchmen, for Napoleon had just been fighting in Italy to secure liberty for Italians. Moreover, the Empire's Roman policy had turned many Catholics against Napoleon and he needed to offset this loss by Liberal support.

An attempt was also made to win workingmen to his cause. In 1862, the state sent a delegation of French workers to the Exhibition in London and published a report of the delegates' observations that included a plea for labor unions. This was followed by a manifesto of French workers in 1864—a document that was not the concoction of theorists but the expression of the desires of ordinary laboring men —which showed clearly a sentiment of class consciousness and the need for labor action.[139] The Government was impressed by these statements, as well as by numerous strikes, and in the same year abolished the law that made concerted industrial action a crime. In 1865, a French branch of the International, which had been founded in London in 1864, was set up in France. The Government continued, moreover, its reform of labor laws; in 1868 it allowed the right of assembly, which included strikes and picketing; it abolished the *livret*, extended free education to the age of twelve, and tolerated labor unions.

In spite of these gestures, opposition to Napoleon continued to grow—opposition that was increased by the Mexican affair and the Austro-Prussian War. January 19, 1867, Napoleon gave Parliament the right of interpellation and in 1868 tempered the press laws and granted the right to hold political gatherings. This so-called "liberal" period of the Empire gave way in 1869 to the "parliamentary" period, with the Senate discussing and voting bills and the *Corps Législatif* having the right to overthrow ministers.[140] Hardly had this reform been consummated, however, before war was declared. Napoleon III was ignominiously captured at Sedan, confined in Germany, and died in England shortly after. The parliamentary Empire had no opportunity to start on a new national economic tack; that was left for the Third Republic.

CHAPTER VII

THE THIRD REPUBLIC[1]

AFTERMATH OF THE FRANCO-PRUSSIAN WAR—THE COMMUNE

NAPOLEON III's capitulation to the Germans on September 2, 1870, inaugurated what was perhaps the most disastrous year in French history since the passing of the first Napoleon. It was a year of defeat, uncertainty, insurrection, and discouragement. Calamity followed calamity with such speed that the usual optimism of the nation turned into despair. Yet throughout this terrible twelve-month efforts were made continuously to salvage the nation from its dejection.

Two days after the Emperor's débâcle at Sedan, a Parisian mob invaded the *Corps Législatif;*[2] announced the Empire dissolved; and, at the Hôtel de Ville, proclaimed the republic. As in 1848, members of the middle class (especially Gambetta, Jules Favre, and Jules Ferry) dominated the situation sufficiently well to control the newly constituted Government of National Defense—to eliminate from it socialist members. This Government did its best to stave off the invaders, but all to no avail. Paris was encircled by the Germans and starved into submission.[3] On January 28, 1871, further resistance seemed unfeasible and an armistice was arranged with Bismarck. Provision was made for the surrender of Paris and the election of a National Assembly with which an authoritative peace could be made. Selection of representatives to this new body was proceeded to at once. The main, if not the sole, issue was peace or war: monarchists supported the former stand; republicans, the latter. The nation voiced its desire for the cessation of hostilities and incidentally chose a majority of politically unknown agriculturalists, industrialists, and soldiers who desired a restoration of the monarchy.[4] These "cow fanciers," as they were derisively called by Parisian republicans, elected Thiers, the ablest statesman among them, "head of the executive power of the

200

French Republic until the political institutions of France are decided upon." Thereupon the Assembly moved from Bordeaux to Versailles and prepared for the signing of a treaty of peace with Germany.

In the meantime, however, all was not well in Paris. The armistice had been unpopular with the radical republicans and socialists, who had been ultra-patriotic during the siege.[5] Socialist organizations boasted considerable strength; the French section of the International had 200,000 members in 1870[6] and its power increased during the days of turmoil. The course of events played into its hands. Before the siege of Paris began, the well-to-do had sent their families to the provinces and many had themselves left the capital. The National Guard was thus depleted of conservative elements and at the same time was greatly swelled with working-class members. All kinds of persons were admitted to its ranks and the salary paid to the guardsmen was looked upon by the poor as a dole. After the fall of Paris, soldiers from the defeated French armies of the provinces swarmed into the city and bolstered the number of malcontents. Work was scarce; the Parisian laborer was in a demoralized stupor. The victory of the conservatives in the election of the National Assembly made radical Paris more fearful than ever.

This fear was well founded, for before economic activity had become normal the new Government abolished payments to all but indigent National Guardsmen and decreed that the moratorium on private debts be ended.[7] The decision to make Versailles the seat of government instead of Paris was, moreover, unpopular among all classes of Parisians and especially so among the lower classes, for they felt deprived of power to control policies by direct action. The discontent thus heaped up overflowed on March 18, 1871, when the Government, attempting to seize cannon in the possession of the National Guard of Paris, as a first step in the disarmament of that force, met with strong resistance. Thiers believed that the best strategy for coping with this emergency was to withdraw the Government's troops from the city and to await the moment when he could clean house thoroughly.[8] Paris, thus abandoned, fell into the hands of the insurrectionists, who placed the government of the city in the hands of an organization which had grown up within the National Guard—

the central committee of the *Fédération républicaine de la garde nationale*. This was the beginning of the Commune—a movement that in its origin was not socialist, but that was rather the result of disastrous war, a long siege, and opposition to the conservative national government.

The appearance of the Commune presented France with a situation reminiscent of 1848. Once again the working class of Paris was making a bid for power and its triumph would have been important in framing new economic legislation. Nevertheless, there is not much evidence to show that the Commune would have advanced in a strictly socialist direction, for although socialist writers have endeavored to claim the Commune as a great epoch in the history of their movement,[9] it was, in fact, "only indirectly and very tenuously related to conscious and expressed desires for a socialist society."[10] Elections on March 26 for a Municipal Council gave the majority to bourgeois democrats of the stamp of 1793 rather than to socialists. Consequently the policies of the Commune did not aim to overthrow the capitalist system. Measures were taken to alleviate the pinched conditions of the proletariat—the restoration of pay to members of the National Guard, prohibition of night work in bakeries, remittance of debts for rents, prolongation of the period for satisfying other debts, permission to make gratuitous withdrawals from pawnshops of goods worth less than twenty francs pawned before April 25, abolition of fines in private factories, the revision of contracts for National Guard uniforms in order to transfer them to workingmen's associations, and the assistance of labor organizations. It was also suggested by some that factories be taken over by the Commune, but the committee charged with this subject never realized the reform.

Although incontestably there were germs of socialism in the Commune, they never leavened the whole. Private business was generally left untouched and even the Bank of France was respected. What might have developed in time cannot be said, for within two months the Commune was at an end. The proletariat of the provinces, with the exception of a few uprisings in industrial centers, remained cold to the movement in Paris. On May 21 and 22 troops from Versailles entered the city and, in what was probably the bloodiest street fighting of the century, took over the capital.[11] By May 28 the episode of the Commune was at an end.

THE PEACE TREATY—PAYMENT OF THE INDEMNITY

The failure of the working classes of Paris to take control of things cleared the field for other political developments and for the rehabilitation of the nation. France was faced with serious problems, for she had lost 139,000 men killed and 143,000 wounded in the war, not to mention those who had perished in the Commune, her expenditures had exceeded the budget by 2,700,000,000 francs,[12] and she had only a provisional government. The united efforts of the French were necessary to cope with the situation.

The most pressing problem, however, was to fulfil the terms of the peace treaty which was signed at Frankfurt-am-Main, May 10, 1871. The treaty required that France surrender Alsace with the exception of Belfort[13] and North Lorraine including the city of Metz—a territory with a population of 1,500,000 persons.[14] Moreover, she had to pay 5,-000,000,000 francs to the victors. This was a large sum. Bismarck intended to demand enough to weaken France, but not so much that she would be unable to pay.[15] A large current of opinion in Germany, however, expressed a desire to force France to surrender a substantial part of her capital resources.[16] The figure that was ultimately decided upon was not an indemnity in the ordinary sense of the word, for the war had cost Germany only about 2,000,000,000 francs. It was tribute.

The national economic import of the peace provisions was obvious. Germany wanted the highly industrialized districts of the Upper Rhine[17] and the metallurgical industry and iron deposits of Lorraine—iron mines that were to become of prime importance after the invention of the Thomas and Gilchrist method of smelting phosphorus ore in 1878. Germany wanted also to get French capital in order to weaken her late enemy and to finance her own economic development. Such demands invited economic retaliation, but Germany prevented France from resorting to the easiest form of reprisals—tariff discriminations. By article eleven of the treaty both contracting powers guaranteed to the other most-favored-nation treatment—a provision to which we shall return later.

For the moment, the most burdensome part of the treaty was that which required the payment of 5,000,000,000 francs, for twenty-one departments were to be occupied by German troops at French expense until the bill was paid. The treaty stipulated that the first payment of 500,000,000 francs should be made thirty days after the establishment of order in Paris; one billion in 1871; one-half billion May 1, 1872; and the remaining three billion, bearing interest at 5 per cent, March 2, 1874. The schedule of payments was not altered in any major fashion except that Germany, desiring to lengthen her occupation of a part of France in the hope of preventing, on the one hand, a radical government under Gambetta and, on the other, a reactionary Catholic monarchy, granted an extension for the last billion to March 2, 1875.

But even under this condition speed was necessary and speed was shown. The total monetary circulation of gold and silver in France amounted only to five or six billion francs. France immediately realized that the sum demanded by Germany would have to come from extension of government credit. Therefore a loan of two billions was offered to the public on June 27, 1871 (the bonds issued at 82.50 bore 5 per cent interest[18]), which, much to the surprise of the Government, was oversubscribed—the public demanded a total of 4,897,000,000 francs. The state kept only 2,225,994,000 francs of this sum, but this was enough, with advances from the Bank of France, to meet the first installment of half a billion by July 10 and, with a credit of 325,000,000 francs for the railways of the lost provinces,[19] to pay off the first two billions by March, 1872. On July 15, 1872, another loan was floated to cover the remaining three billions (5 per cent bonds issued at 84.50), that was oversubscribed thirteen times. This permitted the French to satisfy the demands of Germany by September 5, 1873, and French soil was free from occupation by September 13 of the same year. With interest included, France had paid in only a little over two years 5,301,-145,078 francs!

This remarkable feat was not accomplished without difficulty. In order not to injure the credit of the state, a great effort was made to balance the budget. To this end vigorous economy was urged in the administrative branches of government and new taxes were voted. Stamp taxes were levied on certain types of business and on legal transactions; taxes were increased on sugar, telegraph messages, tobacco, and matches and those on spirits more rigidly enforced; license fees were augmented; a tax on income from stocks and bonds was resorted to, much to the consternation of Thiers; customs duties were placed on raw materials and ships; and the *droit d'entrepôt* was re-established.[20] With these and still other measures, receipts and expenses were gradually made to balance—real equilibrium was attained in the budget voted in 1875.

The transfer of the indemnity to Germany was another vexatious problem—a problem which plagued Germany in making her payments after the World War. At first, payment in French currency and purchases of foreign money threatened the value of the franc. Consequently, direct payments in francs were limited (they did not exceed 510,000,000 francs). French bankers co-operated in buying foreign exchange in small quantities all over the world. Thus the market was not flooded with French currency and the franc was maintained at par. It was found that foreign credit could be obtained more advantageously in other ways than by direct purchases. French exports, the expenditures of foreign tourists in France, and the interest on investments abroad provided an important source for foreign currency.[21] However, sums obtained in this fashion were insufficient to meet the demands of the indemnity. The state was obliged to purchase foreign securities held in France and to sell them, as well as its own bonds, abroad. Thus the transfer problem was overcome, and the state's credit was held intact. The loss of currency was not enough to impair the value of the franc nor the loss of capital enough to curb for long French economic activity.

REPUBLICAN FORM OF GOVERNMENT ADOPTED

After Germany's demands had been satisfied, France could concentrate on internal affairs. First and foremost a decision had to be reached concerning the form of government that was to be established. Already on August 31, 1871, the famous Rivet law, proposed by Charles Rivet, a friend of Thiers, had given Thiers the title "President of the French Republic" and had conferred upon the National Assembly, which had been elected only to make peace, the attributes of a constitutional convention. Monarchists predominated in this body, but they were badly divided between the Legitimist and Orleanist groups. Their differences and constant bickerings delayed any definite action and antagonized many of their sympathizers. Thiers, himself one of them, wearied of their petty squabbles. Forced finally by the republican attacks of Gambetta to take a stand, he declared on November 13, 1872, "The republic exists. It is the legal government of the country. To wish anything else would mean a new revolution and the worst one of all."[22]

This republican declaration of their chief turned the monarchists against Thiers and in spite of the statesmanlike fashion in which he had made the peace and paid the indemnity, they forced him to resign, May 24, 1873. The same day a loyal monarchist, Marshal MacMahon, was elected to the presidency; a restoration seemed in the offing. Already the Legitimist candidate, the Count of Chambord, was calling himself Henri V and royalists were shouting victory. But their triumph was not to be, for their candidate definitely refused the crown (October 27, 1873), unless it brought with it the white flag, traditionally the banner of the Bourbons, in place of the revolutionary tricolor upon which the Orleanists insisted. Petty as this issue may have been, the Count stood firm, and the royalists had to accede to his decision. They did not give up hope, however, for the Count was not a young man and if the negotiations could be delayed, the way might still be clear for the Count of Paris, of the house of Orleans, to ascend the throne. It was with this hope in mind that MacMahon's term of office was fixed at seven years,[23] November 19, 1873, and that the Assembly delayed the establishment of a new régime. Yet this law that determined the length of the president's incumbency was a constitutional law—the first one toward the erection of the Third Republic.

There was further delay in voting other constitutional provisions, but finally on January 30, 1875, enough Orleanists co-operated with republicans to provide a majority of one for a law that definitely fixed the term of election and the eligibility of the president. Thereafter constitution-making went rapidly forward and inasmuch as the parliamentary tradition was fairly well ingrained in France, and both Thiers and MacMahon had, in the main, followed its precepts, parliamentary government after the English model formed the basis of the constitutional legislation.[24] As in England, practically all authority was placed in the legislative branch of government rather than being divided among the executive, judicial, and legislative powers. Provision was made, still following English example, for a bicameral legislature. The lower house, the Chamber of Deputies, was to be elected directly by universal manhood suffrage.[25] Royalists feared that such a body would be republican and tend to act rashly. They insisted upon a senate of "graybeards"—members over forty years of age indirectly elected by electoral colleges.[26] The powers of these two bodies were almost identical. Both had to pass on all legislation.[27] Sitting together at Versailles they formed a constitutional convention for amending the fundamental laws of the land.

In actual practice, the Chamber proved to be the more important body, for upon its complexion came to depend largely the choice of ministers, and governments were to be overthrown usually, but by no means always, by the lower house.[28] Through the influence of the monarchists, who wanted the king to be able to rule as well as to reign, if a restoration took place, the president of the republic was endowed theoretically with great power. Gambetta said that the executive was the strongest one ever established in a democracy and, from a strictly legal standpoint, this was only a slight exaggeration of the case. In the course of time, however, the president became little more than a figurehead. Only once has he used his authority to dissolve the Chamber with the consent of the Senate (1877); his acts are countersigned by ministers; and he may be forced to resign as was Millerand in 1924. Executive power rests with the cabinet, which is dependent upon a fluctuating majority in the Chamber and, to some degree, upon the conservative Senate. French cabinets have been notoriously unstable; a fact that has weakened the executive.[29] In the last analysis, the Chamber is the bulwark of the French government. On its shoulders rests the burden of directing the course of public affairs.

THE REPUBLICAN GOVERNMENT IN OPERATION

The machinery of government that was set up by the constitutional laws of 1875 creaked and groaned at first under the strain of party strife. Thiers had governed with a coalition of the center, which, although not very reliable, served as a working basis for a parliamentary majority. MacMahon, however, was not such an astute politician as his predecessor and soon found himself in hot water. The elections of 1876 resulted in a slight monarchist majority in the Senate and in a large republican majority in the Chamber. At first, the President selected his ministers from among the republicans, but later replaced them (May 16, 1877) with monarchists on the ground that they were responsible to him and not to parliament. He then proceeded to dissolve the Chamber and to call for new elections.

In this test the republicans were overwhelmingly victorious and MacMahon accepted, after another futile attempt at crossing the Chamber, the doctrine of ministerial responsibility to the lower house. Up to this time royalists had presented a stubborn resistance to republican strength, but henceforth their political power diminished rapidly. They lost control of the Senate in the elections of January 5, 1879, and their royalist President resigned January 30 of the same year. Except for a flurry during the Boulangist movement, which came to a head in 1889, monarchists have had little more than social and extra-parliamentary influence. They have not been a threat to republican domination.

When the republicans got control of the two houses of the legislature and the presidency (1879), differences of opinion among them, which had been displayed previously, became accentuated. They were soon split into several groups; and multiple parties have continued to be characteristic of the political life of the Third Republic. The result has been that no one party has ever held a majority in the Chamber, and government by coalition—with the attendant weakness of frequent change of cabinet and dilatory action—has been the rule. Political parties have been, for the most part, loosely organized, which has made it difficult for leaders to keep their supporters in line or to exert much authority over their parliamentary followers. Nevertheless, French parties reflected and still do, in a general way, reflect the demands of the electorate.[30] An analysis of political groups and of their influence in the affairs of state provides some general notion of what economic classes and what ideas are dominant in determining the course of politics in France. To undertake a detailed analysis here would be an unpardonable digression,[31] yet it is important for our purposes to have some conception of the force of economic ideas and interests in affairs of state.

From the beginning of the republic, the fan-shaped Chamber of Deputies has been filled with parties that stretch from left to right—that blend harmoniously into one another. In 1871, the group on the extreme left was the Republican Union, led by Gambetta. It was composed of "radicals" who represented the petty bourgeoisie. This party was the only one that was interested in social reform and it subordinated its mild demands to republicanism. All other parties represented capitalists, who were divided among themselves by a score of non-economic issues—religion, form of government, foreign policy, and the like.[32] In the course of time, the monarchical parties of the right disappeared and their places were taken by the early bourgeois republican groups of the left. So complete was this transition that today there are no parties in the Chamber with "rightist" names, and groups with "left" in their titles, like the Left Republicans, sit well to the right.[33] On the left, however, there have been newcomers. The Radical Party, led by Clemenceau, split off from Gambetta's following, but it demanded nothing much more far-reaching in the economic order than an income tax! The Radical Socialists appeared next at the outer fringe of the left, they were followed by the Socialists, whose representation was important after 1893 and became still larger after the union of socialist groups in 1905. The Socialists gave way on the left to the Communists in 1919.

Of all these parties, the Radical Socialist became the strongest. Since 1898 it has been nearly always a "government party" with the notable exception of its half-hearted opposition to the National Bloc, 1919–24, and to Poincaré, 1928–29. Up to the election of 1936 it was the largest single party.[34] It represents the lower middle class and, although its platform pays homage to the socialist ideal, in practice it has offered no serious threat to the capitalist system nor, for that matter, to capitalist interests. The Socialists, who increased their representation until it was second largest in the Chamber of 1928, and the largest in 1936, have never had sole control of a cabinet nor as a unit have they governed in coalition with bourgeois parties except during the first part of the War and in the Popular Front coalition with the Radical Socialists after the

elections of 1936. The Communists, for their part, have been political
outcasts and have had little direct influence in determining the conduct
of public affairs except under the Popular Front cabinets of 1936–
1937. Thus government in France has been mostly by parties to the
right of revolutionary groups; the mildly reformist Radical Socialists
have been fused in coalitions with more conservative or more radical
elements and this has tended to keep governments from going to extremes. The result has been that during the entire period of the Third
Republic capitalist interests, whether industrial, commercial, or agricultural, have practically dominated the political arena. Evidence of this
domination is ample, but one significant indication of it is that no successful attempt has been made to alter the character of the conservative
Senate. Control of politics by moneyed persons has been so complete that
Frederick Schuman in his excellent book, *War and Diplomacy in the
French Republic,* was led to exclaim:

"The Third French Republic rests securely on a social and political
foundation of businessmen, merchants, manufacturers, and all the petty
proprietors and tradesmen who constitute, along with the professional
classes and the *fonctionnaires,* the bulwarks of *bourgeois* respectability
and conservative republicanism. Other classes there are—and they are
by no means politically negligible: the ghosts of the old aristocracy;
the religious and tradition-bound peasantry . . .; the workers of the
factories, mills, and mines, often sullen, resentful, clinging to the red
memories of '93, '48, and '71, and hoping and planning for the new
revolution which is to transmit power to the proletariat. These groups
are all alive and vital in the political life of *bourgeois* France. But the
largest share of political power rests with the beneficiaries and masters
of the economic order of capitalism, based as it is upon private property, personal and individualistic economic initiative, the profit motive
to productivity, the employment and control of labor by the owners of
the means of production, and relatively unrestricted competition between large numbers of producers and traders."[35]

INTENSIFICATION OF NATIONAL PATRIOTISM

Economic interest is one of the controlling forces in modern French
politics; national sentiment is another. There is little doubt that French

love of country became intensified after 1870. The participation of the masses in public affairs, even if only to exercise the right of suffrage, quickened popular interest in the welfare of the nation. Moreover, the disastrous results of the war with Prussia stirred the French to the need of a profound national rejuvenation. France, which had been the strongest power on the Continent, had suffered defeat. Love for the nation could not condone the acceptance of such a humiliation. All Frenchmen wanted to eradicate those weaknesses which had been responsible for the military fiasco and some, like Paul Déroulède, desired an ultimate war of revenge. Obligatory military service for five years was instituted in 1872 (it was reduced to two years in 1889 and increased to three in 1913), in an effort to bring France's army to at least a par with Germany's; the Ferry education laws established obligatory and gratuitous primary education and aimed to improve more advanced instruction in order that France should suffer no inferiority in this regard; and numerous efforts were made, as we shall soon see, to strengthen the economic structure of the state.

These measures not only attained their appointed ends, but contributed incidentally to stimulating national sentiment. The Frenchman who was made to give up five years of his life for the military prestige of his country was perforce made to believe that his sacrifice was for a great cause—for the grandeur of France. The children who were sent to school were taught the glories of the nation. And when they left their schoolrooms, upon the completion of the grades, they had an equipment sufficient to allow them to absorb gullibly, but not to analyze critically, national propaganda that was forever being shoved upon them. This was particularly significant, for under the Third Republic there developed the popular newspaper and other forms of cheap printed matter which could be and were used for national purposes.[36] Littérateurs, like Maurice Barrès, turned their talents to nationalist ends. Patriotic societies, such as the League of Patriots, came into being and drove home the emotional appeal of patriotism.[37] International competition and friction sharpened the edge of patriotic devotion. The entire course of development was toward the intensification of national sentiment. The French believed more firmly than ever that French culture had made so many contributions to civilization and that French historical traditions had been so rich that France had a mission to lead all peoples in the onward march of mankind. Increased patriotism combined with bourgeois control of politics has led one American author to suggest that the French motto *Liberté, Egalité, Fraternité* would be much more realistic if it read *Patriotism, Power, Profits*. These are the factors that have conditioned French national economics most fundamentally during the Third Republic.[38]

A RETURN TO HIGH TARIFFS BEGUN

Evidence of these forces was seen almost immediately after the Franco-Prussian War. Thiers personified them: he was a conservative in economics, a supporter of the interests of business, and an arch-patriot. National sentiment drove him to extraordinary activity in paying the indemnity to Germany and his schemes for meeting fiscal demands were shot through with sound bourgeois ideas. He insisted first and foremost on keeping France's credit good by paying interest regularly on the loans that were contracted. In order to do this, it was necessary to raise taxes, but, instead of levying direct imposts and then placing the burden on those with property, he sought revenue by indirect taxation.[39] Being an ardent protectionist and having for his finance minister a man of like conviction, Pouyer-Quertier, he saw in the extremities of the financial situation the possibility of undoing the liberal tariff system of the late Empire. Consequently in the budget of 1871, it was proposed to increase the duty on sugar and coffee, to impose a few export taxes, to increase the *droits de quai* (harbor dues), and to permit the Government to restore the *droits de pavillon et d'entrepôt* which had been abolished in 1866. Finally, it was suggested that a duty of between 10 and 20 per cent be levied on a great number of raw materials, but in order that this provision might not injure French production for export, drawbacks equal to the duty, to be paid upon the re-export of these goods either in their original or manufactured form, were provided for. The National Assembly voted immediately the rates on coffee and sugar along with others on cocoa, wine, tea, mineral oils, etc. (July 8, 1871), and shortly thereafter approved the re-establishment of the *droit de pavillon* (January 30, 1872).

The legislature balked, however, at duties on raw materials. Industrial protectionists wanted tariffs to apply only to their articles of manufacture and not to the materials that they employed. On this occasion they did not make common cause with agricultural circles to establish a national tariff. In fact, they repudiated protectionist leaders and, aided by those who were in favor of the *status quo* or of low duties, they established a committee of fifteen to investigate Thiers' proposals. The President, who himself was not very enthusiastic about the duties on raw materials, but who believed they were necessary for fiscal reasons, castigated industrialists for their selfishness. Bitter at their refusal to support him, he presented his resignation to the Assembly. This was not accepted and a compromise tariff was arrived at (law of July 26, 1872). A duty of about 3 per cent on raw materials was agreed upon, a compensating duty on imported manufactured goods was promised, and the drawback provision of Thiers' original scheme was maintained. These measures were contrary to France's commercial commitments to Belgium and Great Britain, so the treaties with these powers were denounced and new ones negotiated.

The results of Thiers' protectionist program were not very happy. The revenue from the duties was much less than had been anticipated and the drawback was abused so that manufacturers received sometimes more upon the re-export of goods in finished form than they had paid at the time of importing the raw materials. The *droits de pavillon et d'entrepôt* were found to be in contradiction to terms of a treaty with Austria which were extended to other countries by the most-favored-nation clause. Austria was asked to surrender her rights and she would probably have been willing to do so (her interests at stake were very meager except in the Mediterranean), had it not been for pressure brought to bear on her by Bismarck to make no concessions. After Thiers' fall from power, the need for revenue was somewhat less pressing and MacMahon decided to give up the tax on raw materials. In this he was unanimously supported by the *Conseil supérieur de l'agriculture, du commerce, et de l'industrie,* although agriculturalists were loath to see a change. The new treaties with Belgium and Great Britain were abrogated and there was a general return to the *status quo ante.* Only the *droits de quai* remained as evidence of Thiers' protectionist plans.[40]

PROSPERITY, 1871-73; DEPRESSION, 1873-79

The failure of manufacturers and agriculturalists to act together accounts in large measure for this unsuccessful attempt to discard the tariff system of the Empire. The course of events, however, was ultimately to play into the hands of the protectionists. Shortly after the War of 1870, it did not seem that this would be the case, for France enjoyed a business boom that exceeded all expectations. In 1873, discounts of the Bank of France were double what they had been in any year during Napoleon III's régime and the amount of money in circulation exceeded what it had ever been previously or what it was to attain in the next ten years. Factories were running at full speed, consuming about 25 per cent more than they had under the Empire; salaries were going up; and the price index rose from 144 in 1869 to 159 in 1872 and 1873.[41] Abroad similar conditions existed; the United States was enjoying a railway boom; Germany was indulging in industrial expansion and in excessive building which was stimulated, in part, by the indemnity;[42] Austria was in the throes of speculation.

Tension was great on the financial cables that hold the business world together and they finally snapped with the failure of Jay Cooke in New York (1873). France endeavored to relieve the situation by raising the discount rate, but to no avail. The crash came and a slump set in. Discounts of the Bank of France went so low that from 1876 to 1879 they did not exceed 58 per cent of those of 1873. Prices declined steadily to an index of 130 in 1879 and salaries followed suit. Industrial production fell off[43] and agriculture, which had suffered during the war, was ailing. The harvests of 1878 and 1879 were poor in both quality and quantity. Grain imports, which had never exceeded 14 million hectoliters, jumped to over 29 million in 1879. The specter of American grain inundating the country was a real one; and French farmers were in an extraordinarily embarrassing position because imports had staved off the normal price rise. Moreover, a disease was destroying cattle and phylloxera was causing so much havoc to grapevines that wine production fell from 84 million hectoliters in 1875 to 34 million in 1881, with the result that wine began to be imported, hitherto an unheard-of thing. The silk industry was beginning to feel the pressure of Far Eastern competition and other industries feared English goods. Foreign-trade statistics indicate that some of this trepidation was founded on fact, for exports declined after 1873 and imports, after a momentary drop following the crash, increased steadily to the end of the decade.

SPECIAL COMMERCE IN MILLIONS OF FRANCS[44]

Year	Imports	Exports
1871	3566.7	2872.5
1872	3570.3	3761.6
1873	3554.8	3787.3
1874	3507.7	3701.1
1875	3536.7	3872.6
1876	3998.7	3575.6
1877	3679.8	3436.3
1878	4176.2	3179.7
1879	4595.2	3231.3
1880	5033.2	3467.9

TARIFF OF 1881

All evidence seems to show that the period from 1871 to 1879 was not a flourishing one[45] and it is not strange that under the circumstances business interests in French legislative halls began to consider tariff increases. A questionnaire sent to chambers of commerce in 1875 indicated a desire to revise the tariff and to abandon the most-favored-nation clause. In 1877, the Superior Council of Commerce, Agriculture, and Industry proposed new schedules, but they never came to a vote.[46] A senatorial commission which was appointed to investigate the state of industry concluded (1877) that conditions were bad and that to better them tariff rates should be increased. Hearkening to this sentiment and egged on by Bismarck's adoption of a protectionist policy and by tariff increases in other countries, the Government proposed that the general tariff be replaced by rates on the average 24 per cent higher than those in the commercial treaties, which, by the way, were about to expire. The Chamber was on protection bent, as its refusal to renew France's treaty with Italy (1878) indicated, but, to be sure of its ground, it appointed a commission to study the tariff situation. The investigation of the commission was extensive and comparatively impartial.[47] It showed that metallurgists and cotton spinners wanted prohibitive rates; that woolen manufacturers asked for increases; that agriculturalists wanted protection; and that only silk industrialists seemed satisfied with the existing situation. This information was confirmed by the agitation carried on by the *Association de l'industrie française pour la défense du travail national,* the *Société des agriculteurs de France* (founded 1867), and the free traders.

With the preliminary investigations out of the way, the Chamber began discussion of the proposed increases (January 31, 1880). The minister of agriculture and commerce opened the debate by explaining that France had a favorable balance of trade with England and that the products of that country should not be feared. This argument started a statistical battle in which both sides cited, juggled, and interpreted figures to prove their contentions. Theory, too, found its place, for both the liberal and protectionist schools had their protagonists in the Chamber. Among the latter was Félix Jules Méline, representative of the department of the Vosges, supporter of Thiers, journalist and lawyer. He was a conservative in economics and was to play an important rôle in the restoration of high protection in France. As a member of the Chamber's investigating commission, he was familiar with the problem before the house and presented his case in these terms:

"All of us here, gentlemen, whatever our economic doctrines may be, have only one desire: that is to seek the economic régime which can contribute the most efficaciously to the grandeur and the prosperity of France. (*Très bien! très bien!* from several benches.)

"What is this régime? How are we to recognize it and how are we to determine what it is?

"It seemed to your commission that the reply to this question is dictated by certain principles of political economy which can be considered true and which I am authorized to place even above free trade, for if free trade is questioned, at least its principles are not.

"The first of these principles is that labor is the source of everything; that it is labor which creates capital; and the more labor there is, the more capital will increase and the more public wealth will be augmented. (*Approbation.*)

"The second of these principles is that the more capital increases, the higher salaries will be; and the higher they are, the more the working class, for which we have so much solicitude, gains in well-being and morality. (*Again approbation.*)

"National labor—that is the idea which your commission had ever before it in its long task; that is the flag which I have the mission to place on this platform, and towards it I shall ever have my eyes turned during the course of this long and laborious debate. (*Très bien, très bien.*)"[48]

In the Senate, the persistent protectionist Pouyer-Quertier labored long and diligently for extreme protection for agriculture, but the Chamber undid his work. Finally the Government measure was passed, becoming the law of May 7, 1881. The new tariff favored industry more than it did agriculture. Specific rates amounting to between 10 and 30 per cent *ad valorem* were levied on manufactured products,[49] while grain was burdened only with a statistical tax; cattle were taxed 3 per cent; and raw materials were admitted free. The general increase in the tariff was about 24 per cent, but this advance was soon reduced by trade treaties to a point where rates were only a little higher than they had been before 1881.[50] Moreover, most of the treaties were to run for ten years, which meant that the customs duties established by them could not be changed until the beginning of the next decade. Only agricultural products were free from such a predicament, for they were generally omitted from the treaties.

PROSPERITY, 1880–82; ECONOMIC CALM, 1883–93

The tariff of 1881 was enacted in the midst of a business recovery. By 1879, the effects of the crisis of 1873 had worn off and reports indicated good times except in agriculture. In 1880 and 1881, economic activity improved; the Bank of France paid a dividend of 25 per cent and some industrial establishments far exceeded that. Pig-iron production jumped from 1,400,000 tons in 1877 to 2,069,000 in 1883; railway building under the enthusiastic drive of Freycinet was extensive; the bourse was feverish with speculation; new companies were founded; and credit was greatly expanded.[51] This flurry of prosperity was followed by a crash in 1882 with a series of bankruptcies and losses (the

Crédit Lyonnais lost in the neighborhood of 40 million francs). This was the beginning of a long period of economic calm. Until 1893, business was, with few exceptions, to wallow in a slough of despondency, small profits, and restricted margins. Discounts of the Bank of France fell from 11,374 millions in 1881 to 8269 millions in 1887; consumption of coal remained stationary from 1882 to 1888; and pig-iron production decreased until the year 1891. The value of imports did not exceed until 1906 what it had been in 1880 and the value of exports was greater only in a few years before 1899 than it had been in 1881. These figures reflected restricted activity, although it should be noticed that this was a period of declining prices—the index was 133 in 1880, 122 in 1883, 111 in 1890, and 91 in 1896.

SPECIAL COMMERCE IN MILLIONS OF FRANCS[52]

Year	Imports	Exports
1880	5033.2	3467.9
1881	4863.4	3561.5
1882	4821.8	3574.4
1883	4804.3	3451.9
1884	4343.5	3232.5
1885	4088.4	3088.1
1886	4208.1	3248.8
1887	4026.0	3246.5
1888	4107.0	3246.7
1889	4316.8	3703.9
1890	4436.9	3753.4
1891	4767.9	3569.7
1892	4188.1	3460.7
1893	3853.7	3236.4
1894	3850.4	3078.1
1895	3719.9	3373.8
1896	3798.6	3400.9
1897	3956.0	3598.0
1898	4472.5	3510.9
1899	4518.3	4152.6
1900	4697.8	4108.7
1906	5627.2	5265.5

Agriculture was especially hard hit. Although grain crops were good from 1882 to 1887, imports were large and prices were low.[53]

Year	Production of wheat in France	Excess of imports over exports of wheat	Average price
		Hectoliters	
1886	107,287,082	9,586,987	16.5
1887	112,456,107	12,084,587	17.7
1888	98,740,728	15,356,830	18.8
1889	108,391,770	15,311,060	18.1
1890	116,915,880	10.466,448	18.9
1891	77,657,568	19,593,472	20.5
1892	109,537,907	18,833,960	17.8

Production per acre increased only slightly, taxes were higher than they had been in 1860, and wages of agricultural labor had gone up. Disease was raising havoc with the grape and silk-worm industries, and sugar-beet growers felt the impact of bounty-fed Austrian and German sugar.

AGITATION FOR HIGHER TARIFFS

In order to alleviate their economic hardships, agriculturalists sought aid from the state in the form of protection. They took the lead for higher tariffs, as the agriculturalists had done in Germany, and with Méline, minister of agriculture from 1883 to 1885, as their champion, they attained many of their objectives. American lard and ham were excluded in 1881 under the guise of sanitation and did not reappear on the French market in any quantity until 1890.[54] Sugar, which had been allowed in 1880 to come in upon the payment of a very moderate rate,[55] was kept out by an act of 1884[56]—an act that was aimed primarily at the subsidized sugars of Austria and Germany. But the most important legislation concerned wheat. The duty on it was raised to 3 francs in 1885, to 5 francs in 1887, and to 7 francs in 1894[57]—a figure which was maintained until the World War. Contrary to the sliding-scale corn laws of the Restoration, which had aimed to stop importations of grain only when prices were low, these rates applied at all times. Thus the price of wheat in France was higher than in England, that is, in the world market. In 1883, the price differential was 2 shillings 8 pence, in 1886, 7s. 6d.; and in 1890, 12s. 2d.[58] Any social virtue that there might be in cheap foodstuffs was ignored; the interests of agriculturalists were given first consideration. Nor did the protectionist wave ebb with the wheat duties. The year 1885 saw new rates placed on other grains, livestock, and alcoholic liquors; in 1888 more protection was given to cattle; and in 1890 an excise was established for certain wines made from raisins—an excise being resorted to in this case because an augmentation of duties was prevented by treaties.

These many tariff changes indicated a definite trend in France toward protection—a trend that had its counterpart in most other countries in the decade of the 1880's.[59] Economic conditions, increasing national sentiment, and bourgeois domination in politics all forced French commercial legislation in this direction. There were other factors in the situation, too, that bear mention—one of which, economic theory, was not the least significant. At this time the leading exponent of national economy in academic circles was Paul Louis Cauwès (1843–1917). Professor at the University of Nancy from 1867 to 1873, he was called to the *Faculté de Droit* at Paris in the latter year. Here he taught political economy for many years and from 1910 to 1913 was dean. In 1878 he published his famous *Cours d'économie politique,* which subsequently went through three editions. Greatly influenced by the German historical school and by Friedrich List, Cauwès regarded the nation, as did his German predecessor, as the acme of political development. He defined nation as a "union of men inhabiting the same territory and forming by their customs and their interests a real social and economic unity."[60] He accepted, moreover, List's picture of the ideal nation:

"It possesses a language and a literature, a large territory full of varied resources, a considerable population; agriculture, industry, commerce, and navigation are developed together; arts and sciences, means of instruction, and general culture are at the same level as material production. The political constitution, laws, and institutions guarantee to citizens a high degree of safety and liberty, keep up religious sentiment, morality, and well-being and have as a goal the comfort of all. It [the nation] possesses land and sea forces sufficient to defend its independence and to protect its foreign commerce. It exercises an influence in the development of other nations less advanced than it; and with its surplus population and capital it establishes colonies and rears new nations."[61]

"Patriotism is," Cauwès maintained, "an immense moral force and precious guarantee of independence." It can be turned in economic matters toward making the nation, France, the ideal or normal nation described by List. How this can be done is explained in detail in the four stout volumes which describe Cauwès' system. In the first place, no nation can be great, if its production is not great. It should aim at increasing its economic activity. There is solidarity of interests within the nation. Industrialists should not oppose agriculturalists; nor laborers, capitalists. All should work together to make of the nation a stronger entity and a place in which it is good to live. Free trade is a chimera, for if goods for consumption are imported, national production must of necessity decline. Labor will be thrown out of work and capital will have no use at home. International reciprocity is also dangerous, although it should not be discarded entirely, for once a nation obtains monopoly of a market, it will abuse its power. National production must endeavor to achieve self-sufficiency as a guarantee of economic welfare and defence. This is much more important than the temporary satisfaction of wants by importation. The state must intervene in economic matters to guarantee this condition. Whatever may be necessary—high tariffs, subsidies, credit advances, or the like—must be provided. The nation must be great.

Cauwès furnished much of the economic theory for the protectionists of his day. He worked hand in hand with Méline. He founded the *Société d'économie nationale,* of which Méline was honorary president, and wrote for the *Revue d'économie politique,* while Méline directed the *Travail national,* the most influential of protectionist organs.[62] Together they threw the seeds of national economic propaganda on fertile ground. They did not have, however, the field exclusively to themselves. French academic halls had been filled throughout the century with free traders and it was not to be expected that the situation would change overnight. Gustave de Molinari[63] and Yves Guyot,[64] editors of the *Journal des économistes,* were two of the stanchest advocates of economic liberalism; others were Frédéric Passy of the *Société d'éco-*

nomie politique and Léon Say. Later their cause was carried on by
Emile Levasseur[65] and Clément Colson.[66] But an extreme view of the
free exchange of goods seemed to be waning. Liberal theorists like
Paul Leroy-Beaulieu,[67] who was well grounded in practical business
affairs, leaned toward an opportunist course. Charles Gide[68] and the
group behind the *Revue d'économie politique* were supercritical of
all nostrums—an attitude that seemed to be finding more and more
adherents.

A reaction toward protectionist theory fitted well into the plans of
capitalists. Both agriculturalists and industrialists, who had been somewhat divided by the vote for the tariff of 1881, drew together. The
president of the Association of French Industry stated, "We demand
. . . that our sister, the industry of agriculture, be treated on the same
footing as manufacturing. . . . The union is made; it is solid."[69] Protectionism penetrated even the ranks of socialism. Jules Guesde and
his Marxist followers and Edouard Vaillant and his Blanquist supporters remained, to be sure, comparatively immune, but Jean Jaurès
leaned strongly in its favor. He had in him a deep love for France[70]
and a conviction that under the existing circumstances many economic
problems must be worked out on a national basis. According to him,
protection is necessary but it should not redound to the sole benefit of
a grasping bourgeoisie as it had all too frequently in the past. Protectionism is necessary to save the peasant farmer,[71] whose vote Jaurès
was anxious to catch, and to prevent wage reductions to the level of
Hindu coolies in cut-throat international competition.[72] But, he maintained, once a protective tariff is voted, the state must see to it that
labor gets its share of the benefit and that what profit might accrue to
capital owing to such legislation be taken away by taxation.[73]

THE MÉLINE TARIFF OF 1892

The stage was thus well set for higher customs duties. The Government took cognizance of the trend of opinion and in 1890[74] submitted
a tariff bill to the Chamber of Deputies. Its object was, so stated the
preamble of the document, not to proscribe foreign products from
French soil but to guarantee to French producers the ability to compete on equal terms with foreigners. Rates had been worked out to ac-

complish this end in co-operation with the Superior Council of Commerce, Industry, and Agriculture which had conducted one of its inevitable *enquêtes*. The tariff commission to which the bill was presented was composed of a majority of protectionists. Instead of making an investigation as had been its wont, the tariff commission referred to its members that section of the bill over which they had special competence. The result was that they were usually directly interested financially in the rates on whose merits they were ordered to pass. Their decisions, therefore, had a tendency to favor higher protection rather than moderate duties.

The report[75] of their findings was presented by Méline, secretary-general of the commission, who played such an important rôle in the subsequent proceedings that the tariff, when adopted, became known as the Méline tariff. In his hands, the report became an encomium of national economics. Protectionism was found, he stated, to be the best system to provide for the nation the greatest amount of labor, "for the more labor there is, the more capital there is, and consequently a larger wage fund for the working masses." He cited the growth of Germany's economic structure under the ægis of protection and compared it with the relatively humble advances made by France. Prohibition was a dead issue, but French producers needed security—security that could best be provided by protection. The tariff of 1881 had provided some security for industry; the new tariff was to provide more and was to include agriculture in its scope. The commission believed that this was absolutely necessary and wise, for it recognized what had not been recognized in the earlier law, that agricultural products are those that benefit the country most. If some agricultural goods were not given much protection, it was because under existing circumstances the French market was adequate to absorb them at advantageous prices.

The commission had to consider other problems in addition to the increased rates. There had been agitation for the abandonment of commercial treaties and of most-favored-nation treatment. *La Société des agriculteurs* was especially forceful in its demands for such a change and its position was supported by many industrialists. They argued that treaties, which run for ten years, make for instability, because technical improvements and economic crises alter the economic

relationship of nations. Also treaties, during the course of their existence, deprive a nation of the right to raise rates and a nation should
always have authority over its tariff in order to meet any emergency.
Most-favored-nation treatment makes a policy of reciprocity impossible, for no special advantages can be given to any one state.[76]

Although these contentions were flatly contradicted by free traders,
the problem was brought to the attention of the nation by France's
commercial relations with Germany. Most-favored-nation treatment
had been guaranteed to both nations by Article 11 of the Treaty of
Frankfurt. This arrangement had been proposed by one of the French
negotiators, the ultra-protectionist Pouyer-Quertier, in lieu of renew-
ing the former Franco-German commercial treaty. He thought at the
time that France would abolish her commercial treaties under the
leadership of Thiers and that therefore most-favored-nation treatment
would not be particularly advantageous to Germany. When the treaty
was negotiated, France could compete favorably with her rival, so
most-favored-nation treatment worked to her advantage rather than to
Germany's.

In the course of time, however, conditions became profoundly altered. Germany's economic development, particularly in the decade of
the 1880's, made her a serious competitor and France did not abolish
commercial treaties. To the contrary, Germany abandoned from 1878
to 1888 the policy of making commercial treaties and when she began
to make them again, she avoided, in so far as possible, granting favors
which France could enjoy. The classic example of her efforts in this
direction was her treaty with Switzerland in which she gave reductions on livestock raised at an altitude of one thousand or more me-
ters—a condition that prevented French farmers from profiting by the
concession.[77] The French sought a means of getting around their
agreement with Germany, which, of course, had no time limit, because
it was incorporated in a treaty of peace.

Two ways out of the predicament were discovered: one, a very high
tariff; the other, a double tariff. The former method was discarded for
fear of reprisals and economic isolation. The latter was regarded with
more favor. A minimum tariff could be established that would be
granted to those nations with which France had most-favored-nation

treaties and a maximum tariff to other states. Such a system would do away with specific rates in treaties and would hence allow France to change her tariff duties whenever she desired. It would, moreover, not lead easily to reprisals, would do away with excessive reciprocal concessions, and would be an advantage in treaty negotiations. It had been proposed by Waddington in 1881, but was not adopted. Now it was brought forward by the Government and readily approved by the Chamber's tariff commission.

Parliamentary debates on the new tariff bill began shortly after the commission had made its report. Protectionists and free traders expounded their beliefs in the usual fashion, employing arguments that by this time had become hackneyed. Perhaps a little more attention than usual was given to the benefits to be derived from the two systems by the working classes and this fact reflected, in part, the growing political importance of these elements of the population. The protectionists stressed the necessity for guaranteeing work and wages to labor and for seeking cheaper prices by improving national production; free traders insisted upon the need for buying in the cheapest market. Commercial interests criticized the new arrangements as an injury to trade; most industrialists and agriculturalists insisted upon them if their businesses were to prosper. National strength was appealed to frequently and most lyrically by one deputy who exclaimed, "Never forget that industry and agriculture are twin sisters which push with their robust shoulders the imperishable chariot of the nation along the infinite route of progress."

Upon the conclusion of the oratory, which failed undoubtedly to change the minds of but an infinitesimal number of representatives, the new tariff bill became law, January 12, 1892. It provided for increases of approximately 80 per cent over the old rates. Manufactured goods enjoyed more protection and agricultural duties, when reduced to an *ad valorem* basis, averaged about 25 per cent. France was now mistress of her tariff by the institution of minimum and maximum rates;[78] she was practically free from duties that had been fixed by commercial treaty. Finally, the tariff of 1892 established definitely the policy of tariff assimilation of the colonies—a policy which had already shown signs of developing.

RESULTS OF THE MÉLINE TARIFF

The effects of the Méline tariff on the economic and social condition of France are extremely difficult, if not impossible, to ascertain.
The revival of prosperity that followed its enactment was eagerly
seized upon by protectionists as proof of the validity of their contentions, but free traders were ready to point out that there was probably
no cause-and-effect relationship between the two facts. The tariff did
have the effect of raising agricultural prices in France and of maintaining them at a level higher than the world market prices. It did
much to save French agriculture from declining, as had English
farming, in competition with the virgin lands of the Americas and
Australia. The incomes of agriculturalists were increased, which meant
increased consumption of industrial products, but whether or not
this was a greater advantage to industrial capital and labor than cheap
food would have been is a question probably impossible of solution.
To what extent manufacturing interests and labor benefited either
directly or indirectly from the tariff is shrouded with uncertainty. It
is true that through the gaps left by the tariff of 1892 foreign goods
poured in large quantities, but whether or not France would have
been able to meet competition by means of improved productive
equipment, if there had been no protection, is problematical. The
unknowns in the situation are so numerous that it is little wonder
that theorists resorted to dogma to maintain their respective positions. One thing is very certain, however, and one which concerns
this study particularly: the tariff of 1892 was an important step in
the national economic history of France. It aimed toward self-sufficiency; it was a step in developing all branches of production on a
national basis; it showed her fear of having to give way to countries
better endowed by nature and better equipped technically than she.

Another definite result of increases in customs rates was tariff war.
The most serious conflict of this nature in which France became embroiled was the tariff war with Italy. It came about as a consequence
of protectionist measures adopted by the two countries in the 1880's.[79]
A commercial treaty, signed by both powers in 1881, was to last
until 1892, but each reserved the right to terminate it in 1887. Before

that date arrived, Italy had ample reason to be aggrieved at France. Tunis had been snatched from her grasp; she had joined the Triple Alliance; and France had raised her agricultural rates. Italy, therefore, took advantage of her right to abrogate the treaty with France and immediately established a tariff that averaged nearly 60 per cent *ad valorem*.[80] France raised some rates in 1887 and made plans for further increases.

Efforts to arrive at a conciliatory position failed in 1888. Italy, therefore, applied her general tariff to French goods, and the French reciprocated in kind, adding a few surtaxes on Italian goods to equal the Italian duties. Surtaxes were also applied by each nation to the other's shipping. In 1889 the intensity of reprisals was lessened to some degree, but until 1898 both countries applied their general tariffs (maximum tariff in the case of France after 1892) to the other's goods. Trade between the two nations fell appreciably. French exports to Italy decreased by one half and Italian exports to France by nearly two thirds. Some goods evaded the tariff barriers by passing through Switzerland, but it was obvious that both nations were suffering at the expense of their competitors. France was somewhat better able than Italy to find new outlets for her goods, as is testified by the fact that her total exports did not decrease during the "war," but she, as well as her rival, was anxious for a cessation of hostilities. Finally, better feeling developed between the two nations, for Italy was allowed to become interested in other colonial conquests and France went out of her way to win Italy from a seemingly illogical alliance with Austria. In 1898 Italy and France signed a new commercial treaty that eased the tension between them and restored economic exchanges to normal.

A similar conflict between France and Switzerland resulted from the tariff of 1892.[81] When negotiations for a commercial treaty were undertaken after the passage of the Méline tariff, the Swiss refused to grant concessions in return for France's minimum tariff and the Chamber refused to make exceptions. The result was that both nations submitted the other's goods to their highest rates and even established some special ones for the occasion. Trade between the two countries declined by over one third. Injury to both states was great and after two years and a half of bickering, they signed a commercial agreement. Difficulties were also encountered with Spain and Portugal, but they were overcome without serious trouble. With a few nations commercial treaties were made that extended the favor of the minimum tariff, but these accords could be changed every year, which allowed France to raise her rates almost at will. To about twenty other states, minimum tariff rates were granted without commercial treaties.

Whatever the other results of the tariff of 1892 may have been, it is a fact that trade prospered immediately after its passage. As has already been stated, the enactment of the Méline law coincided with a general revival of business activity. Imports were held down and exports grew.

SPECIAL COMMERCE IN MILLIONS OF FRANCS[82]

Year	Imports	Exports
1891	4767.9	3659.7
1892	4188.1	3460.7
1893	3853.7	3236.4
1894	3850.4	3078.1
1895	3719.9	3373.8
1896	3798.6	3400.9
1897	3956.0	3598.0
1898	4472.5	3510.9
1899	4518.3	4152.6
1900	4697.8	4108.7
1901	4369.2	4012.9
1902	4394.0	4252.2
1903	4801.3	4252.2
1904	4502.3	4451.0
1905	4778.9	4866.9
1906	5627.2	5265.5
1907	6223.0	5596.1
1908	5640.5	5050.7
1909	6246.1	5718.1
1910	7173.3	6233.8
1911	8065.8	6076.9
1912	8230.8	6712.6
1913	8421.3	6880.2
1914	6402.2	4868.8

If the imports of foodstuffs be isolated, it will be found that they dropped from 1,652,500,000 francs in 1891 to a low of 783,900,000 francs in 1901 and did not surpass the former amount until 1911.

FURTHER TARIFF INCREASES

In these figures protectionists found ample justification for their tariff views and argued that further increases would produce still more beneficial results. In the ten years following the Méline tariff, some thirty laws were passed reforming the tariff or giving aid to business. One of the most noteworthy changes was the so-called Cadenas law (December 13, 1897). This law provided for the application of new rates immediately upon their proposal and not when they were approved by Parliament in order to prevent excessive importation before proposed increases in the tariff were voted. Another governmental move was to grant direct export bounties to sugar,[83] and to increase indirect bounties, which included a reduction of taxes and duties in proportion to the distance sugar travelled favors which aided in about trebling by 1901 the production of 1884. These measures were part of an international movement to aid sugar and became so excessive that, in free-trade England, beet-sugar growing practically disappeared. The extreme cost of waging a sugar war brought the nations to terms. They signed the Brussels convention in 1902 by which they guaranteed to abolish export bounties, to tax all sugar produced at home, and to levy import duties equal to bounties given by non-signatory powers.[84] Although this agreement put an end to export bounties on sugar, France did not give up the practice of direct money aids to industry. She voted subsidies in this period to shipbuilding,[85] to silk-worm growing and silk spinning,[86] and to the raising of flax and hemp.[87]

There was almost a continual cry for government aid to business. Pressure groups were better organized than previously for raising their voices in pleas for assistance. Chambers of commerce were declared public institutions in 1898[88] and provision was made for the establishment of at least one in every department. They were raised to the level of official advisory bodies and through the National Assembly of Chambers of Commerce, which met every two months in Paris, they could bring more concerted power to bear on the government than hitherto. Agriculturalists, also, were much better organized than ever before. The law of March 21, 1884, which had permitted the formation of economic unions, was taken advantage of by peasants and landed proprietors for the creation of agricultural syndicates. By 1912, 900,000 farmers had grouped themselves together into 2550 syndicates. The primary purpose of these institutions was for the co-operative purchase and use of farm equipment, but they soon entered politics to defend the "rights of farmers." The *Union des Syndicats des Agriculteurs de France,* founded 1886, which united local bodies into a national federation, and the *Société des Agriculteurs* gave voice to their demands.

Industrial trade associations, life the *Comité des Forges,* were also growing in strength and influence. Many of them, or their members, co-operated in such lobbying groups as the *Fédération des industriels et des commerçants français* (founded in 1903) and the *Alliance syndicale du commerce et de l'industrie.*[89] Societies like the *Société d'encouragement pour le commerce français d'exportation* and various colonial groups aimed to facilitate French sales abroad. In this work, the Government lent a helping hand. In 1898 the *Office national du commerce extérieur*[90] was set up to furnish French exporters with information concerning export trade and commercial counsellors were appointed as agents in the field to find opportunities for the marketing of French goods.[91] Even consuls were ordered to devote more attention to the economic aspects of their tasks.

There was, however, no lessening of the desire for protection and numerous reasons were found in the first decade of the twentieth century for tariff increases. Other nations were augmenting their customs rates in a tariff race. The German tariff of 1902 and the United States Payne-Aldrich tariff, which was to go into effect April 1, 1910, were particularly disconcerting.[92] France also realized that other states were developing much more rapidly than she. After the long period of stagnation, which lasted in France from 1882 to 1893, there was a rapid expansion of foreign commerce. But from 1869 to 1909 French special foreign trade increased only 90.6 per cent, whereas Germany's grew from 1872 to 1909 172 per cent; the United States', 303 per cent;

and the United Kingdom's, 105 per cent. In total foreign trade, France slipped from second to fourth place as the following figures indicate:[93]

TOTAL SPECIAL COMMERCE, 1909

IN MILLIONS OF FRANCS

United Kingdom	25,078
Germany	18,890.4
United States	16,514.5
France	11,964.5
Netherlands	11,111

An analysis of France's trade with individual states was not reassuring. She did most business with Great Britain in 1909, exporting to that country merchandise valued at 1261 million francs and importing, for a value of 886 million francs. This apparent favorable balance of trade was somewhat illusory, however, for many of the French exports were not destined for consumption in Britain, where they would have had to compete with English goods, but were to be transported in English ships to overseas markets. With Germany the character of French imports changed from foodstuffs and raw materials to manufactured goods, yet France exported to Germany more than she imported in 1909. The greatest excess of imports over exports resulted from trade with the more backward nations—Japan, India, Egypt, etc.—which led the French to believe that their organization for marketing goods in more remote parts was inefficient, especially their shipping services.

Nor was there much consolation in comparing French industries with those of other countries. In 1913 France produced 41,000,000 tons of coal as compared with Britain's 292,000,000 tons and Germany's 279,000,000. She steadily imported half as much as she mined. Of "worked" iron and steel she produced 5,000,000 tons in 1913, as compared with Britain's 7,500,000 tons and Germany's 17,000,000, and in the same year she exported 10,000,000 tons of the 22,000,000 tons of iron ore she mined. In 1910 she had a steam merchant marine of 816,000 net tons, while the United Kingdom had 10,400,000 net tons. In the cotton industry she had in 1912 7,600,000 spindles and 140,000 looms; while Great Britain had 57,000,000 spindles and 725,000 looms; and Germany had 10,500,000 spindles and 230,000 looms. In the chemical and electrical industries, France was hopelessly behind. Concentration of industrial manufacture and the application of mechanical power to machines were not highly developed. A survey of 1896 showed that 534,500 of 575,000 industrial establishments employed less than ten persons (the average was 5.5) and data for 1912 indicated that the average horsepower per establishment (63,000 factories considered) was 51.3.[94] In agriculture France seemed to hold her own in comparison with her industrialized neighbors, but even here per-acreage yield indicated backward methods and the use of marginal lands. Perturbed by these signs of fundamental economic inferiority, the French national economist was further annoyed by such practices as dumping—the selling heavily by trusts and cartels, like the Rhenish-Westphalian Coal Syndicate and the Stahlwerksverband, of their surplus abroad at prices inferior to those demanded at home.

All these factors goaded the French along the route of higher tariffs. Protection was one of the leading issues in the election of a new Chamber of Deputies in 1906 and protectionists entered the legislative halls of France triumphant. The tariff question was immediately taken up and a commission was appointed to study the matter. A questionnaire, sent out to chambers of commerce and business men, reaffirmed once again the demand of capitalists for high tariffs. As in the preparation of the Méline tariff, members of the commission were assigned the task of preparing that part of the report in which they had special competence, which meant that they could suggest rates in conformity with their personal interests. The general report was a hymn of praise for the ideas incorporated in the tariff of 1892. The scheme of minimum and maximum rates was lauded and to protection was attributed the growth of French industry and agriculture.

The commission voiced no desire to change the principles on which French tariff legislation was founded; it wanted solely to reenforce the existing system. To this end certain tariff increases were proposed which, as ultimately revised and enacted into law, resulted in raising the duties on taxable goods from between 12 and 20 per cent to between 15 and 30 per cent. Levasseur in his *Histoire du commerce*[95] maintained that these rates, figured *ad valorem* on *all* imports including untaxable raw materials, averaged 8 per cent *ad valorem,* as compared with 7.6 per cent for the tariff of 1892 and with 8.4 per cent applied by Germany, 9.6 per cent charged by Italy, 13.4 per cent collected by Spain, 23.2 per cent enforced by the United States, and 38.9 charged by Russia. Furthermore, the commission proposed that the difference between France's minimum and maximum tariffs be widened to 50 per cent. The purpose of this was to provide a means for bringing more pressure to bear on foreign powers to grant concessions to France in return for minimum tariff treatment.

In the same order of things, it was provided that the maximum tariff of 1892 might be applied to the articles of some countries which did not subject French goods to a differential treatment—a provision designed to facilitate a satisfactory arrangement with the United States. Moreover, weapons were forged in the bill for fighting tariff wars and for preventing dumping. Power was given to the executive authority to double the rates of the maximum tariff on goods from countries placing surtaxes or exceptionally high duties on French exports and to place 50 per cent *ad valorem* duties on articles imported free. The executive was empowered to order, as retaliatory measures, formalities, taxes, duties, rules, etc., identical with those used by foreign nations to impede the importation of French products. An anti-dumping clause provided further that the government could increase the rates on imports enjoying bounties, subsidies, or favors of any kind, direct or indirect (including favors obtained by cartel agreements), to a sum equal to these bounties, subsidies, or favors. The bill continued the practice of allowing the executive to suspend certain duties, as, for example, that on wheat, in time of crisis and to collect provisionally duties proposed in a bill, even before it was enacted into law. Finally, to be sure that nothing had been overlooked, the extraordinary authority was given the government to take "all dispositions which would be appropriate to circumstances."

This bill, implemented with all conceivable provisions for making France's tariff position impregnable, went to the Chamber for discussion, June 15, 1909. The economic crisis of 1907 had spurred on the commission and had improved the protectionist background against which it worked. Moreover, the fear that the Payne-Aldrich tariff in the United States would be applied before the new tariff was enacted into law urged the Chamber and Senate to action. Both houses, however, trundled out the well-worn arguments for protection and free trade for a new exhibition. The latter seemed to be weakened by a feeling of hopelessness, but the protectionist views rang with the conviction of approaching victory. Business elements, for the most part, favored the measure. Jaurès and his socialist friends supported it in the hope that labor would be benefited. Vaillant and his more radical labor group opposed it as the work of the devil. After more than ample oratory, the bill became law, March 30, 1910. This was the final important tariff revision prior to the World War.

France's new tariff was accepted by most countries without any serious difficulties. The minimum tariff was granted to most states; Chile, Peru, and some of the English colonies were among the few who had to pay the maximum rates. France negotiated commercial treaties with sixty-two countries, thus returning, in a degree, to the régime that the double tariff had aimed to abolish. The most-favored-nation clause, which did away with special reciprocity agreements, was included in thirty-five of these accords, and fixed rates, which lessened France's tariff autonomy, were also provided for in some. There was, just before the World War, a movement toward long-term commercial accords of the type in existence under the Second Empire. There was, however, no decline in protectionist feeling. On the contrary, a proportionately greater increase of imports than of exports and a decidedly unfavorable balance of trade made many wonder what else could be done to protect the home market. Nothing was done, however, until the war, and then a new set of circumstances profoundly altered the entire situation.

RAILWAY EXPANSION WITH STATE AID

Protectionism aimed to preserve France's internal market for French goods. National economists approved this policy, so far as it went, but they maintained that it, in itself, did not suffice—expansion of the home market was equally essential to the growth of the nation's economic system.[96] It was believed in those days that the primary necessity for the development of internal commerce was the building of railways. Canals and roads served an important purpose, but railways were the instruments of transportation which would most readily and most extensively widen the demand for goods and permit the exploitation of formerly unattainable natural resources. It was believed that France had by no means done all that should be done in this direction. In 1870 she had 18,500 kilometers of lines in comparison with Germany's 19,500 and the United Kingdom's 24,500; and even Belgium surpassed her in proportion to area. Her inferiority in railways had been driven home with a vengeance during the war with Prussia and now military necessity was added to purely economic reasons for more extensive construction.

In spite of the obvious need for more railways and regardless of the popular demand for them after the signing of the peace in 1871, construction was slow. Bankers and railway interests feared that the new Government would not assist them as bountifully as had the Second Empire and that the future of privately owned railways was insecure. In fact, the purchase of railways by the state was seriously considered by the National Assembly, and although this idea had to be given up for the moment because of the expense,[97] the issue was not dead. The proponents of state ownership still hoped to drag the government into the railway business, if only by the back door. Consequently, they advised the state to purchase several small companies, with a total of 2615 kilometers in the southwest, which speculators had unsuccessfully endeavored to amalgamate for the purpose of competing with the older lines. When these companies became financially embarrassed in 1875, the state took them over (1876) and thus added to the fright of private interests.[98]

As though this triumph of the proponents of state ownership was not enough to scare off private entrepreneurs, Freycinet, the minister of public works, conceived a vast plan for *outillage de la paix* (national equipment in peace time) in which state railway construction loomed large. He proposed, in addition to building or improving bridges, canals, roads, and ports, to create a third railway network of 10,000 kilometers. Many parliamentarians had their qualms about the project, but they suppressed their opposition and made the scheme even more ambitious by seeking "pork-barrel" favors for their districts. The Freycinet plan was adopted July 17, 1879.

The execution of this plan was energetically pushed. In 1880, 1881, and 1882, 3000 kilometers were built at the cost of 274 million, 328 million, and 378 million francs, respectively, not counting expenses for rolling stock in the parts opened for use. This placed a heavy financial burden on the national treasury and gave the state a number of short, unconnected lines, hemmed in by the large companies. Estimates for the completion of the third network were increased, moreover, from 3 billion to 6 billion francs, which seemed more than the state could manage. When the crisis of 1882 burst, with the failure of the *Union Générale* bank, the state decided to run to cover. It decided that it would try to shift its Freycinet-plan railways on to the shoulders of the old companies.

In order to do this peace had to be made between the republican Government and the railways. Steps had already been taken in this direction by the Government, for it had reached an understanding with high finance. By 1882, Gambetta's power had been broken and Leon Say, who was personally connected with the house of Rothschild, had been taken into Freycinet's cabinet. Say was strongly opposed to the plan for state railways and urged economy for the sake of a balanced budget. His presence in the Government gave confidence to railway builders and facilitated the signing of some conventions with them in 1883.

These agreements, which mark the beginning of a new collaboration between the state and private railway companies after an interim of hostility, provided that the lines projected under the Freycinet plan should be amalgamated with the lines of the big companies and that, by a system of swapping, the remaining state lines should form a homogeneous network. The state agreed to carry the main cost of constructing the roads of the third network, but the companies would have, for their part, to contribute a fixed sum per kilometer, provide rolling stock, and construct the stations. The companies were to oversee the construction[99] and to loan money to the Government for the state's share in the enterprise up to a given maximum. In return for these advantages, the state agreed to abolish the former distinction between old and new networks and to guarantee interest on the capital invested in *all* railways, including those of the third network.[100] The treasury was to receive ultimately a larger share than had been provided for previously of the surplus earnings of the railways and the railway companies were placed in a more secure financial position than formerly.[101] In this way, the new railways, necessary for economic development and war purposes, were built; and the state was relieved of the burden it had undertaken.

The fact that the public treasury could be relied upon to make certain the payment of capital charges stood the railway companies in good stead during the succeeding years. The period of economic stagnation that lasted from 1882 to 1892 saw railway receipts dwindle and the annual sums advanced by the public treasury, as guarantees of earnings on capital invested, mount from 5,797,000 francs in 1883 to 94,500,000 francs in 1893. With the coming of better times the financial burden on the state in this respect became less heavy. By the end of 1913, the *Nord, P. L. M.,* and *Est* had paid back all that had been advanced them as guarantee of interest and the demands of the *Orléans* and *Midi* were less than the state received in excess earnings from the three former lines.[102]

The company which had given the most trouble had been the *Ouest.* It had received sums as guarantee of interest in excess of the value of its rolling stock, which was security for these advances. This situation gave advocates of government ownership of railways an opportunity to press their case. The election of seventy-five socialists to the Chamber in 1906 and the triumph of the left republicans at the same time augured well for the success of a plan to take over the *Ouest.* After a general airing of the arguments for and against state ownership, a decision was reached to buy the *Ouest* (July 13, 1908) at a price agreed upon by the two parties—a sum sufficient to service the outstanding obligations of the line. This purchase permitted the amalgamation of the state's railway holdings and allowed the trains of its network to come over its own line to Paris. The fortunes of the state's venture in railway operation were at first none too brilliant, but in the course of time, as will be shown, the enterprise was reasonably successful.

Agitation for the purchase of other networks was carried on in the period before the World War, but it was unsuccessful.[103] According to the terms of the concessions, French railways were to become property of the state without cost between 1950 and 1960[104] and many persons were willing to await these dates rather than to act prematurely with an excessive expenditure by the treasury. So the exponents of government intervention had to console themselves with such measures as control of railway rates. When reductions were made, especially in 1892, it was curious to hear voices raised in complaint because cheaper transportation would offset the custom duty increases of the same year on foreign goods seeking to compete in the French market. Especial criticism was aimed at the *P. L. M.* for its policy of *tarifs de provenance*—special low rates on Australian wool, for example, coming to Marseilles and destined for the woolen centers of the East. These rates, which were established for the purpose of securing more traffic and eliminating the English as middlemen, were actually lower than those on French wool from the Midi to the industrial centers of the North and East and militated, so it was claimed, against the use of native products. Even though this practice was counterbalanced, to a degree, by *P. L. M. tarifs d'exportation*—reductions on goods for markets beyond the Suez, which were granted in an effort to bring merchandise to Marseilles for shipment rather than to let it go to Antwerp—vested interests were always ready to point out the slightest injury done them. Such is the way in national economics.[105]

The state's rôle in the railway development in the nineteenth century was great. Up to the end of 1910, the public treasury had paid out for this purpose 5,700,830,000 francs in comparison with the 16,307,867,057 francs raised by private companies through the sale of stocks and bonds.[106] In 1910 France had 49,500 kilometers of lines; Germany had 61,000, and the United Kingdom 38,000. Although her carrying did not equal that of the two aforementioned nations, the number of passengers carried one kilometer had jumped from 1 billion in 1853 to nearly 17 billion in 1910 and the number of tons of freight carried one kilometer had jumped from 1 billion in 1854 to 22 billion in 1910.[107] In view of these figures, there is no doubt that railways played a leading part in the growth of French economic enterprise. They not only made hitherto inaccessible markets available to French producers, but they tapped new resources, made possible the exchange of heavy products between distant parts of the country, and introduced a wide variety of new products that required rapid transportation. Yet it is interesting to note that in the matter of railways, as in most industries, France did not have a pre-eminent international position. This fact is especially important in considering that great test of economic strength which was the World War.

Other means of transportation and communication were not neglected by the Third Republic before 1914. The mileage of national roads, however, was not extended, although improvements were made upon them. About 684 kilometers of new canals were constructed, following the Freycinet plan, which brought the total to 4940 kilometers, and those already built were deepened and their locks were lengthened. The result was that the number of tons of freight carried one kilometer on them and on rivers increased from 2 billion in 1869 to about 5½ billion in 1909. The postal service was increased from 358 million letters and 334 million pieces of printed matter carried in 1869 to 1062 million letters and 1368 million pieces of printed matter in 1903, not to mention 196 million post cards sent in the latter year. From 1878 to 1910 the number of telegrams sent increased 500 per cent and the telephone system, made a state monopoly in 1889, was greatly extended. All indications led to the conclusion that France was enjoying tremendous growth of commercial activity, but compared with other countries she was unable to hold her own.

SHIPPING SUBSIDIES

Important as the development of the home market and home production was, national economists looked ever with great favor upon the conquest of foreign markets—upon the amount of French exports. This phase of national economic life was closely related to the merchant marine and under the Third Republic strenuous efforts were made to bring it to a par with France's rivals. The task was herculean. In 1870 France did only 34 per cent of the shipping in French ports and she had a merchant marine of but one million tons as compared with the United Kingdom's six million. In this extremity those interested in France's shipping appealed to the state—the one entity that represented common national welfare—for aid.[108]

The classic French manner of assisting the merchant marine had been to levy, as we have already seen, surtaxes of various kinds upon foreign shipping. Thiers attempted to return to this system, but international treaties prevented the realization of his project.[109] Consequently, a commission was appointed to study what could be done, but during the seven years of its existence matters only got worse. By 1879 French ships were carrying only 28 per cent of the commerce in French ports and, as one member of the commission remarked, France thus paid an annual "tribute" of 345 million francs to foreign merchant marines.[110] This was the time when wooden ships were being supplanted by iron and steel vessels and France found that she could not make the change easily. Not only was she recovering from an exhausting war and torn by internal political strife, but she did not have the technical equipment nor supplies of cheap raw materials necessary for the new industry. The haul of steel and coal to the construction centers at Nantes, St. Nazaire, and Le Havre was long and costly. French ports were poor and were so situated that other nations could use them as ports of call, while French ships had to use them as home ports and could not call in the harbors of her European economic rivals without making a return trip. Finally, France's policy of economic self-sufficiency, particularly as regards agriculture, militated against carrying, and her lack of bulky export cargoes deprived French vessels of remunerative hauls to foreign lands.

The investigating commission took cognizance of these hardships and early came to the conclusion that drastic measures were needed. It realized that maritime mortgages, established in 1874, and the removal of customs duties on the importation of shipbuilding materials would not suffice. It reported that the state would have to resort to direct money subsidies to the industry, if it were to prosper. This was like music to the ears of shippers. Yet, they felt that this was only their due, for if businessmen on land were to get assistance from protective tariffs, they believed that they should get aid of some kind for their business on the seas. A spirit of bargaining pervaded their thinking, and that of others as well. In fact, the subsidy laws of 1881, 1893, 1902, and 1906 coincided almost exactly with the tariffs.

The law of 1881 really initiated the practice of granting bounties to shipping in France.[111] It provided for financial aid to both shipbuilders and carriers. For construction, it granted 60 francs per gross ton to iron and steel ships, and from 10 to 20 francs for wooden ones, and, in addition, sums for the employment of steam engines and boilers. For carrying, it gave 1 franc 50 per ton for each 1000 nautical miles covered, provided the ship were constructed in France, and half that sum if it were of foreign origin—sums which diminished annually with the age of the vessel.

Many excuses were made to the public for this legislation. In the Chamber much emphasis was placed on the increased cost of construction which could result from the new tariff and on the fact that carriers had to train French seamen for the navy. But the object was clear to every one: the law aimed definitely at improving France's position upon the seas. The results were not entirely unsatisfactory. Construction of sailing vessels increased from 9176 tons in 1881 to 40,655 tons in 1884, and of steamships from 11,559 tons to 16,507 tons. Meanwhile, French shipowners increased their percentage of the carrying to and from French ports only from 33.12 per cent of the total to 34.37 per cent. Moreover, a time limit of ten years from the passing of the law was placed upon subsidy-giving and as the year 1892 approached both shipbuilders and carriers began to curtail their activities.

This fact spurred French legislators to renew their efforts in seeking succor for the merchant marine. They reserved shipping with Algeria (1889),[112] and the carrying of certain articles from Tunis for French vessels.[113] But what was more important, they voted a new subsidy law, January 30, 1893. In order to meet the most important of contemporary criticisms,[114] the construction bounties were increased to offset the difference in costs between England and France and shipbuilders were allowed to collect subsidies on orders from foreigners as well as from French citizens. An effort was also made to correct the error of the 1881 law in respect to the time limit during which carrying bounties could be received. The limit was now set, not as previously at ten years from the time of the enactment of the law, but at ten years from the date of a ship's being put in service, provided it was constructed in France. Foreign ships were excluded from the benefits. Shipowners complained of this latter provision, for either they could not get deliveries of French-built vessels or the quality and costs of them were less satisfactory than those which could be obtained abroad.[115]

By all odds, however, the worst feature of the law was that larger carrying bounties were given to sailing vessels than to steamships, with the result that the more antiquated and inefficient branch of the industry prospered. Ships were sailed in ballast, or carried goods on long hauls at extremely low rates, as, for example, English coal to Chile with nitrate as a return cargo, in order to obtain bounty payments. One company is reported to have secured more income from subsidies than from actual freight charges. The practice resulted in cheap carrying to foreigners but in little national benefit to France. Furthermore, although newly constructed tonnage increased from 20,-000 in 1893 to 100,000 in 1901, the tonnage of steam construction only slightly exceeded 10,000 tons per year,[116] and the amount of French carrying done by nationals was around 30 per cent.

Thus another rectification was made in the subsidy legislation (April 7, 1902). According to the new law, bounties were arranged definitely to favor steam, steel ships and an equipment subsidy (*prime d'armament*) was established to assist French owners of foreign-built vessels. Provisions were made, moreover, to curb the practice of getting carrying bounties by sailing in ballast or with a very small cargo. Henceforth, it was necessary to have a given amount of freight for every voyage in order to tap the coffers of the state.

As impeccable as the Government had endeavored to make this new legislation, it, too, had a flaw. Because the sums to be paid in subsidies were limited, *entrepreneurs* took an early plunge but then grew frightened for fear that no more assistance would be forthcoming. Consequently, new construction dropped from 205,000 tons in 1902 to 58,000 tons in 1905 and French carrying of the nation's overseas trade declined to 26 per cent of the total. Therefore, one more attempt was made to secure a successful subsidy law (April 16, 1906). Construction bounties, based upon the difference of English and French prices,[117] were made more generous and were allowed to run for twelve years. Subsidies for equipment were to be given for twenty-four years on French-constructed ships only. And no limits to the amounts that might be spent under this law were fixed.[118]

At last French legislators had devised a measure that was really efficacious. After a long period of fits and starts the French merchant marine was to make steady progress. This is not surprising, for the direct subsidies amounted to about $5,000,000 a year and the mail contracts, given to the French line, the *Compagnie des Messageries Maritimes, Chargeurs Réunis,* and the *Compagnie Fraissinet,* totaled a similar sum.[119] France constructed in 1913, 110,000 tons, almost all of which was steam, and had in 1912 a total gross tonnage of 2,450,000. Still she did but 26 per cent of her carrying and was hopelessly outdistanced by Great Britain.[120] She was definitely on the road towards improving her condition when she was rudely stopped by the events of the World War.

IMPERIAL EXPANSION

Closely connected with the efforts to develop the merchant marine was the colonial policy of the Third Republic. Immediately after the War of 1870, expansionist sentiment in France was at low tide. The exigencies of war had consumed all French energy and resources and the nation concentrated on the necessity of repairing the damages and settling her indemnity. What dreams there were of active foreign policy were centered on taking revenge on Germany for the recent defeat. Moreover, Napoleon III's imperialist adventures had required large investments in men and money on which there appeared to be little chance of return. His liberal trade policy with the colonies had caused their commerce to slip gradually from French control into the hands of foreigners. Only two thirds of the total trade of French colonies was with France, yet France had to expend at least 30 million francs a year (27 millions of which were sent to Algeria), to support her colonial domains, not one of which was actually prospering. Eminent economists, with the exception of Paul Leroy-Beaulieu[121] and Paul Cauwès,[122] disapproved of colonial expansion. Many statesmen and politicians, among whom Clemenceau and Déroulède were perhaps the most militantly outspoken, opposed colonization, heaping epithets as strong as "traitor" upon those who dared to suggest that France turn her attention from seeking a just rectification of the eastern boundary to overseas imperialist endeavor.[123] Nor was there any noteworthy popular demand for colonial expansion. Colonial societies did not exist; the press was quiet on the subject; and the slowly growing population saw no necessity in Malthusian arguments for colonies.

In spite of all this opposition to colonization in the decade of the 1870's, the Third Republic was to engage in one of the greatest imperialist expansions in French history. The discovery of reasons for this development would seem difficult in view of what has just been said, yet there were vital forces at work which explain why France obtained colonies.

There were, in the first place, fundamental economic factors that must be taken into consideration. In the earlier part of the nineteenth century, French capital, enterprise, energy, and techniques had been engaged in exploiting the money-making possibilities of the homeland itself, but by the 1880's, so it seemed, they had reached the point of marginal return. The economic crisis of 1882 and relatively poor times from that date to 1894 convinced at least some Frenchmen that France had reached the apex of her internal economic development. If industry was to grow, if the almost static population was to increase, and if France was to keep pace with all countries, particularly with Germany, she must seek advantages from overseas. She must increase her markets, obtain colonies possessing basic raw materials, and achieve greater economic self-sufficiency. Colonies thus obtained and developed would serve as supply stations along the routes of empire and as bases for the launching of trade offensives in distant parts. Technical improvements in transportation and in warfare would make comparatively easy the subjugation and exploitation of hitherto almost inaccessible territories.

Another economic factor in favor of colonies was the exportation of capital. From 1882 to 1895 Frenchmen found some difficulty in securing satisfactorily remunerative employment for their excess funds at home and there was a general wave of foreign investment.[124] A portion of this capital found its way into territories that were regions of potential colonization. The schemes thus financed paid high interest rates, but were risky; and sometimes French investments had to be protected by the armed forces of the state. Such action resulted in colonial acquisitions, causing many Frenchmen to rejoice that there were territories, over which France exercised political suzerainty, in which they could invest their savings.

In the second place, there were very important political reasons why

France should desire to engage in colonial adventures. New information about central Africa, resulting from the explorations of de Brazza, an Italian who was naturalized French, of Stanley, of Livingstone, and of numerous others, opened up a field for expansion that appeared to promise satisfactory returns. After the Berlin Conference (1884–85), attended by all the leading nations of Europe, had fixed the rules whereby the merry game of seizing colonies should be played in Africa, it was only to have been expected that there would be a rush for the grab bag. Individual nations which proceeded to take their portions were not necessarily convinced that their new holdings were Eldorados, but they wanted to be certain that they kept pace with their rivals in obtaining what might be of strategic or economic advantage.

This fear of getting left behind, or hope of surging ahead, made France along with other states rush almost blindly into enterprises of the most questionable economic value. The mere thought that another nation desired a colony made France anxious to possess it. National pride was a powerful motivating force in imperialism. France gloried in seeing that particular pastel shade which her cartographers used for coloring her possessions[125] spread over the map and enjoyed boasting that she had the second largest empire in the world.

Furthermore, the international diplomatic situation was such as to encourage France, after the 1870's, to add to her overseas dominions. Prince Bismarck was anxious to divert the attention of his enemies in the West from the lost provinces of Alsace and Lorraine and thought that this could be done by dangling colonial plums before their eyes. Although his rôle in this matter should not be exaggerated, he employed deftly the machinery of diplomacy to indicate that he would not be opposed to French expansion and was instrumental in embroiling France and Italy over the Tunis affair, thus winning the latter power to the Austro-German alliance.

The internal political situation had, likewise, certain elements in it conducive to colonial expansion. With the definite triumph of the Republican party in 1879 and with peace made between that group and high finance, especially after the fall of Gambetta in 1882,[126] there came to the helm of the Government a group of men who represented big business interests—the only interests that stood to profit very much from the acquisition of colonies. Republicans needed to achieve success to add prestige to their cause and there were those among them, although only a minority at first, who looked upon colonial victories as one of the easiest ways of securing political glory in foreign affairs.[127]

Among the new political leaders who took an interest in colonialism were Jules Ferry, Admiral Jauréguiberry, and Freycinet. Ferry was the real hero of France's return to an active policy of expansion. He was a cool, calculating Lorrainer, who could hew closely to the line amidst the cries and catcalls of his opponents. A man of this quality was necessary, for there was bitter opposition to imperialism. Monarchists opposed it; Clemenceau, presenting the radical viewpoint, was hostile to it; Gambetta, the Left Republican spell-binder, could not be counted upon to support it; and Ferry's own followers were not wholeheartedly in favor of it. To play a lone hand under these circumstances required courage and fortitude; these Ferry possessed in bountiful measure.[128] The first definite steps under the Third Republic toward the acquisition of colonies were taken during his ministries—1880 to 1881 and 1883 to 1885.

Ferry was a shrewd enough politician, however, not to act without some rationalizing of his policies and he provided the country with a philosophy of colonization that received some popular support. He founded his argument on an economic base. He believed that national economic power depended upon production; production upon industrialization; and industrialization upon markets. The home market must be protected, but the home market was not sufficient.[129] Colonies afforded the only sure and practical outlet for surplus products. For the principles of free trade, Ferry had no use; they had become antiquated. France needed colonies for markets and places for the investment of surplus capital; she must get them or reconcile herself to the position of a second-rate power.

It was with this reasoning, fortified by a desire to see French culture brought to backward peoples, that Ferry appealed to the country to support his colonial projects. This is not the place to retell the political history of French acquisitions, a story that has already been told adequately in other places.[130] Only the highlights of that narrative need to be recalled to mind. Ferry's first colonial project was in

Tunis. Here French economic interest was concerned with land hold-ings, certain telegraph and railway concessions, and with bonds which had gone into default. From a political point of view, France looked with disfavor upon Italy's obvious desire to seize Tunis, for that would have meant a weakening of France's position in the Mediter-ranean and in North Africa. The stake seemed important to Ferry and a border incident between a Tunisian tribe and Algerians gave him an opportunity to act. A cautious parliament voted the credits which he demanded to "protect" the Algerian colony and then adjourned. Without a declaration of war and with reassuring words to the Italian and Turkish Governments, Ferry sent his troops into Tunis and de-clared a protectorate over the country (1881). For national, economic and political reasons the imperialist Ferry overstepped his rights. He even exceeded the demands of popular opinion in initiating his colo-nial projects.

When parliament met again, it had learned the real motives of the Tunis expedition and turned furiously upon the premier. It forced him out of office and took a definite stand against imperialist adven-tures in the future. So strong was this feeling that when, in 1882, an occasion presented itself for joining Great Britain in an armed inter-vention in Egypt, credits necessary for France's participation were re-fused—an action that was tantamount to the abandonment of hope to extend French political dominion to that country. Even in 1883 when Ferry returned to the premiership, enthusiasm for colonial undertak-ings was at the ebb. Undismayed by this state of affairs, Ferry busied himself with propagating his faith in colonization and in developing plans for further acquisition.[131] He took measures to tighten France's hold on Tunis; he furthered French interests along the Guinea coast, in the Congo, and in Madagascar; and, at the Berlin Conference in 1884, he was instrumental in paving the way for the further partition of Africa and in coming to an understanding with Germany and Great Britain concerning their attitudes toward French colonial policy.

Ferry's outstanding achievements during his second ministry were the re-occupation of Tonkin and the war with China. France had sought trade in this part of the world and in 1874 had made a treaty with Annam which gave her special commercial privileges in the

country. Close adherence to the terms of the treaty, especially as regards protection from pirates on the Red River, was practically impossible, and, over this and the question of a protectorate, France and
Annam came to blows. Ferry's course did not run smoothly. He was
early confronted with an unyielding Chinese foreign policy and with
a parliament that only grudgingly voted financial support for the execution of his plans. He had to use force against the former to attain
his ends; he had to evade the latter by fighting without a legal declaration of war and by asking for occasional small sums. Finally, when
defeat had come to his expedition in Annam and it was necessary to
ask for large credits in order to cope with the situation, parliamentary
opposition led by Clemenceau attacked him unmercifully and threw
him out of office. But Ferry had remained in power long enough to
accomplish his end in the Tonkin affair; he had practically agreed to
terms with China and virtually secured for France a free hand in the
territory of Annam (1885). The succeeding Government was faced
by a *fait accompli* which it refused to repudiate.

The seven years following this episode were ones of uneasiness. At
home, France was torn by the Boulanger affair, the Panama scandal,
the resignation of President Grévy, and labor troubles. Foreign affairs
were almost equally disturbing—made tense by the Schnaebelé incident, Germany's conversion to a policy of imperialism, the renewal of
the Triple Alliance, and colonial rivalry with Great Britain. In spite
of these troubled times, however, the idea of colonization made steady
progress. Numerous books on colonial subjects were published in this
epoch—books that included: Paul Leroy-Beaulieu, *De la colonisation
chez les peuples modernes* (1874); A. Rambaud, *La France coloniale*
(1886); J. L. de Lanessan, *Principes de colonisation* (1895); L. De-
schamps, *Histoire de la question coloniale en France* (1891); M. Dubois and A. Terrier, *Un Siècle d'expansion coloniale* (1902); Gabriel
Hanotaux, *Fachoda* (1909); Christian Schéfer, *La France moderne et
le problème colonial* (vol. I, 1907), etc.[132] Colonial societies also appeared—*Union Coloniale Française* (1893), *Comité Dupleix* (1894),
Ligue Maritime et Coloniale Française (1899), and the *Comité de
l'Afrique Française* (1890)—as did colonial publications, such as
L'Afrique Française and *La Quinzaine Coloniale*.

These creations were at once the reflection and the agent of an altered colonial sentiment in France, but they were not alone responsible for the change that was taking place. A growing need for raw materials, as well as an increased hope that in the long run colonies would be strong economic entities, tended to weaken the opposition of many economists to colonial enterprise. The rapid exhaustion of unclaimed territories and the necessity of consolidating holdings already staked out encouraged action even in a world tense with international friction. A more intensive demand for markets, more capital for investment, and intensified national feeling contributed toward the same end. The result was that the twenty years after 1892 were filled with colonial conquests.[133]

In this period of expansion, popular public opinion never once took the initiative in demanding war for imperialist purposes, but it opposed earnestly only those enterprises that seemed hopelessly unprofitable or turned out to be unsuccessful. The rank and file of French citizenry could usually be brought into line, once a crisis occurred, by an appeal to patriotism and so acted only as a very feeble check on imperialistic businessmen and ambitious statesmen. Particularly was this true when strong leaders like Hanotaux, Delcassé, Poincaré, and Clemenceau were directing the destinies of the French state. A strong current of militant imperialism had, moreover, begun to flow through the French people and it could always be counted upon to sweep before it large sections of popular opinion. Even under these conditions, however, French governments had to use caution. In the case of Madagascar and in the extension of French power in certain other places, the true aims of policies had to be kept from the public and action had to be taken without prior consent of Parliament.[134]

There were really no insurmountable impediments to imperialist policies and French power was extended without much opposition at home. The Ivory Coast, Guinea, and French Sudan were established as colonies in 1893 and Dahomey in 1894, which, with the older holdings of Senegal and Upper Senegal and Niger, were joined together to form French West Africa (1895-99)—a colony that was increased by the addition of Upper Volta and Mauretania. French Equatorial Africa was formed around the nucleus of the French Congo and

Gabon and expanded, especially after 1890, to include Cameroon, Ubangi-Chari and the Chad territory. France declared a protectorate over Madagascar in 1895 and promptly annexed it as a colony; she made war on Siam in 1893, thus adding Laos to her Far Eastern holdings in Indo-China; and she established a protectorate over Morocco in 1912. These territories, along with those obtained during the Ferry decade of the 'eighties, increased France's colonial empire from less than one million square miles to a grand total of 6,314,582 square miles with a population of over 55,000,000 persons[135]—an empire in size and importance second only to Great Britain's. National ambition, national economic theory and practice, and desire for private gain were largely responsible for this great growth.

THE "NEW" COLONIAL SYSTEM

The mere acquisition of colonies was, of course, not an end in itself —it was a fundamental precept of the imperialist philosophy of the republic to make colonies enhance the economic power of the motherland. An obvious step toward the realization of this desire was to regulate colonial trade for the benefit of France. Under the Second Empire the "colonial pact" had been weakened by Napoleon III's liberal economic policy. A large amount of tariff autonomy had been given to Martinique, Guadeloupe, and Réunion in 1861 and 1866. This reform had led these colonies to place *octrois de mer* on all imports—a measure that hit French as well as foreign goods. Gradually France's trade with these colonies declined and that of foreign powers grew.[136] Increased military expenditures and sums spent in bringing French culture and civilization to backward peoples fell so heavily on the homeland that agitation for some change by which part of the burden would be placed on the colonies became insistent. Economic crises and the contemporary movement towards protectionism in France added to this sentiment and there was a decided trend toward the establishment of what was closely analogous to the old colonial system.[137] Evidence of the trend is to be found in the curbing of the power of the three privileged colonies to tax French goods (1879 and 1885), the assimilation of Algeria into the French customs system in 1884—that is, the establishment of the French tariff on foreign imports into Algeria and the free exchange of goods between Algeria and the homeland[138]—and the practically similar assimilation of Indo-China in 1887.[139]

Assimilation became the watchword of the new policy and preparations were made for applying it more generally. To this end French chambers of commerce, trade associations, and businessmen were asked for an opinion. They voiced approval of it. Significantly enough the attitude of the colonies themselves was not canvassed, and the diminution of trade in those colonies to which the policy of assimilation had already been applied was ignored. France wanted to reserve her colonial markets for herself and this she aimed to do by the law of January 11, 1892. Thus the principle of assimilation was applied to Algeria, Martinique, Guadeloupe, Guiana, Saint-Pierre and Miquelon, Réunion, Mayotte, Gabon, French Indo-China, and New Caledonia.[140] Only a very few of their products, notably sugar, tea, coffee and cocoa, had to pay duties upon entering France and a still smaller number of goods were charged export taxes when sent to foreign powers. The other colonies remained "non-assimilated" either because of international agreement, as in the case of the Congo and later of Morocco, or because of the small size and widely scattered nature of certain holdings, as in India, or because of the impracticability of customs collections, as in some parts of West Africa. As regards these non-assimilated colonies, however, France endeavored to establish a policy of imperial preference and whenever possible, as in Tunis, to aim at assimilation.[141]

In the opening years of the twentieth century, approximately three-fourths of the external commerce of French colonies was done under a régime of assimilation. The effects of this policy were not beneficial to the colonies, with the possible exception of Algeria. Most of the assimilated colonies complained that their interests were being sacrificed to those of France. In truth, in most of the small colonies, as in Gabon and New Caledonia, assimilation meant an increase in prices equal to the import duties; and in others, like Madagascar and the Antilles, a curbing of trade and business turnover. The only French industry to profit much from the system was cotton and even this industry might have benefited to a greater degree if colonial enterprise had been allowed to develop under a more liberal system.[142] Nevertheless, the total amount of the external commerce of French colonies (exclusive of Algeria and Tunis) increased from a total of 533 million francs in 1891 to 1242 million in 1911, and the share of France and other French colonies in that trade grew somewhat larger.

FRENCH COLONIAL TRADE IN 1911
(Exclusive of Algeria and Tunis)[143]

	Millions of francs
Imports from France	261.3
Imports from French colonies	16.5
Imports from foreign countries	323.4
Total	601.2
Exports to France	273.4
Exports to French colonies	10.4
Exports to foreign countries	357.2
Total	641.0

The use of the tariff was not the only method employed nor the only reform effected to make the colonies less of a burden and more of a boon to France. To reduce the amount of financial aid that the homeland had to give its colonies, a reform of 1900[144] granted to each colony an autonomous budget and required that each one meet its own civil and police charges. The Government was willing to help meet only military expenditures in the future.

More fundamental than this administrative reform, however, was the development of the economic possibilities of the colonies. Here private capitalists[145] and the state worked side by side. By 1914, the former had invested about 4 billion francs, or about one-tenth of all French foreign investments, in the empire. This sum was employed in all kinds of projects, but primarily in those of a commercial or industrial nature. At the same time, the state had thrown its weight behind colonial exploitation. Its largest expenditures had been for military purposes, but it had spent large sums upon roads, railways, ports, water works, and subsidies to colonial shipping. Unfortunately, most of its activity had not been very remunerative, for opposition to state ownership had been so great that private concerns had obtained a hold over "paying" enterprises and the state had had to indulge in public works of a social or political, rather than of a profit-making, nature. In Algeria, for example, railways most likely to pay had been built by private companies, interest on the capital of which had been guaranteed by the state, and the state had been left to build and operate the poorest lines. The best instance of co-operation of state and private interests was perhaps in the erection of the eight colonial banks. These institutions were private, joint-stock companies, but in return for the right to issue notes the state reserved the power to name their governors. The state was a party to the extension of the activities of the *Crédit Foncier* to Algeria and subsequently to the establishment of colonial land banks and mutual agricultural societies.[148] An earnest effort was made to put the colonies on a paying basis and to make of them real assets to the national economy. Just how successful governmental policies were in attempting to realize this end is an almost insoluble problem, but it is one that will be discussed in Chapter IX.

FOREIGN INVESTMENTS AND NATIONAL INTEREST

In addition to colonial expansion, French economic power was reflected during the Third Republic in a large increase of foreign investments. In 1880, total French investments abroad were about 13,-170,000,000 francs; in 1913, they were 44,640,000,000 francs.[149] The means by which France amassed this large, so-called "surplus capital" for investment outside the national confines is difficult to understand in the face of commercial statistics that reflect a large excess of imports over exports.

SPECIAL COMMERCE IN MILLIONS OF FRANCS[150]

Year	Imports	Exports
1871	3566.7	2872.5
1880	5033.2	3467.9
1885	4088.4	3088.1
1890	4436.9	3753.4
1895	3719.9	3373.8
1900	4697.8	4108.7
1905	4778.9	4866.9
1910	7173.3	6233.8
1913	8421.3	6880.2

There are, nevertheless, various reasons to make one believe that the unfavorable balance of trade was not so great as these figures indicate. No allowance was made in them for shipments of precious jewels, border exchange of agricultural products, smuggling, or French goods in the possession of travellers leaving France. Moreover, goods in transit, which had been warehoused in France, were included in the special trade statistics; parcel-post packages were given an arbitrarily low value; and exports were almost always evaluated at less than the real value in order to decrease the amount of *ad valorem* import duties collectable in the importing country. A questionnaire sent to members of the *Commission permanente des valeurs en douanes* indicated that the import figures should be increased by about 3 per cent and the export, from between 5 and 15 per cent to arrive at the true totals. If this correction be made, France's balance of trade for the years 1880–1913 would be improved by 10 billion francs, which would represent nearly one-fourth of French foreign investments in the period.[151] If specie transfers, receipts from tourists, transportation earnings, and all other invisible items are taken into consideration, it is probable that France received enough capital from abroad to offset her foreign investments.[152]

Difficult as an accurate analysis of the balance of French trade and payments is, France obviously had large sums available for investment abroad. It has been estimated that from one-third to one-half of all French savings found an outlet for investment in foreign lands.[153] The tendency of French entrepreneurs to finance their enterprises out of surplus, and the policy of the Bank of France to discount commercial paper for small sums, lessened the national demand for capital and kept internal rates low,[154] while the high returns on foreign loans overcame a traditional French hesitancy to take risks. Finally, the development of large banks, with their elaborate machinery for placing capital, accelerated what otherwise would have been a slow process.[155]

The political significance of foreign investment was recognized early in the nineteenth century. In 1823, the Government undertook to supervise the listing of the securities of foreign states on the Bourse and in 1873 reaffirmed its policy. Then as the stocks and bonds of foreign private companies began to be quoted on the exchange (1858), the Government by a decree of 1880 insisted on control over them.[156] This control proved in operation to be a powerful weapon in foreign policy: the government encouraged loans to France's friends and placed an almost complete ban on investments to her enemies. Thus Belgium found it easy to secure French capital, but Germany discovered it to be almost impossible. Investments were used to wean Italy away from Austria-Hungary and Germany, to secure a foothold in Morocco, and to keep Russia in the Gallic sphere of alliances. To the latter power was lent 25 per cent of all French foreign investments, a sum so great that after 1887 a borrower had frequently to satisfy both the French and Russian foreign offices before securing any French capital.[157] The geographical distribution of French foreign loans indicates in a general way the political use to which they were put:

GEOGRAPHICAL DISTRIBUTION OF FRENCH FOREIGN LONG-TERM INVESTMENT[158]

Country	Billions of francs 1900	Billions of francs 1914
Russia	7.0	11.3
Turkey	2.0	3.3
Spain and Portugal	4.5	3.9
Austria-Hungary	2.5	2.2
Balkan States	0.7	2.5
Italy	1.4	1.3
Switzerland ⎫ Belgium ⎬ Netherlands ⎭	1.	1.5
Rest of Europe	0.8	1.5
Total (Europe)	19.9	27.5
French Colonies	1.5	4.
Egypt ⎫ Suez ⎬ South Africa ⎭	3.	3.3
U. S. A. ⎫ Canada ⎬ Australia ⎭	0.8	2.0
Latin America	2.0	6.
Asia	0.8	2.2
Total	28.	45.

Over one-half of the total French foreign investment was in foreign government securities—in fact, France was more willing than any other state to lend to governments. The private investor was attracted by high interest rates paid on these bonds and by their freedom from taxation. Much of the capital thus invested went to weak and corrupt states, where there was less competition for making loans than in the more stable ones, and to nations which were spending beyond their means. Perhaps only a half of these government loans were used for productive purposes (railways, canals, public works, etc.); the rest were employed to meet current expenses.[159] The political significance of this procedure is obvious; it was possible largely because of close co-operation between the French government, French banks, and the Bourse.

The effect of foreign investments on French national economy was at first looked upon as beneficial, provided, of course, the investments were sound. Unfortunately, the risk was frequently very great. The theory that the reputation of the banks negotiating loans would be a guarantee of their safety was soon seen to be fallacious. Banking institutions made a profit from floating foreign securities and inasmuch as the earnings from risky undertakings were larger than those on conservative investments and the risk was passed on to the banks' customers, the bankers frequently threw caution to the winds. When a foreign loan was too precarious, the government sometimes intervened, but its action in this sphere was unimportant. Hence, losses on foreign investments were great and counterbalanced the benefit of high interest returns.[160] Moreover, default on foreign loans resulted in a net loss to the nation, for in this case the homeland had nothing to show for its trouble except paper, whereas a default on domestic loans resulted in the nation's having something tangible left in the way of production equipment.

Lastly, the theory that foreign loans would cheapen imports and increase exports was also not substantiated in French practice, unless very indirectly. France could buy and did buy her foreign supplies in the cheapest market, which was not necessarily that to which capital had been loaned, and her borrowers followed the practice of making their purchases in the world's markets and not necessarily from

France.[161] After 1909, the government attempted to get orders for French goods in return for loans (common stock of the United States Steel Co. was kept off the Bourse because of the corporation's refusal to grant such concessions), but comparatively little could be accomplished in this respect to secure beneficial results.[162]

Foreign loans, instead of bringing new business to France, helped to develop production in other states which were in direct competition with the French. French-financed enterprises abroad were generally not staffed by Frenchmen, because the French did not emigrate in large numbers, and they were not managed with the idea of increasing business with the homeland.[163] Furthermore, capital exports meant a depletion of the savings available for the development of French production and caused interest rates to be higher than they otherwise would have been. They had the effect of keeping wages low, as was pointed out by the socialists; this fact reduced the domestic market for goods on which entrepreneurs made a profit;[164] and there was not a compensating reduction of prices. The total effect of French foreign investments was, therefore, not very beneficial in increasing French production or in raising the standard of living in France. Nevertheless, there was no strong opposition to lending abroad before the World War and even the extensive defaults of the 1914–18 period did not curb for long the export of capital. The usefulness of loans in winning political allies and the hope for gain have caused France since the re-establishment of peace to pursue much the same policy that she pursued before 1914.

THE WORKER AND NATIONAL INTEREST

Analogous to the neglect of France's national interest in the export of capital was the disregard shown for the welfare of the working classes. Only a comparatively few persons in the middle of the nineteenth century believed that the state should intervene in economic affairs to improve working conditions with the aim of establishing a healthier and more powerful national economy. Economists of the liberal school taught that the individual laborer could best work out his salvation if left to his own devices, and, because this doctrine coincided so well with the selfish interests of businessmen, it was closely followed in practice.

There were, however, certain currents wearing away the opposition to social legislation. National economists, like Cauwès, declared that state action was necessary for the amelioration of working conditions, if French economy were to grow stronger.[165] Some liberals were converted by humanitarian arguments to this view[166] and many bourgeois statesmen were impressed with the importance of social legislation for national economy, as exemplified by the functioning of the German social insurance laws.[167] The growing importance of socialism, both as a theory and as a movement, forced to the attention of public opinion the case for labor.[168] The case had its logic, for increased industrialization with its long hours of labor, unhealthy living and working conditions, the absolute dependence of the proletariat on wages for existence, accidents, strikes, periodic business depressions accompanied by unemployment, and a standard of living for workers that had improved but little since the middle of the century were to be seen on every hand.[169]

From 1841 to 1874, practically nothing of a lasting nature was done by the state to ameliorate the conditions of workers. In the latter year, however, the spell of lassitude was broken. Then the employment in factories of children less than twelve years of age was prohibited; the working day for those between the ages of twelve and sixteen was limited to twelve hours; and factory inspectors, paid by the state, were appointed to oversee the execution of these provisions. In 1892, the working day for children under sixteen was limited to ten hours, for those between sixteen and eighteen years and for women to eleven hours, and for men to twelve hours. In 1900, the maximum working day for all persons was reduced to ten hours—a limit that was not altered before the World War. In 1898, a law on labor accidents established the responsibility of the employer to compensate the victim according to a fixed schedule in proportion to the seriousness of the accident, and, in 1910, a *Caisse des retraites* (optional social insurance) was created. Other less important laws provided for the abolition in its entirety of the workers' passbook (*livret*) (1890), mine inspection (1890), safe and hygienic conditions of labor (1893, 1903), a six-day week (1899, 1906), the conciliation of labor disputes (1892), the creation of an *Office du travail* (1891), and of a *Conseil supérieur du travail* composed equally of employers, employees, and politicians (1891, 1899), and old-age relief (1905).[170]

National interest was probably not a primary consideration in the voting of these laws, but inadvertently, at least, the French state resorted to interventionism for the improvement of social conditions. With some exceptions, French workers were willing to accept reform on a national basis. They ignored, as their syndicalist friends indicated, the interests of the world proletariat and the revolutionary ideal in admitting the wisdom of national legislation in social matters. As has already been stated, Jaurès favored protective tariffs, if something could be obtained by them for French labor. The labor class generally found in the protectionist arguments a logical basis for the exclusion of foreign laborers who hoped to better their lot by immigrating to France. It was largely because of the demands of labor that foreign workers were limited to 10 per cent of those employed on public works (1894), and that the registration of foreigners was required in France (1888, 1893)—a requirement by which the foreign labor supply was to be controlled.

To a degree, then, social conditions and labor welfare were recognized as part and parcel of the national economic system. The importance of this fact is greater than might appear at first sight. It meant, if carried to a point where it dominated socialist thought, that effort should be concentrated on a national revolution rather than on a world revolution and that the resulting socialist state should be founded on a national base. It meant that under the present system labor could expect some consideration and that its affairs would be regulated with thought for the good of the national economic system. It was a stage in labor thought that was an immediate precursor of fascism.

CHAPTER VIII

ECONOMICS OF THE WORLD WAR[1]

CHARACTER OF THE PROBLEM

THE World War broke out in a Europe in which national economic policies were in the ascendency. *Laisser-faire* and free trade, the dogmas of the so-called "classical economists," were being supplanted by state interventionism and protectionism.[2] Social legislation, control of foreign investments, national equipment programs, subsidies, capital advances by the state to private concerns, investment of state funds in economic enterprises,[3] and high tariffs gave ample evidence of the trend of the times. The basic theory of national economists, that national economic strength is measured by productive capacity and that productive capacity can be increased by state aid, was gaining ground. So well established and so favorably regarded was this doctrine, that businessmen and workers appealed to it frequently when they desired legislation for their own benefit.

These principles and practices conditioned the course that war economy took. In general, the war may be said to have accelerated and accentuated the developments which had been in evidence prior to 1914. But the exigencies of the war crisis, as well as the temper of the times, were important factors in determining the formation of policies. The intense national feeling that the war engendered and the necessity of using every ounce of national strength for stemming an invasion that was thought to endanger the very existence of France and of civilization led to a degree of state economic control that previously would have been thought impossible of attainment. In many respects, a nice parallel can be drawn between the situation with which the French Revolutionary Convention was confronted and the one with which France was faced from 1914 to 1918. In both cases critical military circumstances, national patriotism, and extraordinary economic needs gave rise to programs that were in their essence strikingly similar. The Revolution and the World War mark, indeed, the high spots of national economics in French history. War has proved to be the largest of state economic enterprises.

In view of the enormity of the war-time economic problem, it is strange that France had made almost no preparations for it. The economic machine which came into being during the conflict was not pre-arranged. Its parts were forged and assembled and its operation tuned up as necessity demanded. Consequently, the economic history of the war does not fall into any very rational scheme—it is confused and complicated. In spite of this fact, however, it is possible to discern three major organizing principles—first, an effort to restore some order in an economy that was disrupted by the advent of war; secondly, an endeavor to harness and develop national economic power; and thirdly, an attempt to realize interallied economic co-operation.

The first of these principles, the restoration of economic order, characterized the period from July, 1914, to the first months of 1915. This was the time when each side was endeavoring to secure an immediate and complete military advantage over the other and when little thought was given to a long-range economic conflict. France muddled through these months with her main economic concern a return to a modicum of normal activity. But when it became apparent that the struggle was to drag on and that the economic strength and resources of nations would be as important as military proficiency,[4] the French began to realize that, if they were to meet the crisis successfully, they would have to obtain the maximum amount of power from their economy. They saw that they would have to have sufficient credit to finance necessary undertakings; that they would have to have adequate transportation facilities; and that they would have to regulate the commerce in and speed up the production of the necessaries of war and of life. From the spring of 1915 to the end of the war, France devoted her energies to the accomplishment of these tasks. The impossibility of achieving them without foreign assistance, however, became apparent in 1916. From the fall of that year, a definite effort was made to secure interallied economic co-operation and by the end of the conflict considerable progress had been made in this direction. It is around these problems and the measures taken to solve them that the economic history of the World War centers.[5]

The evolution of the state's war-time economic policy can hardly be understood without a knowledge of the kinds of government which France had from 1914 to 1918. The fact that the French executive was weakened by all manner of vicissitudes in the first part of the war and that a virtual dictatorship was established in November, 1917, sheds much light upon the development of the economic program. A close relationship existed obviously between the power of the Government and the economic measures which were taken. Thus it seems advisable to make a brief survey of war governments before attempting a description of the national economics of the war.

The opening of hostilities in 1914 found a ministry headed by the Radical-Socialist Viviani in power and the Parliament concerned with the levying of a heavy income tax and the repeal of the three-year military service law. The declaration of war, however, adjourned immediately all issues except those of invasion—party policies were left in abeyance after Jaurès' peace action failed. The one issue before the nation was to meet the invader; all parties and all statesmen recognized the imperativeness of the danger. After the first defeats in the field, Viviani reorganized his Cabinet, and formed a *union sacrée* of all political elements. Delcassé, Briand, and Millerand were brought into his new ministry and even the Unified Socialists, who previously had refused all Cabinet co-operation with bourgeois politicians, delegated the anti-militarists, Guesde and Sembat, to represent the revolutionary working classes.

The oneness of purpose that lay behind this action was conducive to dictatorial action and, in fact, the constitutional order was set aside from August 4 to December 22, 1914. The legislature abdicated to the executive. It gave the Government the power to open credits by decree, to modify contracts, to establish financial moratoria, and to continue the autocratic powers constitutionally accruing to the executive through the declaration of a state of siege. In this period, the ministry took those measures which were necessary to meet the crisis without con-

sulting the legally delegated representatives of the nation; and while
at Bordeaux the ministers, in their turn, surrendered much of their
authority to the military. From the last of August to the first of October, 1914, "the civil power allowed itself to be eclipsed by the military power."[6]

The *de facto* dictatorship that was thus established did not, however, continue with its authority unimpaired. From January, 1915,
to November, 1917, Parliament gradually regained some, but never
all, of the prestige and power that it had enjoyed in peace time. In
August, 1915, Millerand resigned as Minister of War as a result of investigations conducted by parliamentary committees, and, in October
of the same year, Socialists withheld their support of the Cabinet. This
situation led to the formation of a new Government under Briand
(October, 1915)—a government of "all the talents"—and to sharper
parliamentary attacks. An attempt was made to allow Parliament to
exercise its right to criticize the Government by having Cabinet members appear before parliamentary committees, but this device soon
proved unsatisfactory. Many of the deputies were not members of
committees, and those who were realized that their hands were tied.
They could criticize, advise, and argue with the Government under
this system, but they could not direct its policies nor overthrow it.

For these reasons a new solution to the war relations between the
Cabinet and the representatives was sought. During a short period the
Chamber, sitting as a secret committee, was allowed to interpellate
the ministry and to have commissioners at the front. But this arrangement, although it allowed criticism of the conduct of affairs, was
not satisfactory. It was necessary to have a strong executive, and parliamentary control enfeebled it. Briand endeavored to overcome the
difficulty by setting up a "war committee," but this body was unsuccessful in cutting through the dilemma, and in the extremity, he asked
that legislative power be delegated to the Council of Ministers. Parliament refused the request and Briand resigned, March, 1917. He
was followed by the veteran Ribot; and Ribot was succeeded by
Painlevé. Both men encountered the same difficulty that their predecessor had experienced. Parliament made the life of the executive almost unbearable. Finally, when Socialist opposition to the Govern-

ment undermined the *union sacrée,* it was almost impossible to carry on. Painlevé resigned November 14, 1917, after a formal vote of Parliament. This was the first Cabinet since the beginning of the war that had been cast out by such action.

The return of Parliament to a semblance of its former power created a situation of governmental inefficiency and impotency that neither Parliament nor the nation wanted. Strong action and stern measures were obviously necessary. The times required a man who could make capital of the fundamental temper of the country and escape being hamstrung by Parliament. The man who was found to perform this task was Georges Clemenceau. He came to the premiership in November, 1917, and held office until January, 1920; his was one of the longest-lived ministries in the history of the Third Republic. From the first, he was able to restore the authority of the executive. He did not have to make constitutional changes to accomplish this end—he imposed his will upon Parliament and upon the nation. Unlike his predecessors, he made no concessions to the Socialists of the opposition; he recognized their hostility and ran roughshod over it. He had the confidence of the country—that sufficed. The most extraordinary power that he asked was the right to legislate "by decree in the whole domain of the country's economic life,"[7] and that demand was granted to him February 10, 1918. Under Clemenceau, the powers of the executive reached their acme; under him, too, the national economic action of the state attained its height.

FINANCIAL POLICIES

The same factors that permitted the development of an authoritative government are reflected in the economic history of the war, especially in the financial phase of it. Early in 1914 a credit crisis had threatened and the outbreak of the conflict precipitated it. French and Russian bonds fell rapidly and brokers indulged in short-selling of both stocks and bonds. In view of these developments the Bourse was closed, July 31, 1914, and the settlement of brokerage accounts was postponed to August 30. This move contributed to creating a shortage of liquid capital and to runs on banks. To avert the impending panic, the state declared moratoria on debt payments (July 31,

1914) and the Bank of France suspended specie payments.[8] The financial world was in great confusion. The state measures did not remedy the situation much; they only altered its character.

The greatest difficulty was the immobilization of the money and credit markets and no one was anxious to risk his fortune in breaking the jam. In the emergency, private banks shied away from making discounts and businessmen were embarrassed in meeting their current obligations. Such conditions could obviously not be allowed to continue and to the Bank of France must be given much of the credit for the re-establishment of private financing. This institution had a reserve of over four billion francs in the spring of 1914—a reserve that constituted a veritable war chest—and it did not hesitate to use its funds for patriotic purposes. It liberally rediscounted pre-moratorium commercial paper, which private banks fearfully refused to keep; it issued new bank notes to refurnish the depleted supply of cash;[9] and it made advances to the government for the financing of the war.

Largely owing to the Bank's activity, business dragged itself laboriously from the morass into which the war had plunged it. The Bourse was opened on December 7, 1914, for cash trading and the Bourse moratorium was declared at an end in October, 1915. Restrictions on the withdrawal of bank deposits were made less stringent and after January, 1915, were not taken advantage of by most of the big banks. The moratorium on debts was limited to persons who had been called to arms; only the moratorium on rents remained virtually intact. Thus a semblance of normality was restored to the money market. Business experienced financial difficulties after this, but it encountered nothing so severe as the crisis in the first months of the war.

In public finance, there was a similar period of confusion at the beginning of the war. At that time, no one had any conception of the total expenditures the state would have to make before peace was declared. The general belief that the war would last but a few weeks, or at most several months, did not lead many Frenchmen to give the matter serious thought. Concern was shown for the situation of the moment—the future could take care of itself. This was the attitude of the Government, as well as of the rank and file of the nation; it was a position reinforced by a capitulation of power to the military in 1914. Thus it was that at first no serious measures were taken to raise taxes to meet the new expenditures nor to draft a rational plan for borrowing. Recourse was had to the simplest means at hand for getting money—the immediate payment to the state of tax and other public moneys held by various bureaus; advances on tax anticipations; advances from the Bank of France; and the sale of short-term National Defense Bonds that were essentially treasury bills. From the last two sources came 3,900,000,000 francs and 1,288,334,000 francs, respectively, in 1914. These were enormous sums when one considers that the budget for that year was only 5,192,000,000 francs.[10] Yet, when added to ordinary receipts, these amounts were not sufficient to cover expenditures. The annual cost of running the war mounted rapidly from 10.4 billion francs in 1914 to 22.1 billion in 1915, to 36.8 billion in 1916, to 44.6 billion in 1917, and to 56.6 billion in 1918.[11]

These staggering figures precluded the possibility of a "pay as you go" policy. The temporizing measures of the first year of the war indicated the financial policy that France was to adopt. Haphazardly the country drifted into a position where it had to raise money for carrying on the conflict largely by borrowing instead of by taxation. The following table for the period from the beginning of the war through 1919 makes this amply evident:[12]

1. Budgetary receipts.   *Millions of francs*
   a. Permanent budgetary receipts 32,194
   b. Exceptional budgetary receipts
        (war profits tax and sale of stocks) 2,666
                                                                    ———
                   Total 34,860
2. Borrowings, less reimbursements (which is probably
   30,000,000,000 too low because of an official error)......... 175,520
                                                                    ———
                   General total 210,380

Taxation, as a source of revenue, was of course not ignored. An income tax was applied January 1, 1916; a war-profits tax was established July 1, 1916; a turnover tax was set up July 31, 1917; a luxury tax was levied December 31, 1917; and tax rates were raised on De-

cember 30, 1916, July 31, 1917, December, 1917, and June 29, 1918.[13]
In spite of these new taxes and increased rates, however, the yield
of French taxes during the war period was small:[14]

	Billions of Paper Francs	Billions of Pre-War Francs
1913	4.1	4.1
1914	3.4	3.4
1915	3.3	2.4
1916	4.1	2.2
1917	5.7	2.2
1918	7.0	2.1

It is no wonder, therefore, that borrowing had to be resorted to.
The advances from the Bank of France amounted to a total of 25,-
500,000,000 francs and those from the Bank of Algeria to 235,000,000
francs by the end of 1919.[15] The amount of outstanding war-time,
short-term National Defense Bonds and treasury paper was 48,052,-
200,000 paper francs in December, 1919;[16] the internal funded debt
increased from 1914 to the end of 1919 by 71,474,000,000 paper
francs;[17] and the foreign debt was 67,076,000,000 paper francs at the
end of 1919.[18]

The use of these tremendous sums for purposes of destruction meant
a great loss to the national wealth of France. Capital that had been
amassed through a long period of labor was destroyed in four short
years. France's position as a creditor nation was exchanged for a debtor
one. A large portion of her foreign investments was sold. Those who
had held foreign bonds or private domestic ones were now loaded
down with government paper. The individual investor may not have
lost immediately by the transaction, but the nation certainly had.

Ultimately the problem of settling an enormous debt had to be
faced. Obviously this could only be done over a long period of time
in three ways—by taxation, or by inflation, or by repudiation. Repudiation might strike out the debts, but except for foreign ones, it
would be of no advantage to the nation. Inflation would put the
debtor (the state) in a more favorable position to pay and would reduce the debt—thus acting as a form of taxation on previously saved

capital. Taxation was politically difficult, but had to be looked forward to as a mortgage on the future. Only if France had financed the war to a greater extent by foreign borrowing and then resorted to repudiation, could she have escaped from the predicament she was in. As it was, the war consumed vast amounts of capital. France's financial position was much weaker in 1919 than it had been in 1914.[19]

Nor did these billions which passed through the French treasury represent by any manner of means the total cost of the war to the nation. Losses in property and men and decreased production for several years must be included in the balance sheet. If everything is taken into consideration, the cost, that is at best a rough estimate, reaches fantastic heights.[20]

MEASURES TO INCREASE PRODUCTION

As the shock of war threw confusion into the financial life of the nation, so, too, it disrupted the productive processes. The calling of 2,887,000 reservists to the colors between August 1 and August 15 so depleted the personnel of factories, offices, and shops that 47 per cent of such establishments closed their doors and those which remained open had only 34 per cent of their former payrolls employed.[21] Farms, already to begin harvest, were faced with a shortage of male labor and had to do the best they could with the services of women and children.

In these early days of the great military drama, the common belief that hostilities would not last long caused the authorities to think that army stores, supplemented by those articles which could be procured in a routine way or be purchased abroad, would be sufficient to meet the demands of the military. Therefore, at first, no great effort was made to harness the economic power of the nation for war. No control was exercised over the use of raw materials; non-essential luxury manufacturing was allowed to continue; and little state assistance was offered to French producers aside from permitting advances to them for three-fifths of the value of an order.[22] In January, 1915, industrial establishments of the non-invaded regions had only 57 per cent of the personnel which they had had prior to July, 1914, and their production had declined by more than 50 per cent.

As the war dragged on and assumed more and more the character of an economic struggle, the attitude of the French toward production changed. They began to place more credence than ever in the national economic theory that productive power was the basis of national power. Production, in fact, came to be considered the real sinews of modern warfare. Moreover, in addition to the obvious need of providing the fighting machines with adequate supplies, there were other reasons for placing emphasis on production. Goods manufactured in France would keep prices down, so it was believed; allied nations would be able to get a larger share of the war materials produced in neutral countries if French demands were reduced; and home manufactures, by restricting imports, would prevent the exchange rate from going against the franc. Hence the French did much to accelerate the speed and to increase the volume of their production.

A noticeable change in France's policy toward production was effected toward the middle of 1915. By a decree of July 15 of that year a definite effort was made to stimulate the national output of goods—to effect an "industrial mobilization." The aim of this move was not to deprive capitalists of their property or of their profits nor to curb high salaries to French workers—private interests proved too powerful all through the war to realize such ends. The purpose of it was to get war supplies, especially munitions, from industrial establishments which had not previously produced them. To make the transformation in plant equipment necessary for the production of new goods or to construct new factories was costly and risky, and with the tightness of the money market, especially in moments when things looked black, as in 1917, private concerns found the obtaining of capital for such purposes difficult. It was to meet this need that the state agreed to make capital advances or to give subsidies to war industries up to the following limits:

Artillery	130,000,000 francs
Powder	35,000,000 francs
Aeronautic	3,500,000 francs
Engineering	300,000 francs
Total	168,800,000 francs[24]

As time went on, it became apparent that government aid in financing war industries was not sufficient to obtain the desired results. Private initiative proved inadequate to meet the emergency and the state had to intervene to provide direction, discipline, and control. Even those persons who, under normal circumstances, opposed government interference in business, declared state intervention in the crisis inevitable, necessary, and even "inspired by genius."[25]

The complicated nature of the Government's economic action makes treatment of it difficult. Bureaus and committees were created, reorganized, and abolished with alarming rapidity; rules were laid down, contradicted, and ignored as conditions changed; controls were established, enlarged, and altered. But out of this maze of regulation a general trend of development may be discerned. The goal at which the Government aimed was the production of war materials and of the essentials of life; and however confusing measures taken may have been, the attainment of the goal was the main concern. This fundamental idea must ever be kept in mind.

At the beginning of the war, official bodies were charged with the investigation and study of economic problems. The Ministries of Commerce, Agriculture, Labor, and Foreign Affairs, especially, expanded rapidly to cope with the problem of securing economic information; and the Ministry of War frequently duplicated their endeavors. As the problems became more and more technical, new bodies, which included men of affairs, were created alongside the central departments. These new organs, of which there were 291[26] at the end of the war, were called "commissions," "committees," or "offices." An "office" in theory usually enjoyed a government subsidy and financial autonomy; it could go into the market and do business. For example, the Office of Agricultural Reconstruction, created in December, 1917, was given the task of loaning money to farmers for the purchase of livestock, seeds, and fertilizers, and the Central Office for Agricultural Chemicals, set up February 4, 1918, was instructed to obtain machinery and chemicals.[27] "Committees" and "commissions," on the other hand, were consultative bodies which in some instances might take administrative measures on their own initiative. "The interdepartmental Commission on Cotton . . . composed of representatives of

the principal ministries and of the Headquarters Staff, and of manufacturers and dealers" could ascertain the needs of the industry, determine the quantities of raw material to be imported, and fix sale
prices.[28]

Then, as economic problems became still more complicated and
their solution more pressing, a closer co-operation between the state
and the business man was sought. This was obtained by the creation of
"consortiums." These were associations of manufacturers or commercial men interested in a certain industry who were brought together
under state supervision to control the securing, the distribution to
manufacturers, and the working up of raw materials. The first organization of this kind was established in 1916 and others soon put
in their appearance. They had funds of their own, so that, except in
rare instances, they did not rely upon the state for financial resources.
They put order into the purchase and distribution of raw materials.
Moreover, they could see to it that only those industries producing
war goods or necessities could obtain supplies. Finally, that local resources might be better exploited and flexibility given to orders from
the central government, regionalist consultative economic committees were established, August 31, 1915, and regionalist Associations of
Chambers of Commerce were organized, August 25, 1917.[29] It was
thus through the functioning of these bodies that the state endeavored
to control capitalist enterprise and to harness the industrial production for one end—victory.

LABOR IN THE WAR

In no small measure the success of the production program depended
on labor. This was a very vital problem in view of the man power
that was needed for military duty. During the course of the war,
France mobilized 7,935,000 men, or 20 per cent of the total population
of the country—a tremendous drain upon her productive labor supply. Moreover, the withdrawal of large numbers of men from civil
occupations by the first mobilization orders resulted in the closure of
many establishments, and these shut-downs caused, in turn, the unemployment of about 2,000,000 civilians.[30] Finally, this large group of
people without work was swelled by 900,000 refugees from the war

zones. France was faced with the anomalous situation of having factories closed because of loss of employees, and workers who were
placed on relief because no jobs were to be had.[31]

Under such circumstances state intervention appeared necessary.
To meet the crisis occasioned in 1914, the Government established the
Office Central de placement des chômeurs et des réfugiés (November, 1914). The duty of this organization was to allocate the unemployed and the refugees to sections where there was a labor shortage.[32] As adjustments of the first serious labor problem were made,
and regional, departmental, and municipal employment agencies were
established, the *Office Central,* instead of actually placing workers in
jobs, directed the activities of the local organizations with a view to
the labor needs of the entire nation.

In 1915 the Government was presented with a problem that was
almost the complete reversal of the previous situation. Instead of having to find jobs for the unemployed, it had to secure workers to meet
the demands of increasing production. One of the measures taken by
the state to cope with this new emergency was to encourage feminine
labor to lend its aid to industry. In this matter, it was not entirely unsuccessful, for by July, 1917, 29 per cent more women were employed
in industry than in 1914; and in armament manufacturing and government services the increases were many times greater.[33] Helpful
as this new supply of labor was, it was not sufficient to meet the need,
and beginning in 1916 the Government brought foreign laborers to
France.[34] From July 1, 1916, to January 1, 1919, industry received 81,-
897 of these workers and agriculture 133,000 (men, women, and children). And these numbers were increased by the importation of 140,-
407 colonial laborers.

Most of these workers were fit only for manual labor; skilled workers were still in great demand, especially in munitions plants. It was
decided, therefore, to bring back from the front many of the highly
trained men, who had been drafted in the wholesale mobilization of
1914, and to place them in industry. This practice was begun on a
large scale in the summer of 1915. It was controlled by the Under-
Secretary of Artillery and legalized by the Dalbiez Law (August 17,
1915). In a few months about half a million formerly mobilized men

were employed in the manufacture of war supplies—a number that did not fluctuate greatly to the end of the war. Other mobilizable men were allocated to agriculture, railroads (especially to handle American troops and supplies in 1917), mines, and the marine; and in harvest season, an additional number of soldiers was given temporary leave. On January 1, 1918, nearly a million and a half men, who might have been in the trenches, were employed outside the army.[35]

One of the results of this practice was to place on agriculturalists more than their share of actual fighting. After 1915, the number of industrial workers killed in action was much less proportionately than the losses of agricultural workers—a condition that gave rise to a certain amount of bitterness.[36] Ill-feeling also developed because the men from the army in civil production were paid the same wages as civil workers, while soldiers received a mere pittance. The Government thought it unwise, however, to alter either of these practices for fear of lessening production. It could not gamble with creating labor troubles. Under the existing circumstances, there were plenty with which it had to cope.

One characteristic difficulty concerned the working conditions and hours of female labor. Existing laws regulating these matters were set aside in the interest of greater production, but as abuses developed, it was obvious that the Government would have to intervene. The Ministry of Munitions, therefore, set up the Committee of Female Labor (April 21, 1916) which, by an enlightened policy of social welfare, handled most of the issues at stake.

Another problem concerned wages, for they failed to advance as rapidly as prices, and labor knew that it could secure increases because of the emergency. To avert disputes concerning them, the Minister of Munitions established minimum-wage scales (January, 16, 1917) for all the industries with which the Government had made contracts. Finally, and most important of all, there was the question of strikes. They were not very numerous until 1917, but then they became a real menace. The establishment of minimum wages was, of course, one way to avert difficulty, but the Government did not stop there. It created, January 17, 1917, permanent arbitration and conciliation commissions to which all disputes in industries important to the prosecution of the war had to be taken before there could be either strikes or lockouts. These commissions, which numbered sixty-one in November, 1917, performed important services in correcting conditions that might have led to trouble and in settling controversies that had attained an acute stage.[37] It was essential that nothing interrupt the production of materials destined for the front.

FOOD CONTROL

Hardly less serious than the problem of providing war materials for the army was the question of supplying the nation with food. Such a grave concern was it, in fact, that the government could not trust it to private enterprise; it had to deal with it directly. Four avenues of attack were open—regulation of consumption, increase in agricultural production, prohibition of the exportation of foodstuffs, and purchases abroad. Into all four of these the government entered with vigor. At the very beginning of the war customs duties on foodstuffs were suspended in order to encourage their importation; grain was bought by the state abroad; and the exportation of food and other products vital to the life of the nation was forbidden.[38] Simultaneously the *Service du Ravitaillement* was created to give direction to the control of food. The importance of this organization developed rapidly and it became a ministry, September 15, 1917. It was given charge of military food-supply, December 21, 1917, and was connected for greater efficiency with the Ministry of Agriculture, December 24, 1917.

The *Service du Ravitaillement* attacked with resourcefulness and energy the problems before it.[39] Four important laws regulated its activity: the law of July 19–22, 1791, which gave the state the right to fix prices of bread and meat—but of no other articles; the law of October 16, 1915, which authorized the Government to requisition French grains at an arbitrary price for the civil population and to make purchases of wheat in the colonies and foreign countries; the law of April 20, 1916, which permitted the fixing of prices for and the requisitioning of sugar, petroleum products, potatoes, milk, margarine, alimentary fats and oils, dry vegetables, fertilizers, copper sulphate, and sulphur, and the creation of a separate treasury account for the purchase and sale of these goods; and finally the law of February 10, 1918, which gave the state complete control over combustibles, the merchant marine, and the production, commerce, and consumption of foodstuffs. By virtue of these laws various restrictions were placed upon consumption. There was in the first place price regulation of bread and meat. Then wholesale prices of the articles enumerated in the laws of 1915 and 1916 were fixed; and finally, when this move proved to have an undesired effect on production, the 1918 law led to the establishment of maximum prices.

Thus the cost of living was to some extent regulated and kept down. But the limited supply of goods would have resulted in greater increases if rationing had not been resorted to. Beginning in 1917, bread and sugar were rationed and curbs were placed upon the use of meat, milk, eggs, wine, olive oil, etc. Some of these foodstuffs could not be sold on certain days of the week; others could not be used by manufacturers; others were reserved for invalids and children; and some were sold under restrictions in bakeries and restaurants. Propaganda was used for the purpose of reducing the wasting of bread and encouragement was given for eating more of the cheaper articles of consumption, like potatoes, beans, and lentils. The percentage of the whole grain of wheat which could go into bread was increased considerably and rye, barley, and buckwheat were used for flour.[40]

In these ways, much was done to make what stores of food France had suffice; but the providing of a bare minimum at a reasonable price was not always easy. The need for greater agricultural production was always present. The invaders occupied agricultural territory that produced in normal times 50 per cent of the French sugar-beet crop, 20 per cent of her wheat, 25 per cent of her oats, etc.;[41] other factors caused a decline in production that amounted to nearly 60 per cent for wheat, 37 per cent for oats, and 67 per cent for sugar beets in 1917;[42] and food consumption increased to unprecedented heights.[43] The situation necessitated government intervention and the Government did not ignore its duty.

The problem that confronted the state was a particularly difficult one; it was believed necessary to increase production, but at the same time to keep prices down. These two aims were antithetical, for to fix prices of agricultural products at a low figure naturally discouraged farmers from raising more produce. Thus the establishment of a low price for wheat in 1914 led to a decrease in wheat acreage in 1915, but to an increase in the acreage of oats.[44] It seemed that the government attempts at trying to provide cheap food were going to deprive the nation of the very things it needed. The difficulty was partly overcome after 1916 by establishing fixed prices for all leading agricultural products; and yet prices were kept so low (lower than prices in the world market which the state was paying for foreign purchases)[45] that there was little profit-making incentive for agricultural expansion. Farmers endeavored to force the government to raise prices by keeping their products off the market, but their attempt was foiled by the laws of October 16, 1915, and August 3, 1917, which authorized the state to requisition crops for feeding the civil population.

Harsh as the lot of farmers was in the face of this situation, it was made much worse by the fact that they had to pay war-time prices for machinery, fertilizers, and labor. Therefore, the state tried to help them out of their difficulties. Mention has already been made of the efforts to provide an adequate labor supply for the nation, and agriculture, of course, benefited from the measures taken—the establishment of employment offices, the employment of women, and the importation of foreign labor. Agriculture was served especially in this matter by the *Office National de la Main d'Œuvre Agricole,* which was opened March 15, 1916. It was aided further by a governmental policy of using prisoners, wounded soldiers, and certain other classes for farm labor; by giving soldiers leave in harvest time; and by sending out soldiers in gangs to perform such tasks as plowing and harvesting.

There was, however, a shortage of farm labor throughout the conflict and efforts were made to overcome the deficiency by the use of machinery, employment of more fertilizers, and the cultivation of abandoned lands. Subsidies were given to farmers' syndicates for buying machines, instruction in their use was provided for, and special allotments of gasoline were permitted to owners of tractors.[46] The *Office Central des Produits Agricoles,* not established until June 20,

1918,[47] endeavored to secure adequate supplies of fertilizers (an impossible task at the time) and to control their distribution. The law of October 6, 1916, allowed the state to requisition abandoned lands and to give the use of them to farmers who would work them. This scheme had, however, scant success, because the newcomers usually had no financial resources. It was not until May 4, 1918, that a fund was established for making loans to these people, but the entire undertaking was outrageously expensive and added but little to production. All these measures, to say nothing of minor aids like the providing of seeds for planting, coal for running threshing machines, restrictions on slaughtering, etc., did not achieve, however, the desired result. France was forced to buy large quantities of foodstuffs as well as other goods abroad—and this necessity led to government control of foreign commerce.

GOVERNMENT CONTROL OF FOREIGN COMMERCE

French imports nearly doubled from 1914 to 1915,[48] so great was the need for supplies of all kinds. This tremendous influx of goods, which was to increase rapidly to 1920, placed an almost insupportable strain on French resources. There was difficulty in securing enough shipping tonnage to handle the traffic; there was the problem of financing purchases without devaluating the franc in foreign exchange; there was competition with Allied countries in buying abroad; and there was the danger of importing unnecessary articles. How France endeavored to overcome these obstacles makes an extremely complicated story, but one in which certain measures stand out as high lights of a fairly consistent policy.

In order to insure imports of materials needed for the prosecution of the war and the elimination of non-essentials, Parliament granted the Government, first, the right to raise customs rates and to establish prohibitions by decree (May 6, 1916), and then forbade the bringing to France of any foreign merchandise except that purchased by the state (March 22, 1917). These laws, particularly the second, gave the Government complete control over the import trade, yet they were not stringently applied. In fact, a *Comité des Dérogations* was created to grant exceptions to the rules, and it provided some leeway by classifying imports into the following categories: (1) those which could be imported without hindrance; (2) those which had to come in under a quota system; and (3) those which had to secure a special license.[49]

The task of determining what goods should be allowed to enter the country fell at first to the lot of the committees referred to above. They endeavored not only to decide what the needs of the nation were, but also to centralize purchases and to allocate goods to those who could put them to the best use. These rather loose organizations performed a useful function, but the need for more efficiency and greater accomplishments led to the establishment of *consortiums*. These bodies were in many respects like the committees, but they had the additional power of making direct purchases and of distributing goods by the control of sales. They covered metallurgy, cotton, petroleum, paper, jute, and many other articles.

The activities of the consortiums, committees, and offices frequently overlapped and their efforts were often confused. In order to correct these faults, the Executive Committee on Importations was set up, December 15, 1917, and the Superior Commission on Foreign Purchases, March 8, 1918. They endeavored to prevent any consortium from purchasing too much of one article, to see that shortages were met, to establish import priorities, and to keep purchases within limits financially practicable. Thus the state, through its agencies, became the sole importer in France; it had complete control over the goods which were brought in, over their purchase abroad, and over their distribution within the country.

Great as were the advantages resulting from this centralization of, and planning for, imports, the foreign-trade problem was only partially solved by these measures. There was, for instance, the drain on the franc occasioned by these imports. To have allowed the franc to sink would have meant paying more for goods obtained abroad, so the state took measures to protect its currency. In the second half of 1914, when action was needed to bolster the foreign-exchange rate of the franc, the Bank of France used 400,000,000 francs of its gold to establish foreign credit for importers.

The Bank realized, however, that this process could not go on for long, for its supplies of bullion were limited. So when the franc began to decline in February, 1915, recourse was had to other measures. In the first place, Great Britain and France agreed to co-operate in the use of their gold reserves for regulating exchange, and London, with all its experience, equipment for handling capital, and world-wide connections, was made the center for the settlement of Allied accounts. This agreement, which dates from April, 1915, simply provided a better means of employing available gold, but gold still had to be used. In order that the state might most advantageously employ the supplies at hand, private export of gold was prohibited (July 3, 1915) and bankers were urged to prevent the expatriation of capital or to provide exchange for other than necessary commercial transactions. A more strict control was established over foreign exchange by the laws of August 1, 1917, and April 3, 1918, so that it was almost impossible for private individuals to export capital.[50] At the same time an effort was made to mobilize French capital resources that could be used for establishing foreign credits. A campaign was instituted to bring gold out of hiding to the Bank of France— a campaign that netted 2,400,-000,000 francs; foreign stocks and bonds were bought up by the state; and loans were made in foreign countries. These measures had undoubtedly the desired effect. The franc which had an exchange value for the dollar of a par at 5.18 was quoted at 5.45 in December, 1918.

At the beginning of the war it was hoped that an extension of France's export trade would suffice to pay for imports and that thereby the franc would not be endangered. The *Office National du Commerce Extérieur* gave information to French citizens concerning markets, which the Germans and Austrians could no longer supply. Fairs for the display of French goods were opened in Paris and Lyons; French industrialists were encouraged to imitate German and Austro-Hungarian export articles; and a ship, loaded with samples of French and English products, went to South America in the hopes of securing the erstwhile German markets there.

This desire to take advantage of the military situation for securing new markets, however, was soon eclipsed by the necessity of war production, and the export problem took on another complexion.[51] From the spring of 1915 to the end of the war, the Allies exerted every effort to keep from their enemies any goods that could be of use to the military or civilian populations. France forbade the importation of enemy goods (September 27, 1914) to injure enemy trade, and she established new contraband lists, and finally prohibited all exports to her opponents (April 4, 1915). As a further precaution to prevent supplies from reaching the Central Powers and to retain necessary goods for themselves, the French joined the Allies in establishing importing companies in Switzerland (*Société Suisse de Surveillance Economique*) and in the Netherlands (*De Nederlandsche Oversee Trust Maatschappij*), and agreements were made with other groups, like the *Corporation des Négociants de Copenhague* and the *Chambre des Industriels Danois* in Denmark to receive all goods exported from Allied countries and to see to it that these goods did not find their way to the enemy.[52] These measures and the maritime blockade of the Central Powers were extremely effective in arresting enemy foreign trade.[53]

OFFSETTING THE INADEQUACY OF TRANSPORTATION

Closely connected with this problem of regulating foreign commerce and with the task of stimulating production was the question of transportation. The war placed new and extraordinarily heavy burdens on French carrying equipment both on land and sea. At the beginning of the conflict, transportation, like all other branches of economic life, suffered an upheaval. The railways were requisitioned and placed under military control (August 4, 1914) according to plans that had been drawn up long prior to the outbreak of war,[54] but the moving of troops and war supplies was the only thought in the minds of the men then in charge and they suspended for a time all commercial traffic. The long continuance of this situation was impossible and measures were soon taken to make possible ordinary carrying over the lines that remained outside the army zones.[55] By the end of November, 1914, attention was being given to commercial transportation and by the end of March, 1915, "normal" conditions for the war period were nearly established. The state made a serious attempt to control and integrate the railways for national use.

The history of railways in this period had a parallel in the case of the merchant marine. At the inception of hostilities, many French ships were frightened off the seas and a partial stop was put to overseas transport. The Ministry of the Marine endeavored to assuage the anxieties of ship-owners by explaining (August 17 and 29, 1914) that the danger was not great, for German men-of-war were bottled up by the superior British and French fleets, and that the profitable carrying formerly done by Germany was awaiting the coming of French vessels.[56] Most important of all, perhaps, the state guaranteed to insure ships up to 80 per cent of their value, provided they were insured in regular commercial companies for 25 per cent of their value (August 11, 1914). These measures, in addition to others that aimed to provide sufficient man power for the crews, aided the *reprise* of maritime carrying. A few requisitions were effected in this early period,[57] but the state was not successful in assuming immediately complete direction, control, and use of the merchant marine for the best interests of the nation.

The immense importance of maritime commerce to France necessitated a change in this state of affairs. Whereas Germany was forced to rely largely on her own resources for war materials, France drew heavily upon neutral and Allied countries for the products she needed. Fortunate as she was to be able to pursue such a course, she was embarrassed from the early days of the war at providing sufficient shipping for her imports. The necessity of transporting colonial troops to France and of importing war supplies in 1914 was met by the navy's requisitioning ships, that resulted chiefly in a reduction of the postal and passenger services.[58] With the beginning of the German submarine campaign[59] that took a toll of 300,000 tons up to 1916[60] and with the increased need for food and war materials from overseas a premium was placed upon ships and upon the national use of available tonnage.

In an effort to meet this new challenge, a *Section du Transit Maritime et des Affrêtements Généraux* was established, September, 1915, in the Ministry of War. Its services were valuable, but the pressure for more stringent control increased continuously. France lost by war causes 442,167 tons in 1917 and for the entire war period from all causes 1,088,668 gross tons—a tremendous proportion of a fleet that amounted in July, 1914, to 2,498,285 gross tons.[61] These losses threatened disaster. In a frantic endeavor to ward it off, one official maritime body after another was set up—each with more power than the last. Finally, a virtual dictator of transports was created by the establishment of the Under-Secretariat of Transports, December 27, 1916.[62] This organization was supplanted by the Under-Secretariat of Maritime Transports, June, 1917, directed by de Monzie, and over it was established, January 29, 1918, the Commission of Maritime Transports.

These administrative organizations indicated an earnest attempt to extend state control over shipping; but the real test came in meeting the problems that arose. In the first place, there was the task of replacing lost tonnage. Shipyards, which had been at first turned into munition plants, were encouraged by the extension of easy state credit[63] and by being supplied with specialized workers to return to shipbuilding; and although they were handicapped by lack of materials, especially steel plates, they managed to construct 155,792 gross tons during the war. Purchases of 188,837 tons were made abroad and 92,383 tons were constructed on French order in foreign countries. This tonnage, augmented by 60,000 tons of sequestered enemy vessels and by 342,947 tons in the French state fleet (acquired by purchase and construction), gave France a total of 2,249,000 tons at the conclusion of the war. This figure was only 250,000 tons short of what it had been in July, 1914.

Important as the replacement program undoubtedly was, it was subordinated to the control of carrying for war purposes. In the spring of 1916 measures were taken to prevent French vessels from engaging in commerce that was not of specific value to the prosecution of the fight. The autumn of the same year witnessed the introduction of official control over departures and the establishment of priority lists. On August 15, 1917, French ships leaving the homeland had to have a license—a regulation that was extended to Allied and neutral vessels, September 17, 1917. Shipping officials co-operated with the Executive Committee of Importations, after it was created (December 13, 1917), in allocating carriers for the goods most needed. All ships were placed under the orders of the Under Secretary of Marine Transports, December 22, 1917, and finally all French vessels were requisitioned by the state, March 10, 1918. Gradually the state established itself as the sole shipper in France. Its clients were the various government organizations which needed materials—consortiums, food-supply administration, war department, etc. It was only by creating such an organization, it was believed, that available equipment could be made to render its maximum.

INTERALLIED ECONOMIC CO-OPERATION

Import demands of France were so great, however, that the monopoly of shipping, the replacement program, control of trade and all the other measures which were taken did not suffice. Tremendous obstacles were in the way of France's securing the goods she needed and it ultimately became apparent that those obstacles could only be overcome by Allied economic co-operation. Slow as the Entente powers were to realize this fact, its truth was forced upon them and they achieved a unity of effort that was vital to the final victory.

The first evidence of a willingness of France and Great Britain to co-operate in economic matters was presented early in the conflict. On August 15, 1914, these two nations created the *Commission Internationale de Ravitaillement* (C. I. R.) for the purpose of exchanging information concerning the purchase of army supplies—especially the purchase by France of goods in England—in order that there might be no increase of prices resulting from competitive bidding. Soon the Commission was making joint purchases for the two countries; and then Italy was admitted (September, 1915), so that its buying could be handled in the same fashion. An extension was given to this Interallied co-operation by an Anglo-French accord of August, 1915, for the purchase of wheat in common, by Anglo-Franco-Italian agreements for the joint buying of sugar, February, 1916, and by a Franco-Russian deal for the exchange of basic articles.[64]

Useful as these measures were, however, they did not cope adequately with the problem of securing materials for the Entente belligerents, or of allocating them where they were most needed, or of shipping them. Many Allied statesmen realized this inadequacy and urged a pooling of economic resources. This point of view was made clear at the Preparatory Allied Economic Conference, March 27-28,

1916, but at the Paris Allied Economic Conference, June 14-17, 1916, the most vital issues were dodged. Nevertheless, the idea of common economic action made progress. In May, 1916, the French and English made an arrangement for the supplying of coal to France at reasonable rates; Great Britain consented to aid her Allies in their maritime carrying; an Allied Chartering Committee was established to secure neutral tonnage;[65] and Allied gold stocks were pooled in an effort to maintain favorable exchange rates.[66]

A somewhat slow but unmistakable evolution toward Allied economic co-operation took place in 1915 and 1916, as these acts indicate, but up to the autumn of 1916 this development had definite limitations. No *guaranties* were given for mutual assistance in supplying raw materials and tonnage—all action in these spheres was based on friendly agreements—and Great Britain showed little willingness to co-operate with France for providing for more than military needs. The demands of the civil population had to be met by individual action in a free market. The next move to be made to effect Interallied economic unity was, therefore, to get guaranteed mutual assistance in supplying materials and tonnage for civilians.[67]

An encouraging step in this direction was the creation of the Interallied Wheat Executive, November 27, 1916. This organization, which was one of the earliest and best examples of Allied economic union, resulted from an agreement among France, Great Britain, and Italy to pool their buying of wheat, to allocate supplies according to needs, to pay the same mean price, and to use available ships in proportion to requirements.[68] The principles involved in this accord were extremely significant, for they indicated a willingness on the part of the three powers to make individual sacrifices for the welfare of others. This same spirit of co-operation was given further expression, December 3, 1916, by an agreement between Great Britain and France. The former power consented to send more coal to France, to ship railway cars and locomotives across the channel in order to facilitate moving stocks from the ports, and, most significant of all, to use her shipping in co-operation with her Allies.[69] This last concession meant, in reality, the employment of British ships in the carrying of goods to France and Italy and consequently a diminution in the amount of tonnage available for transporting necessaries to the British Isles. Such a sacrifice on the part of the British was of the deepest import.

Unfortunately, however, the first attempt at effecting an Allied pool of shipping proved unsuccessful. The Interallied Shipping Committee, created in January, 1917, to survey carrying needs and to ration tonnage among the three great powers, discovered that there was not sufficient control over shipping in the individual countries concerned to permit effective super-control and that the Committee lacked the authority necessary to carry out its recommendations. Consequently, the body vanished from the scene, but the need for co-operation was so great that hope for its realization did not die. In March, 1917, France had a wheat reserve sufficient for only twenty-two weeks and England's supply was capable of meeting demands for only eight weeks. Moreover, the Allies had lost by the autumn of 1917, 17,000,000 tons of shipping (Great Britain's loss alone was 10,000,000 tons) and the British construction program was not well under way.

In the face of such extremities, it is not surprising that Allied representatives met frequently throughout 1917 in an effort to overcome the obstacles to economic co-operation. Nor were these meetings entirely unsuccessful. In August the Meat and Fats Executive was created to perform the same task for meats and fats that the Wheat Executive was performing for wheat, and plans were drawn up for more bureaus of a similar kind for other products. Moreover, Great Britain consigned ships for French carrying in moments of great need and fulfilled the terms of earlier agreements. Finally in November, 1917, lengthy conferences of Allied representatives, including American delegates, were held that resulted in the establishment of organizations that would definitely effect the pooling of Allied economic resources. One of these organizations was the War Purchase and Finance Council,[70] the purpose of which was to pool Allied financial power and to obtain credit from the United States' treasury. The second was the Allied Maritime Transport Council, which was at last to realize the much-needed amalgamation of all Allied shipping and the disposal of that shipping where the need was greatest.

The organization of the Allied Maritime Transport Council profited much from the experience of the abortive Interallied Shipping Com-

mittee. It was composed, unlike its predecessor, of ministers or responsible agents of Allied states who could take authoritative action
for their respective governments. Nor did the Council encounter the
difficulty which had handicapped the Committee of being faced with
the inability of the various states to control their shipping, for individual nations had by now established complete jurisdiction over their
merchant marines. Therefore, the Council did not have to attempt
the actual operation of fleets, save for about 500,000 tons of chartered
neutral shipping,[71] but could pass on its recommendations to the co-
operating countries with an assurance that its wishes would be carried out. The Council, working through its Executive in London, arrived at decisions concerning the whole maritime situation which
would result in the best use of vessels for the entire Allied cause. A
construction program was laid down, purchases of ships were made,
and tonnage was allocated for duty where the need was most pressing.[72]

For an intelligent use of ships it was necessary to have authentic information concerning Allied requirements. To obtain it, "program
committees," similar to the Wheat Executive, were established for
various goods, as is shown by the accompanying chart. In each country corresponding bodies were created, if not already in existence, to
determine national needs. Subsequently some of the program committees were placed, for greater efficiency, under centralized authorities, like the Food Council and the Munitions Council, but all of them
co-operated in preparing schedules of requirements and in scaling
down their demands to conform to available shipping facilities. These
organizations were extremely important, but because the realization
of their programs was usually contingent upon maritime carrying, the
A. M. T. C. soon attained a dominant place in Allied economic co-
operation. Its key position gave it control over the main sources of
supply. The Council met periodically throughout 1918 to discuss problems as they arose and to make alterations in schedules as demands
changed. Between the meetings of the Council, the Executive handled
the day-to-day issues that were presented to it. A detailed account of the
Council's activities would be out of place here. Suffice it to say that
France profited greatly from them. When the Armistice was signed,

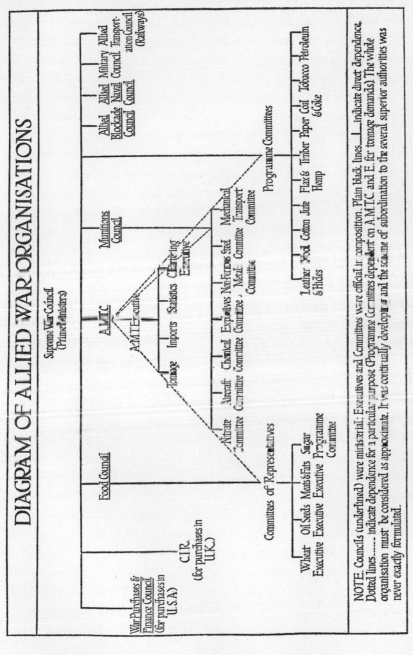

DIAGRAM OF ALLIED WAR ORGANISATIONS

NOTE. Councils (underlined) were ministerial. Executives and Committees were official in composition. Plain black lines ___ indicate direct dependence. Dotted lines...... indicate dependence for a particular purpose (Programme Committees dependent on A.M.T.C. and E. for tonnage demands.) The whole organisation must be considered as approximate. It was continually developing and the scheme of subordination to the several superior authorities was never exactly formulated.

Reprinted with permission. From J. A. Salter, *Allied Shipping Control* (Oxford: Clarendon, 1921); *Economic and Social History of the World War* (Ed. by James T. Shotwell for the Carnegie Endowment for International Peace).

she was using 780,183 tons of English shipping, 315,000 tons of American shipping, and 962,987 tons of neutral shipping. These vessels were carrying about three-fourths of all her maritime commerce. Without them she would probably have been unable to carry on. Undoubtedly Allied economic control performed an absolutely essential task.

In the last months of the war, those who had Allied co-operation close at heart were looking forward to the problems of reconstruction. Orders were issued some time previous to the Armistice instructing shippers to cease loading the goods needed for war immediately upon the cessation of hostilities. But a much more fundamental question was the chief concern of the Allied powers. Would the Allies continue to pool their resources after the signing of the Armistice? The French and to a degree the English were anxious for them to do so, but the United States wanted a free market in which to operate. This was amply shown in negotiations carried on in December, 1918 and January, 1919.[73] The European needs for food were so pressing, however, that an Allied Supreme Council of Supply and Relief was set up in January, 1919, in Paris, which was replaced by the Supreme Economic Council in February. These bodies supplanted in a large measure the Allied Maritime Transport Council as the central administrative, economic organ, but they lacked its experience and efficiency. Evidences of the disruption of Allied economic solidarity were apparent on every hand, for the victory had been won and the binding forces of a common cause had been torn away. In December, 1919, America and Britain refused to provision France with foodstuffs and coal out of an Allied pool. This decision marked the end of close economic co-operation among the victors; and the remaining Allied organizations were soon allowed to disappear. The French were dismayed at this course of events, but could do little but lament it. Clémentel expressed well the sentiment of his countrymen when he wrote:

"We believe that because of this error the peace is incomplete. It lacks the spirit of high altruism, of disinterested co-operation among the Allies which ought to be brought to bear against ex-enemies and to permit during the long and perilous period of national and world economic reconstruction the continuation of the generous effort which contributed to the victory."[74]

CHAPTER IX

POST-WAR NATIONAL ECONOMICS

THE IMMEDIATE AFTERMATH

As the "generous effort" which had marked Interallied economic co-operation during the war disappeared with the defeat of Germany, so, too, victory destroyed the economic organization within France that had been established for patriotic purposes. October 24, 1919, was fixed as the official date for the end of the war and marked the death of those decrees, laws, and organizations which had been created "for the period of the war." Fixed prices and requisitions were terminated, July 1, 1919, except for the wheat supply. Railways were returned to their former owners, January 2, 1919. Consortiums, "offices," and committees were washed away by a wave of reaction against state control. Economic freedom was generally re-established by February 24, 1921. Only a very few of the war-time creations—such as the public employment agencies and the petroleum service, to which reference will be made later—were continued, but in a reorganized form. Yet most French economists, in spite of everything, realized that in time of national crisis state intervention is imperative. But the degree of that intervention, it was felt, should be in proportion to the seriousness of the emergency and, in the flush of victory after four years of terrible stress, the emergency did not seem to be very great.

The state's abandonment of its war-time economic measures did not mean that the French government was to adopt a thoroughgoing policy of *laisser-faire*. What it did mean, however, was that although France would relinquish her strict supervision of the conduct of business and permit a comparatively free interplay of economic forces at home, she would lend her support to increasing national production and, in correct national economic fashion, would aid French inter-

ests in their competition with foreigners. Ample proof that this was
to be the new policy was provided at the Peace Conference when definite efforts were made to diminish the economic strength of the Central Powers, especially that of Germany, and to augment the production of the Allies, particularly that of France.[1]

ECONOMIC BOOTY IN THE PEACE TREATIES

The French demands at the Peace Conference for economic spoils
were great, too great indeed to secure the approval of some of the dele-
gations who had to rely upon the future to settle many of the questions that could not be decided at Paris. In the problem of reparations
this situation was well portrayed. The French supported the English
contention that Germany should be held for the meeting of all "war
costs," while the Americans insisted that she should be responsible for
paying only "war damages."[2] Although the French finally conceded
this point, after it had been decided to include pensions and separation
allowances in "damages," they refused to fix a definite sum that Germany should be required to pay. They argued that it was impossible
to determine at that time the amount of "damages," but, while there
was much truth in this belief, other reasons conditioned this point
of view. France wanted relief in the near future for her reconstruction burdens and she wanted to demand the maximum possible from
her vanquished foe.[3] The task of fixing the amount of the indemnity
was therefore left to the Reparations Commission which presented a
war bill far in excess, as experience has shown, of Germany's ability
or willingness to pay.

France looked to her needs also in determining the nature and
amounts of deliveries in kind. She insisted that Germany give her at
once certain articles as compensation for the destruction which had
taken place and for the requisitions which had been made in occupied
territory. To this end she secured provision in the treaty for Germany's
sending to her reconstruction materials, livestock, machinery, and
equipment of various kinds.[4] She shared favorably in the partition
among the Allies of German shipping and she benefited, like her
Allies, in the decision to maintain in force war measures that in-
fringed on German patents.[5] Moreover, she secured the delivery of

coal from Germany for ten years to an amount equal within limits to the difference between current production and pre-war production of destroyed French mines and, with Belgium and Italy, she obtained an option on German coal equal to pre-war exports of coal to these countries. Finally, she was to receive an option for five years on German exports of chemicals and dyestuffs. It was hoped that these provisions would allow France rapidly to regain her place in the international economic sun and at the same time would serve as brakes upon Germany's industrial revival.

In the territorial settlement at the Peace Conference, France's position was also conditioned by economic ambitions. This was true of her demands for that part of French Equatorial Africa which had been ceded to Germany in 1911 and of her desire to obtain a portion of the Cameroon and Togoland. In Syria, she had her eye not only on trade but also upon Mosul oil, as was shown by her attempt to divide with Great Britain the petroleum resources of the Near East by the San Remo agreement (1920). In the case of Alsace-Lorraine, France's claim was largely sentimental, political, and strategic, but it was fortified by economic considerations. Alsace had important potash deposits, a well-established textile industry, and in Strasburg an inland port of the first order. Lorraine possessed one of the finest iron-ore fields of Europe as well as an important metallurgical industry. All of these things France wanted in order to fortify her national economy. But the securing of them did not satisfy her ravenous appetite. She made a strong plea for the acquisition of the Rhineland with its important coal and iron deposits and its industry. When this demand failed, she insisted that at least she obtain the Saar basin with its coal —an almost indispensable complement to the iron of Lorraine. So tenaciously did Clemenceau cling to this demand that President Wilson threatened to withdraw from Paris if he did not moderate his attitude.[6] In the *impasse* a compromise was reached whereby France was given ownership of the coal mines, the territory was to be administered by the League, and at the end of fifteen years a plebiscite should determine the political future of the district.

In these ways France extended her territorial possessions with the hope of augmenting her economic power. But she did not stop here.

She lent her weight at the Peace Conference to policies which deprived Germany of important industrial or commercial areas, like part of Upper Silesia and the Polish Corridor, and she obtained certain guarantees concerning commercial relations with her ex-enemy. According to the terms of the Armistice, Germany was kept in a state of blockade until the signing of the peace and France hoped to limit the amount of certain raw materials which would be sent her even after that.[7] The realization of this particular hope was blocked at Paris by other nations, especially by the United States, but France secured plenty of palliatives for her disappointment in this failure. She benefited from a provision in the treaty which required Germany to apply her most favorable duties as of 1914 to Allied goods for a period of six months; she profited from an extension of this requirement for thirty months for goods that were most important in German imports before 1914; and she had the option to renounce bi-lateral treaties with Germany by simple notice within six months. For a period of five years, Germany had to receive products originating in Alsace-Lorraine free of duty up to the average amount sent annually to Germany from 1911 to 1913. Germany was also forbidden to discriminate against Allied exports and imports for a period of five years or to indulge in unfair competition (dumping and the like). Luxemburg was not to remain in the German customs union; the Rhineland, which was to be occupied for fifteen years as a guarantee for the faithful fulfilment of the terms of the treaty, was to have a tariff régime imposed by the Allies; and the Saar was to be included within the French tariff boundaries pending a definite settlement of that territory's destiny. Finally, free navigation of the Rhine River was established, which, although of benefit to the Netherlands, Belgium, and Switzerland, was of especial moment for shipping from Alsace.

ECONOMIC ILLS OF THE WAR: THE PROPOSED REMEDIES

By these provisions in the treaty of peace, France hoped to protect herself from discrimination and to augment her economic strength. The position which she took at Paris is comprehensible in the light of her suffering and the ravages of war. The index of her industrial production, which according to the normal rate of increase should have gone from 100 to 130, had fallen during the war to 60 and her agricultural production, which had remained stationary in the years prior to 1913, had fallen to 70.[8] In the devastated regions, which were largely industrial districts, 900,000 buildings (9300 of these were factories employing ten or more workers), 200 coal mines, and 34 iron mines had been damaged or destroyed, 85 per cent of the arable land had been devastated, and 94 per cent of the cattle had disappeared,[9] one half of the roads had been put out of commission, and 6000 bridges, 1500 miles of railway lines, and 700 miles of canal routes had been partially or wholly demolished.[10] The population of France had decreased from 39,200,000 in 1911 to 37,100,000 in 1921, a loss of 5.4 per cent, but there had been a loss of 11 per cent in the number of males between the ages of 15 and 50.[11] French foreign commerce had shrunk to the point where exports were only 25 per cent and imports 87 per cent of the weight of those in 1913,[12] and internal commerce, judged from the 41 per cent decline in railway and the 59 per cent decline in canal transportation, had shrunk considerably.[13] The franc had lost about 70 per cent of its purchasing power,[14] the net amount of French lendings abroad of 38 billion gold francs had turned into a net indebtedness to foreign powers of 6.8 billion gold francs,[15] and the financial position of the state treasury had become burdened with net borrowings amounting to 60.6 billion gold francs.[16] In fact, except for a few advances in the metallurgical, chemical, canning, rayon, and shipbuilding industries and in the development of hydro-electric power, the war had left France from the point of view of economic strength in a condition of extreme feebleness.

The proposed cures for the economic ills that had befallen France as a result of the war were numerous. At least each social class had its remedy, and then there were a few others for good measure. In the first place, there was the economic theory of business men—men of affairs—who knew what they wanted and worked energetically to get it. A fairly accurate conception of their opinions may be obtained by studying the programs and activities of the two most important associations of industrialists—The National Association of Economic Expansion and the General Confederation of French Production.[17] These two closely related organizations join together the leading trade associations and regional business groups of France (the latter claims to unite twenty-one general associations and 1500 trade syndicates). They declared their faith in "the same doctrine of economic liberty,"[18] but insisted that the state should aid French industry and commerce at home and abroad, because prosperity of businessmen means prosperity for all.[19] They favored protective tariffs, government aid in establishing export credit insurance, and the exploitation of the French colonial empire. They opposed cut-throat competition in the domestic and international markets, for they believed that private initiative should deal with these problems by cartels.

This position was essentially that of the Union of Economic Interests—the association of businessmen that has been most active in bringing pressure to bear in politics since the war.[20] It has maintained with vigor a defense of private property and private initiative and has opposed government control, state monopolies, and graduated taxes. It has held that social classes should co-operate rather than fight and before each election has put up alarming posters concerning the effects of socialism. It has insisted that the tax burden should be equally distributed, that there should be collaboration of businessmen in drawing up social legislation, and that the tariff of France should benefit both agriculture and industry.

The stand of the Union and of the National Association of Economic Expansion, which is characteristically capitalist, has been subscribed to since the War by any number of less important groups. Agriculturalist societies, like the Central Union of Syndicates of Agriculturalists of France,[21] have regularly passed at their annual congresses resolutions demanding higher protective rates on farm products, tax relief, and more governmental co-operation on all questions pertaining to their industry. *Le Redressement Français,* founded by businessmen, professors, and publicists, had, during its brief but active existence after 1926, a platform which included the protection of private property but called for government assistance in developing the nation economically. It published a series of inexpensive books which provided technical information for the drafting of an "economic plan" for France.

Among other organizations, which have been active in encouraging economic development on sound capitalist lines, may be mentioned the Republican Committee of Commerce and of Industry (the so-called Committee Mascuraud),[22] the lobbying organization of Radical-Republican businessmen; the Association of French Industry and Agriculture,[23] which has advised protectionist tariffs, and the closely allied *Société d'Economie Nationale;*[24] *Association pour la Propagande et la Défense des Produits Français,*[25] which, with its slogan *Achetez Français,* has encouraged the purchase of goods "made in France"; the *Société d'Encouragement pour l'Industrie Nationale,*[26] an organization for aiding inventors and stimulating technological improvements; and finally the Committee of Economic and Tariff Action,[27] which, because it has numbered among its members those who can compete successfully in foreign markets, has demanded a tariff that will allow the entry of those goods which France lacks and exclude those which she has in abundance.

Among the members of the laboring class in France there has been less unanimity of opinion concerning the economic policies which should be pursued by the state than among the capitalists. Even after the federation of French unions in the *Confédération Générale du Travail* in 1902, there were two distinct schools of thought in the organization. The one stood firm for the forceful overthrow of capitalism in a world-wide revolution and for the solidarity of workers of all nations. It would make no compromise with patriotism, refusing to support national measures, like protective tariffs that might benefit French workers. It would only be content with a classless society of the world. The other school believed that the final goal should be one of a collectivized society, but it was willing to temporize, to compromise, and to go slowly. It supported national policies that would improve the conditions of French workers, even if these same measures worked a hardship on foreign laborers.

The division between these two schools of labor thought, which was based essentially on methods of reform and on patriotism, was accentuated by the events of the war. It became so serious that a definite split of the *Confédération Générale du Travail* took place in 1922. Those who adhered strictly to the Marxian doctrine of world revolution, the use of violence, and internationalism formed the Communist *Confédération Générale du Travail Unifié*. It became affiliated with the Third International of Moscow and, as can easily be imagined, preached the establishment of a world soviet system.

The parent organization of trade unions, the C. G. T., retained those elements which were inclined toward gradual socialist reforms in the existing political states of the world.[28] This position was definitely reflected in the platform of the C. G. T., which after the usual demands for better working conditions and heavier taxes on capitalists, proposed that the state should exploit all natural wealth (mines, water power, etc.), for the profit of the collectivity and that all production should be reorganized according to a scheme of industrialized nationalization.[29] This plan envisaged the purchase, with capital advanced by the state, of all "large public services and industries of national interest" and the placing of them under the control of bodies composed of producers (workers), consumers, and representatives of the state. These managing boards would enjoy administrative and financial autonomy, but they would operate their industries to serve best the collectivity.

As temporary expedients before the realization of general socialization, the platform held that the state should control all industrial cartels and trusts and that it should support the economic interests of France in world markets. Although the C. G. T. pays lip service to internationalism and holds a membership in the International Federation of Trade Unions of Amsterdam, it is likely that, if national states become business concerns, as is suggested by the C. G. T., national economics will live on in a new form. In fact, the C. G. T. proposes what, in its early stages at least, might be the acme of economic national organization.

POLITICAL PARTIES AND ECONOMIC CURES

The economic programs of the groups noted above have been reflected with almost mirrorlike accuracy by French political parties since the War. To obtain this reflection, however, is not easy, for French political parties are numerous, have loose organizations, have titles which give a false notion of their character, and sometimes employ names for parliamentary groupings different from the ones used for electoral purposes.[30] But if analysis is limited to the most important political groups, the confusion is minimized—the parties are seen to have economic programs which are based on class differences.

The chief political organizations of the upper bourgeoisie have been since the War the Republican Federation of France[31] and the Republican Democratic Alliance,[32] formerly known as the Democratic and Social Republican Party. The programs of these two groups have differed only in that the platform of the latter has reflected a mild form of anti-clericalism, while that of the former has been Catholic. Both have been extremely patriotic and in international relations and international economics have assumed a chauvinistic attitude. They have stood for the fulfilment of the economic terms of the treaty of Versailles and for the payment of heavy reparations even to the point of forcing the debtor into bankruptcy. In domestic economic affairs, the two parties have adopted the same position as the large associations of businessmen. They have lauded the doctrine of economic freedom and have insisted that the state should not control profit-making institutions, or enter business, or give labor aid that will result in higher taxation. Nevertheless, when capitalist interests have needed the support of the state, they have not hesitated to demand it. They shroud the obvious contradiction with a halo of patriotism. They argue that the productive power of France must be increased if the nation is to maintain its place in the sun; and productive power will not be augmented if their interests are endangered.

The most important of those parties which have held an intermediary position between conservatives on the right and socialists on the left has been the Radical Republican and Radical Socialist Party[33]— a party that has not been nearly so wild as the number of "radicals" in its title would seem to indicate. In its ranks have been found members of the *petite bourgeoisie,* city workers, intellectuals, and here and there rural, anti-clerical groups. Since 1898, as was pointed out in a previous chapter, this party has almost always been represented in the cabinet, and hence has been one of the most important political groups. Its platform has included many suggestions for state intervention in economic matters that smack of socialism and in 1927, in fact, it signified its approval of the program of the *Confédération Générale du Travail*. The party has maintained that the state should continue the operation of its monopolies; should place a controlling hand on all those industries which are monopolies in fact; and should participate in the exploitation of natural resources by forming joint stock companies for their development, as was done in the case of Alsatian potash. The state should pursue a vigorous social program consisting of improving the conditions of labor, of building houses for the poor, of extending education, and of instituting an extensive system of social insurance.

The Radical-Socialists have had the economic interests of the nation close to heart. They would dare do nothing that would not increase the productive power of France, but they have given evidence that they consider the problem of distribution essential to the economic welfare of the nation. In actual practice the Radical-Socialists have bridged the gap between socialism and capitalism. Whether in a government coalition with the right or the left parties, they have furnished a leaven that has tended to keep French economic policies from going to extremes.

On the left of the Radical-Socialist Party is the Socialist group—the *Section Française de l'Internationale Ouvrière* (S. F. I. O.).[34] This party, like the C. G. T., was divided before the war by divergent schools of socialist thought—and over patriotism there was difference of opinion. During the first years of the war, however, there was relative unanimity of sentiment for *la patrie en danger*. But as the conflict wore on the former divisions were re-affirmed; and after the cessation of hostilities, they became even greater. Then the problem arose as to whether or not French socialists should follow the dictates of Moscow. On this issue the party split at the Congress of Tours in 1920. A majority of the delegates at this convention favored co-operation with the Russians, but they managed to win only a minority of the rank and file of the party to their standards. Therefore, they organized a Communist Party, the *Section Française de l'Internationale Communiste* (S. F. I. C.), which adopted a strictly non-national and workingman's program, and left their former colleagues to carry on the less drastic program with the Socialist Party.

The platform of the Socialist Party has been very similar to that of the C. G. T., for, although the two organizations have remained separate, the leaders of one have been influential in the executive circles of the other. The Socialists, like the trade unionists, have expressed a belief in the possibility of changing the existing capitalist order by evolutionary methods. They have supported the C. G. T. plan for nationalizing industry and have held that nationalization should be applied first to insurance, to petroleum and its products, to sugar, mines, fertilizers, and railways. Furthermore, the party stands for the extension of credit to farmers and the nationalization of mortgages.

The national implications of such a program, as has already been suggested, are obvious. Reform would take place within the nation, France, and there is no reason to believe that the collectivized nation could not vie with foreign powers for economic advantages as strenuously as private nationals do under a system of private capitalism. France would undoubtedly protect her home market as rigorously then as she does now because of her inability to pay for imports or for fear of becoming dependent on foreign supplies. She would almost certainly desire to keep production at a high pitch for the creation of goods necessary for war, because the danger of international conflict would surely not pass at once. Like members of other economic or political groups in France, the Socialists expect that in the struggle for control of the tremendous power which is inherent in the state, they may be successful at some time, even if it be at a distant date, to use that power for their own interests. As far as the intensity of economic patriotism is concerned, it seems as though there would be little change, if the state were used for the benfit of the many rather than for the interests of a few.

WHO GOVERNS FRANCE?

In the period since the war, however, this particular problem has not been put to a test, for Socialists have not been able to realize all their reforms. A brief review of France's post-war political history shows how general the domination of bourgeois parties has been. From 1919 to 1924, the *Bloc National,* which aimed to unite all political factions in the Chamber, as the *Union Sacrée* had done during the war, but which soon became a coalition of bourgeois parties, governed France. In the elections of 1924, however, the Radical-Socialists and Socialists, not to mention some of the smaller groups of the left, joined forces in the *Cartel des gauches* for a mass attack on the right. This group of left parties took advantage of the system of semi-proportional representation then in effect to concentrate their electoral strength on one left ticket. This manœuvre prevented the dissipation of left-wing voting power and resulted in a decisive defeat of the *Bloc National*.

The victory of the *Cartel des gauches* in 1924 proved to be relatively hollow. The Socialists refused to join the Radical-Socialists in a cabinet and subsequently abstained from voting or directly opposed the Government. This situation made it necessary for the Radical-Socialists to seek support from the right-center and prevented the giving to national policies of a real leftist character. The Cartel Government led a precarious life, for it did not have strong parliamentary support and it had to face extremely embarrassing problems, the most troublesome of which was the fall of the franc. It was, therefore, not surprising that the Cartel was overthrown and that a cabinet of National Union, formed from parties of the right-center and led by Poincaré, came to power, July 23, 1926.

The success of this definitely bourgeois government in meeting the monetary crisis won for it enough political prestige to enable the more conservative groups to emerge victoriously from the elections of 1928. They governed until the elections of 1932, when the parties of the left rose up again in their might. This time the *Cartel des gauches* succeeded once more in combining the voting strength of the left, except for the Communists, but made use of that strength in a different fashion from that in 1924. A new electoral law of 1927 had re-established the district system of election in order to avert a recurrence of the 1924 landslide, but it provided, in case no candidate received a majority in the election, that a week later a second balloting should take place in which a plurality of the votes cast would be sufficient for election. This allowed the *Cartel* to throw all its strength behind single candidates in each district in the second balloting and thereby to win a strong majority. But, as in 1924, the left victory was a pyrrhic one, for Socialists refused to join with Radical-Socialists in forming a cabinet. Once more the Radical-Socialists were faced with the problem, which had weakened them after 1924, of not having sufficient parliamentary support.

Frequent cabinet changes, excessive parliamentary bickering, several scandals involving politicians, of which the Stavisky case was the most famous, and the inability to get things done spelled the undoing of the *Cartel's* power. The economic depression and the resulting difficulty in obtaining necessary revenue complicated the situation. Extreme parliamentarianism was the object of sharp criticism; even the parliamentary form of government had its opponents. The trend of this sentiment was illustrated at the time by Doumergue's proposals for constitutional reform that would increase the power of the cabinet and by the rapid growth of fascist leagues. It seemed as though a new period in French political history was about to begin. It appeared that the bourgeoisie, which had championed political liberalism in order to break the power of the nobles and to get power into its own hands and which had been able to control the political life of the nation under a parliamentary system, had come to the realization that it could no longer maintain its dominant position by the old methods and that it would have to resort to measures of force. For the moment, many of its members supported the fascist *Croix de Feu*—an organization that attracted also some members of the proletariat with its appeal of patriotism. This group envisaged the possibility of seizing power by a *coup d'état*.

The parliamentary crisis finally came to a head on February 6, 1934, when the *Croix de Feu* staged a demonstration in the Place de la Concorde against the inefficiency of the Chamber. Whether a march on the Palais Bourbon was intended or not, it is difficult to say, but leftists evidently thought that this was the plan and prepared to prevent it by force. Serious rioting broke out in which several persons were killed, but there was no attack on the Chamber. The danger passed, but the events of February 6 brought home to the French the necessity of a strong government. The size and strength of both the *Croix de Feu* and the extreme left parties indicated that the possibility of establishing a fascist régime, which would preserve private capitalism and prevent class conflicts by force, or a communist dictatorship was not entirely illusory.

One of the immediate results of the political crisis of February, 1934, was to cast new aspersion on the *Cartel des gauches*. Numerous cabinet crises during periods of *Cartel* domination, seven from May, 1924, to July, 1926, and six from May, 1932, to February, 1934, seemed to indicate a fundamental weakness in government by the left. Moreover, the *Cartel* had failed in 1926 to settle a financial problem and it seemed impotent to meet the challenge of the economic crisis. Political and economic instability appeared, unjust as the presumption may have been, to be an inevitable consequence of *Cartel* government. Such a state of mind resulted in a swing to cabinets more to the right. They governed France until the elections of May, 1936.

The left realized the predicament into which it had fallen and made desperate efforts to strengthen its position. The move, which was most obviously necessary, was to effect a closer union among the Radical-Socialist, Socialist, and Communist parties—a union that would be willing to co-operate not only in elections but that would also be ready loyally to support a left cabinet. Although previously Communists and Socialists had refused such collaboration, they decided that, in the face of existing circumstances, it was their only salvation. The concrete results of this decision were the creation of the *Front Populaire* and a fusion of the communist trade unions with the C. G. T. The political importance of these moves was tremendous, for it made possible a new triumph of the left in the elections of May, 1936.[35] The *Front Populaire* secured a strong parliamentary majority and created a Radical-Socialist and Socialist cabinet under Léon Blum that was supported by the Communists. But after a year's time there was a drift to less radical Radical-Socialist control in ministries headed in succession by Chautemps, Blum, and Daladier—a drift that led to the destruction of the *Front Populaire* at the time of the general strike (November 30, 1938).

The immediate program of the *Front Populaire* government was less radical than might be imagined. It proposed to improve the conditions of the proletariat, to increase agricultural prices, to "nationalize" war industries, and to alter the statutes of the Bank of France in order to deprive the few largest stockholders of absolute power. Very little was said about the collectivization of private property. This issue would certainly have found a hostile reception in the Senate, where the strength of the Government was none too great, and would probably have split the *Front* asunder. The *Front Populaire,* therefore, was forced to preserve the institution of private property and, what is of particular importance for this study, envisaged reforms of an almost exclusively national character.

For the most part, therefore, bourgeois parties have been able to control the French Government since the war. In applying their will they have had the support of the higher ranks of the administrative branch of government, which is extremely powerful.[36] When the left has been in power, it has been unable to free itself from national interests. Thus no fundamental change has taken place since the war in the character of state economic measures. They have been for the most part colored by the wishes of the bourgeois, but may in the future become more highly tinged with the demands of the workers. In any case, they have maintained a definitely national complexion.

MORE NATIONAL ECONOMIC THEORY

The economic policies which France has pursued since 1918 have been conditioned not only by the fortunes of political parties but also by current economic theory, problems of reconstruction, and difficulties of the economic crisis. The interrelations of economic conditions, political control of the state, and economic theory are extremely intricate and yet they throw indispensable light upon the formation of national policies. In order that our consideration of French national economic history may benefit from that light, let us turn to these subjects in turn, with our attention first given to economic theory.

One of the leading national theorists immediately after the war was Henri Hauser. Profound and careful student of the pre-Colbertian and Colbertian periods, he had concentrated his efforts before the war on the study of sixteenth and seventeenth-century France and of mercantilism. The war, however, saw him, like many of his colleagues, drawn into the service of the state and placed in a position where he was in touch with economic reality. This experience, added to his mercantilist study, led him after the war to ally himself definitely with national economists. This was apparent from the publication of his *La nouvelle orientation économique* in 1924.[37] In this book he declared that there are no universal, eternal, and immutable economic laws, as the classical economists and their followers would have us believe, but rather that every economic situation requires its own solution.[38] A fear of famine in the centuries previous to the nineteenth gave rise to a belief in and the developing of a highly regulated and rigid economic organization. An ample supply of goods in the nineteenth and the beginning of the twentieth centuries justified credence in the theory of freedom of exchange and economic liberty.[39] But times have changed; the war devoured the world's supply of goods and left Europe in a state of famine [poverty]. This being the case it is only natural that one should lose faith in *laisser-faire* and should advocate neo-mercantilism. Economic liberty may be wise for the rich nations and will be suggested by them[40] (witness the third of Wilson's fourteen points), but it is not the policy for European nations to pursue. It may even be ideally the best thing for them, but just as one would not say to a paralytic, "Football is good for me, why don't you play?" so one should not say to the impoverished nations of Europe, "Abolish economic nationalism." "Economic nationalism is an obstacle to the circulation of goods and it is a permanent danger for the peace of the world. But it exists."[41]

"As long as peoples form closed economic entities, it will be necessary under pain of death to have a national economy; that is to secure from the national and colonial domain the maximum of foodstuffs and of raw materials that it can furnish in order to get the least possible from states which wish to have a fruitful monopoly of them; to buy the least possible from nations with dear money and the most possible from those whose exchange is equal or inferior to our own; to prevent waste by a complete utilization of raw materials and by-products, by a renewal of equipment, by a more rational organization of labor; to distribute tasks by a kind of industrial mobilization among the different elements of the nation and by a geographic division of work among the different regions; to organize the system of transportation to make cheaper and more rapid the circulation of goods in the country, the importation of raw materials, and the exportation of merchandise; to promote scientific research, both the study of pure science and the study of the economic and social conditions of production and of expansion; to insure this expansion by the presence and the action of our producers and of their representatives in foreign markets and also by treaties with other peoples based on reciprocal exchanges and reciprocal advantages. . . . In the struggle in which we are obliged to engage—since we live in a period of history in which the law is a law of struggle—a discipline is necessary, and it must be severe. Who can exert this discipline? No other authority than the state. . . ."[42]

Among French academic economists the late Professor Lucien Brocard of the University of Nancy has been one of the chief exponents of national economics in the post-war period.[43] As a student of Paul Cauwès at the Faculté de Droit in Paris, he early became convinced of the wisdom of national economic policies, but only recently put in print the result of his economic thinking. His contentions are that the region, the nation, and the world are individually *solidaire* in an economic sense; each has economic interests of its own that are in part, at least, exclusive of and sometimes contrary to the interests of the others.[44] In the course of economic history technical improvements and the desire for gain have made possible an expansion of the concentric circles of economic exploitation, and life has thereby become richer.[45] Relations among regions became closer and closer until finally larger economic units—the nations—were formed.[46] Now relations among nations are continually developing, but up to date have fallen far short of attaining the importance of relations within national boundaries.[47] Before international economy can obtain a position comparable to national economy, it must go through a period of travail as onerous as that through which interregional economy went in its development into national economy.[48] This will take considerable time because international economy is handicapped by the lack of political, juridical, and psychological supports analogous to those enjoyed by national economy.[49] The most that one can hope for is a gradual evolution of international economy along paths of peace.[50]

The main task, at all events, is to improve the condition of the individual and not the condition of any one class.[51] This can best be accomplished in the field of national economy, for "between regional economy, which has been partially supplanted . . . by national economy, and the slowly developing international economy, national economy appears to be the most coherent, the most autonomous, and the most powerful, the one whose smooth operation means the most to the other [economic systems] and to the progress of civilization."[52] Already this seemingly paradoxical realization of individualism by means of the action of the collectivity has been attempted. Unscrupulous practices, harmful foreign competition, and the exigencies of the business cycle have forced the state toward a policy of regulation, protection, and planned economy.[53] This development is in the right direction, but the nation should not let itself be dragged into state socialism,[54] nor be guided by false economic doctrines. The state should above all things develop its productive power to the limit of its resources.[55] This will necessitate the exploitation of the state's natural resources; it will mean the protection of the home market for goods produced at home and the collaboration with foreign powers for the purchase of those things obtainable only abroad; it will necessitate the surveillance of the national population and its physical, intellectual, moral, and social conditions; it will require in some cases the acquisition of new territory, although not by the use of violence,[56] and it will demand a fiscal policy that will provide a stable medium of exchange,[57] furnish nationals with sufficient capital, and encourage wise investment abroad.[58]

As can be readily seen, Brocard stands in the List-Cauwès tradition of national economic theory—a position in which he has a certain amount of company. Yves Le Trocquer, several times Minister of Public Works since the war, placed himself in the group of Cauwès followers in 1914 by the publication of *De la politique économique, administrative et financière à suivre en matière de travaux publiques.*[59] He held that the state ought to develop and co-ordinate the productive forces of the nation and to preserve its national unity—an essential factor of its power—against all disintegrating forces.[60] André Marchal, post-war student of Professor Brocard, has likewise given evidence of his approval of the fundamental concepts of this school.[61] Camille Perreau, professor of economics at the Faculté de Droit, Paris, has expressed his sympathy for the contentions of national economy. In the preface to the second edition of his *Cours d'économie politique*,[62] he maintained that although these doctrines had few partisans before 1914, "it is no longer possible to ignore their very high value and it is wise that one keep in mind, when analyzing a problem, solutions which will serve best the present and future needs of the nation." He has remained loyal to the method of Cauwès, itself influenced by that of Schmoller, of minimizing abstract and deductive theory and of substituting for it the consideration of concrete problems. This method in itself, given the national character of our times, has proved conducive of conclusions in harmony with national economics.[63]

Among French economic theorists strong strains of classical economic theory are still to be found,[64] but it is interesting to note even here a decided infiltration of national theory. W. Oualid was so impressed with this fact that in his article on Cauwès in the *Encyclopedia of the Social Sciences* he maintained that nearly all French theorists have a touch of national economics in their work. This has been illustrated by the case of Charles Rist, who, although far from being an avowed supporter of Friedrich List, has found much in the man's writings to admire[65] and by the case of Professor H. Truchy of the Paris Faculté de Droit who has maintained, "There is in the theory of free trade a gap which comes from losing sight of the fact that the nation is a collectivity which lasts, an *ensemble* of productive forces which can develop and find in protectionism a means of development."[66]

An analogous seepage of national economic theory has found its way into socialist theory. The most extravagant, but by no means the most important case of this kind is that of Gustave Hervé. Before the war he was a fiery internationalist, but during the conflict he became an equally vehement nationalist. Since the peace he has carried on a romantic campaign for nationalist socialism and has been ever ready to defend French economic interests.[67] A much more sober writer, Edmund Laskine, although perhaps not correctly classed any longer as a socialist, has endeavored to show the national forces at work which prevent proletariats of various countries from burying their differences. He has insisted especially that capitalists and laborers are tied together by common interests in production. Without production there would be no jobs for labor and no profits for capital. Hence it is that the two classes unite on national economic policies for the purpose of increasing economic activity to their mutual benefit. Capital and labor are at loggerheads concerning the distribution of wealth, but the imminent necessity of production usually overshadows this difference. At all events, the common interest of the world proletariat in distribution is a weak foundation for socialist internationalism; national forces far surpass it.[68]

The weight of this contention has been recognized by Henri De Man, the Belgian socialist. But he adds to it a belief that the increased political influence of the socialists in certain countries has resulted in concessions, social laws, and collective enterprises which give proletarians an economic stake in the preservation of their country.[69] "The more socialism becomes the embodiment of the idea of the State, the more does it also become the embodiment of the idea of the nation which is itself incarnate in the State."[70] Moreover, the working class is subject to all the forces that tend to make patriots—language, culture, historical traditions, fear of war, national school systems, and the like. National sentiment is an integral part of the emotional content of the socialism of each country. It grows in strength in proportion as the lot of the working masses of any country is more closely connected with the lot of the country itself; in proportion too as the masses have won for themselves a larger place in the community of national civilization.[71]

CONCENTRATION OF WEALTH; CLASS CONFLICT; "FASCISM"

Nevertheless, concentration of wealth has reached a point where a wide distance separates the proletarians and the upper bourgeois. Although it is almost impossible to determine with accuracy the degree of this concentration, certain available statistics provide an indication of its extent. Returns from inheritance taxes in 1902, 1903, and 1904 showed the following division of real and personal property: 98 per cent of the inheritance taxpayers owned 40 per cent of the inherited wealth; 1.7 per cent owned 34 per cent; and .12 per cent owned 25 per cent.[72] The inheritances for the year 1933 were distributed as follows:[73]

Categories (Size of inheritances)	Number of Inheritances	Net Total of Inheritances Francs
From 1 to 500 francs................	27,466	7,334,035
" 501 to 2000 francs	46,724	59,602,412
" 2001 to 10,000 francs	111,283	622,630,047
" 10,001 to 50,000 francs	119,774	2,667,885,315
" 50,001 to 100,000 francs	25,808	1,715,260,194
" 100,001 to 250,000 francs	14,838	2,223,452,626
" 250,001 to 500,000 francs	4,709	1,598,528,323
" 500,001 to 1 million francs	2,032	1,391,903,138
" 1 to 2 million francs	947	1,289,164,560
" 2 to 5 million francs	404	1,195,448,389
" 5 to 10 million francs	94	626,189,516
" 10 to 50 million francs	66	838,365,242
Above 50 million francs	2	254,091,250
	354,147	14,489,855,197

If the returns for 1926 of the general income tax, a flat 30 per cent levy which is graduated by exemptions, be taken as indicative of wealth concentration in France, it will be found that .06 per cent of those paying the tax or about .0033 per cent of the total population of the country pay 32 per cent of the amount obtained by the tax.[74]

Whatever the exact degree of wealth concentration may be, it is certain that the partition of capital is such as to provide the basis for economic classes that are poles apart. Political alignments are determined in a rough way by these classes. Among the political parties and hence among social classes a spirit of antagonism has developed. This fact has been complicated by the great number of political parties, the harsh and hostile propaganda of the partisan press, the necessity for coalition government, consequent parliamentary inefficiency, and finally the periodic inability of the state to perform its functions. Pitched battles between members of right and left wing groups, like those of February, 1934, have occurred when the government in power has been especially inefficient in getting things done.

Such circumstances have given rise to a desire to unite France socially and to create a strong government to keep recalcitrant citizens in line. Some Frenchmen have come to this position because of the great waste, procrastination, and inefficiency of parliamentarianism —especially the hopeless antics of the Chamber. Members of the bourgeoisie incline towards it because they fear the overthrow of private capitalism and because they see the possibility of not being able to control the state under a liberal, parliamentary constitution. Some members of the proletariat believe that such a reform would provide the best method of securing advantages for labor because it would strengthen the nation. Something must be done, it is thought, about these fundamental problems or France will be torn asunder by civil strife and so weakened by governmental inertia that she will not be able to maintain her high position in the family of nations.

One of the first political groups to preach the necessity of liquidating the class struggle and parliamentarianism in the interests of the nation was the royalist *Action Française*. Although this party has not made social and economic questions the real issue of its agitation, it has been drawn by its doctrine of integral nationalism to a serious consideration of them. The hope of the *Action Française* is in a plan, inspired by La Tour du Pin, to organize French society into corporations or gilds for the more rational production of goods and for the abolition of class conflict. Its economic expert, Firmin Braconnier, has taken a consistent nationalist attitude toward economic problems. He has opposed ownership and operation of economic enterprises by the parliamentary state and has sought in corporatism the salvation of the French.[75]

From out the *Action Française* stemmed a short-lived Fascist group —*Le Faisceau*—that advocated the creation of a corporative state in France. The leader of this party was Georges Valois,[76] who broke with the royalists in 1925. For a time Valois waged an energetic battle for his ideas. He insisted that the French should be organized into employer and employee syndicates; that the economic activity of the syndicates should be run by a superior economic council on the basis of an economic plan; and that the political life of the state should be in the hands of a group that would not be hamstrung by Parliament. This ambitious program, the roots of which run back through French socialist thought, won few adherents. The Fascist Movement, which was at its height during 1925-26 in the period of weak Cartel government, soon vanished from the scene.

The idea was not lost sight of, however, and a new Fascist movement—*La Croix de Feu,* directed by Colonel de la Rocque—soon lifted its head. This organization was, at first, a war veterans' society, but it and its affiliated groups—*Volontaires Nationaux* and *Regroupement National autour des Croix de Feu*—gradually assumed the character of a political body. Its members believed that the military victory of 1918, which they had helped to win, was being lost by governmental inertia and parliamentary weakness. France was divided by rival classes and rival parties. The oneness of purpose which had characterized the period of the war had been forgotten. Selfishness and sloth had taken its place. France was becoming through her own incapacity a weak prey of other nations.

De la Rocque believed all this. In a little book, *Service Public,*[77] he pointed out that serious rivalry had grown up between economic classes and that something ought to be done about it. He proposed to eliminate class friction by organizing French society into corporations or syndicates, and to achieve domestic peace by substituting for the weak, dilatory, parliamentary system a strong government. He hoped that all differences among Frenchmen would be fused in mystical faith in the *Croix de Feu* and in love for the fatherland.

The riots of February, 1934, played into the hand of the *Croix de Feu*. Its membership grew considerably during the year and it became a real force in the country. Its failure to achieve any concrete success gradually weakened it. When the Popular Front government disbanded political leagues, June, 1936, the *Croix de Feu* was transformed into the *Parti Social Français.* If it is forced to confine itself to purely political action, its future does not seem bright.

The passing of Colonel de la Rocque's movement would not, however, mean the death of Fascism in France. The concept is making progress. A steady procession of books on the subject indicates that it is securing a large following among intellectuals[78] and the continual appearance of political groups that write the principles of corporatism into their platforms shows that it has caught the imagination of some of the "men in the street," as brief mention of the leagues will show.

The *Jeunesses Patriotes,* formed in 1924 by Pierre Taittinger to fight Bolshevism and to maintain government by the right, evolved gradually toward the concept of a corporate organization for the nation.[79] Although it was disbanded with other leagues in June, 1936, it continued to carry on its propaganda through its organ *L'Ami du Peuple* and to keep its followers united in the *Rassemblement Social et National.* Closely related to this group are two leagues that owe their parentage in part to the political action of the perfume manufacturer François Coty: *Parti du Rassemblement Populaire Français,* formerly the *Solidarité Française,* led by Jean Renaud and the *Francisme* directed by Marcel Bucard.[80] The cohorts of these "leaders," dressed in blue shirts that are differentiated only by an insignia, mince no words about their willingness to use force to attain their ends—a strong nation of corporations. Equally vehement in its determination to defend the sacred rights of the peasant from Marxist tendencies is the *Comité Central d'Action et de Défense Paysanne,* formerly the *Front Paysan* or *Green Shirts,* led by Henri Dorgères—a group that suffered severe defeat in the elections of May, 1936. And equally pledged to corporatism is the *Union des Comités de Défense des Jeunesse Françaises Ouvrières et Paysannes* and its organ *La Nation Reveillée.*

These leagues or parties are usually said to be of the right, although many of their members come from the lower classes. But as in Italian Fascism and German National Socialism, the concept of corporatism in France, with its strong appeal to patriotism, has won support from proletarian leaders. Within the ranks of the Socialist Party (S. F. I. O.) there formed a group that was won to the corporate national ideal and that broke off from its parent to form the *Parti Socialiste de France.* Among Communists, too, there were those who came to disapprove of being directed by Moscow. These *Communistes Dissidents* wanted a national communist party and one of their members, Jacques Doriot, founded (1936) an organization, the *Parti Populaire Français,* and a paper, *L'Emancipation Nationale,* that virtually embraced the corporative scheme.

The creation of all these so-called Fascist leagues indicates a certain vigor of an ideal. Individual groups may come and others go, as is the case with such organizations, but the movement seems to have taken firm root. Up to the present the action of Fascist leagues has been weakened by the division among them. Appeals for union have been made and a few attempts tried. The most noteworthy effort to effect this end that was being made in the summer of 1936 was directed by the *Comité de Rassemblement Français Antisoviétique*. If it should succeed in its task, it would have at its command a force of no mean strength.

At the foundation of the economic theory behind these political organizations and in the writings of national theorists since the war, the idea that national strength and prestige are determined by productive capacity remained fundamental. The war had undermined the very base of economic power—it had left France's productive machinery in a wrecked and wornout state. All economic theorists joined in urging the necessity of a general overhauling and the French generally attacked the problem with spirit. Their energy soon produced results which had been considered impossible. To the astonishment of all, reconstruction of the devastated regions was completed by 1927,[81] and what was still more unexpected, France, in rebuilding what had been destroyed, did more than return to the *status quo ante* —she actually increased her ability to produce, for the new equipment was more efficient and more productive than the antiquated machinery which it replaced. Thus the industrial renovation of the war areas, plus the advances made during the war in other parts of the country, particularly in the metallurgical, chemical, canning, automobile, and hydro-electric industries, placed France in a strong position for international economic competition.

The recovery of France in view of the general conception of the catastrophic effect of the war was remarkable.[82] The index of industrial production[83] which stood at only 60 in 1919, reached 125 in 1926,[84] that of agricultural production (including Alsace-Lorraine), which was 70 in 1919, attained 100 in 1925, but fell back to 82 in 1926, that of railway transportation (including Alsace-Lorraine) went from 59 in 1919 to 122 in 1926, although that of internal waterways for the same period went only from 41 to 79,[85] and that of weights of exports and imports (including Alsace-Lorraine since 1919 and the Saar after 1925), increased as follows:[86]

Exports	Imports
1913.....100	1913.....100
1919..... 25	1919..... 87
1922.....103	1922.....116
1927.....166	1927.....117

Finally, the balance of trade and payments, which was very unfavorable on the morrow of the war, became favorable in 1924 and on an average remained more favorable than it had been in the years previous to 1914.[87]

The recovery of France from the abyss into which the war had plunged her was astonishing. Reconstruction brought not only a return to an economic *status quo ante,* but an increase in the nation's productive power. The years 1928 to 1930 were extraordinarily prosperous—the index of general industrial activity reached 127[88] in the former year and agricultural production was maintained at high pace. This prosperity had in it, however, the germs of an impending depression. France had increased her productive power to a point where it exceeded national consumption. "About 40 per cent of her iron and steel output and nearly half her woolen and silks" had, for instance, to be exported under normal rates of manufacture.[89] But while France had been increasing her productive capacity, other nations had similarly been expanding theirs. France could not reduce below a certain margin her prices on industrial products in order to compete in the world market, because a protective agricultural policy had aided in establishing high costs of living that necessitated relatively high wages. The possibility of increasing home and colonial consumption was limited. The most important potential purchasers of goods were workers, but they had little surplus for satisfying expensive wants and their wages little more than took care of their fundamental needs. High prices, reduced purchases by the rich, and ultimately reduced production restrained Frenchmen from making forward commitments.

These factors, undoubtedly accompanied by innumerable other causes, ushered the depression, even if somewhat tardily, into France. Beginning in 1931, evidences of a crisis were apparent on every hand. The index of industrial activity declined as follows:[90]

1929	139
1930	140
1931	124
1932	96
1933	107
1934	99
1935	94

Agricultural production did not vary greatly, but the prices of agricultural products fell to ruinous levels. Railway freight-car loadings suffered:[91]

	Daily Average (in thousands)
1930	65.4
1931	53.9
1932	47.3
1933	45.2
1934	42.5
1935	40.1

The volume of foreign trade was 11 per cent and 28 per cent less, respectively, for the years 1931 and 1932 than it had been for 1929.[92] The number of foreign tourists decreased from 1,911,107 in 1929, to 944,400 in 1932. The number of those receiving unemployment relief, which by no manner of means included all the unemployed, increased from around 1000 in 1930 to 351,000 at the end of February, 1934, and to 503,502 in February, 1935.[93]

The situation portrayed by these figures is one of crisis—of crisis in which it is natural to demand the intervention of the only collective agency to which every citizen may appeal in time of trouble—the state. Thus, directly upon the heels of the reconstruction problem, which had required the controlling hand of public authority, came a new problem that necessitated state action. The post-war economic history of France has been, therefore, highly colored by governmental economic action and, because the nation is now coterminous with the state, by national economics.

FINANCING RECOVERY—INFLATION

State action in dealing with the problem of reconstruction was vigorous from the very beginning of the post-war era. Belief in the national necessity of revived production and in Germany's paying the costs of restoration caused things to move with speed. Agencies were established to handle industrial and agricultural reconstruction, to buy goods for returning refugees, and to handle German deliveries in kind. The Ministry of Public Works undertook the replacement of destroyed roads, bridges, and public buildings. The state began, through the *Crédit National,* which was especially created for the purpose, to indemnify private persons for their war losses. This task was of prime importance, for it amounted almost to financing the reconstruction of the war districts. The *Crédit National,* which was a joint-stock company, obtained resources by appropriation from the public treasury and by selling bonds, the principal and interest of which were guaranteed by the state.[94]

The sums necessary to meet the costs of reconstruction were enormous. Up to the end of 1926, when most of the big claims had been met except pensions, which of course were to continue for a long time, total expenditures for pensions, damage to private property, damages to state property, and interest payments on unpaid damage claims amounted to 130,157,000,000 francs.[95] This figure was far greater than what France realized from reparations. The Reparations Committee credited Germany with the payment of 10,426 million marks up to September 1, 1924,[96] and Germany paid from that date (beginning of the Dawes Plan), to June 30, 1931 (Hoover moratorium which ended actually if not legally reparation payments), 10,481.2 million marks. France got 5986.5 million marks of the latter sum,[97] and a little over one-half of the former, and in addition she realized something from other debtors, but she had to pay out a goodly portion of this income to her war-debt creditors.[98] The balance which she had left for reconstruction purposes was not sufficient to pay the bill and she had to rely on other sources.

Three methods were used to raise the required sums: taxation, borrowing, and the issuing of paper money. Taxation was the least important of all, for, although increases were registered in 1920, little success in securing extra funds for reconstruction was possible when new imposts were needed to care for the ordinary expenses of government.[99] Borrowing proved more successful in raising funds for reconstruction —from 1919 to the end of 1925, bonds amounting to 44,000,000,000 francs were floated for this purpose.[100] But borrowing did not satisfy the ravenous hunger of the agents of reconstruction—the issuing of paper money held out the greatest hope.

Recourse had been had to this method of financing during the war and although the foreign exchange rate of the franc had been kept down by strong control the wholesale price index had risen 356 per cent from 1913 to 1919. Soon after the war, but only for a short period, from January, 1919, to April, 1920, there was rapid inflation. Advances of the Bank of France to the state increased 28 per cent, the bank-note circulation rose from 31.8 billion to 37.3 billion francs, and the wholesale price index went up 69 per cent. Then until 1925, inflation was not resorted to on an important scale. Finally, however, the failure of a *Crédit National* loan (January, 1924) indicated that the borrowing power of the Government had reached its limit; the financial failure of the Ruhr occupation caused the French to lose confidence in making Germany pay; and increased taxes in March, 1924, although heavy, did not yield enough to cover "extraordinary" expenditures.

Thus when the *Cartel des Gauches* took the helm in 1924, either heavier taxation, which proved impossible, or inflation was necessary. Hence a new inflationary movement began. From January, 1925, to July, 1926, the note circulation rose 38 per cent; government borrowings from the Bank of France went from 21.2 billion francs to 37.5 billion; the wholesale price index increased from 514 to 836; and the exchange rate for the dollar from 18.5 to 41. Poincaré, who came to power in July, 1926, was able to vote new taxes and to bring the situation under control in 1927. Circulation remained around 52 billion francs; the exchange rate for the dollar was established and kept at 25.52; and the wholesale price index fluctuated between 600 and 650.[101]

This inflationary movement was undoubtedly not the result of a preconceived plan but of immediate financial necessity and for this reason should perhaps not strictly be classified as a national economic policy. Nevertheless, its effects on national economy were significant. In the first place, inflation cut the public debt so that the debt charge on the French budget needed to be a sum only "sufficient to cover the increase on an amount of indebtedness approximately one-third (32.3 per cent) greater than that which was outstanding in 1913."[102] This remarkable reduction of a public debt which had been swelled by the costs of war and by reconstruction to many times its 1913 size was not accomplished, however, without some one's making a sacrifice. The burden fell on those who owned francs, who were paid money salaries, or who had their fortunes in paper the value of which was represented in francs (mortgages, bonds, savings accounts, etc.).

It is usually recognized that inflation helped temporarily to make the economic wheels of the country turn faster, a condition which has come to be regarded as a state of prosperity, although such febrile activity in the long run may not prove to be advantageous. The low value of the franc in terms of foreign exchange encouraged exports, limited imports,[103] and attracted tourists to France. It encouraged buying within the country, because people feared to hold money that was constantly being depreciated. It allowed industries to pay off their indebtedness in cheap money, although manufacturers experienced a scarcity of capital in the last years of the inflationary process. Finally, and most important of all, inflation permitted the rapid reconstruction of the devastated regions. To the rebuilding of these districts[104] may, in turn, be attributed a part of the exceptional industrial activity and economic expansion of the inflation years.

The cheapening of money aided considerably the rapid growth of the productive power of the nation. From the national point of view, inflation seemed to have many of the advantages of subsidies, export aids, and protective tariffs—and, at the same time, it had the virtue of being a tax policy. So useful did inflation or devaluation appear to be that it frequently was advocated as a national policy. Cheap money, it was argued, would provide, at least temporarily, favorable prices for national goods in the much-competed-for markets of the world and would thereby stimulate economic activity or bring prosperity at home.

Moreover, it would make easier the settlement of private debts, which might not otherwise be paid, and it would allow governments to lessen the load of their public debts. Certain nations (eleven in the summer of 1936) endeavored to secure some of the advantage of devaluation by providing especially favorable exchange rates to persons who would spend money within their borders and by controlling rigidly the exportation of capital for foreign purchases. This practice, known as "blocked currency" or "currency control," aimed essentially to attract tourists, to restrict imports, and to prevent the outflow of gold.

Other states shied away from this restrictive policy and resorted to devaluation usually when a warning was sounded by the withdrawal of gold to safer havens. The pound sterling, accompanied notably by the currencies of the three Scandinavian countries and of Japan, fell in 1931, and the dollar abandoned the gold standard in 1933. These moves were followed by the creation of the British Equalization Fund and the American Stabilization Fund for the purpose of maintaining foreign-exchange rates favorable to the exporters of these two countries.

The advantages in foreign trade that accrued to the nations with devalued currencies did not improve conditions in other states already depressed by economic crisis. In France this was especially noticeable, and the situation was made worse by a general deflationary policy from 1932 to 1936 that resulted in lower prices and lower real wages. There was, moreover, a decline in exports, a freezing of internal private debts, an increasing national debt, that grew from 264 billion francs at the close of 1930 to 370 billion at the end of 1936, and finally a lack of confidence in the franc and a flight of capital. Under these circumstances, France abandoned the previous gold standard in October, 1936, and was followed in this action by Switzerland, Holland, Italy, and Czechoslovakia.

This move was accompanied by an agreement among France, the United States, and Great Britain to maintain their currencies within certain limits. But even then there were many indications that further change would be necessary. Strikes in the summer of 1936 increased labor costs; prices went up; the Government spent money with a lavish hand; and there was no great improvement in the trade balance.

Hence it was not surprising to see the franc go down again in July, 1937, and once again to a level of 2.79 cents in May, 1938.

What the end of devaluation may be, it is difficult to say. But it should be borne in mind that the stabilization of currencies requires a balancing of international accounts with goods, while nations, in order to increase their economic power and to keep their economic balls rolling, have placed all manner of barriers in the way of imports. Furthermore, stabilization could be more easily maintained if markets were expanding and if governments did not amass great public debts that are not self-liquidating. It is not unreasonable to imagine, under existing circumstances, an international race toward devaluation with each nation jockeying for an advantageous position. But because the good to be obtained from such a policy is temporary, serious efforts may be taken to prevent a bitter international currency contest.

TARIFFS AND QUOTAS

Inflation was not and could not be relied upon to carry permanently the burden of protectionism and of subsidy for French economy. From the termination of hostilities the more traditional weapons for waging the economic battle were resorted to. Among these weapons, tariffs proved to be popular. In considering tariffs immediately after the war, the French decided that a change in their pre-war policy was necessary. They felt that the granting of most-favored-nation treatment to other peoples had been a mistake, for France imported especially raw materials, the duty on which was in any case low, and exported finished products, the duty on which, even when France enjoyed most-favored-nation advantages, remained high. They also believed that no rates should be fixed by commercial treaties which they would not be able to change easily in a short space of time.

Therefore by the decree of April 23, 1918, commercial treaties which included these two features were denounced and the Government was instructed to negotiate new commercial treaties on the basis of reciprocity.[105] That is, the Government was authorized to grant foreign nations, in return for special favors, reductions calculated in percentages of the difference between French maximum and minimum rates.

But no guarantees were given as to what these rates would be over a period longer than a year. The difficulties encountered in executing such a plan were great. France wanted to get most-favored-nation treatment, but she was unwilling to give it. The result was that she was virtually forced to grant it by giving her minimum tariff rates in exchange for favors. The "scheme of 1919" was not the success that had been expected.[106]

In the meantime, other tariff problems harassed the French. The fall in the value of the franc automatically reduced the tariff, for rates were paid in terms of the monetary standard per import unit rather than *ad valorem*. Measures, therefore, had to be taken to offset the decline of the franc. The most general practice to overcome the difficulty was a system of "coefficients of increase," which were multiplied by the existing rates. From 1919 to 1922, sixty-five decrees increased the customs duties by this method. As a protection against "exchange dumping," the large exportation of goods by countries with depreciated currency, France put up special rates and prolonged the right of the Government to raise rates by decree. The most noteworthy act taken in this regard was the decree of March 28, 1921, which raised maximum rates 400 per cent and provided a 300 per cent difference between them and the minimum rates. This measure was aimed primarily at Germany, but it hit also nations like Czechoslovakia, friends of France, with whom no commercial treaties had yet been made. With all these increases, however, the French tariff level index was 12 in 1925 as compared with 18 in 1913 and France had fallen from fourth to twelfth in the rank of nations having the highest tariffs.[107] Thus, when the record wave of post-war inflation became serious, rates (coefficients included) were increased by 30 per cent April 6, 1926, and again by 30 per cent August 14, 1926.

These rather hit-or-miss increases, the unsatisfactory working of the new commercial treaties, and changed conditions of many industries made imperative a general overhauling of French tariffs and the establishment of a more rational system of commercial exchanges with foreign powers. The difficulty of coming to a working arrangement with Germany, which was freed after January 10, 1925 from the treaty provision of granting France most-favored-nation treatment, hastened the French in an attempted accomplishment of the task. A tariff-reform bill was distributed in the Chamber, February, 1927, but because the deputies believed they had not had time to study it adequately and because they feared their special interests might suffer, they defeated it. A commercial impasse with Germany threatened and the French effected under great pressure a tariff *coup*. The Government was given power for three months (July 27, 1927) to raise rates by decree as a preparation for negotiations with Germany. This it did; negotiations were begun; and a Franco-German trade agreement was soon signed, August 17, 1927. This new treaty provided reciprocally for most-favored-nation treatment, prevented the changing of rates on some goods during the life of the accord unless there was a 20 per cent variation in the wholesale price index, and could not be denounced until March 31, 1929. The French rates which were raised before the treaty was signed and which were accepted by Germany applied exclusively to industrial goods. French agriculturalists, of course, complained of the treatment which they had received, so an "additional tariff" was passed March 2, 1928, that completed for the moment France's customs duties.

The importance of the Franco-German accord was great, for it marked France's return to an avowed policy of granting most-favored-nation treatment, of making relatively long trade agreements, and of fixing some rates for the term of the treaties. The theories which had governed French negotiations immediately after the war were, therefore, definitely thrown overboard.

On the basis of these new principles many commercial treaties were signed. The most-favored-nation clause was inserted in them and 72 per cent of the rates in the French tariff were fixed by them.[108] While this new customs régime, which extended favors to competitors and made it more difficult than formerly for France to raise her rates whenever she wanted, was being established, events were taking place that made embarrassing the position into which France was putting herself. Other nations were engaged in raising their rates and many went off the gold standard, which meant that it was easier than before for them to sell their products in the French market and more difficult for them to buy from France. Moreover, the general economic crisis came just at the crucial moment to add its weight to the burden placed on French export trade. The effects of these difficulties were reflected in France's foreign-trade statistics:

SPECIAL COMMERCE

	Imports		Exports	
	(in millions of francs)	(in millions of tons)	(in millions of francs)	(in millions of tons)
1928	53,644	49.3	52,104	41.1
1929	58,220	59.5	50,139	39.9
1930	52,511	60.9	42,835	36.7
1931	42,206	58.1	30,436	30.3
1932	29,808	47.6	19,705	23.6
1933	28,430	48.5	18,473	25.
1934	23,097	45.8	17,850	28.4
1935	20,974	44.6	15,496	29.3
1936	25,398	47.9	15,454	28.9

The predicament in which France found herself was awkward. To denounce all existing commercial treaties and to make new agreements, which was the logical way out, would have been an enormous task and would have caused delay. An easier solution to the problem was sought; and the quota system was hit upon as the most satisfactory way of settling the matter.[109] France had already had some experience with this system, for she had restricted the showing of American films in France (1924–27) and she had subjected some Russian goods to licenses (1930). The quota system was also inherent in the law of December, 1929, which limited to a fixed percentage the amount of foreign wheat that could go into bread and in controls placed on petroleum imports.

Although these measures had not proved eminently satisfactory because of the retaliation which they invoked, the influx of foreign goods became so great, in spite of tariffs, that a definite limit had to be established. Therefore in July, 1931, quotas were placed on certain goods irrespective of French demands or the ability of these goods to compete in the French market. Gradually this system was extended to cover 1800 classes of industrial goods and many agricultural products.[110] So strict and so all-inclusive did it become, that it was reminiscent of war-time practice. The entire policy was indeed a crisis measure. It is interesting to surmise what the result will be if the number of such acts increases. If it is true that unexploited markets are becoming fewer and productive capacity has exceeded present market demand, the possibility of more frequent crises and hence of more crisis measures is very good. Nations will thereby be driven willy-nilly toward self-sufficiency—toward more intense national economic policies.

REPARATIONS

Closely allied to this problem of defending the home market is the question of reparations. France had imagined at the Peace Conference that German payments would enrich her and would automatically result in a second blessing—the keeping of her vanquished foe prostrate. There might have been some foundation for the former belief, if Germany had been able to pay the indemnity out of accumulated surpluses and France had found ways for spending the money without raising costs of production of her goods so that they could not compete in the world market. It was soon discovered, however, that Germany could only pay the large sums demanded of her if she had a favorable balance of trade and payments, for she could not settle this debt by those two very important invisible items in international balances —inflation and bankruptcy. She had, in the long run, to pay the debt with goods[111] and the Allies showed no great willingness to receive German products or to stand back while the Germans sold to the world market. Even reparation payments in kind were ultimately frowned upon by France. Germany had been required, for example, to build ships for the Allies, but when the shipyards of the victorious nations were thus deprived of business, a halt was called on German ship deliveries. The capitalist system required maintenance of building operations to provide profit on specific invested capital and salaries to definite groups of workers.

The nation could not simply accept gifts without having her economic system thrown out of gear. Even the delivery of coal, which France did not mine in sufficient quantities to meet her needs, was not entirely welcome. The supplies from Germany forced the price of domestic coal down and France received such large shipments that she was able to re-export coal, thus cutting into British exports.[112] Deliveries in kind, which figured large in the Dawes plan, were for these reasons reduced in the Young plan. France, also, changed her ideas about 1924 concerning the desirability of a prostrate Germany, for the German market was vital to her export trade. Finally, she gave up without too strenuous a fight the possibility of securing further payments (Lausanne agreement, 1932). The idea of collecting huge reparations ran into and foundered on the snag of national economics.

STATE AID TO EXPORTERS

The defense of the home market, whether from the sale or from the gratuitous delivery of foreign goods, has only been one side of France's task in attempting to regulate her external commerce since the war. She has been actively engaged in assisting her citizens with their problems of selling their wares abroad. To perform this function France has had numerous organizations and agencies. There has been, in the first place, the Ministry of Commerce with all its administrative branches and services. Its general line of action has been largely laid down by the National Committee of Councillors of the Foreign Commerce of France, a body composed of leading industrial and commercial men.[113] Then there has been the National Office of Foreign Commerce.[114] This body has provided information concerning all matters of foreign trade, has served as a link between foreign buyers and French producers, has aided French firms in quoting prices that will compete with foreign bids, and has planned itineraries for the shipment of goods. Thirdly, there have been commercial attachés and agents,[115] who have represented French exporters in foreign fields and have kept the National Office of Foreign Commerce informed of interesting developments in their territories.[116] Fourthly, to stimulate not actual exports, but the foreign tourist trade in France, there has been the National Office of Tourism. And finally there has been the French National Bank of Foreign Commerce,[117] capitalized at 75,000,000 francs, which the government pledged to aid with advances bearing no interest up to a total of 25,000,000 francs and subsidies for five years not to exceed 2 million francs a year.[118]

In addition to the services rendered by these state or semi-state institutions, other aids have been granted by the government for making the capture of export markets easier. Although the state has not indulged in direct export bounties, it has provided or encouraged indirect subsidies of various kinds. Nearly all assistance which has been given industries—assistance that will be treated in some detail later—might be classified as indirect export subsidy; but there has been a category of public aid that has been definitely for stimulating exports. This assistance has taken such forms as reductions in the price of state coal to metallurgical establishments which produce for exportation,[119] as exemptions to exporters from paying the turn-over and luxury taxes,[120] and as especial transportation rates on goods shipped via specified routes.[121]

Then there has been government export credit insurance administered by the French National Bank of Foreign Commerce[122] which has aimed to allay the political risk of credit on exports. Whenever a French concern sells goods abroad to any foreign nation, public service, or municipality, the bank will insure the credit up to 60 per cent of the total.[123] Under the circumstances created by these provisions, it is inevitable that the government will bring all possible pressure, both diplomatic and financial, to bear on foreign debtors whose credit has been insured.[124] When the depression became really serious, the terms for export credit insurance were made more liberal. In 1936 the Popular Front Government promised to make advances to exporters to counterbalance the wage increases of June and July and to aid them in getting their credits from countries with "blocked currencies."

The assistance thus given, although for the most part indirect, has been none the less real or none the less national. The patriotic implication of the measures has been made doubly clear, in truth, by the fact that the French Government has the power to raise customs rates by decree to offset similar advantages given by foreign states to their exporters—an anomalous position that is characteristic of much of modern economic nationalism.[125]

COLONIES—DO THEY PAY?

A further stimulus to export trade since the war has been furnished by the development of the colonial empire. France was able, as has already been pointed out, to acquire control of new territories at the Peace Conference and to obtain (1920) a share of Mosul oil. But in recent years the nation has been more concerned with the exploitation of lands already occupied than with the acquisition of new holdings, and policies of *mise en valeur* rather than of conquest[126] have characterized French colonial history since 1919.

During the war, when France was pushed to the limit for supplies of all kinds, an economic census of the colonies was made which became the basis for action after the establishment of peace. Public funds and reparations were used to develop railways, roads, ports, electrical power plants, etc., and attention was given to agricultural and general industrial development. In every plan for "national equipment"[127] since the war, exploitation of the colonial domain has figured large. Under the impulsion of state aid and a renewed activity of private interests, production in the colonies has gone forward.

France's hope of profiting from her empire has conditioned her colonial commercial policy since the war. Algeria has been treated as an integral part of the motherland; goods have been exchanged between the two territories as they have been between any two parts of Continental France. Tunis has had the right to make its own tariffs in accord with the home government, but most important French exports have been received in the colony free of duty. French goods have also been permitted to enter free in the so-called assimilated colonies (Indo-China, Madagascar, Guadeloupe, French Guiana, Martinique, and Réunion) and preferential rates have existed in most of the other parts of the empire. Morocco has been the most notable exception to this rule, for international agreement has precluded special favors to French exports, but even here a movement is under way to effect a change. The Colonial Economic Conferences in 1933, 1934, and 1935 endeavored to iron out the problems arising from this system of imperial preference and at the same time to study how to make the economics of the colonies and of the homeland complementary. Although they were not especially successful, they resulted in the formation of the state *Crédit Colonial* bank for financing colonial commerce and industry, and in the establishment of a permanent bureau for colonial economic conferences.

Attempts at increasing colonial trade have not been entirely unsuccessful. Imports from the colonies, expressed in percentage of total French trade, were twice as much in 1932 as in the period 1909-13, and exports two and a half times as much. Imports from the overseas empire exceeded in 1931 the combined imports from the United Kingdom and Germany, and in 1932 exports to the colonies were greater than sales to France's three best customers (Belgium, the United Kingdom, and Germany). Trade with the empire, which was 11.8 per cent of France's total trade in the 1909-13 period, rose to 15.1 per cent of the total in 1929. When the depression came, colonial trade stood up much better than commerce with foreign lands. In 1934, colonial imports were 25.3 per cent, and exports 31 per cent, of the nation's total commerce.

These statistics have been the pride of colonial enthusiasts, but they are not to be taken uncritically. National economists, who believe that there is some significance in an excess of exports over imports, were quick to point out that the colonial balance of trade was favorable from 1900 to 1913, but that it became very unfavorable in the years 1932-36. Thus the relatively large percentage of total French trade which the colonies had in the depression years was to be accounted for by tremendous imports of colonial goods. And these imports were exorbitantly high-priced because of the high valuation of the franc and the quota-tariff controls. Moreover, it was recalled that some of the imported colonial products, especially Tunisian and Algerian wines and Indo-Chinese coal, iron, and steel goods, competed with French products either domestically or in the world market. It was believed that these facts should be squarely faced and not obliterated by juggling figures. It was suggested that the then current form of subsidizing colonies (by paying high prices for imports) should be replaced by more direct aids, and that a rational distribution of markets should be attempted in order to avoid the competition of French national and colonial products.

Such conditions and divergent points of view suggest that the old debate as to whether or not colonies pay has been kept alive in post-war France. This is certainly the case, and much ink has been spilled trying to resolve the problem. From a strictly business point of view, it is difficult to show that the French colonies in the aggregate have provided a net asset. The accomplishment of such a task would require answers to certain very knotty, but essential, questions. What percentage of the total colonial trade attributable to political ownership of colonies may be, for instance, considered as gain to France?[128] How much has the possession of an empire increased foreign commerce and what are the potential factors for further augmentation? What has been the profit on private national investments in the colonies which may be regarded as a direct result of political domination?[129] To what extent have the colonies contributed to the costs of operating the home government? How significant is it to have trade carried on in the monetary unit of the home country to avoid a drain of gold? And how important have the expenditure of money and the settlement of Frenchmen in the colonies been to the economy of the mother country? If, which is doubtful, exact and concrete data could be obtained concerning these and many other questions, the total benefits could, perhaps, be set off against the total costs.

Efforts which have been made to strike such a balance have resulted in conclusions discouraging to imperialists. In the case of France, it is maintained that with the exception of certain colonies, especially Algeria and Tunis, the empire is, as a purely business venture, unprofitable.

Such conclusions, however, have not dampened appreciably French colonial ardor. Enough favorable factors have been found to keep alive a belief that the empire is of national advantage. It is pointed out, in the first place, that if the "business" test were applied to the colonies of every country, the development of backward areas would never have taken place and the civilized nations would have been deprived of innumerable articles which make modern life more agreeable. In the second place, it is maintained that the potential economic value of the colonies cannot be estimated, and that in the long run they may be of tremendous profit. Thirdly, some French trade with foreign countries has been made possible by the possession of colonies. Fourthly, the cost of empire will gradually be shifted from the home-land to the colonies themselves. Fifthly, in case of crises, like the war, the colonies provide wealth which may be tapped, as was done dur-ing the years 1915-20, when French colonies subscribed to national loans for about one billion francs and provided nearly 700,000 men to the French army and about 240,000 laborers to the cause of national production.[130] And sixthly, it should be recalled that strictly business methods of drawing a balance sheet do not do justice to an issue like the present one.

If, however, it cannot be shown in any way that the empire is an economic advantage to France, the business aspect of the enterprise may be disregarded, so argue the imperialists. The civilizing mission of France is sufficient to justify all the expenses of empire.[131] The frequency with which the "white man's burden" and the national-prestige arguments, rather than the economic argument, are used to glorify colonization indicates that there is little profit from all the colonies. The remarks of Gabriel Hanotaux in the conclusion to the most extensive modern history of French colonization furnish an ex-cellent illustration of this point. This eminent historian and colonial protagonist advises:

"Let us get away (God helping us) from the fatal error of base and immoderate avarice which demands, 'How much does [colonization] pay?' From it comes an embellishment of living, an enlargement of inspirational force: the Empire. May the lesson of history enlighten us. Let us create a greater France."[132]

BALANCE OF TRADE

In the minds of national economists "a greater France" implies a growth of foreign trade in which exports exceed or at least nearly equal imports. Protective tariffs, export aids, and coloniel expansion are all aimed to attain this end. From 1875 to 1900 the total value of French foreign trade increased only 20 per cent, but from 1900 to 1913 it rose by almost 75 per cent,[133] and in the latter year was 7.82 per cent of the world's international commerce.[134] The war severely upset this growth, however, and in the years immediately following the signing of the peace other disturbing elements—extraordinary demands for stock replacements, annexation of Alsace-Lorraine, reconstruction, and inflation—gave trade statistics an abnormal appearance. If the franc is reduced to its 1913 purchasing power, the trade statistics from 1919 to 1927 are as follows:

	Exports	Imports
	(in billions of francs) [135]	
1913 not including Alsace-Lorraine	6.9	8.4
1919 including Alsace-Lorraine and Saar	3.3	10.1
1920	5.3	9.8
1921	5.7	6.4
1922	6.5	7.3
1923	7.3	7.8
1924	8.5	8.2
1925	8.2	8.1 (Saar excluded)
1926	8.3	8.5 " "
1927	8.8	8.6 " "

It will be noted that imports were heavy immediately after the war, when France replaced depleted stocks, especially coal, but that they soon became about normal. Exports, on the other hand, were very low in 1919–21, but exceeded the 1913 amount during the period of inflation. Measured in terms of weight, exports increased from 22.1 million tons in 1913 to 36.6 million tons in 1927 and imports from 11.2 million tons to 51.9 tons in the same years.

These figures indicate the remarkable recovery which France had made since 1919 and to a degree the efficacy of her paternal policies. Her industrial equipment was producing so efficiently that its products competed favorably in the foreign market and her purchases abroad were kept down to a healthy level. The growth of foreign trade was an encouraging index of the development of national economy. Unfortunately the enthusiasm aroused by the statistics was to be short-lived, for the economic depression soon put a term to the expansion of foreign trade.

The turn taken by foreign trade with the coming of the depression was discouraging in view of the remarkable development to 1929. The balance of trade now showed a great excess of imports over exports, whereas earlier a slight excess of exports over imports had been registered. When all items in the balance of trade and payments—services, bullion, and goods—were taken into consideration, France was found to have had a debit international account from 1919 to 1923, but from 1924 to 1928 she had a net credit. In 1929 the annual settlement of accounts indicated again a net loss.[187] Although the accuracy of such generalizations may be doubted, for the amount of some invisible items has to be estimated, the trend indicated is probably correct.

FOREIGN INVESTMENTS

At all events, it is improbable that France had a credit balance in international payments to warrant the investment of capital abroad in the same ratio as such placements were made before the war. The costs of reconstruction after the war were so great that much available capital for investments went into state bonds. Moreover, the instability of the franc made the floating of foreign issues difficult; taxes on foreign investments were high; colonial investments increased; a large part of French capital sought protection from inflation in short-term foreign investments that were soon repatriated;[138] and from 1918 to 1928 the exportation of capital was prohibited. Finally, a much larger proportion of French savings went for taxes after the war than prior to it.[139] From a national point of view, this may have been a good thing, for, as was indicated in an earlier chapter, such a tendency indicates a strengthening of the nation rather than a financing of rival states.

However this may be, French foreign investments shrunk from 45 billions in 1913 to about 30 billions in 1919 on account of losses incurred in certain countries, especially Russia, and in the repatriation of some holdings. In 1929, France had approximately between 90 and 118 billion francs in foreign securities, although, if this figure is reduced for purposes of comparison by the proportion of the decline of the franc during these years, it will be seen that French foreign investments were in the neighborhood of one-half what they had been in 1914.[140] These foreign placements, although relatively small, did, however, maintain the character of pre-war investments.[141] Most of them were loans to states whose political friendship France hoped to win.[142] Sometimes the placing of foreign loans was used for strictly diplomatic purposes. The most notable example of this fact was France's refusal in 1931 to lend money to Austria to save a large Austrian bank, the *Kredit Anstalt,* unless Austria pledged not to join Germany in a proposed customs union. Indeed, there is little evidence of any fundamental change in the nature of French foreign investments. Only in their amounts has there been any serious alteration.

STATE FINANCIAL AID TO AND CONTROL OF BUSINESS

Capital used for foreign investments has to come from a favorable balance in international accounts and this favorable balance results only if a nation has great productive capacity. Production has always been stressed in national economic theory and it is always present in national practice. One of the time-honored means of stimulating production has been the granting of direct subsidies. Gradually this particular policy has gone out of vogue, but it is still employed in France for two types of industries those which are failing and those that are necessary for national defense. Among the former, the natural silk industry is perhaps the most characteristic. It has suffered because of the development of cheap substitutes and the direct competition of Eastern silks. To allow it to decay would be to throw out of employment a great many persons and to weaken France's position in the styles trade. Therefore, the state has endeavored to save it by direct grants, having paid to it between 1892 and 1910 140,000,000 francs.[143]

Among industries needed for defense, the industry to benefit the most from direct subsidies since the war has been aviation. Airplanes played an important rôle in the last war and everything points to their playing a still more vital part in the next one. Largely for this reason, France has granted large sums to commercial aviation companies. The budget appropriation for civil aviation subsidies in 1934 was 160,000,000 francs.[144] In order to receive aid from the state, aviation companies had to be French; their capital be owned by Frenchmen; their officers be French; their ships must be constructed in France; and their aviators must also meet certain requirements of nationality.[145]

Direct subsidies have, however, given way to other forms of state financial assistance—especially to state loans at low rates of interest. This is particularly noticeable in the case of the merchant marine. The last construction bounties provided for by the law of 1906 were paid in 1920 and the last navigation subsidies in 1930–31. Although the shipbuilding industry derived some benefit from being able to receive certain construction materials from abroad free of duty[146] and four of the large shipping companies were aided by fat mail contracts,[147] France's merchant marine was not keeping pace with its rivals. From 1927 to 1932 its total tonnage did not increase much beyond 3,500,000 tons; it ranked sixth among the merchant marines of the world; and it carried only 40 per cent of French sea-borne foreign trade.[148]

If conditions in the shipping industry were to be improved, it seemed that the state would have to lend a hand.[149] This it did beginning in 1928 by extending easy credit to shipbuilders. The *Crédit Maritime* was established within the semi-state *Crédit Foncier* bank and given sums which could be advanced to builders up to 85 per cent of the cost of a ship.[150] It was believed, because of the interlocking nature of shipping and shipbuilding concerns, that the system would provide adequate aid for the main branches of the industry.

This might well have been the case, if the economic depression had not come just when the force of state financial aid should have made itself felt. Under the circumstances, however, the entire shipping industry was severely affected by the decline in business activity. The *Compagnie Transatlantique* was especially hard hit. Its situation became so bad that collapse threatened; and in the extremity it appealed to the state for assistance. This was, after much haggling, forthcoming upon the condition that the state have a voice in the affairs of the line. Similarly, the government has come to the financial support of and has obtained a measure of control in all the important French shipping companies—*Messageries Maritimes, Compagnie Générale Aéropostale, Compagnie Frayssinet,* and *Sud-Atlantique.*[151]

Direct state assistance has also been given to certain branches of agriculture in order to keep them from foundering. The fall of prices in the world market with the advent of the depression and increased production resulting from improved agricultural methods placed a heavy burden on French farmers. The wine growers were particularly hard hit—prices fell precipitously and huge stocks were carried over. To meet the emergency the state enacted a law, July 4, 1931, which required: (1) That wine growers should declare the amount of their production and that the state should "block" those who produced more than 400 hectoliters from putting their surplus on the market without authorization; (2) That a certain amount of wine should be used for distilling alcohol; (3) That proprietors with more than 10 hectares in vines should not increase their plantings; and (4) That vineyards which produced more than 100 hectoliters per hectare (theoretically low-grade wine) should be heavily taxed. These measures were by no means platonic ones, for the *"blocage"* policy affected 50 per cent of the production of those who produced over 50,000 hecto- liters. Nevertheless, prices continued to fall and other schemes had to be attempted. By the decrees of June 26 and July 30, 1935, the state agreed to purchase alcohol distilled from low grade wines up to a given amount; it offered to remunerate wine growers who would pull up their vines; and through the *Crédit Agricole* it facilitated the financ- ing of the wine industry.

Wheat growing also suffered so severely with the depression that the state had to provide it succor. At first (January 26, 1933) it tried to increase the price of wheat by making purchases; but when this move seemed unefficacious, it promised export bounties; fixed the price of wheat; required that mills use a certain percentage of the carry-over; encouraged the reduction of lands sown to wheat and the use of wheat for industrial purposes; tried to regulate the amount of wheat thrown on the market at any one time; and encouraged better elevator facilities for storing wheat. These measures and a relatively poor crop in 1935 helped to ameliorate conditions, although they did not restore good times. The *Front Populaire* government in 1936 finally enacted a law for the creation of an *Office du Blé* that would regulate the trade. It would especially fix the price of wheat for vari- ous regions and would encourage the establishment of co-operatives which would serve as middlemen and hence reduce speculation.[152] Such policies mean that the collectivity has to support the cost of keeping certain industries alive—a practice that is in line with national economic doctrine.

This manner of the state's entering into business was not new to France, for the government had frequently been called upon to pull the chestnuts of capitalists out of the fire. The history of French railways had been marked by such procedure; and after the war the railways again made an appeal to the public treasury for aid—an appeal that resulted in closer government control of them. Upon the conclusion of the war the condition of the railways was not an enviable one. Costs of operation had mounted so greatly that huge deficits piled up. This meant that the state had either to furnish the sums necessary to guarantee interest on the capital investment, as provided for in the 1883 agreements, or to cover the losses, as in the case of the Nord and P. L. M. lines.[153]

Thus both the government and the companies were anxious for a new solution of their problems. It was suggested, especially by socialists, that the state purchase the lines, but this proposition was turned down because of the heavy financial obligation which it would have placed on the treasury. A less thorough and more conventional solution was found which was embodied in the law of October 29, 1921. The state agreed to cancel the debts owed it by the railways for sums advanced during the war as guarantee of interest or to cover losses and to accept the cost of putting the lines in a condition corresponding to that of 1914. The companies, for their part, had to surrender their position of receiving state money as a guarantee of interest and to accept tariff schedules which would provide net earnings sufficient to finance all the roads. A common railway fund was established to operate so that the richer companies would finance the poorer ones and so that the state would be free from financial responsibility except in unusual circumstances. A Superior Railways Council, composed of representatives of the railways and of the state, and its subordinate Direction Committee were set up to fix rates, suggest reforms, effect savings, control the common fund, and, in short, to be a clearing house for matters of interest to all the lines.[154]

The plan worked well until the depression set in, but this "unusual circumstance" placed an added burden upon the state's finances. The government suggested that unification was necessary to effect the economies required to save the railways, but the private companies refused to concur in this opinion, proposing instead higher rates and lower taxes.[155] The situation led to an agreement (July 6, 1935) which allowed the state to nominate two directors to the board of each company and to exercise closer control over contracts. But when this did not suffice, the *Front Populaire* government pushed through a merger of all the railways. They were united in the *Société Nationale des Chemins de Fer,* August 31, 1937, with the state holding 51 per cent of the stock and the remaining 49 per cent being given to the holders of stock in the former private companies. This latter block of stock will be retired gradually to 1982, when the railways will become entirely state-owned.

THE OIL POLICY

In the oil industry the state has played likewise a large rôle. The importance of the internal-combustion engine both in times of peace and times of war makes it imperative for the nation to have adequate supplies of petroleum. Until recently, however, France did little to foster the industry. After the War of 1870 and the Commune a high tariff was established on refined petroleum products mainly because it was feared that these articles would be used for incendiary purposes. The exorbitant duties resulted in the development of a refining industry, controlled by the *Cartel des Dix,* that manufactured about 80 per cent of the oil consumed in France. In 1903 the tariff rates were changed to favor the importation of refined instead of crude oil. The *Cartel* became fundamentally a distributing agent for Standard Oil products and refining decreased until in 1928 it supplied only 10 per cent of the nation's needs.

The dangerous nature of this situation was made abundantly apparent during the World War. Fortunately France was able to obtain supplies from America in this crisis, but it was obvious that something should be done to avert the possibility of a future calamity. It was believed necessary, first, to get control of oil reserves; secondly, to develop a refining industry in the country, which incidentally would increase the nation's productive power; and, thirdly, to maintain large stores of oil in France. Considerable satisfaction concerning the first of these desiderata was obtained as a result of the Sykes-Picot and San Remo agreements which gave France a 23.75 per cent share of the oil of Iraq.[156] But what should be done about the other problems was not clear. There was considerable pressure for a continuation of the war-time state monopoly of oil and the creation of a nationalized refining industry, but these schemes were not adopted, for, as in the case of the railways, the initial financial burden was considered too great.

No very positive action was taken, in fact, until the "Petroleum Charter" was issued on January 10, 1925.[157] This important document provided for the creation of an *Office National des Combustibles Liquides*—a body that should map out a "plan" for the development of the oil industry in France. Although the *Office* could not go into business itself, it was allotted sums accruing from customs duties on oil for the purpose of subsidizing the construction of tankers, of prospecting, and of encouraging technological improvements. The Charter required, moreover, oil companies to maintain reserves equal to 25 per cent of the amount sold in the preceding year and it indicated that France was going to do everything possible to encourage the development of refining at home.

One of the first acts of the government towards this latter goal was to concede its share of Mosul oil to a holding company, *Compagnie Française des Pétroles*. The state then obtained a 25 per cent interest in this concern[158] and a 10 per cent interest in its subsidiary, the *Compagnie Française de Raffinage*. According to the terms of the agreement between these companies and the state, the government was to take the necessary measures to assure 25 per cent of the refining business to the companies or, in other words, to give its companies a large share of the trade by legislation.[159] This was made possible by placing (March 30, 1928) all importers under a license and quota system. The result was that by 1931 the *Compagnie Française de Raffinage* had been given the privilege to import 21.62 per cent of French consumption; the *Société Franco-Américaine de Raffinage* (Standard Oil interests), 21.34 per cent; the *Société des Pétroles Jupiter* (Royal Dutch Shell), 15.12 per cent; the *Société Générale des Huiles de Pétroles* (Anglo-Persian), 9 per cent; and the Vacuum Oil Co. and *Compagnie*

Industrielle des Pétroles, 8.09 per cent.[160] The licenses for crude oil were issued for a twenty-year period; those for refined products for only three years. So not only did the license system favor the company in which the government was interested, but it also encouraged foreign interests, because of the short-term nature of the licenses for refined oil, to build refineries in France. As a further inducement to this end, high customs duties were placed on refined products and comparatively low ones on crude.[161]

The effects of these national economic measures were exactly those desired. Refineries were built with such rapidity that by the end of 1934 nearly two-thirds of the oil products consumed in France were refined on national soil. Pressure was brought to bear upon the British-controlled Iraq Petroleum Company, which exploits the Mosul holdings, to hasten the deliveries of oil from its wells. A branch of the pipe line from the fields to the Mediterranean was constructed to a French-controlled seaport in Syria and oil began to flow through it in 1934. The tonnage of French oil tankers was increased from 30,000 tons in 1920 to 400,000 tons in 1933. Extensive prospecting for oil in France has been carried on in the hope of finding supplies which will allow the nation to produce more than its present 1 per cent of the annual consumption;[162] and a quest for resources has been conducted in Morocco, Algeria, Madagascar, and French Equatorial Africa. If oil within the political dominion is found, French national oil policy will largely have achieved its aims. In any case, it has accomplished much in the refining and transport divisions of the industry—accomplishments that probably would not have been realized without state aid.

THE STATE IN BUSINESS

The increasing importance of the state's rôle in economic affairs is perhaps no better illustrated than in the field of banking. The Bank of France has played a leading part in recent financial history, especially in helping to finance the war and in the reconstruction of the country. Other state or semi-state institutions have grown in power and prestige. The *Crédit Foncier,* with its task of financing urban properties, floating public loans, and of handling the *Crédit Maritime,* has become the second financial institution in France. The eight colonial banks, the postal savings system, the *Caisse des Dépôts et des Consignations,* which is the depository for certain public funds,[163] and the *Caisse Nationale du Crédit Agricole*[164] have grown in strength and importance through the performance of their appointed duties.

Important as the services of these institutions are, the state has thought it wise to supplement their activity by creating new financial organs. The *Caisse Autonome d'Amortissement* was set up in 1926 to manage and gradually to redeem the national debt. The *Crédit National,* which was instituted originally to make state compensation payments to war victims, has been continued as an agency for granting loans to manufacturers and merchants. The *Banque Nationale Française du Commerce Extérieur* was established[165] to aid the export trade; the *Crédit Hôtelier,* to assist in improving hotels; *Banques Populaires,* co-operative short-term credit societies, to provide a service for small enterprises; the *Crédit Artisanat,* to furnish credit to craftsmen who employ at most two persons; and the *Crédit Colonial,* to finance colonial enterprises. As though these institutions were not sufficient to care for the state's responsibility in financing business, the government has in certain cases aided private banks that were on the verge of collapse.

These various state or semi-state institutions and the state's interest in private banks which it has saved from ruin (*Banque d'Alsace et de Lorraine* and *Banque Nationale de Crédit*) have made the nation financially interested in many private businesses. They have dragged the state into the market place by the devious routes of finance. But the state's economic activity is by no means limited to its banking interests; it is an owner and operator in its own right. The tapestry manufactories of Gobelins and of Beauvais, the porcelain manufactory at Sèvres, and some of the thermal establishments like Vichy, are time-honored state enterprises. The state maintains monopolies of the gunpowder, match, and tobacco industries;[166] owns large tracts of forests; has plants for manufacturing munitions and other military and naval stores; in 1936 decided to nationalize all war industries and in 1937 took over the largest arms plant, Schneider-Creusot, and aviation companies; operates the postal, telephone, and telegraph systems; owns two railway lines; and through the Ministry of Public Works engages in the construction of bridges, canals, roads, hydro-electric plants, harbors, and irrigation dams. Nearly all the state ministries that have to do even incidentally with economic matters lead the state into business. So widespread is their interest that some seventy-eight "national offices," which are administrative bureaus, have been created to handle special matters. Among the more important of them may be mentioned the National Liquid Fuel Office, the National Industrial Nitrates Office, the National Office of Social Hygiene, and the National Office of Navigation.

Furthermore, the state has become involved in business ventures as a result of the spoils of war. A good example of how this came about and how the state was pushed more deeply into business by it is furnished by the potash mines of Alsace—*Mines Domaniales de Potasse d'Alsace*.[167] These mines reverted to France by the terms of the peace and it was decided that the state should operate them. It was soon discovered necessary for the state to extend its activity and interests to allied concerns. It obtained, for instance, a 70 per cent interest in the *Société Commerciale des Potasses d'Alsace* which markets potash; a 70 per cent interest in the *Société des Potasses et Engrais Chimiques* which manufactures potash fertilizers; and a 70 per cent interest in the *Société d'Études pour la Fabrication des Engrais Chimiques*.[168] Another example of a similar nature was the shipping on the Rhine and Danube. The state received by the peace treaties fleets on both the rivers. The National Office of Navigation did not have the legal right to operate them, so state companies, *Compagnie Générale pour la Navigation sur le Rhin* and *Société de Navigation Danubienne,* were established for the purpose. These resulted in turn in the state's securing interests in a tug-boat company and in a hotel concern for lodging French pilots![169]

Finally, as has been mentioned before, the state has entered business for the purpose of improving the nation's economic equipment. Immediately after the war, in spite of the great costs of reconstruction, the government lent its support to the development of industries which had not developed rapidly or which were not remunerative enough to attract private capital. The impulsion given to oil refining is a case in point, but there are other noteworthy examples. Especially is this true of the hydroelectric industry which had a tardy development. The government stimulated its growth by subscribing to large blocks of stock in private concerns or by taking mortgages on their property.[170] Similarly the state, through the *Office National de la Navigation,* has given an impetus to canal and river shipping by investing in towing companies.[171]

Important as such action was, however, no comprehensive scheme of national equipment was advocated by the government until 1926, when reconstruction had been nearly completed and the energetic Poincaré was in power. Neither the plan that was drawn up at this time nor the more ambitious project of the Tardieu Government in 1929 bore immediate fruit. With the coming of the economic depression, however, France, like other nations, was forced to work out her economic difficulties largely on a national basis. The exigencies of the situation gave an impulse to the concept of self-sufficiency and made *outillage national* seem more rational, more useful, and more pressing. Consequently in 1931, 4,146,000,000 francs were allocated for national equipment and although much of this money was used for current needs, for roads, education, air force, mercantile marine, etc., about 40 per cent of it was employed for new *outillage* projects. This important beginning initiated a campaign for still larger expenditures, with the result that in 1934 a plan was adopted to spend ten billion francs in the ensuing six years[172]—a plan that was further enlarged by an ambitious arms program.

THE LABOR POLICY

One of the fundamental reasons for the use of these large sums was to reduce unemployment, which, according to official statistics, increased from less than 2500 in the period 1926–30 to 351,000 in February, 1934, and to 503,502 in February, 1935.[173] This fact indicates that the modern nation accepts responsibility for providing at least the minimum of subsistence for its proletariat. The condition of labor under a capitalist national economic system has not been particularly brilliant, for the interests of the workers have been subordinated to those of the capitalists in the bourgeois-controlled state. Labor is not paid enough to enable it to buy the goods which it produces; surplus production has to find an outlet in the world market; and labor has to compete in this trade with the low wage scales and reduced standards of living of other states. Nevertheless, national economists, like their mercantilist predecessors, realize that it is necessary to have a sufficient and efficient labor supply in times of peace and a numerous and healthy army in times of war.

For national reasons, then, and also because of a certain amount of political power which labor wields, Western European nations have taken measures to protect their workers. France had before the war a less highly developed body of social legislation than Germany or England, owing in part, no doubt, to the fact that she was less highly industrialized than these neighbors. Immediately after the war, however, a law was passed establishing the eight-hour day and the forty-eight-hour week.[174] Public employment agencies (*Offices Publics de Placement*), which had been established during the war, were continued; and a campaign was carried on for an extension of social insurance.

In this latter field, France was particularly backward, a fact that was brought forcefully to her attention by the workers of Alsace-Lorraine, who, when these provinces were returned to France, refused to surrender the extensive social-insurance benefits that they had enjoyed under German rule. The best solution for the problem thus presented appeared to be an extension of social insurance in France and this was done by the law of April 5, 1928, that went into effect July 1, 1930. Insurance was now made available against sickness, premature infirmity, old age, and death, and the state participated in providing maternity and unemployment insurance.[175] The government has also taken measures to increase the notoriously low birth rate of France.[176] Its most noteworthy action in this regard was a law of March, 1932, which made it compulsory for employers to give workers, in addition to their salaries, a "family allowance" in proportion to the number of their children.

All that was done to increase the native population prior to the depression was not enough to provide the necessary number of workers, however, and France had to encourage immigration of foreign labor-ers. Official statistics indicate that from 1922 to 1931 nearly 1,750,000 foreign workers came to France, but to this total should be added those who evaded the authorities and seasonal laborers.[177] When business activity began to decline, bars were put up against the entry of more workers, and impediments to employment were placed in the way of those already in the country. Consequently nearly half of the foreign laboring population, it has been estimated, left France. This exodus provided a handy safety-valve to unemployment, but it did not entirely solve the problem caused by the crisis. The state therefore endeavored to create employment, as we have seen, by extending its public-works program, to alleviate suffering by unemployment benefits, and by instituting a "share the work" or "short time" plan.[178]

The *Front Populaire* government, that came to power in June, 1936, was more favorably disposed toward labor than its immediate predecessors. When widespread strikes broke out just after it took office, it accepted the responsibility of trying to re-establish industrial peace. As peacemaker the Government succeeded in securing the signatures of representatives of capital and labor to accords signed in the Hôtel Matignon which provided for a forty-hour week and for increased wages. That the new wage burden on capital should not result in unreasonably higher prices or in the closure of factories, and hence more unemployment, the Government established a price commission to prevent illicit price increases and provided assistance in the form of loans to those industries which could prove that they could not bear the added charge. It also proposed to reduce unemployment by retiring state employees at lower age limits, by requiring children to attend school to the age of fifteen instead of thirteen, and by new public works. Furthermore, it was empowered by the legislature to provide for compulsory mediation and arbitration in order to prevent the strike situation from getting out of hand. In these ways, France has tried to keep her laboring class from becoming demoralized during the depression. By her social laws she has endeavored to raise the level of French workers to a position where even the lowest classes would be worthy of the ideal set by the standards of patriotism.

The labor policy of the *Front Populaire* did not meet, however, with a kind reception from all quarters. There were those who pointed out its cost to the state and those who insisted that its provision for a forty-hour week increased prices and reduced national production. Even many of the workers were inclined to believe that their gains had been hollow, for higher living costs offset advances in wages. Finally, when it seemed apparent that production—the touchstone of national strength —had suffered, an attempt was made by the Daladier Government to lengthen the working week. This action met with resistance from the *Confédération Générale du Travail* and a general strike was called for November 30, 1938. The government met the challenge by mobilizing vast numbers of workers, as it had done in 1910, and forcing them to carry on under military rule. This measure broke the strike and France resumed work in a patriotic endeavor to keep pace with her rivals. Under a system of national economics labor is not allowed to shirk its duty.

STATE ECONOMIC PLANNING

The state has reached out in every direction in an effort to pull its economy together into a well-integrated, powerful whole. This task has been difficult, for it requires much foresight and exacts a tremendous amount of technical information. France has entrusted, for the most part, its "economic planning" to the tender mercies of a parliamentary system that in several respects is inadequately equipped and technically incapable of doing this work efficiently. The need for a master organization, a national economic council, was seen to be imperative before the war by several political philosophers and was preached ardently in the last years of the great conflict and just after its close by men who, like Walter Rathenau[179] in Germany, had been engaged in forming national economic policies. The *Confédération Générale du Travail* became in France the great champion of economic planning,[180] writing into its platform a plank for the creation of a national economic council. The *Bloc National* Government did not take kindly to this idea, however, so that C. G. T. established a council of its own, the *Conseil Economique du Travail*,[181] which worked out a scheme for France's economic life and developed a plan for "industrialized nationalization."

The idea of planned economy was thus kept alive after the war and, following the victory of the *Cartel des Gauches* in 1924, the proposed council for planning was set up as the National Economic Council.[182] This new institution was not to be a new parliament or a new economic ministry, nor was it, as the syndicalists hoped it would be, endowed with power to force the adoption of its recommendations.[183] Its duty was to study the economic interests of the nation, of consumers, laborers, and employers, and to work out proposals for action by Parliament. Its members were chosen by economic associations and represented all categories of economic thought and interests.[184] The Council has investigated colonial and housing problems, is engaged in making an economic survey of France, and has prepared plans for national equipment. Although the Council is still relatively impotent, if developed to its logical end it will plan the entire economic life of France.[185] Impediments to such a development are, however, numerous and important. Under a system of private capitalism in which the profit motive is always strong, it will be difficult to secure the approval of measures which subordinate private interests to those of the nation. Economic planning under present circumstances will be limited by the benefits which accrue to those classes whose representatives make the plans. It is doubtful whether or not it can regulate what is perhaps the most pressing of problems—the problem of distribution.[186]

There is, however, considerable evidence in addition to the existence of the National Economic Council, that a modicum of economic planning is necessary and feasible. The various national offices, the ministries which handle economic matters, and other governmental bureaus endeavor to establish rational schemes for the development of the particular industries with which they are concerned. An effort has been made to harmonize their economic activities by the creation in 1929 of an Under-Secretariat of National Economy, which in 1936 became the Ministry of National Economy.[187] Furthermore, Parliament has virtually approved planned economy by enacting a law that will allow the state absolute control of economics in case of war. It provides that in times of war "all Frenchmen and French subjects, as well as all legally constituted bodies, are to participate . . . in the defense of the country or in the maintenance of the country's material life and morale.

"When war is declared the state may contract for or requisition industries, may exploit mines, may take over all private business, may use inventions, may demand the co-operation of trade unions and other societies, and may require the active service of any or all Frenchmen."

If such action may be taken in the crisis of war, it is possible that it may be taken in peace crises too. If this is ever done, it will mean that national economics has reached its highest development. Even collectivization may be achieved in this way, not, as the socialists hoped, for the improvement of society, but for the strengthening of the state.

WHAT NEXT?

Practically every nation of Western Europe and many others besides are today pursuing more or less assiduously policies of national economics. The *sovereign* state is used to secure what seem to be immediate benefits.[188] Strictly national policies, as has been seen in the case of France, tend to lead in the long run toward autarchy—toward attempted economic self-sufficiency. Thus far the industrialized nations of Western Europe have profited by selling manufactured articles to agricultural nations and by buying from the latter the raw materials and foodstuffs which they needed. If the foreign-trade statistics for 1925 of the United Kingdom, France, Belgium, Holland, Denmark, Norway, Sweden, Germany, Switzerland, Czecho-Slovakia, and Austria are grouped together the following picture will be obtained.[189]

	Imports	*Exports*
Foodstuffs	$5,319,213,000	$1,682,344,000
Raw materials	6,346,021,000	2,155,476,000
Manufactured articles	2,888,940,000	6,998,523,000
Total	$14,554,174,000	$10,836,343,000

How long a balance sheet of this nature can be continued is a query. Will the national policies of the "backward" nations allow the continued importation of manufactured articles? Will the spread of technological knowledge and the development of industry throughout the world destroy the markets for European manufactured goods? Will Western Europe cease to be the workshop of the world? These are questions for the prophet to ponder. Their very nature, however, seems to indicate a trend toward self-sufficiency. If autarchy is the end toward which national economy is drifting, the nations that are most bountifully endowed by nature will become, other things being equal, the most powerful.

The wheels of history, however, grind slowly. Long periods of time elapse before the conclusions obtained from such an analysis of given conditions become actualities. Moreover, this is not a static world, nor is it one over which man has no control. What may happen to change the course of events can seldom be foreseen. But if mankind can be brought to realize that it is not headed in the right direction, the course may be changed.

It should be clear that at present the economic life of the modern world is full of contradictions.[190] In international economic relations, not to mention the perhaps more important domestic problems, interexchange of goods is obviously necessary for a fuller life, yet national economics has put literally thousands of impediments in the way of international commerce. The World Economic Conference in 1927, held under the auspices of the League of Nations, resolved that—

"Recognizing that the maintenance of world peace depends largely upon the principles on which the economic policies of nations are framed and executed:

"Recommends that the governments and peoples of the countries here represented shall together give continuous attention to this aspect of the economic problem, and looks forward to the establishment of recognized principles designed to eliminate those economic difficulties which cause friction and misunderstanding in a world which has everything to gain from peaceful and harmonious progress."[191]

Comparatively little has thus far been done to remove the economic causes of international discord. To be sure reciprocal trade agreements have been signed; international trusts have been created; international cartels, to lessen cut-throat competition, have been formed;[192] statistics on world production have been amassed; and the Bank of International

Settlements has been established. But the force of these institutions has not been great enough to leaven the whole loaf. Internationalism needs many more international economic agreements and institutions and a freer exchange of goods and populations. The World Economic Conference recognized this; but is it possible? The nonchalant way in which nations disregarded the Conference's recommendations,[194] the failure of the London Conference in 1933, and intensified national economic policies of the depression are discouraging. Can anything constructive be done without abolishing or controlling those forces—political patriotism, insecurity, capitalism, capitalist-dominated governments, the national state system, etc.—which make for national economics? Something undoubtedly can be done, but the task will be slow and arduous. It will be a long time before the economic resources of all the world will be exploited and managed for all mankind.

CHAPTER X

RECAPITULATION

THE NATURE OF NATIONAL ECONOMICS RESTATED

THE study of national economics is an inquiry into the problem of the economic power of national states. It implies an investigation (1) of what constitutes national economic power; (2) of what policies have been pursued to increase that power; and (3) of what the effects of these policies have been.

It may not be amiss, before a summary of these three questions is attempted, to recall to the reader's mind what a national state is and to endeavor to indicate why so much emphasis is placed by contemporaries upon national strength.

The national state may be defined as a "nationality" that has achieved political independence and political unity. This point is clear, but it suggests that the concept of "nationality" is well understood. Unfortunately, this is not the case; even political theorists differ in their interpretation of it. But what the author means by "nationality" (and in this definition he owes much to the researches of Professor C. J. H. Hayes) is a group of people who are bound together by such unifying forces as a common language or closely related dialects, a common culture, common historical traditions, geographical ties, and similar economic interests, so that they constitute or believe that they constitute a homogeneous body. A nationality equipped with a sovereign political organization is a national state.

Today the national state holds a position of tremendous importance. But it is not difficult to explain why this should be the case. The very factors which gave birth to nationalities have provided common interests and ideals that have been admired and cherished. This fact has given rise to national sentiment—to national patriotism. In the course of time this love for the nation has reached a high emotional pitch, for

it has been nurtured by foreign wars, struggles to effect territorial unification, economic conflicts and cultural triumphs, which in themselves arouse emotions. National feeling is, moreover, militant and
anti-foreign. It will brook no interference with national interest. The
foregoing chapters have given ample evidence that this is the case in
France. In that country there is a strong belief that French culture
has made so many contributions to civilization and that French historical traditions have been so glorious that France has a mission to
lead all peoples in the onward march of mankind. For these reasons,
it is essential that no harm come to the nation, whether it be by military invasion or economic attack. In fact, if France is strong economically, she will be in a position the better to fulfill her calling.

The national state has become the object of the ultimate allegiance
of most citizens. In this matter, forms of government make little difference. Under institutions of democracy, individuals consider themselves to be the nation, so that injury or insult to the nation is a personal affront and not to be tolerated. Under institutions of dictatorship, national interest is looked upon as superior to, not entirely sy-
nonymous with, personal welfare, so that individual well-being must
be sacrificed to the good of the nation. The national state is to be
loved, cherished, and obeyed.

It is not alone to national sentiment, however, that may be attributed
the important position to which the national state has attained. Political
theory and political practice have played their rôle. The doctrine, so
clearly expressed by Hugo Grotius, that the state is sovereign has fortified the modern attitude toward the nation. No other political entity
is superior to the national state; it is absolute master in its own territory and of its own affairs. The state, thereby, becomes the one collective agent to which citizens may appeal in case of need. If anything
goes wrong, it is the state that is looked to for setting it aright. If anything requires improvement, it is the state that is turned to for reform. The action of the state is therefore very extensive. And inasmuch as the state is coterminus with the nation, it acts in theory for
the national interest.

The fact that the state is quasi-omnipotent, that it is the sole organization to which *all* may have recourse in matters of public interest,

and that it operates on a national scale, must ever be kept in mind in studying national economics. But it must not be forgotten that the political organization which is the state is not an automaton. It is operated by human beings who do not live in a vacuum. Once they have obtained political power, they may use it for personal interests and cloak their actions under a shroud of national propaganda. The subject requires an understanding not only of what the national state is and with what love the citizens cherish it, but also a knowledge of who runs the state and for what purpose. The formation of public policy is, however, a study in itself and constitutes but one phase of the problem of national economics. The main issue of a history of national economics must be to determine the good of public policy as regards economics, to chronicle the measures that have been taken to attain that goal, and to analyze the effects of these measures. From what has preceded, it is abundantly obvious that the aim of national economic policies has been to strengthen the state.

The criterion of national economic power has been productive capacity. So well entrenched has this idea become that national greatness is frequently measured in terms of output. Nor is it strange that this should be the case. Large production led either to the amassing of economic reserves or to the providing of those goods that decided long international conflicts. It made possible also the wherewithal to sustain a large population—another adjunct of national strength. Furthermore, in the period under consideration there was great expansion of markets which placed a premium upon the production of goods to satisfy demands. Inability to take advantage of the opportunities that presented themselves meant national retrogression.

France, like other nations, has therefore concentrated her efforts on augmenting her production. Unlike Great Britain, which had definite superiority in certain branches of manufacture, France did not specialize in the production of any small number of goods and rely upon foreign trade to procure other articles of consumption. Without definite advantages of production and control of the seas, such a policy would have been impractical, especially in case of war, as would have been also a policy of free trade. France endeavored to develop *all phases* of her economy simultaneously. She aimed at developing, if not economic self-sufficiency, at least a well-rounded productive economic machine.

Productive capacity as a yardstick of national power has never been pushed into the background, but at times another problem, closely related to production, has come to the fore as vital to national economics—the problem of maintaining "prosperity." It is not easy to define prosperity in a manner that will be immune from attack by economists, yet some notion of what it is exists and needs statement. Under the system of private capitalism, capitalists, who have reserves of wealth to use, must make profits, and proletarians, who are dependent upon a daily wage for a living, must have work. Prosperity under the capitalist system would then seem to be in proportion as these requirements are met. In more general terms, prosperity exists when the wheels of the economic machine turn fast enough to provide profit for capital and work for labor.

In the larger part of the time-span from 1815 to 1914, the steady opening up of new markets, the creation of new wants, and rising prices made the economic system function generally at a rapid pace. In certain periods, especially from 1846 to 1848, from 1873 to 1896, with the exception of two or three years, and from 1929 to 1937 the wheels of business turned slowly. Capitalists saw their incomes decline and workers were thrown out of employment. In such periods production, the criterion of national economic strength, suffered. Moreover, these depressions had in them the germs of civil strife, and civil strife would *ipso facto* be a national calamity. Under such circumstances, it is not strange that the state has taken remedial action. It has endeavored to save capitalists from bankruptcy and it has attempted to provide work for labor. It has made efforts to deal with one of the fundamental factors of economic crises—the unequal distribution of wealth—by providing means for placing purchasing power in the hands of those whose wants are great. If buying can thereby be stimulated, the "pump is primed." But before the pump is working properly again, the state has been dragged into business activity on its own account and has established various forms of economic controls. The national state goes to great lengths to restore prosperity—to make the economic machine function well.

National economic policies aim, therefore, to build up productive capacity to a point equal or superior to the production of its rivals. It tries to insure prosperity. Everything that the national state does to realize these two purposes is a proper object of a study of national economics.

ORIGINS OF NATIONAL ECONOMICS—MERCANTILISM

It is a far cry from present-day Europe, organized into national states, back to the Europe of early medieval times when nationalities did not exist and when political overlords exerted but a tenuous authority over their subjects. A history of the rise of national states would require a consideration of the development of all the factors that led to the formation of nationalities and of the organization of nationalities into political entities. It would be necessary, in order to accomplish this task, to study the formation of national languages, the development of national literature, music, art, and philosophy, the growth of historical traditions, the binding ties of geographical environment, and the evolution of common economic interests. It also would be necessary to explain how one feudal lord established his supremacy over other lords, how he brought the territory of the nationality under his sway, and how he set himself up as the absolute ruler of the sovereign, monarchical state. Interesting as such a study would be, it is not possible to include it in this book. Some knowledge of the formation of the French national state to 1789 has been taken for granted.

The origins of national economics reach far back into the past, too, but again the history of its beginnings exceeds the compass of this work. Some attention has been given, however, to the period from approximately 1500 to 1789, because these three centuries saw changes that deeply affected the nature of national economics. It was this epoch that witnessed the extension of commerce over large areas, the development of manufacturing not only for increased local consumption but also for distant markets, and the rise of modern capitalism. Entrepreneurs of the new economic activity required the support of strong political organizations to protect and to aid their interests. For this reason they supported kings in their attempts at consolidating power and secured some political recognition themselves, even though they were seldom able to dominate the political scene.

The centralized monarchies, which evolved during the sixteenth, seventeenth, and eighteenth centuries, took cognizance of these economic changes and developed policies in regard to them that have been usually indiscriminately lumped together under the rather misleading term of mercantilism. The essential aim of mercantilist practice was, as was pointed out in the first chapter, to increase the economic power of the state and thereby to augment its political prestige. The measures which were taken to get power varied greatly from place to place and from time to time. Mercantilism was highly empirical in its details.

In France, production was generally considered to be the touchstone of national power. State policy, therefore, aimed at increasing production. It included the giving of subsidies to industry, the introduction of new industries, an attack on indolence, regulation of manufacturing, and protective tariffs. Stimulus was given to production by opening up new markets at home, by removing internal trade barriers, and abroad by the establishment of trading companies, development of the merchant marine, and colonial expansion and exploitation. Other aids to business, such as the establishment of standard systems of weights and measures, a central banking system, a sound national currency, and a uniform commercial code, were also cherished as ideals, if not realized at once. Such measures had the effect of economic unification, but unity, like commerce, was regarded as a handmaiden of production.

To what extent mercantilism represented class interests, it is difficult to say. The issue is somewhat obscured by the fact that emphasis was placed upon increasing the economic power of the state and not upon augmenting the wealth of the individual. Nevertheless, no matter how much a statesman like Colbert might fume and fuss about the selfishness of businessmen, it is clear that mercantilist measures endeavored to stimulate economic activity. This was exactly what members of the bourgeoisie who were engaged in industry and commerce wanted. It may be concluded, therefore, that mercantilism redounded to the benefit of the middle class.

Another problem on which there is no unanimity of opinion is to what extent the economic program of French statesmen in this period from 1500 to 1789 was purely *étatiste,* that is, had no direct bearing on augmenting the power of the nation, as, for example, increasing the revenues of the monarch, and to what extent it was national, that is, aimed definitely at strengthening France as a cultural, historical, political, and economic entity. This is a nice question and can perhaps never be answered to the satisfaction of all. Nevertheless, it seems safe to say that the idea of "national state" had arisen in the seventeenth and eighteenth centuries, even though perhaps in an embryonic form, and that certainly Colbert and some of his followers had specific intentions of increasing the economic power of the nation—France. Be that as it may, an economic policy of obtaining power persisted to the verge of the French Revolution.

THE FRENCH REVOLUTIONARY AND NAPOLEONIC PERIODS

The French Revolution is one of the most significant periods in the history of French national economics. It is important, in the first place, because it marks a decided increase in national fervor. Prior to 1789 national sentiment was limited largely to "intellectuals," much as in some present-day minority movements. The masses had little consciousness of nationality. Allegiance was first to the King and only secondarily to the nation. Beginning with the Revolution, when the King disappeared and democratic principles were established, and continuing up to our own day, there has been an ever-increasing tendency for the nation to be the object of the all-consuming and intolerant love of every man, woman, and child in it. Secondly, the Revolution marks the rise to political power of the middle class. To be sure, the bourgeoisie was not able to maintain the position which it secured during the early Revolutionary years against rulers like Napoleon I, Charles X, and Napoleon III, but gradually by persistent effort, which included recourse even to revolution, capitalist interests obtained political control of the state. Thirdly, the Revolution proved to be a great laboratory for national economic experiments. The old policies were carried on with an intensity that gave them a new character.

The *cahiers,* which were prepared prior to the calling of the Estates-General in 1789, demanded the economic unification of France and a more lavish use of mercantilist policies for increasing business activity. The Constituent Assembly began the realization of this program and succeeding governments continued it. Economic depression, the conviction that France could not compete in many branches of production with England, foreign war, and the coming to power of the bourgeoisie in 1792 speeded up the process. The Convention established a high tariff on British goods and a navigation act in 1793 in order to bring injury to the "isle of shopkeepers" and at the same time to enhance the economy of France. Under the stress of invasion, it declared not only a *levée en masse* of fighting forces, but also a *levée en masse* of the economic forces of the nation. All manner of effort was expended to stimulate production to a point which would provide the nation with the goods that it needed.

With the passing of military danger these aggressive economic measures were moderated or allowed to fall into desuetude. When the war began again, however, the Directory was very generous in granting industrial subsidies and in offering prizes for the invention of new machines, of which one was for an invention that would cause the greatest loss to Britain. Napoleon, also, endeavored to build up the economic strength of France. He caused to be written a national commercial code, established the Bank of France, built roads, and encouraged technological improvements. But not until the World War did France experience again popular economic activity for national ends comparable to that of the Convention period. Napoleon might have been able to arouse the masses to such a feverish pitch, but he expended most of his energy on war. He hoped that the Continental System, by providing France with the markets that formerly had been exploited by Britain, would make French industry supreme as well as subdue England, but such was not to be the case. England was able to withstand the attacks on her economy and France suffered from being deprived of foreign raw materials—especially cotton. The Revolutionary and Napoleonic periods did, in fact, cause great injury to French foreign trade. Moreover, the French were unable to develop their technological equipment as fast as the English. Although spared in economic matters the ravages of omnivorous victors at the Congress of Vienna, France found at the beginning of the Restoration that she was not, as she had been on the eve of the Revolution, a formidable economic rival to Great Britain.

ECONOMIC CLASSES AND NATIONAL ECONOMICS

A study of the Revolutionary and Napoleonic periods shows that increased national sentiment, class interest, economic depression, foreign competition, economic theory, and the exigencies of war accounted for the direction of French national economic policy. These same factors were predominant in subsequent French history and, because space does not permit a chronological recapitulation of what has taken place since 1815, let us consider these forces and the nature of the national economy to which they have given rise.

Enough has already been said about national patriotism to make further insistence upon it unnecessary. Sentiment for the nation has been whipped up by all kinds of propagandist methods, so that France is veritably a "nation of patriots." This is well known and has been discussed in detail in other scholarly studies.

The class in France which has given most vehement expression to national theory has been the capitalist. This may be explained by the facts that its members have been, for the most part, the intellectual leaders in France and that they have had the most in a material way to lose by the weakening of the nation. In the *ancien régime* capitalists were divided between the nobles, theoretically those who had their fortunes in land, and bourgeois, those who had their wealth in industry or commerce. The former enjoyed political supremacy, privileges of taxation, and social superiority. Bourgeois were jealous of nobles for their advantages and waged a campaign to establish equality between the two groups. The aims of the bourgeoisie were supported by the political philosophy of liberalism—of liberty, equality, and fraternity of all capitalists. Liberalism was in its historical setting a class philosophy. It provided a *rationale* whereby middle-class people might get political power. After it had accomplished its appointed task, a distinction between capitalists interested in agriculture and capitalists interested in industry and commerce began to disappear. By the time of the

July Monarchy all capitalists had fused, as far as national economics was concerned, into one class. Henceforth it was not uncommon to refer to them as bourgeois—a practice that has frequently been resorted to in this book.

Gradually the bourgeois class obtained virtual control of politics. By limiting the franchise on the basis of property during the Restoration and the July Monarchy and the establishment of responsible ministerial government, the wealthy classes were able to enact those laws, at least in matters of national economy, which were to their advantage. Of course, they had the autocratic Charles X and Louis Philippe, in the later years of his reign, with whom to contend, but they succeeded in removing both by revolution. Napoleon III attempted a personal rule, but he, too, had to bow to many of the capitalists' wishes and finally to admit of parliamentary government. With the coming of the Third Republic, upper bourgeois feared the establishment of universal suffrage, but the earlier experience of 1848 had shown that this did not mean the destruction of their political power. Until recently they dominated the political scene and used the state as they desired. In matters of national economics, their interests usually coincided with what was accepted as national interest. At all events, they rationalized their action by arguing that national wealth or power depends on production and that if production decreases, they will not only suffer but the strength of the nation will be impaired.

From an early date, it was held, moreover, that decreased production would throw workingmen out of employment and into the direst misery. Many proletarians accepted this argument. They felt that capitalists and workers in France had more in common—that is, the maintenance of production—than did the workers of the world. Among those who took a national stand was Jean Jaurès. He did not want French labor to have to compete with Chinese coolies and to have its standard of living forced down to the lowest in the world. He was willing to tackle the labor problem on a national basis. He insisted, however, that national economic policies should benefit the workers and strengthen the nation and not be exploited by capitalists for private gain.

It is not strange that proletarians under the system of capitalism should have taken this stand, but large elements of the working class saw a better life for themselves only in the overthrow of that system and the establishment of socialism. At the beginning of the twentieth century socialists developed some political strength—strength that has been steadily growing. But they have never acquired enough power completely to unseat the capitalists—only to wring concessions from them. Their strength has become great enough, however, to have put fright into capitalist ranks and their use for their own ends of some parts of the old bourgeois doctrine of liberalism has become embarrassing enough to bourgeois, so that many capitalists have deserted the philosophy of liberty, equality, and fraternity. They have turned to ideas of dictatorship as a means to protect their property—a dictatorship that would provide a "square deal" for both classes. This new stand is capped with a halo of national sentiment. It is an appeal to do everything for the glory of France and to do nothing that would weaken her in any degree. This is essentially a Fascist position.

FOREIGN COMPETITION; ECONOMIC CRISES; WAR; NATIONAL ECONOMIC THEORY

In addition to the control of politics by the wealthy classes and intensified national feeling, the economic policies of France have been conditioned in the nineteenth and twentieth centuries by increased foreign competition, violent economic depressions, war, and economic theory. Acute foreign competition was felt immediately upon the morrow of Napoleon's abdication by an influx of British goods. The French realized at once that they had lost ground during the Revolutionary and Napoleonic eras and trade statistics supported their realizations. If official reports on the volume of exports and imports may be taken as an indication, French foreign commerce during the Restoration did not surpass that of 1788 until 1825, and even then remained far behind British. From the Restoration onward, France felt herself on the defensive in the cost of producing most goods. In manufactured articles, she had to compete with cheap British, and later with cheap German and American goods, and in agricultural products with the crops grown on virgin soil in the New World or with those from the rich steppes of Russia. In only a few products, such as silks, wines, women's clothing, and luxury articles, did France have a real superiority. France had to have protection in order to preserve her own markets for home-produced articles.

The weight of this foreign competition was usually most keenly felt in times of economic depression, especially in those that were of a productive rather than of a financial nature. In the absence of sound and thorough historical studies of French economic crises, only the most tentative generalizations can be made about them. But it would seem that most of the depressions of the first three centuries of modern European history resulted from famines, wars, and financial extravagances. In the nineteenth and twentieth centuries, crises have had more generally their basis in the actual operation of the economic system. Stresses are set up by accumulative changes—increasing costs of production, the inability of proletarians to purchase the goods that they have produced, increasing inefficiency of management, etc. These factors in the business cycle which bring on depression usually make themselves most apparent following periods of over-expansion, speculation, high prices, and war. When depressions come, there is at least a temporary decrease in production, the closing of manufacturing establishments, and unemployment. Those very things that theorists have held to be the aim of national economic policies are thus threatened. The result has been for the state in such periods to rush in with remedial legislation to save business and care for the unemployed. The most striking examples of these phenomena may be found in the crises of 1846–48, of 1883–96, and the present one. National workshops, public works, and relief have been granted to the labor class, and subsidies, loans, easy credit, tariffs, and even government operation have been resorted to as aids to business. It is probably safe to say that during crises national economic policies have become more highly developed than under any other circumstances except war.

Military conflict has led always to state economic action for the strengthening of the nation. But while this has been true even of short wars, like the War of 1870, it is more extensive in struggles that are long drawn out. From the Napoleonic wars to the World War, France was not engaged in an armed conflict that gave rise to a real test of economic prowess and that resulted in mobilizing the economic forces of the country for victory. But in the last war, the long duration and seriousness of hostilities made the economic problem a vital one. At first it was believed that the emergency could be met in a routine fashion, but soon it was seen that extraordinary measures had to be resorted to. The state set up a virtual monopoly of foreign trade, recruited and allocated labor, controlled production, fixed prices, rationed food, and stimulated production. Whether government action was wise in all details or not is open to discussion, but that it was necessary can hardly be seriously denied. At all events, the experience of the World War has caused France to draft elaborate plans for economic mobilization in the next war and a law has been enacted that permits the state to take economic matters almost completely into its own hands.

Conditions, like war, that have been conducive to the pursuance of national economic policies have had an important handmaiden in national economic theory. From the beginning of the Restoration to the present time there have been numerous economic writers who have preached national economy. Under the Restoration there was Louis Say, brother of Jean Baptiste Say; during the July Monarchy there was Lestiboudois; under the Third Empire there was Gouraud; and under the Third Republic there was before the war Cauwès and since the war Lucien Brocard, to mention only a few. Many of these theorists were quite overshadowed in their own day by members of the liberal school, like J. B. Say, Bastiat, Chevalier, Leroy-Beaulieu, and Molinari, who became well entrenched in academic circles, and by theorists of the proletariat from Sismondi to Jaurès or De Man, who attracted attention by the freshness of their views. Nevertheless, there has always been a strong undercurrent of national economic doctrine flowing steadily from the pens of ofttimes minor writers and of business men themselves.

Nor did French liberal economists take an anti-national position. The premises of their arguments were entirely national, that is, they wanted to increase the economic welfare of the nation. But they believed that this could best be achieved by the free operation of natural economic laws without government interference. If their advice were followed, they contended, individuals would become more wealthy and the nation would thereby be stronger. In recent times the French classical school has gone to great pains to harmonize liberal theory with national interest and has made certain concessions to state intervention.

National economists have, unlike most *laisser-faire* theorists, placed emphasis upon state rather than individual interest and have lauded the virtue of political economic action. In this respect they have had much in common with their mercantilist predecessors. Nor does the similarity between theorists of these two schools stop here. National economists have maintained that national strength depends upon the ability of the nation to produce. Production should not be for the ultimate acquisition of bullion, as some mercantilists believed, but for raising the standard of living and providing in case of war those goods that the emergency might require. As regards other mercantilist principles, the modern national economists have come to look upon bullion as of use mainly as a backing for currency. Currency must be used and credit extended to aid production. Concerning the balance of trade, these theorists hold that an excess of exports over imports is good, for it indicates that the nation is able to compete with foreign countries in the world markets. At least, a nation ought to have a favorable balance of trade and payments; otherwise, it is living on its principal and not on its income. Fundamentally, production is the basic concern of national economists. Productive power is the criterion of national economic strength.

POLICIES TO DEVELOP NATIONAL ECONOMIC POWER

The policies that have been pursued to achieve the desired degree of productive capacity have smacked, like national theory, of mercantilism. The most common of all these policies is the protective tariff. At the beginning of the Restoration ultra-high import rates, including many prohibitions, were established and, with minor changes, remained in force until the treaty with England in 1860. This agreement, urged upon Napoleon III by Michel Chevalier, who believed that free exchange of goods between countries would be the best policy for France, was opposed by industrialists and was never ratified by Parliament, but went into effect by imperial decree—the only method possible for such extreme reductions in the tariff schedules. Similar treaties were made with other countries, and France had for a short period comparatively low rates but never absolute free trade. With the defeat in 1870, an intensification of national patriotism, and the depression of 1873 there was a recrudescence of national economics that brought with it higher tariffs. After the World War there were still greater increases and with the coming of the Great Depression in 1929 France resorted (1931) to the quota system that amounts to partial prohibitions of foreign goods.

High tariffs have not worked to the advantage of all undertakings and especially not to shipping, because they tended to curb international commerce. The importance of a large merchant marine from the national viewpoint was, however, recognized by most Frenchmen and it was felt that something had to be done for the carrying trade. In place of the Navigation Act of 1793, there were substituted early in the Restoration such aids to shipping as the *droits de pavillon, droits d'entrepôt, droits de tonnage,* the reserving of coastwise and colonial shipping to French vessels, and the prohibition of registering foreign ships in France. The advantage of the *droits de pavillon* was practically abolished by treaties from the 1820's to 1840's, and the *droits de tonnage,* the restricting of colonial shipping to French bottoms, and the reserving of French registry to French-constructed vessels were abolished under the Third Empire. An offset to this decline of aid to shipping was sought with the beginning of the construction of steamships in subsidies, tariff exemptions for naval materials, and even by state operation of shipping services. Subsidies were especially important under the Third Republic, but have been supplanted of recent date by government extension of easy credit.

Closely connected with the shipping industry has been French colonial policy. The attitude toward colonies has always been that they should supplement the national economy of the motherland. Under the Restoration, colonies were looked upon much as they had been in the age of mercantilism and the policy of *exclusif* was adopted toward them. This attitude was somewhat modified in later years, but nevertheless overseas possessions have been judged primarily as lands to serve the economy of France. Under the July Monarchy, there was some opposition to colonies as being of economic disadvantage—a contention that had its counterpart in the "Little England" agitation across the Channel—but, for the most part, colonization has been in favor in France. It is interesting to note, however, that not one single French colonial adventure in the nineteenth or twentieth century started as a popular movement but as the agitation of small groups that had some particular axe to grind.

Financial policy in the interest of the nation has undergone considerable change since mercantilist times. The old theory of bullionism has gone by the board and it has been supplanted by concepts of money aimed to facilitate the operation of the economic machine. Finance is thought of more as a means to an end than as an end in itself. For this reason, financial policy has varied according to circumstances. Dear money is no longer considered to be the *sine qua non* of economics; cheap money, which means cheap prices for national goods, has been looked upon at times as necessary to secure a larger share of the world's markets. Credit for the productive forces of the country has been one of the national state's main financial concerns. To provide this credit, France has established under government supervision one of the best central banking systems of the world. It has fathered the creation of and it has subsidized such institutions as the *Caisse Nationale du Crédit Agricole,* the *Crédit Foncier,* the *Crédit National,* and the *Banque Nationale Française du Commerce Extérieur*—banks which provide services that private enterprise failed to give or gave inadequately.

Attention should also be drawn to foreign investments which have an important national economic implication. French investments abroad have been considered an addition to the national strength of the country. They have been used effectively to win and to bind political friendships, but from a purely national economic viewpoint, they were perhaps unwise. Their interest yield was not greater than that on domestic loans, when defaults are taken into consideration, and the repudiation of a foreign loan means a complete loss to the nation, whereas in the case of domestic default, the nation still possesses the property created by the investment. Moreover, foreign loans helped other nations to build up economies that in many cases competed directly with the French and they probably did not, as classical theory maintained they would, cheapen goods that France imported. Finally, foreign investments drained from the nation capital necessary for development or for improving the standard of living.

Foreign investments, that took annually from one-third to one-half of French savings in the pre-war era, made difficult the financing of social programs and the equipment of the nation for greater production. Despite this handicap, France established, although somewhat later than Germany and Great Britain, social insurance, which was held to be necessary from a national viewpoint in order to guarantee an adequate and healthy labor supply. France has also done much in the matter of national equipment. She has constructed roads, bridges, canals, and hydro-electric plants. But her most formidable undertaking was subsidizing the construction and operation of the railways, which were essential, so said their protagonists, for national purposes —to allow France to develop as fast as other countries and to move troops rapidly to the frontiers in case of danger. It was stress on *outillage national* and the extension of credit that formed the basis of Napoleon III's national economics and that he hoped would be more beneficial than the protectionism which he surrendered. It was scarcely a sufficient substitute, however, but it has remained an important adjunct to protection and at present is being pushed to the fore.

RESULTS OF FRENCH NATIONAL ECONOMIC POLICIES

What the effects of such policies as high tariffs, navigation laws, colonialization, financial services, social measures, and national equipment have been on the national economy of France is very difficult to estimate. In every economic cause-and-effect relationship, the situation is so complex that no easy and simple statement of the case will do it justice. Some estimate of the results of French national economic policies has been attempted in the preceding chapters, and space permits only the briefest of summaries here.

Inasmuch as national economic policies have aimed primarily at increasing production, it is necessary to consider whether or not they have been successful in this regard. The conclusion of the author is that they have been. France seems to have achieved greater national economic power by the policies that she pursued than she otherwise would. At least, state aid in developing natural resources, in extending markets, in providing means of transportation, and in establishing new industries appears to have accelerated the pace by which France attained her present productive strength. To what extent private initiative would have accomplished the same results without state intervention can only be guessed. Classical theorists maintain that the natural laws of economics, if they had been allowed to operate without hindrance, would have brought even greater prosperity to France. That may be true, but it is only a hypothesis; and opposed to it is concrete evidence of the benefits to national production of some state aid, as, for example, in the building of railways.

The inalterable opposition of some economists to state intervention almost forces them to conclude that national economics is detrimental. They rest their case on the naturalness, and hence on the virtue, of economic laws which should be allowed to operate automatically without man's conscious control. It may be, however, that it is "natural" for man to use what agencies he has in his power to better his economic conditions.

One of the most striking effects of French national economics, and one about which there is little disagreement, has been that the policies pursued have led to a diversified economy. There has been production of a great variety of articles rather than concentration on the production of a few specialties. This does not mean that France has achieved self-sufficiency, but it does mean that she has approached it. This diversification is, from a strictly national point of view and given the political and economic conditions of the world as they are, probably an advantage.

Another result of the protectionist phase of national economics has been higher prices for some goods than would otherwise have prevailed. Under the capitalist system, work and income are more important than low prices. As a matter of fact, the capitalist system seems to operate best when prices are rising. It is curious to note in this regard that prices in terms of a unit of gold have shown a general upward trend throughout the history of modern capitalism. Low prices are hence not the only criterion for the successful operation of a nation's economy. The French have not had a position in production of most articles advantageous enough to compete successfully with foreign goods in the world market. Hence they have hesitated to abolish protective measures for fear of suffering economic decline, even though they would be able thereby to buy some goods more cheaply.

Protectionism has resulted further in the maintenance of antiquated machinery, but a highly technical and detailed investigation would be necessary to show to what extent this has been true. Protection has served as a kind of insurance against sudden change. It has contributed to stability and to a certain feeling of security. Undoubtedly some protection has been unnecessary and has been exploited for private gain, but now all classes feel that it must be resorted to. If their demands seem too brazen, they simply invoke national interest.

Whatever the results and whatever the wisdom of national economics may be, it is certain that the national system of economics is firmly established. French statesmen show no signs of casting it aside. To the contrary, they seem bent on intensifying it. The political development of national states and the functioning of the capitalist system point in the same direction. France, along with other nations, is going to greater and greater lengths in speeding up and improving her economy for the welfare of her citizens and for her national prestige and glory. So long as there is no agency for settling many of our social and economic problems on an international scale, they will have to be handled by the state on a national scale. So long as this is the case, national economics will be with us.

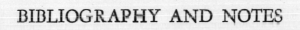
BIBLIOGRAPHY AND NOTES

BIBLIOGRAPHY AND NOTES

CHAPTER I

(1) There is no good monograph in any language on the general theory and practice of national economics from 1500 to 1900. The works on mercantilism come nearest to filling the want, but, for the most part, they are very brief, sketchy, and unsound. The best general treatment in English is probably J. W. Horrocks, *A Short History of Mercantilism* (London: Methuen and Co., 1925), viii, 249 pp. It attempts to trace the phenomena of national economics from ancient times to the present in every Western European country. Its treatment is therefore necessarily very summary. The present author concurs in most of Horrocks' generalizations. It should be noted that Horrocks feels that the word "mercantilism" is a misnomer for the material under discussion, but employs it for want of a better term. His remarks about the national economics of the nineteenth century are particularly noteworthy.

The best-known work on mercantilism in English is undoubtedly Gustav Schmoller, *The Mercantile System and its Historical Significance. Illustrated Chiefly from Prussian History* (New York: Macmillan Co., 1896; a new edition was brought out in New York by P. Smith, 1931), viii, 95 pp. This work is a translation of the introduction to Schmoller's *Studien über die wirthschaftliche Politik Friedrichs des Grossen* (1884). It is a most suggestive pamphlet; its most significant thesis is that mercantilism was not an economic philosophy of bullionism, balance of trade, or productivity, but was a philosophy of state-making. It contains very little detail, and much of the illustrative data is taken, as its title states, from Prussian history.

One of the longer studies on mercantilism is that by Eli Heckscher, *Mercantilism* (London: Allen and Unwin, 1935), 2 vols. This is an informative book, but it does not consider Portugal and Spain. Professor Heckscher's comparison of *laissez-faire* and mercantilism is stimulating. See also Heckscher's article "Mercantilism," *Economic History Review,* November, 1936.

In French, the most competent survey in the form of a monograph is J. Morini-Comby, *Mercantilisme et protectionnisme. Essai sur les doctrines interventionnistes en politique commerciale du XVᵉ au XIXᵉ siècle* (Paris: Alcan, 1930), xx, 217 pp. This book, which has an extensive bibliography, deals largely with economic theory and minimizes the economic policies of the growing national states of Europe. It, too, may be criticized for its brevity and failure to reduce national economic phenomena into categories for

371

different times and places. There is also Laurence Bradford Packard, *The Commercial Revolution, 1400–1776, Mercantilism—Colbert—Adam Smith* (New York: Henry Holt and Co., The Berkshire Studies in European History, 1927), vii, 105 pp., which is of the character of a textbook. The article on mercantilism in Ludwig Elster, Adolph Weber, and F. Wieser, *Handwörterbuch der Staatswissenschaften* (Jena: Fischer, 1925); the one by W. A. S. Hewins in R. H. I. Palgrave's *Dictionary of Political Economy* (London: Macmillan Co., 1925); and that by Eli Heckscher in the *Encyclopedia of the Social Sciences* (New York: Macmillan Co., 1930) are worthy of note. For the position of labor under mercantilism see E. S. Furniss, *The Position of the Laborer in a System of Nationalism* (New York: Houghton Mifflin Co., 1920).

Perhaps the best treatment of national economic theory may be found in general histories of economic theory. The section on mercantilism in L. H. Haney, *History of Economic Thought* (New York: Macmillan Co., 1920), xix, 677 pp., however, is not well organized nor lucidly presented; J. K. Ingram, *A History of Political Economy* (London: Black, 1915), xix, 315 pp., is to be used with care; Othmar Spann, *The History of Economics* (New York: W. W. Norton & Co., 1930), 328 pp., devotes only twenty-four pages to "The Mercantile System"; and Edwin Cannan, *A Review of Economic Theory* (London: P. S. King & Co., 1929), x, 448 pp., dismisses mercantilism in seven pages. One of the best surveys to be had is found in René Gonnard, *Histoire des doctrines économiques. Doctrines antérieures à Quesnay* (Paris: Librairie Valois, 1928), vol. I. A brilliant and informative account is A. Dubois, *Précis de l'histoire des doctrines économiques dans leurs rapports avec les faits et avec les institutions. L'époque antérieure aux physiocrates* (Paris: Rousseau, 1903), 342 pp. His approach to the problem—the linking together of the practical and theoretical sides of the phenomena—is highly commendable. August Oncken, *Geschichte der Nationalökonomie* (Leipzig, 1902), part I, which covers only the period to Adam Smith, is of primary importance, as is W. Roscher, *Geschichte der Nationalökonomik in Deutschland* (Munich, 1874), 8, 1085 pp. Of the many other books of a similar nature, attention should be called to the short but brilliant work of A. Espinas, *Histoire des doctrines économiques* (Paris: Colin, 1891), 359 pp.; Luigi Cossa, *Introduzione allo studio dell' economia politica* (3rd edition; Milan: Hoepli, 1892), which is highly stimulating and refreshing, and has excellent bibliographies; and Paul Mombert, *Geschichte der Nationalökonomie* (Jena: Fischer, 1927), ix, 557 pp., which, although uneven in its treatment of mercantilism, has a good account of Netherlandish and German mercantilists. There are a few monographs on mercantilist theory in general. H. I. Bidermann, *Über den Merkantilismus* (Innsbruck: Wagner, 1870), 58 pp., of which 26 pp. are devoted to notes, is largely an attempt to show that mercantilist writers were concerned mostly, not with discovering ways by which the national store of precious metals might be increased, but with regulations by which the circulation of money, and hence industrial production and commerce, might be stimulated. A discussion of the same idea consumes a large part of the highly suggestive book by Emilio Cossa, *L'interpretazione scientifico del mercantilismo* (Messina: Nicastro, 1907), 65 pp. Attention should also be called to the very brief article by C. Supino, "La giustificazione storica del mercantilismo," *Festgaben für Ad. Wagner* (Leipzig, 1905), pp. 99–102. Concerning the balance-of-trade question, it might be well to mention Edmund von Heyking, *Zur Geschichte der Handelsbilanztheorie* (Berlin: Puttkammer und Mühlbrecht, 1880), v, 90 pp., which endeavors to unite the development of theories of commercial balances with the growth of national states; and T. H. Boggs, *The International Trade Balance in Theory and Practice* (New York: Macmillan Co., 1922), viii, 221 pp.

There are almost innumerable books on special phases of national economic theory and practice. The outstanding ones which have come to the author's attention will be mentioned in the footnotes.

(2) See especially the works of Carlton J. H. Hayes, *Essays on Nationalism* (New York: Macmillan Co., 1926), 279 pp.; *The Historical Evolution of Modern Nationalism* (New York: R. R. Smith, 1931), viii, 327 pp.; and *France, a Nation of Patriots* (New York: Columbia University Press, 1930), x, 487 pp.; and Bernard Joseph, *Nationality: Its Nature and Problems* (New Haven: Yale University Press, 1929), 380 pp. See also the series in civic training published under the editorship of Charles E. Merriam by the University of Chicago Press, especially Samuel N. Harper, *Soviet Russia* (1929), xvii, 401 pp.; H. W. Schneider and Shepard B. Clough, *Making Fascists* (1929), xv, 211 pp.; and Charles E. Merriam, *The Making of Citizens. A Comparative Study of Methods of Civic Training* (1931), xv, 371 pp. One should also consult Waldemar Mitscherlich, *Nationalismus, Die Geschichte einer Idee* (Leipzig: Hirschfeld, 1929), and his other works on nationalism; Hans Kohn, *A History of Nationalism in the East* (New York: Harcourt, Brace & Co., 1929), xi, 476 pp.; Frederick L. Schuman, *War and Diplomacy in the French Republic* (New York: Whittlesey House, 1931), xvii, 452 pp.; G. M. Stratton, *Social Psychology of International Conduct* (New York: Appleton and Co., 1929); Koppel S. Pinson, *A Bibliographical Introduction to Nationalism* (New York: Columbia University Press, 1935).

(3) *Labor Charter* of April 21, 1927, Article II.

(4) Arnaldo Mussolini, brother of Benito Mussolini, in his article *Ordinamento corporativo e iniziativo privato,* quoted in Fantini, *La politica economica del Fascismo* (Rome: Tiber, 1929), pp. 21–22. See also my article,

"The Evolution of Fascist Economic Practice and Theory, 1926–30," *Harvard Business Review,* April, 1932.

(5) For a further study of modern national economics one would do well to inspect M. B. Amzalak, *O néo-mercantilismo* (Lisbon, 1929), 30 pp.; Charles A. Beard, *The Idea of National Interest* (New York: Macmillan Co., 1934); N. Boukharine, *L'économie mondiale et l'impérialisme* (Paris: Editions Sociales Internationales, 1928); Lucien Brocard, *Principes d'économie nationale et internationale* (Paris: Recueil Sirey, 1929–31), 3 vols.; W. S. Culbertson, *International Economic Policies—A Survey of the Economics of Diplomacy* (New York: Appleton and Co., 1925); Laurent Dechesne, *Économie mondiale et protectionnisme* (Paris: Recueil Sirey, 1927); L. Denny, *America Conquers Britain* (New York: Knopf, 1930); John Donaldson, *International Economic Relations* (New York: Longmans, Green & Co., 1928); Edward Mead Earle, "The New Mercantilism," *Political Science Quarterly,* vol. XL, No. 4, December, 1925; O. Fantini, *La politica economica del Fascismo* (cited above); Conrad Gill, *National Power and Prosperity: A Study of the Economic Causes of Modern Warfare* (London: T. F. Unwin, 1916); Joseph Grunzel, *Economic Protectionism* (Oxford: Carnegie Foundation, 1916), and *Handbuch der Internationalen Handelspolitik* (Vienna: Universitätsbuchhandlung, 1898); Henri Hauser, *La nouvelle orientation économique* (Paris: Alcan, 1924), and *Les origines historiques des problèmes économiques actuels* (Paris: Vuibert, 1930); W. A. S. Hewins, *The Apologia of an Imperialist. Forty Years of Empire Policy* (London: Constable, 1929); Martin Sogemeier, *Die öffentliche Hand in der privaten Wirtschaft* (Berlin: Hobbing, 1926); Mihaïl Manoëlesco, *Théorie du protectionnisme et de l'échange international* (Paris: Giard, 1929); Parker Thomas Moon, *Imperialism and World Politics* (New York: Macmillan Co., 1928); J. Morini-Comby, *Mercantilisme et protectionisme* (cited above); Leo Pasvolsky, *Economic Nationalism of the Danubian States* (New York: Macmillan Co., 1928); Theodor Plaut, *Deutsche Handelspolitik* (Leipzig: Teubner, 1929); N. S. Smith, *Economic Control. Australian Experiments in Rationalisation and Safeguarding* (London: P. S. King & Co., 1929); and the reports and proceedings of the International Economic Conference (Geneva: League of Nations, 1927). One will find considerable discussion of the theory of recent economic nationalism in several of the general histories of economic theory mentioned in the first bibliographical note to this chapter. One should add to this list Charles Gide and Charles Rist, *Histoire des doctrines économiques depuis les physiocrates jusqu'à nos jours* (5th edition; Paris: Recueil Sirey, 1926).

(6) For definitions of nation, nationality, national, state, nationalism, *et cetera,* consult C. J. H. Hayes, *Essays on Nationalism.*

(7) Victor Brants, *L'économie politique au moyen âge. Esquisse des théories économiques professées par les écrivains des XIIIe et XIVe siècles* (Louvain: C. Peeters, 1895), and George O'Brien, *An Essay on Mediæval Economic Teaching* (London: Longmans, Green & Co., 1920).

(8) On the attitude of Protestants toward capitalism, consult: Richard H. Tawney, *Religion and the Rise of Capitalism* (London, 1926); Ernest Troeltsch, *Die sozialen Lehren der Christlichen Kirchen und Gruppen* (Tübingen, 1912); Max Weber, *The Protestant Ethic and the Spirit of Capitalism* (London: Allen, 1930); H. M. Robertson, *Aspects of the Rise of Economic Individualism* (Cambridge: University Press, 1933); and L. Brentano, *Die Anfaenge des moderne Kapitalismus* (Munich, 1916).

(9) Henri Sée, *Modern Capitalism* (New York: Adelphi Co., 1928), p. 38; Henri Hauser, *Les débuts du capitalisme* (Paris: Alcan, 1927); and Werner Sombart, *Der moderne Kapitalismus* (Munich: Duncker, 1921–27), 3 vols.

(10) See the excellent book by David G. Loth, *Lorenzo the Magnificent* (New York: Brentano's, 1929). Lorenzo believed that a large export trade was a sign of prosperity, and he encouraged commercial expansion. He took shares in several companies and made Pisa a free port. G. R. B. Richards, *Florentine Merchants in the Age of the Medici* (Cambridge: Harvard University Press, 1932), p. 47. See also Richard Ehrenberg, *Capital and Finance in the Age of the Renaissance* (London: J. Cape, 1928), pp. 233–238; and Henri Pirenne, *Histoire de Belgique* (Brussels: Lamertin, 1900–26, 6 vols.), vol. II, pp. 432–438.

(11) A French decree of 1305 during the reign of Philip the Fair forbade the exportation of grain and wool. See R. Vivier, "La première grande intervention de la royauté dans le domaine économique," *Revue d'histoire économique,* No. 2, 1920. See also N. S. B. Gras, *The Early English Customs System* (Cambridge: Harvard University Press, 1918). James Westfall Thompson, *An Economic and Social History of Europe in the Later Middle Ages* (New York: The Century Co., 1931), pp. 74, 85. A. E. Bland, P. A. Brown, R. H. Tawney, *English Economic History. Select Documents* (New York: Macmillan Co., 1919), p. 186. *Calendar of Letter-Books,* ed. by R. R. Sharpe (London, 1899–1912); *Letter-Books A to L; Letter-Book E,* fol. CLXVII (1326). 11 Edward III c. i: and c. 5 1336–37. See also H. S. Lucas, *The Low Countries and the Hundred Years' War, 1326–1347* (Ann Arbor: University of Michigan Press, 1929).

(12) See the account of the theories of Buridan in Dubois, *Précis de l'histoire des doctrines économiques,* p. 92.

(13) *Opere inedite* (Florence: Barbera, Bianchi e Comp., 1857), vol. I, pp. 61–62.

(14) Machiavelli, *Ritratti delle cose dell'Alamagna.* Also see Karl Knies, "Machiavelli als volkswirtschaftlicher Schriftsteller," *Zeitschrift für Staatswissenschaft,* vol. VIII (1852), pp. 251–256; and Jean Thévenet, *Les idées économiques d'un homme d'état dans la Florence des Médicis* (Villefranche: Réveil du Beaujolais, 1922), p. 23.

(15) Dubois, *op. cit.,* p. 193. E. R. A. Seligman, "Bullionists," *Encyclopedia of the Social Sciences* (New York: Macmillan Co., 1930), vol. III, pp. 60–64.

(16) F. Isambert, A. Jourdan, Decrusy, Armet, and Taillandier, *Recueil général des anciennes lois françaises* (Paris: Belin-Le-Prieur, 1821–33), vol. IX, p. 118.

(17) Bland, Brown, and Tawney, *English Economic History. Select Documents,* p. 222.

(18) It is still called in French *économie politique,* and in German *Nationalökonomie.*

(19) Gustav Schmoller, *The Mercantile System* (edition of 1896), p. 50.

(20) W. A. S. Hewins in his extremely interesting book, *The Apologia of an Imperialist,* pp. 35–36, shares this opinion about national economics:

"I have defined its object as the creation of an industrial and commercial state in which by encouragement or restraint imposed by the sovereign authority, private and sectional interests should be made to promote national strength and efficiency. We can contrast this system of policy with that of the free trade or *laissez-faire régime* by substituting in this definition for 'encouragement or restraint imposed by the sovereign authority,' the operation of free competition, and for 'national strength and efficiency,' the pursuit of wealth.

"The mercantilist statesmen held that private interests did not necessarily, or even usually, coincide with the interests of the community. The Mercantilist or National System was not theoretical, it was political economy, a branch of the science of statecraft, and that statecraft was not inspired by abstract aims. The end in view was clear, but the means of arriving at that end were questions of expediency. Our forefathers believed in what they called 'regulation,' but not in any doctrinaire system. There was no belief in what in our time we call protection, for its own sake. Theoretically, at any rate, if we may use such expressions of those times, protective duties were not necessarily involved—the end might be attained by regulation and control by the central authority, and many of the mercantilist writers admit numerous cases for free importation and exportation, and write with admiration of the lightness of customs imposed by the Dutch Republic. In fact the tariff schedules invariably appeared, but not as a tariff worked out in conformity with some abstract principle. They were devised, according to the circumstances of the times, to meet a definite and actual situation. Freedom of trade in the modern English sense of the term was not known or desired. That is a phrase, used in at least a dozen different senses, but not in the modern English sense of a general policy of free importation."

Gustav Schmoller, *op. cit.,* pp. 50–51, maintains:

"The whole internal history of the 17th and 18th centuries, not only in Germany but everywhere else, is summed up in the opposition of the economic policy of the state to that of the town, the district, and the several Estates; the whole foreign history is summed up in the opposition to one another of the separate interests of the newly rising states, each of which sought to obtain and retain its place in the circle of European nations, and in that foreign trade which now included America and India. Questions of political power were at issue, which were, at the same time, questions of economic organization. What was at stake was the creation of real *political economies* as unified organisms the centre of which should be, not merely a state policy reaching out in all directions, but rather the living heartbeat of a united sentiment.

"Only he who thus conceives of mercantilism will understand it; in its innermost kernel it is nothing but state making—not state making in a narrow sense, but state making and national economy making at the same time; state making in the modern sense, which creates out of the political community an economic community, and so gives it a heightened meaning. The essence of the system lies not in some doctrine of money, or of the balance of trade; not in tariff barriers, protective duties, or navigation laws; but in something far greater:—namely, in the total transformation of society and its organization, as well as of the state and its institutions, in the replacing of a local and territorial economic policy by that of the national state."

Wilhelm Roscher in his *Zur Geschichte der englischen Volkswirthschafts-lehre* (Leipzig, 1851), p. 122, holds that:

"Unsere weitverbreitete Gewohnheit, die ganze Entwickelungs-Periode der Volkswirthschaftslehre, welche den Physiokraten voraufgeht, mit dem Namen des Merkantilsystems zu bezeichnen, ist allerwenigstens eine sehr ungenügende. Das Bekannte Bild, welches die Lehrbüchertradition von einem Merkantilisten zu entwerfen pflegt, passt immerhin auf manche unbedeutendsten Schriftsteller des 17 und 18 Jahrhunderts; aber die bedeutendsten werden keineswegs dadurch getroffen. . . ."

J. W. Horrocks in *A Short History of Mercantilism,* p. 1, states that:

"The term 'Mercantile System' is not a satisfactory one. It does not accurately describe or even aptly suggest the essential nature of the complex of theory and practice which it is used to designate . . ."

Yet he does not throw over the use of the expression.

"In the absence of a satisfactory, recognized substitute, therefore, the familiar name is retained as a convenient term for the matter in hand." Pp. 3–4.

E. Lipson, *The Economic History of England* (5th edition; London: Black, 1929–31), 3 vols., also maintains that "the use of this term [mercantilism] is apt to be misleading: it suggests the systematic working out of a national policy based on precise and definite principles . . ." Vol. III, p. 1.

(21) Consult especially K. G. Jayne, *Vasco da Gama and his Successors, 1460–1580* (London: Methuen and Co., 1910). This work has a good critical bibliography. See also R. S. Whiteway, *The Rise of the Portuguese Power in India, 1497–1550* (London, 1899); E. Prestage, *The Portuguese Pioneers* (New York: Macmillan Co., 1933); and M. B. Amzalak, *Do Estudo et do evolucão das doctrinas em Portugal* (1928).

(22) For a further discussion of Spanish national economic policies of the sixteenth century, see José de Veitia Linaje, *Norte de la contratación de las Indias Occidentales* (1672), the only treatise on the organization of Spanish colonial commerce prior to the eighteenth century; C. H. Haring, *Trade and Navigation between Spain and the Indies in the Time of the Habsburgs* (Cambridge: Harvard University Press, 1918); E. G. Bourne, *Spain in America, 1450–1580* (New York: Harper Brothers, 1904); R. B. Merriman, *The Rise of the Spanish Empire in the Old World and the New* (New York: Macmillan Co., 1918–1925), 4 vols.; Henri Bérindoague, *Le mercantilisme en Espagne* (Paris: Imprimerie Union, 1929); E. J. Hamilton "Spanish Mercantilism before 1700," *Facts and Factors in Economic History* (Cambridge: Harvard University Press, 1933); W. Roscher, *The Spanish Colonial System* (New York: Henry Holt & Co., 1904); and M. Colmeiro, *Historia de la economia politica en España* (Madrid: Lopes, 1863), 2 vols.

(23) Gonnard, *op. cit.*, vol. I, pp. 118–119; and Bérindoague, *op. cit.*, p. 122.

(24) On the amounts, consult C. H. Haring, "American Gold and Silver Production in the First Half of the Sixteenth Century," *The Quarterly Journal of Economics,* May, 1915, pp. 433–479, and *Trade and Navigation between Spain and the Indies in the Time of the Habsburgs.* He reduces considerably the earlier estimates of the precious metals taken from America. See more especially E. J. Hamilton, *American Treasure and the Price Revolution in Spain, 1501–1650* (Cambridge: Harvard U. Press, 1934) and "Imports of Gold and Silver into Spain, 1503–1660," *The Quarterly Journal of Economics,* May, 1929, pp. 436–473. For an idea of earlier beliefs of the amounts imported, see M. M. Knight, H. E. Barnes, F. Flügel, *Economic History of Europe,* pp. 308–311. The figures in this book are based largely on the work of Soetbeer.

(25) C. E. Chapman, *A History of Spain* (New York: Macmillan Co., 1918), p. 330; Damian de Olivares, *Memorial para prohibir la entrada de los generos estranjeros* (1621).

(26) Andres V. Castillo, *Spanish Mercantilism. Gerónimo de Uztáriz-Economist* (New York: Columbia University Studies, 1930).

(27) Concerning the national economic policies and practices of the Dutch, consult: P. J. Blok, *History of the People of the Netherlands* (New York: Putnam, 1898–1912), 5 vols.; Ernest Baasch, *Holländish Wirtschaftsgeschichte* (Jena: Fischer, 1927); H. T. Colenbrander, *Koloniale geschiedenis* (The Hague: Nijhoff, 1925–26), 3 vols.; E. Laspeyres, *Geschichte der volkswirth-schaftlichen Anschauungen der Niederländer* ... (Leipzig: Hirzel, 1863; and J. G. van Dillen, *Bronnen tot de geschiedenis der wisselbanken* (The Hague: Nijhoff, 1925), and *Geschichte der wirtschaftlichen Entwicklung der Niederlände und die Amsterdamer Wechselbank*, 1609–1820, ed. by Brodnitz (Amsterdam, 1929); T. P. van der Kooy, *Hollands stapelmarkt en haar verval* (Amsterdam: H. J. Paris, 1931).

(28) Baasch, *op. cit.*, pp. 253–256 and Mombert, *Geschichte der National-ökonomie*, pp. 130–133.

(29) Carl Ballhausen, *Der erste Englisch-Holländische Seekrieg (1652–1654) sowie der Schwedisch-Holländische Seekrieg (1658–1659)* (The Hague: Nijhoff, 1923).

(30) M. A. S. Hume, *The Great Lord Burghley; A Study in Elizabethan Statecraft* (London: Nisbet and Co., 1898), xv, 511 pp.

(31) The Dutch economic position was glamorously presented to the English, notably by R. Coke, *Discourse on Trade* (1670), and by Sir William Temple (1628–1699).

(32) James A. Williamson, *A Short History of British Expansion* (second edition; New York: Macmillan Co., 1931) vol. 1, *passim*. Williamson, vol. 1, p. 258, states:

"The Commonwealth, by the ordinances of 1650 and 1651, had sketched out a maritime policy which, as we have seen, was in itself a recapitulation of ideas previously existing in a vague and uncorrelated condition. The foreign wars of 1652–9 have obscured the evidence bearing upon the actual utility of the Puritan legislation. All that we can say with certainty is that contemporary thought was unanimously in favour of its continuance. . . ."

See also Br. Suviranta, *The Theory of the Balance of Trade in England; A Study in Mercantilism* (Helsingfors, 1923), iv, 171 pp.; and Hjalmar Schacht,

Der Theoretische Gehalt des Englischen Merkantilismus (Berlin: Mann, 1900), 106 pp.

(33) Consult G. Cawston and A. H. Keane, *The Early Chartered Companies* (London: E. Arnold, 1896); and W. R. Scott, *The Constitution and Finance of English, Scottish, and Irish Joint Stock Companies* (Cambridge: University Press, 1910–12).

(34) William Cunningham, *The Growth of English Industry and Commerce in Modern Times,* part 1, *The Mercantile System,* pp. 176–7 (Cambridge: University Press, 1921). See also E. Lipson, *The Economic History of England.*

(35) There had been insistence upon a profit for the nation in every single transaction. This was the "balance of bargains," a term used by Richard Jones in his "Primitive Political Economy of England," *Edinburgh Review,* April, 1847, and by Luigi Cossa, *Histoire des doctrines économiques* (Paris: Giard & Brière, 1899), pp. 213–217.

(36) This difference of opinion between the two groups of economists is exemplified with great clarity by the somewhat acrimonious debates concerning the practices of the East India Company. Gerard Malynes protested against the Company's export of bullion for the purchase of oriental luxuries in his pamphlet *The Canker of England's Commonwealth* (1601) and in his other writings: *St. George for England Allegorically Described* (1601); *England's Views on the Unmasking of Two Paradoxes* (1603); *The Maintenance of Free Trade* (1622); *The Centre of the Circle of Commerce* (1623); *Lex Mercatoria* (1622).

George Weymouth suggested the forcing of a northwest passage in the hope that in a colder clime would be found people who would take English products instead of bullion in exchange for oriental goods. To the supporters of the Company, however, the export of bullion to the East presented no difficulty at all. Thomas Mun, the hero of Adam Smith's treatment of the mercantile system, pointed out in his *Discourse of Trade from England into the East Indies* (1621) and *England's Treasure by Forraign Trade* (1664) that, although a certain amount of bullion was exported by the Company to the East, a still greater quantity was imported by the sale of Oriental products to Continental powers. Nor was this the only advantage of the Eastern Trade to England. The carrying trade and maritime insurance netted Englishmen neat profits every year, and England's commerce, in its demand for goods that might be offered in exchange for overseas luxuries, stimulated national production.

Mun's theories, however, did not hold for long the front stage in English economic thought. So far as commercial doctrines went, supporters of trading interests had to take a new stand, for by no stretch of the facts could they prove that the Eastern trade resulted in an eventually favorable balance of trade. Josiah Child (1630–99), a director of the East India Company, contended that the best test of a nation's wealth is low interest rates and that the best criterion of a favorable balance of trade is the condition of the merchant marine. To increase the wealth of England based on these standards, Child advocated, perhaps not without selfish motives, the establishment of an English colonial empire, increased commercial capital, the reduction of the legal rate of interest to four per cent, the protection of national commerce, and the opening up of trade with other nations. Another supporter of the Company, Charles Davenant, criticized sharply the bullionist theory, holding that "money is the servant of trade—at bottom no more than the counters [with] which men in their dealings have been accustomed to reckon—" and that "he who would compute with any good effect in matters relating to trade must contemplate the wealth, stock, product, consumption, and shipping, as well as the exportations and importations of the country." And an unknown writer with remarkably prophetic acumen contended that the overseas commerce would lead to an industrial renaissance and the application of machines to the art of manufacture.

"The East India trade is no unlikely way to introduce more articles, more order and regularity into our English manufactures. . . . [It] procures things with less and cheaper labour than would be necessary to make the like in England; it is therefore very likely to be the cause of the invention of arts, and mills, and engines, to save the labour of hands in other manufactures. . . ."

See the excellent work by P. J. Thomas, *Mercantilism and the East India Trade; An Early Phase of the Protection v. Free Trade Controversy* (London: P. S. King & Son, 1926), p. 10. Thomas Milles in *Customers' Apologie* (1601), and *Customers' Replie* (1604) took the same stand as Malynes. Lewes Roberts (1596–1640), a member of the East India Company, championed foreign trade. In his *Treasure of Traffike,* or *A Discourse of Forraigne Trade* (1641), he concluded that there were three ways by which a kingdom was enriched; (1) by arms and conquest, which he condemned as "bloody and hazardable," (2) by planting colonies, building well-situated cities, etc., and (3) by foreign trade. And the greatest of these was foreign trade:

"These two points thus considered and granted, and that neither the naturall commodities of a countrey, be they ner'e so rich or precious, nor yet the artificiall commodities of a Kingdome, be they never so many or excellent, can of themselves, without the assistance of Traffike, benefit a common-weale, or bring plenty or abundance thereto; and consequently inrich the same. Come we in the next place to the third point, which is this trade it selfe, which of it selfe and by it selfe, can supply all defects, either of naturall or artificiall commodities, and that without the assistance and helpe of either, can yet produce both, and is alone effectuall to accomplish and perfect the same, though in a barren place, affording nether in the prosecution, preservation, and augmentation thereof."

A Select Collection of Early English Tracts on Commerce (London: Political Economy Club, 1856), p. 65.

(37) There were in England many advocates of less government control prior to Adam Smith. David Hume and Josiah Tucker are worthy of note in this connection. Concerning the latter, see R. Schuyler, *Josiah Tucker—A Selection of His Economic and Political Writings* (New York: Columbia University Press, 1931). Concerning Hume, see James Bonar, *Philosophy and Political Economy* (London: Allen and Unwin, 1922), pp. 116 ff.; Max Klemme, *Die volkswirtschaftlichen Anschauungen David Hume's* (Jena: Gustav Fischer, 1900), pp. 7 ff.; and Hermann Thies, *David Hume als wirtschaftlicher und politischer Schriftsteller* (Cologne: H. Kuhn, 1929), pp. 19 ff.

(38) *Wealth of Nations,* Book IV, chap. II, entitled, "Of Restraints upon the Importation from Foreign Countries of such Goods as can be produced at Home." See also Joseph Shield Nicholson, *A Project of Empire: a critical study of the Economics of Imperialism with special reference to the ideas of Adam Smith* (London: Macmillan Co., 1909).

(39) L. H. Jenks, *The Migration of British Capital* (New York: Knopf, 1927).

(40) There are several interesting books on the decline of *laisser-faire* in Britain. See especially C. R. Fay, *Great Britain from Adam Smith to the Present Day* (New York: Longmans, Green and Co., 1928), particularly the first hundred pages; William Cunningham, *The Rise and Decline of the Free Trade Movement* (Cambridge: University Press, 1905); J. M. Keynes, *The End of Laissez-Faire* (London: Woolf, 1926), 53 pp.; Charlotte Leubuscher, *Liberalismus und Protectionismus in der Englischen Wirtschaftspolitik seit dem Krieg* (Jena: Fischer, 1927), vi, 224 pp.; and Herman Levy, *Der Liberalismus in England* (Jena: Fischer, 1928).

(41) French trade with the Levant was considerable, but it was hardly to be compared to the Portuguese commerce with the East.

(42) Isambert, *Recueil général des anciennes lois françaises,* vol. XII, pp. 695–6.

(43) Isambert, vol. XII, p. 834. Similar regulations, called sumptuary laws, were made in 1547, 1549, 1563, 1565, 1573, 1576, 1577, 1583, 1594, 1600, 1601, 1606, 1613, 1623, etc. The frequency of these laws indicates not only that they were

not rigorously effective, but also that the principle behind them continued to be held by the government.

(44) Isambert, vol. XIV, pp. 241–244. Similar decrees were made in 1627, 1629, etc.

(45) E. Levasseur, *Histoire des classes ouvrières et de l'industrie en France avant 1789* (Paris: Rousseau, 1901), tome II, p. 239, explains that royal manufactories comprised three categories of establishments: (1) manufactures of the state which belonged to the king; (2) factories which belonged to companies and had received royal privileges; and (3) private undertakings which had received patent letters of royal manufacture.

(46) See, for a complete and scholarly treatment of this economic activity of the state, P. Boissonnade, *Le socialisme d'état, l'industrie et les classes industrielles en France pendant les deux premiers siècles de l'ère moderne* (1453–1661) (Paris: Champion, 1927). A good example of state encouragement of industry was the granting of letters patent in 1531 to an Italian who wished to make Venetian lace in France. Isambert, vol. XIII, pp. 184–5.

(47) A. Dubois, *Précis de l'histoire des doctrines économiques dans leurs rapports avec les faits et avec les institutions,* pp. 226–7.

(48) The Compagnie de la Nouvelle France (1627) was the only successful one.

(49) F. C. Palm, *The Economic Policies of Richelieu* (University of Illinois, Studies in the Social Sciences, 1920). This work should be used with the greatest care, as its author seems to have used his sources in an uncritical manner.

(50) Perhaps the best work on Bodin is H. Baudrillart, *J. Bodin et son temps* (Paris, 1853).

(51) For a treatment of the economic thinking of this man, see Charles W. Cole, *French Mercantilist Doctrines before Colbert* (New York: R. R. Smith, 1931); H. Hauser, *Les débuts du capitalisme;* "Le Colbertisme avant Colbert et la liberté de travail sous Henri IV, Lyon et Tours, 1596–1601," *Revue Bourguignonne de l'ens. sup.,* vol. XIII, pp. 3–69; and "Le système social de Barthélemy de Laffemas," *Revue Bourguignonne de l'ens. sup.,* vol. XII, pp. 113–131.

(52) C. W. Cole, *op. cit.;* André Vène, *Montchrétien et le nationalisme économique* (Paris, 1923); and Paul Dessaix, *Montchrétien et l'économie politique nationale* (Paris, 1901).

(53) For further information concerning Colbert, see *Lettres, instructions,*

mémoires de Colbert, ed. by Pierre Clément (Paris, 1861–70); Pierre Clément, *Vie de Colbert* (Paris, 1846), 2 vols.; Ernest Lavisse (ed.), *Histoire de France* (Paris: Hachette, 1900–11), 9 vols., the section on Colbert by Lavisse himself, vol. VII, part I; A. J. Sargent, *The Economic Policy of Colbert* (London: Longmans, Green and Co., 1899); S. L. Mims, *Colbert's West Indian Policy* (New Haven: Yale University Press, 1912); P. Boissonnade, *Colbert; le triomphe de l'étatisme, la fondation de la suprématie industrielle de la France, la dictature du travail (1661–1683)* (Paris: Rivière, 1932); and Charles W. Cole, *Colbert and a Century of French Mercantilism* (New York: Columbia University Press, 1939), 2 vols.

(54) François Simiand, *Recherches anciennes et nouvelles sur le mouvement général des prix du XVIᵉ au XIXᵉ siècle* (Paris: Domat Montchretien, 1931), p. 194, and Henri Hauser, *Histoire des prix en France* (Paris: Presses Modernes, 1936).

(55) Gonnard, *Histoire des doctrines économiques,* vol. I, p. 190.

(56) On Colbert's attitude toward idleness, see *Lettres, instructions, mémoires,* vol. II, pp. cclxx, 515, 584.

(57) Punishment for the infraction of the rules for manufacturing was severe. On the first offense, the defective goods were exposed in a public place with an explanatory note and the name of the manufacturer. On the second offense, the manufacturer was blamed publicly. On the third offense, he was exposed with the defective goods in a public place.
Concerning internal customs, see S. Elzinga, "Le tarif de Colbert de 1664 et celui de 1667," *Economisch-historisch Jaarboek* (1929).

(58) *Lettres, instructions, mémoires,* vol. VI, p. 269. See also vol. IV, p. 264.

(59) *Ibid.,* vol. VII, p. 230. See also vol. II, pp. 677 and 739.

(60) Paul Harsin, *Les doctrines monétaires et financières en France du XVIᵉ au XVIIIᵉ siècles* (Paris: Alcan, 1928), and Georges Dionnet, *Le néomercantilisme au XVIIIᵉ siècle et au début de XIXᵉ* (Paris: Giard et Brière, 1901). Dubois, *Précis de l'histoire des doctrines économiques,* p. 27, maintains that these inflationists were anti-mercantilists. See also Paul Harsin, *Dutot, Réflexions politiques sur les finances et le commerce* (Paris: Droz, 1935), 2 vols.

(61) His most important work was *Money and Trade Considered: with a Proposal for Supplying the Nation with Money* (1705).

(62) See *Essai politique sur le commerce* (1731).

(63) In order to secure an idea of the extent of these regulations, see the

lettres patentes of May 5, 1779; those of June 4, 1780; and the decree of August 28, 1783, in Isambert, vol. XXVI, pp. 77, 340; and vol. XXVII, p. 324. Heckscher maintains in his *Mercantilism,* vol. I, p. 173 that some 16,000 persons were put to death as a result of enforcing laws against cotton prints between the years 1686 and 1759.

(64) Charles Ballot, *L'introduction du machinisme dans l'industrie française* (Paris: Rieder & Cie., 1923), p. 3, and Henri Sée, *L'évolution commerciale et industrielle de la France sous l'ancien régime* (Paris: Alcan, 1925) and *Esquisse d'une histoire économique et sociale de la France depuis les origines jusqu'à la guerre mondiale* (Paris: Alcan, 1929), p. 338.

(65) Ballot, *op. cit.,* pp. 43–5.

(66) Ballot, pp. 247–248.

(67) Ballot, p. 398.

(68) Ballot, pp. 436 ff. The memoirs of Jars were published in the *Journal d'Agriculture* (October, 1770), and in the *Mémoires de l'Academie des Sciences* for 1769 (published in 1773). They are entitled *Manière de préparer le charbon minéral, outrément appelé houille, pour le substituer au charbon de bois dans les travaux métallurgiques, mise en usage dans les mines de Saint-Bel* . . .

(69) Ballot, p. 69.

(70) Ballot, pp. 117–118, 27–28.

(71) Hazel Roberts, *Boisguilbert, Economist of the Reign of Louis XIV* (New York: Columbia University Press, 1935).

(72) This essay, written originally in English and translated into French for the use of a friend, was completed about 1730, but was not published until 1755.

(73) George Weulersse, *Le mouvement physiocratique en France de 1756 à 1770* (Paris: Alcan, 1910), vol. I, pp. 78–9. See also the works of G. Schelle: *Du Pont de Nemours & l'école physiocratique* (Paris, 1888); *Le Docteur Quesnay, chirurgien, médecin de Madame de Pompadour et de Louis XV, physiocrate* (Paris, 1907); *Turgot* (Paris, 1909); *Vincent de Gournay* (Paris, 1897).

(74) Weulersse, *op. cit.,* vol. II, pp. 683 ff.

(75) G. Martin, *La grande industrie sous Louis XV* (Paris, 1899), p. 57.

(76) Circular letter sent to the inspectors of manufactures April 26, 1775.

(77) *Lettres patentes* of May 5, 1779, and of June 4, 1780.

(78) E. Levasseur, *Histoire du commerce de la France* (Paris: Rousseau, 1911), vol. I, pp. 449–450.

(79) J. Necker, *De l'administration des finances de la France* (1784), vol. II, p. 170.

(80) Roger Picard, *Les cahiers de 1789 au point de vue industriel et commercial* (Paris: Rivière et Cie., 1910), p. 115.

(81) Henri Sée, *Esquisse d'une histoire économique et sociale de la France,* pp. 322–3.

(82) E. Levasseur, "Les traités de commerce entre la France et l'Angleterre," *Revue d'économie politique,* vol. XV, 1901, pp. 970–971; and Charles Gouraud, *Politique commerciale de la France et de son influence sur le progrès de la richesse publique depuis le moyen âge jusqu'à nos jours* (Paris: Albert Durand, 1854), vol. I, p. 305.

(83) F. Dumas, *Étude sur le traité de commerce de 1786 entre la France et l'Angleterre* (Toulouse: Privat, 1904), pp. 3–5.

(84) Article XVIII of the Treaty of 1783. See also the annex to the treaty, in which the French specified that the negotiations should endeavor to rectify those portions of the trade agreement of the Treaty of Utrecht which seemed unacceptable.

(85) See also P. de Ségur-Dupeyron, *Histoire des négociations commerciales et maritimes de la France aux XVIIe et XVIIIe siècles* (Paris: Ernest Thorin, 1872–73), 3 vols.

On the French side, the negotiations were carried on by Vergennes, Controller General of Foreign Affairs, who believed that France should make some concessions to the English to keep them from retaliating for their recent defeat and who was sympathetic to the *laisser-faire* idea of the Physiocrat Dupont de Nemours, and by Gérard de Rayneval, an honest servant, who was not well-versed in commercial questions, but who followed the orders of his superior. On the English side the chief negotiator was William Eden, an able statesman with a brilliant record, who made his preparations for the conferences with the French with meticulous care. He sent out questionnaires to English manufacturers in an effort to learn their desires concerning a trade agreement with France, and he dispatched investigators across the Channel to study the state of French indusry. Thus he was able to present specific demands based not, as has often been thought, on the theories of Adam Smith or of any other economist, but on the practical needs of English manufacturers. He went to seek concessions for the import of English goods into France, and to offer advantages for the import of French goods into England on only those products which England did not produce. The French preparations for the negotiations were, on the other hand, very meager, for Vergennes, in view of his Physiocratic tendencies and his desire to please the English, was ready to grant such large favors that he even feared to consult French industrialists.

So certain was Eden of what he wanted that he was able, a few days after his arrival in Paris, to present a tentative treaty to Rayneval. Dumas, *op. cit.*, 40–43; Levasseur, *Histoire du commerce*, vol. I, p. 537; see also, G. F. von Martens, *Recueil des traités* . . . (2nd edition, prepared by Charles de Martens; Göttingen: Dietrich, 1826–35), vol. IV, p. 155.

(86) Dumas, *op. cit.*, p. 160.

(87) Camille Bloch, *Études sur l'histoire économique de la France (1760–1789)* (Paris: Picard et Fils, 1900), pp. 268–9, held that the treaty was not well received in England. This point of view has been adequately refuted by Dumas, *op. cit.*, chap. VI.

(88) A. M. Arnould, *De la balance du commerce et des relations commerciales extérieures de la France dans toutes les parties du globe, particulièrement à la fin du règne de Louis XIV et au moment de la Révolution* (2nd edition; Paris: An III), vol. I, pp. 172–180. Compare these figures with those found in *Statistique de la France publiée par le ministre des travaux publics, de l'agriculture, et du commerce* (Paris: Imprimerie Royale, 1838). Arnould's figures are in proportionate agreement, although they do not correspond exactly, with English figures. See Auguste Arnauné, *Le commerce extérieur et les tarifs de douane* (Paris: Alcan, 1911), p. 108.

(89) F. Dumas at the end of his *Étude sur le traité de commerce de 1786* concludes that the treaty had a salutary effect on French industry; that, although it caused an industrial crisis, the crisis was necessary and beneficial; and that, because of the industrial changes which it effected, competition with England became easy.

Auguste Arnauné in his *Le commerce extérieur et les tarifs de douane* states that the treaty caused great progress to be realized by French industry. This is also the opinion of P. Clément, *Histoire du système protecteur en France* (Paris: Gillaumin, 1854), p. 90.

On the other hand, see the judgment of Charles His de Butenval in his *Précis historique et économique du traité de commerce entre la France et la Grande Bretagne, signé à Versailles le 26 septembre, 1786* (Paris: Dentu, 1869), and of Charles Gouraud, *Politique commerciale de la France et de son influence sur le progrès de la richesse publique depuis le moyen âge jusqu'à nos jours*, vol. I, pp. 43–4.

(90) Henri Sée in his *Évolution commerciale et industrielle de la France sous l'ancien régime* (Paris, 1925), pp. 299 ff., and his *Esquisse d'une histoire économique et sociale de la France,* pp. 323-4, and Charles Schmidt, "La crise industrielle de 1788 en France," *Revue historique,* vol. XCVII (1908), pp. 78-94, maintain that the treaty had much to do with bringing on the crisis of 1788, and do not cite any particular industrial progress that resulted from it. Charles Ballot, *L'introduction du machinisme dans l'industrie française,* p. 12, agrees that the treaty contributed to the crisis, but cites one contemporary witness to the effect that English competition drove French manufacturers to greater efforts.

(91) They are based on Arnould, *De la balance du commerce* and, for the India trade, on L'Abbé Raynal, *Histoire philosophique et politique des établissements et du commerce des Européens dan les deux Indes* (Geneva, 1780-81). Arnould's figures are expressed in *livres tournois* which were established by the financial reform of 1785. At the Archives Nationales there are series of trade statistics. Those prepared by Bruyard are given in *livres tournois* at their mean value during each period for which the statistics are quoted. The statistics of Bruyard do not agree with those of Arnould. At the Archives there is also another series that does not correspond with the figures of Arnould or those of Bruyard. Necker in the *Administration des finances* gives still another set of figures. See E. Levasseur, *Histoire du commerce,* vol. I, pp. 510-11.

(92) See the remarkable work of C. Labrousse, *Esquisse du mouvement des prix et des revenus en France au XVIII*e *siècle* (Paris: Dalloz, 1932), pp. 361-2. In this same connection one would do well to consult, but to use with great caution, G. d'Avenel, *Histoire économique de la propriété, des salaires, des denrées, et de tous les prix en général depuis l'an 1200 jusqu'en l'an 1800* (Paris, 1894-1926), 7 vols.

(93) Labrousse, *Esquisse du mouvement des prix et des revenus en France au XVIII*e *siècle,* pp. 640-642; Georges Lefebvre, Raymond Guyot, Philippe Sagnac, *La Révolution française* (Paris: Alcan, 1930), pp. 9-10; and Philippe Sagnac, *La Révolution (1789-1792),* in E. Lavisse (ed.), *Histoire de France contemporaine* (Paris: Hachette, 1920), vol. I, p. 68.

(94) Roger Picard, *Les cahiers de 1789 au point de vue industriel et commercial,* pp. 149-173.

(95) Condillac, *Le commerce et le gouvernement considérés relativement l'un à l'autre* (1776), part I, chap. XXIX; part II, chap. XVII. See Auguste Lebeau, *Condillac, économiste* (Paris: Guillaumin & Cie, 1903).

(96) Author of *De la balance du commerce.*

(97) F. L. Nussbaum, *Commercial Policy in the French Revolution: A Study of the Career of G. T. A. Ducher* (Washington: American Historical Association, 1917), pp. 38–39:

"If a state is the most populous of Europe; if the soil is fertile and the manufactures numerous; if it has rich possessions all over the globe—that state ought to cut itself off and ought to open its markets to foreign goods only on great inducements. No power can give it the equivalent of its own internal market for its own manufactures. The outlets which will be opened to it among foreign powers cannot be useful except when it receives only specie or raw materials, and not manufactured goods, in return.

". . . The interest of commerce demands that a patriotic barrier should be raised at the frontiers to assure to French industry the greatest possible share of the products of its own activity. . . .

". . . the new tariff ought not to leave any imposts in any of the ports of France, except on the vessels and goods of foreigners. . . .

"An industry that deserves particular encouragement is the construction and navigation of ships. Navigation is another manufacture . . . to buy vessels of foreign construction and not to limit the participation of foreigners in the carrying trade is to renounce two very important industries. The commerce of France demands that it should be ordained that no vessel will be reputed French or be entitled to the privileges of French vessels if it has not been built in France . . . and is entirely manned by Frenchmen. Our interest requires us to ordain that no foreign commodities, productions, or goods can be imported except directly by French vessels or vessels belonging to subjects of the sovereign of the country of growth, production, or manufacture, or of the ordinary ports of sale and first exportation."

(98) *Dialogues sur le commerce des blés* (1768–69).

(99) Gonnard, *Histoire des doctrines économiques,* vol. II, p. 146. See also Gignoux, "L'Abbé Galiani et la querelle des grains au XVIIIᵉ siècle," *Revue d'histoire économique et sociale,* vol. X, 1922, pp. 17–37.

(100) No attention has been given to German economic theory and practice in this brief sketch. This was done because the Germanies were not united into a nation, and because the German states did not contribute anything to national economic theory and practice different from that of other states. It should be noted that the economic policies of Colbert received wide publicity in Europe in the seventeenth century. In the Germanies the theories of the Kameralists, so-called because they concocted economic procedure for the "chancelleries" to follow, are analogous in many respects to those of France, but are perhaps more political than the French, if that is possible. J. J. Becher (1625–82) preached the necessity of a large population, the importation of raw materials and the exportation of manufactured products, an active commerce, a German *Zollverein,* and a great national industry.

Wilhelm von Horningk (1638–1712) in his *Oesterreich über alles, wann es nur will* argued for Austrian economic self-sufficiency. And Wilhelm von Schröder (1640–89) maintained that gold and silver should be obtained in order to speed up production. In Prussia the Great Elector pursued policies not unlike those followed by France, and Frederick the Great was a thoroughgoing productionist. In Russia Peter the Great's economic program was definitely national. As time went on, German economists refined their views of Kammer economics. J. H. G. von Justi (1741–91) argued that states must control private economics for the welfare of the collectivity, and Josef von Sonnenfels (1732–1817) supported the theory of national production and the doctrine that the favorableness of trade balances should be judged in productionist terms. There were many other Kameralists, but those mentioned are typical. See the treatment in Mombert, *Geschichte der Nationalökonomie,* pp. 157–192, and bibliography, p. 192.

CHAPTER II

(1) Carlton J. H. Hayes, *The Historical Evolution of Modern Nationalism.*

(2) See, for instance, Shepard B. Clough, *A History of the Flemish Movement in Belgium* (New York: R. Smith, 1930).

(3) For a comprehension of the *ancien régime* the following books will be found to be of especial service: A. de Tocqueville, *L'ancien régime et la Révolution* (Paris, 1956); A. Chérest, *La chute de l'ancien régime* (Paris, 1884); H. Taine, *L'ancien régime* (Paris, 1876); E. Lavisse (ed.), *Histoire de France,* vol. IX; H. Sée: *Economic and Social Conditions in France during the Eighteenth Century* (New York: Knopf, 1927), a poor translation of *La vie économique et les classes sociales en France au XVIIIe siècle* (Paris, 1924); *L'évolution commerciale et industrielle de la France sous l'ancien régime* (Paris, 1925); *Les idées politiques en France au XVIIIe siècle* (Paris, 1920); and *L'évolution de la pensée politique en France au XVIIIe siècle* (Paris, 1925).

(4) They numbered 131,000 and 400,000, respectively, out of a total population of between 23,000,000 and 24,000,000. Abbé Coyer, *Noblesse commerçante* (1756).

Henri Sée, *Economic and Social Conditions in France during the Eighteenth Century,* p. 60; Necker, *De l'administration des finances;* Calonne, *L'état de la population du royaume* (1787); Henri Sée, "Les essais de statistiques démographiques en Bretagne à la fin de l'ancien régime," *Études sur la vie économique en Bretagne* (Paris: Imprimerie Nationale, 1930); and E. Levasseur, *La population française* (Paris: Rousseau, 1889–92), 3 vols.

(5) This class was growing rapidly with the concentration of industry and the extension of commerce. One coal mining company employed 4000 laborers, 600 horses, and 12 steam engines before 1789. See the foreign trade statistics cited in chapter I. See also Knight, Barnes, and Flügel, *Economic History of Europe,* p. 328.

The bourgeoisie was not very large numerically. The entire urban population of France was but 2,000,000, and, in the provinces, only one city, Lyons, had more than 100,000 inhabitants.

(6) Sée, *Economic and Social Conditions in France during the Eighteenth Century,* p. 28.

(7) C. Labrousse, *Esquisse du mouvement des prix et des revenus en France au XVIIIe siècle,* p. 608; concerning his method, the author states:

"Le mouvement général des prix, tel qu'il ressort de nos 24 séries d'indices partiels—représentatives de la production nationale, constituées dans leur masse d'après une documentation administrative sérieuse que ne paraît affecter aucun vice systématique: mercuriales, extraits de mercuriales, taxes municipales, états de l'inspection des manufactures; exprimant des amplitudes auxquelles on peut attacher, en droit, pour les articles les plus importants, la signification d'un ordre de grandeur certain ou simple, en fait, pour la plupart, une valeur fonctionnelle apparemment sérieuse, et dont les erreurs, indépendantes et peut-être assez faibles, comme permet de le supposer la concordance des mouvements comparables, doivent se compenser en partie; reproduisant au reste remarquablement des caractères généraux des variations des prix—peut donc être tenu, dans l'ordre qualitatif et quantitatif, pour l'esquisse, d'intention plus proprement budgétaire et sociale que monétaire et économique, annoncée au début de ce travail." Pp. 360–361.

(8) There were crises in 1725, 1740, 1759, 1766–68, 1772–76, 1784–85, and 1789.

(9) Albert Mathiez, *La vie chère et le mouvement social sous la terreur* (Paris: Payot, 1927), p. 16. Georges Lefebvre in *Documents relatifs à l'histoire des subsistances dans le district de Bergues pendant la Révolution* (Lille: Robbe, 1914), vol. I, p. xxxviii, states:

"If bread had been cheap, the forceful intervention of the lower classes, which was indispensable for the overthrow of the *ancien régime,* would perhaps not have taken place and the bourgeoisie would have triumphed less easily."

(10) Labrousse, *op. cit.,* pp. 539–541:

"La grande crise industrielle de 1788–1789, qui présente le même caractère de généralité que celle de 1770, est antérieure au maximum cyclique des prix des céréales enregistré en 1789. Il faut en chercher l'origine dans le traité de commerce franco-anglais: la chute de la production se manifeste presque aussitôt, dès 1787. Mais c'est surtout au cours du second semestre de l'année suivante qu'elle s'accélère, avec la rapide montée des prix agricoles. Le maximum cyclique, frappe la France entière, apparaît simultanément dans presque toutes les régions. La crise est nationale. L'effondrement industriel, national aussi.

"On paraît retrouver au cours du XIXᵉ siècle, et notamment jusqu'à la crise de 1847, une corrélation cyclique du même ordre entre le prix des céréales et le mouvement de la production textile. Valable par delà le XVIIIᵉ siècle, la corrélation l'est également au delà des frontières françaises et présente un caractère international. On a déjà signalé l'influence des variations des prix des céréales hindoues sur l'activité industrielle anglaise. De même l'exportation des toiles crées de Bretagne dans la péninsule ibérique dépend des fluctuations de la récolte espagnole ou portugaise et de leur action sur le marché. L'année 1768, par exemple, a été, en France comme en Espagne, une année de faible productivité: 'Les récoltes one été mauvaises l'année dernière en Espagne; le peuple espagnol qui seul consomme de ces toiles [crées], n'a pu en acheter, ce qui a fait tomber les prix dans la fabrique . . .' écrit en 1769 l'inspection des manufactures de Bretagne. Si, en France, comme on l'a vu, 'le prix du pain est la boussole des fabriques,' 'le thermomètre du commerce des toiles crées est la récolte des grains et des fruits en Espagne . . .' La chute de la productivité cyclique et la hausse des prix agricoles qui en est la conséquence provoquent une crise de sous—consommation génératrice de chômage dans le pays exportateur."

Labrousse, *op. cit.*, pp. 640–1:

"Nous l'avons déjà noté à plusieurs reprises: l'explosion révolutionaire qui survient en juillet 1789 dans les villes et les campagnes cöincide non seulement avec l'année, mais, approximativement, avec la période de l'année où le prix du blé atteint son maximum depuis le début du mouvement de longue durée, et même depuis la seconde décade du siècle. La hausse cyclique a été d'une soudaineté exceptionnelle. L'amplitude du mouvement, exceptionnelle aussi. Le maximum cyclique est atteint à la fois dans la presque totalité du Royaume, dans 27 généralités sur 32. Soudaine, virulente, générale, la crise agricole de sous-production éclate dans un pays frappé déjà par une grave crise industrielle. . . . Mais la crise agricole va réagir, comme c'est la règle, sur l'activité industrielle, et notamment sur l'activité textile, la grande industrie de l'ancien régime économique. . . ."

(11) Justin Godart, *L'ouvrier en soie de Lyon* (Lyons, 1901).

(12) In spite of the Family Pact that united France with Spain, and as part of a campaign to resurrect Spanish industry and to increase Spanish national production, the King of Spain issued (1778) a decree which increased import duties and virtually closed the Spanish market to certain

French goods—especially to textiles that came in large part from Brittany. Henri Sée, *Esquisse d'une histoire économique et sociale de la France,* p. 326. A. Girard, "Une négociation commerciale entre l'Espagne et la France en 1782," *Revue historique,* vol. CXI, 1912, pp. 292 ff.

(13) For most of what follows on the industrial crisis, see Charles Schmidt, "La crise industrielle de 1788 en France," *Revue historique,* vol. XCVII, 1908, pp. 78–94.

(14) Sée, *Economic and Social Conditions in France,* pp. 208–9.

(15) A. Mathiez, *La Révolution française* (4th edition; Paris: Colin, 1930), vol. I, p. 22.

(16) About 2,000,000,000 *livres* were expended by the French during this struggle.

(17) Marcel Marion, *Histoire financière de la France depuis 1715* (Paris: Rousseau, 1914–1928), vol. I, *loc. cit.*

(18) The fact that not one of these men was a financier, with the possible exception of Necker, who was more of an accountant than a statesman, did not matter.

(19) The meeting of the Estates General was called for May, 1789. It was the first meeting of this body that had been held since 1614.

(20) Roger Picard, *Les cahiers de 1789 au point de vue industriel et commercial,* pp. 132–134. See also Beatrice Hyslop, *French Nationalism in 1789 according to the General Cahiers* (New York: Columbia University Press, 1934).

(21) J. Letaconnoux, "La question des subsistances et du commerce des grains . . . au XVIIIᵉ siècle," *Revue d'histoire moderne et contemporaine,* vol. VIII, pp. 409–445; and *Les subsistances et le commerce des grains en Bretagne au XVIIIᵉ siècle* (Rennes: Oberthür, 1909).

(22) Picard, *op. cit.,* pp. 128–9.

(23) Picard, pp. 131–2.

(24) Picard, p. 142.

(25) Picard, p. 125.

(26) *Archives parlementaires–Besançon,* vol. II, p. 343.

(27) Nobility of Béziers, *Archives parlementaires,* vol. III, p. 348.

(28) Picard, p. 142.

(29) The Chambers of Commerce in France were founded at the beginning of the eighteenth century and by the end of the century had become important institutions. See Fournier, *La chambre de commerce de Marseille d'après ses archives historiques* (Marseilles, 1910); G. Pariset, *La chambre de commerce de Lyon* (Lyons, 1887); and H. Wallon, *La chambre de commerce de la province de Normandie (1703-1791)* (Rouen, 1903).

(30) Dumas, *Traité de commerce de 1786*, pp. 152-157. Also see Arthur Young, *Voyages en France en 1787, 1788, et 1789*, translated by Henri Sée (Paris: Colin, 1931), vol. II, pp. 928-950.

(31) See above, p. 34.
The Intendant of Maritime Commerce, in a probably greatly exaggerated report on trade with England during the first eight months following the application of the treaty, maintained that the increase of English manufactured imports into France was tremendous, and that France only sold to England raw materials that were bought back as finished products. The Chamber of Commerce of Amiens pointed out that competition with English textiles was impossible in the *Provinces Réputées Étrangères* because, while English goods paid a tax of 12 per cent, French goods from the *Cinq Grosses Fermes* paid 7½ per cent, which resulted in a net protection of only 4½ per cent. This, it was held, was absolutely insufficient. See Dumas, *op. cit.*, pp. 157-158.

(32) Dumas, *op. cit.*, pp. 160-162.

(33) Cited in Picard, p. 159.

(34) Cited in Picard, p. 161.

(35) Cited in Picard, p. 160.

(36) "Que l'on représente au souverain le tort, peut-être irréparable, que le traité de commerce fait avec l'Angleterre, a occasionné aux manufactures françaises: traité funeste, où 24 millions de consommateurs traitent avec 8 millions, et qui, dans une supposition égale d'importation et d'exportation, fait sortir de la France 24 millions contre 8, ce qui fait les deux tiers de perte réelle, lesquelles pertes augmentent encore bien d'avantage par l'anglomanie qui perd les Français, et leur fait honteusement tirer de nos voisins toutes sortes de marchandises indistinctement, sans aucun égard pour les ouvriers français abandonnés à la détresse, sans égard pour ces belles manufactures qui assuraient à la France la supériorité dans l'Europe; tandis que ces mêmes Anglais, par un amour patriotique qui devrait nous enflammer comme eux, ne tirent rien de la France que nos vins, dont les riches Anglais ne peuvent se priver et qu'ils consommeraient même sans ce fatal traité." Ch. L. Chassin, *Les élections et les cahiers de Paris en 1789* (Paris, 1888), vol. II, p. 64.

(37) Picard, pp. 153–154.

(38) Picard, p. 156.

(39) Picard, pp. 252–254.

(40) Picard, p. 101.

(41) Picard, p. 260.

(42) Picard, pp. 169–170.

(43) Isambert, vol. XXVII, p. 459. Arnauné, *Le commerce extérieur et les tarifs de douane,* pp. 216–47.

(44) Picard, p. 166.

(45) As it was, such measures availed but little, for the Revolutionary and Napoleonic Wars injured French foreign commerce so badly that the level of 1788 was not attained again until 1825. Sée, *Economic and Social Conditions in France in the Eighteenth Century,* p. 154.

(46) The following books will be found particularly useful for a general study of the Revolution: L. R. Gottschalk, *Era of the French Revolution* (New York: Houghton, Mifflin & Co., 1929); C. D. Hazen, *French Revolution* (New York: Holt & Co., 1931), 2 vols.; F. V. A. Aulard, *French Revolution, a Political History;* translated from the French of the 3d edition (1910), 4 vols.; A. Mathiez, *La Révolution française* (Paris: Armand Colin, 4th edition, 1930), 3 vols.; Georges Lefebvre, Raymond Guyot, Philippe Sagnac, *La Révolution française;* P. Sagnac, "La Révolution (1789–1792)" and G. Pariset, "La Révolution (1792–1799)," in E. Lavisse (ed.), *Histoire de France contemporaine* (Paris: Hachette, 1920); J. Jaurès, *Histoire socialiste* (Paris, 1901–1905), 5 vols.; A. Mathiez, *La réaction thermedorienne* (Paris, 1929); Henri Sée, *Évolution et révolutions* (Paris: Flammarion, 1929); Crane Brinton, *A Decade of Revolution, 1789–1799* (New York: Harper & Brothers, 1934); and Henri Sée, "L'influence de la Révolution sur l'évolution industrielle de la France," in *In Onore e ricordi di Giuseppe Prato* (Turin, 1931), pp. 103–110.

(47) Mathiez, *La Révolution française,* vol. I, pp. 44–46.

(48) The constitution provided that Louis XVI, who had been "Louis by the grace of God, King of France and Navarre," should be in the future, "Louis by the grace of God and the Constitution of the State, King of the French." Montesquieu's principle of the separation of powers was applied. The king was allowed administrative power, but his legislative power was reduced to a suspensive veto. There was only one house, because, if an

upper house had been created on English lines, it would have placed the noble class in a favored position, which was just what the Revolution was trying to avoid. The franchise was based on a property qualification; elections were indirect and so arranged that poorer citizens would be eliminated; and public office was limited to those who fulfilled comparatively high property qualifications.

(49) For what follows on the peasant question and the abolition of feudal dues, consult: Henri Sée, *Französische Wirtschaftsgeschichte,* ed. by G. Brodnitz (Jena, 1932), vol. II, pp. 20 ff.; P. Sagnac, *La législation civile de la Révolution française* (Paris, 1898); A. Aulard, *La Révolution française et le régime féodal* (Paris, 1919); and P. Sagnac and P. Caron, *Les comités des droits féodaux et de législation et l'abolition du régime seigneurial* (Paris, 1906).

(50) Georges Lefebvre, *La grande peur de 1789* (Paris: Colin, 1932).

(51) Decree of August 5 and 11, 1789. There was further trouble in the winter of 1789-90, and the decrees of March 15, 1790, and of May, 1790, abolished certain feudal rights without indemnity, but others only on payment of twenty or twenty-five times their annual value.

(52) Decree of July 17, 1793. This decree stated that commons belonged to the inhabitants of the town in which they were located. Most of them were not divided. See Georges Bourgin, *Le partage des communaux* (Paris, 1910). Commons and *vaine pâture* (the right to pasture one's flocks in any fields after harvest-time) were not abolished until about 1840.

(53) February 9, 1792. The land was put up for sale and sold by preference in exchange for *assignats.* Although the peasants as a class bought from one-half to two-thirds of the land thus disposed of, except in districts near cities, which went mostly to the bourgeoisie, the majority of them secured no land at all. This fact proved to be the hardest blow of the Constituent Assembly to revolutionary enthusiasm. J. Loutchisky, *Quelques remarques sur la vente des biens nationaux* (Paris, 1913); M. Marion, *La vente des biens nationaux* (Paris, 1908); and P. Sagnac, "La division du sol pendant la Révolution et ses conséquences," *Revue d'histoire moderne et contemporaine,* vol. V, 1903-04, pp. 457-470.

(54) Marion, *Histoire financière de la France,* vols. II and III; S. E. Harris, *The Assignats* (Cambridge: Harvard University Press, 1930); J. Morini-Comby, *Les assignats, Révolution et inflation* (Paris, 1925); R. Stourm, *Les finances de l'ancien régime et de la Révolution* (Paris, 1885), 2 vols.

(55) Decree of September 27–October 16, 1791.

(56) March 17, 1791. An indemnity was given to the masters, for they had paid dearly for their rights. The amounts finally paid them were often derisory on account of the fall in the value of the *assignats*.

(57) The Le Chapelier law, June 14, 1791. Passed following labor troubles —and demanded by manufacturers. E. Levasseur, *Histoire des classes ouvrières et de l'industrie en France de 1789 à 1870* (2d edition; Paris: Rousseau, 1903–04), vol. I, pp. 49–56. See also Grace M. Jaffé, *Le mouvement ouvrier à Paris pendant la Révolution française, 1789–1791* (Paris, 1924); a work in Russian by E. Tarlé on the working class in France during the Revolution but given in a résumé by Karéiev in *Révolution française,* vol. LXII, 1912, pp. 333 ff.; and E. Tarlé, *Studien zur Geschichte der Arbeiterklasse in Frankreich während der Revolution* (Leipzig, 1910).

(58) October 30–31–November 5, 1790. Provinces were abolished December 1, 1790. The *octrois* were also suppressed, May 1, 1791, but were resurrected later.

(59) With the abolition of feudalism.

(60) Commission established May 10, 1790. The metric system was adopted in 1793, but it was slow in being taken up by the people and was not generally employed until 1800. Lefebvre, Guyot, Sagnac, *La Révolution française,* pp. 478–480.

(61) August 29, 1789.

(62) Levasseur, *Histoire du commerce de la France,* vol. II, pp. 37–38. Pierre Caron, "L'enquête sur l'état des routes, rivières, et canaux au début de l'an II," *Bulletin d'histoire économique de la Révolution* (1917–1919).

(63) Law of March 18, 1791.

(64) Law of June 22, 1791.

(65) September 11, 1793. J. Saintoyant, *La colonisation française pendant la Révolution (1789–1799)* (Paris: La Renaissance du Livre, 1930), 2 vols. The Constituent appointed a committee to study trade between France and French colonies. The committee reported too late for discussion by the Constituent, but the report indicates the temper of the body:

"We ought to have a monopoly of the commerce with the colonies; foreigners ought not to be admitted; we can furnish all their [the colonies'] requirements. . . . The absolute exclusion of foreigners—that is the most infallible means to make our commerce with America prosper."

(66) A commission had been appointed in 1767 to study the question.

(67) Levasseur, *Histoire du commerce,* vol. II, p. 11; Sée, *Französische Wirtschaftsgeschichte,* vol. II, pp. 65–6.

(68) March 2–15, 1791.

(69) See the discussion of Jacobin nationalism in Carlton J. H. Hayes, *The Historical Evolution of Modern Nationalism,* chap. III.

(70) March 1, 1793.

(71) Levasseur, *Histoire du commerce,* vol. II, p. 16; Eli F. Heckscher, *The Continental System: an Economic Interpretation* (Oxford: Clarendon Press, 1922), pp. 25–26. Some exemptions had to be made on account of France's dire needs for certain goods. Decree of May 19, 1793.

(72) F. L. Nussbaum, *Commercial Policy in the French Revolution,* p. 109.

(73) Saintoyant, *La colonisation française pendant la Révolution,* p. 356.

(74) October 18, 1793, a supplementary decree was issued.

(75) A French ship was defined, after January 1, 1794, as being one that had been built either in France or the colonies, or taken from the enemy and manned by a crew of which the officers and three-fourths of the men were French. Because of France's great needs for certain goods, breaches had to be made in the Navigation Act. See Nussbaum, *op. cit.,* pp. 287–9.

(76) This is the first time in history that the entire civil population of a nation was treated as besieged. Lefebvre, Guyot, Sagnac, *La Révolution française,* p. 181.

(77) November 6, 1793, to January 8, 1794. On this latter date, instructions required the neutralization of French colonial goods by passing through a neutral port. In January, 1798, a new order required that a ship from French colonies had either to pass via a port of its homeland before sailing for France, or to pass via a British port. This regulation remained in force until the peace in 1802.

(78) Heckscher, *op. cit.,* p. 44.

(79) Heckscher, *op. cit.,* p. 32.

(80) Heckscher, *op. cit.,* p. 42.

(81) As our study progresses, it will become more and more evident that in times of peace men are, for the most part, economic individualists, and that, in times of national danger, they display the greatest willingness to coöperate. In this respect they are like monkeys. Mr. S. Zukerman in his very

remarkable *The Social Life of Monkeys and Apes* (New York: Harcourt, Brace and Co., 1932) states that in the primate world "mutually coöperative behavior occurs only when a group is attacked or threatened. . . . Every animal obtains such social and material advantages as he can in a predominantly hostile environment. Except in some situations of attack it is usually every monkey for himself."

(82) Quoted in Hayes, *The Historical Evolution of Modern Nationalism,* pp. 53–54. *Moniteur,* April 4, 1793, p. 420.

(83) This work in time became so enormous that the Committee was incapable of attending to it all. To supervise much of the work, it set up a Commission des Armes et Poudres de la République, whose name was later changed to the Commission des Armes, Poudres, et Exploitation des Mines. The Commission was divided into several "Agencies" for various branches of economic activity.

(84) Barère's enthusiasm pictured the future activity:

"Paris va voir dans peu de jours une manufacture immense de tout genre s'élever dans son sein. Dépositaire de tous les arts, cette cité a des ressources immenses que le Comité . . . a déjà mises en activité, en se concertant avec des patriotes très habiles . . . Le Paris de l'ancien régime vendait des modes ridicules, des hachets nombreux, des chiffons brillants et des meubles commodes à la France entière et à une partie de l'Europe; le Paris de la République, sans cesser d'être le théâtre du goût et le dépôt des inventions agréables et des productions des arts . . ., va devenir l'arsenal de la France . . . Les plans s'exécutent dans ce moment par des articles renommés et des administrateurs d'un patriotisme prononcé. . . ."

(85) C. Richard, *Le Comité de Salut Public et les fabrications de guerre sous la terreur* (Paris: Rieder, 1921), p. 99.

(86) *Ibid.,* p. 343.

(87) *Ibid.,* pp. 362 ff.

(88) *Ibid.,* p. 447.

(89) *Ibid.,* p. 459.

(90) Quoted in Richard in full, p. 460.

(91) G. Lefebvre, "Le commerce extérieur en l'an II," *La Révolution française,* vol. LXXVIII, 1925, pp. 132–155; 214–243.

(92) Archives Nationales, A. F., II, 218, d. 1882.

(93) It is interesting to note that private banks contributed to the inflation

by issuing *medailles de confiance,* which could be exchanged for *assignats* when they were issued. A. Mathiez, *La vie chère et le mouvement social sous la terreur,* p. 52.

(94) A. Mathiez, *La Révolution française,* vol. III, p. 222. André Lichtenberger, *Le socialisme et la Révolution française* (Paris, 1899).

(95) To meet current expenses it had to issue paper money, *mandats territoriaux,* similar to the *assignats.*

(96) Mathiez's judgment of the inflation in his *La vie chère sous la terreur,* p. 613, seems too severe.

"By means of inflation [the bourgeoisie] conquered its enemies at home and abroad. By means of the inflation this class equipped at cheap cost its war factories. By means of the inflation it domesticated the lower classes for a century."

(97) Law of Nivôse (December 24, 1794).

(98) Particularly those made at Lille.

(99) C. L. Lokke, *France and the Colonial Question* (New York: Columbia University Press, 1932), pp. 182 ff.

(100) A Girondist naval officer, Kersaint, had declared in 1793 that:

"The credit of England rests on fictitious riches. The real riches of that people are scattered everywhere and are essentially mobile. On her own soil the national wealth of England is to be found almost exclusively in her Bank, and the whole of that structure is supported by the prodigious activity of her maritime commerce."

(101) July 2, 1796 [14 Messidor, Year IV]; January 18, 1798 [29 Nivôse, Year V].

(102) 10 Brumaire, Year V.

(103) Bonaparte, shortly after his coming to power, put a stop to the war on neutral trade.

(104) This was a really gigantic sum for the period. At the outbreak of the World War in 1914, Britain's debt was only £587,000,000.

(105) They were not resumed until after the Napoleonic wars.

(106) As early as 1795 there had been talk of extending the blockade.

"The alliance with Holland offers the most important result of all, namely, to exclude the British from the Continent, to shut them out in war time from Bayonne to north of Friesland and from access to the Baltic and North Seas. The trade with the interior of Germany will then return to its natural channels. . . . Deprived of these immense markets, harassed by revolts and internal disturbances which will be the consequences, England will be greatly embarrassed by her colonial and Asiatic goods. These goods, being unsaleable, will fall to low prices, and the English will find themselves vanquished by excess [vaincus par l'abondance], just as they had wished to vanquish the French by shortage."

Cited in Heckscher, *op. cit.,* p. 57.

(107) Sée, *Esquisse,* p. 395. R. Schnerb, "La dépression économique sous le Directoire," *Annales historiques de la Révolution française,* 1934, pp. 27–49.

(108) Levasseur, *Histoire du commerce,* vol. IX, p. 42.

(109) *Statistique de la France, commerce extérieur* (1838).

(110) Silk manufacturers at Lyons profited most, perhaps, from these benefactions, although a large grant was given to a certain Barneville, who had founded a muslin factory at Versailles, and a substantial sum was placed at the disposition of Leblanc, the inventor of artificial soda, for the exploitation of his invention.

(111) Lefebvre, Guyot, Sagnac, *La Révolution française,* p. 444. See circular of October 15, 1795.

(112) December 16, 1797.

(113) The action was also called a *coup d'état.* It was the third one under the Directory. See Albert Meynier, *Les coups d'état du Directoire* (Paris: Presses Universitaires, 1927–28), 3 vols.; and Albert Mathiez, *Le Directoire du 11 brumaire an IV au 18 fructidor an V* (Paris: Colin, 1934).

(114) Lefebvre, Guyot, Sagnac, *op. cit.,* p. 441.

CHAPTER III

(1) On Napoleon and the Napoleonic era, consult, for general works: F. M. Kircheisen, *Napoleon* (New York: Harcourt, Brace and Co., 1932); Ed. Driault, *La vraie figure de Napoléon* (Paris: A. Morance, 1928); J. H. Rose, *Life of Napoleon I* (New York: Harcourt, Brace and Co., 1924); Albert Sorel, *L'Europe et la Révolution française* (Paris: Plon, 1887–1911), 9 vols.; A. Thiers, *History of the Consulate and the Empire of France under Napoleon* (1893–4), 12 vols.; Georges Lefebvre, *Napoléon,* in the collection *Histoire des peuples et des civilisations* (Paris: Alcan, 1935); A. Fournier, *Napoleon I* (New York: Longmans, Green, 2nd edition, 1912); G. Pariset, *Le Consulate et l'empire,* in Lavisse (ed.), *Histoire de France contemporaine,*

vol. III; E. Tarlé, *Bonaparte* (New York: Knight, 1937); and G. Bruun, *Europe and the French Imperium* (New York: Harper & Bros., 1938).

(2) Turkey and the Two Sicilies were also joined to the Second Coalition against France. Spain was engaged in making war on Portugal in France's behalf.

(3) Treaty of Lunéville, 1801.

(4) The Armed Neutrality of the North, composed of Sweden, Denmark, Russia, and Prussia, was aimed largely at the British. It was broken up by Nelson. Denmark was thrown definitely into the arms of the French by Lord Nelson's bombardment of Copenhagen (April 2, 1801).

(5) Pitt fell, in part, because he was intransigent for war and had failed, when the occasion had presented itself, to make a victorious peace. The Addington-Hawkesbury Ministry, which took office in March, 1801, favored peace, but on condition that Malta would not be surrendered, which meant also the subsequent loss of Egypt to the French. Napoleon also wanted peace, but at what terms! He frequently issued pacific pleas, but their transparency is so obvious that it is strange that they have been taken seriously. He wanted a peace based on England's complete submission. One of his familiar statements is his proclamation of March 8, 1800:

"Français, vous désirez la paix, votre gouvernment la désire avec plus d'ardeur encore. Ses premiers vœux, ses démarches constantes ont été pour elle. Le ministère anglais a trahi le secret de son horrible politique. Déchirer la France, détruire sa marine et ses ports, l'effacer du tableau de l'Europe ou l'abaisser au rang des puissances secondaires, tenir toutes les nations divisées pour s'emparer du commerce de toutes et s'enricher de leurs dépouilles, c'est pour obtenir cet affreux succès que l'Angleterre répand l'or, prodigue les promesses, et multiplie des intrigues."

(6) This plan to attack England should not be confused with the "Boulogne Campaign."

(7) The Commercial Code was published in complete form March 21, 1804, and put in force January 1, 1808. The Civil Code confirmed the abolition of feudalism and of *ancien-régime* privilege, forbade workers' or employers' associations, ordered, in cases concerning labor contracts, that the master's word be taken as final (Article 1781), and provided that, on the Councils of Prud'hommes, which were established to arbitrate labor disputes, labor be not given representation equal to that of capital.

(8) September, 1806.

(9) The greatest of Napoleon's roads were Mont Cenis, Simplon, Cor-

niche (along the French Riviera), Paris-Hamburg, Paris-Amsterdam, and Paris-Madrid. See Blanchard, *Les routes des Alpes occidentales à l'époque napoléonienne* (1796–1815). (Grenoble: Allier, 1920.)

(10) The bankers saluted Bonaparte with bourgeois felicitations on this occasion. "He belongs [to the Government] which has contributed so powerfully to giving us great success as a warrior nation and to making known that this nation is also to be admired and respected by the results of a good economic policy and a sane administration." Cited in Levasseur, *Histoire du Commerce de la France,* vol. II, p. 60.

(11) Bonaparte gave the Bank the state's current account. By a law of April 14, 1803, the Bank was given exclusive right to issue money. In 1806, Napoleon took unto himself the right to appoint the Bank's powerful Governor and two Vice-Governors, and to fix the discount rate. He encouraged the founding of the Bank of France, which, as its act of association testifies, was looked upon from the first as a nationalist economic institution.

"The undersigned, considering that, as the inevitable result of the French Revolution and of a long and costly war, the nation has experienced the displacement and dispersion of the capital which served her commerce, the changing of public credit, and the slowing up of the circulation of wealth;

"That, in similar circumstances, many nations have experienced the same difficulties and have found great resources in banking establishments;

"That the French nation, accustomed to exert the greatest efforts in the conquest of freedom, ought not to let herself be held down by forces that she can overcome;

"That, finally, one ought to expect that public and private interests converge in a real and powerful manner for the success of the proposed establishment;

"Have resolved and decreed the following articles, as fundamental statutes of a bank."

See Gabriel Ramon, *Histoire de la Banque de France* (Paris: Grasset, 1929).

(12) Concerning French colonies during the Napoleonic period, see: J. Saintoyant, *La colonisation française pendant la période napoléonienne* (1799–1815) (Paris: Renaissance du Livre, 1931); Gustav Roloff, *Die Kolonialpolitik Napoleons I* (Munich: R. Oldenbourg, 1899); Carl Ludwig Lokke, *France and the Colonial Question* (New York: Columbia University Press, 1932); Lothrop Stoddard, *The French Revolution in San Domingo* (Boston, 1914); François Charles-Roux, *France et l'Afrique du nord* (Paris: Alcan, 1932); M. Dubois et A. Terrier, *Un siècle d'expansion coloniale* (1800–1900) (Paris, 1901); and Georges Hardy, *Histoire de la colonisation française* (Paris, 1926).

(13) Saintoyant, *La colonisation française pendant la période napoléonienne,* p. 239.

(14) Saintoyant, p. 68.

(15) Treaty of Saint-Iledefonso, October 1, 1800.

(16) Quoted in Saintoyant, p. 282. See also E. W. Lyon, *Louisiana in French Diplomacy, 1759–1804* (Norman, Oklahoma: University of Oklahoma Press, 1934).

(17) This is the judgment of Saintoyant. See his *La colonisation française pendant la période napoléonienne,* p. 461.

(18) March 18, 1800.

(19) March 21, 1801.

(20) September 29, 1801.

(21) October 8, 1801.

(22) On June 25, 1802, the capitulations were renewed and navigation in the Black Sea was made free to French ships.

(23) J. H. Rose, "Napoleon and English Commerce," *English Historical Review,* vol. VIII, 1893, p. 712.

(24) This is the opinion of Émile Levasseur, *Histoire du commerce de la France,* vol. II, pp. 74, 84.

(25) Saintoyant, *op. cit.,* p. 19.

(26) December 2, 1804.

(27) Discounts at the Bank fell from 630 millions in 1804 to 255 millions in 1805. See M. Marion, "La Fondation de la Banque de France et ses premières années (1800–1814)," in J. G. Van Dillen (editor), *History of the Principal Public Banks* (The Hague: Nijhoff, 1934).

(28) Jean G. M. Montgaillard, *Mémoires diplomatiques (1805–1819),* ed. by Clément de Lacroix (Paris: Ollendorff, 1896), p. 81. See also F. L. A. Ferrier, *Du gouvernement considéré dans ses rapports avec le commerce* (1804). Also J. Henri Lassalle, *Des Finances de l'Angleterre* (1803), and Comte d'Hauterive, *Le l'Etat de la France à la fin de l'An VIII.*

(29) Audrey Cunningham, *British Credit in the Last Napoleonic War* (Cambridge, 1910).

(30) A statement of August 24, 1807, taken from his survey of the position of the Empire, *Correspondance,* No. 12,187.

(31) He stated, to justify his belief that England was vulnerable through her credit system, "History of all time confirms that fatal experiences [of inflation] occur only under emasculated governments." *Correspondance,* No. 9,929.

(32) *Archives Nationales,* A. F. IV, 1241, No. 342. Cited by E. Tarlé, "Napoléon et les intérêts économiques de la France," *Napoléon,* March-April, 1926, p. 119.

(33) July, 1803.

(34) August 9, 1804.

(35) Concessions were made to ship captains who "through forgetfulness of forms or in consequence of change of destination" failed to provide themselves with such certificates. They were allowed to land their cargoes, if they would take in return an equal value of French goods. June 20, 1803.

(36) Decrees of February 6, 1805; February 22 and March 4, 1806; and the codification of these decrees, April 30, 1806.

(37) Charles Schmidt, *Le Grand Duché de Berg (1806-1813), étude sur la domination française en Allemagne sous Napoleon Ier* (Paris: F. Alcan, 1905); Robert Hoeniger, *Die Kontinentalsperre und ihre Einwirkungen auf Deutschland* (Berlin, 1905).

(38) J. Pelet de la Lozère (compiler), *Opinions et discours de Napoléon au conseil d'état* (Paris, 1833), p. 238.

(39) This Berlin Decree was presumably an answer to the British Orders in Council of May 16, 1806.

(40) Eli F. Heckscher, *The Continental System, An Economic Interpretation* (Oxford: Clarendon Press, 1922), p. 22. See also: Wilhelm Kiesselbach, *Die Continentalsperre in ihrer oekonomisch-politischen Bedeutung: ein Beitrag zur Handelsgeschichte* (Stuttgart, 1850); W. E. Lingelbach, "Historical Investigation and the Commercial History of the Napoleonic Era," *American Historical Review,* vol. XIX, 1914, pp. 257-281; J. H. Rose, "The Continental System," *Cambridge Modern History,* vol. IX, pp. 361-389; and W. A. Philips and A. H. Reede, *Neutrality. The Napoleonic Period* (ed. P. Jessup) (New York: Columbia University Press, 1936).

(41) Contrary to the belief of some historians, Napoleon knew at least the approximate contents of the Order in Council of November 17, 1807. There had come to his attention well-established rumors of the measures to be taken; these reports had been circulating in London before the Order was issued.

(42) F. E. Melvin, *Napoleon's Navigation System* (New York: Appleton and Co., 1919), p. 17.

(43) *Correspondance de Napoléon* I, 12,899.

(44) And also lost Finland.

(45) *Correspondance des Napoléon* I, 16,824.

(46) E. Tarlé, "L'union économique du continent européen sous Napoléon," *Revue historique,* vol. CLXVI (1931), gives the impression that the Continental System did work toward a continental economic union. This is true only in the sense that different parts of the Continent were more economically independent and, despite the title of Professor Tarlé's article, it is this view that the author upholds.

(47) E. Tarlé, "Napoléon et les intérêts économiques de la France," *Napoléon,* March–April, 1926, p. 124.

(48) E. Tarlé, *Le blocus continental et le royaume d'Italie* (Paris: Alcan, 1928), pp. 366–368; Heckscher, *op. cit.,* p. 298.

(49) Tarlé, *Le blocus continental et le royaume d'Italie,* p. 86.

(50) Heckscher, *op. cit.,* p. 297.

(51) Heckscher, *op. cit.,* p. 299.

(52) Heckscher, *op. cit.,* p. 311; Charles Schmidt, *Le Grand Duché de Berg, passim.*

(53) Heckscher, *op. cit., passim;* Melvin, *op. cit., passim.*

(54) Darmstädter, "Studien zur napoleonischen Wirtschaftsgeschichte," *Vierteljahrschrift für Sozial- und Wirtschaftsgeschichte,* 1905, pp. 116–117.

(55) *Ibid.,* p. 121.

(56) *Ibid.,* p. 135–136. This is also the judgment of other writers on the Continental System. See, for instance: Heckscher, *op. cit., passim,* and E. Tarlé, "Napoléon et les intérêts économiques de la France," p. 124, and *Le blocus continental et le royaume d'Italie,* p. 20.

(57) Max Schäfer, "Bremen und die Kontinentalsperre," *Hansiche Geschichtsblätter,* vol. XX, 1914.

(58) Napoleon charged Bernadotte with corruption.

(59) Louis A. F. de Bourrienne, *Mémoires sur Napoléon* (Paris, 1829), vol. VII, pp. 291 ff.

(60) Axel Pontus von Rosen, Governor of Gothenburg, informed the Swedish minister of state that he had confiscated ten oxen destined for the English fleet, and added: "I entreat that this be put in the papers, so that I, wretched that I am, may for once wear the nimbus of continental zeal in the annals of Europe. Saumarez (British fleet commander) was informed beforehand so that he will not be annoyed." Heckscher, *op. cit.,* p. 160.

(61) Duboscq, *Louis Bonaparte en Hollande d'après ses lettres* (Paris, 1911), No. 182. Dated October 1, 1808.

(62) Duboscq, *op. cit.,* p. 48.

(63) Melvin, *Napoleon's Navigation System,* p. 146.

(64) After the defeat of Austria, Napoleon wrote to Fouché the following letter:

"If the [commercial] department had done its duty, it would have taken advantage of my march into Vienna to encourage merchants and manufacturers to export cloth, pottery, and other goods which pay considerable duties in Austria, cloth alone paying sixty per cent. I should, as a matter of course, have released them from these dues and filled the warehouses of Vienna chock-full of French goods. But that department thinks of nothing and does nothing."

This indicates Napoleon's interest in having his military victories followed up by economic victories. A week after his letter reached Paris, French manufacturers dispatched goods to Vienna.

(65) See note 95.

(66) Allowance was not made in these figures for smuggling. The figures are not infallible, but probably represent a decline that was real.

(67) Quoted in Melvin, *op. cit.,* p. 48. See also Henri Sée, *Le commerce de Bordeaux à l'époque napoléonienne d'après la correspondance d'Honorat Lainé* (Paris: Librairie des Sciences Économiques et Sociales, 1933).

(68) Darmstädter, "Studien zur napoleonischen Wirtschaftsgeschichte," *Vierteljahrschrift für Sozial- und Wirtschaftsgeschichte,* 1904, p. 585.

(69) See the prices of raw cotton given in Heckscher, *The Continental System,* p. 274.

(70) Liévin Bauwens, a cotton manufacturer of Ghent, employed 1269 workmen on May 1, 1808, and only 230 on November 1. Prices of cotton rose during the same period from 5.25 francs to 11 or 12 francs a pound, and then fell to 6 or 7 francs.

(71) Decree of Alexander I, December 31, 1810.

(72) Levasseur, *Histoire du commerce,* vol. II, p. 99.

(73) Darmstädter, *op. cit.,* p. 585.

(74) *Ibid.*

(75) E. Levasseur, *Histoire des classes ouvrières et de l'industrie en France de 1789 à 1870,* vol. I, p. 727.

(76) Melvin, *op. cit.,* pp. 57 ff. This plan dates from 1808.

(77) *Ibid.,* p. 16. In characteristic fashion, Napoleon thought that if one frigate were sent out, it could carry 3000 tons of flour and bring back sugar worth 1,200,000 francs. "Judge what an immense sum." Unfortunately, Napoleon did not give enough consideration to the possibility of realizing his dream.

(78) Darmstädter, *op. cit.,* p. 593. Decree of January 8, 1811.

(79) J. A. C. Chaptal, Count de Chanteloup, *Mes souvenirs sur Napoléon* (Paris, 1893), p. 280. Tarlé, "Napoléon et les intérêts économiques de la France," *Napoléon,* 1926, p. 131, says that he was unable to find figures that confirmed Chaptal's statement in the Archives. That large sums were expended in this way, however, is a well-established fact.
These subsidies were given, in part at least, to provide work for the unemployed whom Napoleon feared. Chaptal relates that Napoleon said to him, "I fear these disturbances based on lack of bread; I should have less fear of a battle against 200,000 men."

(80) An earlier imperial decree of July 15, 1806, aimed to relieve Breton farmers. It permitted the export of grain from Nantes. Exports ceased after the Milan Decree.

(81) Melvin, *op. cit.,* p. 87. His judgments are based on material in the Archives Nationales, F^{12} 2051. The plans for licenses were perfected in March, 1809. A new form of license was adopted December 4, 1809.

(82) The list was extended by the decree of December 4, 1809. Under the liberal license decree of February 14, 1810, no licenses were granted, according to Melvin, p. 126.

(83) Prize decree of January 12, 1810. Certain British manufactured goods, such as cotton textiles, were exempt from the provisions of the decree.

(84) Archives Nationales, A F^{IV} 1243, pièce 209. Napoleon wrote to his brother Louis, April 3, 1808:
"If you need to sell your gin, the English need to buy it. Settle the points

where the English smugglers are to come and get it, and make them pay in money, but never in commodities."
Quoted in Heckscher, p. 192. This indicates Napoleon's adherence to the bullionist doctrine.

(85) Napoleon I, *Lettres inédites de Napoléon I,* ed. by Léon Lecestre (Paris, 1897), vol. II, pp. 52–54, No. 652.

(86) The so-called License Decree of St. Cloud, July 3, 1810, and its amendment, the decree of July 25, 1810. Provision was made for the neutralization of French vessels. Coastwise trade was opened to foreign bottoms, but they had to be bonded on leaving port. Ships could not leave France without a license, and high prices were charged for the papers. Licenses would be granted for trade only in specified goods.

(87) A letter reproduced by Lanzac de Laborie, *Paris sous Napoléon* (Paris, 1905–1913), vol. VI, which is alleged to have been written by Napoleon, is more specific in the reasoning against colonial products. It was addressed to Junot, who was governor of Paris.
"Your women must drink Swiss tea, which is as good as the tea of the East, and chickory, which is as healthy as the coffee of Arabia. They must set the style for these things in their *salons* instead of bothering about politics like Madame Du Staël. They must also take care that I do not notice that they wear gowns made from English stuffs." This letter is dated November 23, 1806.

(88) This information is taken from the report by Montalivet on the license system. Of the 1153 licenses signed, 494 were delivered, 466 expired unused, and 193 remained to be delivered.

(89) Ninety thousand, five hundred twenty francs still remained to be paid by license holders of the state.

(90) The last figure is based on an estimate by Thiers.

(91) Heckscher, p. 204.

(92) Las Cases, *Journal de la vie privée et des conversations de l'empereur Napoléon à Sainte Hélène* (Stockholm, 1823–4), vol. IV, p. 200.

(93) See the deliberations of the Council of Commerce and Manufactures for January 13, 1812; Napoleon's *Correspondance,* 18,431; and the document cited below.

(94) Ministerial report of March 10, 1812.

(95) Napoleon was undoubtedly urged on by other motives than the desire to enforce the continental blockade in Russia. He also wanted to keep Russia

in his political orbit and perhaps even dreamed of the grandeur of oriental conquests. Fouché has written, "The Russian war was not, as the common people at first believed, a war of sugar and coffee." *Mémoires de Joseph Fouché,* vol. II, p. 90. For what pertains to Russia and the Continental System, see E. Tarlé, "Russland und die Kontinentalsperre," *Zeitschrift für die gesamte Staatswissenschaft,* vol. XCIV, February, 1933.

(96) *Correspondance,* No. 19,391.

(97) Heckscher, *op. cit.,* p. 154. In the moment of crisis, Napoleon did not relax his attitude toward his vassals. Chaptal advised him to try to win them by establishing ordinary economic relations with them. Napoleon refused to take Chaptal's advice. Chaptal, *Mes souvenirs sur Napoléon,* p. 278.

(98) Pierre Paul Viard, "Les conséquences économiques du blocus continental en Ille-et-Vilaine," *Napoléon,* January–February, March–April, 1926. In 1807 the Conseillers d'Arrondissement de Fougères, in comparing the economic situation in France and Great Britain, concluded that both countries were suffering from an abundance of goods—France with agricultural goods, and England with manufactured products, p. 57.

(99) Russia prohibited French silks in 1810.

(100) Charles Schmidt, "Les débuts de l'industrie cotonnière en France, 1760–1806," *Revue d'histoire des doctrines économiques et sociales,* 1914–19, vol. VII, pp. 26 ff.

(101) A. N. Rambaud, *Naples sous Joseph Bonaparte,* 1806–1808 (Paris, 1911), p. 437.

(102) Chaptal, *De l'industrie française* (Paris, 1819), vol. II, pp. 7, 15.

(103) Quoted by Tarlé, *Kontinental naja Blokada* (Moscow, 1913), vol. I, p. 513.

(104) Chaptal was a staunch protectionist. A letter by Brentano, the German economist, to Charles Gide, which is reproduced in Chaptal's *Mes souvenirs de Napoléon,* p. 51, footnote, is interesting in this respect.

"J'ai l'impression que Chaptal était un réorganisateur, un Colbert du 19ᵉ siècle, avec beaucoup de traits semblables à ceux de son grand prédécesseur, mais plus moderne en technique, comme en philosophie. Enfin, Chaptal me semble être l'homme qui, le premier, a donné aux peuples continentaux du 19ᵉ siècle l'exemple d'une organisation économique sur une base nationale, qui a inspiré List et tous les continentaux qui, plus tard, ont prêché l'organisation nationale de la vie économique.

"Il me semble que l'orthodoxie économique qui a régné jusqu'ici en France est la cause que l'on ne sait rien, ni des mesures pour réorganiser l'économie politique de la France sous le Consulat, le Directoire, et le premier Empire, ni de l'homme réorganisateur."

(105) Chaptal, *Mes souvenirs sur Napoléon,* p. 279.

(106) C. K. Webster, *The Foreign Policy of Castlereagh* (London, 1925), p. 74.

(107) S. Charléty, *La Restauration (1815-1830)* in Lavisse (editor), *Histoire de la France contemporaine,* vol. IV, p. 74.

(108) France recognized the independence of Haiti, her former Santo Domingo, in 1825.

(109) Webster, *op. cit.,* pp. 82 ff., and Charléty, *op. cit.,* p. 74 and A. Nicolle, *Comment la France a payé après Waterloo* (Paris, 1929).

CHAPTER IV

(1) The Restoration was part of *La Monarchie Censitaire.* This is a term frequently applied to the Restoration and the July Monarchy because suffrage was granted only to those who paid a direct tax (cens) of a certain sum. It connotes rule by the wealthy.

General Works:

Frederick B. Artz, *France under the Bourbon Restoration, 1814-1830* (Cambridge: Harvard University Press, 1931).

Frederick B. Artz, *Reaction and Revolution:* 1814-1832. (New York: Harper and Brothers, 1934.)

S. Charléty, *La Restauration (1815-1830)* in *Histoire de la France contemporaine* edited by E. Lavisse (Paris: Hachette, 1921).

G. L. Dickinson, *Reaction and Revolution in Modern France* (London: G. Allen, 1892, second edition, 1927).

Pierre de la Gorce, *La Restauration* (Paris: Plan, 1926-28), 2 vols.

J. R. Hall, *The Bourbon Restoration* (London: A. Rivers, 1909).

Henri Sée, *La vie économique de la France sous la monarchie censitaire (1815-1848)* (Paris: Alcan, 1927).

Alfred Stern, *Geschichte Europas seit den Vertragen von 1815* (Stuttgart: J. Cota, Second edition, 1905-1929).

Alfred Stern and others, *Die französische Revolution, Napoleon, und die Restauration, 1789-1848* (Berlin: Propylaën-Verlag, 1929).

René Viviani, *La Restauration (1814-1830)* in *Histoire socialiste* edited by Jean Jaurès (Paris: Jules Rouff et Cie, 1900).

Georges Weill, *L'Eveil des nationalités et le mouvement libéral* (1815-1848) in *Peuples et Civilisations* edited by L. Halphen et P. Sagnac (Paris: Alcan, 1930).

Georges Weill, *La France sous la monarchie constitutionnelle* (1814–1848) (Paris: Société Française d'édition d'Art, Second edition 1912).

(2) S, Charléty, *La Restauration (1815–1830)* in Lavisse (editor), *Histoire de France contemporaine,* vol. IV, p. 74, and E. Levasseur, *La Population française* (Paris: Rousseau, 1889–1892), vol. I, pp. 326 ff.

(3) H. Sée, *La vie économique de la France sous la Monarchie censitaire* (Paris: Alcan, 1927), pp. 11 and 12, states this fact. The *annuités successorales,* an inheritance tax, seem to prove it. *"Ainsi, en 1826, les immeubles représentent 880 millions de francs, contre 457 aux biens mobiliers soit 66 per cent de l'ensemble."* In 1848 the percentage was 61 per cent and in 1869 55 per cent. It was not until 1896 that there was a balance between the annuities on *immeubles* and on *biens mobiliers.* Consult also E. Besson, "La progression des valeurs successorales et le développement de la fortune mobilière de la France," *Journal de la Statistique,* May, 1899.

(4) M. Marion, *La vente des biens nationaux* (Paris, 1908).

(5) J. Loutchisky, *Quelques remarques sur la vente des biens nationaux* (Paris, 1913); R. Laurent, *L'agriculture en Côte-d'Or pendant la première moitié du XIXe siècle* (Dijon, 1931); and *Les Bouches du Rhône, Encyclopédie départementale,* vol. VII. *Le mouvement économique* by Paul Masson and E. Estrangin (Paris, 1928).

(6) J. H. Clapham, *The Economic Development of France and Germany* (Cambridge: University Press, 1928), Chapter III, *passim.*

(7) *Statistique de la France*—Commerce extérieur (Paris: Imprimerie Nationale, 1838). Retrospective, pp. 6–7. These figures are not identical with those in more contemporary statistical reports, but as all of the data available are open to criticism these sums may be taken as giving an approximate idea of the change.

(8) L. C. A. Knowles, *The Industrial and Commercial Revolutions in Great Britain during the Nineteenth Century* (New York: E. P. Dutton, third edition 1924), p. 26, footnote, and p. 136. The figure for 1788 should be taken as approximate; that for 1815 is the declared value of goods. Some modification of the latter figures should be made because of a rise in prices.

(9) Emile Levasseur, *Histoire du commerce de la France de 1789 à nos jours,* p. 107.

(10) J. H. Clapham, *The Economic Development of France and Germany,* 1815–1914 (Cambridge: University Press, 1928), p. 71.

(11) Ordinances of April 23 and 26, 1814.

(12) This indemnity was never granted.

(13) Quoted in S. Charléty, *La restauration (1815–1830)* in Lavisse, *Histoire de France contemporaine,* vol. IV, p. 273.

(14) The replies are to be found in the Archives Nationales under the series F^{12} 633–637 and F^{12} 638, *Enquête sur le régime commercial de la France 1814.*

(15) The General Council of Manufactures was created by Napoleon June 26, 1810. It was composed of sixty members. Similar bodies assisted in the *ancien régime* and have continued to the present day.

(16) The General Council of Commerce dated back to the *ancien régime* in form and name. It had twenty members who were named by the Minister of the Interior on recommendation of the Chambers of commerce.

(17) *Archives Nationales,* versement du ministère du commerce pour 1899, No. 10.

(18) Deputies had to be at least forty years of age. They were chosen through an indirect election system of two stages. Voters had to be at least thirty years of age.

See Maurice Deslandres, *Histoire constitutionnelle de la France de 1789 à 1870* (Paris: Colin, 1932), 2 vols.

(19) Charléty, *op. cit.,* p. 272.

(20) This body had been forced into servility by the Emperor, yet had won the esteem of the bourgeoisie and a reputation for some independence by voting almost unanimously in 1813 a report that condemned Napoleon's bellicose policies and that demanded a strict observance of laws. It had approved by formal vote the overthrow of the Emperor and the restoration of the Bourbons. It had usually been servile to the new régime, but on November 15, 1814, had voted a law favoring sheep growers, granting the right to export French wool. This was a privilege contrary to the Colbertian policy of retaining national raw products for manufacture at home and one that had been strictly abrogated by Napoleon's blockade tariff of 1806.

(21) The chairman of the tariff commission reported, "It is a principle of political economy that customs are established to guarantee the prosperity of manufacturers and to enhance national industry. . . . The institution [of protection and prohibition] will become really national when a million workers produce what they need and when production keeps out foreign

goods that would otherwise enter the home market." Quoted in E. Levasseur, *Histoire du commerce de la France*. Second part, *de 1789 à nos jours,* p. 114.

(22) The free transit of goods had been prevented by the Revolutionaries. Transit was allowed for goods going from Holland through Alsace and Switzerland in 1793 and other exceptions were made as France's frontiers were extended. The law of December 17, 1814, established the modern idea of transit in France. It was extended by the laws of March 27, 1817, etc., and especially the law of February 9, 1832, that allowed the transit of prohibited articles. See Georges Pallain, *Les douanes françaises* (Paris: Paul Dupont, 1913), vol. I, pp. 478–483.

(23) 10 Brumaire, year V. See above p. 56.

(24) Law of April 30, 1806.

(25) Thus nicknamed by Louis XVIII in the first flush of his pleasure at seeing such a royalist body elected. He was soon to change his attitude toward this Chamber; it became so violently anti-Revolutionary that he dismissed it on September 5, 1816.

(26) By the law of March 27, 1817, a few new restrictions were placed on foreign commerce. In the debate preceding the passage of the bill, agriculturalists expressed their belief in high industrial protection, because such a system brought industrial prosperity and increased the purchasing power of those who bought agricultural products.

The main feature of the law of April 21, 1818, was the establishment of free transit through Alsace in order to regain for that province the carrying trade between the Rhine and Switzerland that it had enjoyed before the Revolution. It had then been a *province d'étranger effectif* and as such was able to trade freely with foreign states. With the Revolution it was incorporated in the French customs union and this fact forced the above mentioned traffic to the right bank of the Rhine.

(27) The Chamber numbered about two hundred and seventy seats at this time. In the election of 1819 when one-fifth of the Chamber was up for election, the Liberals won thirty-five of the fifty-four seats.

(28) Ordinance of July 26, 1814, and law of December 2, 1814.

(29) Robert Marjolin, "Troubles provoqués en France par la disette de 1816–1817," *Revue d'histoire moderne,* November–December, 1933.

(30) Subsidies were given from November 22, 1816, to September 1, 1817.

(31) Thus testified Comte Decazes, the head of the cabinet.

(32) The mean price for wheat from 1800 to 1814 was 21 francs 36.

(33) See above, p. 90. Her most notable loss was Santo Domingo, which had revolted.

(34) The Duc de Richelieu, Louis XVIII's first premier, wrote to the French ambassador at London:

"You understand perfectly that it would be impossible to yield to the demands of Portugal [concerning Guiana] not so much because of the real interest there is for us to keep a territory which offers very few advantages except in the distant future, but because the dignity of the king and of the state would be wounded by a concession which cannot be justified on the part of Portugal."
Quoted in Georges Hardy, *Histoire de la colonisation française*, p. 146.

(35) Ministerial instructions in 1816 stated:
"The purpose for establishing colonies being essentially to favor and develop the commerce of the Metropolis, it would be a ruinous prudence to tolerate anything which would break down the régime of the *exclusif*. . . ."

(36) Professor Christian Schéfer has referred to part of French colonial history as the "policy of merchants" or "the reign of Bordelais."

(37) Count Thierry de Hogendorp, a former officer in the Dutch East India Company and a French general under Napoleon, carried on enthusiastic propaganda for the Dutch system of colonial *mise en valeur*. His ideas were put down in *Le système colonial de la France*.

(38) Johannès Tramond and André Reussner, *Eléments d'histoire maritime et coloniale contemporaine (1815–1914)* (Paris, 1924), p. 14.

(39) René Viviani, *La Restauration (1814–1830)* in *Histoire socialiste,* edited by Jean Jaurès (Paris: Jules Rouff et Cie, 1909), p. 250.

(40) In 1826, because of a shortage of certain goods, small quantities of American products were sold in the French West Indies.

(41) Agriculturalists and industrialists stated frequently in their pleas for protection that high customs rates were a boon to the working classes. Expressions of opinion on the part of labor in this connection are scarely to be found.

(42) See above, p. 46.

(43) Pallain, *Les douanes françaises,* vol. II, pp. 65 ff. and René Verneaux, *L'Industrie des transports maritimes au XIXe siècle et au commencement du XXe siècle* (Paris: Pedone, 1903), vol. I, pp. 41 ff.

(44) That is, in the fishing of certain districts and certain fish well removed from French coasts. Pallain, *op. cit.,* vol. II, pp. 276 ff.

(45) Laws of July 5, 1836, and May 6, 1841, Pallain, *op. cit.,* vol. II, p. 74, and F. Guérin, *Précis de législation maritime,* II partie (Paris: Gauthiers–Villars et Cie., 1928), *passim.*

(46) W. Roscher, *System der Volkswirtschaft,* vol. III, sixth edition, p. 646.

(47) *Essai politique sur la revenue des peuples de l'antiquité, du moyen âge, des siècle modernes et spécialement de la France et de l'Angleterre depuis le milieu du XVe siècle jusqu'au XIXe siècle,* 3 vols. (1804). *Des systèmes d'économie politique* (1809); *Théorie d'économie politique* (1815); and *Dictionnaire analytique de l'économie politique* (1826).

(48) *Du gouvernement considéré dans ses rapports avec le commerce,* first edition 1804; third edition 1822; *De l'enquête commerciale* (1829).

(49) Louis Say (1774–1840). Works:
Principales causes de la richesse ou de la misère des peuples et des particuliers (1818);
Considérations sur l'industrie et la législation sous le rapport de leur influence sur la richesse des États et examen critique des principaux ouvrages qui ont paru sur l'économie politique (1822);
Traité élémentaire de la richesse individuelle et la richesse publique et éclaircissements sur les principales questions de l'économie politique (1827);
Études sur la richesse des nations et réfutations des principales erreurs en économie politique (1836). See André Desmazières, *Louis Say* (Lille: Robbe, 1911).

(50) Published in 1819.

(51) Published in 1823.

(52) *Le commerce au 19e siècle,* 2 vols. (1825).

(53) *Du commerce de la France en 1820 et 1821* (1822).

(54) *Forces productives et commerciale de la France, 2 vols.* (1827); *Progrès de l'industrie française depuis le commencement du XIXe siècle* (1824). See Léon Duvoir, *Recherche des tendances interventionnistes chez quelques économists libéraux français de 1830 à 1850* (Paris: Rousseau, 1901), chap. VII.

(55) Speech: the Chamber of Deputies, February 14, 1817.

(56) A report presented in conjunction with the bill which became the tariff of 1822.

(57) 1822.

(58) Charléty, *op. cit.,* pp. 286–288.

(59) Taken from *Documents statistiques sur la France publiés par le Ministre du Commerce* (Paris: Imprimerie Royale, 1835), pp. 45–49.

(60) The price of goods on which English customs were figured was established in 1696. These prices were far from the actual value during the early part of the nineteenth century. In addition to the "official evaluation," English customs show a real or declared value of exports.

(61) Comte de Vaublanc, *Du commerce de la France en 1820 et 1821* (Paris, 1822), *passim.*

(62) S. Charléty, *La Restauration* in *Histoire de la France contemporaine,* edited by E. Lavisse, p. 289.

(63) *Ibid.,* p. 290.

(64) *Ibid.,* p. 312.

(65) *Ibid.*

(66) Such is the work of Charles Dupin, *Forces productives et commerciales de la France,* 2 vols. (1827).

(67) According to a statement made by the General Director of Customs, Baron St. Cricq.

(68) Clapham, *Economic Development of France and Germany,* p. 61.

(69) Mining statistics were prepared periodically by the Services des Mines and are relatively trustworthy.

(70) Nevertheless, in 1820 sixty-five industrial establishments employed steam engines; in 1830 this number had increased to six hundred and twenty.

(71) The population of Roubaix was 5000 in 1789, 15,000 in 1830, and 34,000 in 1850.

(72) Clapham, *op. cit.,* p. 65.

(73) Levasseur, *Histoire du commerce en France,* Second Part, *De 1789 à nos jours,* p. 217.

(74) Power was not applied to looms manufacturing plain silk until 1843–44.

(75) See above, p. 93.

(76) It has been estimated that the sugar imported from French colonies cost 33 per cent more than it would have if it had been purchased from foreign sources. The consumption of sugar in France was four pounds per person; in England fourteen; and in the Netherlands twenty-two.

(77) Sée, *Esquisse d'une histoire économique et sociale de la France*, p. 423. Charléty, *op. cit.*, p. 293, gives the number of beet-sugar factories in 1827 as one hundred and one with a production of 5 million kilograms.

(78) Levasseur, *Histoire du commerce*, Second Part, *De 1789 à nos jours*, pp. 154, 242.

(79) Levasseur, *op. cit.*, p. 154. G. R. Porter, *The Progress of the Nation* (1851), p. 403.

(80) *Ministère du Commerce et des Manufactures. Commission formée pour l'examen de certaines questions de législation commerciale*, 2 vols. (Paris, 1828). *Rapport de la commission libre nommée par les manufacturiers et négociants de Paris sur l'enquête relative à l'état actuel de l'industrie du coton en France* (Paris, 1829).

(81) The suggestion of the investigating commission was for a gradual reduction of the iron duties. L. Amé, *Études sur les tarifs de douane et sur les traités de commerce*. (Paris: 1878), vol. I, p. 175. The bill was presented to the Chamber May 21, 1829. See the *Moniteur*. A celebrated statement in this connection was that made by Siryeis de Mayrinhac, General Director of Customs, in the Chamber, 1830; "La France produit trop." France produced so much that he felt high protection was unnecessary.

(82) Georges Weill, *L'Éveil des nationalités,* vol. XV in *Peuples et Civilisations,* edited by L. Halphen and P. Sagnac (Paris: Alcan, 1930), p. 79;

Marcel Marion, *Histoire financière de la France depuis 1715* (Paris: Rousseau et Cie., 1928), vol. V, p. 86;

Léon Dubreuil, *La vente des biens nationaux dans le département des Côtes-du-Nord (1790–1830)* (Paris: Champion, 1912); and especially André Gain, *La Restauration et les biens des émigrés* (Nancy: Société d'Impressions Typographiques, 1928), 2 vols.

(83) Antoine A. Cournot, *Souvenirs* (Paris: Hachette, 1913), p. 129.

Marcel Marion, *Histoire financière de la France depuis 1715* (Paris: Rousseau et Cie., 1928), vol. 5, p. 86.

CHAPTER V

(1) General Works: In addition to the books cited at the beginning of Chapter IV, one may consult with profit the following volumes:

S. Charléty, *La Monarchie de Juillet* in *Histoire de France contemporaine,* edited by E. Lavisse (Paris. Hachette, 1921).

E. Fournière, *Le Règne de Louis-Philippe* in *Histoire socialiste,* edited by J. Jaurès (Paris: J. Rouff et Cie, 1906).

Ernest Hamel, *Histoire du règne de Louis-Philippe (juillet 1830–février 1848)* (Paris: 1889–1890), 2 vols.

G. Hanotaux, *Histoire politique de la nation française de 1804 à 1929* in *Histoire de la nation française,* edited by G. Hanotaux (Paris: Société de l'histoire nationale, 1929), vol. V.

Karl Hillebrand, *Geschichte Frankreichs von der Thronbesteigung Louis-Philipp's zum Fall Napoleon's III* (Gotha: Perthes, 1877–1879), 2 vols.

Alexandre Pilenco, *Les mœurs électorales en France. Régime censitaire* (Paris: Imprimeric Graphique, 1928).

Paul Thureau-Dangin, *Histoire de la monarchie de Juillet* (Paris: Second edition, 1888–1892), 7 vols.

(2) Georges Weill, *L'Eveil des nationalités et le mouvement libéral (1815–1848),* p. 103.

(3) In the first years of the July Monarchy, two thousand members of the national guard were killed in action. The national guard was the main support of Louis-Philippe. Once it deserted him, he fell from power.

(4) The expression is Armand Carrel's.

(5) Alexis De Tocqueville, *De la classe moyenne et du peuple,* a pamphlet published in October, 1847.

(6) F. P. Guizot, *Mémoires pour servir à l'histoire de mon temps* (vol. V, chap. XVIII, p. 31).

(7) S. Charléty, *La monarchie de Juillet* in *Histoire de France contemporaine,* edited by E. Lavisse, vol. V, p. 347.

Inasmuch as the franchise was based on direct taxes and most of such taxes were collected on land, there was a tendency for professional men, especially lawyers, to buy land in order to play a political rôle. In the above analysis, such persons were not classed as proprietors and justly so, because their main interest was not the same as that of owners of large estates.

Marx analyzed the situation later on as follows:

"Not the French Bourgeoisie ruled under Louis Philippe but only a faction of the same, bankers, kings of the stock exchange, railroad kings, owners of coal and iron mines, of forests, a part of the land-owning element allied with them—the so-called aristocracy of Finance. . . .

"The July monarchy was nothing but a stock company for the exploitation of the French National wealth, the dividends of which were divided among ministries, chambers and the 240,000 voters . . . Louis Philippe was the director of the Company, Robert Macaire on the throne. . . . Commerce, industry, agriculture, shipping—the interests of the industrial bourgeoisie—all these were constantly menaced and injured under this system. . . ."

From Karl Marx, *Class Struggle in France, 1848–1850* (New York, 1924), pp. 34, 37, 38. (Translated from the German by Henry Kuhn.)

(8) J. P. Proudhon, *"La Justice dans la Révolution et l'Eglise," Œuvres complètes de Proudhon,* new edition under the direction of G. Bouglé and H. Moysset (Paris, 1932), vol. III, p. 139.

(9) This body was composed of the presidents of the three general councils, eleven members appointed by the King, and one appointed by the Minister of Finance.

(10) Law of February 9, 1832. By the law of June 5, 1845, transit duties were abolished.

(11) Laws of February 9 and 27, 1832.

(12) Comte d'Argout endeavored to reassure protectionists by a statement he made in presenting his bill.

"The present tariff protects numerous interests. Some of these interests are easily alarmed. . . . When we presented the bills concerning transit and bonded warehouses, these interests expressed their fear. They attributed to the Government the intention to destroy, or at least to weaken severely the protective system under which our industry has made such singular progress. . . . It is the duty of the Government to declare most solemnly that it wishes sincerely, strongly, and with perseverance, the maintenance of this system. . . . But it wishes at the same time to free this system of all that is useless, annoying, and exorbitant. . . ." *Moniteur,* 1832, p. 2075.

(13) Thiers approved of national economics but wanted a prudent and gradual downward revision of the tariff. *Moniteur,* 1833, p. 1186.

(14) This right was granted by the tariff law of 1814 and by a law voted May 24, 1834. The ordinance had to be issued between sessions of the Chamber and to be ratified at the next session.

(15) Ordinance of June 2, 1834.

(16) The results of the investigation are to be found in *Enquête relative à diverses prohibitions établies à l'entrée des produits érangers, commencée le 8*

octobre, 1834, sous la présidence de M. T. Duchâtel, ministre du Commerce (1835), 3 vols.

(17) *Enquête,* vol. I, pp. 87 ff.

(18) *Enquête,* vol. II, p. 213.

(19) Treaty of July 25, 1840.

(20) Law of June 9, 1845.

(21) Law of April 26, 1833.

According to an article in a newspaper of the period, *Tribune,* benefits of the bounty accrued to six large refineries. The paper was fined 10,000 francs for the article, the responsible editor was thrown into prison for three years, and the paper had to close its doors. See E. Fournière, *Le règne de Louis-Philippe* in *Histoire Socialiste,* edited by J. Jaurès, p. 240.

See also W. Lexis, *Die französischen Ausfuhrprämien in Zusammenhange mit der Tarifgeschichte und Handelsentwicklung Frankreichs* (Bonn, 1870)

(22) Law of July 18, 1837.

(23) Ordinance of August 21, 1839.

(24) Law of July 3, 1840.

(25) By the law of July 2, 1843.

(26) For what follows see Charles Schmidt, "Un projet d'union économique de la France et de l'Allemagne du Sud," *Revue Rhénane,* 1923–1924.

(27) See Léon Faucher, *L'Union du midi, association de douanes entre la France, la Belgique, la Suisse, et l'Espgagne* (Paris: Paulin, 1842), p. X. His opinion was that:

"It is high time for France to build a dike against this invasion. In the interest of Europe as well as in our own, the German association ought not to be left without a counter-weight. It is necessary to constitute French unity; and this cannot be done without associating more closely for the commercial struggle all the peoples that Napoleon led with us to war."

(28) Issue of March 1, 1837.

(29) A parliamentary investigation was conducted by the Belgian Government in 1840 to determine the attitude of the country toward protection.

(30) Charléty, *La monarchie de juillet* in *Histoire de France contemporaine,* vol. V, pp. 183–184.

(31) Speech by a manufacturer of Rheims. Quoted in Amé, *Étude économique sur les tarifs de douanes et sur les traités de commerce,* vol. I, p. 221.

(32) Faucher, *L'Union du midi,* p. cxxxviii.

(33) The preface to the Germain Garnier translation includes an interesting guide to the *Wealth of Nations.*

(34) Say was the author of *Traité d'économie politique* (1803); *Catéchisme d'économie politique* (1817); and *Cours d'économie politique* (1828-1829), 6 vols.

(35) Author of *Cours d'économie politique* (1840), which is an exposition of the theories of Malthus, Ricardo, and Say.

(36) Author of *De la liberté du travail* (1825); this was his principal work.

(37) Other names that might be mentioned are Charles Comte, Wolowski, and Hippolyte Passy. Bastiat's works included *Les sophismes économiques; Cobden et la Ligue; Les harmonies économiques;* and *Les petits pamphlets,* all published between 1844 and 1850.

(38) The preamble to its statutes read:
"The object of the Association is to propagate the principle of free-trade; to enlighten public opinion on the damage to the interests of the country of the protectionist system which can give special advantages to certain branches of industry only at the expense of all others and of all the consumers of protected goods; finally to demonstrate that the interest of the government and of the country is that of consumers, moderate duties being the only ones which, ceasing to be prohibitive, become a source of wealth for public finances."

(39) The Association endeavored to establish connections with free-trade organizations in other countries. In 1847 an international congress of economists was held at Brussels for this purpose, but it led to no substantial results.

(40) This letter was reproduced in the *Libre Échange,* December 6, 1846, p. 10.

(41) See M. A. Calmon, *Discours parlementaires de M. Thiers* (Paris: C. Lévy, 1878-89).

(42) Adolf Wurst, *Thiers volkswirtschaftliche Anschauungen* (Sammelung nationalökonomischer Abhandlungen der staatswissenschaftlichen Seminars zu Halle, 1893), pp. 10-18.

(43) Thiers expressed most of his national economic theories in the tariff debate of 1836.

Calmon, *op. cit.*, vol. III, pp. 269 ff.

(44) C. J. H. Hayes, *Essays on Nationalism* and the *Historical Development of Modern Nationalism, passim.*

(45) Thém. Lestiboudois, *Économie pratique des nations* (1847).

(46) *Ibid.,* pp. 43–44.

(47) *Ibid.,* p. 512.

(48) Mathieu de Dombasle, *Économie politique* (Paris, 1843) and *Avenir industriel de la France* (1834). See G. Schelle, "Un adversaire de la théorie des débouches," *Revue d'Histoire Économique et Sociale,* vol. 7, 1914–1919, pp. 87–99. See also Hantute, *Du libre échange et résultats que l'adoption de ce système aurait pour l'agriculture, le commerce, l'industrie, et la marine de la France* (Paris: Joubert, 1847).

This author was strongly opposed to free-trade theories, although he admitted the wisdom of tariff reform. He concluded his argument as follows:

"En résumé, si on admettait ce système, sous le rapport de l'agriculture, la France, en arrière de plusieurs nations, verrait une grande partie de ses terres en friche, car on sait que, par les méthodes de culture en usage dans nos départements, la terre est loin de produire autant que dans quelques pays voisins; ce qui, en définitive, met des frais plus considérables à la charge du cultivateur français; l'introduction du bétail étranger aurait en outre pour résultat de diminuer la quantité de fumier nécessaire à toute bonne culture (ce qui est en grande partie la cause de l'infériorité du rendement de nos terres) et il en résulterait aussi que le progrès de l'éducation de la race chevaline et des troupeaux seraient arrêtés dans leurs développements.

"Sous le rapport du commerce et de l'industrie, trop de causes d'infériorité subsistent, principalement vis-à-vis de l'Angleterre, même de l'aveu des libre-échangistes. Ajoutons, que ce sérait nous mettre, en cas de guerre, dans un état d'infériorité qui nous placerait à la merci de l'étranger pour quelques produits essentiels à la défense du pays, comme le fer, le charbon, les chevaux pour notre cavalerie. Ce serait en outre, comme nous l'avons dit, et nous ne saurions trop le répéter, plonger la classe ouvrière dans une affreuse misère, qui amenerait forcément à sa suite cette alarmante criminalité qu'on remarque en Angleterre.

"Sous le rapport de la marine, notre infériorité est aujourd'hui désespérante, le système du libre échange, avec toutes ses conséquences funestes, amenerait assurément l'anéantissement complet de la force navale de la France. Ce système serait plus fatal que les fautes qu'on a reprochées aux ministres de Louis XV avec tant d'amertume, mais non sans raison."

(49) There are a great many works on Frederick List. See of the more recent books H. Dietzel, *Lists nationales System und die nationale Wirtschaftspolitik* (1912) and *Die Bedeutung des "Nationalen Systems"* (1925),

A. Sommer, *Fr. Lists System des politischen Okonomie* (1926) and "A. Muller and F. List," *Weltwirtschaftliches Archiv,* vol. 25, heft 2; the *Mitteilungen der Fr. List Gesellschaft;* and Paul Mombert, *Geschichte der Nationalökonomie,* pp. 453–465.

(50) A second edition of the translation appeared in 1857.

(51) See any history of economic doctrines, for example Gide and Rist, *Histoire des doctrines économiques,* chap. IV.

(52) For March, 1831.

(53) In addition to Thiers, Lestiboudois, and List, the July Monarchy produced one other anti-free trader who is worthy of mention—Augustin Cournot, author of *Recherches sur les principles mathématiques de la théorie des richesses* (1838). This work received little attention when it was published, but has since become celebrated. Cournot is better known, however, as a mathematical economist than as a protectionist.

(54) For this discussion of statism or *étatisme,* see the remarkable work by Henri Michel, *L'idée de l'état* (Paris: Hachette et Cie., third edition, 1898).

(55) *Cours de philosophie positive,* published between 1830–1842; *Discours sur l'esprit positif* (1844); and *Discours sur l'ensemble du positivisme* (1848); *Système de politique positive* (1851–54). Comte was a historical economist and the originator of the term sociology.

(56) See G. Weill, *Un précurseur du socialisme, Saint Simon et son œuvre* (Paris, 1894) and *L'école saint-simonienne, son histoire, son influence jusqu'à nos jours* (Paris, 1896); and S. Charléty, *Histoire du Saint-Simonisme* (Paris, 1896).

(57) Blanc's principal book was *Organisation du travail* (1839).

(58) *Des améliorations matérielles dans leurs rapports avec la liberté* (1839) and *Théorie nouvelle d'économie sociale ou politique* (1842).

(59) *De la répartition des richesses ou de la justice distributive en économie politique* (1846) and *Vivre en travaillant* (1848).

(60) See especially *Nouveaux principes* (1819) and *Études sur l'économie politique* (1837–38).

(61) *Essais sur les relations du capital et du travail* (1846); *L'individu et l'état* (1857); and *La centralisation* (1868).

(62) Among the works of Villeneuve-Bargemont see *Histoire de l'économie politique* (1841) and *Le livre des affligés* (1841).

Gonnard, in characterizing French socialism just prior to 1848, says that: "It remained in general utopian, that is, it placed its confidence in moral forces, love, fraternity, justice; it did not exclude patriotism—it was sometimes even chauvinistic."

Gonnard, *Histoire des doctrines économiques,* vol. III, p. 65, footnote. See also Laskine, *Le socialisme suivant les peuples,* p. 94.

(63) See A. Colin, *La navigation commerciale au XIXe siècle* (Paris: 1901).

(64) For railways in France consult P. C. Laurent De Villedeuil, *Bibliographie des chemins de fer* (Paris, 1903); L. J. Gras, *Histoire des premiers chemins de fer en France* (St. Etienne, 1924–1929).

Richard von Kaufmann, *La politique française en matière de chemins de fer* (Paris: Béranger, 1901); Alfred Picard, *Les Chemins de fer* (Paris: Dunod et Pinat, 1918); Alfred Picard, *Les Chemins de fer français* (Paris, 1884–1885), 6 vols.; and R. Thévenez, M. Hérouville, and E. Bleys, *Législation des chemins de fer* (Paris: Rousseau et Cie., 1930), 2 vols.

(65) That is, in kilometers of railways per square kilometer. Great Britain was using a total of 2521 kilometers; Germany 627; France 569; and Belgium 378.

See G. Lefranc, "Les chemins de fer devant le parlement français (1835–1842)," *Revue d'histoire moderne,* September-October, 1930, pp. 338–339 and an article by the same author in the *Journal of Economic and Business History,* February, 1930.

(66) Adolphe Blanqui, *Cours d'économie,* p. 431.

(67) This is contrary to the statements found in most treatises on railways. Thiers voted usually, however, for railways. See G. Lefranc, "Les chemins de fer devant le parlement," *Revue d'histoire moderne,* September-October, 1930, p. 348.

(68) Chambre des Députés, speech delivered April 21, 1836.

(69) Arago held also that the cost of railway freight transportation being two-thirds cheaper than horse-drawn rates, foreign goods passing through France would be carried for two-thirds less, thus depriving the country of nearly 2,000,000 francs a year.

(70) See the articles in the *Globe* beginning December 1, 1833.

(71) E. Arago and M. Alboy, *Les Chemins de fer,* a vaudeville revue; presented in 1832. Quoted in G. Lefranc, "La construction des chemins de fer

et l'opinion publique vers 1830," *Revue d'histoire moderne,* July-August, 1930, p. 271.

(72) See Perdonnet, *Notions générales sur les chemins de fer, passim.*

(73) Quoted in Alfred Picard, *Les chemins de fer,* p. 255.

(74) Speech in the Chamber of Deputies, May 10, 1837.

(75) Quoted in E. Levasseur, *Histoire du commerce de la France de 1789 à nos jours,* vol. II, p. 202.

See Louis M. Jouffroy, *Une étape de la construction des grandes lignes de chemins de fer en France. La ligne de Paris à la frontière d'Allemagne (1825-1852)* (Paris: Barreau, 1932), 3 vols.

Also L. M. Jouffroy, *Recherches sur les sources d'une grande ligne de chemin de fer aux XIXᵉ siècle* (Paris: J. Barreau, 1932).

(76) Michel Chevalier, a leader among the Saint Simonians and a future adviser to Napoleon III, was a member of this group. He published as a result of this trip, *Lettres sur l'Amérique du Nord* (1836), published in the *Journal des Débats.* He was also the author of *Intérêts matériels de la France,* in which the importance of railways was stressed. This book went through four editions in 1838-1839.

(77) Law of July 7, 1833. See Ernest Charles, *Les chemins de fer en France pendant le règne de Louis-Philippe* (Paris: Fontemoing, 1896).

(78) Law of April 21, 1832.

(79) Law of July 9, 1835.

(80) Chamber of Deputies, May 10, 1838.

See G. Schlemmer and H. Bonneau, *Recueil de documents relatifs à l'histoire parlementaire des chemins de fer français* (Paris: Dunod, 1898), p. 53, and G. Guillaumot, *L'organisation des chemins de fer en France* (Paris, 1899).

(81) Law of July 7, 1838.

(82) By Law of July 15, 1840. The interest was to be 3 per cent and 1 per cent for amortization on a capital of 40 million francs. The government guarantee was to last for forty years.

(83) Several other concessions were not acted upon. The state itself undertook the building of a line from Lille to Valenciennes to connect France with Belgium.

(84) According to the original law, towns and departments through which

the lines passed were to reimburse the state two-thirds of the cost. This provision, which aimed to appease those districts that the new lines did not traverse, was dropped in 1845.

(85) Law of June 11, 1842.

(86) Some companies went out of existence during this depression; others secured state aid. To the line Paris-Rennes, the state guaranteed interest on private investments.

(87) The amount of freight carried by railways increased from one million tons in 1841 to 3.6 million tons in 1847 and the number of passengers from 6,300,000 to 12,000,000 over the same period.

(88) See above, Chapter IV, footnotes 78, 79.

(89) Pallain, *Les douanes françaises*, vol. II, p. 130. The ships of those nations that levied a tonnage charge on French bottoms had to pay similar charges when entering a French port.

(90) Law of May 3, 1841.

(91) Twenty-five million francs appeared in the budgets of 1841, 1842, and 1843 for this line.

(92) In 1844 a Frenchman, Dupuy de Lôme, went to England to study iron ship construction. Iron ships were not built in France until after the July Monarchy.

(93) In 1846, foreign ships did nearly twice as much of the carrying to and from France as French ships did. This does not include, however, trade reserved to the French merchant marine.

(94) See above, p. 102.

(95) Speech by Comte de Sade, quoted in Levasseur, *Histoire du commerce de la France de 1789 à nos jours,* p. 225.

(96) November 11, 1835.

(97) For the following discussion of industry and agriculture during the July Monarchy see especially, Henri Sée, *La vie économique de la France sous la monarchie censitaire* (1815–1848), and by the same author, *Esquisse d'une histoire économique et sociale de la France,* part seven.

(98) Levasseur, *op. cit.,* p. 217.

(99) See above, p. 102.

(100) Clément Juglar, *Des crises commerciales et de leur retour pério-*

dique en France, en Angleterre, et aux Etats-Unis (Paris: Guillaumin et Cie., 1889), pp. 415 ff.

(101) Villermé, *Tableau de l'état physique et moral des ouvriers employés dans les manufactures de coton, de laine et de soie* (Paris, 1840).

See also François Simiand, *Le salaire, l'évolution sociale et la monnaie; essai de théorie expérimentale du salaire* (Paris: Alcan, 1932), 3 vols., especially vol. III.

(102) The Chapelier law of 1791 and the law of 1834.

(103 Pierre Quentin-Bauchart, *La crise sociale de 1848. Les origines de la révolution de février* (Paris: Hachette, 1920), p. 132.

S. Charléty, *La Monarchie de Juillet,* in Lavisse (ed.) *Histoire de France contemporaine,* vol. V, p. 246; and Donald C. McKay, *The National Workshops. A Study in the French Revolution of 1848* (Cambridge: Harvard University Press, 1933), p. XI.

CHAPTER VI

(1) Concerning the Second Empire see the standard French histories: Charles Seignobos, *La révolution de 1848—Le Second Empire,* and *Le déclin de l'empire et l'établissement de la 3ᵉ république,* vols. VI and VII of Lavisse (ed.), *Histoire de la France contemporaine* (Paris: Hachette, 1921), and Gabriel Hanotaux, *Histoire de la nation française (Histoire politique de 1804 à 1926)* (Paris: Plon, 1929). See also Pierre de la Gorce, *Histoire du Second Empire* (Paris: Plon, Nourrit, 1905–07), 7 vols., emphasizes political history; Taxile Delord, *Histoire du Second Empire (1848–1869)* (Paris: Beillière, 1869–75), 6 vols., from the republican standpoint; Albert Thomas, *Le Second Empire,* vol. X of Jean Jaurès, *Histoire socialiste* (Paris: Rouff, 1907); Philip Guedalla, *The Second Empire* (London: Constable, 1922), having to do largely with the person Napoleon III; Émile Ollivier, *L'Empire libéral* (Paris: Garnier, 1895–1918), 18 vols.; René Arnaud, *The Second Republic and Napoleon III* (London: Heinemann, 1930), popular; F. A. Simpson, *Louis Napoleon and the Recovery of France 1848–1856* (London: Longmans, Green, 1923); and Georges Weill, *Histoire du mouvement social en France* (Paris: Alcan, 1924). Other more specialized books will be found mentioned in the footnotes.

(2) Pierre Quentin-Bauchart, *La crise de 1848. Les origines de la révolution de février* (Paris: Hachette, 1920), p. 143.

(3) Lamartine read off the names on the list at the Chamber and did some censoring on his own part. Pierre Quentin-Bauchart, *Lamartine, homme politique; la politique intérieure* (Paris, 1903).

(4) The mob had not demanded that the names be added to the list of *Le National* either at the Chamber or at the Hôtel de Ville. The four new members were candidates of a Jacobin republican paper, *La Réforme*. *La Réforme* was tardy in getting its list drawn up and was presented by the *fait accompli* of a provisional government. Its candidates were not exclusively radicals but included some of the names proposed by *Le National* and even that of the editor of *Le National*, Marrast.

(5) A million francs were to be devoted to the workshops. This sum was to be obtained by the abolition of the civil list. The declaration drawn up by Louis Blanc was signed only by himself and Garnier-Pagès from among the members of the provisional government. The names of the others were placed on the document but were not individual signatures.

(6) The demand for the red flag, which had appeared in the barricades during the revolution of 1848, was repelled by Lamartine's brilliant appeal. "Je repousserai jusqu'à la mort ce drapeau de sang, et vous devriez le répudier plus que moi. Car le drapeau rouge que vous nous apportez n'a jamais fait que le tour du Champ de Mars traîné dans le sang du peuple en '91 et '93, et le drapeau tricolore a fait le tour du monde avec le nom, la gloire et la liberté de la patrie."

(7) Louis Blanc, *Histoire de la révolution de 1848* (ed. 5, Paris, 1880), I, 133.

(8) *Marchandage* was of various kinds. The *marchandeur* was an intermediary between workers and employers. In the case most in view in 1848, he operated in the building trades. He would contract to do part of a job and hire labor at the cheapest possible wage. Another practice was making loans to workers. These loans were marked on the workers' *livrets* and workers had to pay these loans before they could secure new employment or else have it taken out of their wages by their new master. This gave the *marchandeur* a hold over labor which he frequently sold to employers.

(9) The commission's official title was *"Commission du Gouvernement pour les Travailleurs."* See especially G. Cahen, "Louis Blanc et la Commission du Luxembourg," *Annales de l'école libre des sciences politiques,* XII (1897).

(10) The 5 per cent state bonds fell from 116 on February 23, 1848, to 75 on March 8; the 3 per cent state bonds from 73 to 47 in the same period.

For further details see Clément Juglar, *Des crises commerciales et de leur retour périodique en France, en Angleterre, et aux États-Unis* (ed. 5, Paris: Guillaumin, 1889), pp. 415 ff.

(11) The luxury industries were also injured by the departure of many of the wealthy from Paris who feared a socialist revolution. See also G. Renard, *La République de 1848 (1848–1851)*, vol. ix of Jean Jaurès (ed.), *Histoire socialiste* (Paris: Rouff, 1906), p. 329, and Quentin-Bauchart, *La crise sociale de 1848,* p. 241, note 1.

(12) At the first meeting, the organization of the commission was loose. About two hundred workers, representing the various trades of Paris, were present. Their elections of the delegates were irregular and in some instances no elections were held.

(13) Charles Seignobos, *La révolution de 1848—Le Second Empire,* in Lavisse (ed.), *Histoire de la France contemporaine* (Paris: Hachette, 1921), VI, 47. During the reaction following the "June days" the maximum working day was increased to twelve hours.

(14) The reorganization of the commission was effected for the session held on March 10. Three workers were elected from each trade (*corporation*), making a total of 242. One delegate from each was to attend the daily sessions and the other two, the general assemblies. Employers elected three delegates for each trade, choosing a total of 231. Two permanent commissions, composed of ten delegates each, were established. One represented labor, the other capital. Usually they met separately, but held joint sessions to debate important questions. There was thus set up a corporate commission suggestive of the Italian Fascist corporations.

(15) Cited in Quentin-Bauchart, *La crise sociale de 1848,* p. 281.

(16) Louis Blanc, *Organisation du travail* (Paris, 1839).

(17) Aimé Chérest, *La vie et les œuvres de A. T. Marie, avocat, membre du gouvernement provisoire* (Paris, 1873). Marie himself said, "I was not a socialist. I never believed in the right to work. . . . The decree which proclaimed the right to work could not find in me a devoted and obedient servant. The decree of February 27, the execution of which was placed in my care, could not therefore be understood in that sense."

(18) At first, the men had three days off each week.

(19) Émile Thomas, *Histoire des ateliers nationaux* (Paris, 1848). Thomas had been a student at the *École centrale des arts et manufactures.*

(20) This was more than half the estimated male working population of Paris at the beginning of 1848.

(21) Donald C. McKay, *The National Workshops. A Study in the French Revolution of 1848* (Cambridge: Harvard University Press, 1933), p. 130, and Appendix I.

(22) A. Antony, *La politique financière du gouvernement provisoire* (Paris, 1910). The new paper money fell below par almost at once, but it soon rose to its nominal value. The increased taxes were increases in direct taxes which were unpopular in the rural districts. The public debt of France was increased by 48,670,376 francs in 1848, which was a greater increase than had been effected during the entire reign of Louis Philippe. See Marcel Marion, *Histoire financière de la France depuis 1715*, V, 279.

(23) The capital for these institutions was furnished in the following proportions: one-third by the state, one-third by the city in which the bank was located, and one-third by stockholders. Inasmuch as the state's contribution was in the form of government bonds and the city's in the form of notes, the working capital came mostly from private individuals. In three years, sixty-two *comptoirs d'escompte* were established throughout France. A bank of this nature had been set up in 1830, but it lasted only two years.

(24) Decree of March 21, 1848.

(25) By decree of April 27, 1848, the banks of Lyons, Rouen, Le Havre, Toulouse, Orléans, and Marseille were united to the Bank of France, and by decree of May 2, 1848, the banks of Nantes and Bordeaux were also joined to it.

(26) The franchise was granted to all males, twenty-one years of age or more, who had been residents of one locality for six months. Decree of March 2, 1848. Voting was to take place in the chief town of the canton instead of in the chief place of the arrondissement. Thus the obstacle of distant travel was removed.

(27) During the *monarchie censitaire,* that is from 1814 to 1848, members of parliament were not paid. Now the remuneration was fixed at 25 francs a day, a sum supposedly sufficient to maintain a bourgeois standard of living. The amount of the stipend was not increased until 1906.

(28) The reasons for Louis Blanc's attitude are well summed up in McKay, *op. cit.,* p. 39, note 20.

(29) McKay, *op. cit.,* pp. 38–40.

(30) The National Guard of Paris was increased from 56,751 members to

190,299 by March 18 and similar increases took place in other cities. By May it was estimated that three-fourths of the men in the National workshops were enrolled in the National Guard. The National Guard was also allowed to elect its own officers.

(31) By decree of February 25, 1848. The suggestion for organizing this force came from Lamartine, who argued that it was better to have the emotional youth fight for the provisional government than against it.

(32) Enlistments in the regular army were made more popular by reducing the term of service to two years and by promising that promotion would be only on the basis of merit. Troops were brought into Paris under the guise of the *Fête de la Fraternité* (April 20). Pierre de la Gorce, *Histoire de la second république française* (Paris, 1887), I, 201.

(33) Louis Blanc, *Histoire de la révolution de 1848* (Paris, 1870), II, 12.

(34) Not a single member of the workingmen's Luxembourg list was elected. Louis Blanc and Albert, the two most radical members of the provisional government, were elected simply because they were included among the candidates of other parties. Of the 880 representatives chosen, 500 were Moderate Republicans, less than 200 were *Orléanistes ralliés,* that is, supporters of Louis Philippe who were willing to accept the republic, 100 were Legitimists, and 100 were Democratic and Social Republicans. These figures are merely approximations. See Seignobos, *La Révolution de 1848—Le Second Empire,* in Lavisse (ed.), *Histoire de la France contemporaine,* VI, 83. The election was conducted on the principle of the *scrutin de liste* by department as opposed to the *scrutin d'arrondissement.*

(35) According to A. Chaboseau, "Les constituants de 1848," *La Révolution de 1848,* VII–VIII (1910–12), 779 of the representatives could be classified as follows:

over 325 lawyers
99 officers or former officers
53 physicians
160 landed proprietors
53 men in commerce
65 industrialists
6 foremen
18 workers

There were a few ministers, priests, and teachers in the assembly. The bourgeois character of the body is evident from the foregoing analysis. It was obvious that the lower classes had not used the ballot for class interests and also that the provinces were cool toward the social struggle that was going on in Paris.

(36) The condemnation took place in 1849.

(37) P. Loustau, *Louis Blanc à la Commission du Luxembourg* (Paris, 1908), p. 30.

(38) Quentin-Bauchart, *La crise sociale de 1848,* p. 272.

(39) This was the work of Vidal and Pecqueur. In addition to proposing the establishment of producers' coöperatives, it was suggested that the state buy up the railways, establish a monopoly of insurance, set up a state bank and state stores, fix prices, and improve housing.

(40) Only a central committee of its delegates remained as evidence of the commission's prior existence. This committee centered its attention on political action. It should be noted that some other cities besides Paris had their "Luxembourg Commissions"—Lyons, Lille, Marseilles, Anzin, Creusot, etc. Their main task seems to have been the settlement of labor disputes. Georges Renard, *La république de 1848 (1848–1852),* p. 274. One measure taken at this time supposedly in favor of workers was the reorganization of the *Conseils de prud'hommes.* These councils, which had existed previously, were arbitration commissions or courts to settle labor disputes. The reform made concerned the election of *prud'hommes.* Workers were to elect a panel of labor members; entrepreneurs a panel of employers. Then the workers would elect the employer members from the panel of entrepreneurs; the employers the workers' members from the panel of laborers. This system, created by the decree of May 27, 1848, did not function smoothly, and was changed by Napoleon III, decree of March 2, 1852, and law of June 1, 1853, so that employers would elect employers and workers would elect workers.

(41) McKay, *op. cit.,* pp. 38 ff. Émile Thomas, director of the workshops, had kept his men out of the demonstration of March 17. The workshops appeared thus as a safety valve. On March 23, Thomas was encouraged to enlist all the workers he could control. As regards finances, he was told, "Spare no money; if necessary, it will be provided to you from secret funds." As part of the scheme to influence the workshop members, a "company union," *Réunion Centrale des Ateliers Nationaux,* was set up March 25. Its members were chosen from the brigades of workers and students of the École Centrale des Arts et Manufactures. See McKay, *op. cit.,* pp. 41–43, and Émile Thomas, *Histoire des ateliers nationaux,* which is vol. II of J. A. R. Marriott, *The French Revolution of 1848 in its Economic Aspects* (Oxford: University Press, 1913), pp. 174–79.

(42) McKay, *op. cit.,* pp. 52–53, and Seignobos, *La Révolution de 1848— Le Second Empire,* p. 70.

(43) Upon his refusal to obey, Thomas was taken prisoner and hurried off to Bordeaux. The orders comprised: (1) the dismissal of all workshop members who were not residents of Paris prior to May 24; (2) dismissal of workers refusing positions in private enterprises; (3) the organization of workers into units and their dispatch to the provinces for public work; (4) substitution of piece work for day work; (5) the taking of a census.

Already on May 13 it had been decided to allow unmarried men from eighteen to twenty-five years of age in the workshops to enlist in the army. Those who refused were to be dismissed. An order to this effect was made public during the demonstration of May 15.

(44) Among those elected were Cabet, chief of the *Icariens,* Proudhon, the anarchist, and Leroux, an associationist and probable inventor of the word "socialism." Gide and Rist, *Histoire des doctrines économiques,* ed. 5, 1926, p. 276, footnote.

(45) See Octave Festy, *Les associations ouvrières encouragées par la Deuxième République* (Comité des travaux historiques, section d'histoire moderne et contemporaine), vol. IV, 1915. Among the notable successes were jewellers, chair makers, and type-setters. The tailors of Clichy had to close their shops, but some of them opened again and carried on. See also Jean Gaumont, *Histoire générale de la coöpération en France* (Paris: Fédération nationale des coöpératives de consommation, 1923–24), II, 242–46. The main reason for the collapse of so many coöperatives seems to have been mismanagement.

(46) Those courageous souls who endeavored to present socialist schemes for the consideration of the constituent assembly were either ignored or laughed off the floor. Socialist leaders had been banished from the assembly after the June days; only the theorists remained. Considérant presented the philosophy of Fourier; Lerroux, that of Louis Blanc; Proudhon, his own.

A handy manual of French constitutions is L. Duguit and H. Monnier, *Les constitutions . . . de la France depuis 1789* (Paris: Librairie de droit, 1915).

(47) Cavaignac, candidate of the *Réunion du Palais National,* composed of moderate republicans, got 23 per cent of the vote; Raspail, candidate of the socialists, and Ledru-Rollin, candidate of the Solidarité républicaine, received only a handful of votes.

(48) For the background of Louis Napoleon see especially F. A. Simpson, *The Rise of Louis-Napoleon* (London: Murray, 1909); B. Jerrold, *Life of Napoleon III* (London, 1879–82), 4 vols.; H. Thirria, *Napoléon III avant*

l'empire (Paris, 1895–96); H. N. Boon, *Rêve et réalité dans l'œuvre économique et sociale de Napoléon III* (Paris, 1936).

(49) *Rêveries politiques* and an appended *Projet d'une constitution* (1832); and *Les idées napoléoniennes* (1839).

(50) *Extinction du pauperisme* (1844) and *Analyse de la question des sucres* (1842). The works of Louis Napoleon in this early period have been collected and published: *Œuvres de Napoléon III* (Paris, 1856).

(51) Seignobos, *La révolution de 1848—Le Second Empire,* p. 126.

(52) M. Chevalier, *Cours d'économie politique* (ed. 1, 1842, ed. 2, 1858). See also Pierre Labracherie, *Michel Chevalier et ses idées économiques* (Paris: Picart, 1929), and Louis Reybaud, *Économistes modernes* (Paris, 1862). Chevalier was considerably influenced by a visit to the United States (1833–35). His American letters, published in the *Journal des débats,* show his admiration for the economic activity in the New World. They offer an interesting source for students of American history of that epoch.

(53) Labracherie, *op. cit.,* pp. 103 ff. France should not endeavor to attain complete freedom of trade at once. England took twenty-two years to accomplish it; France might require a similarly long period. Chevalier, *Examen du système commercial connu sous le nom de système protecteur* (Paris: Guillaumin, 1852).

(54) The appointment to this body required Chevalier's resignation of his post at the Collège de France, because a member of the council could not hold another salaried state position. The *Conseil d'État* had as its duty the drafting of all bills and was, therefore, a very important body.

(55) The relationship between banking and national economic development has been treated briefly for France and Germany in Walter Huth, *Die Entwicklung der deutschen und französischen Grossbanken im Zusammenhange mit der Entwicklung der Nationalwirtschaft* (Berlin: Siemenroth, 1918). See also C. K. Hobson, *The Export of Capital* (London, 1914), and A. Sartorius von Waltershausen, *Das volkswirtschaftliche System der Kapitalanlage im Auslande* (Berlin, 1907).

(56) André Liesse, *Evolution of Credit and Banks in France from the Founding of the Bank of France to the Present Time* (Washington: Government Printing Office, 1909), pp. 110 ff.

(57) By decrees of December 3, 1852, it became the *Crédit foncier de France.* It took over other smaller institutions of its kind and extended its business to the entire nation.

(58) At first the state did not have the right to appoint its highest officials. It took that power July 5, 1854. The original name of the institution was *Banque foncière de Paris*.

(59) Haussmann was prefect of the Seine from 1853 to 1869.

(60) It extended its business to Algeria in 1860. After July 6, 1860, it was authorized to lend money to departments, towns, and land owners' associations without mortgages.

(61) Chartered by decree of February 16, 1861.

(62) Founded in 1852. Its firm name was *Société générale du credit mobilier français*. The Pereire brothers were natives of Bordeaux. J. Plenge, *Gründung und Geschichte des credit mobiliers* (Tübingen, 1903).

(63) These included the *Caisse des actions réunies, Caisse et journal des chemins de fer,* and *Caisse générale des chemins de fer.*

(64) Its firm name was *Société générale pour favoriser le commerce et l'industrie en France.*

(65) For histories of French banking see Alphonse Courtois, *Histoire de la Banque de France et des principales institutions françaises de crédit depuis 1716* (Paris: Guillaumin, 1875); F. François-Marsal, *Encyclopédie de Banque et de Bourse* (Paris: Crété, 1929), 5 vols.; André Liesse, *op. cit.;* Eugen Kaufmann, *Das französische Bankwesen* (Tübingen: Mohr, 1923).

(66) The law of May 23, 1863, recognized the usefulness of limited liability companies; the law of July 24, 1867, removed capitalization limits from the companies, abolished requirements for governmental authorization, and provided for stockholders supervision of them.

(67) See P. Dupont-Ferrier, *Le marché financier de Paris sous le Second Empire* (Paris, 1926). One hundred and forty-eight were founded from 1852 to 1859. Some of them were naturally not very sound investments.

(68) See a contemporary book by Oscar de Vallée, *Manieurs d'argent,* and Ponsard's *La Bourse,* which were hostile to speculation and which were approved by the Emperor. See also *Ten Years of Imperialism in France. Impressions of a "Flaneur"* [pseudonym of C. B. Derosne] (London, 1862), chap. vii.

(69) Greece joined in 1866. See H. P. Willis, *History of the Latin Monetary Union* (Chicago, 1901). There had been a considerable influx of gold to Europe following the discovery of that metal in California (1848) and Australia (1851). According to an estimate of Émile Levasseur, *La question*

d'or, prices in France increased about 20 per cent. Gold became cheaper and silver relatively dearer, which required changing the silver and gold content of coins. The Latin nations vied with each other in this process until the formation of the union.

(70) Decree of November 18.

(71) It is said that one-half of private capital in French railways prior to 1847 was British. See L. H. Jenks, *The Migration of British Capital to 1875* (New York: Columbia University Press, 1927), p. 148. French foreign investments amounted to about 2,500,000,000 francs in 1850. Dupont-Ferrier, *op. cit.,* p. 7.

(72) Dupont-Ferrier, *op. cit.,* p. 163, and Herbert Feis, *Europe, the World's Banker 1870-1914* (New Haven: Yale University Press, 1930), p. 47.

(73) The reason for small investments in England was not political but economic—the English market was well taken care of by English financiers.

(74) The financial side of the Mexican incident is a most romantic affair. A Swiss banker, Jecker, became seriously involved by financing erstwhile Mexican presidents. His bank failed and he appealed for aid to his friend, the Duc de Morny, half-brother to Napoleon III and one of the Emperor's most influential advisers. The Duc was offered a handsome profit for Jecker's salvation. Jecker became a French citizen and the French Government pressed Jecker's claim. As a matter of fact, it provided an excuse, if not the reason, for the French expedition to Mexico. Two Mexican Empire loans were floated with the encouragement of the French Government in Paris and London. The first amounted to 272,000,000 francs, which was more than enough to satisfy Jecker and other Mexican creditors—more than enough by only 34,000,000 francs! The second loan for 250,000,000 francs was subscribed for only 170,000,000 francs, and but 70,000,000 francs of it ever reached Maximilian. In addition to service on these loans, the Mexican Government had to pay the French Government high prices for the military assistance that was sent out. When the bubble of the enterprise burst and the French holders of Mexican bonds found out what rich royalties the bankers had been paid and what advantage the Mexican loans had been to men in high office, they stirred up so much trouble that Napoleon III's government thought it wise to pacify them with a gratuity for their losses. See Egon Caesar, Count Corti, *Maximilian and Charlotte of Mexico* (New York: Knopf, 1929), 2 vols.; Percy F. Martin, *Maximilian in Mexico* (London, 1914); W. H. Chynoweth, *Fall of Maximilian* (London, 1872).

(75) Navigation on the Seine was given particular attention. Sunken chain

towing was introduced in places where the current was swift. Dams, locks, and port facilities were constructed.

(76) The organic law for telegraphs was dated September 21, 1851. In the 1860's cables were laid.

(77) See above, pp. 147–148.

(78) The concessions ran from twelve to ninety-nine years. The average was about forty years.

(79) "Exposé des motifs du projet de loi du 17 Mai 1848," printed in the *Moniteur universel,* May 19. The executive commission of the constituent assembly felt that concessions had been granted by Louis Philippe to personal friends.

(80) See *Moniteur universel,* June 23, 1848; G. Schlemmer and H. Bonneau, *Recueil de documents relatifs à l'histoire parlementaire des chemins de fer français* (Paris: Dunod, 1898), p. 131.

(81) Upon the refusal of the Government to buy up the railways, the credit of the lines suffered. Some of them were aided by larger concessions and by reducing their obligations to the state. The Paris-Lyons road was taken over by the Government (August 17, 1848), but was conceded again to a private company, January 5, 1852. Only one new concession was granted in the period 1848–1851. It was for the Paris-Rennes line.

(82) René Thévenez, Maurice d'Hérouville, and Étienne Bleys, *Législation des chemins de fer* (Paris: Rousseau, 1930), p. 10.

(83) See the report on railway concentration by the Duc de Morny, *Moniteur universel,* June 27, 1852.

(84) These companies existed until 1937. The *Ouest* was, however, bought by the state in 1908 and there was a partial merger of the *Orléans* and *Midi* lines.

(85) The Government promised that it would do what was necessary for the economic health of the nation. *Moniteur universel,* April 13, 1858. Railway companies found themselves pinched in this period. See the *Journal des chemins de fer,* December 11–25, 1858, and the *Semaine financière,* September 25, 1858. See Marcel Blanchard, "La politique ferroviaire du Second Empire," *Annales d'histoire économique et sociale,* 1934, pp. 529–549.

(86) Only to the *Midi* was granted a guarantee of earnings of 4 per cent on the old lines. In practice, the 4 per cent guarantee on the new networks

amounted to 5.75 per cent, because of other charges. See Thévenez, d'Hérouville, and Bleys, *op. cit.,* p. 13.

(87) A. Audiganne, *Les chemins der fer* (Paris, 1862), II, 118.

(88) A. Picard, *Les chemins de fer* (Paris, 1918), p. 175. The average value of exports by land in the period 1827–1836 was 192,400,000 francs; in the period 1867–1876, 1,299,700,000 francs. Tons of freight carried one kilometer by railways in 1854 was 2 billion; in 1863, 4 billion.

The attempt made in 1868–69 to get control of the Luxembourg railways is an example of the imperialist aims of Napoleon by means of rails.

(89) The review of the association, *Le libre échange,* foundered in 1848. The *Journal des économistes* continued to appear and favored free trade.

(90) Quoted in A. L. Dunham, *The Anglo-French Treaty of Commerce of 1860 and the Progress of the Industrial Revolution in France* (Ann Arbor: University of Michigan Press, 1930), p. 19. Refusal to discuss Ste. Beuve's bill was voted by 428 to 199.

(91) Auguste Arnauné, *Le commerce extérieur et les tarifs de douane* (Paris, 1911), p. 245.

(92) Author of "Tendance de l'économie politique en Angleterre et en France," *Revue des deux mondes,* April 15, 1852; *Essai sur la liberté du commerce des nations ou examen de la théorie anglaise du libre échange* (Paris: Durand, 1853); and *Histoire de la politique commerciale de la France et de son influence sur le progrès de la richesse politique depuis le moyen âge jusqu'à nos jours* (Paris: Durand, 1854), 2 vols. The ideas indicated as being those of Gouraud are to be found in the first chapter of vol. I of the last-mentioned book.

(93) "Agriculture, industry, shipping, and consumers are interested in the manufacture [of beet sugar]. Foreign trade alone and the treasury would find an advantage in its suppression. It is a question of knowing what interests have the most importance for the prosperity of France. The Emperor Napoleon made the following classification which shows the bases on which the political economy of France ought to be founded.

" 'Agriculture is the base and the force of the prosperity of a country.

" 'Industry is the ease, the happiness of the population.

" 'Foreign trade, the super-abundance, the good use of the other two.

" 'This last is made for the other two; the two others are not made for it. The interests of the three essential bases are divergent, often opposed' . . .

"Agriculture and industry are the two causes of vitality, while foreign trade is only the effect. A wise government ought never to sacrifice the major interests of the first for the secondary interests of the last. One is able to

admit, therefore, in principle, that the manufacture of beet sugar, a source of wealth for agriculture and industry, ought not to be sacrificed for a commercial interest. Especially it ought not to be sacrificed for a fiscal interest, for . . . one thinks of the condition of Spain, which fell from being the empire of the world because she abandoned her industry and her agriculture for her commerce."
"Analyse de la question des sucres," *Œuvres de Napoléon III,* III, 235, 237–39.

(94) *Senatus consulte* of December 25, 1852. The laws of 1814, 1818, and 1836 empowered the monarch to reduce rates by decree, but they had to be ratified by the legislative bodies.

(95) Decree of August 18, 1853.

(96) These decrees were issued from 1853 to 1856. The reduction on iron and steel was great enough to permit large quantities of English rails to be imported.

(97) Acts of July 26, 1856, and April 18, 1857. Concerning the improvement of business activity see Marcel Marion, *Histoire financière de la France,* V, 317.

(98) The Government's statement issued October 18, 1856, read as follows: "The progress of French industry had been shown so clearly at the Universal Exposition of 1855 that the moment seemed opportune for replacing the prohibitions in our tariff laws by protective duties. This was a great step toward the goal which should be sought by all peoples. In fact, the development of commercial activity and of international relations paves the way for the progress of civilization. Profoundly convinced of this, the government had introduced in the *Corps Législatif* a bill repealing all the prohibitions. This bill could not be brought to a vote in the last session and the government, desiring adequate advice, decided to begin an official investigation of these questions. Alarmist reports were, however, spread throughout the country and made use of by the interested parties. His Majesty wished to have a very careful study made of the complaints which had reached him and, therefore, directed the minister of commerce to examine them. Having been enlightened by the minister's report on the true position of French industries, the emperor decided to modify the bill introduced in the *Corps Législatif* so as to have the repeal of prohibitions take effect only after July 1, 1861. A bill to this effect has been sent to the council of state. French industries, warned of the firm intentions of the government, will have ample time to prepare themselves for the commercial régime." Quoted in Dunham, *op. cit.,* pp. 24–25.

(99) *Ibid.,* chap. iii.

(100) The interview took place on October 27, 1859. Chevalier saw the

emperor in the morning, and prepared the way for Cobden, whose visit took place in the afternoon. During the audience with Cobden, Napoleon is said to have exclaimed, "Je serais enchanté et flatté de l'idée d'accomplir la même œuvre en France [that Peel accomplished in England]; mais les difficultés sont bien grandes. Nous ne faisons pas de réformes en France; nous ne faisons que des révolutions."

(101) "The Encouragement of trade through the multiplication of the means of exchange will follow as the natural consequence of these measures. The progressive decrease of the tax on foodstuffs of general consumption will, then, be a necessity, as will the substitution of protective duties for the system of prohibitions which restricts our commercial relations. Through these measures agriculture will find a market for its products; industry, freed from obstacles within the country, aided by the government, stimulated by competition, will fight successfully against foreign goods, and our commerce, instead of languishing . . . will have a new and vigorous growth."
Letter of Napoleon III to Fould, Dunham, *op. cit.,* pp. 83–84.

(102) Ernest Feray, *Du traité de commerce de 1860 avec l'Angleterre* (Paris, 1881), pp. 11–12.

(103) Other articles on which there was an excise tax in Great Britain were to be charged a duty equal to that tax and a slight additional surtax to offset the cost of the excise to the British producer.

(104) The full text of the treaty and supplementary conventions may be found in H. Reader Lack, *The French Treaty and the Tariff of 1860* (London, 1861).

(105) John Morley in his *Life of William Ewart Gladstone* (London, 1911), II, 23, cites Gladstone's belief: "It was and it is my opinion that the choice lay between the Cobden Treaty and not the certainty, but the high probability, of a war with France."

(106) April and May, 1860.

(107) *Enquête de 1860 sur l'état de l'industrie en France* (Paris, 1860). The seventh volume is to be found only at the ministry of commerce, Paris. Information concerning the investigation itself and how it was conducted is to be found in *Historique du traité de commerce de 1860 et des conventions complémentaires* (Paris, 1861).

(108) Edgar Allix, *Les droits de douane* (Paris: Rousseau, 1932), 2 vols., I, 40.

(109) May 23, 1860.

(110) The dates of these accords were with Belgium, May 1, 1861, with an additional convention May 12; with the German Zollverein, August 2, 1862; with Italy, January 17, 1863; with Switzerland, June 30, 1864; with Sweden and Norway, February 14, 1865; with the Hanseatic towns, March 4, 1865; with the Netherlands, July 7, 1865; with Spain, June 18, 1865; and with Austria, December 11, 1866. See Léon Amé, *Étude économique sur les tarifs de douanes* (Paris, 1876), II, *passim*.

(111) Clapham, *The Economic Development of France and Germany*, p. 112.

(112) Agreement of February 28, 1851. The subsidy was to be 3,000,000 francs a year for ten years and then to be decreased in the next ten years of the twenty-year contract. As a matter of fact, the subsidy was increased to 4,776,118.40 francs in 1857, during the crisis, and later diminished.

(113) This sum was reduced by about one-half because of the abandonment of one of the services to South America.

(114) Decrees of August 25, 1861, and February 5, 1862, applicable to Canada and the United States. Other nations who made commercial treaties with France on the basis of the most favored nation secured the privilege. See footnote 110.

(115) It was held in 1862. Another was granted in 1866.

(116) Law of July 3, 1861.

(117) Decree of July 9, 1868. Earlier decrees had extended the privilege to certain colonies.

(118) By treaty with Austria, December 11, 1866.

(119) He was governor-general of the colony with one slight interruption from 1854 to 1865. The conquest was not completed until 1880.

(120) On March 4, 1848, about 500,000 slaves were emancipated. Their owners were given an indemnity of 126,000,000 francs for this reform—a sum that did not compensate them completely for their loss. About 120,000,000 francs of the indemnity were paid in state bonds which were low at the time. The freeing of the slaves led to labor turmoil. At first an effort was made to replenish the labor supply by negroes from Africa and Hindu coolies, but gradually the negroes already in the islands were brought under control. Some, detained as vagabonds, were put to work. Others worked as members of "associations," supposedly of the 1848 type, and still others were hired as laborers at very low wages. Sugar production fell to less than one-third normal in 1848, but was back at par in 1853.

(121) Decree of March 27, 1852.

(122) Decree of May 3, 1854.

(123) Arthur Girault, *The Colonial Tariff Policy of France* (Oxford: Clarendon Press, 1916), p. 68.

(124) Law of July 17, 1867. Foreign cotton goods, for example, were especially favored. See Girault, *op. cit.,* pp. 79–80.

(125) These figures are from the *Annuaire statistique* (Paris: Imprimerie nationale, 1931), Résumé rétrospectif, *passim.* A very rosy picture is given in the official *Exposé de la situation de l'empire présenté au sénat et au corps législatif* (Paris: Imprimerie impériale, 1861–69).

(126) United States consular reports.

(127) See footnote 125. The increased value of foreign trade must not be taken at its face value, for there was a considerable augmentation of prices following the discovery of gold in California and Australia. This increase was probably in the neighborhood of 20 per cent from 1847 to 1857. Levasseur, *Histoire de commerce de la France,* II, 265, footnote 2.

(128) These figures are from Marcel Marion, *Histoire financière de la France,* V, 317.

(129) See Dunham, op. cit., chap. ix, and *La sidérurgie française, 1864–1914,* privately printed by the *Comité des forges* in 1920. This little book is exceedingly difficult to find, but is available at the *École normale supérieure* in Paris.

(130) Dunham, *op. cit.,* chap. x, and Alphonse Cordier, *La crise cotonnière dans la Seine Inférieure* (Rouen, 1864).

(131) L. Roux, *Les régimes successifs de la construction navale et de la navigation maritime en France* (Paris: Payot, 1923), p. 97.

(132) These are the figures for special commerce which exclude transit trade.

(133) This does not necessarily mean a reduction in the standard of living because of invisible items in the trade balance.

(134) Dunham, *op. cit.,* chap. xvii.

(135) Du Mesnil-Marigny, *Le rôle de l'industrie française et les interpellations qu'il a provoquées au Corps législatif* (Paris: Lacroix, 1868). This book is largely a compilation of complaints against Napoleon's economic policies by French industrialists.

(136) J. M. S. Allison in his *Monsieur Thiers* (New York: W. W. Norton, 1931), pp. 40 and 89, has quite misunderstood Thiers' interest in and knowledge of economic matters. See Adolf Wurst, *Thiers volkswirtschaftliche Anschauungen* (Halle, 1893) (*Sammelung nationalökonomischer Abhandlungen der staatswissenschaftlichen Seminars zu Halle*).

(137) This is the opinion of Dunham, *op. cit.,* p. 297. *Enquête parlementaire sur le régime économique en France* (Paris, 1872). It covers cotton, wool, linen, and to some degree silk.

(138) Marion, *Histoire financière de la France,* V, 491–92. Among the books criticizing government expenditures see: Horn, *Le bilan de l'empire* (1868), and *Salut au troisième milliard;* Allain Targé, *Déficits* (1868); Boudon, *La vérité au peuple français sur la situation économique et financière de l'empire en 1867;* and Merlin, *L'empire et ses principes financières* and *Progression comparée des budgets de 1853 à 1866.* In defense of the Emperor's expenditures see Vitu, *Finances et l'empire,* which is a glorification of Napoleon's wars and his policy of national equipment.

(139) This manifesto, issued February 17, 1864, marked an important step in the development of French socialism.

(140) This reform was approved by a plebiscite, 7,350,000 to 1,538,000.

CHAPTER VII

(1) Among the general histories of the Third Republic, the following will be found useful:

J. E. C. Bodley, *France* (London: Macmillan & Co., 1900).

J. C. Bracq, *France under the Republic* (New York: Scribner, 1916).

Gabriel Hanotaux, *Histoire de la France contemporaine,* Vol. I–V (Paris: Combet & Cie., 1904–1908).

J. Labusquière, *La troisième république* (1871–1900) (Paris: Publications Jules Rouff et Cie., 1909) in Jaurès (ed.), *Histoire socialiste.*

Michel Lhéritier, *La France depuis 1870* (Paris: Librairie Félix Alcan, 1922).

Maxime Petit, *Histoire de France contemporaine de 1871 à 1913* (Paris: Librairie Larousse, 1916).

Propylaën–Weltgeschichte, vols. VIII, IX, and X (Berlin: Propyläen Verlag, 1930–1933).

R. Recouly, *The Third Republic* (New York: Putnam, 1928).

Ch. Seignobos, *Le Déclin de l'empire et l'établissement de la 3ᵉ République*

(1859–1875) and *L'Evolution de la 3ᵉ République* (1875–1914) in E. Lavisse (ed.), *Histoire de France contemporaine,* vol. VII and VIII (Paris: Librairie Hachette, 1921).

E. A. Vizetelly, *Republican France 1870–1912* (Boston: Small, Maynard & Co., 1912).

Alexandre Zévaès (pseudonym for Gustave Alexandre Bourson) *Histoire de la Troisième République* (1870–1926) (Paris: Impr. Amiard, 1926).

E. Zévort, *Histoire de la troisième République,* 4 vols. (Paris: Félix Alcan, 1899).

(2) This move was permitted without resistance by the bourgeois National Guard.

(3) January 28, 1871. Prices of food had soared to tremendous heights and supplies had run low. In January, the people of Paris were eating up horses at the rate of seven hundred a day. Dogs, cats, and animals at the Jardin des Plantes had been resorted to as means of sustenance; prime rats had brought three francs a head. Long lines of women had waited hours outside distributing centers for rations of bread and vegetables. Churches had been broken into for firewood. The cry of "Give us bread or give us lead" had been heard repeatedly.

(4) There were about 330 Republicans and 450 Monarchists in the National Assembly.

(5) Two of the leaders in the Commune, Delescluze and Félix Pyat, contributed to two patriotic journals, *Le Réveil* and *Le Combat,* respectively. Blanqui had edited *La Patrie en Danger,* excerpts from which were published in a book by that title (Paris: Chevalier, 1871). He wrote, pages 19–20:

"La gloire de Paris est sa condamnation.

"Sa lumière, ils veulent l'éteindre; ses idées, les refouler dans le néant. Ce sont les hordes du cinquième siècle, débordées une seconde fois sur la Gaule, pour engloutir la civilisation moderne, comme elles ont dévoré la civilisation greco-romaine, son aïeule.

"N'entendez-vous pas leur hurlement sauvage: 'Périsse la race latine!' Ils entonnent le chant de la tribu zélandaise autour de son festin cannibale: Heureux qui brise de son tomahawk les têtes de la tribu ennemie et qui se repait de sa chair et de son sang.

"C'est Berlin qui doit être la ville sainte de l'avenir, le rayonnement qui éclair le monde. Paris c'est la Babylone usurpatrice et corrompue, la grande prostituée que l'envoyé de Dieu, l'ange exterminateur, la Bible à la main, va balayer de la face de la terre. Ignorez-vous que le Seigneur a marqué la race germaine du sceau de la prédestination? Elle a un mètre de tripes de plus que la nôtre.

"Défendons-nous. C'est la férocité d'Odin doublée de la férocite de moloch, qui marche contre nos cités, la barbarie du Vandale et la barbarie du Sémite. Défendons-nous et ne comptons sur personne."

In socialist clubs, schemes for a *sortie torrentielle*—a mass movement from Paris, for turning the wild animals of the zoo on the Germans, for protecting the virtue of French women by the Prussic finger, and for a last-ditch stand had been concocted. Concerning these clubs, see Molinari, *Les Clubs rouges pendant le siège de Paris* (Paris, 1871) and Henri d'Almeras, *La Vie parisienne pendant le siège et sous la commune* (Paris, 1927).

(6) *Enquête sur l'insurrection du 18 mars,* 3 vols. published by The National Assembly, vol. II, p. 573. Most of the socialists at this time were followers of Proudhon or Blanqui; other theorists had few disciples.

(7) It is estimated that 150,000 Parisians unable to pay their debts were thus made liable to legal action.

(8) This was the plan that Thiers had proposed in 1848.

(9) Marx, Engels, Lenin, Trotsky, and Kautsky have all written about it. Marx's *Civil War in France* was finished two days after the defeat of the Commune. In his work, the Commune appears as an uprising of the proletariat of Paris. In Soviet Russia, the eighteenth of March is a holiday and streets all over the country are named for it. In the French socialist movement, the Commune is also considered as an important historic moment; the Mur des Fédérés in the Cemetery Père Lachaise, where one hundred and fifty of the communards were shot, is still a socialist shrine. See Edward S. Mason, *The Paris Commune; an Episode in the History of the Socialist Movement* (New York; the Macmillan Co., 1930) which minimizes the socialist nature of the Commune. Among other scholarly works may be mentioned G. Bourgin, *Histoire de la commune* (Paris: Cornély & Cie., 1907); L. Fiaux, *Histoire de la guerre civile de 1871* (1879); and Georges Laronze, *Histoire de la commune de 1871 d'après des documents et des souvenirs inédits* (Paris: Payot, 1928). Books that present the case of the *Fédérés* are: P. O. Lissagaray, *History of the Commune of 1871* (Eng. trans. London, 1886); L. Dubreuilh, *La Commune,* vol. XI of the *Histoire socialiste,* edited by Jaurès; and E. Lepelletier, *Histoire de la commune de 1871* (Paris: Mercure de France, 1911–1913), 3 vols. See also the recent work by Frank Jellinek, *The Paris Commune of 1871* (London, 1937).

(10) Mason, *op. cit.,* p. 242 and Lepelletier, *op. cit.,* vol. III, p. 30.

(11) The Communards took hostages, like the Archbishop of Paris who was murdered, and resorted to extensive burning as they retreated before the national forces. It is estimated that 15,000 men were killed in the action

and that 15,000 were taken prisoners, many of whom were killed or imprisoned.

(12) Michel Lhéritier, *La France depuis 1870* (Paris: Alcan, 1922), p. 19. Some of the excess had been raised by an internal loan of 750,000,000 francs, a loan from the house of Morgan in London, of which 202,024,770 francs went to the treasury and 6,875,000 francs to the bankers in commissions and carried interest amounting to 7.42 per cent, and by advances from the Bank of France. For estimates on the cost of the war, see Marcel Marion, *Histoire financière de la France,* vol. V, p. 519. Thiers said that the war had cost between 7,800,000,000 and 8 billion francs, but he was trying to cut the figure in order to make a good impression.

(13) A "rayon" or circle of ten kilometers around Belfort was given to France in exchange for a district next to the Luxemburg frontier that had iron ore. The French attached value to Belfort for patriotic reasons. One of the negotiators, Pouyer-Quertier, succeeded in saving for France a village in which lived some of his relatives!

(14) People in the ceded territory could declare their desire to retain French nationality. About 150,000 in the territories opted for France. An equal number of natives of Alsace-Lorraine who were domiciled in France expressed the same desire. Germany insisted on a real transfer of domicile to France in case a person wanted to retain his French nationality, which ruled out 110,240 of the optants.

(15) Marcel Marion, *op. cit.,* vol. V, p. 516.

(16) Lhéritier, *op. cit.,* p. 19.

(17) Partly because the Saxon textile manufacturers feared the competition of Alsatian textiles and because France could use products from her lost provinces, France agreed to allow goods from these district to enter the country without paying the full duty until the end of 1872.

(18) Therefore an actual interest rate of 6.25 per cent.

(19) France had to reimburse the Compagnie de l'Est for the railways. This was done by paying interest on the investment for the life of the concession.

(20) The *surtaxes de pavillon* were also voted, but were not enforced because they violated a treaty with Austria.

(21) Just how much this sum was, it is difficult to state with accuracy. The export of French goods was over 10 billion francs in the three years 1871–1873; the interest on foreign investments amounted to between 6 and 7

hundred million francs a year; and tourist expenditures between 2 and 3 hundred million francs. As no foreign investments were made in these years, there was only the drain of payments for imports and French tourist expenditures abroad to compete with government needs for foreign currency. See the illuminating treatise by Léon Say, *Rapport sur le paiement de l'indemnité de guerre* in his *Les finances de la France sous la Troisième République* (Paris: Lévy, 1898), vol. I, section IX.

See also Marcel Marion, *Histoire financière de la France,* vol. V, pp. 571–579. According to Say, vol. I, p. 372, France paid her indemnity as follows:

CREDITS TO FRANCE

Chemins de fer de l'Est	325,000,000
Moneys owed City of Paris by Germany	98,400

PAYMENTS

Billets de la Banque de France	125,000,000
Or français	273,003,058.10
Argent français	239,291,875.75
Numéraire et billet de banque allemands	105,039,145.18
Thalers	2,485,313,721.04
Florin de Francfort	235,128,152.79
Marcs banco	265,216,990.40
Reichsmarcs	79,072,309.89
Florins de Hollande	250,540,821.46
Francs de Belgique	295,704,546.40
Livres Sterling	637,349,832.28
	4,990,660,453.29

(22) Thiers added that the Republic would have to be conservative or it could not be.

(23) This was a compromise between the ten-year term demanded by the monarchists and the four-year term proposed by the republicans.

(24) For what follows, see:

H. Leyret, *Le gouvernement et le parlement* (Paris, 1919).

J. Barthélmy, *Le gouvernement de la France* (Paris, 1919).

Lindsay Rogers, *The French Parliamentary System* (New York: Columbia University Press, in preparation).

L. Duguit and H. Monnier, *Les constitutions de la France . . . depuis 1789* (Paris, 1915).

L. Duguit, *Traité de droit constitutionnel* (Paris, 1924), 5 vols.

A. Esmein, *Droit constitutionnel français* (Paris, 1921), 7 vols.

E. M. Sait, *Government and Politics of France* (New York, 1920).

The chief constitutional laws were, in addition to that concerning the presidency, the Law on the Organization of the Senate, February 24, 1875; Law on the Organization of Public Powers, February 25, 1875; and Law on the Relation of the Public Powers, July 16, 1875.

(25) The electoral law of November 30, 1875, provided for the election of deputies in single-number constituencies (*scrutin d'arrondissement*). By the law of June 16, 1885, this procedure was replaced by *scrutin de liste*—each department being a constituency for the number of representatives allocated to it by population. On February 13, 1889, the *scrutin d'arrondissement* was reintroduced. July 12, 1919, a modified proportional-representation system was inaugurated. This was replaced in turn by single-member districts in July, 1927. The shifts have been the result of attempts of the parties in power to gain more strength by a new system. Deputies are elected for four years. They must be twenty-five years of age. There are over six hundred of them. To be chosen in the first election, a candidate must have a majority, not a plurality, of votes cast. In case this does not occur, another election is held a week later in which a plurality is sufficient. The result is that in the first election the voter expresses his real preference; in the second, he may cast his vote for the candidate who has the best chance of victory among those of the general political nuance with which he sympathizes. There are also frequently coalitions for the second balloting.

(26) To begin with it was provided that 75 of the 300 senators should be appointed by the National Assembly for life. Each vacancy among this number should be filled by the Senate itself. The other 225 were apportioned to the departments on the basis of population. They were to be elected by colleges which were composed of the deputies from the department, the departmental general council, the arrondissement councils, and 1 to 24 members of municipal councils, depending on size of the city. Life membership was abolished December 9, 1884. A senator is elected for nine years, one-third of the senate is renewed every three years. To be chosen on the first ballot, a candidate must receive a majority, not a plurality. This results in considerable vote-swapping for successive ballotings.

(27) The Chamber has the right to consider fiscal bills before the Senate; the Senate may sit as a judicial body to try cases of treason or ministers accused by the Chamber.

(28) The Senate stands in fairly high regard in the country, perhaps in higher esteem than the Chamber.

(29) Frequent ministerial changes do not necessarily mean a change in policy. It often happens that the Government is defeated on a single rather unimportant question and is reconstituted without a very great change of personnel.

(30) André Siegfried, *France, a Study in Nationality* (New Haven: Yale University Press, 1930), chap. II makes light of this opinion. Nevertheless, I consider it to be the case.

(31) Besides such an analysis has already been made. See G. Bourgin, J. Carrère, and A. Guérin, *Manuel des parties politiques en France* (Paris: Rieder, 1928).

(32) Seignobos, *Le déclin de l'Empire et l'établissement de la 3ᵉ République (1859–1875)*, p. 322–3.

(33) Seignobos, *Histoire sincère de la nation française,* pp. 479–484.

(34) G. Bourgin, J. Carrère, A. Guérin, *Manuel des partis politiques en France* (Paris: Rieder, 1928), p. 139.

See also Armand Charpentier, *Le parti radical et radical-socialiste à travers ses congrès* (1901–1911) (Paris, 1920).

(35) Schuman, p. 366.

The composition of the French legislative bodies following the election of 1928 and including by-elections to October 20, 1929, was as follows:

Senate		Chamber	
Right	9	Belonging to no group	45
Republican Left	22	Popular Democratic	19
Republican Union	77	Republican-Democratic Union	97
Democratic and Radical Union	32	Left Republicans	64
Democratic Left	150	Unionist and Social Left	17
Socialist	15	Democratic and Social Action	30
Belonging to no group	8	Radical Left	52
	313	Independent Left	15
		Republican Socialist	35
		Radical and Radical Socialist	118
		Socialist	100
		Communist	10
		Not inscribed	7
			609

Total authorized by law 612

Schuman, *op. cit.,* p. 17.

(36) C. J. H. Hayes, *France—A Nation of Patriots* (New York: Columbia University Press, 1930). See the chapter concerning the press and the appendix.

(37) *Ibid.*

(38) For a discussion of this phenomenon see C. A. Beard, *The Idea of National Interest* (New York: Macmillan Co., 1934), chap. I, and F. Meinecke, *Die Idee der Staatsräson* (Munich: Oldenburg, 3d edition, 1929), see the Einleitung.

(39) See above, pp. 204–205.

(40) Arthur L. Dunham, "The Attempt of President Thiers to Restore High Protection in France (1871–1873)," *The Journal of Economic and Business History,* vol. I, pp. 302 324 (1929).

(41) Figures from the *Annuaire Statistique.* This index was based on prices during the period 1891–1900, which were given the index 100.

(42) W. H. Dawson, *The Evolution of Modern Germany* (London: T. Fisher Unwin, 1919), p. 7; and H. H. O'Farrell, *The Franco-German War Indemnity and its Economic Results* (London: Harrison and Sons, 1913).

(43) *Annuaire statistique* for 1931 (1932). *Résumé rétrospectif,* pp. 60 ff.

(44) *Ibid.,* p. 102. It should be remembered that prices decreased.

(45) In Great Britain this was the beginning of a long depression which was not over until about 1896. See H. L. Beales, "The 'Great Depression' in Industry and Trade," *The Economic History Review,* October, 1934, vol. V, No. 1, pp. 65–76. In France, as we shall see, this same period was not very brilliant, but there were moments of prosperity. During the entire span, statistics indicate economic growth.

(46) L. Amé's *Étude sur les tarifs de douane et sur les traités de commerce,* 2 vols., 1876, was prepared for the Council at this time.

(47) Published, three volumes in four (1879).

(48) *Journal Officiel, Chambre, Débats.* February 3, 1880.

(49) All rates were made specific at this time in place of *ad valorem* which had been subject to abuse.

(50) Efforts to make a treaty with England failed, but nevertheless France granted her most-favored-nation treatment. Germany had this same favor by article 11 of the Treaty of Frankfurt.

(51) As is usual on the eve of crises, discounts increased considerably.

(52) *Annuaire statistique,* vol. 47 for 1931 (1932), p. 102*.

(53) The following table is from A. von Brandt, *Beiträge zur Geschichte der französischen Handelspolitik* (1896), p. 231.

(54) Decree of February 18, 1881.

(55) July 19, 1880. This measure was to increase the consumption of sugar in France.

(56) July 29, 1884. A new system of taxing sugar in France, which granted considerable exemptions, served as a kind of bounty.

(57) These increases were dated March 28, 1885; March 29, 1887, and January 27, 1894, respectively.

(58) Percy Ashley, *Modern Tariff History* (London: Murray, 1904), p. 332. Ashley cites B. Franke, *Der Ausbau des Heutigen Schutzzollsystems in Frankreich* (1904), in this connection.

(59) Tariff increases were registered in Germany in 1879, 1885, and 1887; in Italy from 1877 to 1888; in Austria, 1882 to 1887; in Russia, 1881–82; in Belgium, 1887; and in the United States by the McKinley tariff of 1890.

(60) *Cours d'économie politique* (Paris: Larose et Forcel, 3d edition, 1893), vol. I, p. 134.

(61) Quoted *ibid.*, p. 136.

(62) Other protectionist organs were the *Réforme économique* edited by Doumergue and the *Economiste européen* edited by Edward Théry.

(63) Molinari (1819–1912). Principal works: *Cours d'économie politique* (1863); *Lois naturelles de l'économie publique* (1887); *Morale économique* (1888); *Viriculture* (1897); *Grandeur et décadence de la guerre* (1898); *Organisation politique et économique de la société future* (1899); *Economie de l'histoire* (1909); etc.

(64) Principal works: *L'économie de l'effort; La morale de la concurrence; La tyrannie socialiste; La propriété; La science économique; La gestion par l'état et les municipalités.*

(65) Levasseur (1828–1911). Principal works: *Le système de Law* (1854); *L'or* (1858); *Histoire des classes ouvrières* (1867); *Précis d'économie politique* (1883); *La population française* (1889–1892); *L'ouvrier américain* (1898); *Questions ouvrières et industrielles sous la troisième République* (1907); *Histoire du commerce de la France* (1911).

(66) See especially *Cours d'économie politique professé à l'Ecole nationale des ponts et chaussés* (1903).

(67) *La question ouvrière au XIXe siècle* (1872); *De la colonisation chez les peuples modernes* (1874); *Science des finances* (1877); *Essai sur la réparti-*

tion des richesses (1881); *L'état moderne et ses fonctions* (1890); *Le travail des femmes au XIXe siècle* (1873); *Le collectivisme* (1884); *Traité d'économie politique* (1895); etc.

(68) His chief work was *Cours d'économie politique* (1909). See his *Rapport sur l'économie sociale à l'exposition universelle de 1900* and the statement of faith in the first number of the *Revue d'économie politique* (1887).

(69) Quoted in Levasseur, *Histoire du commerce de la France,* vol. II, p. 578.

(70) In a speech before the Chamber February 17, 1894, Jaurès declared:
"There is a historical group that is called France, which has been created by centuries of common hopes and fears.
"The slow monarchical formations slowly placed together and soldered the parts and the severe trials of the Revolution fused them into one metal. It is the French nation.
"Yes, the nation exists, independently of the struggles which may be produced in the interior among individuals. Yes, there are struggles, hates among citizens, rivalry between families, passionate party rivalries; there are also, believe me, and we say it because we always declare what we believe to be the reality—professed antagonisms of class. But whatever political struggles, economic diversions, or social antagonisms there may be, they cannot destroy the idea of the nation, the unity of the nation, as it has been constituted."
See Jean Jaurès, *Discours parlementaires* (Paris, 1904), p. 557.
"If tomorrow France were invaded, all who, like the socialists, do not like the actual constitution would defend the *patrie* with the thought that afterwards this constitution would be changed. In the same fashion, no matter how unevenly property is divided at the present time, no matter how unreasonably and how unjustly wealth is distributed in our country, it is first necessary to defend French property, national wealth, in a common effort against invasion with the thought of modifying later by profound reforms the partition of property and of wealth."
La Dépêche de Toulouse, July 10, 1890.

(71) Speech in the Chamber, March 8, 1887.

(72) Speech in the Chamber, February 17, 1894.

(73) *La Dépêche,* July 10, 1890, and April 16, 1890. Harold Weinstein, Jean Jaurès. *A Study of Patriotism in the French Socialist Movement* (New York: Columbia University Press, 1936).

(74) October 20.

(75) Presented March 3, 1891.

(76) For a discussion of these problems see Edgard Allix, *Les droits de douane* (Paris, 1932), vol. I, pp. 47 ff.

(77) Cited in Allix, *op. cit.,* vol. I, pp. 56–57. See also A. Sartorius von Walterhausen, *Der Paragraph elf des Frankfurter Friedens* (Jena, 1915).

(78) The minimum and maximum rates were the same on some articles, notably wheat and cattle.

(79) *Foreign Office Report on Tariff Wars* (London, 1904).

(80) *Ibid.,* p. 14.

(81) Grete Eysoldt, *Der Zollkrieg zwischen Frankreich und der Schweiz (1 januar 1893 bis 19 august, 1895)* (Stuttgart: Cotta, 1913).

(82) *Annuaire statistique* (1932), p. 102*.

(83) Decree of July 26, 1896, and law of April 7, 1897.

(84) Convention signed March 5, 1902. Applied by France September 1, 1903. The powers which co-operated in this move were Germany, Austria-Hungary, Belgium, Spain, France, Great Britain, Italy, Netherlands, and Sweden. Some of the nations dropped out, but the majority continued to adhere to it until the World War. The only bounties that were allowed under the convention were distance bounties actually equal to the cost of transportation.

(85) April 9, 1906. See below, p. 242.

(86) April 2, 1898.

(87) March 31, 1894.

(88) April 9, 1898.

(89) See Le Comte de Rocquiny, *Syndicats agricoles et leurs œuvres* (Paris, 1900); and G. Lécolle, *Les Associations agricoles—syndicats, coöpératives, mutualités* (Paris, 1912). See also Etienne Villey, *L'Organisation professionnelle des employeurs dans l'industrie française* (Paris: Alcan, 1923) and the bibliography contained in his book, p. 3. See also G. Giraud, *Le Comité des Forges de France. Étude monographique* (Paris: Sagot, 1922); and Bézard-Falga, *Les syndicats patronaux dans l'industrie métallurgique de France* (Paris, 1922).

(90) Law of March 4, 1898.

(91) Decree of May 21, 1898.

(92) In this period, there were the German tariff of 1902, which was to be

applied in 1906; the Swiss tariff of 1902–1903; the Russian of 1903–1905; the Roumanian, 1904; the Austro-Hungarian, 1906; the Spanish, 1906; the Canadian, 1907; the Danish, 1908; the Australian, 1908; and the American, 1909, to be applied in 1910.

(93) See Levasseur, *Histoire du commerce de la France,* vol. II, chaps. VI and VII.

(94) These figures are from Clapham, *Industrial Development of France and Germany,* chap. X, *passim.*

(95) Vol. II, p. 601.

(96) Paul Cauwès, *Cours d'économie politique,* vol. IV, pp. 65 ff.

(97) The Montgolfier Law of March 23, 1874, did, however, provide for a new condition of purchase of the railways by the state on terms generally favorable to the companies.

(98) Law of May 18, 1878, and decree of May 25, 1878.

(99) With the exception of Midi.

(100) Those sums advanced as guarantees of interest had to be repaid.

(101) For the many other provisions in these conventions, see René Thévenez, M. d'Hérouville, and E. Bleys, *Législation des chemins de fer,* vol. I, pp. 22 ff.

(102) The debt of guarantee in 1908 was 1208 millions; in 1913 it was 652,983,000 francs.

(103) The Canal du Midi was bought from the *Midi* railway company in 1897.

(104) Thévenez, etc., *op. cit.,* vol. I, p. 154.

(105) Clément Colson, *Cours d'économie politique* (Paris, 2nd edition 1910), vol. VI, p. 266. Concerning the French method of controlling railway rates in this period, see W. H. Buckler, "The French Method of Controlling Railway Rates," *The Quarterly Journal of Economics,* vol. XX (1906), pp. 279–286.

(106) Alfred Picard, *Les chemins de fer* (1918), pp. 247 and 252.

(107) *Ibid.,* p. 238.

(108) F. Guérin, *Précis de législation maritime* (Paris: Gauthiers-Villars et Cie., 1928), II partie, p. 244.

(109) See above, pp. 212–213.

(110) Lucien Lefol, *La protection de la construction navale en France et à l'étranger* (Paris: Les Presses Modernes, 1929), p. 37, table.

(111) There had been, to be sure, bounties on fish shipping previously, but they had had little effect upon the merchant marine as a whole. The law of 1881 was dated January 29.

(112) This law could not be applied until 1893 because of treaties with foreign powers.

(113) July 19, 1890.

(114) M. Siegfried, Minister of Marine, in his report of 1893, said:
"So far as French ship-building is concerned, the results of the act of 1881 have not been satisfactory. . . . It is true that we have constructed in France 307,626 tons of iron and steel steamers, but from this should be deducted 124,-000 tons for steamships belonging to subsidized government mail lines, the construction of which in France is obligatory. . . . On the average we estimate that an ordinary steamship in England costs 300 fr. ($57.90) per gross ton, while the same vessels cost 420 fr. ($81.06) in France. Besides this average, English ship-builders have numerous advantages in the magnitude of their plants, the large number of vessels they build, often from the same model, and the shorter time for construction than is required in France. These reasons show why the act of 1881 has given insufficient results, but I hasten to say that without this act our ship-yards would have completely disappeared. Our average annual expenditure of 2,679,766 francs for the last ten years has not been wasted; it has merely been insufficient. Until French ship-yards shall have grown and secured large and regular contracts, it is impossible for them to build on equal terms with foreign yards. The latter and especially British yards obtain their raw materials on much more advantageous terms; indeed at the moment steel and iron plates cost in England 15 francs per 100 kilograms, against 23 and 25 francs in France, while the price of their coal is much below ours.
"Undoubtedly labor is cheaper in France, where fitters (*ajusteurs*) and riveters (forgerons) are paid from 5 to 6 francs ($0.96½ to $1.158) a day, while in England they earn an average of 12 to 15 francs ($2.316 to $2.895), but the British workman, usually paid by the piece, turns out a large amount of work, and thus by efficiency compensates in great measure for the difference in wages. Finally general expenses, which are an important element in cost of naval construction, are much less in England. . . . We estimated that general expenses are one-half in England what they are in France. Competition on equal terms is thus impossible. Experience shows that the construction bounty of 60 fr. ($11.58) per ton under the law of 1881, even with the aid of a larger navigation bounty for vessels built in France has been insufficient. . . . So far as navigation is concerned it can be affirmed that the

results of the bounty act of 1881, without being very great, have been satisfactory."

He noted that in 1881, besides mail-contract steamships, France had 47 steamers of 380,433 gross tons. But of this amount 332,627 tons of large iron and steel steamers were purchased. This statement is taken from Meeker, *History of Shipping Subsidies,* p. 46.

(115) Meeker, *op. cit.,* p. 55, and *U. S. Consular Reports,* vol. 18 (1900), p. 36.

(116) Lefol, *La protection de la construction navale,* p. 21.

(117) Bounties on ships for foreign purchase were 70 per cent of those destined to sail under the French flag.

(118) Saugstad, *Shipping and Shipbuilding Subsidies,* p. 150.

(119) Edwin M. Bacon, *Manual of Ship Subsidies* (Chicago: A. C. McClurg & Co., 1911), p. 36.

(120) Lefol, *op. cit.,* p. 27.

(121) The first edition of Paul Leroy Beaulieu's great work on colonial history, *De la colonisation chez les peuples modernes,* was published in 1874. Later on Charles Gide took a stand for colonization, *A quoi servent les colonies* (1886).

(122) The first edition of Cauwès' *Cours d'économie politique* appeared in 1878. Against colonization see Yves Guyot, *Lettres sur la politique coloniale* (Paris: C. Reinwald, 1885).

(123) The story is told that Ferry said to Déroulède, "You will end by making me think that you prefer Alsace-Lorraine to France. Must we hypnotize ourselves with our lost provinces, and should we not take compensations elsewhere?" Déroulède replied, "That is just the point. I have lost two children, and you offer me twenty servants." Quoted in G. P. Gooch, *Franco-German Relations, 1871–1914* (1923).

(124) See below, pp. 253 ff.

(125) Stephen H. Roberts, *History of French Colonial Policy 1870–1925* (London: King and Son, 1929), vol. II, p. 634:

"The starting-point of any comparative study of French colonization must be to note the peculiar position in which France stood from the commencement. The whole of French colonial organization was coloured by certain influences which did not come in so clearly with any other Power. In the first place, France was not under the same imperious necessity of colonizing as was England. She was not sea-girt and confined to a small area: her population was not increasing at a menacing rate: and she did not experience overweening difficulties in feeding her people. . . . Colonization therefore, while a matter of economic life and death to England, was to France only an outlet of her energies. So much was this so that, at first, French theorists agreed with Bismarck that it was a weakening vice of a great nation. . . . In any case it was a venture not directly connected with the problem of national welfare. It was only a hazard—Mexico over again—expressing the pent-up exuberance of the Gallican spirit or a nation chafing under the grind of its conventional life."

(126) C. Seignobos, *L'évolution de la 3ᵉ République (1875-1914)*, Lavisse (ed.), *Histoire de France contemporaine,* vol. VIII, pp. 91–92 and 52–53.

(127) *Ibid.,* p. 57, and George Hardy, *Histoire de la colonisation française* (Paris: Larose, 1931), p. 228.

(128) A. Rambaud, *Jules Ferry* (1903), and Stephen H. Roberts, *History of French Colonial Policy,* vol. I, pp. 13 ff.

(129) *Journal Officiel,* Senate, December 11, 1884.

(130) See especially F. L. Schuman, *War and Diplomacy in the French Republic.* Concerning Tunis, pp. 57 ff., and his footnote references.

See above, S. Roberts, *op. cit.;* G. Hardy, *op. cit.;* G. Hanotaux and A. Martineau, *Histoire des colonies françaises et de l'expansion de la France dans le monde* (Paris: Plon, 1929–1933), 6 vols.; P. T. Moon, *Imperialism and World Politics* (New York: Macmillan Co., 1928); and numerous monographs suggested in the bibliographies of these works.

(131) See the *Discours et opinions de Jules Ferry* (Paris: A. Colin, 1893–98), 7 vols. For Ferry's views, see his speech of July 28, 1885, and his preface to Léon Sentapéry, *Le Tonkin et la Mère-Patrie* (Paris: Havard, 4th edition, 1890), from which the following is quoted:

"La politique coloniale est fille de la politique industrielle. Pour les Etats riches, où les capitaux abondent et s'accumulent rapidement, où le régime manufacturier est en voie de croissance continue, attirant à lui la partie sinon la plus nombreuse, du moins la plus éveillée et la plus remuante de la population qui vit du travail de ses bras,—où la culture de la terre elle-même est condamnée pour se soutenir à s'industrialiser,—l'exportation est un facteur essentiel de la prospérité publique, et le champ d'emploi des capitaux, comme la demande du travail, se mesure à l'étendue du marché étranger. S'il avait pu s'établir entre les nations manufacturières quelque chose comme une division du travail industriel, une répartition méthodique et rationelle des industries, selon les aptitudes, les conditions économiques naturelles et sociales des différents pays producteurs, cantonnant ici l'industrie cotonnière et là la métallurgie, réservant à l'un les alcools et les sucres, à l'autre les lainages et les soieries, l'Europe eût pu ne pas chercher en dehors de ses propres limites les débouchés de sa production. C'est à cet idéal que tendaient les traités de 1860. Mais tout le monde aujourd'hui veut filer et tisser, forger et distiller. Toute l'Europe fabrique le sucre à outrance et prétend l'exporter. L'entrée en scène des derniers venus de la grande industrie: les Etats-Unis, d'une part, l'Allemagne, de l'autre, l'avènement des petits Etats, des peuples endormis ou epuisés, de l'Italie régénérée, de l'Espagne, enrichie par les capitaux français, de la Suisse, si entreprenante et si avisée, à la vie industrielle, sous toutes ses formes, ont engagé l'Occident tout entier; en attendant la Russie, qui s'apprête et qui grandit, sur une pente que l'on ne remontera pas.

"De l'autre côté des Vosges comme au delà de l'Atlantique, le régime protecteur a multiplié les manufactures, supprimé les anciens débouchés, jeté sur le marché de l'Europe de redoutables concurrences. Se défendre à son tour en relevant les barrières, c'est quelque chose, mais ce n'est pas assez. M. Torrens a fort bien démontré, dans son beau livre sur la colonisation de l'Australie, qu'un accroissement du capital manufacturier, s'il n'était pas accompagné d'une extension proportionelle des débouchés à l'étranger, tendrait à produire, par le seul effet de la concurrence intérieure, une baisse générale des prix, des profits et des salaires. (Torrens, *Colonisation of South Australia*.)

"Le système protecteur est une machine à vapeur sans soupape de sûreté s'il n'y a pas pour correctif et pour auxiliaire une saine et sérieuse politique coloniale. La pléthore des capitaux engagés dans l'industrie ne tend pas seulement à diminuer les profits du capital: elle arrête la hausse des salaires, qui est pourtant la loi naturelle et bienfaisante des sociétés modernes. Et ce n'est pas là une loi abstraite, mais un phénomène fait de chair et d'os, de passion et de volonté, qui se remue, se plaint, se défend. La paix sociale est, dans l'âge industriel de l'humanité, une question de débouchés. La crise économique qui a si lourdement pesé sur l'Europe laborieuse, depuis 1876 ou 1877, le malaise qui s'en est suivi, et dont des grèves fréquentes, longues, malavisées souvent, mais toujours redoutables sont le plus douloureux symptôme, coïncidé, en France, en Allemagne, en Angleterre même, avec une reduction notable et persistante du chiffre des exportations. L'Europe peut être considérée comme une maison de commerce qui voit depuis un certain nombre d'années décroître son chiffre d'affaires. La consommation européenne est saturée: il faut faire surgir des autres parties du globe de nouvelles couches de consommateurs, sous peine de mettre la société moderne en faillite, et de préparer, pour l'aurore du vingtième siècle, une liquidation sociale par voie de cataclysme, dont on ne saurait calculer les conséquences."

France renewed her interest in Somaliland at this time (1883 and 1888).

(132) See the list in Roberts, *op. cit.,* vol. II, appendices. Even Jaurès thought France had a right in Morocco. See his speech in the Chamber of November 20, 1903.

(133) Roberts, *op. cit.,* vol. I, p. 10.

(134) *Ibid.* and Schuman, *op. cit.,* pp. 338–340.

(135) These figures include all of France's colonies.

(136) In 1890, France imported from her colonies goods of a value of 101 million francs and sold to them for about 71 million francs; foreign powers imported from them but 87½ millions and sold to them 136½ millions.

(137) Arthur Girault, *The Colonial Tariff Policy of France* (Oxford: Clarendon Press, 1916), pp. 81 ff. Extra-parliamentary commissions of 1878 and 1882 supported this policy.

(138) Law of December 29, 1884.

(139) Law of February 26, 1887, mitigated somewhat by Law of March 30, 1888.

(140) To this list of assimilated colonies were added the Comores (May 23, 1896) and Madagascar (April 16, 1897). See also *Colonial Tariff Policies,* United States Tariff Commission, 1922.

(141) Girault, *Colonial Tariff Policy of France,* pp. 132–133.

(142) Girault, *op. cit.,* p. 285 and *passim.*

(143) Compare with footnote 136.

(144) April 13, 1900.

(145) Paul Restany, *Le problème des capitaux dans les colonies françaises* (Paris, 1924) and Feis, *Europe, the World's Banker* (New Haven: Yale University Press, 1930), p. 56.

(146) Harry D. White, *The French International Accounts, 1880–1913* (Cambridge: Harvard University Press, 1933), p. 122, and Herbert Feis, *Europe, the World's Banker, 1870–1914.*

(147) From 1830 to 1891, about 5.3 billion francs were spent on the colonies, of which 1.7 went for public works. L. Vignon, *La France en Algérie* (Paris: Hachette, 1893), p. 286. See also Constant Southworth, *The French Colonial Venture* (London: P. S. King and Son, 1931), pp. 41 ff.; and Levasseur, *Histoire du Commerce de la France,* vol. II, pp. 491–492.

(148) F. Selnet, *Colonisation officielle et Crédit Agricole en Algérie* (Alger: Minerva, 1930); and Robert Delacourt, *Les relations économiques de La France avec ses colonies au lendemain de la Guerre* (Paris, Thesis of the Faculté du Droit, no date).

(149) Harry D. White, *The French International Accounts, 1880–1913,* p. 122. The net foreign investments for these years were 9,120,000,000 francs

and 39,345,000,000 francs, figures that are arrived at by subtracting foreign investments in France from the total figures.

(150) *Annuaire statistique, 1931. Résumé rétrospectif*, p. 102*.

(151) White, *op. cit.*, p. 42.

(152) *Ibid.*, p. 301.

(153) *Ibid.*, p. 269.

(154) Henri de Peyerimhoff, *Entreprises et capitaux français à l'étranger* (Paris: Société des Sciences Politiques, 1915), p. 111. Recently 75 per cent of the discounts made by the Bank of France were for sums under 1000 francs. The discount rate of the Bank has been kept lower than in most countries. G. Ramon, *Histoire de la Banque de France*, pp. 424-426.

(155) Jean de Montéty, *Les banques et la politique de placement à l'étranger de l'épargne nationale* (Paris: Editions de la Vie Universitaire, 1923).

(156) This supervision applied to the Coulisse or curb exchange as well as to the Bourse.

(157) The Government refused to sanction a loan to Austria-Hungary in 1909 because of that state's political alliance with Germany. See Feis, *Europe, the World's Banker*, p. 134 and *passim*.

(158) Feis, *Europe, the World's Banker*, p. 51.

(159) *Ibid.*, p. 58.

(160) White, *op. cit.*, p. 273. In this connection see also Lysis (pseudonym for M. Letailleur) *Contre l'oligarchie financière en France* (Paris: La Revue, 12th ed. 1908).

(161) White, pp. 295-296.

(162) Feis, pp. 125-127. See also *Bulletin de la Fédération des Industriels et des Commerçants Français*, February–March, 1909.

(163) Peyerimhoff, *op. cit.*, p. 100.

(164) White, p. 294.

(165) Paul Cauwès, *Cours d'économie politique*, vol. III, pp. 98 ff. This is also true, to a degree, among those who teach the solidarity of interests between social classes. See Léon Bourgeois, *La Solidarité* (1897).

(166) Among others, there were Wolowski, Charles Gide, and Levasseur.

See E. Levasseur, *Questions ouvrières et industrielles en France sous la troisième République* (Paris: Rousseau, 1907), p. 448.

(167) This was true of Méline and Paul Deschanel. Georges Weill, *Histoire du mouvement social en France* (1852–1924) (Paris: Alcan, 1924), pp. 432 and 446, and Levasseur, *op. cit.,* p. 498.

(168) Paul Louis, *Histoire de la classe ouvrière en France de la Révolution à nos jours* (Paris: Rivière, 1927), p. 408, and by the same author, *Histoire du socialisme en France de la Révolution à nos jours* (Paris: Rivière, 1925).

Trade-union membership was 60,000 in 1881, 402,000 in 1893, and 1,064,000 in 1912. In 1906, the Socialist party obtained 878,000 votes and 52 seats in the Chamber; in 1914 it got 1,400,000 votes and 103 seats.

The Catholic socialist movement was also important in this regard. See P. T. Moon, *The Labor Problem and the Social Catholic Movement in France* (New York: Macmillan, 1921). The author thinks that social legislation was delayed by Anti-Clerical legislation, pp. 289–294.

(169) For detailed information on these conditions, see Paul Louis, *Histoire de la classe ouvrière en France, passim,* and the official publications *Salaires et durée du travail* (1906), *Salaires et coût de l'existence jusqu'en 1910, etc.,* cited in the above, p. 412.

(170) Paul Pic, *Traité élémentaire de législation industrielle* (Paris: 5th edition, 1922). The labor laws were codified 1910–1912.

CHAPTER VIII

(1) Concerning the economic history of the war, see especially the collection, edited by James T. Shotwell, published under the auspices of the Carnegie Endowment for International Peace—*The Economic and Social History of the World War*. See Camille Bloch, *Bibliographie Méthodique de l'histoire économique et sociale de la France pendant la guerre* (New Haven: Yale University Press, Carnegie Endowment Publication, 1925); G. Olphe-Galliard, *Histoire économique et financière de la guerre* (1914–1918) (Paris: Rivière, 1925); John Bates Clark (editor), *Effects of the World War on French Economic Life* (Oxford: Clarendon Press, 1923); Delemer, *La Bilan de l'étatisme* (Paris: Payot, 1922); Trustee (anonymous), *Le bilan de la guerre* (Paris: Plon-Nourrit, 1921); and Pierre Renouvin, *La Crise européenne et la grande guerre* (1904–1918) (Paris: Alcan, 1934).

(2) See as evidence of this trend, W. Cunningham, *The Rise and Decline of the Free Trade Movement* (Cambridge: University Press, 2nd ed., 1912); J. M. Keynes, *The End of Laissez-Faire* (London: Hogarth Press, 1926); Wilhelm Röpke, *German Commercial Policy* (New York: Longmans, Green & Co., 1934); and Arturo Segré, *Storia del commercie* (Turin: Lattés, 1933), vol. II.

(3) M. Sogemeier, *Die öffentliche Hand in der Privaten Wirtschaft* (Berlin: Hobbing, no date).

(4) See the excellent statement on this point by John Bates Clark in the introduction to *Effects of the World War on French Economic Life* (Oxford: Clarendon Press, 1923).

(5) E. Clémentel, *La France et la politique économique interalliée* (New Haven: Yale University Press, 1931), p. XV.

(6) Pierre Renouvin, *The Forms of War Government in France* (New Haven: Yale University Press, Carnegie Endowment, *Economic and Social History of the World War*, 1927), p. 151, and Gaston Jèze, *L'Exécutif en temps de guerre. Les pleins pouvoirs* (Paris: Girard et Brière, 1917).

(7) Renouvin, *op. cit.,* p. 155.

(8) G. Olphe-Galliard, *Histoire économique et financière de la guerre* (1914-1918) (Paris: Rivière, 1925), chap. I and B. M. Anderson, Jr., *Effects of the War on Money, Credit and Banking in France and the U. S.* (New York: Oxford University Press, Carnegie Endowment Publications, 1919).

(9) H. Truchy, *Les Finances de guerre de la France* (New Haven: Yale University Press, Carnegie Publication, 1926), p. 3, and Gabriel Ramon, *Histoire de la Banque de France,* pp. 427-453.

(10) Bertrand Nogaro, "The Effect of the War upon French Finance," *Effects of the War upon French Economic Life* (Oxford: Clarendon Press, Carnegie Endowment Preliminary Economic Studies of the War, 1923), pp. 84-85.

(11) Robert Murray Haig, *The Public Finances of Post-War France* (New York: Columbia University Press, 1929), p. 26.

(12) Henri Truchy, *Les Finances de guerre de la France* (New Haven: Yale University Press, Carnegie Publication, 1926), p. 6.

(13) See Haig, *op. cit.,* pp. 27-40; Truchy, *op. cit.;* and Nogaro, *op. cit.*

(14) Haig, *op. cit.,* p. 25.

(15) Truchy, *op. cit.,* pp. 45, 48; and Haig, *op. cit.,* pp. 190–191. The advances from the Bank of Algeria were paid up in their entirety in 1920.

(16) Haig, *op. cit.,* p. 235.

(17) *Ibid.,* p. 257.

(18) *Ibid.,* p. 279. The discrepancy between the sum of these figures and those cited from Truchy may be explained by a mistake of 30,000,000,000 francs in French published figures and in different rates of exchange used to get paper-franc totals.

(19) Truchy, *op. cit.,* chap. VIII.

(20) See Gaston Jèze, *Les Dépenses de guerre de la France* (New Haven: Yale University Press, Carnegie Endowment Publication, 1926), and Charles Gide and William Oualid, *Le Bilan de la guerre pour la France* (New Haven: Yale University Press, Carnegie Endowment Publication, 1931).

(21) William Oualid and Charles Picquenard, *Salaires et tarifs, conventions collectives et grèves* (New Haven: Yale University Press, Carnegie Endowment Publication, 1928), p. 4.

(22) Gaston Jèze, *op. cit.,* p. 125.

(23) A. Fontaine, *L'Industrie française pendant la guerre* (New Haven: Yale University Press, Carnegie Publication, 1925), pp. 96 ff.
"It should be remembered that the most highly industrialized parts of France had been occupied by the enemy. The invaded regions had provided 62 per cent of France's pig iron production and 62 per cent of her steel; they contained 85 of the 170 blast furnaces of the country, 48 of the 164 Martin furnaces," etc.

(24) Jèze, *op. cit.,* p. 160.

(25) Delemer, *Le Bilan de l'étatisme* (Paris: Payot, 1922), p. 184, and Olphe-Galliard, *Histoire économique et financière de la guerre (1914–1918),* p. 183.

(26) *Tableau général de la composition des Ministères.*

(27) Renouvin, *The Forms of War Government in France,* p. 59.

(28) *Ibid.,* p. 60.

(29) Henri Hauser, *Le problème du régionalisme* (New Haven: Yale University Press, Carnegie Publication, 1924).

(30) William Oualid and Charles Picquenard, *Salaires et tarifs* (New Haven: Yale University Press, Carnegie Publication, 1928), p. 4.

(31) Unemployment doles began to be paid August 24, 1914.

(32) A. Créhange, *Chômage et placement* (New Haven: Yale University Press, Carnegie Publication, 1927).

(33) Fontaine, *L'Industrie française pendant la guerre*, pp. 74-75.

(34) Service de la Main-d'Œuvre Etrangère. Fontaine, *op. cit.*, p. 68.

(35) Fontaine, *op. cit.*, pp. 59-61 and William Oualid, *The Effect of the War upon Labor in France* (Oxford: Oxford Press, Carnegie Publication, 1923), p. 155.

(36) Fontaine, *op. cit.*, pp. 56-58, and Michel Augé-Laribé, *L'agriculture pendant la guerre* (New Haven: Yale University Press, Carnegie Endowment, 1925), p. 66.

(37) William Oualid, *op. cit.*, pp. 183-185, and William Oualid and Charles Picquenard, *Salaires et tarifs*.
The law of July 10, 1915, established a plan for fixing the minimum wages for those in the clothing industry who worked at home and the law of June 11, 1917, gave clothing workers a half-holiday on Saturday. These are examples of attempts at keeping the industrial peace outside of war industries.

(38) Those on wheat were abolished July 31, 1914. Michel Augé-Laribé, *L'Agriculture pendant la guerre. Carnegie Endowment. Economic and Social History of the World War* (New Haven: Yale University Press, 1925), pp. 119-120.

(39) Pierre Pinot, *Le Contrôle du ravitaillement de la population civile* (New Haven: Yale University Press, Carnegie Publication, 1925), pp. 284 ff.

(40) *Ibid., passim.*

(41) Michel Augé-Laribé, *L'agriculture pendant la guerre*, p. 95.

(42) *Ibid.*, p. 56.

(43) P. Pinot, *Le Contrôle du ravitaillement*, p. 36; Augé-Laribé, *op. cit.*, p. 123; and G. Olphe-Galliard, *Histoire économique et financière de la guerre*, p. 310.

(44) Augé-Laribé, *op. cit.*, pp. 121-134, 152.

(45) *Ibid.*, p. 151.

(46) *Ibid.*, p. 165—Decree of October 7, 1915, and law of January 2, 1917.

(47) January 10, 1917, the Service de la Fabrication des Produits chimiques Agricoles was established. This organization was transformed into the *Office*.

(48) *Annuaire statistique,* 1931, p. 102*.

(49) The lists were established April 13, 1917. They were later changed. See Albert Aftalion, *The Effect of the War upon French Commercial Policy* (Oxford: Carnegie Publication, 1923), pp. 114–115.

(50) Truchy, *Les Finances de la guerre,* pp. 102–104.

(51) Securing foreign markets was not lost sight of entirely. An agreement signed August 24, 1917, between France and England provided for the importation into Great Britain of numerous French luxury articles that amounted in annual trade to 200,000,000 francs. E. Clémentel, *La France et la politique économique interalliée* (New Haven: Yale University Press, Carnegie Publication, 1931), pp. 157–158.

(52) R. Pommereuil, *La Guerre économique (1914–1918)* (Poitiers: Oudin, 1918), p. 12.

(53) C. R. M. F. Cruttwell, *A History of the Great War,* 1914–1918 (Oxford: Clarendon Press, 1934), pp. 187–194; and Louis Guichard, *The Naval Blockade, 1914–1918* (New York: Appleton, 1930).

(54) Laws of July 24, 1873; July 3, 1877, and December 28, 1888. See Marcel Peschaud, *Politique et fonctionnement des transports par chemin de fer pendant la guerre* (New Haven: Yale University Press, Publication of the Carnegie Endowment, 1926), pp. 56 ff.

(55) These were the lines of the "Interior" Peschaud, *op. cit.,* p. 104.

(56) Henri Cangardel, *La marine marchande française et la guerre* (New Haven: Yale University Press, Publication of the Carnegie Endowment, 1927), p. 14.

(57) From the beginning of the war to December 31, 1915, the state requisitioned 202 sloops, 186 cargoes, 17 passenger transports, 64 tugs, and 83 ocean liners.

(58) By a decree of July 31, 1914, ships were requisitioned. The *Commission Centrale des Réquisitions Maritimes* was established August 9, 1914.

(59) Up to April 27, 1915, the losses to Allied and neutral shipping caused by the depredations of the German cruisers were 281,513 tons, which was insignificant when compared with the 25 million tons under the flags of the Allies in this same period.

(60) Henri Cangardel, *La Marine marchande française et la guerre* (New Haven: Yale University Press, Carnegie Publication, 1927), p. 86.

(61) Henri Mazel, "The Effect of the War upon the French Merchant Marine," *Effects of the War upon French Economic Life,* p. 16.

(62) Previously there had been created the interministerial *Comité des Transports Maritimes,* February 29, 1916, to act as a consultative body for the various ministries. It ordered that ships could not sail except for the purpose of supplying the needs of the country (April 4, 1916). In addition to this body was the *Direction Générale des Transports et Importations,* created November 18, 1916. It was to control railway, internal waterway, as well as ocean transportation. It established priorities and controlled sailings.

(63) Law of April 13, 1917. Another factor in ship replacements was the law of April 19, 1917. It required marine insurance. The state agreed to pay at once on the loss of a ship 75 per cent of the insured value and the balance when construction was begun on an equal amount of tonnage or upon the purchase of a vessel.

(64) Etienne Clémentel, *La France et la politique économique interalliée* (New Haven: Yale University Press, Carnegie, 1931), pp. 84–88.

(65) The Chartering Committee was composed of representatives of Great Britain, France, and Italy. Neutrals demanded high prices for carrying. This caused the Allies to use pressure on neutral shippers. The "Law of Angary" was finally employed. This doctrine in international law was a rule used to justify the seizure by a state at war of any property in its territory whether the owner was a national or a neutral. This gave the Allies an excuse to take ships. The "Law" was first used to obtain Danish vessels and later to get Norwegian and Dutch ships. High prices were paid the owners, and hence they did not object very strenuously. Neutral governments, who did not want to antagonize Germany, could plead *force majeure.* See J. A. Salter, *Allied Shipping Control—An Experiment in International Administration* (Oxford: Clarendon Press, Carnegie Publication, 1921), p. 107.

(66) Clémentel, *op. cit.,* pp. 91–92, and H. G. Moulton and L. Pasvolsky, *War Debts and World Prosperity* (Washington: Brookings Institute, 1932), pp. 27–38.

(67) Clémentel, *op. cit.,* p. 92.

(68) *Ibid.,* p. 107.

(69) Salter, *op. cit.,* p. 138.

(70) Clémentel, *op. cit.,* p. 221.

(71) Salter, *op. cit.,* p. 176.

(72) See in addition to Salter, Cangardel, *La Marine marchande française et la guerre,* pp. 60–61.

(73) Clémentel, *op. cit.,* pp. 306–314.

(74) *Ibid.,* p. 318.

CHAPTER IX

(1) Consult in this connection H. W. V. Temperley (editor), *A History of the Peace Conference of Paris* (London: Henry Frowde and Hodder & Stoughton, 1920–1924), 6 vols.; Bernard M. Baruch, *The Making of the Reparations and Economic Sections of the Treaty* (New York: Harper and Brothers, 1920); S. F. Nitti, *Peaceless Europe* (London, 1922), the American edition has the title, *Wreck of Europe* (Indianapolis, 1922), p. 179; *The Decadence of Europe* (London, 1923), pp. 81–82; and J. M. Keynes, *The Economic Consequences of the Peace* (London, 1921); *A Revision of the Treaty* (London, 1922); and Clémentel, *op. cit.,* pp. 337–348.

(2) Baruch, *op. cit.,* pp. 20–32.

(3) *Ibid.,* pp. 47–48.

(4) It is interesting to note that France refused a German offer to reconstruct part of the devastated area. France wanted that business for herself because it would stimulate national production and afford profits for certain French citizens.

See Max Sering, *Deutschland unter dem Dawes-Plan* (Berlin: Gruyter, 1928), p. 37.

(5) Article 306 of the Treaty of Versailles.

(6) R. S. Baker, *Woodrow Wilson and World Settlement* (New York: Doubleday, Page & Co., 1922), vol. II, pp. 18–19, 23 ff.

(7) Clémentel, *op. cit.,* p. 344.

(8) W. Ogburn and W. Jaffé, *The Economic Development of Post War France* (New York: Columbia University, 1929), pp. 101, 105.

(9) J. R. Cahill, *Reports on the Economic and Industrial Conditions in France,* 1920–1925 (London: British Department of Overseas Trade, 1923–27), *passim.*

(10) Ogburn and Jaffé, *op. cit.,* p. 20.

(11) The birthrate of males was so low during the war that when the males who were born at that time were called to perform their military training, the size of the army was diminished by 50 per cent. See C. J. H. Hayes, *France, a Nation of Patriots* (New York: Columbia University Press, 1930), p. 70.

(12) Ogburn and Jaffé, *op. cit.,* pp. 523–527.

(13) From 1903 to 1913 foreign commerce had grown by 66 per cent and it is fair to suppose that under normal conditions its growth would have been at a similar rate. It has been estimated on the basis of incomplete information furnished by the French Chambers of Commerce that internal commerce is about six times as great as foreign commerce. See *Evaluation de la production française d'après les renseignements fournis par les chambres du commerce* (Paris: Ministère du Commerce, 1917), *passim.*

(14) The total number of francs in circulation had increased but not enough to affect the depreciation. James Harvey Rogers, *The Process of Inflation in France, 1914–1927* (New York: Columbia University Press, 1929).

(15) Robert M. Haig, *The Public Finances of Post-War France* (New York: Columbia University Press, 1929), pp. 276 ff.; H. G. Moulton and Cleona Lewis, *The French Debt Problem* (London: Allen and Unwin, 1925), pp. 18, 20, 42.

(16) Ogburn and Jaffé, p. 22. These figures were computed from the *Rapport du Comité des Exports* (Paris: Imprimerie Nationale, 1926), pp. 148–149. See also Haig, *op. cit.,* p. 185.

(17) Association Nationale de l'Expansion Economique was founded in 1915; the Confédération Générale de la Production Française was founded in 1919. Their headquarters are located at 23 Avenue de Messine, Paris. The executive machinery of the two bodies has become so fused that it is difficult to determine where one leaves off and the other begins. The two groups share offices in the same building; they publish together a monthly review entitled *Production Nationale et Expansion Economique;* and some of their chief offices are filled by the same persons.

On the subject of employers' syndicates, see Etienne Villey, *L'organisation professionnelle des employeurs dans l'industrie française* (Paris: Alcan, 1923).

(18) Speech by the president of the confederation at the tenth anniversary celebration in the Confederation's *Annuaire 1929,* p. 29.

(19) *Ibid.,* p. 6.

(20) Its full title is Union of Economic Interests for the Freedom of

Trade and of Industry, the Defense of Private Initiative, and against the Extension of Private Monopolies. It was founded in 1911. Headquarters: 16 Place de la Madeleine, Paris. See the pamphlets of the Union and G. Bourgin, J. Carrère, and A. Guérin, *Manuel des partis politiques en France* (Paris: Rieder, 1928), pp. 243–244.

(21) Headquarters: 8–10 rue d'Athène, Paris. Organ: *Revue des Agriculteurs de France.*

(22) Founded 1898.

(23) Headquarters: 42 rue du Louvre, Paris. Organ: *La réforme économique.*

(24) Organ: *Revue des questions économiques et financières.*

(25) Headquarters: 92 rue de Courcelles, Paris.

(26) Headquarters: 44 rue de Rennes, Paris.

(27) Founded 1925. Headquarters: 60 rue Taitbout, Paris. Article 2 of the Committee's bylaws states that the purpose of the organization is "to take all measures of an economic nature to increase production and to facilitate commercial relations between France and her colonies and foreign nations."

(28) For more information concerning the C. G. T. consult the works by Paul Louis; Georges Weill, *Histoire du mouvement social en France (1852–1924)* (Paris: Alcan, 3d edition, 1924); Louis Levine (Lewis L. Lorwin), *Syndicalism in France* (New York: Columbia University Studies, 1914); and David J. Saposs, *The Labor Movement in Post-War France* (New York: Columbia University Press, 1931). Headquarters of the C. G. T. are located at 211 rue Lafayette, Paris.

(29) *Nationalisation industrialisée.* See J. Duret, *Sens et portée du plan* and other publications of the Institut Supérieur Ouvrier to be obtained at C. G. T. headquarters.

(30) French political parties are not particularly well understood either inside or outside of France. There remains much to be written concerning the French party system before all aspects of it can be understood. The following references will, however, be found helpful: G. Bourgin, J. Carrère, and A. Guérin, *Manuel des partis politiques en France* (1928); André Siegfried, *France, a Study in Nationality* (New Haven: Yale University Press, 1930); C. J. H. Hayes, *France, a Nation of Patriots,* pp. 199–206; the article by Lindsay Rogers in *Current History,* December, 1929; the forthcoming book (Columbia University Press) by the same author; E. P. Chase, R.

Valeur, and R. L. Buell, *Democratic Governments in Europe* (New York: Nelson & Sons, 1935); B. M. E. Léger, *Les opinions politiques des provinces françaises* (Paris, 1934); and Fernand Corcos, *Catéchisme des partis politiques* (Paris: Montaignes, 1932). The bourgeois groups differ mostly on such matters as clericalism, foreign policy, education, and social legislation. Their real opponents are the socialists and at times and on some questions the Radical-Socialists just to the right of the socialists.

(31) Founded in 1903. Headquarters: 36 rue de Varennes, Paris.

(32) Founded in 1901. Headquarters: 17 rue de la Rochefoucauld, Paris.

(33) Headquarters: 17 rue de Valois, Paris.

(34) Founded in 1905 by the Union of French Marxists under Jules Guesde, revisionists or reformists under Jaurès, and revolutionary syndicalists (Blanquists) under Edouard Vaillant. It should be noted that there is also the Social Catholic Party founded in 1924—the Popular Democratic Party.

(35) The composition of the Chamber of Deputies in January, 1934, was as follows:

Indépendants	12
Groupe républicain et social	17
Action économique sociale et paysanne	5
Fédération républicaine	42
Centre républicain	33
Républicains du centre	6
Démocrates populaires	16
Républicains de gauche	32
Gauche radicale	44
Indépendents de gauche	23
Gauche indépendente	14
Radicaux et radicaux-socialistes	157
Républicains socialistes	13
Socialistes français	11
Groupe socialiste de France	30
Socialistes (S. F. I. O.)	98
Unité Ouvrière	9
Communistes	10
Isolés	27
Total	599

Official results of the elections of May, 1936:

Communistes	72
Pupistes et communistes dissidents	10
Socialistes S. F. I. O.	146

Elections of May, 1936—*Continued*

Socialistes U. S. R.	26
Socialistes indépendents	11
Radicaux socialistes	116
Républicains indépendents	31
Républicains de gauches	84
Démocrates populaires	23
Républicains U. R. D.	88
Conservateurs	11
Total	618

(36) Chase, Valeur, Buell, *op. cit.,* p. 343. This is an exaggerated statement of the case, but has a basis in fact. See also Walter R. Sharp, *The French Civil Service* (New York: Macmillan, 1931) and Joseph Barthélemy, *Le gouvernement de la France* (Paris: Payot, 1925), chap. IX; and *Encyclopédie française,* vol. X.

(37) Paris: Alcan. He also published *Propos d'un ignorant sur l'économie nationale* (Paris: Nathan, 1923).

Similar to Professor Hauser's case is that of Professor Serruys. Before the War he was a classical scholar; he was called to an official capacity during the War and he afterwards became the chief negotiator of French commercial treaties. See his *Traités de commerce; systèmes tarifaires et méthodes contractuelles* (Paris, 1928). He is one of the protectionist theorists in France at the present time.

(38) *La nouvelle orientation économique,* p. 185.

(39) *Ibid.,* pp. 184–6.

(40) Ray Stannard Baker, *Woodrow Wilson and World Settlement,* vol. II, pp. 332–334.

(41) *La nouvelle orientation économique,* p. 186.

(42) *Ibid.,* pp. 194–196.

(43) His views are set forth in the three long volumes *Principes d'économie nationale et internationale* (Paris: Recueil Sirey, 1929–1931). See also "Les fondements nouveaux de protectionisme industriel," *Revue d'économie politique,* March-April, 1933.

(44) *Ibid.*

(45) Vol. III, p. 474.

(46) Brocard gives an interesting explanation of the growth of nations, vol. I, pp. 296–393.

(47) Vol. I, pp. 145, 186-7.

(48) Vol. III, p. 484.

(49) Vol. III, p. 482.

(50) Vol. III, p. 488.

(51) Vol. III, p. 493.

(52) Vol. II, p. 675.

(53) Vol. III, pp. 472-479.

(54) Vol. II, pp. 65-66; vol. III, p. 480.

(55) Vol. II, p. 345.

(56) Vol. II, pp. 678-683.

(57) Vol. II, pp. 544 ff.

(58) Vol. II, pp. 280 ff. Professor Brocard does not go so far as to say that a nation should not invest abroad in the production of goods that compete with those produced at home, when the home producers do not need capital. He is more interested in whether the investment abroad pays a safe and good return. From the point of view of economic nationalism, however, it would appear that if productivity is the measure of national strength one should not aid other nations by loans to produce goods which one can sell to them directly.

(59) Paris: Rousseau, 1914.

(60) *Op. cit.,* p. 33.

(61) *La conception de l'économie nationale et des rapports internationaux chez les mercantilistes français et chez leurs contemporains* (Paris: Sirey, 1931), pp. 152-172.

(62) Paris, 1922, p. vii.

(63) *Op. cit.,* vol. I, pp. 144-147.

(64) Gaëtan Pirou, *Les doctrines économiques en France depuis 1870* (Paris: Colin, 2d ed. 1930); René Gonnard, *Histoire des doctrines économiques* (Paris: Valois, 1927), vol. III; and the French economic reviews.

(65) Charles Gide and Charles Rist, *Histoire des doctrines économiques* (Paris: Sirey, 4th ed. 1923), pp. 337-338.

(66) *Cours d'économie politique,* vol. II, p. 68.

(67) C. J. H. Hayes, *France, a Nation of Patriots*, pp. 457–8. Hervé has published a newspaper since the war, *La Victoire*.

(68) *Le socialisme national* (Paris: Renaissance du Livre, 1917), pp. 42–46; and *Le nationalisme suivant les peoples* (Paris: Flammarion, 1920). A similar stand has been taken by Ch. Andler, "D'un nouveau socialisme national," *L'Information ouvrière et sociale,* June 23, 1918. See also Roger Berg, *Le Socialisme entre l'économie nationale et le cosmopolitanisme* (Nancy: Imprimerie Nancéienne, 1934).

(69) *The Psychology of Socialism* (London: Allen & Unwin, 1928), chap. XI. The French edition of this book went under the title of *Au delà du Marxisme* (Brussels, 1927).

(70) *Op. cit.,* p. 311.

(71) *Op. cit.,* p. 325. In order to be complete it is well to mention the rôle of publicists in preaching national economics. Among them may be mentioned Probus (J. Corréard) who organized a small society called *Fédération des Républicains Rénovateurs*. Headquarters: 8 rue de Richelieu, Paris. Organ: *La France Vivante* (weekly). See his *La constitution syndicale de la France* (Paris: Grasset, 1919); *Rénovation* (Paris: Grasset, 1919); and *Des finances modernes pour vivre* (1920).

Mention should also be made of the late Lysis (M. Letailleur), former editor of *La Démocratie Nouvelle*. He was author of *Vers la démocratie nouvelle* (Paris: Payot, 1917); *Pour renaître* (Paris: Payot, 1918); *L'erreur française* (Paris: Payot, 1918).

See also as examples of publicists with national economic leanings the works of Victor Cambon, *Notre Avenir* (Paris: Payot, 1918), and *Où allons-nous?* (Paris: Payot, 1918); and of Ed. Amanieux, *L'armature sociale* (1919).

The Société d'Études et d'Informations Économiques, an institution for the propagation of economic ideas of large capitalists, is also worthy of note. Headquarters: 282 Bd. St. Germain, Paris.

(72) A. de Foleville, "La richesse en France," *Revue économique internationale,* April, 1906.

(73) *Questions financières,* published by *La Société d'Études et d'Informations Économiques,* May 10, 1935. In 1930 there were 357,240 inheritance tax returns. In 1928 there were 674,046 deaths.

(74) See *Annuaire statistique*. Those who pay this tax number 2,486,709. The group taken to form the .06 per cent of those paying the tax comprises those reporting incomes of 50,100 francs or more. There is a considerable evasion of this tax and the evaders are probably those in the lower brackets.

For a discussion of the tax, see R. M. Haig, *The Public Finance of Post-War France* (New York: Columbia University Press, 1929), pp. 315 ff.

See also Charles Rist, *Tableaux de l'économie française* (1935), plate 37.

(75) The *Action Française* has sponsored the *Union des Corporations*. This Union's organ is *Production Française*. Agricultural problems have particularly interested the party. Its attitude toward them is to be found in the weekly *Action Française Agricole*.

It should be pointed out that complete harmony does not exist between the *Action Française* and the pretender—Le Comte de Paris. In 1935 Le Comte de Paris founded his own paper—*Courrier Royal*.

Concerning the trends mentioned in this section, see Harold Laski, *The Rise of Liberalism* (New York: Harper and Bros., 1936), the last chapter.

(76) See C. J. II. Hayes, *France, a Nation of Patriots* (New York: Columbia University Press, 1930), p. 205. Among Valois' writings may be mentioned: *La réforme économique et sociale* (1917); *L'économie nouvelle* (1919); *La revolution nationale* (1924); *La politique de la victoire* (1925); *L'état, les finances et la monnaie* (1925), all published by the Nouvelle Librairie Nationale, now the Librairie Valois. Valois has now returned to his first love—anarchism.

(77) Paris: Grasset, 1934. See also his *Disciplines d'Action* (Paris: Editions de France, 1935); Henry Malherbe, *Un chef, des actes, des idées* (Paris: Plon, 1934); and the party's newspaper, *Le Flambeau*.

(78) See Gaëtan Pirou, *Le corporatisme* (Paris: Sirey, 1935); *Nouveaux aspects du corporatisme* (Paris: Sirey, 1935), pp. 7-9; and *La crise du capitalisme* (Paris: Sirey, 1936), footnote 2, p. 12.

Attention should be called in this connection to the bill proposed to the Chamber by Flandin in 1935, which provided that the state should impose industrial peace on laborers and capitalists. It should dictate terms in case of conflict that would have to be accepted.

(79) Raymond Millet and Simon Arbellot, *Ligues et groupements* (Paris: Temps, 1935), pp. 34-35.

(80) The organs of these two groups are *La Solidarité Nationale* and *Le Franciste,* respectively. They have made famous the cry "*La France aux Français.*"

(81) By January 1, 1926, 8200 of the 9300 factories employing ten or more men which had been destroyed had been reconstructed and at least a thousand had merged to form larger units, all of the 200 coal-mine shafts which had suffered injury had been repaired and improved, iron mines had

been put in working order, textile factories had been reconditioned, and roads, railways, bridges, canals, and houses had been rebuilt or repaired. See J. R. Cahill, *Report on the Economic Conditions in France* (London: His Majesty's Stationery Office, 1923-1927).

(82) Industrial recuperation began in 1921 and was fairly steady to the depression. There were temporary relapses in the early part of 1923, when the Ruhr was occupied, in the early months of 1924, when the franc's decline unnerved businessmen, at the turn of the year 1924-25, and in 1927, when deflation began.

(83) Based on 1913 production.

(84) If it had increased at the same speed that it did from 1907 to 1913, the index would have stood at 150 in 1926 instead of at 125. Ogburn and Jaffé, *The Economic Development of Post-War France,* pp. 92-101. The above index is based on figures compiled by Jean Desserier, statistician at the Statistique Générale de la France. See the *Bulletin de la statistique générale de la France,* July, 1926, and months following. Experts maintain that the increase indicates that the process of industrialization, which had never been so complete in France as it was in Great Britain and Germany, was still going on. The index of British production for the same period follows:

$$1913—100$$
$$1920— 90$$
$$1925— 86$$
$$1926— 68 \text{ (general strike).}$$

These figures were taken from J. W. F. Rowe, "An Index of the Physical Volume of Production," *The Economic Journal,* June, 1927, p. 178.

(85) Ogburn and Jaffé, p. 109.

(86) *Ibid.,* pp. 112-113.

(87) *Memorandum on International Trade and Balances of Payments, 1913-1927* (Geneva: League of Nations, 1928), vol. I, p. 240. Ogburn and Jaffé, *op. cit.,* p. 540.

(88) Sir Robert Cahill, *Economic Conditions in France* (London: His Majesty's Stationery Office, 1934), pp. 628, 652.

(89) *Ibid.,* p. 627.

(90) *Ibid.,* p. 628 and P. Jéramec, "La production industrielle," *Revue d'économie politique,* May-June, 1935.

(91) *Ibid.,* p. 396 and G. Damougeot-Perron, *L'économie française et les décrets-lois* (Paris: Sirey, 1936), p. 41.

(92) *Ibid.,* pp. 468–469.

(93) *Ibid.,* p. 635 and John de Wilde, "Political Conflict in France," *Foreign Policy Reports,* April 1, 1936.

(94) Eight loans were made by the Crédit National between 1919 and 1924. The last one was a failure. James Harvey Rogers, *The Process of Inflation in France, 1914–1927* (New York: Columbia University Press, 1929), pp. 35–36.

(95) R. M. Haig, *The Public Finances of Post-War France,* pp. 302–3. Some 26 billion francs of private claims remained to be met. At the end of 1927, about 85,500,000,000 francs in all had been met, and 9900 millions remained to be settled.

(96) Harold G. Moulton and Leo Pasvolsky, *War Debts and World Property* (Washington: Brookings Institution, 1932), p. 261.

(97) *Ibid.,* pp. 266–7.

(98) *Ibid.,* pp. 299 and opposite 487. From 1924 to 1931, France received from Germany, her principal debtor, 1426 million dollars, which left her a balance of 1998.1 million dollars. Her aggregate scheduled receipts and payments on inter-governmental debts outstanding on July 1, 1931, were, respectively, $13,855,776,000 and $10,498,105,000, which left a surplus of $3,358,671,000. The Hoover moratorium and Lausanne agreement have put a practical end to reparation and war-debt payments.

(99) See Robert M. Haig, *The Public Finances of Post-War France,* pp. 143 ff.; Memorandum on Public Finance, 1922–1926 (Geneva: League of Nations, 1927), pp. 192–218, especially pp. 196–7; and the *International Statistical Yearbook* (Geneva: League of Nations, published annually).

(100) Ogburn and Jaffé, *The Economic Development of Post-War France* (New York: Columbia University Press, 1929), p. 66.

(101) For this material, consult Haig, *op. cit.;* and Ogburn and Jaffé, *op. cit.*

(102) Haig, *op. cit.,* p. 186.

(103) Ogburn and Jaffé, pp. 154–5:
"At the close of 1925 and during the early months of 1926, a period of progressive inflation, there was, contrary to theoretical expectation, an excess of imports. During the latter half of 1925, when deflation was most marked, there was an excess of exports, which is again contrary to theory. These contradictions, however, do not necessarily mean that the export-import ratios

were not influenced by inflation and deflation. It was, in reality, inflation which in the early part of 1926 caused merchants and manufacturers to accumulate stocks, especially of imported raw materials, in anticipation of a further drop in the value of the franc. This, of course, lowered the ratio. Then, in the autumn and winter of 1926, merchants and manufacturers imported no more, but consumed their stocks while waiting for the franc to rise still more and thus make imports cheaper. This caused the ratio to rise at the close of the year.

"In general, the available data of French inflation and trade point to a probable but none too well defined relation between the two phenomena."

For this and what follows, see George Peel, *The Economic Policy of France* (London: Macmillan, 1937).

(104) Ogburn and Jaffé, p. 180.

(105) Law of July 29, 1919.

(106) J. Naudin, *Les accords commerciaux de la France depuis la guerre* (Paris: Sirey, 1928); C. J. Gignoux, *L'après guerre et la politique commerciale* (Paris: Colin, 1924); and Allix, *Les Droits de douane,* vol. I, pp. 92 ff.

(107) Ogburn and Jaffé, *op. cit.,* pp. 542–545.

(108) Pierre Angelini, *La politique du contingentement des importations* (Paris: Presses Universitaires, 1932), p. 25; and F. A. Haight, *French Import Quotas* (London: King and Son, 1935).

(109) In addition there were increases in some rates (Law of March 31, 1932), and special measures were taken against exchange dumping; etc. See Marc Lasserre, *Les nouvelles orientations de la politique commercial française* (Paris: Presses Universitaires, 1933); and the annual article on French tariffs by J. Naudin in the *Revue d'économie politique.*

(110) Cahill, *Economic Conditions in France* (1934), p. 554, points out that the quota figure is determined either by the Government or by trade associations after negotiations with foreign associations. The latter method allows for considerable influence on the quota for selfish purposes. Decrees of December 31, 1933, established 600 new quotas which were to be managed under the Ministry of Commerce by French trade committees—an arrangement that was analogous to wartime committees and consortiums.

(111) Moulton and Pasvolsky, *War Debts and World Prosperity,* pp. 386–387.

(112) This was one of the causes of the British coal strike in 1926.

(113) Prior to 1922 membership in this committee was considered largely

honorary. Since then the committees' activity has made membership of practical value and hence places on it are coveted by leaders.

(114) Founded in 1898 but reorganized in 1919. It publishes the *Moniteur officiel du commerce et de l'industrie* which contains general trade information.

(115) They have sprung into existence since 1919. Before that date French interests were not represented abroad to any great extent, except perhaps by the embassies. The commercial attachés were placed under the jurisdiction of the Ministry of Foreign Affairs until 1929 when they were transferred to the Ministry of Commerce.

(116) There are also French Commercial Offices Abroad. As they are in the process of being abolished and as there are only eight left, they do not seem to deserve mention in the text. They were set up during the war to do approximately what the attachés do at present. Then there are, too, the French Chambers of Commerce Abroad, made up of men of affairs, which receive a subsidy from the Government in recognition of the service that they render to the cause of foreign trade. The estimated subsidies for 1930 were:

National Office of Foreign Commerce	2,897,000
Commercial Attachés and Agents	22,890,000
Commercial Offices	2,295,600
French Chambers of Commerce Abroad	707,500
Trade Fairs and Exhibitions	270,000
Commercial Missions	26,500
Miscellaneous	14,500

See Maurice Duperrey, *Organisation des services d'expansion commerciales* (Paris: Office Nationale du Commerce Extérieur, 1930), *passim*. Also Gignoux, *op. cit.*, pp. 106–111.

(117) Address: 21 Boulevard Haussmann, Paris. Founded by law of October 23, 1919.

(118) Because the Bank entered a field already served by private banks without government subsidies, certain restrictions were placed upon it. It was forbidden to establish branches in France, although it might have "representatives" in the larger French cities, and in foreign cities where French banks already existed except in the latter case by the consent of those banks. When the reserve of the bank is over 25 million francs the state will get 30 per cent of the profits to reimburse it for its advances. When the reimbursements have been completed, that is, when the Bank has paid the state the amount previously advanced, then the state will receive only 20 per

cent of the profits. See *Convention* of May 28, 1919, between the Ministers of Finance and of Commerce and the Bank.

(119) *Direct and Indirect Subsidies. International Economic Conference* (Geneva: League of Nations, 1927), p. 11.

(120) *Ibid.*

(121) Exporters benefit from reduced railway rates on goods to be shipped in French bottoms to East Africa and South America, and 20 per cent reduction in total shipping rates on goods sent on the French Line to England via Saint-Nazaire and New Haven, to New York, and by certain other French merchant lines to the Near and Far East. See Direct and Indirect Subsidies, p. 17, which bases its statement on the *United States Tariff Commission Dictionary of Tariff Information* (1924).

(122) Established by the decrees of November 2, 1928, and June 23, 1929.

(123) The exporter must bear at least 20 per cent of the risk. The other 20 per cent may be covered by insurance with private companics. An extension of this system was made in 1935. See G. Damougeot-Perron, *L'économie française et les décrets-lois* (1936), pp. 143 ff.

(124) The methods which will be employed may be analogous to those used in 1931 when Germany and Austria proposed a customs union. At that time French banks withdrew short-term loans to one of Austria's leading banks, the Credit Anstalt, thus forcing that institution to the verge of bankruptcy, although at the same time they promised loans to Austria if the idea of a customs union were abandoned.

France can wield tremendous influence by throwing her gold in the scales of diplomacy. The Government does bring pressure on the banks to act as it desires. At least, Premier Laval on the occasion of his visit to the United States in October, 1931, said that his Government had taken steps to check the withdrawal of gold from America. *New York Times,* October 26, 1931, p. 1, and continuation.

(125) *Direct and Indirect Subsidies,* p. 23.

(126) The suppression of Abd-el-Krim in Morocco (1926) and of uprisings in Syria might be considered exceptions to this statement, but this action did not add territory to France's colonial empire and hence may be placed in the category of policing.

(127) See below, p. 342. See also Thomas E. Ennis, *French Policy in Indochina* (Chicago: Chicago University Press, 1936).

(128) Constant Southworth, *The French Colonial Venture* (London:

King and Son, 1931), has endeavored to answer this question. He estimates
(pp. 92–93) that 2½ per cent is a generous allowance. Southworth has made
what is perhaps the most serious study of this problem, but his statistical
method is open to criticism. Attention has been given this same problem by
P. T. Moon, *Imperialism and World Politics* (New York: Macmillan, 1926),
p. 532; A. Vallet, *Un nouvel aperçu du problème colonial* (Paris: Berger-
Levrault, 1925); and Melvin Knight, *Morocco as a French Economic Venture*
(New York: Appleton, 1937).

(129) Southworth thinks that the benefits have been very small and
French capital could have been put to better use in other places.

Another anti-imperialist on economic grounds is Grover Clark, *A Place
in the Sun* (New York: Macmillan Co., 1936) and *Balance Sheet of Imperialism* (New York. Columbia University Press, 1936).

(130) Hardy, *Histoire de la colonisation française*, pp. 295–296.

(131) Gabriel Hanotaux and Alfred Martineau, *Histoire des colonies
françaises* (Paris: Plon, 1929), vol. I, p. 1.

(132) Hanotaux and Martineau, *op. cit.*, vol. VI (1933), p. 564.

(133) *Annuaire statistique*, 1926, p. 95.

(134) Ogburn and Jaffé, *op. cit.*, p. 519.

(135) *Ibid.*, pp. 526–527. In francs of current value the trade figures were:

	Millions of francs	
	Exports	*Imports*
1920 including Alsace Lorraine	26,894	49,904
1921	19,772	22,755
1922	21,378	24,275
1923	30,866	32,859
1924	42,368	40,162
1925	45,754	44,095
1926	59,677	59,598
1927	54,924	53,049

(136) The figures in francs should be corrected to allow for a decline in
prices. The general index of wholesale prices during the period was:

1928	634
1929	623
1930	543
1931	477
1932	408
1933	396

Cahill, *op. cit.*, p. 70.

(137) The *Revue d'économie politique* devotes one issue annually to an economic survey of France. The section on the balance of trade and payments has been written since the war by P. Meynial and more recently by L. Rist and P. Schwob. The League of Nations' *Balance of Payments* report relies on the above articles for most of its information.

(138) The huge flight of capital from France during the inflation, which was estimated by Meynial in the *Revue d'économie politique* to have been 37 billion francs in the years 1924, 1925, 1926, was almost entirely repatriated by 1932.

(139) Philippe Bonnet, *Les émissions de valeurs mobilières en France depuis 1926* (Paris: Mechelinck, 1931), p. 147 and Haig, *op. cit.,* pp. 399–401. In pre-war francs, state revenue from taxation increased from 4066 million in 1913 to 7040 million in 1927.

(140) Bonnet, *op. cit.,* p. 136; Eugene Staley, *War and the Private Investor* (New York: Doubleday, Doran & Co., 1935), p. 527; and *L'Europe Nouvelle,* January 11, 1930. French colonial investments, French holdings of securities and capital in French concerns doing business abroad, and treasury loans to governments should be added to these figures for French holdings of foreign securities for a complete picture of French investments abroad. See also J. Malpas, *Les mouvements internationaux de capitaux* (Paris, Thesis, 1934).

(141) Bonnet, *op. cit.,* p. 139.

(142) This is not exclusively true. France's share of the Young Plan loan to Germany may be considered an exception. The largest long-term loans to foreign governments were made to Belgium, Roumania, Poland, Bulgaria, Hungary, Jugoslavia, and Czechoslovakia. See *Le Temps,* March 2, 1932.

(143) The silk industry has not grown in size despite the subsidies. See *Natural Silk Industry. International Economic Conference* (Geneva: League of Nations, 1927), p. 20. In the same category of industries as silk may be placed hemp and flax growing. These industries receive subsidies in France. *Subsidies—Direct and Indirect. International Economic Conference* (Geneva: League of Nations, 1927), p. 11.

(144) The subsidies were based on the tonnage of planes, kilometers covered, and operating deficit. For a detailed treatment see Marian D. Tolles, *A History of French Subsidies to Commercial Aviation* (Northampton, Mass.: Smith College Studies in History, 1933) and Cahill, *op. cit.,* pp. 455 ff.

(145) *Problème de l'outillage national. Rapport de Conseil National Economique. Journal Officiel.* Jan. 17, 1929.

(146) Laws of August 2, 1918, August 1, 1928, and August 10, 1929. The *chiffres d'affaires* tax is not collected on construction and repairs. The ship yards were also granted special rates for the transportation of their materials on state railways. See *Shipbuilding. International Economic Conference* (Geneva: League of Nations, 1927), p. 33.

(147) The mail contracts amounted to a total of 89,000,000 francs in 1928 and to 349,600,000 francs in 1934. Cahill, *op. cit.*, p. 448.

(148) Cahill, *op. cit.*, pp. 446, 450–451. Of French foreign trade, 47.08 per cent was carried by sea, 51.92 per cent by land. French shippers carried 63.92 per cent of sea-borne exports and 35.59 per cent of sea-borne imports.

The nations which ranked above France in total tonnage were in 1931 Great Britain, The United States, Japan, Germany, and Norway. Italy and Holland were close behind.

(149) The costs of construction in France were greater than in Great Britain from between 19.7 and 24.6 per cent. Cahill, *op. cit.*, p. 249, and L. Lefol, *La protection de la construction navale en France et à l'étranger* (Paris, 1929), pp. 93–113.

(150) Law of August 2, 1928, with changes in 1928 and 1931. See Lefol, *op. cit.*; E. Deparès, *Le crédit à la construction navale* (Paris: Presses Universitaires, 1932); and J. E. Saugstad, *Shipping and Shipbuilding Subsidies* (Washington: Gov. Printing Office, 1932).

Only 50 per cent of the value of the ship could be advanced with the ship alone as pledge; 85 per cent if other collateral was used. Cahill, *op. cit.*, pp. 618–19.

(151) Cahill, *op. cit.*, pp. 452 ff.

The *Compagnie des Messageries Maritimes* appealed to the state for aid in 1920 and received it on the condition that a proportion of the Company's earnings go to the public treasury. The state obtained in this fashion a voice in its management.

The *Compagnie Générale Aéropostale* got state financial assistance in 1924 and since 1931 has been managed by a board in which the state has a voice.

The *Compagnie Marseillaise de Navigation à Vapeur* (*Compagnie Frayssinet*) and the *Compagnie de Navigation Sud-Atlantique* have made contracts with the state whereby the public treasury supports a large share of their losses and divides with them their profits, if any. This profit-and-loss-sharing scheme requires the lines to provide stipulated services and allows the state to intervene in their management. See J. E. Saugstad, *Shipping and Shipbuilding Subsidies*, pp. 109–114, 124.

(152) G. Pirou, *La crise du capitalisme* (Paris. Sirey, 1936), pp. 61 ff. and G. Damougeot-Perron, *L'économie française et les décrets-lois* (Paris: Sirey, 1936), pp. 55–69. The state has also helped other branches of agriculture, but this action has been of secondary importance.

(153) The roads were returned to private management in February, 1919.

(154) There were certain other minor provisions such as the proportion of new construction which the state would pay. The length of the concessions was maintained or provided for in 1883. See Thévenez, *Législation des chemins de fer*, pp. 51–53.

(155) In 1933 the Orléans and Midi companies signed a five-year agreement of unification. See also Herbert E. Dougall, "Railway Nationalization and Transport Coördination in France," *Journal of Political Economy*, April, 1938.

(156) The Anglo-Persian, the Royal Dutch-Shell, and Standard interests got equal proportions and M. Gulkenhain 5 per cent.

(157) See the unpublished Master of Arts dissertation (Columbia University) by Nancy Stevenson on the subject, or H. G. Thomas, *Le régime du pétrole en France* (Paris, 1934).

(158) See especially agreements between the state and the company of May 17, 1924, and June 25, 1930. The state had an option to take up a further 10 per cent which it has since exercised.

(159) By agreement of April 1, 1931, the company agreed to sell oil at a discount to the state for public services.

(160) Cahill, *op. cit.*, p. 158.

(161) Laws of March 16, 1928, and April 7, 1932.

(162) The most important wells are at Pechelbronn, Alsace. There are others in the department of the Hérault and in Autun, but their output is very small.

The changing source of oil imports in France is interesting. The percentage of imports from the United States, the principal source, has declined from 40.8 in 1930 to 27.2 in 1932. The U. S. S. R. was second in 1932, having replaced Persia, which took third place. Venezuela and Roumania were the other chief sources.

(163) Savings banks in France must invest their capital in government securities or place their funds in the *Caisse*.

See G. Damougeot, *op. cit.*, pp. 217–226, for the effect of these institutions on the money market. Also M. G. Myers, *Paris as a Financial Center* (New York, 1936).

(164) Created by Law of March 31, 1899. Through its departmental agents it extends credit to coöperatives or to peasants with small or medium size holdings. There is also the National Office of Agricultural Credit, created by the Laws of April 9, 1918, and June 21, 1919, to advance sums to war veterans and victims of the war.

(165) See above, pp. 325–326.

(166) The tobacco monopoly has been administered since October 1, 1926, by the Autonomous Fund for Debt Redemption.

(167) Another example was the coal mines of the Saar.

(168) See the very illuminating anonymous article "Les participations financières de l'Etat dans les enterprises privées," *Revue politique et parlementaire*, March 10, 1933, p. 456.

(169) *Ibid*, p. 159, and *Memorandum on Public Finances: 1922–26* (Geneva: League of Nations, 1927), pp. 192–218. For a list of "Public Undertakings," see pp. 208–210.

(170) For example, the state invested 2,631,500 francs of a total capitalization of 65,000,000 francs in the *Union hydro-électrique à Eguzon* and 6,000,000 francs of a total capitalization of 12,000,000 francs in the *Société de régularisation des Forces motrices de la Vallée de la Romanche*. It also has aided power line companies. See "Les participations financières de l'Etat dans les entreprises privées," *Revue politique et parlementaire*, March 10, 1933, pp. 461–2.

(171) *Ibid.*, pp. 462–3. The state has invested through the *O. N. N.* 2,916,800 francs of a total capitalization of 6,000,000 francs in the *Compagnie Générale de Traction sur les Voies Navigables;* 600,000 francs of a total capitalization of 1,000,000 francs in the *Traction du Nord;* and 2,000,000 francs of 6,000,000 francs in the *Traction de l'Est.*

(172) Cahill, *op. cit.*, p. 644.

(173) These figures are based on unemployment relief payments. Inasmuch as all unemployed do not receive the benefits, the total number of unemployed is much larger than the statistics indicate. Unofficial estimates of unemployment in the spring of 1934 varied from 700,000 to over 1,000,000.

(174) April 3, 1919.

(175) All workers with an annual income of 18,000 francs or less were

required to avail themselves of the law's advantages and all others were allowed to do so, if they so desired, workers without children were not forced to insure themselves if they earned over 15,000 francs. The minimum limit was increased by 2000 francs from 18000 francs for every child beyond two. In order to provide capital for the undertaking a sum equal to 10 per cent of every insured's salary was to be paid into a fund, 5 per cent by the worker and 5 per cent by the employer, unless the worker is voluntarily insured. The unemployment insurance is granted by mutual-aid societies or trade benevolent associations or by municipal or departmental offices known as *Fonds de chomage*. In the department of the Seine, where most unemployment is to be found, the state furnishes about 7 francs of 8 francs 50 which an unemployed person receives. The time limit on the benefits was increased from sixty to one hundred eighty days, but abolished entirely, June 24, 1932. The whole scheme is administered by the National Office of Social Insurance, which was expected to function without state aid. For a complete discussion of the law see David J. Saposs, *The Labor Movement in Post-War France* (New York: Columbia University Press, 1931), pp. 267-279.

(176) Heads of families are given privileges of various kinds—special benefits under the old-age pensions and industrial-accidents acts, reductions on income, legacy, and inheritance taxes, reductions in railway fares, etc.

(177) See George Mauco, *Les étrangers en France* (Paris: Colin, 1932).

(178) In December, 1933, establishments employing at least 100 workers each and a total of 2,414,460 persons, had 36 per cent of their employees on short time. In two years their total number of employed had decreased by only 8 per cent.

(179) See his *Die neue Wirtschaft* (1918), pp. 231 ff.; *Von kommenden Dingen* (1917); and Count H. Kessler, *Walter Rathenau* (1929).

(180) R. Gonnard, *Histoire des doctrines économiques* (Paris: Librairie Valois, 1927), vol. III, pp. 285-288; Pirou, *Les doctrines économiques de France depuis 1870*, pp. 85-86.

(181) Pirou, *op. cit.*, p. 86.

(182) Decree of January 16, 1925; law of March 19, 1936; and decree of July 24, 1936.

(183) If two-thirds of the votes at a meeting of the Council are cast in favor of a suggestion, the Government must consider the proposal and reply to the Council.

(184) Among its members were the famous economist, Charles Gide,

Emile Borel, Fougère, President of the Federation of Silk, Leon Jouhaux of the C. G. T., and M. de Peyerimhoff of the Comité des Forges.

(185) The Council has taken a stand for government control of and aid to industry. See "Avis sur le projet de loi relatif au perfectionnement de l'outillage national," *Journal Officiel,* January 5, 1930.

(186) See the penetrating analysis of this problem by David Mitrany, "The Political Consequences of Economic Planning," *The Sociological Review,* October, 1934.

(187) This office existed for a short time in 1925. It was re-established by the Tardieu Government and has been in existence ever since.

(188) *State and Economic Life* (Paris: International Institute of Intellectual Coöperation, League of Nations), vols. I and II.

(189) Francis Delaisi, *Les deux Europes* (Paris: Payot, 1929), p. 250.

(190) Francis Delaisi, *Les contradictions du monde moderne* (Paris: Payot, 1925).

(191) *The World Economic Conference. Final Report* (Geneva: League of Nations, 1927), p. 48.

(192) French interests are involved in a great many international cartels. One of the most interesting ones is the potash cartel in which the French state mines have joined the Germans. Most of the cartels were not created to overcome strictly national economic policies, but to overcome difficulties resulting from the modern system of national economics, mass production, overproduction, and price-cutting. See Louis Domeratzky, *The International Cartel Movement* (United States Department of Commerce, 1928); Robert Liefmann, *Kartelle, Konzerne und Trusts* (Stuttgart: Moritz, 1930); and Roger Conte, *Auf Veranlassung des Ausschusses für Internationale Industrievereinbarungen* (Paris: International Chamber of Commerce, 1927), No. 46.

(193) For an account of the creation of the B. I. S., see Pierre Mendès—France, *La Banque Internationale* (Paris: Valois, 1930).

(194) *Application of the Recommendations of the International Economic Conference. Report in the period May, 1928 to May, 1929* (Geneva: League of Nations, 1929).

INDEX